THE
GARDENING
ENCYCLOPEDIA

THE
GARDENING
ENCYCLOPEDIA

BLITZ EDITIONS

The material in this book has previously appeared in *Green Fingers*.

© Orbis Publishing Limited 1985, 1992

Published in this edition 1992 by Blitz Editions
an imprint of Bookmart Limited
Registered Number 2372865
Trading as Bookmart Limited
Desford Road, Enderby, Leicester LE9 5AD

Printed in Czechoslovakia
ISBN 1 85605 002 5

50820

Dear Fellow Gardener,

You will probably agree that working on improvements to your garden, whatever its size, is one of life's greatest pleasures. With the advance of technology and the worries of today's world, gardening offers the chance for you to maintain a little contact with nature and appreciate its growth and change. As a pastime gardening is a welcome and relaxing antidote to the rigours of work.

Of course everyone wants to use a garden in their own way; to take care of it as their wants and imagination dictate. So while one person may have a preference for a flower garden, another may enjoy the particular interest of a herb garden.

Our brief was to produce a gardening book which has something to offer to everyone, covering as many aspects of gardening as possible. We hope this book will inform and deepen your gardening knowledge and broaden your gardening capabilities.

It is not intended as a reference or text book in which you will be tutored to produce the perfect garden. It is hoped, instead, that the information it contains will help increase the pleasure you obtain from your garden, encouraging a confident and inspired approach so you can produce a very individual garden which reflects the character of its owner.

Basic Principles in the Garden

In the simplest of terms, gardening is the care and cultivation of plants. It is a therapeutic activity as it involves gentle, healthy exercise in the open air. However, the enjoyment of gardening is in the success of one's work and in this, insufficient knowledge can lead to failure and frustration. Therefore to enjoy gardening to the full you need to understand certain basic principles.

You need to know how to grow individual varieties respecting their preferences for shade or sun, marshy ground or dry. It is much easier and rewarding to grow a plant where the conditions are to its liking than to try and defy the laws of Nature.

Essentially gardening should be a leisurely pursuit but it can only be so if you carefully pre-plan your activity. A vegetable plot need not be demanding if you co-ordinate the weeding and feeding of your plants. Fruit bushes can be easily controlled if you plant a dwarf or semi-dwarf variety. Flowering shrubs are great time-savers – they require little attention once established and are great weed smotherers. They provide a background of colour throughout the winter, flower in the spring and summer and act as living fences.

In planting perennials, you can choose from a wide range of shapes, sizes and colours and they lead a long life. All that is required is the lifting, dividing and re-planting of the plants once every four to five years.

Biannuals and annuals can be grown afresh every year and provide the opportunity for you to ring the changes.

Hardy annuals are of special value to those gardeners without greenhouses. The seeds can be sown in open ground, bloom in the summer and carpet the garden with colour throughout the remainder of the season.

Gardening need not be expensive. If you develop your skills in taking cuttings and offshoots you can benefit from neighbour's plants. Fertilizers too which can be expensive to buy in the shops can be manufactured on your compost heap. By recognising and treating the various pests and diseases which afflict certain plants you can save yourself the expense of replacing them.

Tools are however worth the investment. Good tools together with an understanding of gardening are the basic ingredients to good gardening.

Acid and Alkaline Soils

To grow healthy plants it is vital to provide the right soil conditions. One of the most important tasks is to maintain the correct balance of acidity or alkalinity according to the plants being grown. Some subjects grow better in an alkaline (limey or chalky) soil while others, such as rhododendrons, will grow only in an acid one (free of lime or chalk). The majority of garden plants, however, much prefer a soil that is midway between these two extremes.

Before you prepare your soil for planting it is advisable to carry out a soil test with one of the soil-testing kits that are available from garden centres and good department stores. Such a test will indicate the degree or intensity of acidity or alkalinity. This is measured on a logarithmic scale called the pH scale. On this scale pH 7 is neutral (neither acid nor alkaline) while lower numbers indicate increasing degrees of acidity and higher numbers show increasing degrees of alkalinity. A wide range of commonly-grown plants, including vegetables, fruit, roses, hardy perennials, trees and shrubs, grow best in a slightly acid to neutral soil of pH 6·5 to 7·0.

High acidity or alkalinity

If your soil pH is below 5·5 then many plants may fail to grow. Also the numbers of undesirable organisms increase rapidly.

On the other hand an excessively limey soil, with a pH of over 8·0, can produce many plant disorders. Certain important plant foods, particularly iron and magnesium (but also manganese), are made unavailable to plants if the soil is limey. If a plant cannot absorb sufficient iron then its leaves will turn yellow and it may become stunted and eventually die. This yellowing is known as lime-induced chlorosis. Bushes (particularly fruit bushes, roses and hydrangeas) and fruit trees quickly show symptoms of chlorosis if iron is not available. You can, however, cure this condition with annual drenches of a solution of sequestrene (applied according to maker's instructions); this supplies iron in a readily-available form.

How to make a soil test

When using the soil-testing kit, quarter-fill the test tube (supplied with the kit) with soil and add the lime test solution, following the instructions provided. Then shake the tube to mix the contents thoroughly. Allow the solution to settle. When the soil has settled the clear liquid above will be of a certain colour according to the acidity or alkalinity of the soil. This colour can vary from red (when the soil is very acid) through orange (when only slightly acid) to shades of green (when the soil is neutral or limey). A chart showing the various colours with the appropriate pH number alongside is included in the kit. The liquid in the tube must, of course, be matched as closely as possible with one of these colours in order to ascertain the pH of your soil.

11

INTERNATIONAL SOIL TESTING AIDS

Colours shown on chart are guides and may not exactly match fluid in test tube

LIME TEST (ACIDITY)

A $7\frac{1}{2}$ pH

B $6\frac{1}{2}$ pH

C   6 pH

D $5\frac{1}{4}$ pH

E $4\frac{1}{2}$ pH

NITROGEN TEST

The first figure in the NPK formula for commercial fertilizer

A   2%

B   3%

C   4%

D   6%

E   8%

PHOSPHORUS TEST

The second figure in the NPK formula

A   4%

B   5%

C   6%

D   8%

E   10%

POTASH TEST

The third figure in the NPK formula

A   2%

B   4%

C   8%

D   12%

E   16%

Gardening on alkaline soil

Some plants like a reasonably limey soil (pH of up to 8·0). Examples of these are members of the cabbage family (including wallflowers and aubrietia), carnations and pinks, beech, hornbeam, box, yew, clematis, gypsophila, and scabious. Cabbages and wallflowers suffer far less from club root disease (that causes the roots to swell and the plants to become stunted) if grown in a limey soil. Another interesting fact is that hydrangeas produce blue flowers in an acid soil, but pink blooms in alkaline conditions. If the soil is neutral, the blooms will be mauvish.

To lower the pH of a soil (reduce its alkalinity) you can incorporate heavy dressings of peat, leaf mould, well-rotted manure or garden compost each year. Applying flowers of sulphur will also reduce the pH but a heavy application is needed to reduce the pH by even one unit. For example, to reduce it from 8·0 to 7·0 would necessitate a dressing of about 1kg per sq m (2 lb per sq yd).

In chalky or limey areas it is probably inadvisable to use tap water for pot plants as the water will be alkaline and could result in chlorosis. Instead try to use rainwater collected from a greenhouse or garage roof, or the water obtained from defrosting the fridge or freezer, as this will be soft or acid.

Acid soils

To raise the lime content of an acid soil, treat it with a dressing of hydrated lime or ground chalk. Usually this application is made in the winter after you have finished digging over the garden. Allow the lime to lie on the surface over the winter and then fork it in in the spring. Do not apply manure and lime in the same winter as they interact unfavourably.

On heavy or clay soils apply lime more generously – as much as 500g per sq m (1 lb per sq yd) at one time – but less frequently than on light or sandy types; lime helps to open up and flocculate (create a good crumb structure) the heavier type of soil. Sandy soils are best limed fairly lightly, 135–270g per sq m (4–8 oz per sq yd) annually. On such soils lime is easily leached or washed out by heavy rain. Sandy soils are generally more acid than clay soils and peaty soils are often excessively acid.

If the soil is very acid, say a pH of 5·0 or below, it is inadvisable to apply a large quantity of lime in a single application in order to bring the pH value up to slight acidity or neutral. Instead, apply a moderate dressing – about 500g per sq m (1 lb per sq yd) – regularly each winter over a number of years.

Above: our chart is adapted from Sudbury's soil-testing kit; below: colour of hydrangeas varies with soil balance

How to Improve Difficult Soils

The beginning of winter is the time for digging over the garden so that the elements have a chance to work on the soil before cultivation begins again in the spring. It is during this digging that you can do much to improve difficult soils. 'Difficult' means those that may be hard to work with or those that, because of their poor structure, are either too wet or too dry for good plant growth, or lacking in essential humus or organic matter.

Soils can be divided into four main types: clays, sands, chalk soils and loams. Loams come midway between clays and sands. They are usually easy to work and provide ideal conditions for plants. Clay, sand and chalk each have special characteristics that can make them difficult soils and it may take several years to turn them into easily-managed growing mediums.

CLAY

Clay is commonly known as a heavy soil because it is very hard to cultivate – both to dig and to prepare for seed sowing or planting in the spring. Because of its chemical composition it has a very dense or close structure. It is able to hold large amounts of water within the clay particles, causing them to swell. Water is also held on the surface of the particles, and the particles themselves are held together by electrostatic attraction. It is therefore a very wet and sticky soil and takes a long time to dry out and warm up in the spring.

During the autumn and winter, and in wet weather at other times of year, clay may become waterlogged and this will affect the health of plants. When a soil is holding too much water the oxygen supply to the plants' roots is reduced and if this condition continues over too long a period the plants may die. In hot weather during spring and summer, clay soils can become as hard as rock; for as they dry out the clay particles contract, making cultivation almost impossible.

Opening up clay soils

Dig clay soils in early to mid winter (November to mid December) so that frosts can break them down throughout the winter. Frosts will make a heavy soil more crumbly and therefore far easier to cultivate in the spring. You can also make

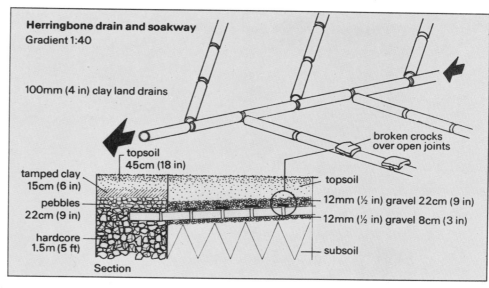

Herringbone drain and soakway
Gradient 1:40

100mm (4 in) clay land drains

topsoil 45cm (18 in)

tamped clay 15cm (6 in)

pebbles 22cm (9 in)

hardcore 1.5m (5 ft)

Section

broken crocks over open joints

topsoil

12mm (½ in) gravel 22cm (9 in)

12mm (½ in) gravel 8cm (3 in)

subsoil

When clay holds too much water, it may be necessary to make a herringbone drain and soakaway before soil is workable

a clay soil more crumbly, and take out most of the stickiness, by applying a top dressing of horticultural gypsum (sulphate of lime) immediately after digging. Let it lie on the surface over the winter, during which time it will be washed into the topsoil by rain. Gypsum can generally be obtained from good gardening shops and centres. Apply it fairly generously each year, at a rate of about 500g–1kg per sq m (1–2 lb per sq yd).

Hydrated lime has a similar effect to gypsum. Again it can be applied as a top dressing after digging. Apply it as evenly as possible. Generally an application every two or three years is adequate for most crops.

It is interesting to note that, though gypsum improves the soil without raising the pH level (increasing alkalinity), hydrated lime raises the pH as well. Both cause flocculation (create a good crumb structure), thus improving the soil texture, drainage and aeration.

During the actual digging, incorporate as much organic matter as possible to 'open up' the soil and to prevent it forming into large clods. This should give better drainage of surplus water and improve aeration. There are various types of organic matter that are suitable, such as well-rotted farmyard or horse manure, garden compost, peat, leaf mould, spent hops, bracken, straw, composted seaweed

and composted sawdust. Try to apply at least one barrowload per square metre or yard. It is best to double dig (see page 17) clay soil as this will enable you to get the organic matter down into the lower soil. When double digging remember to keep the soil in its proper layers; in other words, never mix topsoil with subsoil.

Do not apply lime and manure at the same time, but leave an interval of two or three months between applications. If you are digging in organic material in the autumn, then scatter the lime over the soil surface in early spring.

Spring is also the time to apply a general-purpose fertilizer prior to sowing and planting. It is not much use applying this in the autumn or winter, as most of the plant foods will have been washed too far down in the soil to be of use to the plants when they are needed.

Drainage for clay soils

If clays are constantly waterlogged during wet weather, and none of the other cultural recommendations prove successful, it may be advisable to install a drainage system, although this can be a costly operation and may prove difficult in a small garden.

Basically it involves laying a system of earthenware land drainpipes in the lower soil in a herringbone pattern. The main central pipe, that takes the water from the lateral pipes, should slope gently to a soakaway or ditch at the lowest point of the site. The lateral pipes slope gently to the main pipe.

SAND

Sandy soils are the opposite of clays. They are generally known as 'light' soils because they are easy to work with. Sand has a gritty texture, consisting mostly of grains of silica that are chemically stable. So, unlike clays, the soil particles do not stick together and the soils are very loose in structure.

Because of this loose structure, sandy soils are incapable of holding much water. They warm up quickly in spring but during dry weather they can dry out very rapidly and cause plants to wilt or die through lack of moisture. Again, because of their loose structure and chemical stability, sandy soils cannot hold much plant food and are therefore said to be 'hungry' soils.

Feeding sandy soils

It is not necessary to dig sandy soils as early as heavy clay types, but even so digging should still be completed well before sowing and planting time in the spring. Ordinary single digging to the depth of a spade should be sufficient.

However, in sandy soils an iron pan may form in the lower soil that may be impermeable to air and moisture, and therefore harmful to plants in that it prevents surplus water draining away. An iron pan is a rock-hard layer of soil that, as the name implies, contains a large quantity of iron. Sandy soils naturally contain a large amount of this element that, over the years, is leached (by rain) into the lower soil where it cements sand particles together. If you discover an iron pan, you would do best to break it up by double digging the site. Thereafter you can carry out ordinary single digging as it will probably be many years before a pan forms again.

The main consideration in improving sandy soils is to incorporate as much organic matter as possible to supply humus. Most sandy soils are seriously lacking in humus and so have a very poor structure, the soil being unable to hold water and plant foods. The humus acts as a sponge and ensures adequate moisture during dry periods. Apply plenty of organic matter every year (provided this ties in with the cropping programme) for it quickly disappears in this type of soil. Also apply a general-purpose fertilizer in spring, prior to sowing and planting.

CHALK

In some respects chalk soils are similar to sands. If you have only a thin layer of soil overlying chalk you will often be faced with lack of moisture during dry weather due to the percolation of water down

Dug out trench reveals 'tired' topsoil and subsoil that needs improving with an application of humus

through the chalk out of reach of plant roots. Such a soil will also be lacking in humus and plant foods. An additional problem with chalk soils is high alkalinity that can cause many plants to show symptoms of chlorosis (dwarfing of the plant and yellowing of the leaves). This occurs because the plants are not obtaining sufficient iron from the soil; iron is rendered unavailable to plants in conditions of high alkalinity. Roses, many soft and top fruits, hydrangeas and ericaceous plants (such as rhododendrons, azaleas and heathers, etc.) are prone to chlorosis.

Soils over limestone should be treated as chalk soils; it is often forgotten that chalk is a pure form of limestone.

Improving chalk soils

Chalk soils (especially thin soils overlying solid chalk) need plentiful additions of organic matter; on some types it is almost impossible to apply too much. On such a site you would do best to dig as deeply as possible each year – preferably double digging. This will enable you to get organic matter well down into the soil, so that, over a number of years, you gradually increase the depth of suitable growing soil. Also add organic matter to the topsoil – mix it well in if possible. Any of the kinds of organic matter suggested for clay soils can be used, but very acid materials (such as peat and leaf moulds) are particularly suitable as they help to reduce alkalinity – if only very slightly.

Alkalinity can be reduced by incorporating flowers of sulphur into the soil, but very large applications are necessary to do any good; you would need to use about 500g–1kg per sq m (1–2 lb per sq yd).

As with chalk and sand, apply a general-purpose fertilizer in spring before you begin to sow or plant.

SOIL CHART Recognize your soil type and make the best of it

TYPES	PROBLEMS	ADVANTAGES	HOW TO IMPROVE
CLAY Smooth, not gritty, often wet, sticky and slimy in winter and brick-like in summer	The very small particles stick together when wet, making a solid, almost airless mass. Heavy and difficult to dig and break down. Cold — takes a long time to warm up in spring. Dries out slowly, unevenly and in clods. Seeds germinate poorly (because of lack of air) and plant roots have difficulty in growing (because it is so heavy and solid).	Usually rich in plant food. Can hold water well in dry summers. Is receptive to the addition of plant and animal organic matter, which will decompose by physical, chemical and bacterial activity in the soil. This completely decomposed material is called humus. **Humus** is rich in plant foods, gives the soil 'body' and encourages the retention of food, water and air. In particular, it helps to make clay more workable by breaking down the mass.	Unless already alkaline (chalky), spread garden lime — 375g per sq m (12 oz per sq yd) — all over dug soil in autumn and let the weather work it in. Otherwise fork in during February. Lime makes it easier to dig and cultivate. For lasting improvement dig in large quantities of organic (animal and plant) matter in early spring for several years. This will rot down in the soil and gradually improve its structure and colour. Preferably use 'strawy' farmyard manure, otherwise plenty of peat and garden compost. Continue organic treatment every year, liming every 2–3 years. Do not mix lime with other fertilizers; apply 1 month before, or 2–3 months after, other soil conditioners. If clay is very heavy, artificial drainage may be required.
SAND Light and dry, gritty, crumbly and rough to handle	Poor in plant food. Unable to retain moisture; rainwater passes right through, leaching (washing out) plant foods into the subsoil out of reach of plant roots. Can be very acid due to leaching of lime.	Easy to work at any time of year. Warms up quickly after winter so cultivation can begin early in spring. Plenty of air in soil, allowing plant roots to grow strongly and deeply. Excellent for vegetables, especially root crops, when sufficient organic matter is added to retain water.	Manure, peat and compost must be dug in deeply to increase the soil's organic content. This will add plant foods and increase food- and moisture-retaining abilities. Treatment must be repeated yearly. Also add general fertilizer before sowing or planting in spring and autumn. A light sprinkling of lime should be added every other year if soil is acid. Watering with nitrogenous fertilizer is advantageous throughout the growing season. Artificial watering will probably be necessary during dry spring and summer periods.
CHALK OR LIMESTONE Variable, often shallow, topsoil with recognizable lumps of chalk or limestone, especially in lower soil	Lacks humus and plant food. Difficult to work when wet. Tends to dry out quickly in summer. The calcium in chalk or limestone soil inhibits plants from using many plant foods, and deficiencies may result. Chalky soil is alkaline, and not tolerated by most plants.	Generally light, easy to work, free-draining and warms up quickly in spring. Good for rock garden plants.	Add large quantities of farmyard manure, compost or other organic matter, preferably to the top layer of soil, each spring and autumn. This will break down (into humus) in the soil, improving its condition. Give top-dressings of general fertilizers throughout the growing season.
PEAT Dark brown or black, spongy to touch	Usually waterlogged and may need artificial drainage. May be very acid and sour. Often deficient in plant foods.	Contains plenty of organic matter as it consists mainly of organic material not yet fully decomposed. Easily worked. Too acid for most garden plants but very fertile when drained and limed.	If soil is waterlogged, then a soakaway or drainage pipes may be needed. Liming helps drainage and counteracts acidity. Add lime at 250g per sq m (8 oz per sq yd) every 2–3 years. Add regular, fairly heavy, dressings of general-purpose fertilizers in spring, summer and autumn.
LOAM Dark, crumbly, easy to clean from fingers	Should not be any problem as long as the drainage is satisfactory and the humus and plant food content is maintained.	Ideal garden soil, with a balanced mixture of sand, humus and clay. If humus content is maintained, a well-drained, well-aerated soil rich in plant food will result. Warm enough for early cultivation.	The improvements depend on the proportions of clay and sand in the loam. Sandy loam will require the regular spring and autumn addition of organic matter and fertilizers. Clayey loam may need regular addition of 375g per sq m (12 oz per sq yd) every 2–3 years. Heavy loams will benefit from being roughly dug over in autumn.

Basic Digging

'Single digging' means digging the soil to one spade's depth (one 'spit'); double digging is done to a depth of two spits. The latter was widely practised in private gardens of old, where it was commonly – and more colourfully – called 'bastard trenching'.
If you are unfortunate enough to acquire a garden on a heavy clay soil with poor drainage, then a few years of double digging will help to improve both the soil fertility and the drainage. Otherwise single digging is all you need do.

The object of single digging (which from here on I shall refer to simply as digging) is to turn over the top 20–30cm (9–12 in) of soil; the lower levels are then exposed and aerated. At the same time annual weeds, such as groundsel and chickweed, are turned in and buried so that they will provide valuable humus. Perennial weeds with long tap-roots (like docks and dandelions) will re-emerge if they are buried, so they should be pulled out, left on the path to die, and then placed in the middle of the compost heap. That way every scrap of organic fertilizer that nature provides free is put back into the soil.

Tools for the job

The basic equipment for digging consists of a few layers of warm clothes, stout footwear and a good, strong spade or fork. What you wear on your feet is important. The tendency nowadays is to wear wellingtons but I prefer a robust pair of boots or shoes.

Wellingtons are heavy, tend to chaff the ankles and are inclined to 'sweat'. My gardening boots have thick soles made of some composite material that stands a good deal of rough treatment.

When it comes to the choice of implement you can opt for a spade or a fork. Both are available with two kinds of handle – T-grip and D-grip. I prefer the D-handle because all four fingers of the hand are placed inside the D giving a stronger grip and better leverage.

Whichever you choose it is better to pay a little extra and buy a good-quality tool. A good spade or fork is a sound investment that, properly used and cared for, will last a lifetime. Half- or fully-polished blade or prongs slip more easily into the soil and earth is less inclined to cling to them.

For spring digging you can use either a spade or a fork. If you have a light or sandy soil, or a good loam, a spade will do a better job; but on a very heavy clay, which has lain undisturbed over the winter a fork will make digging easier and the end result will be just as good. So select whichever tool best suits you and your soil.

It is advisable to dig your vegetable plot at least a week or two before you are ready to sow or plant as the soil should have time to settle before you start.

And so to work

For many people the thought of digging is a very off-putting idea. They regard it as a back-breaking slog that must be avoided if possible. But this need not be the case if the job is approached in the right frame of mind. So relax, enjoy it and remember that it takes you out into the open air and that it is a marvellous muscle-toner. Don't set yourself impossible goals and stop before you get exhausted.

First of all dig out a trench one spit deep and about 3–3·5m (10–12 ft) long at one end of the plot. Don't make the trench any longer; it is far better for your morale to finish digging a short strip than to half-finish a longer one. Put the soil from the trench into a wheelbarrow and push it to the other end of the plot (where it will be used to fill in the final trench).

Go back to the start of the row and work your way down the second trench, turning the soil over into the first one. Continue in this manner until you have finished the strip. A word of advice –

Four steps to successful single digging: **1** *marking the spit;* **2** *placing the spade at the correct digging angle;* **3** *turning the soil over into the first trench;* **4** *turning soil from third trench into second one after filling it with manure*

don't try to speed the job up by digging great slices out of the soil. It is much easier, and a lot less tiring, to handle chunks no wider than 15cm (6 in) – at least until you have established a relaxed rhythm. Carry on digging down to the end, fill in the last trench, have a rest and then start on the second strip. Do it this way and you will be surprised how quickly the work gets done.

The newly-turned earth is now an uneven surface of gleaming clods of soil. Leave it like this until the day you are ready to sow and plant, to give it a chance to dry out and settle. Then all you need do on a dry day is shuffle and tramp all over it to break down the lumps before raking it to a fine tilth.

Fertilizers and manures

If you are to get a good, healthy crop fertilizers are absolutely essential. Assuming that none were used in the previous autumn I suggest that a top dressing of general fertilizer, such as Growmore or Fish, blood and bone, or one of the proprietary, concentrated animal manures should be spread over the soil at 70–145g per sq m (2–4 oz per sq yd) before you start digging. Digging the plot puts the fertilizer down into the soil where the plant roots will reach and benefit from it in due course.

I also suggest that you keep some of the fertilizer you use and put a little of it, say about 35g per sq m (1 oz per sq yd) over the whole plot just before you start sowing and planting. This will give the germinating seedlings a boost until their roots reach the main feed below.

Double-digging

Double digging is simply digging the soil two spits deep, that is, to the depth of two spade blades. It should improve the fertility and drainage of a heavy clay soil and is very useful where long-term crops are to be grown or an area is being given over to cultivation for the first time. As in single digging (see page 16), the soil from each succeeding trench is transferred into the one behind it, until finally, the soil from the first trench goes into the last trench.

Digging and filling

The first step is to divide the plot into two and mark out the two sections into 60cm (24 in) wide strips. Starting at the end of the plot dig out the first strip to one spade's depth. The soil should be left next to the adjacent strip in the other half-plot.

Break up the bottom of the trench to the depth of your fork tines and then

1 *Double digging the final trench and turning the soil into the one before.*
2 *Shovelling in the compost and spreading it evenly.* **3** *Mixing compost in with the broken-up second spit.* **4** *Filling final trench with soil left over from the first*

Above: mechanical cultivator with a rotating head helps to make double digging less back breaking. There are various fork tines for the cultivator head to deal with different types of soil

move onto the second strip. Make sure that each ensuing trench is as near as possible the same width as the one before so that the same quantity of soil is removed and a level surface is maintained. The soil from the second digging goes into the first trench, the bottom of the second trench is broken up and the process goes on until the final trench is filled with the pile of soil

which has been waiting to fill the gap.

Compost and manure

If you want to apply compost or manure, it should be spread over the surface of the whole plot. As each trench is emptied, rake in the manure from the next strip and fork it into the broken-up second spit.

Feeding Plants

Ascophyllum nodosum, 'egg' or knotted wrack, exposed on the rocks at low tide

Plants, like people, need a regular supply of food if they are to survive and grow well. The main ways of feeding your plants are by applying fertilizers and bulky organic matter (like manure) to the soil.
Manure supplies some nutrients, but its most important function is to improve the soil structure by adding organic material. This turns the soil into a healthy medium in which plants can thrive. Fertilizers provide some, or all, of the basic plant foods.

When digging, particularly in late autumn or early winter, it is wise to incorporate in each trench well-rotted farmyard manure, garden compost, seaweed or hop manure. These materials will supply bulky organic matter and a variable amount of plant food. None of them, however, supplies adequate nutrients for the plants to make optimum growth; therefore fertilizers will have to be added at planting time to ensure that the plants have sufficient food.

The organic matter is digested by bacteria in the soil and turned into humus. This humus is like a sponge; it holds water and prevents rapid drying-out of light soils. It also helps to break up sticky clay soils by improving drainage. Organic material is, therefore, essential because it improves the soil's structure.

MANURES
Never apply manure at the same time as lime (calcium). This is because the lime can liberate any available nitrogen in the form of ammonia, which may then be lost through evaporation. Also, never grow root crops on ground where fresh manure has been used, for your vegetables may well produce deformed roots.

Seaweed as manure
If your garden is near the coast, use seaweed as a manure. It is excellent for digging – wet or dried – into the soil in the autumn. Seaweed is one of the oldest manures known and contains many plant foods. It is now possible to obtain specially refined seaweed manures from gardening shops.

Manure for mulching
Rotted manure or garden compost makes a good mulch for established plants such as trees, shrubs, top and soft fruit, vegetables, roses, dahlias and chrysan-themums. Place a layer of mulch, 5–8cm (2–3 in) thick, around the plants in spring. It will then provide some food and humus and help prevent evaporation of moisture from the surface soil.

FERTILIZERS
Bulky organic matter is not capable, by itself, of supplying all the foods the plants will require, so fertilizers must also be added to the soil.

As a general rule, dry fertilizers should be applied to moist soil, or else well watered in after application if the ground is dry. Always apply them evenly, and discard or break up any lumps; these can 'burn' roots. Apply all fertilizers carefully and according to maker's instructions. If you exceed the recommended rate of application you may seriously injure your plants.

Before sowing or planting, the usual procedure is to rake in a dry fertilizer which contains the major plants foods (nitrogen, phosphates and potash). There are many of these 'general-purpose' or compound fertilizers on the market. Probably the best known is National Growmore, which is available under numerous brand names. This is suitable for all vegetables, fruit and flowers. You can also apply it as a top dressing in spring or summer by lightly raking it into the soil surface around any of your established plants.

Special dry fertilizers for specific crops (such as roses and tomatoes) are available. These contain the correct balance of nitrogen, phosphates and potash suited to the particular plant.

Lawn fertilizers
There are several proprietary lawn fertilizers which make the lawn 'green up' quickly and grow well due to the high proportion of nitrogen they contain. Feed your lawn once or twice during spring and summer to ensure a lush, deep-green sward. Autumn lawn fertilizer, which is applied in mid autumn (September), contains more potash; this helps to 'ripen' the grass and make it more resistant to hard winter weather.

'Straight' fertilizers
You can also apply 'straight' fertilizers to plants, especially as a supplement to the ready-mixed, general-purpose kinds applied earlier in the growing season; but you must be aware of specific food requirements of individual plants before trying out these fertilizers. Be sure to handle them carefully and accurately.

Sulphate of ammonia and nitro-chalk supply nitrogen which encourages plants to make lush, leafy growth. They are quick-acting fertilizers and should be used very sparingly. They can be used on lawns and also on green vegetables such as cabbage, kale, broccoli and spinach. Apply them in spring and summer only.

Sulphate of potash and muriate of potash both supply the potash (potassium) essential for the production of fruit and flowers. It also helps to ripen the stems, which is necessary for the successful overwintering of all hardy plants. Potash can be applied in summer or early autumn. Wood ashes contain potassium

house, greenhouse and garden. You can apply them most easily with a rosed watering can.

There are many brands of liquid fertilizer on the market, some of which are formulated for specific crops.

Foliar feeding
Foliar feeding is a fairly recent technique of applying liquid fertilizers to plants. The fertilizer is sprayed or watered onto the leaves where it is quickly absorbed by the plants and circulated in the sap stream. The nutrients are made im-

mediately available to plants. This makes them particularly useful to transplanted plants before their new roots have become established.

You can buy special foliar feeds from gardening shops. Alternatively you can apply any liquid fertilizer to the foliage and it will be quickly absorbed.

Sulphate of ammonia can be dissolved at the rate of 3g per litre ($\frac{1}{2}$ oz per gal) of water and applied to leaves to promote growth of foliage. Likewise sulphate of potash will encourage fruiting and ripening of growth.

LIME
Lime is another plant food and this is applied on its own, generally in the winter after autumn digging, in the form of dehydrated lime. It is mainly the vegetable plot that will require lime and an application every two or three years will be adequate.

Lime lowers the acidity of the soil, and as many plants (especially vegetables such as brassicas) do not thrive in an acid soil, liming enables you to grow a wider range of plants. But do not lime if you have a naturally alkaline or limy soil with a pH of 7 or above. Hydrated lime is the type generally used.

Above: applying chemical fertilizer by spoon in small measured quantities
Above right: sieving leaf mould into a wheelbarrow for use as compost
Right: fertilizer spreaders give even results
Far right: applying lime by hand

and, once they have weathered for 3–6 months, can be dug into the soil during autumn digging or raked into the surface.

Superphosphate of lime supplies phosphate (phosphorus). This is also essential for good root production and all-round growth. It is usually applied in spring and summer at the rate of 3g per litre ($\frac{1}{2}$ oz per gal) of water and applied to the soil around plants about once a week. Avoid getting it on the foliage.

Liquid fertilizers
Use liquid fertilizers in conjunction with powdered or granulated fertilizers – not as a substitute. They should be considered as supplementary feeds to boost the growth of plants. They are generally used in the summer when plants are in full growth. Being liquid, they are quickly absorbed by plants and rapidly stimulate growth.

Dilute liquid fertilizers according to maker's instructions, and apply them to moist soil. Use them as frequently as once a week and on all kinds of plants in the

Effects of Fertilizers on Vegetables

As an aid to understanding the role of fertilizers in vegetable growing it is helpful to consider the basic food requirements of plants in general. These are very simple, since all that is needed are supplies of twelve mineral elements. Each of these elements, however, has its own dominant role in plant nutrition so the balance between them affects the type of growth.

Key elements

All the essential plant foods are available in normal fertile soil but the soil stocks of some elements need to be replenished regularly if fertility is to be maintained. In particular, additional supplies of **nitrogen, phosphorus** (phosphate) and **potassium** (potash) are required. Most general garden fertilizers are therefore based on these three elements, although some specialist fertilizers also contain **magnesium.** In addition most fertilizer mixtures have some content of **sulphur** and **calcium** although these are not mentioned on the pack. Use of complete, or compound, fertilizers thus provides an easy way of maintaining suitable levels of the six major plant foods in the soil.

The remaining six key elements are: **iron, manganese, copper, zinc, boron** and **molybdenum** and generally these do not need to be replenished. These are only used in trace quantities by plants so that soil stocks are normally more than adequate. Deficiencies when they do occur are difficult to remedy by the use of solid fertilizer because of the very low levels involved and because of the risk of plant damage by over-application. The best approach in this situation, therefore, is to use either liquid or foliar feeds containing very low concentrations of all six trace elements.

Effects on plant growth

Although all twelve elements are essential for healthy plant growth, each food has its own special function. Nitrogen stimulates vigorous vegetative growth. Potash, on the other hand, favours flowering and fruiting in addition to giving sturdy growth. Phosphorus, whilst essential for most growth processes, is of special importance in root growth. The remaining three major elements, namely magnesium, calcium and sulphur play more general roles in plant physiology.

It is less easy to define the roles of the six minor, or trace, elements but all are involved in important growth processes. Certainly a deficiency of any of them can have serious effects causing leaf damage, stunting or malformed growth.

Choice of principal fertilizer

The food value of a fertilizer is measured by the quantity of nitrogen, phosphate and potash that is available to plants. These quantities are expressed as specific percentages of N for nitrogen (N), of P_2O_5 for phosphate (P) and of K_2O for potash (K). A typical example of a complete fertilizer is Growmore, that contains 7 per cent N, 7 per cent P_2O_5 and 7 per cent K_2O. This information, printed on all fertilizer packages, is of value to the gardener. It not only shows the balance of NPK but also gives a good indication of whether the product is good value for money. Some cheap fertilizers may not be, because of their low food content.

The varying nutritional requirements

Above: correct food balance in the soil and an occasional liquid feed give a crisp healthy lettuce crop
Below: values listed on fertilizer packages

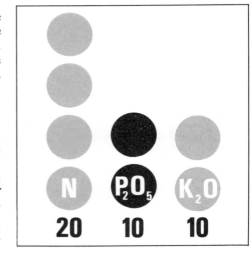

of root crops, brassicas, tomatoes, beans and peas, could be solved by the use of special fertilizer mixtures for each crop. In practice, however, it is simpler and cheaper to use a fairly even balance of NPK as a base dressing and then, where necessary, to vary the feeding by later side dressings or by the use of liquid feeds.

Application of fertilizers

The safe and efficient way of using any fertilizer is to apply it evenly over the growing area at a reasonable rate. For instance Growmore should generally be used at around 140 g per sq m (4 oz per sq yd) just before sowing or planting out. Localized application in seed drills or planting holes must be avoided because of risk of damage to the plant roots. Should later side dressings be needed, these too must be applied evenly over the area. This ensures that the food is available to the whole root system. Rather less care is needed when applying liquid feeds but here it is important to use fairly high volumes. The fertilizer content of liquid feeds is quite low, so plenty of solution is needed to have a worthwhile feeding effect. Generous application of liquid feeds also ensures that the solution penetrates into the root zone.

Fertilizer programmes

In all cases a general NPK fertilizer should be lightly worked into the topsoil before sowing seed or planting out. Proprietary products should be used at the rates recommended by the manufacturers. As a general guide, the rate of application of a product containing 5–7 per cent nitrogen plus phosphate and potash should be about 140g per sq m (4 oz per sq yd).

When using fertilizers with higher or lower nitrogen content the application rate needs to be adjusted accordingly. Subsequent fertilizer treatments vary with the type of crop.

Potatoes Early potatoes should not need any further feeding. In the case of maincrop varieties, however, a second application of NPK fertilizer should be given prior to earthing-up. This ensures adequate supplies of phosphate for root growth and nitrogen for heavy cropping.

Brassicas With these essentially leafy crops the key requirement is to ensure continuity of supplies of nitrogen. So later feeding can be done with straight nitrogen fertilizers. One approach is to use quick-acting sulphate of ammonia (21 per cent N). This fertilizer needs to be applied carefully because of the risk of root damage. Each application therefore should not exceed 35g per sq m (1 oz per sq yd). The first treatment can be given about a month after planting out. A second application can then be made in late summer. An alternative method is to use one of the newer slow-release nitrogen fertilizers. These have an even higher fertilizer content than sulphate of ammonia. So only 35–50g per sq m (1–1½ oz per sq yd) is needed over the whole growing season. A major advantage of these slow-release feeds is that it is safe to apply the whole quantity at one application. This provides a steady supply of nitrogen for several months.

Summer cauliflowers present a special case. With these it is important that growth is continuous since any setback can result in the premature development of small, poor-quality heads. For this reason, regular liquid feeding may be better than the use of solid fertilizer.

Onions and leeks Both these are gross feeders and so benefit from additional feeding. This can be as a single application of sulphate of ammonia or as repeated liquid feeds.

Peas and beans No additional feeding is needed to supplement the base dressing.

Swedes and turnip No additional feeding is needed.

Radish No additional feeding is necessary but regular watering is needed in dry weather to ensure quick growth.

Beetroot A second application of NPK fertilizer should be given when the roots begin to swell to ensure continued growth.

Lettuce This salad crop benefits from liquid feeding.

Outdoor tomatoes With this crop the objective is to encourage flowering and fruit set rather than to stimulate excessive vegetable growth. No further feeding should therefore be given till the first fruits on the bottom truss have set. From then on the plants benefit from regular weekly waterings with a high potash liquid feed. Several good proprietary brands of liquid tomato feeds are available and these should be used in preference to general liquid feeds.

Tomatoes have a special need for magnesium and their leaves tend to yellow if additional quantities of this element are not supplied. One way of remedying this deficiency is to spray the plants at intervals with a solution of Epsom salts using 6g per litre (1 oz per gal). An alternative approach is to use a tomato liquid feed with added magnesium.

Trace element deficiencies These are uncommon in vegetable crops. Boron deficiency may, however, occur if excessive quantities of lime have been applied. This nutrient shortage shows up as dark concentric rings in beetroots, swedes and turnips. It can also cause cracking of celery stalks and hollow stems in brassicas. The remedy is to apply household borax at 17g per sq m (½ oz per sq yd), evenly in solution form, in early to mid spring (February–March).

These easily-recognizable deficiencies – in potassium (above, far left), magnesium (above left) and calcium (left) – can be prevented by using a good liquid feed

Effects of Fertilizers on Ornamentals

planting hole. A few handfuls of bone-meal can also be worked in at this stage to provide long-term supplies of phosphate. Similar fertilizer treatments are even more important in the case of trees planted on a patio. Here it is difficult to apply further fertilizer after the paving has been laid down. Once the tree is established, you need only give a light dressing of an NPK fertilizer each spring.

Shrubs
The great majority of shrubs grow reasonably happily in most soils. All benefit from the use of NPK fertilizer at planting and from annual fertilizer dressing each spring. As mentioned, flowering shrubs respond to high potash. In practice, the best way of meeting this requirement is to use a proprietary rose fertilizer.

Calcifuge shrubs
These are plants that normally only succeed when grown in acid soil – one with a pH of less than 7. Well-known examples are azalea, pieris, magnolia and camellia. Under alkaline conditions the roots of these plants have difficulty in taking up some nutrient from the soil. In particular they suffer from iron deficiency. Because of this the leaves turn yellow, then fall prematurely, and eventually the plant dies. Consequently it is not possible to grow this type of shrub in chalky or limey soil. In cases where the soil is approaching neutrality, however, calcifuges can be grown provided that the soil is drenched each spring with a solution of sequestered iron. This is a very special chemical that enables the roots to take up sufficient iron for its requirements. In addition to the sequestered iron treatment it is of course helpful to give a spring dressing of NPK.

Another approach to the problem of growing calcifuge shrubs where the soil is alkaline is to plant them in raised beds filled with peat. The peat used for this purpose needs to be the acid sphagnum, or moss, type, since the black sedge peat is generally alkaline. If this method of growing is used it is important to realize that the peat itself does not contain plant foods. So regular applications of fertilizers need to be given to support the plant growth. It is also important to mix in, slowly, supplies of trace elements. Suitable products are available from special-

Above: some ornamentals have a special need for magnesium or iron. Discoloured elm leaves indicate an iron deficiency

Below left: an azalea grown in over-alkaline soil; below: apple tree suffering from magnesium deficiency

There are basic elements that contribute towards healthy vegetable growth; here we look at these elements in relation to ornamental plants.

Trees, shrubs, roses, climbing plants, hardy perennials and bedding plants all benefit from being well fed. One way of assuring this is by the regular use of fertilizers. The effects of feeding on the growth of these types of plants, however, are less obvious than is the case with vegetables. Consequently this area of the garden tends to be neglected and the quality of ornamental plant display is often not as good as it should be.

With ornamentals the first essential is to get the soil into good shape. Unless this is done root growth will be restricted and the plants unable to benefit from the fertilizer. Then feeding needs to be adjusted to the growth habit of the plant. So it pays to know a little about what each type of plant requires.

Trees
These are often planted as decorative features in the lawn. This means that in the early stages the young tree can suffer from competition with the grass. So it is important not to plant them in too small a bed, and to mix a general NPK fertilizer into the soil/peat mixture used to fill in the

Potassium-deficient paeony (above) and manganese-deficient blackberry (below) may be cured by an NPK *dressing*

help the ripening of the wood. Roses, however, also have a special need for magnesium. This can be applied as Epsom salt, giving about 1 teaspoonful to the soil around each bush. This treatment needs to be given several times during the season. A simpler method therefore is to use a rose fertilizer containing magnesium in addition to NPK.

Climbers

The soil round house foundations and at the base of walls is generally less fertile than in the rest of the garden. So special care must be taken when planting climbers to improve the physical structure of the soil and to increase its fertility by putting fertilizer in the planting hole. Again, as for other shrubs, annual spring fertilizer dressings should be given to maintain active growth. Don't forget too that overhanging eaves may result in the soil near to the house becoming too dry. So watering is especially important.

Hardy perennials

Here again it is important to get the plants off to a good start by working peat, well-rotted compost or farmyard manure into the soil before planting. Fertilizer, too, should be worked in at this stage. Then in subsequent years all that is necessary is to give an overall treatment to the border using a fairly evenly-balanced NPK fertilizer. Even with this generous treatment, however, the clumps gradually become overcrowded. Consequently the plants should be dug out every three years or so and split up. The hard centres should be discarded and the border planted up again using the younger outward portions of the clumps. This operation is laborious but it is worthwhile. Also it offers an opportunity of correcting any deficiencies in the original preparation of the soil. Finally this replanting ensures that the plants really respond to the fertilizer treatments.

Bedding plants

Before planting out bedding plants, the bed should be forked over and the opportunity taken to work in some peat to ensure good root growth. A light dressing of an NPK fertilizer should then be raked in immediately before setting out the plants. This normally gets them off to a good start. If the plants seem slow to grow at first then they may benefit from foliar feeding. Later, when the roots are established, liquid feeds will maintain the continuity of blooming. The removal of dead blooms also prolongs the flowering period as it stops the growth being diverted into seed production.

ist garden chemical suppliers, but these materials are not in general distribution. An alternative is to mix some neutral or acid soil with the peat when preparing the raised bed.

Roses

Roses respond dramatically to a well-planned fertilizer programme. The modern hybrid rose puts on an enormous quantity of growth each year and so uses up a lot of plant food. Furthermore, unlike other shrubs, it is repeat flowering. That is to say it produces at least three flushes of growth each year and every flush ends in the production of flowers. Clearly the fertilizer usage needs to be planned so as to fit in with this special pattern of growth. This is best done by giving three applications: the first should be applied in spring after pruning, the second when the flower-buds are forming on the first flush of growth and the third when the second flush of blooms is developing. This approach ensures that adequate food supplies are available at the key growth stages. Consequently the quality of the blooms is maintained throughout the summer. A number of good proprietary rose fertilizers are readily available. All contain high levels of potash to encourage flowering and to

Making a Compost Heap

Waste not organic materials from the house or garden and want not for compost is a maxim worth following. Compost, when rotted down, will improve and maintain your soil by adding humus-forming matter, plant foods and beneficial bacteria.

Compost is not difficult or time-consuming to make. Certain types of plant and household waste can be used to make it. Suitable plant waste includes grass clippings, flower and vegetable stems that are not too tough, light hedge trimmings, wet peat, wet straw and annual weeds. Leaves can be used, but not in great quantities as they are more valuable for use as leaf mould. A separate bin can be kept in the kitchen for such household waste as tea leaves, vegetable trimmings, hair, egg shells and vacuum cleaner dust. Bonfire ashes, animal manure, and sawdust are also suitable.

Not suitable for the compost heap are coarse plant material such as cabbage stems and tree prunings, diseased plants, pernicious weeds like docks, dandelions, and bindweed roots, any dead plants on which weedkiller has been used, and cooked matter, such as meat or fish.

Ideal site

As a compost heap is not particularly sightly, it is best situated in the working part of the garden and screened from the house. It should be protected from hot sun or cold winds, but not be against a wall or hedge. An ideal site is beneath a tree. The shape of the heap can be circular or rectangular, although most people find a rectangular one easier to cope with. The best size to aim for is about 1m (3 ft) wide, 1½–2m (5–6 ft) long, and 1–1½m (3–5 ft) high when completed.

Construction

It pays to construct the site of the heap correctly, rather than tipping the waste straight onto the ground. First dig a shallow pit – about 15cm (6 in) deep. Place the soil on one side as you will need it later. Then put down in the pit an 8cm (3 in) layer of broken bricks or stones mixed with coarse tree prunings, woody cabbage stems, straw and similar tough plant material. These will help essential drainage and allow air penetration.

When the base is prepared, begin to build up the compost heap. This should be done roughly as follows:

Layer 1: about 15cm (6 in) of organic material.

Layer 2: a sprinkling of a proprietary compost accelerator according to the manufacturer's instructions. This should supply the essential bacteria, nitrogen and chalk necessary to break down the raw matter into usable compost.

Layer 3: a 2–3cm (1 in) layer of soil, taken from the dug-out heap.
These three layers are repeated until the heap reaches the required height.

Follow these rules for successful composting:
1 Always be sure that each layer of organic material is well firmed down (but not too tightly compressed) by treading on it or beating it flat with a spade blade.
2 If using grass clippings in large quantities, mix them with other materials or they will form a soggy mass in the heap.
3 Check from time to time to make sure that the heap is moist. If it has dried out, either sprinkle water over it or, preferably, hammer stakes into the heap to make holes and then pour water into the holes.
4 To finish off the heap, level the top and put a 2–5cm (1–2 in) thick layer of soil over the top and around the sides to act as a cover.

A properly made compost heap provides material to be used either for digging into the ground or for mulching. Mulch is a top dressing layer on the surface of the soil around the plants. The compost will be ready to be dug in after about 10–14 weeks in summer or 14–18 weeks in winter. When the compost is ready for use the heap will consist of a brownish black, crumbly, pleasant-smelling and easily handled material. If the heap doesn't seem to be rotting down well in the allotted time, something has gone wrong with the construction. If this happens, it is worth the trouble of digging a second shallow pit alongside and rebuilding the first heap into that,

Slotted wood bin

If you lack the space for a compost heap as described, a bin will also give you good results

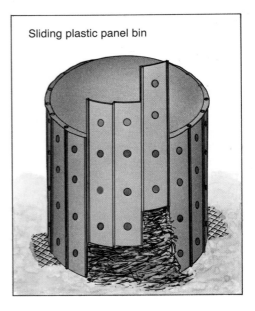

Sliding plastic panel bin

turning the top to bottom and sides to middle and following the sandwich layer principle again. In any case, as one heap is finished, a second one should be started so that there is always a supply of essential humus-forming material ready to add to the soil.

The method of compost-making described here is simple and cheap. If, however, you have a very small garden, it may be easier for you to buy a proprietary bin compost unit, which has its own instructions for use.

The Microclimate in your Garden

Every garden has to endure the general climate of the region in which it is situated, but within that region exposure to sunshine, wind or rain makes weather considerably different from one garden to another. Open hillsides facing south get more sunshine than gardens hemmed in by buildings, hilltops are windier than valleys, and gardens along the banks of rivers or lakes suffer more fog than those quite a short distance away. These inescapable peculiarities combined with cunning contrivance by ourselves create the individual 'microclimate' of a garden or even a corner of a garden.

Heat from the sun

The natural source of all warmth is the sun whose rays warm up any substance they strike. Water is partly transparent to sunshine so that the benefit of heat is spread over a large volume of water, raising its temperature very little in a short period. Glass, when clean, is almost entirely transparent to sunshine and it is objects underneath glass that warm up rather than glass itself. Other solids warm in the sunshine according to the materials of which they are made, and some of the best absorbers of heat in the garden are brick, paving stone and bare soil.

Although the sun is the biggest heat radiator we know, everything on earth is also a radiator in its own small way. On a sunny day, objects no sooner acquire heat from the sun than they re-radiate some for the benefit of anything nearby which hasn't done so well. Hence a south-facing terrace and house wall will be a definite hot spot on a sunny day because of heat radiating from the surfaces. Also vegetables, widely spaced in weed-free soil, will enjoy a warmer microclimate than a crowded flowerbed sited in a lawn.

Heat by conduction and convection

Heat is also distributed by conduction, through brick, downwards into soil and, particularly important, to the air that lies in contact with heated surfaces. Air so warmed becomes lighter and rises upwards to be replaced by colder air from above which then warms in turn. Gradu-

ally warmed air spreads throughout the garden by this convection method, even circulating to areas receiving no direct radiant heat from the sun. On cloudy days, air temperature is pre-determined by its past history and the amount of heating it has received in other parts of the world. Temperatures are similar throughout a garden, except perhaps for special very small areas. A chimney-breast wall can provide a favoured microclimate for a bush whose buds tend to get nipped by late spring frosts. It doesn't hurt so much to lose expensive heat from indoors through brick if you can use it to benefit the garden. But for the best result in creating a warm microclimate at that spot you must trap the heat under a polythene cover or lean-to, otherwise wind – which is only moving air – will whip it away before it accumulates.

The need for water

Wind is a thief of moisture as well as heat. All air contains water vapour, the actual amount depending upon whether its stock has been replenished by journeying across the sea or kept short by travelling across large expanses of land. At any particular temperature air has a maximum possible capacity for vapour and this capacity increases with rising temperature. Moreover, so long as its vapour content is under capacity, air is thirsty for more and drinks from whatever source it can find – washing on the line, soil, or the leaves of plants. Hence rising temperature on a sunny day, or an inherently dry air stream which come from the east, are both likely to denude a garden of moisture and it may be necessary to act the rain-god and alter the microclimate by artificial watering. The same necessity occurs on

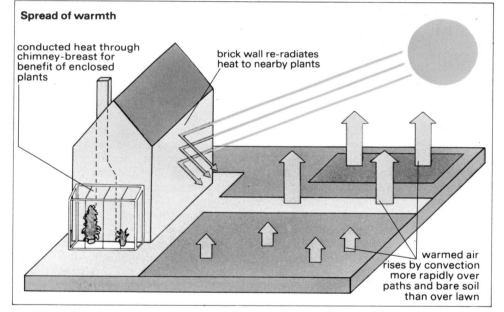

Spread of warmth

conducted heat through chimney-breast for benefit of enclosed plants

brick wall re-radiates heat to nearby plants

warmed air rises by convection more rapidly over paths and bare soil than over lawn

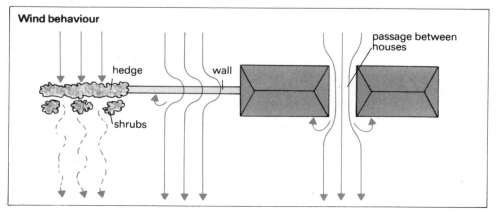

Wind behaviour

hedge

wall

passage between houses

shrubs

Above right: distribution of heat in the garden by conduction and convection
Right: wind control can affect a microclimate with noticeable results

even a cloudy day, if a strong wind, damp or dry, is blowing. That merely means that a great deal of air is passing very quickly and taking lots of gulps of moisture in the process. A strong wind is a blessing to dry out soil after a rainy spell, but in drought conditions it makes already bad conditions worse.

Protection against wind
If you add to these characteristics of wind its sheer brute strength and battering power, protection against it can be seen as a major objective in modifying the microclimate of a garden. Secure staking helps, not because it actually makes a garden less windy but because it tricks plants into thinking it is less windy by giving them extra strength to resist! The trouble is that wind cannot be stopped, only diverted. When it comes across a row of houses with passageways between, it funnels into the constriction and comes out of the exit with increased speed, rather like water forced through the nozzle of a hosepipe. If wind encounters a wall, it either goes round the corners or over the top, giving increased speed in those areas because extra air is crowding through. Moreover, wind eddies backwards in the relatively 'empty' space on the leeward side, sometimes with as nasty effect for plants situated there as if they had received the direct blast of air. A hedge or permeable fence gives better wind protection because it allows enough air through to prevent the eddy space behind, yet breaks the initial force of the blast.

Place for a wind barrier
The choice of site for a wind barrier may be obvious, like the end of a passageway which runs in the same direction as the most frequent winds. Or it may involve a difficult choice between incompatible factors. In Britain the coldest winds come from between north and east, the most drying winds from between north-east and south-east, gales come in any season from any direction but mainly from the western half of the compass. Damaging salt-laden winds in coastal gardens come from whichever direction faces the sea. You can't protect a whole garden from every direction unless you risk undue stagnation of damp air in wet seasons. Gardens on the shoreline have little choice and *must* protect against onshore wind, even if this means some deprivation of sunshine in western and southern districts. Gardens in the middle of such coastal towns possibly have enough buildings between them and the sea to act as a preliminary barrier and have too

great a need for sunshine for you to dare erect another barrier except against cold north winds. East coast gardeners in Britain have less heart-searching to make because by protecting against north and east winds they deal with both the cold, the dry and the salt winds without detracting from their quota of sun.

Glass as a barrier
The ultimate cossetting against the wind is to enclose with glass, remembering that if the wind blows in the same direction as a line of cloches the upwind end must be firmly closed to prevent air funnelling through. Moreover, if it is windy and sunny a watchful eye must be kept for the 'greenhouse effect' on air temperature. Air beneath the glass warms on contact with the heating surface of the ground, and if none can escape the same air gets heated over and over again and air temperatures and moisture evaporation rate increase very rapidly. Such excessively hot microclimates have killed children and dogs left in parked cars in the sun and can even more easily cause the collapse of plants. Some ventilation is essential, and perhaps an opaque wash over the glass as well would help the atmosphere in high summer.

Walls for protection
Although it is relatively easy to make the microclimate of a garden wetter than the general weather pattern ensures, there is little that can be done to prevent excess water in a rainy season except by enclosure and substituting artificial watering for rain. But it is helpful to remember that walls give considerable protection against rain unless it is driving straight onto the wall, and therefore beds alongside walls have different microclimates on all sides of a house. A wall facing south-east strikes a happy compromise between adequate sunshine without excessive rain, but the soil beneath may need topping up with water even in a very wet season. North walls are always very dry, though curious things can alter the microclimate even there. For instance, if you have plants under an overflow pipe, they will flourish better than the others because of their built-in 'rainfall'.

Heat stored at night
When the sun sets at night, gardens lose their principal income of heat but continue as effective radiators themselves, expending heat previously put into storage. On cloudy nights heat radiated from the ground is partly absorbed by the cloud and partly reflected back again so

that temperatures on earth do not fall excessively. But on cloudless nights nearly all radiated heat is lost to space and ground temperature falls rapidly. The air near the ground cools in consequence and thereby becomes heavier. But if a strong wind is blowing the cooled air gets whipped away by turbulence before it suffers an undue fall in temperature.

Warmth at the top
With calm conditions, however, the cooled heavy air hangs stolidly over level ground, continuing to cool as the ground beneath gets still colder. Only gradually is the fall in temperature communicated to the layers of air higher above the ground, resulting in an inversion of the usual temperature pattern. The microclimate enjoyed by the tops of trees is warmer than that experienced by the flowerbeds, a fact that saves much fruit blossom in the ground frosts of early spring.

On sloping ground, heavy cooling air obeys gravity and slithers down to the lowest area, thus creating a down-slope wind of its own. Valleys and hollows become receptacles for the coldest air and it helps create a warmer microclimate in a garden if an easy exit can be ensured for this draining cold air. Keep hedge bottoms free of dead leaves and sticks and set fences or gates a little above ground if they are at the bottom of a slope.

Dew-point
When air cools its capacity for water vapour decreases, even though the actual vapour content has been determined by its past travels. Consequently, cooling air eventually reaches a temperature called dew-point at which its *actual* vapour content is the same as the maximum possible. Air is then saturated and if any further cooling occurs, dew forms on the ground where the air is coldest, or, if dew-point is below 0°C (32°F), hoar frost forms. This is a frequent, if intermittent, feature of most British gardens during the winter and so it is not usually considered worthwhile keeping non-hardy plants outdoors. But in spring gambles have to be taken if a garden is ever to get into summer shape, and frost is possible even up to early mid summer (early June) in some inland areas away from the moderating influence of the sea. The most risky occasions are calm, clear nights when the air is also dry. That means that air temperature can fall far, perhaps down to 0°C (32°F) before any condensation occurs. Though some plants can bear a temperature a degree or so below freezing, such knife-edge conditions are obviously worrying.

Fog versus frost

On still, clear nights when the airstream is moist through some considerable depth, perhaps after a long journey across the sea, a blessed frost protection comes in unpleasant disguise – fog. Very little cooling soon reduces damp air to dew-point temperature through quite a considerable thickness, and the resultant fog blanket prevents any further radiation heat loss and fall in air temperature. While it is likely that greenhouses and cloches will be firmly closed against such fog, you must be on guard against rapidly-changing microclimates under glass next day. A spring sun may clear the previous night's fog during mid morning when many gardeners are away from home. The heat trapped under glass will cause a rapid rise in temperature and arrangements must be made for greenhouses and cold frames to be opened by hand if you are not fortunate enough to have automatic ventilation.

Conserving warmth

Brisk wind and damp air are not, however, weather features which an amateur gardener is likely to be able to summon up for the whole garden, though Californian fruit farmers are having considerable success in manufacturing fog with very fine overhead jets of water. The alternative is to cover individual plants on the same principles that we clothe ourselves. Cover them to prevent loss of existing heat and do it in the late afternoon when there is still worthwhile warmth to conserve.

Glass is only adequate on its own for a very short period and serves best with an additional opaque covering of sacking or blinds. Paper hats for small plants like tomatoes may be adequate and even wigwams of twigs are better than nothing because they cut down exposure to the clear sky. Trees and house walls, likewise, protect against radiation heat loss. All artificial covers must enclose the *whole* plant and not just the base.

Soil is a deep storage unit of heat accumulated during the previous season and particularly after a mild winter it may still have some reserve heat left that can be put to good use in counteracting a ground frost. If this mite of heat is insulated from the foliage by a cover over the soil its value is lost – rather like having a hotwater bottle in bed under the blanket and then lying on *top* of the blanket yourself! Cover completely, cover in good time and, since water is a good conductor of heat, keep the soil moist and clear of interference by weeds or mulch. The best you can do to ameliorate the micro-

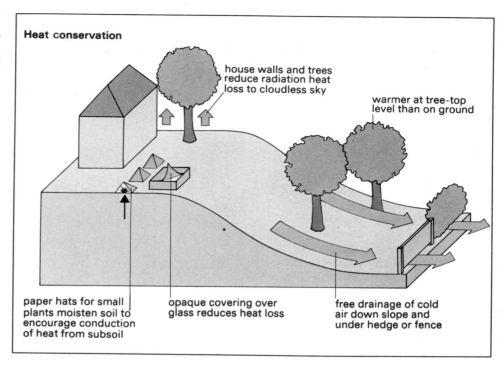

Heat conservation

house walls and trees reduce radiation heat loss to cloudless sky

warmer at tree-top level than on ground

paper hats for small plants moisten soil to encourage conduction of heat from subsoil

opaque covering over glass reduces heat loss

free drainage of cold air down slope and under hedge or fence

Above: some of the methods used to conserve warmth at night-time

climate of large fruit trees is by initial good choice of a site high up on a slope, then keeping air drainage underneath the trees unimpeded by long grass or bushes.

Methods of protection against short frosts are useless when cold air comes with north or east winds because then air temperature can be below freezing level for days on end at all heights that matter to the garden. The cold air-streams are often accompanied by low cloud so there is no chance of the sun raising temperatures during the day. Frost bites deep into the ground and penetrates cloches, cold frames or single-boarded sheds, and the only way to offer frost-shy plants or stored tubers warmer conditions is to take them into an artificially-heated greenhouse or your home.

Treatment indoors

Warmth alone, however, does not make a healthy microclimate and there are dangerous draughts and droughts indoors that need careful watching. The colder it is outside, the faster will the cold air pour through cracks around doors or windows into the cosy warmth indoors. Colloquially we call such draughts 'howling winds' and that is exactly how they will seem to plants standing nearby on windowsills. If you really want to bestow an advantageous microclimate, double-glaze windows (even with polythene in the greenhouse), or put plants somewhere out of the 'wind'. Then think of moisture requirements. When air is warmed to the

extent necessary in very cold weather to make indoor living comfortable, its capacity and thirst for more water increases enormously.

Pot plants provide a ready supply of moisture and it is essential to keep pace with the thieving air by replenishing water. Humidifiers in a centrally-heated room greatly add to the comfort of human beings as well as plants, and you can improve the microclimate of the plants even more by standing them on pebbles almost covered by water in a container of the same depth as the plant pot. The water evaporates steadily into the dry air, enveloping the plant in moist air before it disperses into the room. And as a temporary moist microclimate for wilting cut flowers, try wrapping them in a cylinder of water-soaked newspaper. Half an hour's treatment works wonders on drooping miniature roses.

Watering in the Garden

Plants need water for many reasons. Seeds will not germinate without water and plants can only use the nutrients in the soil if they are in soluble form. Water gives the plant its shape and stiffness; without it the plant becomes limp. If the water loss becomes too great the stomata (holes) in the surface of the 'skin' close and the basic plant processes come to a halt. You must, therefore, ensure that plants always have enough water for all their needs.

During dry weather you must give your plants the water that nature has failed to provide. Too often, however, the mistake is made of watering irregularly and in insufficient quantity. It is essential to give enough water to penetrate the soil down to the layer where the plant roots are growing. If you only sprinkle the surface, the water will simply evaporate in the heat of the sun.

How much water?

Apply sufficient water to penetrate the soil to a depth of at least 15cm (6 in) – preferably more. This means applying at least 2–3cm (1 in) of water, depending on the soil type. The lighter and more sandy the soil, the deeper this amount of water will penetrate. If you are using a sprinkler, you can measure the amount of water being applied by placing a number of tin cans over the area being watered. When there is 2–3cm (1 in) of water on the bottom of the tins you will know it is time to turn off the sprinkler.

If you water with a hosepipe then you will have to dig down into the soil with a hand trowel to see how far the water has penetrated.

Start watering before the soil dries out to any great depth; a good guide is when the top 2–5cm (1–2 in) is becoming dry. In hot, summer weather you may have to water at least once a week.

It is usually best to apply water in the evening, as then none will be evaporated by the sun and it will penetrate the soil to a good depth.

Many people do not realize that wind is a major drying agent (especially in spring

Oscillating sprinkler that will deliver an even spray into a corner

A rotary type sprinkler that waters in a regular circular pattern

and early summer), so watering will be necessary after windy weather.

Sprinklers and hoses

Applying all this water will be very time-consuming if you have to rely on a hosepipe alone. It is therefore a good idea to attach a sprinkler of some kind to the end and let it distribute the water.

There are many types on the market to suit all pockets. The cheapest are those with no moving parts (mini-sprinklers), but which produce a fine circular spray from a static nozzle. Often the base of these is equipped with a spike which you push into the ground to hold the sprinkler firmly.

Rotating sprinklers are slightly more expensive. They have two adjustable nozzles on an arm which is spun round by water pressure, giving a circular pattern. These are probably the most popular for private gardens.

The more sophisticated oscillating sprinklers apply water in a square or rectangular pattern. A tubular bar with a row of nozzles (non-adjustable) moves backwards and forwards, watering a very large area. It is worked by water pressure. Some can be adjusted to water a small or large area.

Sprinkler hoses are perforated plastic hoses of various kinds which are connected to the main hosepipe and produce a gentle spray of water along their complete length. One of these can be laid along rows of crops, or between plants.

You will, of course, want a good reinforced plastic or PVC hosepipe; a 13mm ($\frac{1}{2}$ in) diameter hose is a suitable size for general use.

A perforated hose sprinkler, handy for long borders

Watering vegetables

Most vegetables benefit greatly from regular watering, especially crops like runner, French and broad beans, peas, marrows, lettuce, radish, cucumbers and tomatoes. Vegetables such as cabbages and other greenstuff, and root crops like potatoes and carrots, can get by without regular watering, although their yields will not be so heavy.

All newly-transplanted vegetables must be well watered in if the ground is dry and then kept moist until established. You can water these individually with a watering can.

Germinating seeds
Seeds must be kept moist to encourage them to germinate. This is especially true of the modern pelleted seeds, which will fail to grow if they lack sufficient moisture.

Fruit trees and bushes
Fruit trees, provided they are well established, will not come to much harm if you do not water during dry spells, but the fruits may be smaller than normal. However, black, red and whitecurrants, raspberries, strawberries, gooseberries, blackberries, loganberries and other hybrid berries really do need watering in dry weather if they are to crop well.

Above: use a fine rose for watering cuttings and seedlings

Flowers in beds and containers
It may not be possible to water everything in the garden, especially in a very dry season when there may be restrictions on the use of sprinklers in the garden. If this is the case, the flower garden must take third place – after fruit and vegetables,

which you will be growing to supplement the family budget. However, flowers in containers (such as tubs, troughs, hanging baskets and window boxes) will soon die if not watered regularly. These dry out rapidly in hot weather and may well need watering twice a day – in the morning and again in the evening.

Watering the lawn
Lawns rapidly turn brown in dry weather, although they will green up again once the rains start. To keep a lawn green in the summer you will need to begin watering before it starts to turn brown and continue at weekly intervals, or more frequently, thereafter. Remember also not to cut a lawn too short in dry weather – so raise the mower blades.

Mulching the soil
There is a method of conserving moisture in the soil which will enable you to cut down on watering. It is known as 'mulching' and consists of placing a 5–8cm (2–3 in) layer of organic matter around and between plants – covering the root area. Use garden compost, well-rotted farmyard manure, leaf mould, spent hops, straw, grass mowings or sawdust.

Another method is to use black polythene sheeting. To anchor it to the ground, bury the edges in 'nicks' made with a spade in the soil; then place a few stones or bricks on top. You can buy rolls of special black mulching polythene.

All plants benefit from being mulched, for moisture is conserved and so they do not dry out so rapidly. If you have to limit mulching, however, then concentrate on your vegetables and fruits, rather than on your flowerbeds.

Left: mulching trees and shrubs with compost will conserve moisture

Seed Sowing and Pricking Out

Pricking out seedlings with a dibber

Many different plants are raised from seed sown in containers in a greenhouse: summer bedding plants, flowering pot plants, and vegetables like tomatoes, lettuce, celery, cucumbers and marrows. But the techniques of sowing and subsequent care are similar.

Late winter and spring is the main period for most sowings; more precise timing is usually given on the seed packets. A heated greenhouse, or a propagator, is necessary for germination (that is, starting seeds into life).

Seed trays and pots
Seed trays, approximately 5–6cm (2–2½ in) deep, are available in either wood or plastic. Plastic ones last for many years,

if well looked after, and are easy to clean. Hygienic conditions are important if you are to raise healthy seedlings, so clean the seed trays thoroughly before use.

For very small quantities of seed use plastic pots 9 or 13cm (3½ or 5 in) in diameter. These are also recommended for very large individual seeds, such as marrows and cucumbers. Again, wash all pots carefully before use.

Types of compost
Garden soil is not a very suitable medium in which to grow seedlings as it is full of weed seeds and harmful organisms, and it may not provide the correct conditions required by the seed for successful germination. Instead, buy one of the ready-mixed seed-sowing composts, the most popular being John Innes Seed Compost,

consisting of loam, peat, sand, super-phosphate and ground chalk.

Alternatively there are many brands of seed compost which consist only of peat with added fertilizers; these are known as 'soilless' composts because they do not contain loam. When using soilless compost you have to be especially careful with watering, for if it dries out it can be difficult to moisten again; over-watering may saturate it and cause the seeds to rot. With a little care, however, soilless compost gives excellent results.

Building in drainage
Be sure that surplus water is able to drain from all containers. When using John Innes composts it is essential to

Place a layer of crocks in the bottom of flower pots to provide drainage

place a layer of crocks (broken clay flower pots or stones) at least 13mm ($\frac{1}{2}$ in) deep over the bottom of the pot. Cover the crocks with a little roughage, such as rough peat. If you use seed trays, crocks are not needed, just cover the drainage slits with some roughage.

Soilless compost can be used without any crocking – unless it is going in clay flower pots, in which case you must cover the large hole at the bottom with crocks.

Once you have arranged the drainage material add the compost to about 13mm ($\frac{1}{2}$ in) below the top of the tray or pot, to allow room for watering. Firm it gently all over with your fingertips, paying particular attention to the sides, ends and corners of seed trays. Make sure that the surface is level by pressing gently with a flat piece of wood that just fits into the tray or pot. Soilless compost should not be pressed hard but merely shaken down by tapping the container on a hard surface or lightly firming with the wood.

Very tiny seeds (like lobelia and begonia) should be sown on a fine surface. So before pressing down, sieve a layer of compost over the surface using a very small-mesh sieve. Alternatively you can sprinkle a thin layer of silver sand over the compost before sowing. Do not use builder's sand as this contains materials toxic to plants.

Water the compost lightly, using a fine rose on the watering can, before you sow.

Sowing the seeds

Seeds must be sown thinly and evenly otherwise the seedlings will be over-crowded and you will find it difficult to separate them during pricking out (transplanting). They will also have thin, weak stems and be prone to diseases like 'damping off'.

Small seed is usually sown broadcast (scattered) over the surface of the compost. Take a small quantity of seed in the palm of one hand – just sufficient to sow a tray or pot. Hold your hand about 30cm (12 in) above the container and move it to and fro over the surface, at the same time tapping it with the other hand to release the seeds slowly. If you move your hand first backwards and forwards and then side to side this will help to spread the seeds evenly. You may find it easier to hold the seeds in a piece of paper, instead of in your hand.

It is difficult to sow very small seeds evenly, some being as fine as dust, but if you mix them with soft, dry, silver sand (using 1 part seeds to 1 part sand) this helps to bulk them up and makes them easier to handle.

Large seeds, which are easily handled, can be 'space-sown' – that is placed individually, and at regular intervals, on the surface of the compost. Tomato seed, for instance, can be treated in this way.

Very large seeds, such as cucumbers, peas and various beans, are best sown at two per 9cm (3$\frac{1}{2}$ in) pot. If you use peat pots, they can later be planted, complete with young plant, into the final pot or open ground. When they have germinated, remove the weaker seedling, leaving the stronger one to grow on.

Pelleted seeds

This term describes seeds that are individually covered with a layer of clay which is often mixed with some plant foods. They are easily handled and can be space-sown in boxes or pots. The compost around pelleted seeds must remain moist as it is moisture which breaks down the coating and allows the seeds to germinate.

After sowing

Seeds should be covered with a layer of compost equal to the diameter of the seed. It is best to sieve compost over them, using a fine-mesh sieve. However, do not cover very small or dust-like seeds with compost as they will probably fail to germinate.

If you use John Innes or another loam-

1 *Cover drainage materials with compost, firming it gently with the fingertips*

2 *Level the surface of the compost by pressing with a flat piece of wood*

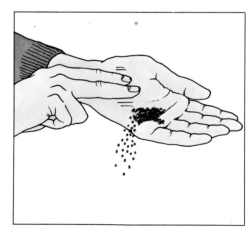

3 *Scatter a little seed into tray by tapping it gently from your open hand*

4 *With large seeds, sow two in a small pot and remove the weaker seedling*

Sieve compost over seeds

Stand tray in water till surface looks moist

Use a dibber to lift the seedlings and transfer them to a new tray where they will have room to grow in

containing compost the seeds should then be watered, either using a very fine rose on the watering can or by standing the containers in a tray of water until the surface becomes moist. (This latter method is not advisable for loam-less composts as they tend to float; moisten them well before sowing the seed.) Allow the containers to drain before placing them in the greenhouse.

A good, or even better, alternative to plain water is a solution of Cheshunt Compound, made up according to the directions on the tin. This is a fungicide which prevents diseases such as damping off attacking seedlings.

Aids to germination

Place the pots or trays either on a bench in a warm greenhouse or in an electrically-heated propagator. Most seeds need a temperature of 15°–18°C (60–65°F) for good germination. The containers can be covered with a sheet of glass that, in turn, is covered with brown paper to prevent the sun's warmth drying out the compost. Turn the glass over each day to prevent excess condensation building up on the inside. Water the compost whenever its surface starts to become dry. As soon as germination commences remove the covering of glass and paper, for the seedlings then require as much light as possible if they are to grow into strong, healthy plants.

Pricking out

Once the seedlings are large enough to handle easily prick them out into trays or boxes to give them enough room to grow. Generally, standard-size plastic or wooden seed trays are used that are 6cm (2½ in) deep; there is no need to put drainage material in the base. The trays are filled with compost in the way described for seed-sowing, again leaving space for watering. A suitable compost would be John Innes Potting Compost No. 1 which can be bought ready-mixed. It consists of loam, peat, coarse sand, John Innes base fertilizer and ground chalk. Alternatively, use one of the soil-less potting composts that contains peat, or peat and sand, plus fertilizers. Make sure the compost is moist before you start pricking out.

You will need a dibber for this job – either a pencil or a piece of wood of similar shape. With this lift a few seedlings at a time from the box or pot, taking care not to damage the roots. Handle the seedlings by the seed leaves – the first pair of leaves formed. Never hold them by the stems which are easily damaged at this stage.

Spacing out

The number of seedlings per standard-size box will vary slightly according to their vigour. Generally 40 per box is a good spacing (5 rows of 8). For less vigorous plants you could increase this to 54 per box (6 rows of 9).

Mark out the position of the seedlings with the dibber before commencing, ensuring equal spacing each way. Next make a hole, with the dibber, which should be deep enough to allow the roots to drop straight down. Place the seedling in the hole so that the seed leaves are at soil level, and then firm it in by pressing the soil gently against it with the dibber.

If only a few seeds have been sown in pots each seedling could be pricked out into an individual 7cm (3 in) pot. But if you have single seedlings, such as marrows, already started in 9cm (3½ in) pots, these will not need to be moved.

After pricking out, water in the seedlings (with a fine rose on the watering can) preferably using Cheshunt Compound. Then place them on the greenhouse bench or on a shelf near to the glass, as maximum light is essential. Continue to water whenever the soil surface appears dry.

Windowsill propagation

If you do not have a greenhouse, heated frame, or propagator, you can still raise seedlings in the house. Ideally the germination conditions should be as similar as possible to those which are recommended for greenhouse cultivation. Windowsills are the best places for raising seeds, and if they are wide ones you can use standard-size seed trays.

However it is usually possible to fit a few pots onto the narrowest of windowsills. For best results use trays or pots that are fitted with propagator tops. The temperature on the sill must not drop below the average room temperature and south- or west-facing sills are obviously best.

Make sure the seedlings are never deprived of daylight or allowed to get cold at night. Never draw the curtains across between the plants and the warm room air on cold nights, if necessary bring them into the room. Finally, to maintain strong and even growth, turn all pots and trays around every day.

Use a pot with a propagator top when starting off seedlings on a windowsill

Potting Off and On

Before placing a pot-bound plant in its new pot, carefully remove old drainage crocks from the base of the rootball

The basic terms used in potting are 'potting off', when young rooted cuttings or seedlings are moved from trays into pots, and 'potting on', when the more advanced plants are transferred to bigger pots.

Nowadays plastic pots are generally used in preference to clay, but whichever type you have ensure that they are clean and dry before using them.

POTTING OFF

As soon as cuttings have developed a good root system they should be carefully lifted from their trays and put into individual pots about 7·5–9cm (3–3½ in) in diameter. When seedlings are large enough to handle easily they can be treated in the same way (as an alternative to pricking out into trays).

For this first potting, use a fairly weak compost, such as J.I. No 1, or an equivalent soilless type consisting of loam, peat, coarse sand, John Innes base fertilizer and ground chalk.

Allowing for drainage

Drainage material is not necessary in plastic pots as the holes are devised so that the compost does not leak. Furthermore, there is a trend towards using less drainage material in the bottom of small clay pots. When there are some drainage holes provided, place a few crocks (pieces of broken clay pots or stones) over the drainage holes and cover with a thin layer of roughage such as coarse peat or partially-rotted leaf mould. If you are using soilless compost, crocks or drainage materials are not normally necessary. Place a layer of compost over the drainage material and firm lightly with your fingers.

Transferring the plants

Hold the rooted cuttings or seedlings in the centre of the pot, with the roots well spread out, and trickle compost all around until it is slightly higher than the rim of the pot. Give the pot a sharp tap on the bench to settle the compost well down and lightly firm all round with your fingers. Make sure the compost is pushed right down to the bottom.

Some soilless composts, however, require little or no firming, so check the manufacturer's instructions first.

Remember to leave about 13mm (½ in) between the surface of the soil and the rim of the pot to allow room for watering.

After potting off, water the plants thoroughly, using a fine rose on the watering can, to settle them in further. Then they can be returned to the greenhouse bench.

POTTING ON

Plants need potting on to prevent them becoming 'pot-bound' (when the roots are packed very tightly in the pot). If this happens the plants will suffer from lack of food, growth will be poor and they will dry out very rapidly and require frequent watering.

However, it is worthwhile noting that some plants, such as pelargoniums, are more floriferous (bear more flowers) when slightly pot-bound.

Plants should be moved to the next size of pot, for instance from a 9cm (3½ in) to a 13cm (5 in), from a 13cm (5 in) to a 15cm (6 in) and so on. The reason for moving only to the next size pot is that plants dislike a large volume of soil around their roots because they cannot absorb water from all of it and, therefore, it is liable to remain wet. This can result in root rot and the possible death of the plant. Small moves allow plants to put out new roots quickly.

Composts and drainage

Richer composts (those containing more plant foods) are generally used for potting on. If you prefer the John Innes type, then use No 2, which contains twice as much fertilizer and chalk as No 1. Some plants (for example chrysanthemums,

To pot on a pot-bound plant: **1** *place crocks and drainage material in bottom of larger pot, then carefully remove plant from old pot;* **2** *half-fill new pot with compost;* **3** *hold plant in centre of pot, add more compost to within 2cm (½ in) of rim;* **4** *firm all round plant*

tomatoes and strawberries for fruiting under glass) like an even richer compost, such as J.I. No 3 – particularly when they are moved into their final size of pot).

Drainage material, as described under potting off, is generally advisable when using soil composts in pots that are 13cm (5 in) or larger. A layer of crocks about 2–3cm (1 in) deep should be sufficient, plus roughage.

Repotting the plant
Remove the plant from its pot by turning it upside-down and tapping the rim of the pot on the edge of a bench. The rootball should then slide out intact. On no account disturb this ball of roots and soil, but remove old crocks, if any, from the base. Scrape off any moss or weeds on the surface with an old wooden plant label or similar object.

Place enough soil in the new pot so that, when the plant is placed on it, the top of the rootball is about 13mm (½ in) from the top of the pot. This will allow for a light covering of compost with room for subsequent watering. Firm the compost lightly with your fingers and then stand the plant in the centre of the

new pot. Trickle fresh compost all round the rootball until you reach the top of the pot. Give the pot a sharp tap on the bench to get the compost well down and firm it all round.

If you are using soilless composts, follow the maker's instructions for firming. You will probably need to add more compost to reach the desired height. Finally, water in the plants, using a fine rose on the watering can.

Potting on is best done when plants are growing actively in spring and summer – or in the autumn, although growth will then be slowing down. Plants potted in spring and summer will quickly root into the new compost because of the warmer weather.

Taking Cuttings

One of the most exciting skills in gardening is to know how to take cuttings. When you can do this, and understand the principles behind the method, you no longer need to buy house plants, shrubs or perennials from a nursery, and you can replace elderly plants in your flowerbeds that are past their prime. And if you have friends who grow plants that you particularly covet, it is easy to persuade them to let you take a cutting.

A cutting is a part of a plant—a piece of stem, leaf or root—which is induced to form roots of its own and thus develop into a young plant that is identical with its parent.

Many plants can be propagated from cuttings but the type of cutting to prepare depends on the plant. A wide range from hardy shrubs to greenhouse plants can be increased from softwood cuttings. These are prepared from very soft young shoots early in the year, generally in the period from late spring to mid summer (April to June), although some may be taken even earlier than this.

Cuttings, whether softwood or any other type, must be prepared with a very

8cm (3 in) in length, and should be cut cleanly just below a leaf joint, or node. Such a cutting is generally known as a 'nodal' cutting.

The lower leaves should be carefully cut off as close to the stem as possible. The bases of the cuttings can then be dipped into a proprietary hormone rooting powder or liquid to encourage rapid root formation.

Softwood cuttings are liable to lose water very quickly and wilt, so they must be inserted in the rooting medium as quickly as possible. The usual compost for rooting is a mixture of equal parts of moist sphagnum peat and coarse horticultural sand.

A small number of cuttings can be rooted in pots of a convenient size, but larger quantities should be inserted in seed trays. The container should be filled with compost to within 13mm ($\frac{1}{2}$ in) of the rim and firmed moderately well with the fingers. Cuttings are placed in holes made with a dibber – a piece of wood shaped rather like a blunt pencil. In fact, a pencil makes a good dibber. The base of each cutting should be in close contact with the bottom of the hole. Firm in with the fingers and when the container is full water with a fine rose on the watering can.

Softwood cuttings of hardy herbaceous perennial plants such as delphinium, lupin, phlox, chrysanthemum, gaillardia and scabious, and of half-hardy perennials like dahlia and glasshouse chrysanthemum, are prepared and inserted in the same way. Remove young shoots when 8cm (3 in) long, from as close to the crown of the plant as possible.

Other plants that can be raised from softwood cuttings are tender greenhouse plants such as begonia, coleus, fuchsia, impatiens and tradescantia. Cuttings of fuchsia can be prepared by cutting the base between two nodes or joints—these are known as 'internodal' cuttings.

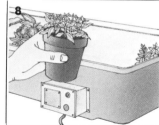

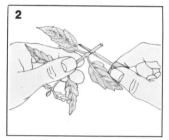
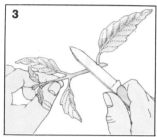
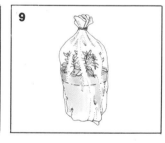

Softwood cuttings: 1 cut shoot from plant with sharp knife or razor; 2 trim cutting cleanly to just below base of leaf joint; 3 cut off lower leaves as close to the stem as possible; 4 dip base of cutting in proprietary hormone rooting powder; 5 using dibber, insert cutting in compost, made of moist sphagnum peat and coarse horticultural sand; 6 firm round cutting; 7 water well in, using fine spray on watering can; 8 place in propagator or mist unit or, 9 put pot in polythene bag

sharp knife or razor blade to ensure clean cuts. Ragged cuts resulting from using a blunt knife may take too long to heal, and could eventually result in the cutting rotting instead of making roots.

Softwood cuttings
Hardy shrubs that can be propagated from softwoods include weigela, deutzia, philadelphus, buddleia, caryopteris, hypericum and many other deciduous kinds. The cuttings of these can be about

Growing conditions
All softwood cuttings need plenty of warmth in which to root, and a humid or moist atmosphere. The simplest method of providing these conditions is to enclose a pot of cuttings in a polythene bag, which should be tied at the top, or place a jam jar over the cuttings, and stand it on a windowsill in a warm room, preferably above a radiator. A more sophisticated approach is to invest in an electrically heated propagating case, which is generally placed on a greenhouse bench. This

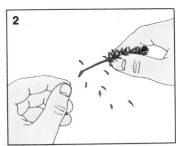

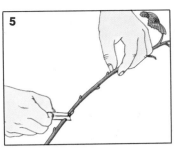

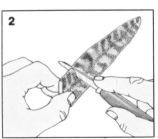

Semi-ripe cuttings:
1 *remove lower stems;*
2 *rub off lower leaves;*
3 *insert cuttings in compost*
Hardwood cuttings:
4 *cut ripe or woody shoot;*
5 *trim to four or five buds;*
6 *put cuttings in prepared,*
V-shaped trench, replace soil
and firm well in

should be set to give a temperature of 52°C (70°F).

The covers should be removed for an hour or two, several times a week, to allow the containers to dry off, because a great amount of condensation forms in these enclosed conditions.

The most adventurous way of rooting cuttings is to install a mist-propagation unit in your greenhouse. This provides heat at the base of the cuttings and sprays the leaves intermittently with water, which prevents the cuttings from wilting and dying. Reasonably simple and cheap units are available to amateur gardeners.

Some softwoods can be rooted simply by standing them in jars of water on a warm windowsill indoors. Plants which respond to this treatment include coleus, fuchsia, impatiens, tradescantia and zebrina – all popular house plants.

Semi-ripe cuttings

Many plants can be prepared from semi-ripe (or semi-mature) cuttings. These are prepared from shoots which are ripening or hardening at the base but are still soft at the tip. The time to take these is late summer to late autumn (July to October).

Evergreen and deciduous shrubs, heathers, conifers and half-hardy perennials like pelargonium (geranium), heliotrope and gazania, can be increased from semi-ripe cuttings.

Cuttings generally vary in length from some 10–15cm (4–6 in), but those of heathers should be only 5cm (2 in) long. These can simply be pulled off the plant, whereas cuttings of other subjects must be nodal and prepared with a knife.

Growing conditions

Preparation and insertion are the same as for softwoods, but less heat is needed for rooting. A cold frame makes an ideal rooting environment, but of course if you have a propagating case or mist unit then root them in these.

Hardwood cuttings

Hardwood cuttings, which are inserted in early and mid winter (November to December), need no heat at all to root. Common examples of shrubs and soft fruits raised from these are privet, willow, shrubby dogwood, Chinese honeysuckle, blackcurrant, redcurrant and gooseberry.

Choose current year's shoots which are completely ripe or woody and cut them into 23–30cm (9–12 in) lengths with sharp secateurs. Cut just above a bud at the top and just below at the base. With redcurrants and gooseberries remove all the buds except the top three or four. Dip the base of the cutting in a hormone rooting powder or liquid.

The cuttings are inserted to two-thirds of their length in a V-shaped trench made with a spade in a sheltered well-drained spot outdoors. Firm them in well. They will be well rooted by the following autumn (September).

Leaf cuttings

Some house, and greenhouse, plants are propagated from leaf cuttings in spring. With peperomia, saintpaulia, strepto-carpus and gloxinia use a whole leaf with

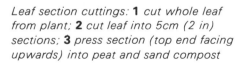

Leaf section cuttings: **1** *cut whole leaf from plant;* **2** *cut leaf into 5cm (2 in) sections;* **3** *press section (top end facing upwards) into peat and sand compost*

Whole leaf cuttings: **4** *cut leaf from plant;* **5** *insert whole leaf-stalk into peat and sand compost, leaving leaf-blade exposed;* **6** *firm compost round cutting*

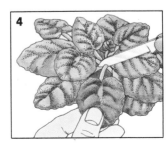

the leaf-stalk attached. The complete leaf-stalk is inserted in a peat and sand compost so that you leave only the leaf-blade exposed.

In the case of a plant like *Sansevieria trifasciata* (Mother-in-law's tongue), one of the long leaves should be cut into 5cm (2 in) sections. Each section is pressed into peat and sand compost to about half its length. Make sure you insert each section the right way up.

Rex begonia can be propagated by removing an entire leaf, cutting through the main veins in several places on the underside and laying the leaf, top side uppermost, on the surface of a tray of compost. Hold the leaf down with small stones. Young plants will form where you have made the cuts.

Like softwood cuttings, leaf cuttings need plenty of warmth and humidity to enable them to root.

Leaf-bud cuttings
A leaf-bud cutting is a portion of stem about 2·5cm (1 in) long, with an entire leaf attached at the top, and a bud in the axil (the point where the leaf joins the stem). Rubber plant, camellia, clematis, passion flower and ivy can be propagated by this method, which should be carried out in late spring (April). Insert cuttings so that the leaf only is above the compost and root in warm, humid conditions.

Eye cuttings
Grape vines and their close relations (parthenocissus and ampelopsis) are propagated from eye cuttings in mid winter (December). You will probably need a propagating case for this method as a base temperature of 52°C (70°F) is required for rooting. Use well-ripened or hardened current year's wood. Cut it into 4cm (1½ in) sections, each with a dormant 'eye' or bud in the centre. Remove a thin slice of wood on the opposite side to the bud. These cuttings are pressed horizontally into pots of peat and sand compost, with the buds uppermost, and just sufficiently deep to ensure that they remain stable. Water in and place in the rooting environment.

Pipings
Pinks are raised from a special type of cutting known as a piping. In late summer or early autumn (July or August) pull out the tops of young shoots: they should snap out cleanly just above a leaf joint or node. Each one should be left with three or four pairs of leaves, after the lower leaves have been carefully pulled off. Using a dibber, insert the pipings around the edge of a small pot containing peat and sand compost. Water well in and then place in a cold frame to root.

Root cuttings
Finally, root cuttings can be used to propagate shrubs like rhus, sambucus, aralia, campsis, celastrus, chaenomeles and rubus; trees such as ailanthus, catalpa, paulownia, robinia and elm; hardy herbaceous perennials like anchusa, echinops, eryngium, gaillardia, Oriental poppy, border phlox, *Primula denticulata*, *Romneya coulteri*, symphytum or verbascum; and the alpines *Morisia monantha* and *Pulsatilla vulgaris*.

The time to take root cuttings is when the plants are dormant, a good period being mid winter (December). Use young roots of no more than pencil thickness; the roots of some plants, such as phlox, primula, morisia and pulsatilla, will be thinner than this.

The roots can be obtained by scraping the soil away from large plants, removing a few roots, returning the soil and firming. Small plants can be lifted, a few roots removed and then replanted.

The roots should be cut into 5cm (2 in) sections with a knife or secateurs. Thick roots are inserted vertically, and to ensure that you keep them the right way up the tops of the cuttings should have a flat cut and the bases a slanting cut. The top of a root cutting is always that part which was nearer to the stem of the plant.

The cuttings can be rooted in pots or boxes of peat and sand compost. Thick cuttings should be pressed vertically into the medium so that the tops are just below soil level. Thin cuttings cannot be pushed in vertically, so are laid horizontally on the surface of the compost and covered with a further 13mm (½ in) layer. Place in a cold frame or greenhouse to root. The top growth will be produced first so do not be in too much of a hurry to lift the cuttings for planting out.

1–3 *leaf cutting using whole leaf laid on compost, with main veins cut;* **4–6** *root cuttings, using thick and thin roots*

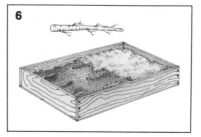
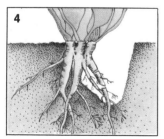

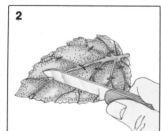

Division and Layering

In nature, where plants must be able to survive all sorts of accidents, they can grow again when split into pieces, or make new roots from the point at which they have suffered an injury. Several techniques have been developed from this natural process.

The simplest method of plant propagation is division, or the splitting of plants into a number of small portions. It is the principal method of increasing herbaceous border plants and other hardy perennials; most of these need lifting and dividing every three to four years to ensure that they remain vigorous and continue to flower well. Many other kinds of plant can also be increased by division.

Perennials and alpines
The best time to carry out this operation is in mid spring (March–mid April), just as the plants are awakening from their winter rest; plants in flower should be left until they finish flowering. Lift the clumps carefully with a fork and shake off as much soil as possible. Large tough clumps can be divided by inserting two digging forks back to back through the centre and pulling the handles apart. The two portions can then be split by the same method. Discard the centre of each clump and replant only the young outer portions. Each division should consist of a number of growth buds and a good portion of roots.

Those perennials that flower early in the year, such as doronicum, pyrethrum, epimedium, symphytum, pulmonaria and primula (including primroses and polyanthus), should be divided immediately after flowering. Some perennials are best not divided at all, as they resent being moved: these include romneya, paeony, helleborus, alstroemeria, echinops, eryngium, *Papaver orientalis*, (Oriental poppy) and Japanese anemone. Plants that grow from a single stem, cannot, of course, be divided.

Many alpine plants form mats or carpets of growth and these too can be lifted and pulled apart to provide a number of smaller plants. Thyme, raolia, sedum, gentian, saxifrage and campanula can all be split in early spring.

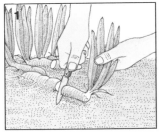

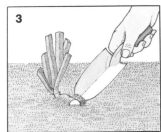

Top: preparing divided perennial plants for replanting; **1** *dividing clump of perennials with forks and trimming damaged roots;* **2–4** *cutting, trimming and replanting young rhizomes;* **5** *corm producing cormlets, and below, bulblets forming round parent bulb*

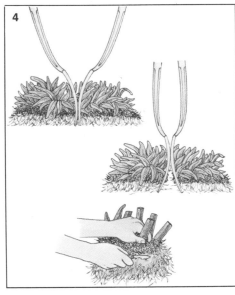

Dividing rhizomes and tubers

Some plants, of which the iris is the best-known example, form 'rhizomes', which are simply swollen stems situated at or just below soil level. There are many kinds of iris, such as the bearded iris, which is a superb border plant, and the dwarf kinds admirably suited to a rock garden.

When you divide iris—which should be immediately after flowering—each division should consist of a short portion of rhizome with some roots and a fan of leaves attached.

Many people keep dahlias from one year to another. Before planting them out in the spring, the dormant clumps can be split into smaller portions. Dahlias are best cut with a knife; make sure that each division consists of a portion of old stem with dormant growth buds at the base, and at best one tuber attached.

Bulbs and corms

Bulbs, such as daffodil, tulip and hyacinth, and corms, for example gladiolus and crocus, form offspring around their bases, and these are known as bulblets and cormlets respectively. If the parent bulbs and corms are dug up after the foliage has died down, these youngsters can be removed and stored dry until the correct planting time, which is autumn (September or October) for most, and mid to late spring (March–April) for gladiolus. Plant them fairly shallowly. Some bulbs and corms may take two or three years to flower, so be patient.

Simple layering: **1** *twist stem sharply to break surface tissue or* **2** *make cut in underside of stem;* **3** *bend stem at wound and peg to soil with wire pin;* **4** *cover pegged section with soil;* **5** *tie end of stem to bamboo cane:* **6** *when roots have formed, sever new plant from parent stem*

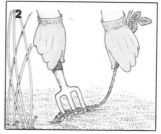
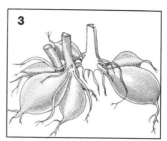

House plants

Some house plants can be split up in spring when they start to become too large, such as ferns, aspidistra, chlorophytum, and other clump-formers. Remove each plant from its pot, shake the soil away and pull apart. Repot each portion, using fresh compost.

Offsets

An even easier method than lifting and dividing is simply to remove offsets from plants complete with a few roots attached. Offsets are small plants found growing around the parent. Carefully tease them away with a hand fork to ensure you do not damage the roots or disturb the main plant.

Sempervivum (houseleek), androsace, some saxifrages, sansevieria and many cacti and succulents form offsets.

Suckers

There are many shrubs that produce 'suckers'—shoots which arise from below ground, usually from the roots. This is one of the ways in which plants increase naturally. With some, such as raspberries, masses of shoots are produced all round the parent plants.

In the winter or in early spring (November–March), when the plants are dormant, suckers can be carefully dug up with some roots attached and planted elsewhere. Shrubs which are often pro-

1 *Removing offsets from sempervivum;* **2** *lifting rooted suckers from raspberry plants;* **3** *dividing dahlia tubers*

pagated by this method include *Rhus typhina*, symphoricarpus, cornus (dogwood) and aralia. It is also the way to increase raspberries.

Layering

Layering is also an easy method of propagating plants. Simple layering consists of pegging down a branch or shoot into the soil, where it will form roots. It can then be detached from the parent plant and planted elsewhere. You may notice, when out in the country, that some plants, such as beech and bramble, layer themselves quite naturally without the help of man.

Almost any tree or shrub can be propagated by simple layering, provided a shoot can be brought into contact with the soil. The best time for this operation is in the spring or early summer when plants are actively growing. Choose young shoots or stems for layering as these will root quicker than older growth. The ground in which the stems are to be layered should be well prepared beforehand. Fork it over and break it down to a fine tilth. Mix plenty of moist peat and coarse sand with the soil to a depth of 15–25cm (6–9 in). Now all is ready.

About 30cm (12 in) or so from the tip of the shoot or stem it should be wounded in some way, so as to encourage quicker rooting. The easiest way to wound the stem is to grip it with both hands and give it a sharp half-twist to break some of the tissue. Another method is to cut diagonally halfway through the stem with a sharp knife, making a cut 4–5cm (1½–2 in) in length. This will result in a 'tongue' in the stem, which should be kept open with a small stone or piece of wood.

Using a piece of galvanized wire bent to the shape of a hairpin, peg the prepared shoot down where it was wounded into a 7–8cm (3 in) deep depression in the soil. Cover with soil and firm with your fingers. Tie the end of the stem protruding through the soil upright to a short bamboo cane. Keep layers well watered whenever the soil starts to become dry.

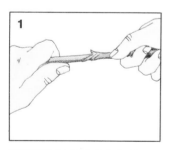

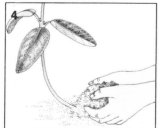
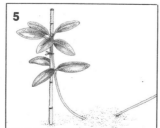

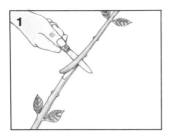

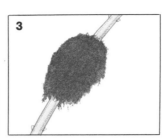

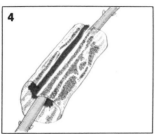
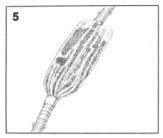
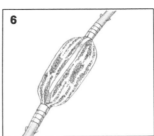

Air layering: **1** *make diagonal cut, half way through stem;* **2** *treat with hormone rooting powder and wedge open with moss;* **3** *bandage cut with moss;* **4** *wrap with polythene sheeting;* **5** *seal lower end below cut;* **6** *seal upper end and join*

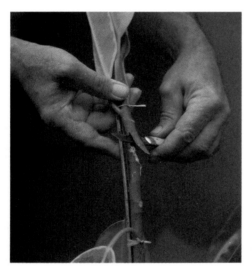

Above: air layering of ficus elastica *rubber plant, showing correct angle of cut*

Some plants, such as the common shrubs forsythia, syringa (lilac), weigela, hebe (veronica), privet and philadelphus (mock orange), will form a good root system in a year. Others may take longer to root well, particularly magnolia, hamamelis (witch hazel), rhododendron, azalea and camellia. When the layers have rooted lift them carefully with a fork and sever from the parent close to the new root area. Set out as soon as possible.

Serpentine layering

This is a minor modification of simple layering, and is done with plants possessing long stems, particularly climbers like clematis, jasmine, lonicera (honeysuckle), wisteria, passiflora (passion flower) and

1 *Serpentine layering;* **2** *pegging down strawberry runners;* **3** *tip layering*

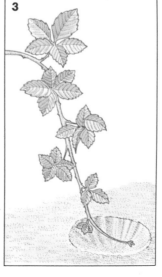

vines. Wound the long stems and peg them down at intervals along the ground, so that you get a number of new plants from one stem. All should have rooted within a year.

Tip layering

Blackberries, loganberries and other hybrid berries are propagated by tip layering. In late summer or early autumn July or August simply bury the extreme tip of a young stem 7–8cm (3 in) deep in the soil. It should be well rooted by the following early winter (November), when it can be planted out.

Air layering

This is a useful method where stems cannot be pulled down to the ground. Again it is suitable for any tree or shrub, spring or early summer (March–May) being a good time to do it.

Use a young stem and cut diagonally halfway through it, making the cut about 5cm (2 in) in length. Make this wound about 30cm (12 in) from the tip and keep the cut open by packing it with moist sphagnum moss. You can first treat the cut with a hormone rooting powder or liquid to speed root production.

The prepared part of the stem should then be 'bandaged' with moist sphagnum moss, held in place by wrapping with a piece of clear polythene sheeting. Each end of this polythene 'sleeve' must be tightly sealed with self-adhesive water-proof tape. The overlapping edge of the polythene must also be sealed with tape.

You will know when roots have formed as they will be seen through the poly-thene. At this stage sever the rooted layer and plant it out.

House plants such as ficus (rubber plant) croton, philodendron, dracaena and cordyline can also be air-layered. It is done in the way described for outdoor plants, making the cut near the top of the plant. If the plant is kept in a warm place, rooting will be a matter of weeks. If the stem of the parent plant is cut hard back after removing the layer, it should produce new growth from the base.

Finally, strawberries are also pro-pagated by layering. In the summer they produce 'runners', or stems which grow along the ground, and at intervals along these new plants are formed. To en-courage these to root quickly, peg the first plantlet (the one nearest the parent) on each runner into a pot of potting compost sunk in the soil. Remove any plantlets beyond the first one. They will quickly root, and in early autumn (August or early September) should be severed from the main plant and planted elsewhere.

Budding and Grafting

Without the techniques of budding and grafting we would have few varieties of rose or rhododendron, and almost no cropping or ornamental fruit trees. These two closely-related methods of propagation are easily-assimilated, and provide a fascinating and richly-rewarding addition to your range of gardening skills.

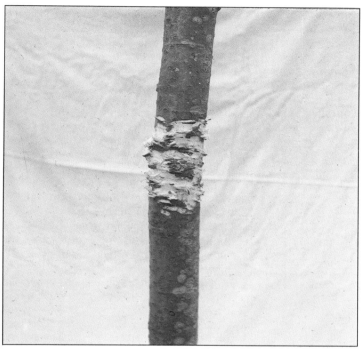

*Bridge grafting stage **1**: tree with diseased or damaged bark*

*Stage **2**: cut away damaged bark before making bridge graft*

*Stage **3**: make slits in bark above and below damaged area*

*Stage **4**: insert scions, taken from tree, to form bridge for sap*

Budding and grafting are both ways of joining permanently together portions of two separate plants to form a complete new plant. One plant provides the root system and is known as the 'rootstock', and the other plant, which is the one we wish to propagate, provides the top-growth. A growth bud, or a piece of stem known as the 'scion', is removed from the plant to be propagated and is inserted in the rootstock, where it eventually unites with it and so a new plant develops. In all cases, it is important to make sure that the 'cambium' (the thin green layer just under the bark) of the stock is in close contact with the cambium of the scion.

Budding and grafting are generally used to propagate plants which are difficult or impossible to increase by other means such as cuttings or seed, or which would not be successful on their own roots. The rootstock generally imparts vigour to the variety budded or grafted on to it; this is usually very beneficial, especially for many roses and fruit-tree varieties which are weak if grown on their own roots. The rootstock is usually of the same species or group as the variety to be propagated. Often it is the naturally-occurring form of which the propagated variety is a cultivar.

T-budding
Budding is a method used to propagate roses and ornamental fruiting trees.
Roses You will have to plant one-year-old root-stocks of *Rosa canina*, the briar, in late autumn (October or November) for budding the following summer or early autumn (from June to early September).

The buds of the variety to be propagated should be plump or well-developed and carried on current year's shoots. Remove one of these shoots with a number of buds attached. Cut off the leaves, leaving the leaf stalks (petioles). Buds should only be removed from this 'bud stick' immediately prior to inserting them in the rootstocks.

Using a really sharp horticultural knife you then cut out each bud on a shield-shaped piece of bark 2–3cm (1 in) long with a thin sliver of wood behind it. This wood should then be carefully removed from the bark. The bud is inserted in the rootstock at ground level. With your knife, make a T-shaped cut in the bark. Lift the bark with the knife blade. Hold the bud by the leaf stalk and slip it down behind the bark. Tie in tightly with raffia, making sure that the bud is exposed.

In the following spring (February or March) cut off the top of the rootstock just above the bud. Soon after, the bud will start into growth. By the autumn you will have a young rose bush.

Ornamental and fruit trees These are budded in the same way, except that the bud is inserted 15–20cm (6–8 in) from the ground. Make sure that you use the right rootstocks; Malling and Malling-Merton apple stocks for apples and crabs; Malling Quince A for pears; *Prunus avium* Mazzard or Gean for cherries; Brompton for almonds, apricots, nectarines, and peaches; and Myrobalan for plums. For other ornamental trees, use the naturally-occurring species as a rootstock.

Chip budding
Although chip budding is performed on roses and fruit trees in exactly the same way as T-budding, you are more likely to achieve successful results.

Remove a bud with a substantial piece of wood about 4cm (1½ in) in length. Make a cut about 20mm (¾ in) below the bud at an angle of 20 degrees into the stem. Then insert the knife about 20mm (¾ in) above the bud and cut down behind the bud to meet the first cut, so that the bud can be lifted out. A corresponding cut should then be made in the stock, so that the bud should exactly fit the cut in

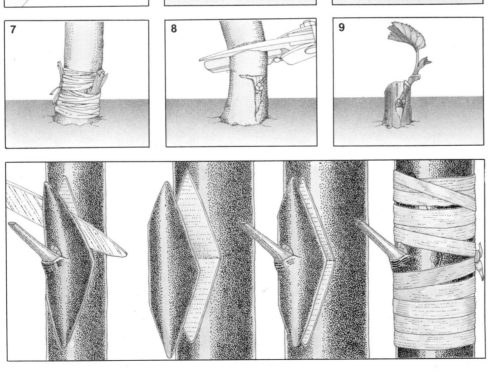

Rose budding: **1** *cut wood from rose to be propagated;* **2** *trim leaves off budstick;* **3** *cut bud from budstick;* **4** *peel away wood from back of bud;* **5** *make T-cut in rootstock;* **6** *insert bud, trimming to fit T-cut;* **7** *tie in place with raffia;* **8** *cut back rootstock in following spring;* **9** *bud coming into growth. Chip budding (left): remove bud; make cut in rootstock; insert bud; tie in bud with raffia*

the stock. Then tie in with raffia or plastic tape above and below the bud, making sure the ties are firm. The bud itself can be left exposed.

Whip and tongue grafting

An alternative method of propagating ornamental and fruiting trees is whip and tongue grafting, which is also carried out in spring (February and March). Use the rootstocks recommended above; plant them in winter or early spring (from November to March), and graft in the second spring (February or March) after having planted the rootstocks.

Whip and tongue graft (below, left to right): prepare scion; make tongue in scion and rootstock; fit scion to rootstock; bind with raffia; treat with tree paint

Cut the rootstock to within 10–15cm (4–6 in) of ground level. At the top make a slanting cut 4–5cm (1½–2 in) long; make a shallow downward v-shaped cut near the top of the first cut to form a 'tongue'. The scion should be four buds in length and prepared from well-ripened shoots produced the previous year. Cut the base with a slanting cut 4–5cm (1½–2 in) long with a shallow downward cut near the top to form a similar tongue. Push the tongue of the scion into the tongue of the stock and then tie in securely ('whip') with raffia, and cover all exposed surfaces with tree paint.

For the graft to be successful, all cuts must be perfectly flat and should match each other exactly, and the cambium layer of the stock must be in close contact with the cambium of the scion.

Saddle grafting

Saddle grafting is used for propagating hybrid rhododendrons, and should be done in spring (February or March) in a heated greenhouse. The stock is two-or three-year-old *R. ponticum* in pots. Cut it down to 2–4cm (1–1½ in) and cut the top into a wedge shape. Cut a previous year's shoot about 10cm (4 in) long with a bud at the top as the scion and cut the base in an inverted v-shape to fit exactly over the stock. Tie in with raffia and keep under glass until the scion is growing well.

Splice grafting

Splice grafting is used for rhododendrons and also for syringa (lilac), for which you should use privet stocks. Graft in spring (February or March) under glass. Cut the stock down to 5cm (2 in) and make a long slanting cut from one side to the other. Make a corresponding cut at the base of the scion. Bind tightly with raffia. Keep under glass until the scion is growing strongly.

Bridge grafting is useful if the bark of a tree has been damaged. Use a few scions from the tree to bridge the damaged area and so ensure that sap continues to flow up the trunk or branch. Use the crown graft (see below) at both ends of the scion. Bind with raffia. Seal exposed wood with tree paint.

Approach grafting

In approach grafting, the scion is united with the stock without first removing the scion from the parent plant; then when the graft has united the scion is severed from its parent. Many trees and shrubs can be propagated by this method.

Generally, stocks are grown in pots and taken to the parent tree. A sliver of wood is removed from both stock and scion and a tongue cut in each as for whip and tongue grafting. The two cuts are pushed together and bound with raffia.

Topworking

There are various grafts that are used to convert old fruit trees to different varieties. This is sometimes necessary if the existing variety is of inferior quality or a poor cropper. First, there is the method known as 'topworking', when the branches are cut back to stumps, to which scions of the new variety are grafted, using either the crown or the cleft graft.

Crown (or rind) graft Prepare scions about four buds in length, by making a slanting cut about 4cm (1½ in) long at the base. Then cut a 4cm (1½ in) slit in the bark at the top of a stump and slide the base of the scion down behind the bark so that the surface of the cut is in contact

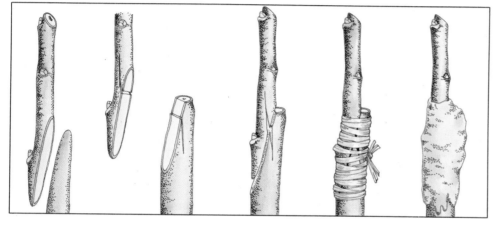

Saddle graft (above): make matching wedge-shaped cuts in scion and rootstock, tie in place and bind firmly

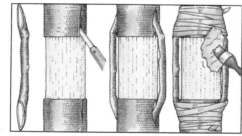

Bridge graft: use scions from tree to bridge damaged bark. Insert as for crown graft and treat with tree paint

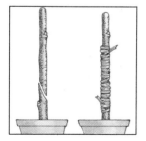

Splice graft (above): make long, slanting cuts in rootstock and scion. Bind tightly with raffia and keep under glass till scion is growing strongly

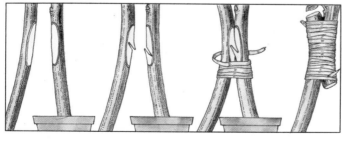

Approach graft (above): unite scion and stock without cutting scion from parent plant till graft has taken. Remove sliver from both, cut tongues and bind

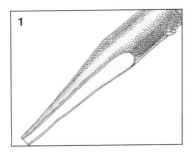

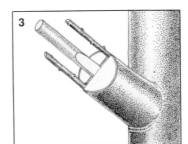
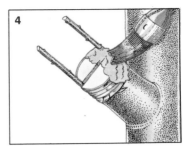

Cleft graft (above): **1** *prepare scions;* **2** *split end of stump;* **3** *insert two scions in cleft;* **4** *bind and apply tree paint.*
Crown graft (right): prepare scion and insert into slit made in bark. Bind with raffia and treat with tree paint

with the wood of the stump. Bind with raffia and cover graft with tree paint.

Cleft graft Cut the base of the scions into a long tapering wedge shape. Prepare the stumps by splitting the ends with a chopper. Keep the splits open with a wedge, and insert two scions, one on each side of a stump. Ensure that the cambium on one side of each scion is in contact with the cambium on one side of the stump. Remove the wedge and cover the graft with tree paint after tying with raffia.

Frameworking

Another method of converting established fruit trees is 'frameworking'. This is probably a better method than topworking because the new tree will crop sooner – indeed it may produce a good crop of fruit in the third year from grafting. The main branch system of the tree is left intact. Scions should be eight buds in length, and well spaced out all over the tree.

Stub graft Leave some side branches 6–25mm ($\frac{1}{4}$–1 in) in diameter on the tree, as the scions are inserted in these. The base of the scions should be cut to a short wedge. Make a 13mm ($\frac{1}{2}$ in) long cut at a 45 degree angle in a lateral branch; pull the branch to open the cut and slip in the scion. Release the branch so that the cut

Inverted-L graft: **1** *prepare both faces of scion;* **2** *cut bark;* **3** *insert scion;* **4** *hold with panel pin;* **5** *treat with tree paint*

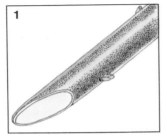
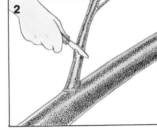
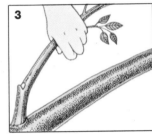

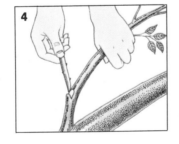
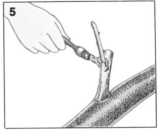

Stub graft: **1** *cut base of scion to a short wedge;* **2** *make angled cut, 13mm ($\frac{1}{2}$ in) long, in lateral branch;* **3** *bend branch to open cut;* **4** *insert scion;* **5** *cut off lateral branch just above scion and treat with tree paint*

closes and grips the scion. Then cut off the side branch close to the graft and cover the wounds with tree paint.

Inverted-L graft This can be used instead of the stub graft, but all small lateral or side branches should be removed. Cut the scions as for crown grafting, then opposite this cut make another, but much shorter, so that you form an unequal wedge. Prepare the branches to receive the scions by making incisions in the bark like an inverted letter L. Lift the flap of bark and insert the base of the scion.

Close the flap of bark and pin in place with a panel pin, inserted through the bark and scion and into the wood. Cover wounds with tree paint.

Inverted-L grafting is done in spring and early summer (from March to May) while crown, cleft and stub grafting should be done in spring (February or March). When you are using these grafts to convert a fruit tree to another variety, a large number of scions will have to be inserted, but once *au fait* with grafting it is a surprisingly quick operation.

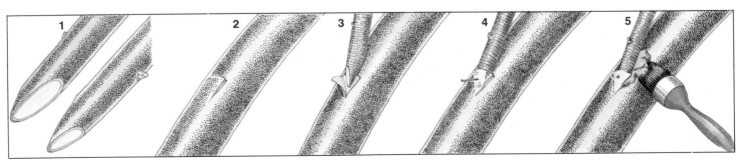

Staking and Tying

One of the most important tasks in the garden – and one that is too frequently left undone – is the provision of adequate support for the growing plants.

Many garden flowers and vegetables have been specially developed to grow taller than their ancestors in the wild. Deprived of their natural support, they may be blown over, or even snap off under their own weight, unless they are properly staked and tied.

Herbaceous plants

Many herbaceous plants or hardy perennials have weak and floppy stems which can easily be knocked to the ground by wind and rain. They do need, therefore, some form of artificial support.

One of the best ways to support plants with several stems is to push twiggy hazel sticks between and around them. This should be done in late spring or early summer (April or May) when the plants are just starting into growth, as the shoots will then grow up through the sticks. Of course, you need to know the ultimate height of the plants so that you can use sticks of the correct length – ideally they should be about 15cm (6 in) shorter than the final height of the plants. By the time the plants have made a good deal of growth and are ready to flower, the sticks will be virtually hidden by stems and leaves.

There are various proprietary supports for herbaceous plants that encircle the stems, but take care that these do not bunch the stems together, so giving an unnatural appearance.

Hazel twigs support bushy plants

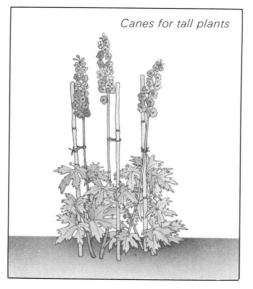

Canes for tall plants

Wire ring supports clump of plants

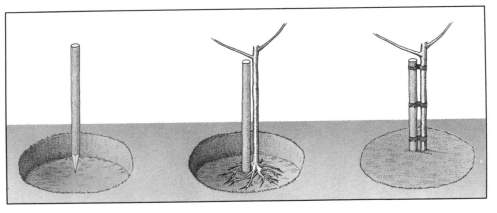

Tall plants with a few stems, such as delphiniums, are best supported by providing a 2m (6 ft) bamboo cane for each stem, and tying in the stems as they grow with soft twine or raffia. Push the canes into the ground behind the stems so that they are inconspicuous from the front of the border.

Hardy annuals
Hardy annual flowers grown from seed are also invariably weak-stemmed, and benefit greatly from the support of twiggy hazel sticks. These must be inserted when the seedlings are fairly small – in the region of 5cm (2 in). Again, you can also buy proprietary supports of the type recommended for herbaceous plants.

Trees and shrubs
It is essential to provide adequate supports for trees at planting time, otherwise they are liable to be rocked about by the wind so that their roots become loose in the soil. This will prevent the trees from easily establishing themselves and if they become too loose they could even die. In addition an adequate support will ensure that the trunk of the tree remains straight.

Chestnut stakes about 8cm (3 in) in diameter are ideal for trees. Cut the base to a point and treat it with a horticultural wood preservative. Hammer the stake into the planting hole *before* the tree is inserted. It should be of such a length that the top comes just below the lowest branch of the tree after planting, with the base inserted about 45cm (18 in) in the ground.

Position the trunk of the tree 2–3cm (1 in) from the stake. When the tree has been planted it can be secured to the stake with proprietary plastic buckle ties specially designed for trees. Position one at the top of the stake and then a couple more lower down, spacing them out evenly. Ensure that the plastic buffer supplied with each tie is positioned between the trunk and the stake, to hold the tree away from its support and prevent the bark from being

chafed. Trees should remain staked for a number of years, until they are really well established in the ground.

Few shrubs require staking after planting, but those that do include cytisus and genistas (brooms) and *Spartium junceum* (Spanish broom). These have small root systems and are liable to be blown over if they are not supported until well established. A stout bamboo cane of appropriate length should be adequate, provided it is inserted some 45cm (18 in) in the ground. Tie the shrub to it with soft garden twine.

Climbers
The modern method of supporting climbers on a wall is to attach trellis panels of plastic-coated metal to it. They should be secured about 2–5cm (1–2 in) away from the wall so that the plants are able to grow through the mesh. Alternatively, special galvanized nails may be used, with wire or string threaded between them.

Vegetables
Climbing vegetables, like runner beans and peas, need adequate supports if they are to grow well and produce nice long pods. Some people still use bean poles for runners, but these are becoming increasingly difficult to obtain. Insert the poles in a double row, with 45cm (18 in) between rows, so that they cross near the top. Then tie them to horizontal poles placed in the forks. The poles should be about 30cm (12 in) apart along the rows. Alternatively, a 'wigwam' of poles or canes tied together at the top can be made. Whatever system is used, allow one pole or cane per plant.

The modern method of supporting runner beans is to use special wide-mesh nylon netting ('bean netting') stretched between posts. It is generally supplied 2m (6 ft) in height and of various lengths. It is even possible to buy a special framework for bean netting which can remain in position from one year to the next and which lasts a very long time indeed.

You can support peas with twiggy hazel sticks of the appropriate height. Push these in on each side of the row when the peas are about 2–3cm (1 in) high. They will then grow up through the sticks. Alternatively, bring yourself up to date and use the special nylon pea netting which is about 1m (3 ft) wide. It should be stretched tight between wooden posts along the side of a row, or it can be formed into a tent shape over a central horizontal wire, so that the peas can grow up both sides.

All nylon netting will last for many years if looked after.

Tomatoes also need some support. Here 1–1·5m (3–5 ft) bamboo canes are adequate, tying in with raffia or soft garden twine.

Fruit
Tree fruits, such as apples, pears, plums and cherries, should be staked at planting time (see under trees and shrubs).

Of the soft fruits, raspberries, blackberries, loganberries and other hybrid berries are the only ones that need supporting. A system of stout posts, with strained galvanized horizontal wires, is needed for these crops. The topmost wire should be about 2m (6 ft) above soil level. The other wires can be spaced about 30cm (12 in) apart below this to within 60cm (2 ft) of the ground. Each end post should be braced with another post driven in at an angle of 45 degrees and nailed firmly to the main post.

If you grow trained fruit trees, particularly cordons, espaliers and fans, these can also be supported by a system of posts and wires, and bamboo poles.

Tidying the Garden

brush you can easily tear plants out of the ground. Other low-growing plants, like heathers, should also be cleared of leaves at the earliest possible time.

Fallen leaves will pollute an ornamental pool. In this case prevention is better than removal, so just before trees and shrubs start shedding their leaves stretch some netting – about 13mm ($\frac{1}{2}$ in) mesh – over the pool, securing it at the edges with wooden pegs. Lift off the netting frequently and remove fallen leaves. Do not let a large quantity of leaves accumulate, or the netting will become too heavy to handle easily. You can also place netting over the rock garden or heather bed for the same purpose; it certainly makes leaf-collecting much easier.

Most gardeners like to rake fallen leaves out of beds and borders for the sake of a neat appearance, although they will do no harm lying between shrubs and other plants – in fact they will add valuable humus to the soil. But leaves that

Above left: clear lawns of fallen leaves
Below: use leaves for composting

As autumn draws to a close it is the time to get the garden into good shape before harsher weather arrives to make the work more difficult. The main task in most gardens will be to clear away the leaves and the remains of summer bedding. But there are many other small jobs that, if done now, will give your plants a much better chance of surviving the winter months in good shape.

Autumn is a beautiful time of year, with trees and shrubs alight with autumn tints and berries. But these colourful leaves are only short-lived and very soon they will be cascading down, covering lawns, rock gardens, beds and borders.

Clearing the leaves

Rake or brush fallen leaves off the lawn as soon as possible after they have fallen, otherwise they will pack down into a solid mat and the grass will quickly turn yellow through lack of light. Also remove leaves, as they fall, from the rock garden before they smother low-growing cushion- and mat-forming alpines and rock plants. In a rock garden it is best to gather up the leaves by hand. If you use a rake or a stiff

Above left: netting over ponds should not touch water; for large areas place a support underneath.
Above: cut down herbaceous plants to ground level.
Below: stake broccoli and other tall vegetables against wind damage.

are diseased should be collected and burned to prevent spread of infection.

Put fallen leaves on the compost heap or, if you have a large quantity, place them in a heap on their own where they will rot down to form leaf mould. This is a useful mulching material and can also be incorporated into soil during digging.

Weeding borders

After clearing leaves, remove all weeds from beds and borders and lightly fork over the surface of the soil between plants. But do not go too deeply otherwise you may damage the roots of shrubs and perennials. Annual weeds can be composted, but burn the roots of perennial weeds as they may not rot down in the heap if insufficient heat is produced.

Cleaning up herbaceous borders

Some people prefer to leave the dead

stems of herbaceous plants until early spring before cutting them down. This is good practice in very cold areas, where they may give the plants some protection over the winter. However, in most areas the dead stems can be cut down to soil level in the autumn before weeding and pricking over the surface of the soil.

Cut down the stems of dahlias to within 10 or 15cm (4 or 6 in) of the ground when frosts have blackened the leaves and stems. Then lift the tubers, clean the earth off carefully and dry them ready for storing in a cool, dry, frost-proof place over the winter.

Pull up all plant supports (such as sticks, canes and stakes) provided they are no longer needed. Dry them off and store them in a dry place ready for use again next year.

If you leave summer bedding plants *in situ* too far into the autumn they start to look very bedraggled; also the beds need to be prepared for spring bedding plants and bulbs. So by late autumn (October) at the latest, clear out the beds and place the old plants on the compost heap. Some summer bedding plants – for example pelargonium, fuchsia, begonia, heliotrope and calceolaria – can be saved if you have a frost-free greenhouse.

Checking plant supports

Examine all climbing plants and tie in the stems where necessary, otherwise winter gales and rain will damage them. Also check plant supports and tree ties to ensure that they are sufficiently secure to withstand winter weather.

Tending the lawn

Lawns can be given a final trim in late autumn (October); do not forget to cut the edges as these can grow long very quickly, even in the autumn. Once you have finished mowing, clean and grease

the mower carefully before packing it away in a dry place for the winter. If the blades need sharpening, or if you consider the machine needs a thorough overhaul, then send it to a local servicing agent.

Tidying the vegetable plot

In the vegetable garden, remove and compost yellow leaves from brussels sprouts and other greenstuff. In windy and exposed areas, and if the soil is light, it pays to stake brussels and other tall greens (such as sprouting broccoli) to prevent them from heeling over. Use stout bamboo canes and soft green garden twine.

When the top growth of the asparagus turns yellow, cut the stems right down and weed the bed. Cut down pea and bean haulms (leaving the roots in the ground) and place them on the compost heap. Dry off nets, sticks and poles used for supports and store them in a shed or garage till required again next year. After clearing away all finished crops, you can make a start on the digging, which you should aim to have completed by mid winter (December), especially if you have a heavy clay soil.

Clearing up the fruit plot

In the fruit plot, clean up strawberry beds by removing and burning dead, diseased and damaged leaves, and lightly hoe off any weeds. Tie in the canes (stems) of raspberries, blackberries, loganberries and other hybrid berries (if not already done) to prevent damage by winter gales. Also check the wooden posts that support the wires. If they are decaying at ground level replace them with new ones.

Above: check fruit canes are secure

48

Lifting and Storing Tubers and Stools

Some of the plants that you grow in your garden are tender or half-hardy and so have to be lifted in autumn, stored in frost-free conditions over the winter and planted out again the following spring.

Various tubers, corms and stools (root clumps) need to be lifted and stored in dry conditions during winter, including dahlias, gladioli, tuberous begonias, tigridias (tiger flower), ixiolirions and outdoor chrysanthemums.

Dahlias

Dahlias are probably the best-known of the tender tuberous plants. Many people wait until the first frosts blacken the stems and leaves before they lift and store. However, if you require the ground for

Cut dahlia stems down to 15cm (6 in)

Lift and clean without damaging tuber

Label tubers with variety and colour

Prop upside down to allow sap to drain

Dust tubers with flowers of sulphur

Store in a box on a layer of peat

Cover tubers with another peat layer

Firm down and store in frost-free place

Alternatively, store in insulated frame

some other purpose, there is no reason why you should not lift them a week or so earlier (early October) while the top growth is still green.

First cut down the stems to within 15cm (6 in) of the ground; the tops can go on the compost heap. Then insert a spade all round the plant, gently pulling back the handle each time, to loosen it. When the tuber is really loose lift it out and clean off the soil. A wooden plant label is a useful tool for this job. Work carefully, as dahlia tubers are easily damaged. Tie a label, stating the variety, to each tuber to save confusion when you come to replant.

Dry off the tubers for a week or two before storing them for the winter. One good method of drying tubers is to suspend them upside down so that sap and moisture are able to drain from the hollow stems. Or you can use wooden or cardboard boxes, with wooden slats placed across the top. Put the tubers on the slats with the stems pointing down between them. Leave them in this position until they feel thoroughly dry.

Before storing, dust any damaged parts of the tubers with a fungicide such as flowers of sulphur to prevent disease penetrating them and causing rot. Stor-age conditions must be frost-proof, but also dry and airy. Avoid storing tubers in a very warm place, otherwise they will shrivel up and probably not come into growth in the following spring. A slightly heated greenhouse, or an unheated spare room, would be ideal.

Tubers are most conveniently stored in open-topped boxes or trays in single layers – or in double or triple layers if space is limited. If you think there is a risk of the tubers becoming frosted, wrap each one in several thicknesses of newspaper, and pack them between more crumpled newspaper, clean straw or some other suitable insulating material. Additionally, you can insulate the whole box with something like straw or old carpet.

Inspect the tubers several times throughout the winter for signs of rotting. Cut out any decaying areas and dust the wounds with flowers of sulphur. If there is any mould on the tubers, then dust the whole lot with sulphur.

Gladioli

These are almost as popular as dahlias for summer display. The corms should be lifted, with a fork, each year in late autumn (October) as the foliage is dying down. You may find small corms around each parent. If you want to increase, or replace, your stock, remove these small corms and store them in dry peat over the winter and then plant them shallowly in the spring: otherwise discard them. Cormlets will flower about two years later, and these can replace the parent corms as they decline in vigour.

Dry off the large corms quickly for a few days in a very warm and airy place. Use a fan heater set at medium, if necessary. When the corms show no trace of dampness, clean off soil and withered leaves. Then store them in a cool, frost-free, well-ventilated place. They are best stored in single layers in slatted boxes or in wire mesh trays to allow good air circulation.

Tuberous begonias

Tuberous begonias that have been bedded out for the summer must be lifted in mid or late autumn (September or October) before frosts commence. Dig up the plant without damaging leaves or roots, and keep it in a dry, frost-proof place. The stems will soon wither and can then be cut off 2–3cm (1 in) above the tuber. Remove any clinging soil from the roots. Place the tubers in flat trays or boxes of dry peat and store in a dry, frost-proof, well-ventilated place, with a temperature of at least 6°C (42°F).

Tigridias and ixiolirions

Some lesser-known plants that need lifting in mid to late autumn (September or October) are the corm tigridia (tiger flower) and the bulb ixiolirion. They are tender specimens as they come from very warm climates. Treat them in the way described for gladioli; you can store them together in boxes or trays.

Outdoor chrysanthemums

The roots of outdoor chrysanthemums are also best lifted after the plants have finished flowering, sometime in late autumn (October). First cut the stems down to within a few inches of the ground and then lift as described for dahlias. These cut-down plants are correctly known as chrysanthemum stools.

Place the stools fairly close together in flat trays or seed boxes of potting compost. Store them in a cool greenhouse or cold frame and keep them just slightly moist during the winter. Under glass the stools are protected from excessive winter wetness that could cause them to rot. In the spring new shoots will be produced. Remove and root these to provide new plants; the old stools can then be discarded.

Lift chrysanthemums carefully with fork

Clean off excess soil from roots

Remove any top growth and label stool

Place close together in boxes and store

Protecting Tender Plants

Plants need to be protected, not only from pests and diseases, but also from the rigours of a winter in the garden. Even quite hardy plants can suffer damage from strong winds and rain, while tender plants are particularly susceptible to cold.
Here we give you some guidelines on preventive care that will help your plants survive whatever the weather.

There are many ways in which you can protect plants from harsh weather conditions. Screens can be placed round them or 'blankets' of litter (such as bracken, leaves or straw) placed over them. Other plants can be brought inside into a frost-free environment, or covered *in situ* with cloches or other types of shelter. Remember however, that all protective materials must be removed in the late spring (about early to mid April).

Protecting shrubs
Even hardy fuchsias can be killed by severe frosts, especially if these occur over a prolonged period. It is the dormant buds that are most prone to the ravages of wind and frost; if these are killed then the plant will not grow. To prevent this, cover the crowns of the plants in late autumn with a 15cm (6 in) layer of soil and leaf mould. Also, leave the dead stems until spring before cutting them down, as they afford further frost protection.

One of the reasons hydrangeas sometimes fail to flower is because the buds have been frosted and killed; so leave the dead flower-heads on over winter.

In cold, exposed and windswept areas many shrubs may be damaged or killed in winter unless protected. These include hebe, cistus (rock rose), some rhododendrons and camellias, coronilla, hypericum hybrids such as Rowallane, *Convolvulus cneorum*, shrubby salvia, evergreen ceanothus, *Romneya coulteri* (Californian tree poppy) and cerato-stigma. Evergreen shrubs are especially prone to having their leaf edges scorched by cold winds.

Many young or newly-planted shrubs, trees and conifers (in particular evergreen species) may suffer during hard weather. Conifers and other evergreens can turn completely brown very quickly through being dried out by cold winds. Therefore it is advisable to protect with screens, as fully as possible, all young shrubs and conifers until they become well established and much tougher.

Protecting with litter
Some bulbs are also rather tender. For instance the belladonna lily *Amaryllis belladonna* should have its young leaves protected from frost with a 15cm (6 in) layer of litter (such as straw, bracken or dry leaves) placed over them. A glass cloche with both ends closed by panes of glass would also be suitable. Other bulbs that would benefit from being protected by these methods are *Nerine bowdenii* and the agapanthus (African lily).

If you are growing the big waterside plant *Gunnera manicata* with its rhubarb-like leaves, protect the crown from frost. Cover the crown first by bending one or two of the plant's own leaves over it, then heap a good quantity of litter on top.

When covering plants with litter, you can hold this material down by inserting thin bamboo canes into the ground, bending them over the litter, and then re-inserting them into the ground. Or you can cover the heap with a sheet of wire

Above: two simple forms of protection; a 'sandwich' made of bracken and netting and an insulating pile of straw

netting, securing it with wooden pegs knocked into the soil.

Shelter from excessive rain
There are various plants that must have their crowns protected from excessive moisture over the winter, otherwise they may rot. For example with kniphofia (red hot poker), draw the leaves up over the crown (like a tent) and tie the ends together. Alternatively pack dry bracken or straw around the base of the plant. To keep eremurus (foxtail lily) dry and safe from frost, place a heap of coarse garden

sand or weathered ashes over the crowns.

You may find that some newly-planted herbaceous plants succumb to very wet soil conditions in winter. These include Japanese anemone, pyrethrum, crocosmia, penstemon, phygelius, dierama (wandflower) and some ornamental grasses. It is best not to plant such subjects until the spring. If you already have the plants they would be far better off in a cold frame over the winter with the glass raised sufficiently to ensure good ventilation, yet keep off the rain.

Some alpines or rock garden plants with woolly, felty or silvery leaves do not like to become excessively wet in the winter, even though they are perfectly hardy: a hard frost will not harm them, only too much rain. Such plants include androsace (rock jasmine), *Leontopodium alpinum* (edelweiss), *Asperula suberosa*, achillea (yarrow), helichrysum (everlasting flower) and sempervivum (houseleek).

To protect these plants, place over them a pane of glass, supported by four corner pegs. An open-ended glass cloche is just as good. Never completely enclose the plants as they must always have a free circulation of air.

Overwintering under glass
Outdoor chrysanthemums dislike cold, wet wintry conditions so cut the stems down in autumn, lift the stools and pack them close together in deep seed trays filled with dry peat or sand. These stools can then spend the winter in a cold frame or greenhouse. Take cuttings from them in spring to provide new plants.

Choosing and Planting Hedges and Screens

To prepare ground for hedge, double dig well in advance, mixing in compost with second spit, **1**, then turning over first spit, **2** and using it to cover compost, **3**. At planting time, dig trench, **4**, after letting soil settle and adding fertilizer. Position first plant at correct depth and firm in, **5**. Space out second plant at correct distance, **6**, and repeat procedure

Most gardens have at least one hedge. You may have grown it as an attractive boundary instead of a wall or fence, or to separate one area of the garden from another. A hedge can also make an excellent background for borders and beds, with dark-leaved types showing off bright flower colours especially well.

A hedge about 1·8–2·5m (6–8 ft) tall is most often required (being a practical height for a boundary), and there are many suitable subjects for this purpose.

First decide whether you would like a formal or informal hedge. A formal one is usually clipped to a regular shape, while informal types need little or no trimming and are just left to grow naturally. Generally flowering and/or berrying subjects are used informally.

Formal hedges

The common hornbeam (*Carpinus betulus*) is used extensively as a hedging plant and makes a thick hedge if planted 30–45cm (12–18 in) apart. It is suitable for clay or chalk soils. Clip it annually in late summer (July), but not for the first two years after planting. Common beech (*Fagus sylvatica*) is similar to hornbeam (except for its smoother leaves) and is cared for in the same way. The foliage persists throughout the autumn and winter at which time it is a beautiful golden-brown colour. Beech, like hornbeam, makes a good background for borders. You may prefer a coloured hedge, in which case you could use the purple- or copper-leaved varieties.

There is probably nothing better for a

formal, evergreen hedge than the common box (*Buxus sempervirens*). Planted 45cm (18 in) apart, it makes really dense growth that stands clipping exceptionally well. It thrives on chalky soils, and its dark-green foliage makes it a good background hedge. Another dense, impenetrable hedge is formed by common holly (*Ilex aquifolium*) with its deep green leaves. Plant 45–60cm (18–24 in) apart and trim annually in early or mid autumn (August or September).

Privet is a very common hedging plant; the golden-leaved variety *Ligustrum ovalifolium* Aureo-marginatum is, perhaps, more interesting than the green-leaved type. It is semi-evergreen, and will tolerate almost any soil and situation. Plant 30cm (12 in) apart and clip as necessary in the summer.

The Chinese honeysuckle (*Lonicera nitida*) is an evergreen shrub with tiny, dark green leaves – like those of the box. It forms a really thick hedge if plants are spaced 30cm (12 in) apart. As it is a fast grower it will need trimming several times during the summer.

Laurels make attractive hedges with their large, glossy, evergreen leaves. The common (or cherry) laurel is *Prunus laurocerasus* that thrives in almost any soil. Plant 45–60 cm (18–24 in) apart and prune with secateurs (to avoid cutting the large leaves in half) during the spring. The Portugal laurel *P. lusitanica* has smaller leaves but is treated in the same way as common laurel.

There are various evergreen conifers that are used for formal hedges, the most popular at the present time being the Leyland cypress (*Cupressocyparis leylandii*). It is the fastest-growing conifer in Britain and has good, deep-green foliage. Plant 45–60cm (18–24 in) apart and clip in late summer.

The Lawson cypress (*Chamaecyparis lawsoniana*) is a similar hedging plant although it is not such a fast grower. A good deep green variety is Green Hedger.

The common yew (*Taxus baccata*) is a very adaptable evergreen plant and makes a good dark background for shrub or flower borders. It grows very well on chalk. Plant 45–60cm (18–24 in) apart and clip in late autumn.

If you want a dwarf, formal hedge – perhaps to surround a bed or a border or to edge a path – then a good plant is the edging box *Buxus sempervirens* Suffruticosa, that will grow only 60cm (24 in) in height, but can be kept lower by clipping in summer. Plant 30cm (12 in) apart.

Informal hedges

There are many attractive shrubs suitable

for planting as informal hedges up to a height of 1·8–2·5m (6–8 ft). Berberis (barberry) forms very thick, prickly hedges and is particularly suitable for boundaries as it will keep children and animals out of (or in) the garden. The most popular ones are B. × *stenophylla* with yellow flowers in spring and *B. darwinii* with deeper yellow flowers. Both are evergreen. They are best not trimmed very much (this applies to all flowering hedges) otherwise flowering will be affected. A dwarf berberis hedge can be formed with *B. thunbergii* Atropurpurea Nana, that has deciduous purple leaves. Plant all 30–60cm (12–24 in) apart.

Evergreen escallonias are very popular, especially on the coast, and should be planted 45cm (18 in) apart. They may be lightly trimmed after flowering. *E. macrantha* and *E.m.* Crimson Spike (both crimson) are excellent for hedging.

Lavenders make fine low-growing hedges (up to 1m or 3 ft) and should be planted 30–45cm (12–18 in) apart. Trim off dead flower-heads. *Lavandula spica* (old English lavender) is most popular.

Pyracantha (firethorn) makes good, informal, evergreen hedges, and produces heavy crops of orange berries in the autumn that last well into the winter. The best is probably *P. coccinea* Lalandei. Plant 45–60cm (18–24 in) apart.

When to plant

Buy bare-root hedging plants whenever possible, as they will be much cheaper than container-grown plants. Many nurserymen grow plants especially for hedging at reasonable prices. The time to plant them is from early winter to mid spring (November to March).

If you buy container-grown plants, you will be able to plant your hedges at any time of the year. And you will find that certain subjects (for instance Leyland cypress and hollies) may be offered in containers rather than as field-grown plants to avoid root disturbance.

Preparing the ground

When preparing the ground, first ensure that it is free of perennial weeds; once your hedge has been planted these will be almost impossible to remove. So treat the site with a suitable weedkiller well before planting time. Once the ground is clean – and free from weedkiller (which can take several months) – you should dig a strip about 1m (3 ft) wide. Double digging (to two depths of the spade) is desirable to ensure that the roots of the hedging plants are able to penetrate deeply; this will give you a stable hedge. Dig in organic matter such as well-rotted farmyard manure or garden compost, at the same time.

Allow several weeks for the ground to settle before planting. Then, just prior to planting, apply a general-purpose fertilizer at 135g per sq m (4 oz per sq yd) and lightly prick it into the surface of the soil. Break down the soil to a reasonably fine tilth that is suitable for planting, and firm it by treading with your heels. Now the site is ready to take your hedge.

How to plant

As hedging plants are planted close together in a line, the easiest way to plant is to mark out a straight row with your garden line and take out a trench. Space out the plants at the correct distance apart in the trench and then replace the soil around them, firming it really well with your heels. Make sure the roots of bare-root subjects are well spread out. If planting container-grown specimens, do not disturb the rootball, just carefully remove the container from around it.

7 Tread in newly-planted shrubs before watering. 8 With correct care and attention, the finished product will soon flourish

After planting, water well in if the soil is dry, and thereafter keep well watered during dry weather. It is a good idea to mulch a young hedge to conserve soil moisture. Use rotted manure, garden compost or peat laid 5–8cm (2–3 in) deep along each side of the hedge. Spray evergreen subjects with an anti-transpirant (such as S. 600) to prevent excessive water loss from the leaves until the plants start rooting into the soil. Use the product carefully, following the manufacturer's instructions.

Trimming hedges

Most formal hedges need trimming regularly to keep them shapely and well clothed with foliage. Start by trimming the sides of a hedge in the early stages and allow it to reach the desired height before trimming the top. Formal hedges can be trimmed to various shapes, but a wedge shape is very practical as it easily sheds heavy falls of snow. It can be flat-topped or round-topped. A wedge-shaped hedge should be about twice as wide at the base as at the top.

The frequency of trimming formal hedges depends on the habit of growth. For example privet and Chinese honey-suckle are very fast growers and you will need to trim them two or three times in the growing season if they are to look neat. Slower-growing hedges, like beech and hornbeam, generally need trimming only once a year.

Tall screens

So far nothing has been said about screens, which are really very tall 'hedges' used to hide unsightly views. They are only suitable for the boundaries of very large gardens as generally they are not cut but left to grow to their natural height. Screens need the same ground preparation and aftercare as hedges, but should have a wider spacing when they are planted. Set the plants 2m (6 ft) apart.

How to trim

Before starting to trim a hedge lay some hessian, polythene sheeting or an an old sheet on the ground to catch the trimmings as they fall. They can then be collected with ease and placed on the compost heap.

To keep a formal hedge perfectly straight and level, use a garden line as a guide. When trimming the sides, place the line along the top of the hedge to the required depth of cutting. When trimming the top, the line should be placed along one of the sides to the required height of cut.

Informal hedges are generally trimmed once a year. Often you will only need to remove over-long or straggly shoots and any dead wood with a pair of secateurs.

Flowering informal hedges usually require that the old flowered wood be cut back immediately after flowering each year. This encourages the growth of strong, new flower-producing shoots from lower down the stems. The time of trimming different kinds of hedge varies tremendously, and suggested times are

included in our chart (see next page).

If formal hedges (or indeed informal types) become out of hand they may need cutting back hard into the old wood. This spoils their appearance for a while as you will have removed a lot of foliage, leaving bare stems. But this is only a temporary situation, as new shoots and foliage will soon hide these stems. Do this hand pruning in early spring just before the plants start into growth. It is amazing how old wood will quickly produce new growth after hard cutting back. However,

1 *Formal use of* Buxus sempervirens *(box)*

2 *Mixed hedge of beech, copper beech, yew, box and hornbeam*

3 Chamaecyparis lawsoniana *(Lawson cypress), a fast grower*

4 *Tall hedging for shade,* Taxus baccata, *(yew)*

5 *Trim laurel hedge with secateurs to ensure leaves are not cut in half*

6 *Cut back old flowered wood on* Forsythia *to just below lowest flower*

GUIDE TO TRIMMING HEDGING PLANTS

Botanical name	Common name	Time	Frequency (per year)	Cutting shape
Aucuba	spotted laurel	late spring (April)	once	formal or semi-formal; use secateurs
Berberis	barberry	after flowering	once	informal or semi-formal; not too hard
Buxus	box	early autumn (August)	as necessary	formal
Carpinus	hornbeam	early autumn (August)	once	formal
Chamaecyparis lawsoniana	Lawson cypress	early to mid summer (May to June)	once	formal
Crataegus	hawthorn	mid summer to early autumn (June to August)	as necessary	formal
Cupressocyparis leylandii	Leyland cypress	early autumn (August)	once	formal
Cupressus macrocarpa	Monterey cypress	late spring (April)	once	semi-formal or informal; dislikes too much, or hard, trimming
Escallonia	escallonia	after flowering	once	informal or semi-formal
Euonymus japonica	euonymus	mid summer to mid autumn (June to September)	as necessary	formal
Forsythia	forsythia	after flowering	once	informal or semi-formal; cut back flowered shoots
Fagus	beech	early autumn (August)	once	formal
Ilex	holly	early autumn (August)	once	formal
Laurus	sweet bay	mid summer to mid autumn (June to September)	as necessary	formal; use secateurs
Lavandula	lavender	mid to late spring (March to April)	once	informal or semi-formal; remove old flowers
Ligustrum	privet	early summer to mid autumn (May to September)	as necessary	formal
Lonicera nitida	Chinese honeysuckle	early summer to mid autumn (May to September)	as necessary	formal
Prunus laurocerasus	cherry laurel	late spring to late summer (April to July)	once or twice	formal; use secateurs
Pyracantha	firethorn	late spring (April)	once	informal or semi-formal
Rhododendron ponticum	rhododendron	mid to late spring (March to April)	once	informal or semi-formal; use secateurs
Viburnum tinus	laurustinus	late spring (April)	once	informal or semi-formal; use secateurs
Taxus baccata	yew	early autumn (August)	once	formal

for ordinary trimming *never* cut into the older wood but always leave a thick covering of leaves.

For small-leaved hedging plants like privet, beech and Chinese honeysuckle (indeed the majority of subjects) use a good pair of hand shears for a really neat finish. An electric trimmer is more practical if you have a lot of hedge to trim.

Large-leaved shrubs, such as laurels, rhododendrons, sweet bay and aucuba are best trimmed with a pair of secateurs to ensure that the leaves are not cut in half. If this occurs, then the cut leaves turn brown and make the hedge look most unsightly. So although it will take longer to trim these hedges with secateurs (as each shoot has to be cut out individually) it is time well spent.

Young hedges
It is sometimes recommended to let young formal hedges grow unchecked for the first few years to attain the required height. However, you will probably find if you do this that your hedge has a bare base. Instead, cut out the tops to ensure that the plants start branching low on the stems and produce foliage right down to ground level. Remember, though, that hornbeam and beech must not be cut for the first two years after planting.

Pyracantha (firethorn) hedge in flower

Autumn Pruning

An annual 'short back and sides' helps to maintain the shape of your trees and shrubs. For neglected specimens, more drastic action, such as bracing, may be necessary to strengthen the plant.

Unless cared for, a young tree starting life with a well-balanced framework of branches can get out of hand. If growing in extra fertile soil, or inadvertently fed with too much nitrogenous fertilizer, it can rapidly form a dense, crowded head of branches, cutting out light to the middle parts and encouraging disease. Lack of light also causes growth of weak, spindly shoots. If the tree was cut back hard in its prime, it may have responded with a forest of sucker or eater shoots – shoots that grow from dormant buds that occur everywhere on stems and branches. These sucker shoots grow vertically, have amazing vigour and can soon swamp the natural spread of branches. Crowded, rubbing, ingrowing and spindly shoots can easily become diseased or suffer physical damage. And once a shoot has contracted an infection such as coral spot (that gives it an orange pimply look) it is not long before it advances to the main limbs of the tree. Within a year or two a fully-fledged tree in its prime can become an aged cripple – rife with dead and broken branches.

Renovating a neglected tree

If you have a tree in urgent need of surgery, tackle it now, while the sap is returning to the roots and the tree is beginning its autumn and winter rest.

Start by observing the tree from a little distance. Note its natural symmetry. Pick out the main branching system, so that when you prune, you do not remove a limb that will upset the balance of the branches. Then, armed with a sharp saw, secateurs and knife, begin the actual cutting.

First remove any obviously dead and dying branches. Shorten them back to live, white, healthy tissues and seal cuts with a fungicidal compound sealant, such as Arbrex. Next, look to find any crossing branches, those growing inwards towards the trunk and any that are sprouting too close to the trunk – within 30cm (12 in) or so – and cut them back to well-placed

Prune to keep your trees in good shape

replacement leaders or sideshoots. Sucker shoots, easily recognized by their alarming vigour and upright habit are torn off the branch from which they arise.

The ground beneath the tree will now be littered with off-cuts. The tree itself will look decidedly thinner. And what about the main branches? Are they all sound? If some are extra long, they may need shortening to prevent them breaking off and tearing away from the trunk. If there are no suitable replacement leaders to shorten them to, consider bracing the branches.

Bracing With a length of cable and one or two bolts, complete with nuts and washers, you can strengthen the framework of a tree by bracing. This is what you do: having decided that a branch is extra long, and has too acute an angle with the trunk and therefore might shear away in high wind, select a point on the branch for drilling a hole to take a bolt. The bolt is fixed to a length of cable

(through an eye on the bolt) and clamped to the branch with a nut and washer. The other end of the cable is similarly attached to another branch facing in the opposite direction, so the two branches are supporting each other.

Dehorning If the tree has grown too tall and thin, dehorning may be the answer. This action consists of lopping off the tops of branches and is invariably followed by a profusion of growth. After a year or two you thin the 'forest', selecting the strongest shoots to form another framework.

A normally healthy tree that is simply too crowded with principal branches should be thinned carefully. Remove unwanted branches flush with the trunk so the tree retains its symmetry but loses that congested look. Large and small cuts should be pared clean with a sharp knife and painted with a sealant.

If you are faced with a rotten tooth of a branch that broke off many years pre-

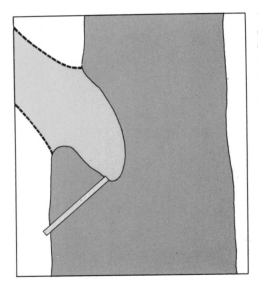

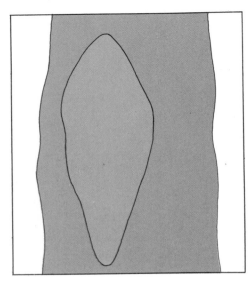

viously, and it is apparent that decay extends into the main trunk itself, the best course of action is to cut off the stump flush with the trunk, then to gouge out the infection with a sharp wood chisel and mallet. Cut out all the diseased wood. This may leave a cavity that could collect water and cause further decay. Overcome this by drilling up the trunk and into the base of the cavity and inserting a drain pipe – a length of 12mm ($\frac{1}{2}$ in) bore metal pipe is usual – so any water that enters drains away quickly. Alternatively, if the cavity is a large one, and the stability of the trunk is jeopardized, fill it with cement. Because of the weight of the cement, this method is more suited for cavities towards the base of the trunk than those higher up. Over the years, as the tree trunk grows, it may loosen the cement filling and allow water to penetrate behind it. An alternative filling is one of a bitumen compound mixed with sawdust; it does not set rigidly and is lighter than cement.

Finally, aim at producing a symmetrical, bowl-shaped arrangement of branches if the tree has a naturally rounded top, or a well-spaced cone of limbs if it ascends sharply.

Removing a large branch

When it is necessary to remove a large limb from a tree, tackle the job in stages, so it does not tear a portion of the trunk away when it falls. Start by sawing off manageable sections, say 45–60cm (18–24 in) long and lowering them to the ground by rope. When you come to the final stump, undercut halfway with a sharp saw, then cut through from the top to meet the first cut. The limb will fall away without ripping any bark from the trunk. Ideally, cut as close to the trunk as possible. Pare the wound clean with a sharp knife and paint with Arbrex.

Pruning roses

Though the main pruning time is mid spring (mid March) roses are better for being trimmed in autumn. Remove seed pods, shortening flowered stems to just above an outward-pointing bud 30cm (12 in) or so beneath the faded blooms. This diverts the plant's energy resources to producing strong new growth.

Cut back by a third to a half any long, whippy stems that increase a plant's wind

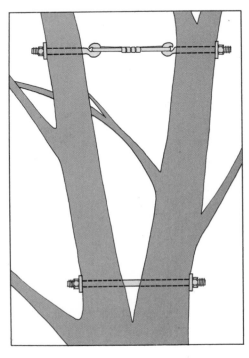

Top left: after cutting off rotten branch, gouge out rotten wood inside trunk and fit metal pipe to drain off water
Centre: if large, fill hole with cement
Left: brace together divergent branches

resistance, causing roots to be loosened and water to collect around the stem at ground level.

Pull up suckers from the stock. Do this by baring the affected root and pulling the sucker away, to prevent it growing from that point any more.

Prune out dead and dying wood, but leave untouched any sturdy new shoots that are not unduly long. By thinning the bushes at this time of year shoots ripen better, there is less wood for pests and diseases to overwinter on and it is easier to spray.

Secateurs There are two main types of secateurs, parrot-billed and anvil.

Parrot secateurs cut with a scissor-like action, that is their blades meet and pass one another. Handles are usually shaped for comfortable use and easy gripping, and are often made in moulded plastic.

Anvil secateurs have one sharpened cutting blade which cuts against a flattened anvil. The disadvantage of some anvil secateurs is that the handles are plain metal and not very comfortable to use. There is a type available with one handle which rotates for easier use.

Anvil and parrot-billed secateurs are made in several sizes, but the small models are really only suited to cutting narrow stems and gathering flowers. Larger models are necessary to cope with thicker stems.

Lopping shears For thicker stems on trees and shrubs. This type will cut stems up to 4cm ($1\frac{1}{2}$ in) thick. Handles come in various lengths, from 20–75cm (8–30 in); the longer ones give better leverage on the blades and so make the cutting easier.

TREES AND SHRUBS TO PRUNE

Apart from conifers, these are mainly deciduous plants that flower from early to late summer (May to July) on shoots produced the previous year. Generally, older non-flowering wood is removed to help the new shoots ripen well and flower strongly the following year.

Conifers and evergreens

This group encompasses *Abies* (silver fir), *Chamaecyparissus* (cypress), *Cupressus* (true cypress), *Larix* (larch), *picea* (spruce), and *Pinus* (pine).

Cut out any dead wood and competing leaders in late summer (July). If the main leader is damaged by insects, or broken by carelessness, do not attempt to train a sideshoot as a replacement: it won't make a satisfactory leader. Wait until the stump sprouts, then select the sturdiest shoot and, if necessary, tie it to a stout cane fixed to the trunk.

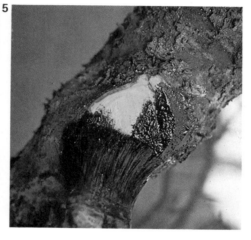

Acer (maple)

Most species make a profusion of twiggy, dense growth. Thin out, preserving symmetry. Shorten long, unbalanced branches to suitable sideshoots. Keep the trunk area free from ingrowing and congested shoots.

Ailanthus (tree of heaven)

Making rapid growth, it can become crowded with thin shoots. Remove these where necessary, and cut back dead and dying wood to clean, healthy tissue.

Alnus (alder)

Can lose its leader or become 'stagheaded' if secondary leaders overtake a damaged central shoot. Take care to preserve its pyramidal or conic shape by judicious thinning and cutting back.

Cornus (dogwood)

Coloured bark types such as *Cornus alba sibirica* and *C. stolonifera flaviramea* are cut back hard to within 15cm (6 in) of the ground in late autumn (October), to sprout afresh the following year and make an inverted cone of shoots valued for their glossy hues when the leaves fall.

Fagus (beech)

Look out for coral spot fungus, when shoots take on an orange pimply appearance. This is a disease to which beech seem prone, so as soon as you see it, cut out and burn all infected wood. Apart from this, thin crowded stems and remove competing leaders.

Fothergilla

Shorten leggy branches to encourage new growth from the base.

Fraximus (ash)

Retain the symmetry by removing ill-placed branches and competing leaders.

Gleditschia (honey locust)

Makes many thin, often spindly, shoots close to the trunk, so thin these out to admit light and air to the middle of the tree. Cut out any shoots growing less than 30cm (12 in) or so from the trunk.

Juglans (walnut)

Autumn pruning is necessary as stems bleed badly if cut in early spring (April) when the sap is rising. Cut out small shoots only. If a large branch has to be removed, and it bleeds, cauterize it by charring the wood with a blowlamp.

Liquidambar (sweet gum)

An upright tree that depends upon a vertical leader to provide character and shapeliness. Seldom needs pruning, then only removal of small branches.

Liriodendron tulipifera (tulip tree)

Retain a sturdy leader and prune branches to upward-facing buds to counter its spreading habit.

Lonicera (honeysuckle)

Thin out old, non-flowering lengths of wood and crowded shoots of late-flowering kinds such as *Lonicera periclymenum* Serotina and *L. japonica*. Train in new shoots for flowering the following year.

Lycium (box thorn)

Cut back extra vigorous shoots to make them branch and remove weak stems.

Magnolia grandiflora (evergreen)

When fan-trained against a wall, shorten unwieldy shoots, thin out crowded ones and tie in growth securely to stop it blowing about in winter gales.

Mespilus (medlar)

Thin out congested growth, shorten long branches to suitable sideshoots and cut out any dead and dying wood.

Platanus (plane tree)

Tolerates severe pruning. Remove weak stems and crowded growth, so light gets to the centre of the tree and encourages vigour.

Potentilla

Remove old non-flowering wood when blooms fade, to encourage strong new shoots to bloom well the following year.

Santolina (cotton lavender)

Shear off flowered growth to induce an abundance of fresh shoots next year.

Above: to remove a branch piece by piece cut halfway from underneath, 1 meet first cut from above, 2 Repeat if necessary so that final cut is flush with trunk, 3 Trim. bark smooth and clean, 4 and seal wood with proprietary sealant 5.

Sowing Lawns

The advantage of making a new lawn from seed is that you can choose the type of grass you want. However, whether it is the sturdy utility grass or the more decorative fine type, it must not be neglected. A perfect lawn is the reward for all your care and effort.

Preparing the ground

So that it has a chance to settle, prepare the soil several weeks before sowing. Dig and manure the site thoroughly and level it by raking the soil in various directions, breaking down any clods of earth and removing stones, weeds and other rubbish.

If the surface is particularly rough you may have to do a more thorough job. Use levelling pegs, a straight 2·50m (8–10 ft) plank of wood and a spirit level. Hammer in one levelling peg to a suitable height and put in the others at 2–2·50m (6–8 ft) intervals. Place the plank on top of the two pegs and check how straight it is with the spirit level. Hammer the pegs in as necessary until the plank is level. Repeat this procedure until all the pegs are at the same height.

Rake the topsoil until roughly the same amount of each peg is showing above the ground. If there are bad bumps or hollows remove some subsoil from the higher to the lower areas, but make sure the topsoil always remains on top.

A few days before sowing, break down the roughly-dug ground with a fork and then firm it by treading over the entire site systematically with your heels. Apply a general-purpose fertilizer, or lawn fertilizer, at 70g per sq m (2 oz per sq yd). Next, rake the site with an iron rake making the soil as fine as possible and removing any large stones and other debris. Then firm and rake the soil again, this time working 'across the grain' of the first raking. Remove any more stones that have reached the surface.

Provided the surface of the soil is dry when you carry out this final preparation, you should now have a really fine surface on which to sow the grass seed. Just before sowing, go over the entire site in every direction very lightly with a rake, drawing it along the surface to produce mini-furrows. This will be a help when you come to cover the seed.

To sow new lawn: **1** remove all debris from site, then dig and manure; **2** break down surface with fork; **3** tread over to firm, then rake; **4** sow seed evenly, releasing slowly; **5** divide ground, and seed, into equal parts for accurate sowing; **6** rake seed in – across previous furrows

Utility lawn mixtures

Next choose your grass seeds: there are mixtures to suit all purposes.

If you require a utility lawn that is very hardwearing and suitable for games and a good deal of foot traffic, choose a utility-grade mixture which includes some really tough grasses. A typical mixture would contain 4 parts Chewing's fescue, 3 parts perennial ryegrass, 2 parts crested dog's tail and 1 part rough-stalked meadow grass.

Chewing's fescue is a fine-leaved dwarf grass which is very drought-resistant and is included in the mixture to help give the lawn a finer appearance. But it will eventually die out and be overtaken by the perennial ryegrass. This is a true utility grass, coarse-leaved, very hardwearing, and especially good on heavier types of soil. It will not stand really close mowing – and indeed a utility lawn should not be closely cut.

Crested dog's tail is another coarse, hardwearing species; it is good on light soils and withstands drought. Rough-stalked meadow grass is of creeping habit and clothes the soil with foliage. It is also a coarse-leaved type and is good on moist, heavy soils.

Luxury-grade mixtures

However, if you prefer a really fine lawn you must choose a luxury-grade mixture containing only fine grasses. Such a lawn is unsuitable for heavy use, but it will provide a beautiful setting for your flower beds and borders. You will have to give it much more attention and more mowing than a utility lawn. Mow it closely: this generally means mowing twice a week in the growing season (spring and summer). You must also feed and water it if you want to keep it looking really good, for it will soon deteriorate if you neglect it; the fine grasses will die out and coarser weed-grasses will take over.

For a fine lawn mixture, choose 7–8 parts Chewing's fescue and 2–3 parts browntop bent. Both are very fine-leaved grasses. Chewing's is a tufted species, while browntop is creeping and covers the surface of the soil with foliage. It is a very drought-resistant species, like Chewing's, but this does not mean that you should neglect to water it in dry weather. This mixture will produce a dense, dark-green sward.

For shaded areas

Normal grass-seed mixtures are unsuitable for shaded areas under large trees or places overshadowed by tall buildings and walls. The grass simply would not grow well and would be thin and patchy. Fortunately, however, it is possible to buy mixtures specially developed for shaded areas. A typical mixture consists of 5 parts rough-stalked meadow grass, 3 parts wood meadow grass and 2 parts creeping red fescue. Wood meadow grass

is very shade-tolerant and is often found growing wild on the edges of woodland and forest clearings. Creeping red fescue is an adaptable species, that is highly drought-resistant and has a creeping habit of growth.

Calculating the quantity

Having decided on a mixture, you must then calculate the quantity of seed you require. You will need to know the sowing rate. For fine lawns this is 35–45g per sq m (1–1¼ oz per sq yd); for others increase the rate to 50–70g (1½–2 oz). Measure the length and width of your site and multiply to calculate the area. It should then be an easy matter to work out the quantity of seed required: multiply the area by the sowing rate.

How to sow

Ideally you should choose a fine, calm day for sowing, when the soil surface is dry. Be sure to sow the seed evenly, otherwise you will have a patchy lawn. Divide the entire site into strips 1m (1 yd) wide by marking out each strip with string, secured by canes at each end.

Then calculate the number of square metres (square yards) in each strip and weigh out sufficient grass seed for each

one. Sow half the seed up and down the strip, and the other half across it. This should ensure even sowing at the correct rate. Repeat the procedure for all the strips until the whole site has been sown.

If you wish to be even more precise you could divide each strip into square metres (square yards) by laying bamboo canes on the soil. Then weigh out the seed into the required number of small lots, sufficient for each square.

When sowing seed by hand, hold it well above the soil, say at waist height, and slowly release the seed as you walk the length and breadth of the area, moving your hand fairly rapidly from side to side. This 'broadcast' method usually ensures very even sowing.

You can also sow the seed with a fertilizer distributor, but only if the machine is adjustable. Obtaining the correct sowing rate is a matter of trial and error. Make practice runs over a sheet of polythene until you find the right setting. Measure out sufficient seed for a given number of square metres (square yards), put this in the distributor and make one run over the measured area of polythene. If the machine runs out of seed before the area is completely sown, or if there is still seed in the machine after running once over the area, then you will need to try other settings. It will only be worth your while using a distributor if you have an exceptionally large lawn; for small gardens, hand sowing is just as quick.

Care of new lawns

After sowing, lightly rake the lawn to cover the seed. Rake across the tiny furrows you made before the seed was sown. You will find that most of the seed is then covered with soil. Don't firm the surface as it may become caked after rain or watering and so inhibit seed germination.

Birds can be a nuisance as they relish grass seed. Some seed is treated with a

bird repellent; otherwise discourage them by stretching black cotton between sticks over the lawn in a criss-cross fashion about 8–10cm (3–4 in) above the soil.

It is very important to water whenever the surface of the soil starts to dry out, both before and after the seeds have germinated. If the soil is allowed to become dry germination will be patchy, and the seedlings can quickly die and wither away. In fact it is essential to carry on watering throughout the summer if you are sowing in spring, or well into the autumn if sowing during early or mid autumn (August or September). Apply the water gently and evenly using a lawn sprinkler on the end of a hosepipe. Always water thoroughly; dribs and drabs do more harm than good, so stand the sprinkler on each portion of the lawn for at least an hour.

The seedlings should appear in two to three weeks if you sow in late spring (April), or within one to two weeks after an early or mid autumn sowing.

Rolling and mowing

Once the seedlings are about 2·5–4cm (1–1½ in) high lightly brush the lawn with a brush or besom to remove any wormcasts. Carry out this task when the lawn is dry. Then you can give the lawn a light rolling – using either a small roller or, preferably, the rear roller of a handmower. This is to firm the surface of the soil which was loosened as the seeds germinated. It also presses into the soil any small stones which might otherwise damage the mower blades. Light rolling induces the grass seedlings to produce new shoots and so speeds up the lawn-making process.

Start mowing when the grass is 5cm (2 in) high. Sharpen the mower blades well as they may tear out the seedlings or severely damage them. Set the blades high so that only the tops of the seedlings are removed.

Weeds usually appear with the new grass but annual weeds soon die out once you start mowing. You can hand-weed a new lawn, but make sure you hold down the grass seedlings with one hand while you pull out the weeds with the other, or you may also pull out the young grass.

On no account should you use the normal hormone lawn weedkillers on a new lawn as they could severely damage or kill the young grass. It is necessary to wait 12 months after sowing before starting to apply them. But there is a special weedkiller (containing the chemical ioxynil) which is suitable if applied according to the maker's instructions.

Laying Turf

The most popular method of making a new lawn is undoubtedly by laying turf, for it creates an immediate effect and the area can be used as soon as the job is complete. Here we detail the preparation necessary before laying the turf and the best conditions and methods in which turfing should be carried out. We anticipate the potential problems and instruct you in the best after care treatment to give your new lawn.

For turf to flourish and produce a successful lawn, thorough soil preparation is necessary and if possible the ground should be prepared a few weeks beforehand to allow for settlement. It is equally important to purchase good, weed-free turfs that are of the same thickness and have them delivered as near as possible to the date you intend to lay them. If they arrive 48 hours before laying, stack them without unrolling; if

there is to be a longer gap between arrival and turfing, unroll each turf and lay it flat.

Marking out curved edges

There has, in recent years, been a breakaway from the traditional square or rectangular lawn in favour of ones with gently curving edges. An irregular lawn site is a bit more difficult to mark out, but the easiest method is to lay out a length of string or rope to mark the outline, then drive in canes or wooden pegs against the string at intervals of about 60–90cm (2–3 ft), and twist the string around them. You will then have quite a durable outline of the lawn to which you can work.

Preparing the site

Thoroughly dig the lawn site to the depth of a spade (single-digging), or, if the subsoil (lower soil) is compacted, to two depths of the spade (double-digging). Be careful not to mix subsoil and topsoil – keep them in their correct layers. A hard subsoil could result in a badly drained or waterlogged lawn if it is not well broken up. During digging incorporate plenty of bulky organic matter in the bottom of each trench, such as well-rotted farmyard manure, garden compost, leaf mould, peat, spent hops or even decomposed straw. This will help to retain moisture in light, sandy or chalky soil during dry weather and will encourage better drainage of surplus water in heavy clay soils.

If you have such a heavy clay soil it would be advisable to incorporate plenty of coarse sand or grit during digging to assist further in drainage of surplus moisture. A good lawn can never be

achieved if the soil holds too much water in the winter. If your site does become very seriously waterlogged in winter, the only satisfactory answer is to have a proper drainage system installed, consisting of tile drains sloping into a soakaway.

Levelling and raking

Once you have completed digging it is best to allow the soil to settle naturally for a few weeks. This is a good time to carry out any general levelling that may be necessary. Then, shortly before laying the turf, final preparations can be undertaken, when the surface of the soil is reasonably dry. Never work on the site when it is wet and sticky or you will end up with a mud patch.

Break down the roughly dug soil with a fork or rake to produce a reasonably fine surface. Then firm the soil by treading systematically over the entire site with as much weight as possible on your heels. At this stage you may apply a general-purpose fertilizer or sterilized bonemeal at 135g per sq m (4 oz per sq yd), which can be incorporated into the surface during final raking.

This raking is to provide a fine, level surface on which to lay the turf, and you should take this opportunity to ensure the site is really level, with no hollows or

5

1 *Begin to lay the turf along one side of the lawn. Be sure the edges are straight*
2 *Turf should be cut with a sharp half-moon edging iron or a sharp knife*
3 *When filling in the turfs, lay them as close together as possible*
4 *Be sure that the turfs are level with the ground or following the slope of the chosen site*
5 *Place more soil under turfs which are too low or remove soil from under those which are too high*
6 *Tamp down the newly-laid turfs to firm them in place*
7 *A newly-turfed lawn has a brickwork pattern which later knits together*
8 *Use a stiff broom to lift the flattened grass and brush in the top-dressing*

bumps. Rake the soil from any high spots into the hollows and firm it well with your heels. The smoother and more level the site, the better the finished job will be.

Laying the turfs

The actual turfing should be done when the surface is reasonably dry. If you have a paved area with a straight edge, this is a good place to start. Lay one row of turfs along, and hard up to, this straight edge. The turfs will generally be 30cm × 1m (12 in × 3 ft) and should be laid lengthways across the site. Allow the turf to overlap your string outline so that when you finish laying you can go round the edges with a knife or half-moon edging iron, cutting them to the required shape, using the string as a guide.

When laying the second row of turfs remember that the joints should be bonded or staggered like bricks in a wall. In other words, the joints of the second row should fall in the centre of each turf in the first row. You should always work over the turf which has already been laid, so it is advisable to stand on a plank to stop your heels sinking into the new turf, especially if it is fairly moist.

Butt the turfs hard up against each other so there are no gaps in the joints. You can push them close together with the tines of a fork used back to front. If the turfs have been well cut and are all of the same thickness they will require little firming. Patting them down with the back of the fork is generally sufficient. If levelling is necessary, do it by adding or removing soil beneath the turfs during laying. Continue turfing the whole site in this way, ensuring that all joints are staggered. To achieve this bonded effect you will need to cut some of the turfs in half at the edges of the lawn.

After turfing, the lawn can be given a light roll if you have a small garden roller. If not, walk up and down the plank, moving this evenly so that the whole lawn is covered eventually.

Adding a top dressing

For a really good finish, brush in a top dressing with a stiff broom. This can be either good, fine topsoil or a mixture of topsoil, coarse sand and fine peat. Apply a 13mm ($\frac{1}{2}$ in) layer over the lawn and work it really well into the grass and joints. Remove any surplus, to ensure the grass is not smothered.

Watering programme

In mid spring it will probably not be necessary to water the turfs after laying as the ground should be moist. But as late spring and early summer approach, with drier weather, you must undertake a regular watering programme. If the turfs are allowed to dry out before they become established or well rooted into the soil, they will shrink and the joints will open up, producing ugly cracks. In addition, the turf will take a long time to become established if it is not watered during dry spells in the spring and summer and it is quite likely the grass will turn brown. It will take a considerable time to recover from this, and weeds may start invading the dried-out patches.

6

7

8

Spring and Summer Lawn Care

You will only achieve a dense lawn of deep green grass, like the rich sward above, by regular maintenance. But spring and summer are the busiest seasons in the lawn care programme when you must mow, feed, weed, rake and water. An oscillating sprinkler of the type illustrated here is a worthwhile investment.

Regular mowing not only maintains the appearance of the lawn, but also helps to get rid of weeds. Feeding puts back into the soil the nutrients that the closely packed roots use up. Weeding is necessary to eliminate moss, clover and other plants that may take over the lawn, and raking clears and cleans the surface.

Watering is essential in hot and dry periods before the shallow roots suffer lasting damage.

How to mow

Start to mow as soon as the grass begins to grow vigorously, which can be mid to late spring (March to April), depending on the weather and the geographical location of your garden. Continue mowing throughout spring and summer, finishing in late autumn (October) when growth stops. Once a week should be sufficient in spring and autumn and during very dry summer spells, but when the grass is growing fast – in late spring and summer – you will need to mow twice a week for a good result.

If the lawn is cut less than once a week during the growing season you will find that, when you mow it, the grass will suffer the sudden loss of a large quantity of leaf, and this can very much reduce its vigour. Also, if you mow infrequently and then shave the lawn too closely, you will quickly ruin it because the fine grasses will be weakened, resulting in a thin, patchy lawn which will rapidly be invaded by weeds such as annual meadow grass, pearlwort, daisies and yarrow.

Remember that mowing does not just ensure a neat lawn, but also encourages dense, healthy growth and helps to reduce weeds and worms. So mow often, but not too closely.

For a utility lawn do not cut the grass any shorter than 3cm (1¼ in) during spring, autumn or in drought conditions. In summer, provided the grass is growing well, cut to 2·5cm (1 in). Fine, luxury lawns can, and should, be mown closer – to 20mm (¾ in) in spring, autumn or during a drought, and to 13mm (½ in) in summer if growth is vigorous.

Mow only when the grass is dry; cutting in wet conditions can pull and bruise the grass and cause mud patches. Scatter wormcasts with a broom or besom before mowing, otherwise the mower will flatten them and produce unsightly patches of mud, inhibit growth and encourage grass seeds to settle. Use a grassbox on the mower so that the cuttings do not build up on the lawn and hamper growth. During droughts, however, a little grass left on the lawn will help keep the roots moist.

If you like a striped lawn mow in parallel (mower-width) strips, slightly overlapping them so that no grass is left uncut. Mow each strip only once, turn, and mow the next in the opposite direction. Next time you cut the grass mow at right angles to the previous cut. This controls the strong shoots of ryegrass that tend to form on the surface and also keeps down weed grasses.

Use of lawn fertilizers

Start feeding once the grass is growing

well, which is generally from late spring to mid summer (April to June). The fertilizer you apply puts back into the soil important plant foods such as nitrogen, phosphorus and potash, which have been used up by the grass. You can apply another dressing of fertilizer in the autumn, but in this case use one of the special autumn lawn fertilizers.

For lush, green grass feed annually – the denser the grass the less trouble you will have from lawn weeds. The best time to apply fertilizer is when the soil is moist; if it is dry you must water the fertilizer well in after application.

There are many excellent lawn fertilizers on the market and all should be used according to the maker's instructions. Apply them evenly and at the correct rate of application. Either scatter by hand or use a fertilizer distributor (a worthwhile implement to buy), being sure to check that the controls are set correctly.

Weeding and raking

Even in the best-kept lawns weeds are bound to appear, generally the rosette-forming, perennial kinds. Unless you can control them they will compete with the grass for food and water. Some, particularly plantains, daisies and dandelions, may also smother the grass.

You can control the majority of weeds with lawn weedkillers that contain the chemicals 2,4-D and fenoprop, or 2,4-D and mecoprop. You must use them strictly according to the manufacturers' instructions, otherwise you may severely damage the grass. Apply them with a watering can kept especially for the job and fitted with a dribble bar. An inexpensive plastic dribble bar can be obtained from any good gardening shop or centre. The best time to apply weedkillers is from late spring to mid summer (April to June), preferably after an application of fertilizer when the grass is growing well. Never apply them during a drought. For persistent weeds you may need a second application about six weeks later.

If there are only a few weeds apply a spot weedkiller, or weed by hand. The best way is to dig them out using a narrow bladed trowel or knife. Try to remove the roots of the weeds without disturbing the soil too much. Fill the holes with a fine soil, firm and sow with the appropriate seed mixture.

Very coarse weed grasses (that have survived mowing) can be controlled by slashing them in various directions with an old knife; weedkillers have no effect on them.

Moss, also, cannot be destroyed by the usual preparations, but should be treated with lawn sand according to the manufacturer's instructions. (Use the same treatment for lichens and algae and also for pearlwort and clover.) Apply it in late spring (April) before you feed the lawn. When the moss has become blackened, rake it off, preferably with a spring-tine lawn rake.

While on the subject of raking, this needs to be done during spring and summer to remove dead, matted grass and other debris which otherwise could choke the grass.

When to water

Water the lawn during dry spells in spring and summer. You will often need to start watering regularly in early summer (May) to keep the grass green and help it to absorb essential plant foods from the fertilizer dressing. Water before the effects of drought are obvious – before the grass starts to turn brown – as it takes a long time to recover and regain its deep green hue.

If the lawn surface has become hard or compacted spike it before watering so that the water is able to penetrate to a good depth. Simply go over the lawn with a fork, pushing it into the soil at 15cm (6 in) intervals to a depth of about 10cm (4 in), or use mechanical spikes.

Watering once a week should be sufficient for most lawns. Increase it to twice a week during very hot, dry weather. It is no use just moistening the surface of the soil, so apply a really good quantity each time using a sprinkler on the end of a hosepipe. The ground must be soaked to a depth of at least 10cm (4 in). This means applying a minimum of 2·5cm (1 in) of water, or 25lit per sq m (4½ gal per sq yd).

Watering can be carried out at any time of day, but if you leave it until the late afternoon or evening, then far less water will evaporate in the sun.

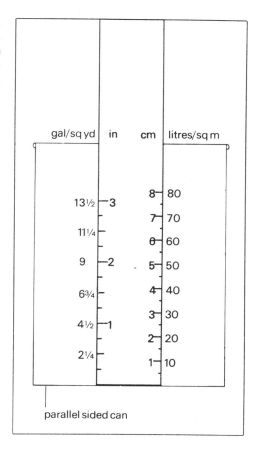

Chart for converting linear units to fluid capacity. If using a ruler (as above) you must allow for any blank space at the start

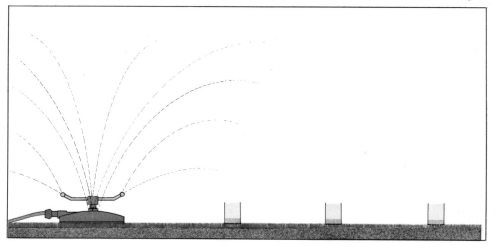

If you arrange 5–6 similar-sized cans in a row, you can easily test the sprinkling time needed for adequate watering (and evenness of distribution) by how quickly and evenly the cans fill with water. In this way you avoid over- or under-watering

Autumn Lawn Care

Autumn is the best time to prepare your lawn for a burst of vigorous, healthy growth in the spring that will be followed by a steady and attractive green throughout the summer. Spiking, top-dressing, fertilizing and general repairs are all best done in mild weather before the onset of winter.

Repairing a hollow in the lawn
1 Straight-edge shows up hollow;

2 using turfing iron to cut through hollow area; 3 lifting off turf; 4 raking level added

soil; 5 checking level before rolling back turf; 6 firming the completed lawn

Continue to mow the lawn about once a week (or as necessary) until growth slows down – usually in late autumn (October). The height of the cut during autumn should be 20mm (¾ in) for fine, luxury lawns and 30mm (1¼ in) for utility lawns.

Avoid mowing the grass when it is wet with rain or dew. First brush it with a besom to encourage the grass to dry quickly. This will also scatter the worm-casts which would otherwise be flattened by the mower. You can mow once or twice in late autumn or winter if the grass is growing, but set the blades fairly high.

Lawn repairs

Autumn is a good time to carry out repairs to the lawn, especially during showery weather so that the repaired areas quickly become established again.

Broken lawn edges are all too common, but fortunately they are very easily mended (see page 385). Using a half-moon turfing iron, cut out a square or rectangle containing the damaged edge. This turf can then be turned round so that the newly-cut part forms the edge, and the old ragged edge now faces inwards. You will now have a hole a few centimetres from

the edge of the lawn, but this can be filled with good topsoil and seeded, or filled with a piece of turf, if available.

Don't forget when carrying out repairs to try to match any new turf or grass seed with the existing grass so that eventually the repaired area merges with the rest of the lawn.

You may have a few bumps in the lawn that are 'scalped' by the mower; now is the time to do something about them. Hollows should also be dealt with at this period as they may hold water, and also prevent the grass from being cut properly.

To cure bumps and hollows, first cut and remove the turf from the affected area, using a knife and spade or a turfing iron. Then remove or add soil as necessary to ensure that the turf will be level. If you have to add soil, use good topsoil – preferably of the same type as the existing soil. It should be well firmed by treading it over with your heels, otherwise it will eventually subside and you will end up with a hollow again.

Once these alterations have been made, replace the turf. Then firm small areas by heavy treading, or large ones with a roller. Fill the joints or cracks with fine, sifted topsoil. This should be brushed well into the cracks and any surplus removed from the lawn.

You may find bare patches on the lawn. These could be due to various things: over-use of the lawn during the summer, an overdose of weedkiller or fertilizer, 'shaving' of high spots by the lawn mower, poor aeration and drainage, or digging out weeds. First correct the cause, if possible, and then carry out repairs. Remove the bare patch of turf and discard it. Try to square up the area if possible. Then loosen the surface of the soil with a hand fork – do not go too deeply. Place some new turfs in the prepared area and firm them by rolling. Fill in the cracks with sifted topsoil.

You may prefer to re-seed a bare patch instead of buying new turf. In this case prick over the affected part with a fork – not too deeply. Add enough topsoil to raise the level of the soil to that of the rest of the lawn. Then rake the area to remove any rubbish and to break down the soil to a fine tilth for sowing. Firm the soil lightly. Sow the appropriate grass-seed mixture at the rate of about 45g per sq m (1½ oz per sq yd). Lightly cover the seed with fine soil and firm it moderately.

If you have tufts of coarse grass in your lawn you may wish to remove them, especially if you have a fine ornamental sward. Dig them out with a hand trowel or sharp knife and re-seed or re-turf as described above.

Autumn fertilizers
Apply an autumn compound fertilizer, containing phosphates, in mid or late autumn (September or October) to encourage the grass to build up a good root system so that it will overwinter well. The best way is to apply it (according to maker's instructions) with a fertilizer

Above: spiking lawn with hollow-tined fork to improve aeration and drainage
Right: a 'true lute' is useful for levelling soil surfaces and working in top dressings

Above right: 'fairy ring' of toadstools caused by the fungus marasmius
Right: brown patch of fusarium fungus disease showing white fungal threads
Left: steel, spring-tined lawn rake

spreader. If you don't have a spreader, apply the fertilizer as evenly as possible by hand, and on a day when there is no wind. Raking (scarification) is one of the most important maintenance jobs as it removes dead, matted grass and other debris that would otherwise build up and retard the growth of the grass. Give a really thorough raking, preferably in two different directions, using a wire lawn rake.

Spiking the lawn

After raking, spike the lawn to improve aeration and drainage; both may be poor if the lawn surface has become hard and compacted due to a great deal of use during the summer. Spiking results in better root growth, and therefore a stronger, healthier lawn that will be more drought-resistant in the summer.

There are special hollow-tine forks for spiking which remove cores of soil. These are highly recommended, especially for heavy soils where drainage is not very good. Alternatively, you can use an ordinary garden fork. If you have an exceptionally large lawn, then a mechanical spiker will save you many hours of work. If using a fork, hollow-tine or otherwise, insert it at 15cm (6 in) intervals all over the lawn. Deep penetration is desirable – at least 8–10cm (3–4 in).

Top-dressing the lawn

After spiking, apply a top dressing. This improves the surface of the soil and results in denser grass. It improves the water-holding capacity of light soils, and will ensure better drainage of heavy, clayey soils by lightening and improving its texture with a higher ratio of sand.

You can easily mix your own top dressing at home. A good general-purpose mixture consists of the following: four parts fibrous sifted loam (or good topsoil), one part fine sphagnum moss peat and two parts coarse horticultural sand. These parts are by volume and you should mix them together as thoroughly as possible.

If you have a very light, sandy soil that is inclined to dry out quickly during dry weather, then increase the quantity of peat and reduce the sand, as for instance: four parts loam, two parts peat and one part sand.

Conversely, for a heavy clay soil, increase the amount of sand and reduce the loam: two parts loam, one part peat and four parts sand.

Apply the top dressing at the rate of 1kg per sq m (2 lb per sq yd). Spread it evenly and brush it well in, using a stiff broom or besom. Work it into the holes produced by spiking. Any surplus should be removed – never leave it lying on the surface of the lawn.

Pests and diseases

Various pests and diseases can be troublesome in the autumn.

Earthworms While not themselves doing any damage to the grass, they make casts of fine, moist soil that are unsightly. If they are flattened by the mower they will cake hard and inhibit growth of grass. So brush off wormcasts before mowing. If you have a bad infestation and wish to eliminate the worms, apply either carbaryl or chlordane in the autumn according to maker's instructions.

Leatherjackets These grubs of crane flies (or daddy long legs) are active in autumn, eating the roots of grass and causing it to die out in patches. Control them by applying BHC dust to the lawn surface.

Fusarium patch Probably one of the most common lawn diseases, it starts off as brown patches, that gradually increase in size and merge together. They are covered in white fungal threads. This disease is worse in poorly aerated turf – so spiking will help to prevent it. To control fusarium patch, apply a mercury-based fungicide according to the maker's instructions.

Corticium disease ('red thread') Seen as pinkish patches on the lawn with red fungus growths on them. Again the control is to apply a mercury-based fungicide, as above.

Dollar spot A less common fungus disease. It appears as small circles, about 5cm (2 in) in diameter, which are brown at first and later take on a bleached appearance. As soon as the trouble is noticed, treat with a mercury-based fungicide.

Toadstools These may appear on the lawn in autumn. If they are growing in a circle of dark green grass with a dead patch in the centre, then they are due to the fungus marasmius. The symptoms are popularly referred to as 'fairy rings'. This disease is difficult to control with chemicals, and the most effective treatment is to remove the turf and soil from the affected area and refill with fresh topsoil. Then re-turf or sow the area with grass seed.

Clearing the leaves

Finally, as it is autumn, the leaves will be falling from the trees. It is advisable to remove these regularly from the lawn by brushing, raking or using a lawn leaf-sweeper. If left too long a layer of leaves can cause the grass to turn yellow. They can also encourage worms.

Weeds and Weed Control

What is a weed? The short answer to that question is: any plant growing where it is not wanted. For instance, a grape seedling germinating in your dahlia bed is a weed – unless you want a vine amongst the dahlias. In a stricter sense, weeds are the native ancestors of our cultivated garden plants; they are undesirable because they are less attractive, generally bear smaller flowers or fruits, and are more vigorous in competition with their descendants. Weeds compete for water, nutrients and light, and often deprive cultivated plants, especially the seedlings and young ones, of their fair share of these necessities, because weeds adapt better to less favourable conditions.

There are two basic types of weeds – perennial and annual: the former are far harder to eliminate.

PERENNIAL WEEDS

Most perennial weeds are quick-growing and tenacious, often re-growing from roots or rootstocks. They are, therefore, very difficult to get rid of. Herbaceous types, such as couch grass, bindweed (convolvulus and calystegia species) and ground elder are often notoriously deep-rooted. They store food in their fleshy roots, rhizomes, stolons, tubers or bulbs. It is easy to remove the visible vegetation but difficult to eradicate the roots. With woody plants, such as brambles and ivy, it is harder to get rid of the growth above ground, but comparatively easy to eradicate the roots, which must be burnt.

Below: daisy (Bellis perrenis)

Manual weeding

Good hand-weeding is still one of the best ways to rid yourself of perennial weeds. Some well-timed work with a trowel will save you much time and trouble later on – providing you don't leave any of the roots in the soil.

If working near decorative or vegetable plants where you don't want to use chemical weedkillers, then manual weeding becomes a necessity. You may need to use a fork, trowel, knife or even a mattock (like a pickaxe). Be careful that you don't just carve them up; this merely helps to propagate them and makes more work in the future. Dig up the weeds, complete with roots, and then burn them or put them in the garbage bin.

When cultivating fresh ground it is essential to remove all the roots and underground storage systems; although hard work, it pays to lift them out by hand. Don't use a rotary cultivator on couch grass or dock-infested land as it will only chop up the weeds and encourage regrowth. Hoeing can have the same effect on a smaller scale unless you take care to remove the root, not just chop off leaves.

Weedkillers

Weedkillers are categorized according to their mode of action, so that you can buy whichever is most suited to your needs.

Total In an area devoid of decorative or culinary plants you can use a 'total' weedkiller, such as aminotriazole, to 'sweep the board'. A total weedkiller will kill all plants with which it comes into contact. You must take great care not to let it drift onto other plants or onto your neighbour's property. There have been many skirmishes over the garden wall as a result of misapplied weedkillers. After using it, remove and burn the debris and plant nothing in the ground for two to three months. If treatment with a total weedkiller is followed by a dose of a residual weedkiller (such as simazine) you will have a weed-free site for several months.

Another total weedkiller is sodium chlorate. It has to be used with great care as it spreads in the soil and can kill plants some distance away from the spot it was applied. Another danger is that, mixed with many other substances, it may be spontaneously inflammable, and it is therefore dangerous to store. It has a residual effect for up to a year.

Total and residual weedkillers are best for clearing paths and driveways.

Residual or pre-emergent These will not kill established weeds but they help to prevent the germination of most weeds for up to three months. There are various degrees of persistence.

Simazine has a long persistence, but it can be harmful to some shrubs (such as deutzia). Propachlor lasts for shorter periods but is less toxic and so is useful for herbaceous borders and shrubberies.

This type remains in a narrow band of the topsoil, so that any weed seeds germinating in this zone take up the chemical and die. It is possible to apply residual weedkiller where bulbs are planted, because their roots are located below the weedkiller band, and they grow quickly through it without suffering any damage. Plants such as runner beans, sweet peas, daffodils and hyacinths will all grow through the weedkiller layer after it has become inactive.

Selective Some weedkillers are termed 'selective' as they kill dicotyledons (broad-leaved plants), but will not damage many monocotyledons – such as grasses. Selective ones like 2,4-D, MCPA, 2,4,5-T or fenoprop (hormone types) kill by causing the plant to overgrow its food reserves so that it literally grows itself to death. Use this kind with great care as the slightest drift will damage crops; tomatoes are especially sensitive to them.

Non-selective The well-known paraquat and diquat weedkillers will only kill perennial weeds while they are still at seedling stage. After a few weeks they become immune and these preparations merely burn off their foliage and allow the roots to re-grow. They are de-activated immediately they meet the soil and are therefore safe to use provided they do not drift. But they must be kept away from children and animals: under no circumstances store them in old lemonade or other misleading bottles.

Methods of application

Always read the maker's instructions on the package and follow them closely; they have been based on years of research. Our recommendations give the chemical name, so when buying proprietary brands check the package label and see that it contains the correct constituents for your purpose. Keep a separate watering can for use with chemical weedkillers, and use a rose fitting or dribble-bar attachment for controlled application.

Specific treatments

Some perennial weeds are particularly stubborn and require special treatment.

Oxalis Remove these plants, which defy all chemical killers, with a sharp knife. Be sure to get up all roots and little bulbs.

Couch grass and perennial oat-grass These persistent grasses, with rhizomes, put up a fight against eradication. The only effective control is dalapon. If they are found in flower or vegetable beds 'spot' apply several doses of dalapon and then dig out the remains.

'Spot treatment' involves applying the weedkiller to the weeds only. It is done most easily by using a bottle with a pourer top or a squeezy-type container.

Docks Repeated action with dichlobenil (not easily obtainable), or spot treatment with 2,4-D, MCPA, fenoprop or mecoprop will keep the plants down. They are difficult to control because the roots, if broken on being dug out, will grow again.

Perennial nettle, bindweed, ground elder and blackberry These tend to grow near hedges or in shrubberies, and once established are likely to remain permanent residents. Apply 2,4,5-T or brushwood killer (usually a mixture of 2,4-D and 2,4,5-T) but avoid spraying onto other plants.

A good way to minimize drift is to make up a solution of this weedkiller in a container and dip the tips of the weeds in it. This will then be taken up through the plant by the sap stream – and kill it. You may need to make several applications over a few days for them to be effective. This method also works on many wild, shrubby plants such as dog rose and ivy (*Hedera helix*).

Thistles These are particularly obstinate weeds that may need pulling out by hand.

Above: bindweed (Convolvulus arvensis)

Below: annual nettle (Urtica urens)
Bottom: creeping thistle (Cirsium arvense)

Above: couch grass (Agropyron repens)
Below: dock (Rumex obtusifolius)

Above: sow-thistle (Sonchus asper)
Below: chickweed (Stellaria media)

Wait till the ground is slightly moist, and be sure to wear gloves. Repeated doses of 2,4,5-T will help to weaken them.

Lawn weeds

The rosette-forming types (such as daisy, dandelion and plantain) are the most successful on lawns as they tend to escape the lawn-mower blades. To spot-apply weedkillers to lawn weeds use a small dropper bottle.

Dandelion, daisy, creeping buttercup, ribwort and plantain Proprietary lawn weedkillers containing MCPA and 2,4-D with mecoprop or fenoprop usually bring quick death, but must be applied in strict accordance with the makers' instructions.
Speedwell Mecoprop/ioxynil mixture is required to check this weed.
Yarrow Use repeated doses of mecoprop. Feeding the lawn with sulphate of ammonia should hasten the expiry date.
Couch grass and perennial oat-grass Two very difficult grasses to remove from lawns. Close and frequent mowing will go a long way towards finishing them off; otherwise you must dig them out with a knife. Effective weedkillers cannot be used as they would kill the lawn as well.

ANNUAL WEEDS

Annual weeds, by definition, mature, flower, seed and die within one year. 'Seed' is the operative word here, because this is the method by which they reproduce and infest the garden. It is also the key to their control; if you can remove the seed before it reaches the soil you can stop the next generation of weeds before it starts.

Many species of annual weeds grow quickly and succeed in completing several generations each year. The seeds seem to be able to germinate at any time of the year, even the middle of winter. So never assume that weeds are 'out of season'; although they may grow more slowly in winter they are always lurking.

Some of the most common annual weeds that you are likely to encounter are: chickweed, speedwell, groundsel, knotgrass, shepherd's purse, annual nettle, charlock, sow-thistle, scarlet pimpernel, goose-grass and wild radish.

Weeding by hoeing

One of the most common, and time-honoured, ways of controlling annual weeds is by hoeing. The secret of successful hoeing is to choose a day that is dry, sunny and, preferably, has a steady breeze. All these factors help to dry out the weed seedlings on the soil surface and prevent them re-rooting.

Persicaria (Polygonum lapathifolium)

Don't just decapitate the weeds when you hoe; make sure the roots are removed.

In a way, you make extra work for yourself by hoeing because you constantly bring more weed seeds to the surface where they germinate. Seeds can remain viable in the ground for years, waiting until they come near to the surface before starting to grow. Some seeds are very sensitive to the amount of daylight available and can only spring into life when they are in the topmost layer of soil. Regular hoeing, however, will keep weed seedlings under control.

Controlling with weedkillers

Most annual weeds are more easily controlled by weedkillers than their perennial counterparts. A whole range of annuals succumb to applications of dichlobenil or propachlor. Both these weedkillers are residual, but last only a few months. Diquat and paraquat are

Red deadnettle (Lamium purpureum) also known as bad man's posies

very useful for killing germinating weed seedlings. You can spot apply these anywhere provided you take care not to let them drift onto other plants.

Unlike many perennials, annual weeds germinate within the narrow soil-surface band to which the weedkillers have been applied; therefore they die almost as soon as they start growing. So, on the whole, these weedkillers tend to be more effective against annuals. Always remember where these chemicals have been put down and make sure that no horticultural activities 'break the band' as this will allow the weeds to come through unscathed.

Special treatments

There are a few stubborn annual weeds that do not succumb easily to dichlobenil and propachlor. These usually need an application of another type (or mixture) of weedkiller.
Rayless mayweed (pineapple weed) Treat with mecoprop or mecoprop with ioxynil.
Common persicaria Several doses of propachlor or dichlobenil may be required before you eventually get rid of it.
Red deadnettle Repeated applications of mecoprop will be needed.

Annual lawn weeds

As well as the tough perennial lawn weeds, you are also likely to encounter some troublesome annual ones. One good preventive measure is to use a grass-collecting box on the lawn-mower. This will stop many weeds falling back on the lawn and propagating themselves.
Chickweed Best controlled with mecoprop which is often applied with 2,4-D as a general lawn weedkiller.
Lesser yellow trefoil Several applications of mecoprop may be needed; or use fenoprop.
Lesser common trefoil This weed often flourishes where grass is short of nitrogen. Feed the lawn with sulphate of ammonia in spring to lessen the chance of this weed getting established.

Pests – Prevention and Control

The word 'pest' conjures up, for many people, a vision of hordes of greenfly on roses or blackfly on broad beans. The vision is quite justified because both are pests and both tend to infest on an epidemic scale. Agriculturists and horticulturists view any organism that interferes with crops as a pest—whether it be a virus or a predatory animal.

This chapter leaves aside the viruses (and fungi and bacteria) and the animals like rabbits and moles and concentrates on insects and insect-like pests, including also slugs and snails (molluscs) and eelworms (nematodes).

Insects are the largest group of creatures on earth. In evolutionary terms they are highly successful, and have proved to be man's fiercest competitors. Historically, insects have caused more deaths to mankind than all wars put together.

Insects will attack most plants, whether they live in the garden, the house or the greenhouse. Like all illnesses and disorders, prevention is better than cure and the best way to reduce your losses is to ensure that your plants are healthy when planted and then well cared for. Many physiological disorders of plants (caused, for instance, by too little water or too much nitrogen fertilizer) pave the way for attack by pests. So as soon as you notice any signs of distress or damage—act promptly.

Knowing what to look for

The pest itself may be almost invisible. Eelworms, for instance, are difficult to see under a microscope. But their size bears no relation to the damage they can do. Even visible pests may not always be sitting in full view. You may have to dig underground and study the roots to determine the cause of the trouble, or wait for night to catch such creatures as slugs.

Pests which attack leaves and flowers are the most easily identified because the damage occurs rapidly and is usually quite recognizable. Two main groups of pests attack leaves: those which have biting mouthparts (for example beetles) and those with sucking mouthparts (such as greenfly). They may hide inside or outside the leaves or, like the notorious leaf-miner, burrow between the middle layers of leaf tissue.

Larger pests (like caterpillars) are usually more noticeable but they may attack and run (or fly) away, in which case you should spray, or lay bait, against the next visit.

Fortunately there are many methods of control at your fingertips, providing you diagnose the enemy correctly and act as swiftly as you can.

Understanding the enemy

Knowing something about the life cycles and habits of pests can help you in anticipating and preventing trouble. For instance a major factor in determining how active they are is temperature; the warmer it becomes the busier they get. And up to 35°C (95°F) they breed faster too. Cold winters greatly decrease the numbers overwintering in the garden.

Day length also plays a part in controlling the breeding seasons and migration patterns of many insects. This is why they always become scarce in autumn, even before cold weather arrives. Clear away and burn garden refuse every autumn because it provides ideal shelter for overwintering pests. Many overwinter as eggs which can also be destroyed by the use of insecticides.

Use of insecticides

Most pesticides are sold under trade names, partly because the chemical names and formulae are cumbersome and difficult to remember. You can, however, be sure of getting the right product by reading the contents on the label and checking with the chemical, or proper, name given here. Full chemical names are

often abbreviated, for instance benzene hexachloride is known as BHC. (It is also sometimes called gamma-BHC.)

Always use protective clothing. Rubber gloves are important and be sure always to wash hands and face thoroughly after using insecticides. Never allow children or animals to be with you when sprays are being applied, and don't let them eat anything that has just been sprayed. Also wash out all spraying equipment after use—but not in the kitchen sink.

In some cases you may be able to use physical methods of combat such as picking caterpillars off plants and burning them. These are always preferable to spraying, because all sprays have some adverse effect on the plant. This is why you must adhere strictly to the manufacturer's recommended rate of application.

How insecticides work

Insecticides kill in two main ways; first as a stomach poison, when the pest either eats it with the leaf or sucks it up with the plant sap. Alternatively, if the pest is sprayed directly, the chemical will poison

Left: aphides attack indoor and outdoor plants. Opposite left: cabbage-root fly larvae is a danger in the vegetable garden. Bottom left: onion fly, enemy of the onion bulb family. Below: cabbage white butterfly, whose caterpillars cause such damage. Below centre: cabbage white caterpillar eating brassica leaves. Bottom: the ubiquitous slug, menace of all gardens. Bottom right: potted palm showing red spider mite damage

through the 'skin' or suffocate the pest. The method you choose depends on several factors, such as climate, type of insect and type of plant involved.

Non-systemic ('knock-down') insecticides Many early insecticides killed either by blocking the breathing processes or by poisoning when absorbed through other exterior surfaces. But they did not persist for long and had to be used frequently in order to be effective. However, some are still very useful for certain purposes.

Pyrethrum and derris, for example, are both very effective general insecticides. They are derived from plants and do not persist for long. This means they are safe to use on vegetables—even up to the day before harvesting. Derris, however, is harmful to fish so do not use it near stocked pools.

But DDT, used by gardeners for so many years, has now been withdrawn from the gardening market as other, newer insecticides have proved to be safer and equally (if not more) efficient. Trichlorphon is one good modern substitue for DDT.

Systemic insecticides The systemics are absorbed by the plant and dispersed throughout its entire system; any biting or sucking insect will ingest them while feeding and be killed. These pest-killers remain in the plant for several days (sometimes even weeks) and they act against a wide variety of pests.

But too often spraying can result in the development of pests that are resistant to them. So spray on sighting the enemy rather than 'just in case'.

Dimethoate and formothion are systemic insecticides that control most aphides, red spider mite, scale insect, mealy bug, caterpillars and leaf hoppers. Systemic insecticides are also one of the most successful ways of killing many of the root-feeding insects, such as lettuce root aphid.

PLACE	COMMON PESTS	PLANT AREA	TREATMENT	OTHER ADVICE
GREENHOUSE PLANTS	Aphides Whitefly	Leaves Stems Flowers	Treat as for house plants or fumigate greenhouse with nicotine, dichlorvos or BHC.	Make sure all vents are closed while fumigating. Do not enter until fumes have dispersed.
	Scale insect	Leaves	Wipe off, but if badly infested spray with malathion, nicotine or systemic insecticides.	Scrape insects off where possible.
	Red spider mite	Leaves	Spray malathion, derris or pyrethrum.	Pick off and burn badly-infected leaves.
	Mealy bug	Leaves Stems	Spray with systemic or non-systemic insecticides.	Scrape insects off where possible.
	Leaf hopper	Leaves	Spray with BHC, malathion or nicotine, often available in aerosol or smoke form.	
	Leaf miner	Leaves	Spray with BHC or malathion.	Pick and burn infected leaves.
	Vine weevil	Roots	Remove and destroy grubs found when repotting plants. Drench soil of infected plants with BHC solution.	Incorporate naphthalene or paradichlorbenzene among the crocks when known susceptible plants are repotted.

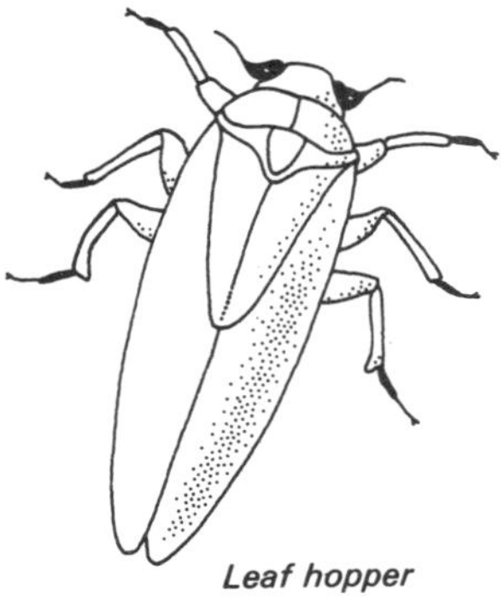

Leaf hopper

PLACE	COMMON PESTS	PLANT AREA	TREATMENT	OTHER ADVICE
HOUSE PLANTS	Aphides Whitefly	Leaves Stems Flowers	Non-systemic sprays: e.g. derris, pyrethrum, are often sufficient. For bad attacks use systemics, e.g. dimethoate.	Check all newly-acquired potted plants and eradicate any pests to prevent them spreading among your existing plants.
	Mealy bug	Leaves Stems	Spray with systemic or non-systemic insecticides, or dab with methylated spirit.	Scrape insects off where possible.
	Scale insect	Leaves	Wipe with a soft cloth dipped in soapy water or methylated spirits, or treat as for aphides and whitefly.	Place your house plants in the greenhouse when you fumigate and do both jobs at once.
	Leaf hopper	Leaves	Spray with BHC, malathion or nicotine (often available in aerosol form).	
	Leaf miner	Leaves	Spray with BHC or malathion.	Pick and burn infected leaves.
	Vine weevil	Roots	See GREENHOUSE PLANTS	

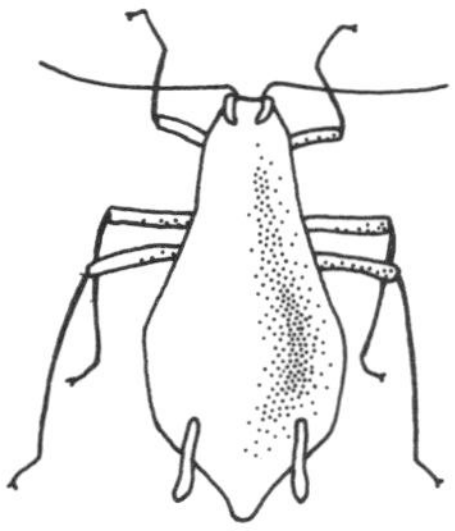

Aphid

PLACE	COMMON PESTS	PLANT AREA	TREATMENT	OTHER ADVICE
FLOWER GARDEN	Aphides Whitefly	Leaves Stems Flowers	Spray with systemic insecticide such as dimethoate or formothion.	Malathion is also effective.
	Scale insect	Leaves Stems	Spray with malathion or systemic insecticide.	Scrape off insects where possible.
	Earwigs	Flowers	Reduce populations by spraying with BHC or trichlorphon prior to flowering.	Place inverted, straw-filled flower pot traps on 1m (3 ft) canes near plants; burn resulting earwig nests.
	Capsid bug	Leaves Stems Flowers	Spray with BHC or malathion as soon as damage appears.	Prompt action is essential.

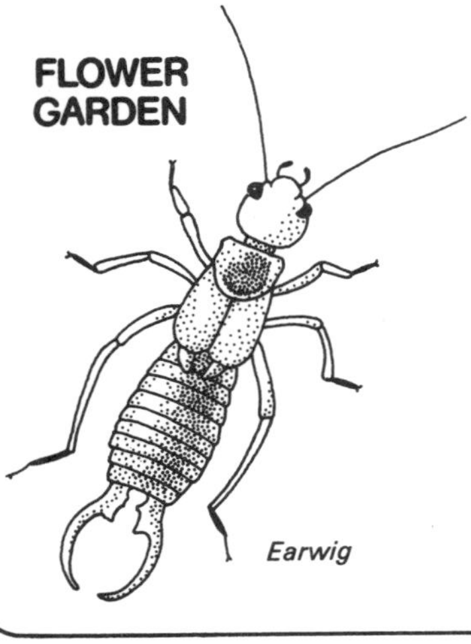

Earwig

PLACE	COMMON PESTS	PLANT AREA	TREATMENT	OTHER ADVICE
VEGETABLE GARDEN	Caterpillars	Leaves	Spray or dust with BHC, malathion or derris.	Pick caterpillars off where possible.
	Cutworm	Roots Stems	Work BHC dust or bromophos into the soil when planting.	Prevention is better than cure.
	Slugs Snails	Leaves Stems	Spray or apply pellets of metaldehyde or methiocarb.	These pests usually attack at night.
	Pea/bean weevil Grubs Thrips	Leaves Pods Peas	Apply BHC dust or fenitrion.	Apply when first flowers open and again 2 weeks later.
	Flea beetle	Leaves	Apply BHC dust when sowing seeds and at seedling stage.	Keep seedlings covered with dust until true leaves appear.
	Aphides	Leaves Shoots	Spray with systemic insecticides or malathion.	Watch for a reinfestation.
	Whitefly	Leaves	Spray with pyrethrum, dimethoate or BHC.	Malathion is also effective.
	Cabbage-root fly Carrot fly	Roots	Dust or spray BHC.	Keep seedlings covered with dust until true leaves appear.

Thrips

PLACE	COMMON PESTS	PLANT AREA	TREATMENT	OTHER ADVICE
FRUIT GARDEN	Caterpillars	Leaves	Spray or dust with BHC, malathion or derris.	Pick caterpillars off where possible.
	Aphides	Leaves Shoots	Spray with a systemic insecticide.	Watch for a reinfestation.
	Woolly aphides	Stems	Spray malathion or a systemic insecticide.	Systemic insecticides can be used, but at least 21 days before harvesting.
	Maggots	Fruits	Spray fenitrothion, BHC or derris.	Spray twice, in mid and late summer, as prevention.
	Gooseberry sawfly	Leaves	Spray thoroughly with derris or malathion.	Attacks usually occur in early summer.
	Capsid bug	Leaves Fruits	Spray with BHC or malathion as soon as damage is noted.	Prompt action is essential.
	Red spider mite	Leaves	Spray malathion, derris or pyrethrum, or a systemic.	Spray systemics 21 days before picking.

Codling moth maggot

PLACE	COMMON PESTS	PLANT AREA	TREATMENT	OTHER ADVICE
FLOWER GARDEN CONTINUED	Caterpillars	Flowers	Spray with BHC or trichlorphon.	Pick caterpillars off by hand.
	Leaf miner	Leaves	Spray with BHC or malathion or use systemic insecticide.	Pick off and burn badly-infected leaves.
	Frog hopper (Cuckoo spit)	Leaves Stems	Spray with malathion, BHC, derris or pyrethrum.	Can be washed off with spray of soapy water.
	Slugs Snails	Leaves Stems	Spray or apply pellets of methaldehyde or pyrethrum.	These pests are most active at night.
	Thrips	Flowers	Spray pyrethrum.	Prompt action is important.
	Red spider mite	Leaves	Spray malathion, derris or pyrethrum.	Pick off and burn badly-infected leaves.

Scale insect

75

Plant Diseases

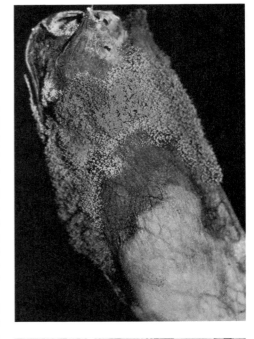

Fungi, bacteria and viruses are the three main causes of plant disease, and of these the most important to the gardener are the fungi. Unlike insects, they can only live in and with the plant they infect, and they are common in all plants, large or small – from the tiniest seedling affected by 'damping-off' to the tall and sturdy elm tree laid low by Dutch elm disease.

Although it is quite often a simple matter to recognise that a plant is diseased – discoloration, distortion of growth, even a general air of listlessness, are all easily observed symptoms – it is usually much harder to diagnose exactly what is wrong with it. It is important, therefore, to learn to recognize the different kinds of fungal infection, so that the right remedies can be applied where possible and without delay.

Propagation of fungi

Most fungi propagate by spores (which are very similar in kind, although not in appearance, to the seeds of plants), and these can be carried from plant to plant by the wind, rain, soil or plant debris, animals and birds, and other means. Each fungus will produce many spores, and this is one of the reasons why they spread so quickly through a bed of plants, a greenhouse, or a whole garden.

Other fungi, and particularly those that attack roots, spread by means of mycelium (a fibrous growth that has much the same function as the roots or stems of plants).

The majority of fungi spread and do most damage in moist, warm conditions. To reduce the likelihood of fungal infection of roots, therefore, it is important to keep the soil well drained; and in the greenhouse adequate ventilation is essential. However, some fungi (of which the powdery mildews are an outstanding example) prefer drier conditions.

Fungus infection of seedlings

'Damping off', or seedling blight, is common when seeds are raised under unhygienic conditions The disease is often due to a complex infection by different species of fungi, some of which are closely related. Pythium species and phytophthora species (sometimes known

as watermoulds) thrive under wet conditions, and their spores are present in all soils. This is why it is essential to germinate all seed in sterilized (and therefore fungus-free) soil or compost, and to use clean pots and trays.

On sterilized soil damping-off will rapidly emerge through a batch of newly-emerged seedlings, and it is worthwhile to water with Cheshunt compound before and after germination. If the disease does take hold, watering with Cheshunt compound, captan, thiram or zineb may check it.

Plants that are growing well are less liable to attack, but even sturdy seedlings will still succumb if they are not well-cared for: over-watering and lack of ventilation are the principal cause of infection at this stage. Seedlings that have been too well nourished with excessive nitrogen may show similar symptoms.

Fungal attack of roots

The majority of species of fungus attack the leaves and other aerial parts of the plant, but there are some that spread through the soil.

Bootlace fungus The mycelium grows to look exactly like a black bootlace, but wherever it encounters dead wood it is

Above right: grey mould (botrytis) attacks many plants, especially in wet weather
Right: damping off (seedling blight) is a fungus infection
Below: bootlace fungus grows from the roots beneath the tree bark

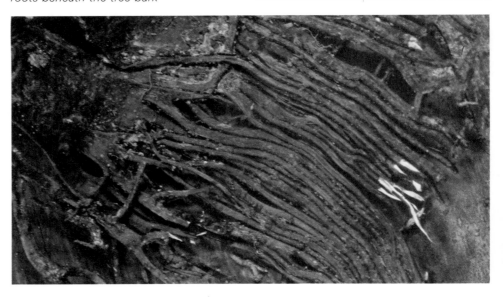

likely to throw up a toadstool, which releases spores into the air. The 'bootlace' grows from the roots beneath the bark of the tree, where it also forms yellowish-white sheets of fungus that have given it the alternative name 'honey fungus'. A tree that is badly affected must be dug up and burnt; and the soil must be sterilized with a mixture of 1 part of formaldehyde to 6 parts of water, applied at a rate of 27 lit per sq m (5 gal per sq yd). Where infection is not too serious, a creosote-like chemical, Armillatox, may be sufficient to control the disease and allow the tree or bush to recover.

Club root Very common and attacks all members of the brassica or cabbage family (and this includes wallflowers). The plants look weak and yellow and the roots are swollen. Liming the soil helps to prevent the disease; so does a crop-rotation system. Calomel dust applied at planting time reduces the likelihood of attack, and dipping the roots in benomyl just before planting has also proved effective.

Crown gall Produces symptoms similar to clubroot, but attacks many different kinds of plant. It is favoured by wet soils: provide adequate drainage, and avoid injury to the roots. Dipping plants in a copper fungicide such as Bordeaux mixture at planting time provides protection.

Brown core Attacks polyanthus and primula roots, and the plants then become weak and sickly. Burn all affected plants and grow no others of the family on that ground for several years.

Above left: conifer gall, a white blight, may affect any conifer tree. Left: club root attacks the brassica family
Below left: roses are susceptible to powdery mildew
Below: downy mildew likes the damp

Violet root rot Affects several plant groups and is easily recognized by the characteristic strands of purple mycelium on the plant roots. Destroy all infected plants and introduce resistant crops. Violet root rot only rarely occurs in land that is in 'good heart' and so attention to drainage and soil fertility is the best means of prevention.

Black root rot Most likely to strike where plants are grown in the same place every year; it also affects pot plants. Drench the soil with captan solution.

Fungal attack of shoots and leaves
Many different fungi attack shoots and leaves, and the following are the most common examples.

Grey mould (botrytis) Prevalent in wet weather, it attacks numerous plants. Remove the infected plants to control spread of the disease, but for really effective control use benomyl, captan, thiram or zineb.

Powdery mildew Found on almost all plants, and there is often a specific species for a particular plant. This is a fungus which favours drier weather for attacks. Plants most commonly infected are roses, gooseberries, apples and Michaelmas daisies. The mildew forms a white powder on the leaves, shoots and flowers. Greenhouse plants also suffer. Cut out infected shoots on trees and shrubs the following autumn, otherwise re-infection can occur. Spray with benomyl, dinocap or thiophanate-methyl. On plants which are not sulphur-shy, sulphur or lime-sulphur sprays may be used. Many varieties of apple are sulphur-shy, for example, so it is important to make sure before using the spray. Generally the container for the mixture lists the plants and varieties for which it is unsuitable.

Downy mildew By contrast with the powdery types, downy mildew thrives in damp, cool conditions. Grey or whitish furry growths appear on leaves and spread very rapidly. Zineb is the best chemical to use.

Potato blight Related to downy mildew, and the treatment is similar. Remove and burn any plants that become very diseased.

White blister Similar to downy mildew, but the spores are liberated from blisters or pustules. The only course is to burn the affected plants, but individual diseased leaves may be removed and burnt if the infection is caught in time.

Silver leaf Affects plums, peaches, cherries and ornamental prunus, turning the leaves silvery. Cut out diseased material and treat all wounds with a protective bituminous paint.

Top left: apple canker spreads along the bark, killing young shoots, and should be treated without delay
Above: the fruiting fungus of silver leaf appears on the bark of affected trees
Centre: rust — a mass of orange, yellow or brown pustules on the leaves
Far right: beware apple scab on leaves, stems or fruit in summer

Fusarium wilt Often the cause of plants looking sickly, with yellowing leaves which appear to wilt, even in wet weather. This fungus blocks the 'plumbing' system of the plant. The spores lie in the soil for considerable periods; it can be sterilized with formaldehyde, but growing on fresh soil is often the only solution.

Apple scab Common throughout the growing season, attacking ornamental malus species such as crab-apple, pears and culinary apples. It infects leaves, stems and fruits, producing olive-green blotches on the leaves, and brown or black scabs on the fruit. Spray with lime-sulphur when flower buds emerge, but do not use on sulphur-shy varieties (see instructions on the spray container). Benomyl, captan or thiram may be sprayed from bud-burst until late summer (July). Rake up all dead leaves and burn them in the winter to prevent further spread.

Rusts Attack many plants, but hollyhocks are particularly prone. All rusts appear as orange, yellow or brown powdery masses. You can obtain resistant varieties which prevent spores germinating on the leaves. Mancozeb, zineb or maneb fungicides sprayed at fortnightly intervals should cure most rust infections.

Black spot Attacks roses and is probably one of the most common of fungal diseases. It starts as dark brown spots which grow up to 2cm (1 in) across. Infected leaves fall during mid summer. It also affects stems and will remain on the plant to re-infect the following season. Burn all diseased leaves and stems, and spray with benomyl, captan or zineb at the initial infection stage.

Cane spot and spur blight Affect raspberries and loganberries. Both form purple blotches; spur blight becomes mottled with black, and cane spot as it develops becomes white. Apply a copper fungicide such as Bordeaux mixture at bud-burst and, in the case of cane spot, again when the fruit has set. Thiophanate-methyl or benomyl may be used throughout the blossom period.

Stem cankers Attack many trees and shrubs. The first signs are poor, weak growth and soft patches of bark. These patches later erupt into unsightly reddish-pink pustules that spread along the bark, causing the shoots to die back. There is no chemical control for the disease, and the only solution is to cut off and burn all infected stems at once. Paint the wounds with a protective bituminous paint, such as Arbrex.

Diseases affecting tubers

These diseases can affect the other storage organ type plants as well as tubers.

Basal rot Often occurs on crocuses, narcissi and lilies. It spreads from the base as a brown rot, eventually rotting the whole bulb. It will attack at any time, even when bulbs are in storage. Cut out infected areas, dust with quintozene.

Smoulder and dry rot Attack bulbs, although smoulder is only usual on narcissus. Dry rot has a wider range and can be stopped by dipping healthy bulbs in solutions of benomyl or captan. Smoulder tends to occur in storage and a cool dry storage place helps to prevent it. If you see any signs during the growing season, spray zineb at fortnightly intervals. Other storage rots and some bulb or corm scabs should be treated in a similar manner to dry rot.

White rot and neck rot White rot is very common on spring onions and on maincrop types during the growing season. It persists in the soil and if your crop has been infected grow onions on a new site the following year. Calomel dust in the seed drills reduces the danger.

Parsnip canker Appears as brown patches and cracks on the shoulder of the parsnip, which can then be attacked by pests. The best remedy is to rotate crops or grow resistant varieties.

Fungicides

All fungicides are phytotoxic to some extent—that is, they affect the growth of the plants which they protect. It is essential that only recommended quantities and dilutions are used. Some fungicides based on lime and sulphur are particularly bad at scorching leaves if over-used. The systemic fungicides like benomyl and thiophanate-methyl are often more effective but cost more.

Removal of infected tissue will often stop the spread of a fungus and this is a point that cannot be over-emphasized. Strict garden hygiene is one of the main ways of preventing infection.

FUNGUS DISEASES OF PLANTS
Non-systemic (knock-down) fungicides

INFECTIONS CONTROLLED	PLANTS COMMONLY INFECTED	CHEMICAL NAME	FORM AVAILABLE
Galls	Azaleas	Bordeaux mixture	Powder
Wilts	Clematis and paeonies		
Peach leaf curl	Many ornamental plants and fruits	Lime-sulphur	Powder or concentrated suspension
Blight	Tomatoes and potatoes		
Cane spot/ spur blight	Raspberries	'Liquid copper'	Concentrated solution
Powdery mildews	Many fruit and ornamental varieties	Sulphur	Powder
Scab	Apples and pears (**Caution**: do not use lime-sulphur or sulphur sprays on sulphur-shy varieties)	Several special formulations of the above are available	
Onion white rot	Onions	Calomel	Powder
Club root	Brassicas and wallflowers		
Moss and turf diseases	Grass/lawns	Other mercury-based mixtures	Mixed with lawn sand
Black spot	Roses	Cheshunt compound	Powder for solution
Leaf spots	Many garden plants	Captan	Wettable powder or dust
Scab	Apples and pears (**Caution**: do not use on fruit to be bottled or used for deep freezing)	Dinocap	Wettable powder, dust, liquid or smoke
Soil-borne infections	Many seeds and seedlings		
Grey mould/ downy mildew/ potato blight	Many plants	Thiram	Concentrated solution
		Zineb	Wettable powder
Rusts	Many ornamental plants and fruits in the garden	Mancozeb	Wettable powder
Spur blight	Raspberries	Several formulations and mixtures of the above are available	

Systemic fungicides

INFECTIONS CONTROLLED	PLANTS COMMONLY INFECTED	CHEMICAL NAME	FORM AVAILABLE
Grey mould	Many fruits and vegetables, growing and in storage		
Leaf spots	Many ornamental plants, soft fruit and celery	Benomyl	Wettable powders
Scab	Apples and pears	Thiophanate-methyl	Wettable powders
Powdery mildews	Roses, other ornamentals and fruit		
Black spot	Roses		

Choosing a Greenhouse

Greenhouses come in all shapes and sizes – and today no garden, however small, need be without one. There are simple and easy-to-erect models; more elaborate and decorative ones; expensive and inexpensive. For those of you contemplating buying a greenhouse for the first time, we give the basic facts about the various types as well as some of the equipment you'll find helpful.
We'll be advising you throughout on how to make the best use of your greenhouse.

The acquisition of a greenhouse opens up an exciting new area of gardening, where you don't have to worry about extremes of weather or damage from cold, wind or excessive rain. You can regulate the amount of water your plants receive and, because fertilizers are not washed away by rain, you can feed them correctly.

Temperature and ventilation can be adjusted and, by applying shading, even the light may be altered to suit plant preferences. Pests and diseases are easier to combat and the plants are protected from damage by birds and small animals.

Every gardener's dream – an extensive greenhouse full of flowering plants

Which type?
Most greenhouse styles offer the choice of a glass-to-ground or a base-wall design. The glass-to-ground type allows very efficient use of space for growing. When staging is fitted, there is enough light beneath for the accommodation of a varied selection of plants. The all-glass house is also ideal for tall subjects like tomatoes and chrysanthemums. By arranging your space carefully you can

grow a wide variety of plants together. For example, you can grow tomatoes along the south side, followed by chrysanthemums – putting the pots on the floor. Your staging can then run along the north side, providing a surface on which to grow and display colourful pot plants, with some space below for plants that like a certain amount of shade (as do many house plants). On the end wall you can train either beautiful flowering climbers or edible crops such as cucumbers.

However, for some purposes a greenhouse with a base wall of brick, concrete or timber boards (usually called a 'plant house') is preferable. This design is more economical to heat artificially and therefore is preferable when the greenhouse does not get much sun. It is also a good choice where high temperatures have to be maintained for propagation or for tropical plants (many of which do not demand much light). There are even plants that positively enjoy deep shade that can be grown below the staging.

Greenhouses with a base wall at one side and glass-to-ground at the other are also available. These should be oriented east-to-west, if possible, with the base wall on the north side.

Planning ahead
Before buying your greenhouse, make sure that you are not infringing any rules or regulations by erecting it in your garden. If you are a tenant you should seek your landlord's permission; should you move, you can take the greenhouse with you. If you are a freeholder, you may normally erect a freestanding greenhouse (of reasonable size) in your garden without seeking permission from your local council. However, if you wish to

erect a lean-to against the house wall – whether a permanent or temporary structure – you may require either planning permission or building regulations approval from your local council.

You must also do some advance thinking about the foundations of the greenhouse. You can lay old railway sleepers or concrete footings, or build a low, cemented brick wall on which the greenhouse can be freestanding or screwed into position. A path of concrete, brick or paving stones down the centre ensures dry feet and clean working.

The best positions
Freestanding, rectangular greenhouses get most benefit from the sun if you orient them east-to-west, with the long sides facing north and south. The 'high south wall' greenhouse *must*, in fact, lie this way to catch as much winter light and sun as possible. Staging, if used, should run along the north side. This 'high south wall' type is often found in old private gardens, set against a south-facing wall. Particularly if the wall is of brick, it will act as a heat store, radiating warmth overnight after accumulating it during the day. This type can become extremely hot, however, and so plenty of ventilation and shading is called for.

With a lean-to, you may have no choice in the siting, but what you grow in it will depend on which way it faces. An east- or west-facing lean-to is usually fairly versatile since it gets some sun and some shade. If north-facing it will be very shady and is best devoted to pot plants (such as cinerarias, cyclamen, primulas and calceolarias) and house plants used for permanent decoration. A south-facing lean-to can be very hot in summer and,

unless you are prepared to install shading, you should choose sun-loving plants such as cacti and succulents.

Types of material
You should consider the cost of subsequent maintenance as well as the initial outlay when deciding which materials to choose for your greenhouse.

Glass or plastic? Glass has the unique property of capturing and retaining solar warmth. It also holds artificial warmth better than plastic. Polythene has a limited life and for long-term use a rigid plastic (such as Novolux) is the wisest choice. Plastic surfaces are scratched easily by wind-blown dust and grit, causing dirt to become ingrained and a loss of transparency over a period of years. Plastic also becomes brittle with weathering and may disintegrate.

However, plastic is advisable if the site is likely to be in danger from children's games – or likely to be the target of hooligans out to break glass; where speedy erection or portability are desirable; or where temporary weather protection is all that's necessary. Moulded fibreglass greenhouses are also available, but tend to be expensive and the fittings have to be freestanding.

Aluminium frames Aluminium alloy (often white- or green-coated) is now tending to replace timber for the frame as it has many advantages. It is lightweight yet very strong, and prefabricated structures are easily bolted together.

Below: barn house with three timber-based walls and one glass-to-ground adds versatility
Below right: 'Dutch light' house with sloping sides to trap sun's rays

Sophisticated glazing, using plastic cushioning and clips instead of messy putty, means that the greenhouse can easily be taken apart for moving. There is no fear of rot, warp or trouble from wood-boring insects, and no need for maintenance, like painting or treating timber. Fitments, however, do have to be specially designed and so tend to be a little more expensive.

Timber frames Undoubtedly, these are the most attractive and certainly look the best in a period-style garden. Select one of the more weather-resistant timbers such as cedar, teak or oak, but remember that all timber needs painting or treating with a wood restorer or preservative (*not* creosote) from time to time.

Providing shade
If your greenhouse receives plenty of sun you will need shading in the summer.

Slatted blinds, run on rails over the exterior of the roof, are the most efficient, but costly. They also have to be specially made to fit. Interior blinds are far less efficient in reducing temperature, since the sun's heat-producing rays have already entered the greenhouse; however, they do help to prevent direct scorch.

The simplest and cheapest effective method of shading here is with an electrostatic shading paint that is not washed off by rain but can easily be removed by wiping with a dry duster.

All-year-round ventilation
Ventilators are usually fitted in the roof and sometimes in the sides as well, reducing excess heat in summer and controlling humidity throughout the year. Thermostatically-controlled units that open and close the ventilators automatically according to the temperature inside the greenhouse are very useful, especially if you have to be away from home all day.

Types of heating
It makes sense to heat your greenhouse, if only just enough to keep out frost, since this greatly widens its usefulness. Whatever heating system you choose, it need not be costly if you don't waste it.

Oil heaters Both oil and paraffin are easy to store and portable heaters are particularly valuable as supplementary heating in periods of extreme cold or during power cuts. Use paraffin heaters that are specially designed for greenhouses: the blue-flame ones are best.

Oil and paraffin, when burned, produce carbon dioxide and water vapour. The carbon dioxide is beneficial to plants, but the water vapour can be a nuisance in winter when you will do better to keep the greenhouse dry. You will need some ventilation to keep down humidity and to supply air for the fuel to burn, but this cold air does mean that some heat is lost.

Electricity is normally trouble-free and gives accurate temperature control, but it can be expensive if used wastefully. Fan heating is very effective providing the fan and heat output are controlled together (preferably with a separate, rod-type thermostat); avoid a heater with a continuously-running fan. Ventilation becomes almost unnecessary with this system, and if you line your greenhouse with polythene to form a kind of double glazing you can cut fuel consumption by up to half.

Convector heaters and electrically-heated pipes are also efficient when used together with an accurate thermostat.

If you decide on electricity you will need to run a cable from the house: be sure to have this – and any other electrical work – installed by a qualified electrician.

Natural gas There are special greenhouse heaters using natural gas, with good thermostatic control. They can also be adapted to work from bottle gas.

However, like oil and paraffin, natural gas produces carbon dioxide and water vapour when it burns – to such an extent, indeed, that a great deal of ventilation is required, resulting in heat loss.

Other types of heating Solid fuel (with the heat distributed by hot water pipes) and oil-fired boilers are still relatively cheap methods of heating. Hot water pipes, linked to a boiler, maintain high temperatures but are costly to install.

Heated propagators You will need some form of heated propagator so that you can germinate seed without heating the whole greenhouse to a high temperature. There is a wide range of electrically-heated models available.

Automatic watering
There is a wide choice of equipment here, too. The water can be fed to the plants by overhead sprays, trickle-feed pipelines, capillary sand benches or capillary matting. In the case of capillary watering, the sand or matting under the pots is kept constantly moist by whatever automatic system is installed. We give more information on these systems later.

One automatic watering system uses a photo-electric cell (connected to a special electric circuit) that registers the amount of sunlight prevailing, and controls the water flow accordingly.

Once you have installed one of these systems you can leave the greenhouse unattended for weeks without worry.

Artificial lighting
A paraffin lamp will give you enough light in the evenings for most jobs, but if the greenhouse has an electricity supply you can install either a lamp-holder and bulb or a fluorescent tube. You can also encourage plant growth with special lighting systems that give artificial daylight. We shall be having a look at these near the end of GreenFingers.

Left: a 'lean-to' can be set against garden house wall to catch the sun

Choosing Frames and Cloches

A frame – or two – costs little to buy, or make yourself and can be fitted into most gardens. Nearly everything you grow in a greenhouse can also be grown in frames, allowing for the restrictions in height and size.
Even if you have a greenhouse, frames can take over much of the work to leave more space for decorative plants and those demanding full greenhouse height.

First you must decide whether to buy a ready-made frame or make one yourself from a frame kit of glass-to-ground design with timber or metal sections. An all-glass frame is suitable unless you want extra warmth for propagation, or for growing cucumbers or melons.

Lids, known as 'lights', can be bought separately and you can place these over your own timber or brick-built sides, or even set one over a pit dug in the ground, adding to it as required. The lights can be easily stored away in the summer, when not in use.

Modern frames are often fitted with sliding glass sides, to give access or for added ventilation, and lights that slide aside as well as lift up so that they can be removed completely for easy working.

Choice of material

Aluminium alloy framework has many advantages: it is long-lasting, requires no maintenance and, being lightweight, is ideal for moving about. If you prefer timber, choose wood that is noted for its weather resistance, because frame sides are likely to come into contact with damp soil for long periods. Avoid soft woods treated with creosote as the vapour continues to be harmful to plants for some time. Green Cuprinol is suitable, but before using any other preservative check the maker's literature to be sure that it is safe for plants.

Plastic, instead of glass, for garden frames is light, easily portable and

A large glass-to-ground frame, with aluminium-alloy framework, being used to house trays of seedlings and plants waiting to be transplanted

obviously advisable where small children are using the garden. From a gardener's point of view, however, glass has many advantages (see previous chapter on choosing a greenhouse). You must use glass if the frame is to be heated, and would be advised to do so in windy areas as plastic can blow away.

Siting the frame

If you use a frame as an adjunct to your greenhouse (and it has vertical sides), you can push the frame close up to one side. This helps to reduce warmth loss from both the greenhouse and the frame.

If using a frame for greenhouse and pot plants, put it in a shady place – against the north side of your greenhouse is ideal. But most vegetable crops, and those alpines which you may be housing

in frames when not in flower, prefer a bright, open position.

With many frames it is often convenient to set them back-to-back, or alongside each other in rows. To obtain more height, stand your frame on a base of bricks or concrete blocks, or place it over a pit (providing you make sure that water does not collect in it).

Electric soil-warming cables

Frames do not have to be 'cold'; you can heat a large one with a small paraffin lamp provided you take great care to see that there is always ventilation. But installing electric soil-warming cables is by far the best method. Lay them in loops across the floor of the frame, making sure that they do not touch each other. Place a little sand on top and keep it moist: this will hold the cables in place and conduct the warmth more uniformly. Use only about 2–3cm (1 in) of sand, then a thermostat can be installed above the sand level to control the frame's temperature.

If you need extra warmth (as for pot plants) run cables round the frame sides as well. With glass-sided frames, fasten the cables to wooden battens with cleats and thrust the battens into the ground.

If you are growing plants to be rooted into a deep layer of compost (such as salad crops, cucumbers and melons) site the warming cables near the bottom of the compost. In this case a thermostat of the rod type should be thrust into the compost. Temperature can also be controlled manually or by a time switch. The considerable bulk of compost will hold warmth over the periods when the electricity is off.

Wattage depends on the size and purpose of your frame; decide after you have consulted the suppliers of such equipment.

You can use small heated frames inside the greenhouse for high-temperature propagation, or for housing a small collection of low-growing tropical plants. An aluminium framework, glass sides and top, and 2–3cm (1 in) or so of sand over the cable, are recommended. The wattage required is usually about 20W per 1000 sq cm (20W per sq ft) of frame floor, and a thermostat is essential.

Frame cultivation

If possible, avoid using soil. Instead, line a trough or pit with polythene sheeting, slitted here and there for drainage, and fill it with a proprietary potting compost. You can grow excellent, high-quality salad and other crops with little risk from pests or diseases.

Where you are moving pots or other

Above left: timber-sided frame, with glass lights, shelters bedding plants prior to planting out. Above: rows of barn cloches protect lettuce that are almost ready for cropping

containers in and out, firm the floor and cover it with polythene, over which is spread coarse sand or shingle. If you keep this damp, it will moisten the air in the frame; the polythene will help to keep out soil pests.

Grow house plants, and pot plants like cineraria, calceolaria, primula and cyclamen, in frames until the decorative stage when they are ready to transfer to the house, conservatory or greenhouse. Use frames to raise bedding plants and for many forms of propagation from cutting and seed. You will also find them especially useful for crops like lettuce, radish, beet and carrots that you want in the kitchen even before winter is over.

Keep plants like dormant fuchsias, chrysanthemums and pelargoniums (that are used for summer garden or greenhouse decoration) in frames during the winter when they often look far from attractive. Store dormant tubers and bulbs there to leave the greenhouse less cluttered. Some crops, like strawberries and violets, lend themselves particularly to frame culture.

Keep glass frames (and cloches) as clean as possible to admit maximum light and discourage plant pests and diseases. Remove any mud splashes by careful use of a hose, if necessary.

CLOCHES

Early cloches were of glass and often held together by clumsy wires that were difficult to manipulate. Modern designs are simpler and often make use of plastics, which are very suitable for this purpose as cloches are frequently used only for weather protection, high temperatures being rarely necessary.

Select your type

There are tent, barn and T-shaped cloches, and a flat-topped 'utility' one. These are usually held together by special metal or plastic clips. Some cloches can be opened for ventilation or for watering, others have perforated tops to allow the rain to enter. Plastic ones with a cellular structure give greater warmth retention.

You can make simple and effective tunnels, ideal for protecting rows of vegetables, by sandwiching lengths of polythene between wire arches at intervals along the row, or by aligning ordinary cloches end-to-end. Anchor your plastic ones carefully in windy areas as they can easily blow away; use stones, bricks, wooden or metal pegs, or some special cloche fitments.

Cloches are most useful from autumn to late spring for providing protection from excessive wet and cold. Set them in place to dry and warm the soil before you dig and fertilize it, in preparation for sowing or planting.

Cloche cultivation

Use individual cloches for protecting isolated tender plants (such as fuchsia) in beds and borders, and protect groups of hardy and half-hardy annuals until they become established. You can also root cuttings directly into the ground of a nursery bed if you use cloches to cover them.

Many flowers grown for cutting benefit from cloche protection, especially low-growing bulbs in pots or bowls. Other favourite cloche flower crops are anemones, hellebore (Christmas rose), lily of the valley, violet and polyanthus. You can harden off bedding plants under cloches if frame space is not available. Also use them to protect sweet peas in the early stages.

In the vegetable garden, cloches give you year-round cropping. If you plan carefully you can move them from one

Top: tunnel cloches of polythene sheeting are versatile. They can be cut to any length, depending on whether you want to cover one plant or a whole row. Above: corrugated plastic cloches are used here to cover strawberry plants; being lightweight these cloches need to be anchored against the wind with wire hoops. End pieces can be added to give the plants greater protection

crop to another as needed, thus putting a limited number to maximum use.

Working with cloches

You do not need to remove cloches for watering; the water that drains off them will seep into the soil provided that it has been well prepared. It should be porous and moisture-retaining, but well-drained. Work in plenty of humus-forming material, like peat or rotted

garden compost. To avoid the wind rushing through your cloche tunnels, block the ends. This also applies to individual cloches used as miniature greenhouses to cover single, or small groups of, plants. When the weather permits ventilation, move the cloches along to leave a small gap between each one and remove the ends of tunnels.

Leave plenty of room between rows for comfortable access and keep the soil along the sides of the cloche rows well hoed to allow water retention. Soluble fertilizers can also be applied along the outside edges of the cloches.

Store glass cloches, and plastic tent and barn types, on their ends and stacked inside each other. For this purpose put down some clean boards (or lay a section of concrete) in a corner of the vegetable plot, and cover it with roofing felt for glass cloches.

Planning a Garden

Our aim in this section is to inform you as to how you can either create a garden from scratch or sensibly modify an existing layout to suit very personal requirements. Design is the basis of any layout, inside or outside the home, and can be summed up as the most practical solution to the problem in hand.

Although most people feel relatively happy when planning a kitchen or living-room, their ideas tend to dry up when they move outside. This is partly due to the fact that we tend to think of house and garden as two separate entities, one for living in the other for everything else. If we think of the garden as an outside room, an extension of the home where each activity can fit into an overall pattern, things would not only work better but they would be more attractive and easier to maintain.

It is fair to say that as homes and gardens increase in number the latter, on average, become smaller. Subsequent demand on use of that space is therefore greater and the need to design it properly even more important. The most difficult thing is knowing where to begin.

The danger lies in overcomplication; the golden rule is not to rush out and start straight away. Whatever the problems, give them time to get into perspective and as an initial exercise try jotting your ideas down on paper, initially in the form of a check-list that indicate both what you want and what you have got.

As a general guide you might include a terrace or patio, lawn, vegetables, shed, greenhouse, fruit, planting, room for access and wheeled toys, sandpit, trees, pool, rockery, room for washing-line or rotary drier, dustbin store, solid fuel bunkers or oil tank, incinerator, compost and even hutches for pets. When your ideas dry up you'll probably find you have catered for most eventualities.

Even when planning a garden with a virgin plot of ground it is worth making a scale drawing of the garden and marking in everything that might affect the future layout. It is worth doing on a piece of squared graph paper, using a simple scale of a small square to each foot. Mark in the house and garage in relation to the boundaries, the position of doors and windows, the length of the boundaries themselves, any change in level, existing shrubs and trees and other features, good views or bad, prevailing winds and most important of all the north point, or where the sun is in relation to the house.

Once all this information is to hand you can see not only what you want to put in the garden, you also see that the components themselves fall into two broad categories; the plants, lawn, hedges and trees, which can loosely be termed the 'soft landscape', and the paths, paving fences, walling, steps and other items that form the 'hard landscape'.

In this section we have taken as a basis the principle of hard and soft landscape. Town gardens, country gardens, odd plots and problem plots as well as the problematic sloping site are covered in detail. Have you considered for instance, using railway sleepers or logs embedded into a bank for steps. We have, together with a great many other stimulating ideas.

From individual gardens we turn our attention to plants and planting – the soft landscape. The planning of borders and island beds, together with the correct use of specific plant material is explained so that it can be used in a controlled rather than a haphazard manner. Just as there are rules governing the design and construction of a garden, so too are there guidelines to planting. Not only should plants provide colour and interest throughout the year but they must also act as screens to block bad views, give shelter from prevailing winds and form divisions within the garden itself. The mechanics of planting design are explained so that you can build up a framework of background plants that give stability to the composition and allow a second stage of filling in with lighter, more colourful material.

It is sensible to use an architectural theme close to the building, so that a brick terrace matches the materials used in the house. Exterior woodwork such as the pergola or overhead beams are painted to link with the colour of existing doors and windows. The layout of the terrace should match the house too and the rectangles here, used in interesting interlocking patterns, will be far more successful than at a point farther down the garden. In fact the farther away from the house we get, the softer and looser the composition should become, thus providing a feeling of space and movement that diverts attention from rectangular boundaries and makes the garden appear larger than it really is.

Planting too can reflect this theme and strongly formed shapes such as yuccas, acanthus, euphorbias and phormium will re-inforce a crisp, architectural setting while softer, looser species will create a feeling of depth and tranquility. Certain plants, such as conifers on a small scale and Lombardy poplars in a larger landscape may act as punctuation marks and should be used to highlight a carefully chosen position. Colour too, both in planting and individual features such as pots or seats, is important. A barrel full of brilliant flowers is fine close to the house but when placed at the bottom of the garden will draw the eye and foreshorten the space.

Not only should colour schemes be intelligently deployed but you also have to remember that flowering times vary. Soil types and the availability of sun and shade will determine what species can be grown.

A garden can offer as much hard work and maintenance as you are prepared to put into it. It can be a full-time concern for the keen gardener or a place of recreation. It can be a dining room, playground, allotment and flower garden.

Design for an Odd Plot

A corner site such as this can provide a challenge, and this plan is the answer. The circular pattern of the layout relates to the house and ignores the outline of the site. The space between house and fence is planted out so that the space of the garden from the terrace is incidental. Nevertheless, the basic ingredients of a standard garden are all present.

The site pictured here is set in the middle of a corner plot. Outside its encircling solid timber fence, all of 1·5m (5 ft) high, there is a pedestrian path and roads that converge on the southern corner of the site. The curving pattern of the layout echoes the flow of movement around the area, although the planting inside the fence blocks out the unattractive view and, surprisingly, much of the noise as well.

The problem inside the garden was that the house faces east and the area farthest away from it gets the afternoon and evening sun, being the time when you are most likely to want to bask in the sun or just sit and have a drink. A terrace was therefore a priority in that area, away from the house but also connected to it so that the children could ride their bicycles on it and wander in and out of the house.

The next priorities were the siting of the dustbins, fuel store and rubbish, and the small vegetable area convenient to both rear door and side service passage. These and the garage are all served with a hard-paved path for easy access. It is in the cold, wet days of winter when going out to cut a cabbage or pick some sprouts that you really appreciate this, and the straight run of path would also allow for a washing line. An evergreen hedge, composed of a mixture of yew, pyracantha and the odd holly, separates the vegetable area from the rest of the garden.

A further hazard in this garden was the fact that the site 'fell away' to a downward slope on the south corner of the house. The lawn pattern could have followed suit but it would have meant that the house terrace would have been at a higher level and the children shooting along on their bicycles might have gone over the end. By stepping the terrace and lawn (as shown in the aerial view), this hazard was avoided and the steps became a feature of the layout. Where they converge they provide another little paved area on the south-east side of the house.

Below these steps the last flat area, although in fact an extension of the lawn, has been gravelled – or rather laid with rounded pea shingle. This is less sharp than gravel when fallen onto, and better than grass for a play area in bad weather.

Between the defined outer lines of the garden and the boundary fence is a thick planting of mixed shrubs with the occasional tree sited into it. Plenty of evergreens are included here – like cotoneasters, large-leaved privets and pyracantha – to block out the noisy world outside. Colour planting, requiring seasonal attention, is confined to the sitting-out terraced area.

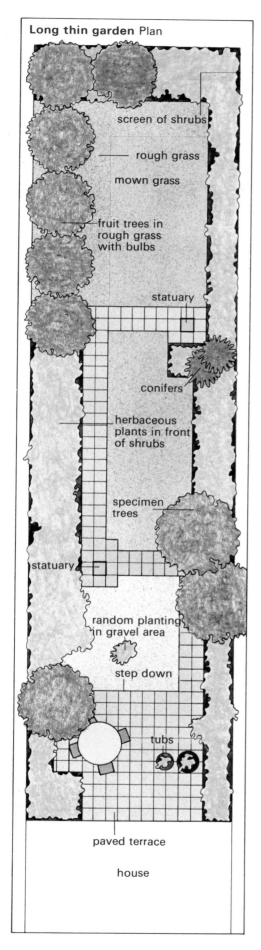

Long thin garden Plan

screen of shrubs

rough grass

mown grass

fruit trees in
rough grass
with bulbs

statuary

conifers

herbaceous
plants in front
of shrubs

specimen
trees

statuary

random planting
in gravel area

step down

tubs

paved terrace

house

Design for a Long, Thin Town Garden

Typical of many town gardens behind the terraces of early Victorian houses, sometimes with a rear access, sometimes not, this site measures 30m long by 7·5m wide (100 × 25 ft). The problem is how not to make the layout seem even longer and thinner – which any sort of straight path down the middle would do – but to create a progression of small areas or 'rooms', staggered if possible, giving the ultimate view a lateral or side-to-side movement, and so apparently increase the width of the garden.

The first of these room areas behind the house is paved and used for many months of the year for eating out since it is so sheltered and surprisingly private with its old pear tree overhanging the area. It would be nice to pave such a setting in brick or old York stone. But if the expense prohibits it, you can use dark precast concrete slabs instead.

The next area, down one small step, is gravelled and planted at random with perennials that seed themselves and look natural in such a setting; alchemilla (lady's mantle) and sisyrinchium (satin flower), for instance. The view is punctuated beyond this area by a piece of statuary (an old urn in fact) again to one side, and this is repeated on the other side of the garden beyond the next mown-

grass room. A staggered path connects all these features and provides a dry, hard access to them.

The bottom room is allowed to be fairly wild with half-standard fruit trees planted in it and rough grass under them where spring and autumn bulbs and wild flowers can be encouraged. The borders on either side of the garden and against the old brick dividing walls are planted with a mixture of shrubs, including *Viburnum tinus* (laurustinus), syringa, philadelphus (mock orange) and choisya. When seen from the house the total effect is green and rather romantic, with the only colour being reserved for the tubs grouped on the eating terrace in the foreground. The view is a static one and planting and statuary are used to compose it. It is a garden for a middle-aged couple who enjoy pottering and the relaxed atmosphere of plants spilling out onto paving or gravel.

A strong lateral pattern progresses down this garden from one small 'room' to another. Near the house is a terrace with a gravel area beyond. A statue breaks up the pattern before the mown grass area and the last 'room' consists of rough grass with bulbs and fruit trees. The boundary fence is hidden by shrubs, and trees frame the general view

Design for a Country Garden Site

An irregular-shaped country garden can present just as many problems as the town gardens described overleaf. Here we look at some possible solutions that would blend in with a less formal rural setting.

This site seemed to be the leftover bit between fields, surrounded by thorn hedges and very boggy at its farthest corner. The back of the period house was sited against the road, with the front door and main living room facing south onto the garden.

The plan shows clearly how the lines of the pattern should first start off with some regard to the shape of the house, usually with straight lines. These can then be continued on in curves to sweep about and encompass existing features and altogether be more gentle than a formal layout that in any case would not sit well within the boundary lines here.

The house is surrounded by a York stone paved terrace, so that the area outside the living room gets a long view down into the curving wild garden under a few old fruit trees. At the rear of the house the formal pattern has been broken down to form a small box-hedged herb garden conveniently near to the kitchen door. The existing hedge on this boundary has been replaced by a white picket fence along the roadside.

Where a house is set within a site the pattern of the garden should more or less follow, or at least compliment, the line of the house when surrounding it. As the pattern gets farther away it can become less regular. In our design the curves make a gentle, wild walk under old apple trees towards a summerhouse

Planting in the garden is mixed and colourful outside the front door, becoming wilder and more rampant as you progress down the length of the garden towards the pretty summerhouse.

At the side of the house facing west the grass is left rough, and bulbs are naturalized in it. The hedge has also been reduced in height so that the feeling of a neighbouring field rolling right in is encouraged and continues right up to the house. This rough grass motif is repeated in circular form to surround an old ash tree nearby. The internal pattern of this garden again pays little service to the existing boundary line, and thick intervening planting screens the discrepancy between the two.

In an old garden you tend to have old existing trees to work around. A feature has been made of the existing ash in this garden by surrounding it with a circle of rough grass containing massed spring and autumn bulbs.

The odd shape of this plot allows the summerhouse at the farthest end to be completely private from the house, approached by a winding, bordered path Below: plan, showing major features

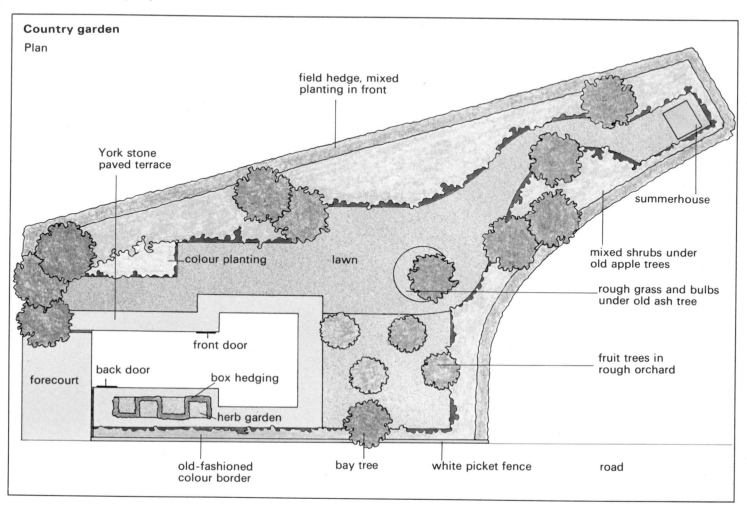

Country garden

Plan

field hedge, mixed planting in front

York stone paved terrace

summerhouse

colour planting

lawn

mixed shrubs under old apple trees

rough grass and bulbs under old ash tree

front door

back door

box hedging

fruit trees in rough orchard

forecourt

herb garden

old-fashioned colour border

bay tree

white picket fence

road

Designs for a Rectangular Plot

A regular-shaped plot with its formal straight lines can be just as much of a challenge as an odd-shaped plot. In the first of our designs for rectangular plots we look at ways of either turning straight boundaries into an asset or distracting the eye from them.

Although many people have odd-shaped gardens, still more possess one of standard rectangular proportions. Gardens on the whole are getting smaller – due to the demands on housing space – and the average size measures about 10m (35 ft) long by 7·5m (25 ft) wide.

With these proportions in mind, whether you start from scratch or inherit an existing garden, the approach should be the same: setting out to create an environment that is not only right for you but at the same time attractive to family and visitors alike.

To many people the ability to 'design' implies a degree of professional skill, so it is often easier to think in terms of reorganization rather than a wholly

original scheme and, again, it is often the simplest solution where an established garden is in existence.

The initial planning can fall into two stages: what you want and what you've got. Your requirements can be tackled in exactly the same way as the family shopping list, but instead of the usual groceries you may list lawn, greenhouse, shed, vegetables, terrace, barbecue, pool, sandpit, swings, roses and so on. As far as existing features are concerned it is best to make a simple scale drawing, using graph paper, and note down the north point, good or bad views, existing planting, trees, positions of doors and windows, changes in level, together with any other relevant information. Your plan might not look as neat as the one shown below but it should be sufficient to give you a good idea of how to use your own available space to the best advantage.

Nor need there be only one solution to the problem, for just as the furnishing and decoration of a room in the house can vary, so can its outdoor counterpart.

For some reason people tend to have a horror of rectangular gardens, probably because most designs involving straight lines fall into the trap of rigid formality. With a small space, however, it is often advantageous to accept the shape of the boundaries, softening them by all means, but using the outline to form a frame for a geometric composition, in much the same way as a contemporary artist might do.

Planning your priorities

An average family, with several children, various pets and busy parents, will have general requirements – from somewhere to sit and have the occasional meal, a vegetable area, shed or greenhouse, flowers for cutting, shrubs and herbaceous material for interest throughout the year, to room for bike riding, games and general children's activities. But above all easy maintenance must be the aim.

Choice of planting

Whether a design is based on rectangles or curves it is sound common sense to keep the areas close to the building reasonably architectural, creating a positive link between house and garden. There are a number of ways of doing this, the most obvious revolving around a paved area that will serve as a background for the many activities that call for an easily maintained, quick-drying surface.

Numerous types of paving are available, ranging from the more expensive natural stones and brick and granite setts,

to pre-cast concrete slabs of various colours and textures. As a general rule crazy paving is not the best material to use close to a house, the conflicting shapes clashing with the cleaner lines of the building. It is also worth bearing in mind that although broken paving is cheap to buy, it is far from cheap or quick to lay. Be wary also of coloured pre-cast slabs: your terrace should be a background, not a gaudy feature in itself. If you are really set on using colours, keep them simple; use two at the most and make sure they don't clash.

DESIGN THEME – RECTANGLES

In our first design we have assumed that the house is built of brick and it is logical, therefore, to use this material on the terrace. A simple squared pattern of

bricks laid flat was evolved, using the corners and projections of the building as starting points. The resulting squares were then filled in with a combination of rectangular pre-cast paving, planting and a raised bed, that might double as a sandpit or pool. As the entire garden is based on rectangles the lines of the terrace were extended on our plan and another series were drawn across the page at right-angles to form a grid. The approximate proportions of the various features we needed were then shaded in: vegetables, lawn, existing shed, swing and clothes drier. A pattern was starting to evolve and by the time we had screened the bad

Left: an imaginative use of pre-cast paving links house with garden. Below: a working design to scale is invaluable

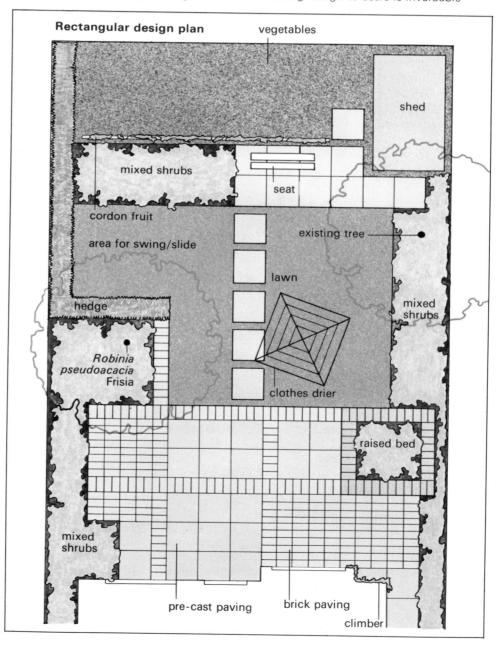

Rectangular design plan

vegetables

shed

mixed shrubs

seat

cordon fruit

existing tree

area for swing/slide

lawn

mixed shrubs

hedge

Robinia pseudoacacia Frisia

clothes drier

raised bed

mixed shrubs

pre-cast paving

brick paving

climber

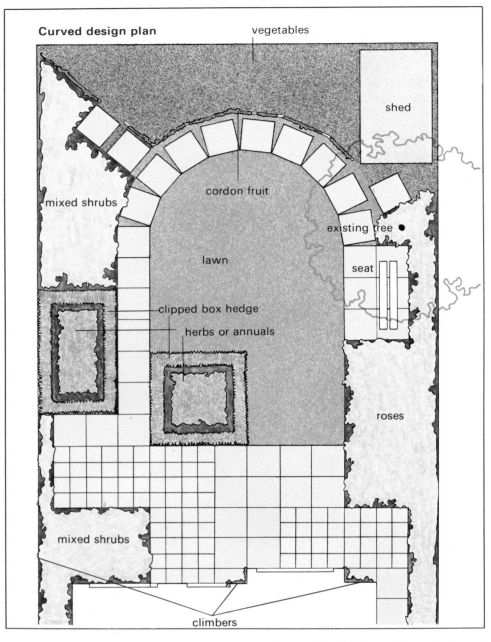

Curved design plan — vegetables — shed — cordon fruit — existing tree ● — mixed shrubs — lawn — seat — clipped box hedge — herbs or annuals — roses — mixed shrubs — climbers

Above: With the rigid outlines of the plot softened by a gentle curve and careful planting, this garden shows the result of good pre-planning.

views, created a focal point and added trees for vertical emphasis the working design was virtually complete.

Planting within the design
Few people realize how quickly planting can soften a composition and it is therefore very important to have a strong ground plan initially, as a weak design very soon loses its line altogether. Planting also helps to reinforce the basic pattern and if you are working with rectangles, these can be linked together and enhanced by bold groupings. Whatever the size of a garden, individual

specimens should be used sparingly and then only as a point of emphasis. Groups of three or four would be ideal in the size of garden shown here, while a large area could use drifts of 15 or 20 for a corresponding effect.

We have already mentioned that there are numerous solutions to a single design problem and having considered a rectangular approach you might prefer the opposite, utilizing curves.

DESIGN THEME - CURVES
Whereas in our first garden the basic idea was to reinforce the ground plan, we can now create a design that positively leads the eye away from the rectangular boundaries, creating a real feeling of space and movement.

Once again it makes sound sense to

keep the area close to the house as an architectural pattern. This time you could omit the geometric grid of brick and concentrate on a simple combination of dark grey and sandstone-coloured precast concrete slabs. Planting interlocks with the paving and directs the eye to the path that sweeps away around the garden, terminating at the white seat that acts as a focal point.

Disguising the manholes
A problem that frequently occurs in paved areas, close to the house, is that of manhole covers. These are invariably sited to create the greatest visual nuisance and people often wonder how they can be hidden. First of all, *don't* place a single tub or statue on top of them, this will only have the effect of drawing the eye and making them all the more obvious. The secret is to conceal them completely, either with a bold group of two or three tubs planted with bulbs and annuals, or to surround them with planting. The latter effect can be quite simply achieved by omitting the adjacent paving slabs, planting several low spreading shrubs such as *Cotoneaster horizontalis* or *Cistus lusitanicus* Decumbens (rock rose), and placing a couple of boulders on top of the cover for sculptural effect. In either event the tubs or boulders can be moved in times of emergency.

A slightly more expensive alternative is to buy specially-recessed covers, into which paving stones can be fitted. This is fine in an area of random rectangular paving but can have the effect of ruining a sequence of carefully-laid slabs. Where manholes are sited in the lawn it is generally best to ignore them. Don't turf them over or the resulting grass will die in dry weather and don't, at all costs, use them as bases for bird baths, sundials or statues, not only for the reason already mentioned but because their siting is unlikely to bear any relationship to the overall composition of the garden. If they are in fact left alone, grass will slowly creep over them and soften the outline. Occasionally you come across the quite horrific spectacle of raised manholes that stand proud of the lawn by anything up to 30cm (12 in). This is generally caused by the builder failing to adjust his finished garden levels and it may be possible to lower the cover by removing the offending courses of brick and resetting the manhole at the new ground level. If in doubt, call in a surveyor, or even the builder if he is still around, to check that any alterations will be in accordance with local authority regulations.

More alternatives for a Rectangular Plot

DESIGN THEME - DIAGONALS

Our third plan for garden plots turns the entire design diagonally across the garden. Diagonal lines are useful for creating a feeling of greater space as they not only direct you away from the main axis of the boundaries but also bring the longest dimensions into play, the distance between opposite corners of a rectangle being the greatest single length available.

In this garden plan the back of the house faces due north, in which case only a minimal amount of paving is needed outside the French doors, just enough in fact to give access for the side passage and room for a single bench seat on which to enjoy the shade during particularly hot weather. A simple buff-coloured pre-cast slab was used, giving a visual link with the pale brown finish of the building.

Siting of focal point

Stepping stones cross the small lawn and draw the eye to the focal point provided by a carefully-chosen urn or statue. Statuary and the like can be delightful ornaments in a garden but remember that they are dominant features in their own right and should be used sparingly as punctuation marks in the overall composition. As a general rule they should be softened and surrounded by planting, a glimpse of a bust or figure being far more subtle than glaring nudity!

Planting within the design

In our design the urn is backed by the soft foliage and flowers of climbing roses, these forming an effective screen to the small vegetable plot beyond. The path changes direction at the urn or statue,

terminating at the main sitting area that is built up from an interlocking pattern of brick and pre-cast slabs. A tree behind the sitting area would be an important element in the design, giving both shade and vertical emphasis.

Few people realize that trees can be bought in a wide range of sizes, from

Our garden with a diagonal design was planned to give a feeling of extra space, while still incorporating most of the features required in the average suburban plot.
The seating area at the end of the path is shaded by a spreading wild cherry, Prunus avium Grandiflora

obviously grow at different rates but when selecting a tree for an important position, such as ours, the size known as 'extra large nursery stock' can be ideal. These trees are most usually grown by specialist nurseries and although large, can be handled by one or two people. They will probably be about 4·2m (14 ft) high and have a girth of anything up to 25–30cm (10–12 in). They establish quickly in a suitably-prepared position and have a far better success rate than the 'semi matures' that can suddenly fail after two or three years in the ground. We chose one of the vast cherry family, *Prunus avium* Grandiflora, a delightful wild cherry tree that bears double white blossoms in late spring to early summer (April to May). Because the tree was large when planted we felt that a seat around

the base would not be out of place. This measured 1·8 × 1·8m (6 × 6 ft) and doubled as a table or even sun-lounger.

The vegetable area was big enough to incorporate a small greenhouse, while the strong pattern of lawn and borders was wrapped in planting designed to give variety of leaf and flower throughout the year.

DESIGN THEME – THE CIRCLE
This fourth alternative plan is a totally different concept; here we take the idea of using curves to create a completely circular pattern. A true circle is not the easiest design element to handle and where a major part of the garden is involved it is best to 'offset' the feature, thus giving the composition a feeling of emphasis in a particular direction.

Choice of paving
As in all our other gardens we needed a paved area at the rear of the house and here again the use of a circular design

semi-mature specimens that are far too big and heavy for the average householder to manage, right down to small saplings that will take many years to show any real potential. Different species

imposed certain restrictions. The shape of the paving was directly related to the geometry of the circle and became an extension of it, radii being extended until they reached and passed the line of the building. Each new circle represented a line of paving and where any circular pattern is involved small modules are the most adaptable. We had therefore a choice of brick, granite setts, stable paviors and cobbles. The last two we rejected on the grounds that they were too uneven for constant walking and the obvious use of tables and chairs. The setts were a possibility but looked a little 'hard' against the pebble dash of the building. Brick was ideal but in order to save expense and also a considerable amount of laying time we evolved a pattern of brick courses that could be filled in with brushed concrete.

For brushed concrete Lay a normal concrete mix of 1:2:3 – one part cement,

Used with care, a circular design brings a refreshing look to a regular-shaped plot. A Japanese note is introduced with the siting of several boulders within the circle, which is surfaced with a layer of gravel on concrete and planted with two Rhus typhina Laciniata *(above far left)*

two parts sand, three parts aggregate – ensuring that the aggregate is made from an attractive selection of small rounded pebbles. Once the job has started to harden, or 'go off', brush with a stiff broom. This will expose the aggregate and produce a striking marbled effect when dry. To stop it drying too quickly in very hot weather cover the surface with damp sacking for a day or two; in frosty weather dry sacking will be sufficient.

The final planting

Climbers and planting soften the outline of the paving and house, and there is room for a small herb bed. As this garden was to be as maintenance-free as possible we decided against a conventional lawn and the main area of the circle was laid

with a weak mix of concrete, over which was spread 13mm (½ in) of washed gravel. Holes were left in the concrete to accept planting, including *Rhus typhina* Laciniata (stag's-horn sumach), while several groups of large boulders provide a sculptural and slightly Japanese feeling.

Stepping stones cross the gravel in a random pattern and lead to the shed that is neatly-screened by planting. A seat is carefully sited to one side of the sumachs, while the main border areas on the outside of the circle help to soften and hide the stiff rectangular line of the fences.

A high proportion of ground-covering plants help considerably in keeping the maintenance at a reasonable level and occasional raking ensures the gravel is free from leaves.

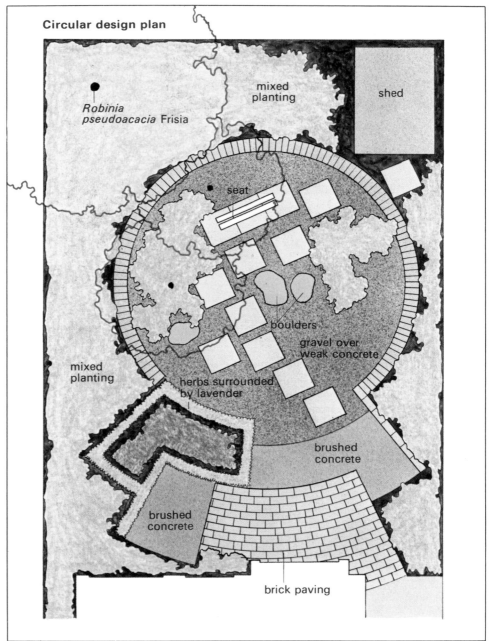

Circular design plan

mixed planting

shed

Robinia pseudoacacia Frisia

seat

boulders

gravel over weak concrete

mixed planting

herbs surrounded by lavender

brushed concrete

brushed concrete

brick paving

The Front Approach

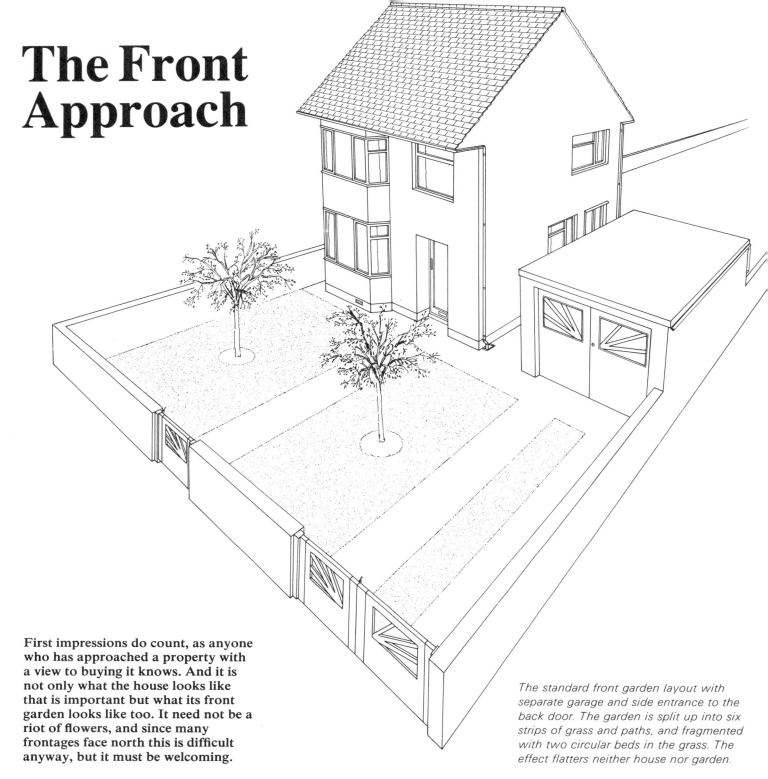

First impressions do count, as anyone who has approached a property with a view to buying it knows. And it is not only what the house looks like that is important but what its front garden looks like too. It need not be a riot of flowers, and since many frontages face north this is difficult anyway, but it must be welcoming.

The standard front garden layout with separate garage and side entrance to the back door. The garden is split up into six strips of grass and paths, and fragmented with two circular beds in the grass. The effect flatters neither house nor garden.

Visitors to the home with a front garden area (and that, don't forget, includes the milkman and the dustman), want a hard, dry, easy access, with a minimum of steps or loose slabs, or eye-height hanging baskets. The driver wants room to park, with space for his passenger and himself to get out easily from his car without landing in a rose bed. If oil deliveries are expected, there must be easy access for the storage tank without the feed-pipe having to trail through areas of planting. The dustman wants his bins as close to his cart

as possible, as do you, to cut down on the inevitable trail of rubbish that is left. The postman, if he is allowed, will beat a path to the next house through your hedge unless he is deterred or directed another way. These are aspects of a front area as seen from the visitors' point of view – for them it is more of a place of arrival and departure than a true garden. With the visitors' needs in mind, now consider what are your own. You wish to present a pleasant face to the world and the materials you use to make up that face

should suit the style of house and location. For the front garden is often public and seen as one of many in a street or close, and while having a character of its own, it should not ruin its neighbours' outlook or strike a jarring note.

Types of enclosure
Consider the types available, and indeed whether you want them at all. Some enclosures will, of course, give you some privacy, will possibly keep your children and pets in and other peoples' out, and

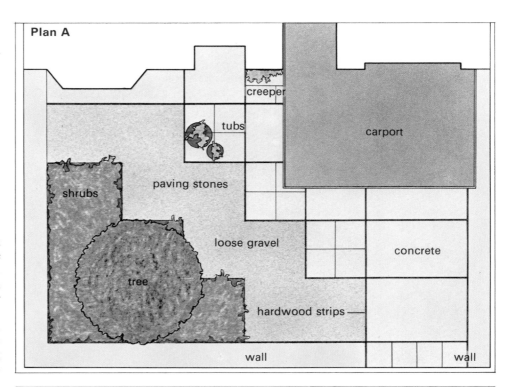

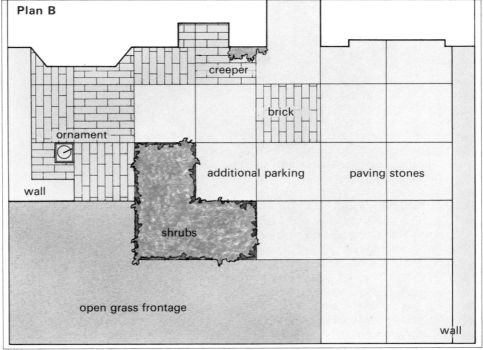

will also help to cut out noise if you are on a busy road.

Walling This is the most expensive form of enclosure, and if built in brick or stone to match your house it looks very smart. Concrete block, rendered, if you like, with a brick or slab coping, is a cheaper version.

Openwork concrete screening You can soften this form of screening with large-leaved climbers like vines rambling through it, but it is too heavy a material to use in conjunction with a small front area.

Fencing Coming down in scale, there are dozens of types of fencing available in timber. You can even try making your own over a small run. Consider, too, a combination low wall and timber fence, which has the advantage of preventing timber rotting along the bottom.

A more open fencing can be obtained by using picket fencing or railings. Fencing is also available in a glass-reinforced plastic such as Fibreglass, that needs little maintenance other than the occasional wash-down.

Hedging If you consider a hedge surround to your garden, think further than privet, which needs endless clipping, and *Cupressocyparis leylandii* (cypress), which will not magically stop growing at the height you want. They become trees 10m (40 ft) high in no time at all!

Other than the traditional type of hedge – beech, hornbeam, thorn or yew – consider holly, which grows slowly, needs little clipping and is a good deterrent for undesirable visiting pets. Or pyracantha, which with minimal clipping will flower and have berries. You could use the upright form of escallonia for a sunny position and even upright rosemary for a looser effect.

Planning out your front area

Within your selected enclosure, list the facilities you require on your site, whether you are starting from scratch or not – front access, side access, garage access and so on. If they can all work as one it means that the garden will not be cut up into masses of little areas with irritating spaces between interlocking paths that need to be filled with plants.

Do you require room to park a second car or a caravan or boat? Will these go in the area at the side of the house, if you have a space there, and if so can they be screened in any way? You may need a washdown area, a hard surface and a tap for this job and some form of drainage so that the surplus water does not flow into the garage. If there is an oil-storage tank at the side of the house, you must allow for access to this, and, of course, to the dustbin area as well.

Now make an accurate plan of the area, marking in the obvious locations for these functions, and join them together with hard surfacing. You should then at least have a practical layout. When moving into a house that the developer or previous owner has already planned, it is worth going through the same exercise even if you have to compromise with what you have inherited and what you really want. Even if this front area does not constitute a garden for relaxing in, your

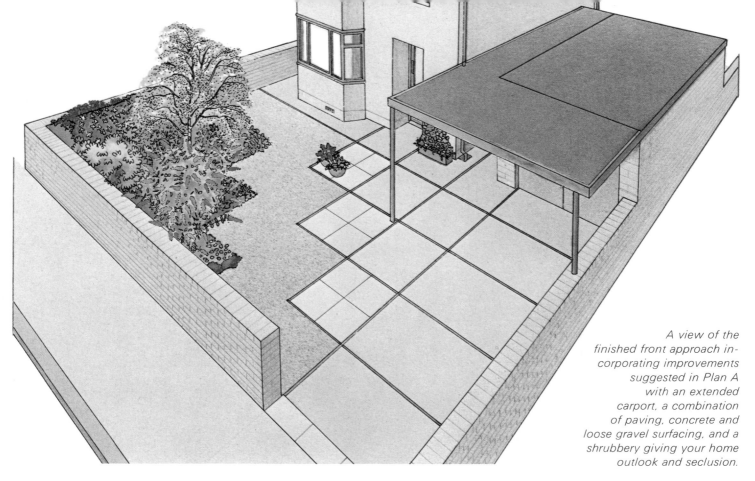

A view of the finished front approach incorporating improvements suggested in Plan A with an extended carport, a combination of paving, concrete and loose gravel surfacing, and a shrubbery giving your home outlook and seclusion.

design should still divide off the more public area from the private.

Types of ground surfacing

Because the front area takes such heavy wear, the materials which you use to build it should be of the best (not necessarily the most expensive) and they should be well laid. Badly-jointed paving – crazy or not – can be lethal when grass comes through the joints, making the surface slippery in rain or with rotting autumn leaves on it. It cannot be over-emphasized that a good surface is the key to a serviceable front area. Stone in a country area and brick in a more sophisticated setting are very handsome as paving materials, particularly if you can use the same as the structure of the house.

Brick For paving, if you buy paviors, (which are slightly larger and thinner than a building brick laid flat and fairly expensive), you need fewer than if you paved with conventional building bricks. It is worth remembering, too, that while the cost of materials like brick, or granite setts, is moderately high, it is the time and labour of laying them that really puts up the price.

Old York stone Where it is available, York stone is ideal paving for a town garden, although it does become stained by oil. To prevent this happening you could insert a cobbled oil-drip area just under where the car usually stands.

Concrete paving stone This now comes in all shapes, sizes and textured finishes. If you are using the straightforward square or rectangular stones, stick to one colour, for it is only a front garden you are laying, not an Italian piazza! New paving stones come textured as granite setts, cobbled, or as stable tiles (rather like slabs of chocolate), and can be attractive in the right setting. The cheaper slabs tend to crack easily and are difficult to cut without breaking. Most of these stones should be laid on concrete if they are to bear the weight of vehicles.

Small interlocking paving stones are available that fit together not unlike a simple jigsaw. They are easy to lay, and being a small irregular element are ideal for a setting that is not totally flat. For a small-scale area, a small paving unit of brick or tile is more attractive than slabs of concrete.

Tarmac On larger areas of frontage you may consider using tarmac, or be talked into re-laying it on an existing drive by door-to-door representatives from small firms offering this service. While some are specialists in this work, many are not. Before parting with any money, obtain a detailed specification of the work they propose to do, ensuring that an adequate base and foundation are laid for the weight of car you put on it. Other possibilities here are coloured tarmac, or rolling a local stone into the surface for a gravelled effect, or just using areas of tarmac within paving. When surfacing with tarmac you will need a curbed edge of brick or concrete, or the surface will break away at the edges because of frost. As you will get a quicker water run-off after rain, you must look to your drainage as well.

Concrete A cheaper broad-scale treatment for the drive-in might well be concrete laid *in situ*, and brushed when nearly dry, or 'green' as it is called, to expose the gravel or aggregate in the concrete. It should be laid in squares to allow for expansion, and these can be broken up with brick or any other small element to make an attractive pattern.

Gravel The cheapest large-scale medium is probably gravel. The disadvantage here is that it is picked up easily and gets carried indoors, but if a foot-scraper is provided you should not suffer from this hazard. Be sure to lay the gravel on hardcore and 'binding' gravel. The latter is unwashed and the clay content hardens and binds it together. If you put the finishing gravel layer on too thickly it will bog you down; to consolidate the finished surface, roll and water it. Gravel comes either as a chipping from a local stone quarry (when it is sharp-edged and not too good for children to fall down on) or preferably rounded (washed by water).

Adding Colour to your Front Approach

We have looked at types of enclosure and suggested varieties of ground surfacing to guide you in planning and structuring your front garden area. Now we give you a selection of suitable plants and shrubs to help you to determine its final appearance.

Top left: evergreen hebe Autumn Glory
Top right: the scented Choisya ternata

Below left: Fatsia japonica *in flower*
Below: Hedera canariensis *on tree stump*

The plantings of the leftovers, the bits between the hard surfacing and against the house and garage should be fairly tough, with a good proportion of evergreen for an all-year-round effect. Evergreen conjures up ideas of laurel and privet (which incidentally are both effective when used well), but there are many other suitable plants, such as cotoneasters, certain viburnums, hebes, fatsia, senecio and choisya which are all attractive evergreens that flower, and some have berries too. These can also survive in an area with not too much sun. The ever-popular conifer, however, being by its shape a point-of-emphasis plant, is not suitable for most frontages.

In your layout, try to avoid little pieces of lawn which are tedious to cut, and consider instead areas of low ground cover. Here you will want something flat. Ivy is suitable in this situation, and hypericum (St John's wort or rose of Sharon), or low juniper would be admirable. Plant boldly and simply for the positive effect that is needed.

Before making your final selection of plants, do some homework on their ultimate size. A weeping willow in the middle of the front garden may look charming for a year or two, but very quickly grows to 10m (30 ft) across. And there is no point in planting shrubs on either side of a path if they need cutting back each year to allow you to walk there.

You could choose a particularly handsome sculptural plant adjacent to the front door, marking its importance. Tubs with bay trees have traditionally been used here, or, more recently, conifers

again. But what about *Mahonia bealei*, or its near relation *M.* Charity? The leaves are an attractive, waxy evergreen, and the yellow flowers smell delicious in the early spring. Euphorbias (or spurges) make another good sculptural plant, or for a sunny situation try the upright-growing rosemary Miss Jessup. A good herbaceous plant in the sun is the beautiful-leafed acanthus.

Scent on entering a garden is always appreciated. Mahonia again is good, as is the evergreen *Daphne odora marginata. Choisya ternata*, the Mexican orange blossom, has scented white flowers and glossy foliage for cutting all year round.

If you are thinking of a climber up the front of the house or on the garage wall, consider a honeysuckle, for its scent. But, whichever climber you settle on, remember that it is the plant you have put

there for display, not its means of support. Use simple wires running along the brick courses rather than complicated patterns of trellis that are liable to rot.

For points of coloured emphasis use window boxes, or pots filled with bulbs and annuals.

Highlighting your home

Lastly, if you provide a serviceable and welcoming frontage to your house, do help your visitors to find it. Put a name or number in a position not only visible to pedestrians but also to car drivers. It helps, too, if the lettering is legible and not too much in the mock Tudor rustic style. Let the name and number be illuminated at night, as well as any change of level at the entrance. With luck this may deter the night intruder, as well as guide the more welcome guest.

A Small Garden in Town

Town gardens are often tiny, and here we look at their possibilities and their limitations with advice on how to make the most of each individual plot.

No two garden designs should look exactly the same, with their size, shape and situation all varying to determine an individual composition. Each site has its own difficulties and town gardens present their own quite distinct limitations.

First, space is likely to be limited, walls of surrounding buildings will cast heavy shade and the views will often be dull and oppressive. On the other side of the coin, shelter is excellent and the chances of severe frost are considerably less than in a garden that stands open to the elements.

Because the area is likely to be small, careful planning is obviously important, but it is also true to say that once completed, a town garden can be a real

asset, acting as an extension of the house and demanding very little maintenance. However, in such a situation people often refuse to take up the challenge, feeling that the problems are either insurmountable or too small to bother about. They may be quite adept at designing the rooms inside the house, but the outside 'room' – probably much bigger – gets neglected.

When space is limited a simple approach is called for. Grass is often

The successful combination of different ingredients is the secret of this pleasant town garden. Brick and pre-cast paving provides an attractive hard surface, while ground cover such as Vinca minor Caeruleo-plena (above right) fills the planting gaps between paving slabs

impossible in an urban area, with shade making growth difficult and concentrated activity quickly producing a quagmire. A hard surface, on the other hand, will provide a solid base for a table and chairs, children's bicycles and even an ironing board for those who like to do their household chores outdoors. Hard surfaces also dry quickly after rain and consequently get maximum use throughout the year.

Planting is important to soften the walls and take the edges off the inevitably rectangular boundaries. Some of the beds will be in shade, meaning that the choice of plant species is important. It is also very helpful to raise the planted areas – this not only gives the young shrubs and herbaceous material initial height, but it makes any maintenance considerably easier.

If views of surrounding buildings are gloomy, rather than increase the height of walls and fences in an attempt to blot them out, it is far better to work on the principle of creating a partial screen, utilizing a possible combination of trellis, planting and perhaps a carefully-chosen small tree. Overhead beams, running out from the house, are useful in this respect

Small Town Garden Plan

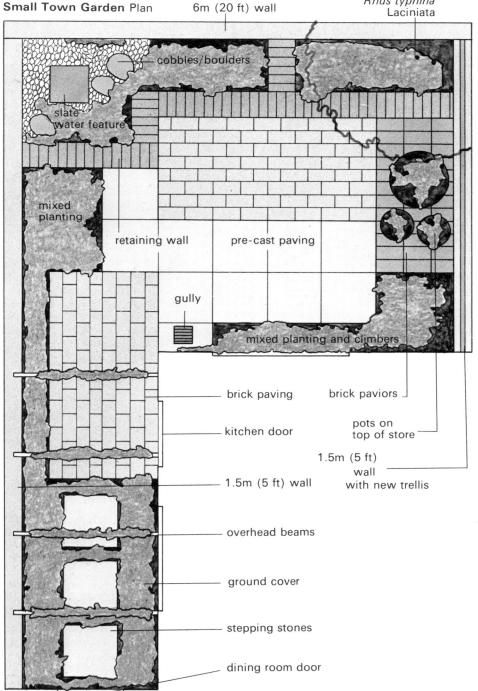

6m (20 ft) wall

Rhus typhina Laciniata

cobbles/boulders

slate water feature

mixed planting

retaining wall

pre-cast paving

gully

mixed planting and climbers

brick paving

brick paviors

kitchen door

pots on top of store

1.5m (5 ft) wall

1.5m (5 ft) wall with new trellis

overhead beams

ground cover

stepping stones

dining room door

as well, giving support for climbing plants and giving a feeling of enclosure without being too dominant. As a general rule it is probably best to leave the beams as an open framework – a canopy of perspex or PVC tends to gather leaves and general debris and dirt.

Water is a definite asset in a town garden where hot summer weather can become oppressive. However, a conventional pool takes up valuable space as well as being a hazard for young children so a small raised pool, tucked into a corner, with a lion's head or other decorative spout, is a traditional solution. But several other interesting permutations revolve around the use of boulders, cobbles and even old millstones, water being pumped through and over them to form a delightful feature. By using these techniques you can emphasize an important fact – it is the sound of running water that really counts in providing a cooling influence on the immediate surroundings.

Perhaps the most important factor of all is the planting. It not only has to undergo close scrutiny throughout the year but also withstand the restrictions of shade and a partially-polluted atmosphere. Plants are easily affected by dust and dirt in the air and this can have the effect of blocking the tiny pores or 'stomata' through which they breathe. Some of the felty, grey-leaved species are particularly susceptible, the hairs on the leaves trapping and holding a thick layer of dirt that is difficult to remove.

These, then, are some of the factors and restrictions that govern the creation of a town garden; but they are by no means insuperable. With careful planning it need not be difficult to create a charming composition.

Planning our town garden
The garden shown here is typical of the 'yard' at the back of many older terraced houses, the main area measuring 3.5×5m (12×16 ft), while a side passage leads to a door out of the dining room. As with all garden design, we first drew up both a list of priorities and a plan of the existing area, marking in the north point, good or bad views, the heights of walls and fences, the position of drains, pipes, manholes, changes of level, doors and windows, as well as any existing vegetation.

If you have just moved in, look out for any seedling trees, particularly sycamore: if they grow to more than, say, 7.5m (25 ft), have them out. There are occasional exceptions when you come across the odd huge tree that, although completely dominant, is the making of a small garden.

The choice of surfacing
Many terraces have no rear or side access, meaning that all materials have to come in and out through the house. This makes careful planning absolutely essential. In our garden the existing surface was an uneven mass of poorly-laid concrete, and under normal circumstances you would think nothing of digging it up and loading it onto a waiting skip or lorry. In a confined space, however, this is a nightmare as every shovel load has to be bagged up and carried through the house. This is where a little forethought is invaluable: raised beds, as we have already mentioned, save maintenance and as the plants will thrive in 45cm (18 in) of topsoil this leaves a considerable height to be made up. Broken concrete makes good hardcore, is sharp-draining and will be an ideal filler for the bottom of those beds.

The raised areas in our design wrap themselves around two sides of the garden, just enough to look after the unwanted material and leave the ground clean. The main part of the 'floor' is given over to paving and measures approximately 3×2.5m (10×8 ft), the size of a reasonable room inside the house. As the house and the surrounding boundary walls were built of brick it seemed reasonable to incorporate at least some of this material in the 'floor'. A good, well-fired, second-hand stock brick is fine for paving, despite the advice of some architects and surveyors. It has the added advantage of an immediate mellow look. Our pattern of brick was based on the main lines of the building and this allowed for a second 'infill' material.

Light, or lack of it, is often a problem in an urban situation and if you can use a pale, reflective material, so much the better. White paving is probably best avoided as it tends to pick up dirt easily. We chose a pale sandstone-coloured precast slab. This mixture of materials ties the composition together while the water feature is emphasized as a focal point.

Devising a water feature
The uses of water in a small garden are legion and as our ground space was limited we decided to try a somewhat different approach. We placed a polythene water tank in the existing raised bed and neatly fitted into this a drilled slate slab. A length of copper pipe was pushed through the hole in the slab and a submersible pump was fitted and the tank filled loosely with large cobbles. When the tank was filled with water and the pump turned on, a steady flow rose through and over the slab, the pressure being just

enough to lift the jet clear of the surface. This looked and sounded attractive and was entirely safe with young children.

Improving the side passage
The side passage was only 1.5m (5 ft) wide, a long narrow space that was difficult to handle. The kitchen window not only looked onto it but was in turn overlooked by the upstairs windows of the house next door. To raise the wall would have cut virtually all the light out and involved considerable cost. An attractive solution was to fit timber beams above the passage; we painted these white to reflect the light and they made an ideal host for climbing plants. The direct view from the neighbouring windows was broken and so was the expanse of brickwork that formed the house itself. The floor of the passage was shady and as the door from the dining room was only used occasionally, we laid a simple stepping-stone path with pre-cast slabs. The gaps between and around the slabs were planted with two tough ground-covering plants, *Epimedium × warleyense* (barrenwort) and *Vinca minor* (lesser periwinkle).

Built-in cupboard for storage
Storage in a small garden is a problem and there are always things to put away, often in a hurry when unexpected guests arrive. Instead of the usual motley shed we decided to build in a double cupboard of ample capacity. This fitted neatly with the raised beds and the top acted as both a worktop and a stand for potted plants. Remember that any storage outside, although dry, is likely to be damp in the long term. Lightly oil all tools and keep your cushions indoors; they quickly grow mould if left out, even in a cupboard.

Furnishing with plants
The planting of the garden finished the picture. Climbers are of paramount importance in a town garden, helping to cover and disguise the walls. Wires for support are neater and need less maintenance than a trellis and should be secured by masonry nails driven into the joints of the brickwork.

Make your selection of shrubs and herbaceous plants with the position of sun and shade in mind. Variations of leaf tones and texture are more effective in a small town garden than brash colour, evergreens being particularly important for winter interest. The whole plant composition should thus act as a backdrop to the completed garden, giving a balanced display that hopefully should belie its urban setting.

Constructing the Garden

We have outlined the methods of planning and the limitations imposed by a small town garden. Here we take a more detailed look at the construction of the various features and describe a choice of planting.

The different materials available and methods of laying paving have already been covered, but it is worth repeating that all paved areas should be given a 'fall' or slight slope away from the house and towards any available gullies. This is particularly important where the whole outdoor area is given over to hard surfacing as puddles and slippery areas are a nuisance as well as being potentially dangerous.

Raising the levels

In order to reduce maintenance and soften the dominating surrounding walls we raised the main areas of planting at the back of the garden. The bricks used for the paving were matched in the raised beds and 230mm (9 in) brick walls. Although this was not essential from a practical point of view, it gives the composition visual stability, linking with the thickness of existing walls and being neatly finished with a brick-on-edge coping. We filled the bottom of the raised beds with broken concrete from the original yard surface and this provided good drainage for the subsequent planting. It is a good idea to leave an occasional open joint in the brickwork that supports raised beds, thus allowing drainage and preventing the soil from becoming sour.

Constructing the water feature

The main focal point is the water feature situated in the corner of the garden at the end of the raised bed. We housed this within a standard polythene water tank, carefully positioned so that its top is 4cm ($1\frac{1}{2}$ in) above the eventual soil level. We built two 230×230mm (9×9 in) brick piers inside the tank, using a 'hard' engineering brick that would not be affected by long immersion in water. The piers stopped short of the top of the tank so that the slate that formed the feature itself stands clear of the rim and the surrounding soil. The slate was a lucky find from a demolition site, but similar materials can usually be picked up reason-

ably from a local monumental mason.

Offcuts of granite, slate or marble can be put to good use in the garden and the mason will usually be able to cut or drill any piece to your specification. Our slate was drilled centrally to accept a length of 12mm ($\frac{1}{2}$ in) copper pipe. This was pushed through the hole so that it was flush with the top, but projected about 5cm (2 in) on the underside, ready to accept the length of hose from the submersible pump. The latter was housed in the bottom of the tank and connected back to the house with the correct combination of exterior cable and sockets.

When laying a paved area it is often possible to incorporate an armoured cable underneath the slabs, thus avoiding a long run of wire above ground. Should you have any doubts concerning electrical work it is wise to seek the advice of a professional, particularly in the garden, where the hazards of moisture and accidental damage are obvious.

We left the final positioning of the slate, boulders and cobbles until the adjoining bed was filled with soil and the other features within the garden were finished, thus allowing any debris to be easily removed from the tank..

The water feature, set amongst planting in the raised bed, makes a delightful focal point and, in the summer, has a cooling effect on the whole garden

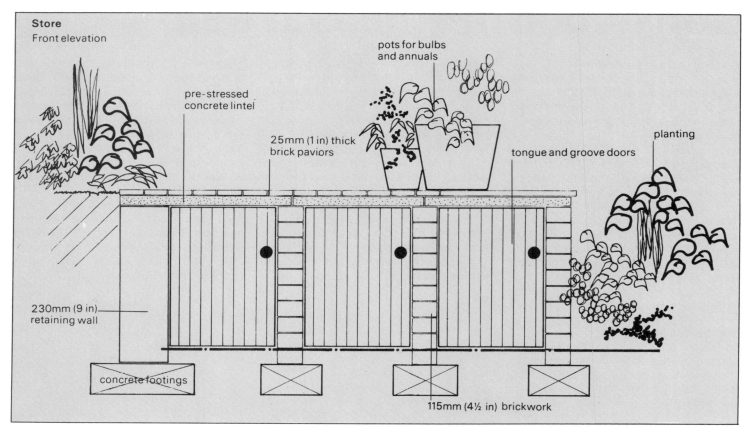

Store
Front elevation

pre-stressed concrete lintel

25mm (1 in) thick brick paviors

pots for bulbs and annuals

planting

tongue and groove doors

230mm (9 in) retaining wall

concrete footings

115mm (4½ in) brickwork

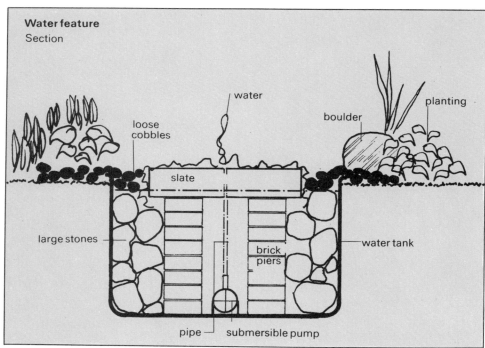

Water feature
Section

water

loose cobbles

boulder

planting

slate

large stones

brick piers

water tank

pipe — submersible pump

Above left: the store cupboard acts as a work bench and a pot plant stand
Left: internal structure of the water feature is not completed until other construction work is finished

paving bricks 25mm (1 in) thick to form the top of the cupboard, the first course overhanging the front by 25mm (1 in).

The doors were constructed with tongue-and-groove boards, and then painted with a primer, undercoat and white topcoat. The hinges, catches and screws are brass, to resist rust.

Decorating the passageway
The white beams that run over the passage to the dining room were hung next. These are constructed from 230×50mm (9×2 in) timbers and supported on the house side by joist hangers while scaffold poles form the uprights into the top of the wall.

In order to help climbing plants onto the beams, we screwed metal eyes into the undersides and passed a wire through them. Once a plant has reached the required height it is simple enough to tuck the stems under the wire and eventually form an attractive canopy of vegetation. The wires also help maintenance as the eyes can be removed and the whole plant lowered when the beams need painting.

Building a worktop store
The next feature to tackle was the store cupboard that doubled as a worktop and stand for pot plants. We built the main framework with 115mm (4½ in) brick walls, each wall dividing the store into sections and acting as support for the lintels. The latter were of the 'pre-stressed' kind that are available from

most large builders' merchants in various widths and lengths. The great advantage of this particular type lies in the thickness – approximately 5cm (2 in), as opposed to a cast lintel that takes anything up to 15cm (6 in) to achieve the same strength. We used three 23cm (9 in) wide lintels, (firmly bedded side by side in mortar) on top of the walls. We then laid glazed

Filling the water tank

Before tackling the planting we finished the water feature by loosely filling the tank with large stones and cobbles. The hose from the pump we connected to the pipe inserted in the slab with a jubilee clip, and then the slate was carefully positioned on top of the brick piers. More loose cobbles and several boulders disguised the lip of the tank, the latter being filled with water to within 8cm (3 in) of the top. When the pump was switched on, water bubbled up through the slate and slid smoothly over the surface to descend into the tank in a continuing cycle.

Small Town Garden
Planting plan

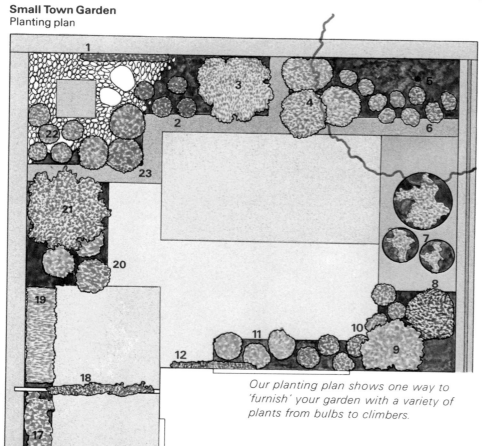

Our planting plan shows one way to 'furnish' your garden with a variety of plants from bulbs to climbers.

The choice of planting

The last major operation involved planting and the preparation of the beds themselves. New soil was absolutely essential as what little there was from the original yard was of poor quality and extremely 'tired'. It is at this point that town gardeners score over their country cousins as they can virtually select the type of soil they need. If you are a lover of rhododendrons, camellias or other acid-loving plants it is easy enough to prepare a soil of the correct pH value.

In town gardens shade is often a limiting factor but it should be re-membered that the range of plants that enjoy these conditions is by no means small. In our garden, as you can see from the suggested planting plan, we have used many shade-lovers, some of which are described here. *Fatsia japonica* (fig-leaf palm of Japanese aralia) with its fine sculptural evergreen foliage is a good choice, together with *Hosta sieboldiana* (plantain lily) that contrasts with the upright form of *Iris foetidissima* Lutea.

Hydrangeas are invaluable and we have chosen one of the prettiest 'lacecap' varieties, *Hydrangea macrophylla* Blue Wave. *Viburnum davidii*, that grows into a compact rounded shrub, is another evergreen with attractive purple berries.

For vertical emphasis we have included *Rhus typhina* Laciniata, a small sumach tree of sculptural habit that can be carefully shaped to enhance its dramatic branch formations.

Climbers too are of paramount importance. *Jasminum nudiflorum* (winter jasmine), or the climbing *Hydrangea petiolaris* are particularly useful on a shady wall as is Virginia creeper, a good variety of which is *Parthenocissus tricuspidata* Veitchii. An unusual climber is featured on one of the beams, *Aristolochia durior* or *macrophylla* (Dutchman's pipe), taking its common name from the oddly-formed flowers. This, too, is happy in sun or semi-shade. Actinidia (Chinese gooseberry) is ideal for a sunny position while the many varieties of lonicera (honeysuckle) are invaluable for their fragrant blooms.

As planting is inevitably small when first introduced to its new home, it is a good idea to fill the initial gaps with bulky annuals and of course, bulbs. Nicotiana (tobacco plant) and matthiola (stocks) give the bonus of scent while helianthus (sunflowers) have more dramatic qualities to add in these early stages.

Imaginative planting clothes the composition, softening the hard line of walls and providing a backdrop to your outside room throughout the year.

Key to planting plan

Numerals after names denote quantities of plants

1 *Parthenocissus tricuspidata* Veitchii (Virginia creeper) ×1
2 *Iris foetidissima* Lutea ×4
3 *Hydrangea macrophylla* Blue Wave ×1
4 *Viburnum davidii* ×3
5 *Rhus typhina* Laciniata (sumach) ×1
6 *Vinca minor* (lesser periwinkle) ×9
7 Bulbs and annuals in plots
8 *Rosmarinus officinalis* Miss Jessop's Variety (rosemary) ×1
9 *Salvia officinalis* Purpurascens (common sage) ×1
10 *Festuca ovina* Glauca (blue fescue grass) ×7
11 *Hebe pinguifolia* Pagei (veronica) ×3
12 *Actinidia chinensis* (Chinese gooseberry) ×1
13 *Hypericum calycinum* (rose of Sharon) ×24
14 *Hedera canariensis* Gloire de Marengo (Canary Island ivy) ×1
15 *Lonicera japonica halliana* (honeysuckle) ×1
16 *Lonicera japonica* Aureoreticulata (honeysuckle) ×1
17 *Pachysandra terminalis* ×24
18 *Aristolochia (durior) macrophylla* (Dutchman's pipe) ×1
19 *Jasminum nudiflorum* (winter jasmine) ×1
20 *Hedera helix* Glacier (common ivy), as ground cover ×3
21 *Fatsia japonica* (Japanese aralia or fig-leaf palm) ×1
22 *Bergenia cordifolia* (pig squeak) ×5
23 *Hosta sieboldiana* (plantain lily) ×3

Before you do any planting at all you will need to prepare the soil thoroughly. Before putting in your climbers, dig the soil deeply and break it up well; if it is heavy you can lighten it by incorporating peat, leaf mould, humus, or well-rotted manure if you can get it. In early spring (February) each year you should top dress the soil with a handful of Grow-more fertilizer to every square metre or yard. Scatter this lightly on the surface, but don't let it come in contact with any green leaves. Once the soil is light and well broken-up the new plants will quickly make roots and grow rapidly. If your soil is just a mass of clay it may be worthwhile importing new soil, in which case you will have to dig out areas about 30cm (12 in) deep and 1·20m (4 ft) square.

The choice in climbers
In selecting plants you will have to be guided by the direction in which the walls face, some plants being suited to a south-facing wall, others to a north-facing one and so on.

If possible your plants should be continuously interesting to look at, or at least have more than one season of interest. One of the best of such plants is pyracantha (firethorn). This is not a climber by nature so in the early stages you will have to tie in the branches against the wall and prune the plant back from time to time. Firethorn is evergreen, and bears heads of white flowers in mid summer (June) that are followed by very brilliant berries which will last through much of the winter. It is one of those convenient plants that will grow in any aspect and even thrive against a north-facing wall where the choice is somewhat limited, and is ideal for one facing east.

Magnolia grandiflora is another ever-green shrub that will require tying in, but no pruning. It is not suitable for very chalky soils but will thrive on walls facing south, east or west. *M. grandiflora* Goliath bears large and waxy, cream-coloured flowers fragrant throughout the summer, and at a much earlier age than most forms. *M. grandiflora* Exmouth also flowers at quite an early age and the leaves have a vivid, cinnamon-brown felt on the undersides, adding to their attractive appearance.

Parthenocissus henryana, a refined relative of the too-vigorous Virginia creeper (*P. tricuspidata*), will support itself against a wall by means of sucker pads and does best against a west-facing one, although it will also grow on a north-facing wall.

Euonymus fortunei, another self-cling-ing, evergreen climber, is a rather weak

Top: evergreen, scarlet-berried pyracantha (firethorn) is easily trained up a wall
Above: a flower of the evergreen Magnolia grandiflora that grows out of a gap left in the brick-paved area of our patio
Right: Clematis montana will cling equally easily to an old tree or a boundary wall

plant of which there are many forms. Although slow-growing it would be suitable for the north-facing wall here. One of the best is Coloratus whose leaves turn purple during the winter months. They are not, however, very exciting during the summer, so you may prefer Variegatus, with grey-green leaves with a white margin which sometimes turn

pinkish in the winter.

Rather unexpectedly, most of the large-flowered clematis do extremely well on north-facing walls, and the earlier-flowering types such as Nelly Moser will do better there than anywhere else. However, these look gorgeous for a short period only and have little attraction later on, whereas the smaller-flowered *Clematis tangutica* not only covers itself with yellow flowers throughout mid to late summer (June–July), but follows these up with very ornamental silky fruits like superior versions of *C. vitalba* (Old Man's Beard) so that it remains attractive for three to four months on end. It does require some direct sunlight, so is best on east-, west- or south-facing walls.

Ampelopsis (or *Vitis*) *brevipedunculata* Elegans is another plant for such a position. This is a rather slow-growing vine, climbing by means of tendrils, with the lobed leaves mottled white and pink.

The honeysuckles, which climb by twining and so must be given something to twine around, do best on east or west walls, as they do not like too much direct sunlight. The showiest is *Lonicera* × *americana*, which produces enormous trusses of fragrant white flowers in mid to late summer (June–July) that turn yellow as they age. Slightly less showy but liable to produce attractive red berries later in the season is the woodbine, *Lonicera periclymenum*, of which

Top left: Lonicera periclymenum *Belgica (Early Dutch honeysuckle), which on our patio twines from a container up the trellis*
Top right: the sweet-smelling Teinturier grape, Vitis vinifera *Purpurea*
Above: hanging blooms of Wisteria sinensis *look well on the pergola*

the Early Dutch and Late Dutch have much redder flowers than the ordinary wild plant.

For the pergola

You will also need climbers for the pergola but here you want a very vigorous plant that can easily be trained, such as a wisteria, and both *W. sinensis* and

W. floribunda are among the most spectacular of all climbers. Once established they grow very vigorously and require hard pruning in winter to keep them within bounds. On the other hand, pruning will delay flowering so some balance must be struck and it is possible that you will have to wait a few years before seeing many flowers. Unfortunately birds can be a great enemy, attacking the unopened buds in early spring.

For a pergola it is hard to do better than grow one of the hardy vines. If you can obtain it, *Vitis riparia* (often sold as *V. vulpina*) has the advantage that the rather inconspicuous flowers smell of mignonette and the black grapes are produced quite freely. The same can be said of Brandt, of which the grapes are pleasant to eat while the leaves usually colour beautifully in the autumn. The so-called Teinturier grape, *Vitis vinifera* Purpurea, has leaves that are reddish, turning later to dark purple.

All these vines are attractive but lack any floral display, so if you want flowers but feel that wisteria might not be suitable you will probably do best with one of the forms of the very vigorous *Clematis montana* which covers itself with flowers in early to mid summer (May–June). Most forms are white, but *C. montana* Rubens has pink flowers and bronzy leaves, while *C. montana* Tetrarose has bronzy leaves and purplish flowers.

Make a Roof Garden

You don't need a ground-level site to experience the joys that gardening can bring: all that is necessary is a suitable roof and a little ingenuity.

The benefits that a roof garden can offer include a warm environment that will appeal to both plants and gardener alike; peace and privacy; and – if you are fortunate – an unhindered view.

Here we introduce our own design, and later on we describe the formation of the basic features.

To create a garden on a roof means a departure from normal gardening techniques, and often involves an entirely new set of rules. As the height above ground increases so, too, do the difficulties – seemingly in direct ratio; access, shelter, irrigation and weight: all will assume quite new proportions.

Certain problems are peculiar to roof gardens. A common one is how to hide the rash of pipes that always seems to be in the most awkward position. Another frequently concerns weight: before undertaking any work you should be absolutely certain that the existing structure is sound and capable of supporting the proposed garden. If you are in any doubt, call in an architect or surveyor to make a professional assessment of the situation – it is better to be safe than sorry!

Apart from technical considerations though, the chief factor affecting your roof garden is likely to be the wind. In a built-up area calm is normally taken for granted. However, what may seem a gentle breeze in the street can be a biting wind three floors up. Providing adequate shelter is therefore of paramount importance, both from your plants' point of view, and your own.

Plan and design

As far as design is concerned, you should tackle the initial survey exactly as you would for a ground-level garden. Views, direction of prevailing wind, aspect, position of doors and windows, and the total dimensions must all be drawn on your basic plan, together with any other relevant information. If you do this on squared paper it will be easy to establish a scale and ensure that the features are correctly related to one another.

It would be wise to position heavy features around the perimeter, where the underlying framework will transfer the load onto the surrounding walls. As soil is usually the heaviest, your planting area will be strictly regulated.

Paving, in the conventional sense, will also present a weight problem. It is usual to find either asbestos tiles or some kind of specially-laid bituminous surface where access has been previously planned, but neither would be particularly attractive over large areas.

The limitations and possibilities should now be falling into some form of pattern, possibly similar to that shown on our detailed ground plan.

Roof gardens, in general, are small and ours is no exception, measuring approximately 10·5 × 6m (35 × 20 ft). It has a high wall on one side, and a lower wall topped by chimney pots on the other. The main view is from directly in front of the doorway leading to the house below. The floor was originally laid with asbestos tiles, and unsightly pipes were visible in a number of places. A television aerial hung from the higher wall, and the prevailing wind tended to sweep over the lower wall, making sitting outdoors impossible in all but the calmest weather.

Our first task, then, was to provide some form of shelter. To this end, we constructed a strong wooden canopy, and used clear corrugated rigid PVC to form the roof. We left the front open, but fitted the side facing the wind with open, horizontally-arranged slats to form a protective screen. The latter, while breaking the force of the wind, still allows some movement of air through the garden, so helping to keep the temperature reasonable on hot days. It also hides the pipes,

Raised beds and wooden seat form focal point of design, while a rigid PVC roof and slatted wall provide shelter

and creates the small utility area that houses the tiny shed and the invaluable water butt for irrigation.

A timber handrail ran along the front of the roof. As children might use the garden we decided to close it in for safety, using plate glass with bevelled edges. This way we retain the view and reduce wind velocity within the garden even more.

Structurally, in addition to the supporting walls around the perimeter, we were lucky enough to have a wall running along the line of the horizontal slats. So we were able to plant along the edges of the roof, and also incorporate a planting feature in virtually the middle of the design. This led to the creation of an interesting composition involving planting on split levels, and a seat that gives definition to the main relaxation area.

Next we turned our attention to the floor. The asbestos tiles measured 23cm (9 in) square and covered the whole roof. After we had scrubbed them with a strong detergent their colour was a uniform grey that, although not unpleasant in moderation, was distinctly oppressive over the entire area.

As already mentioned, pre-cast paving is normally far too heavy for a roof, likewise the more traditional natural

111

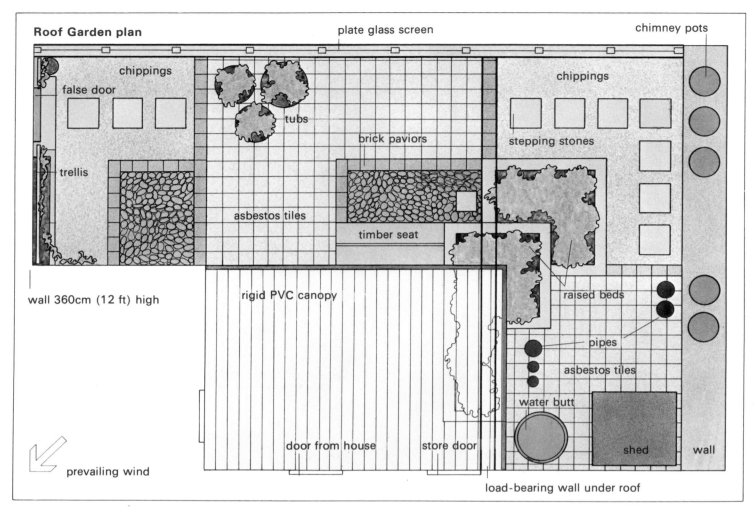

Roof Garden plan

plate glass screen

chimney pots

chippings

false door

tubs

brick paviors

chippings

stepping stones

trellis

asbestos tiles

timber seat

raised beds

wall 360cm (12 ft) high

rigid PVC canopy

pipes

asbestos tiles

water butt

prevailing wind

door from house

store door

shed

wall

load-bearing wall under roof

stone. Thinner paving bricks and quarry tiles are lighter, although where a large area is involved the weight would still be considerable.

In our design we divided the garden area into squares and worked out a simple geometric pattern. Some parts we left as the original surface, and others we edged with black paviors 25mm (1 in) thick. The resulting panels we filled with a thin covering of loose chippings – just enough to cover the tiles. As the stones were laid loose, drainage was unaffected, the occasional joint being left open in the brick surround to allow water to flow on its way to the main gutter. One word of warning: chippings come in a range of colours, but you should exercise particular care over your choice. It is advisable to steer clear of white as it can prove extremely dazzling in such an open situation; the same goes for painted surfaces. Buffs and browns are particularly restful and form a good background for plantings.

We had a bit of fun on the high wall. When the house was being converted a new front door was hung and its predecessor was due to be carted away with the

rest of the rubbish. Instead, we rescued it and screwed it into position on the wall. We laid chippings over the area in front of the door and placed stepping stones to lead up to a small and quite obvious step. With a handle fitted, the door fooled numerous visitors, who either asked what was on the other side, or actually tried the handle. We fitted the wall on each side with squared trellis, and trained climbing plants over this.

After checking with a television engineer we discovered that the aerial could be removed and replaced with an indoor model.

Planting your roof garden
A special lightweight variety of soil is available that you can actually mix in your own home and we tell you more about this on page 114. If you are thinking of using pots or tubs make sure they are of ample size, for they will dry out far quicker on a roof than at ground level, with the combination of greater heat and drying wind in that situation.

It is essential that you water pots every single day in summer, which can lead to obvious problems at holiday time. Raised

Tackle initial survey as for ground-level garden, and draw basic plan on squared paper to establish scale and ensure features relate correctly to one another

beds on the other hand, will hold a greater depth of soil and thus retain moisture longer. You could use timber as a construction material, although it will be costly and require protection from damp on the inside by polythene or asbestos. A far easier method is to use lightweight concrete blocks such as Thermalite, from which you can build beds of any shape; simply bore holes through the blocks for drainage. To protect the blocks from the weather you can render them on the outside, or give them a coat of suitable stone paint, such as Sandtex.

Choose plants that will enjoy a hot sunny position. Cistus, potentilla, senecio, cytisus and yucca will all thrive in a roof setting, provided you erect shelter, while bulbs and annuals will also grow quickly. You can group your plants in the same way as you would in a ground-level garden, choosing species to provide colour and interest throughout the year.

We have not outlined the advantages of high-level gardens, introducing our own Roof Garden design as an easy-to-follow example. We go on to detail the basic features of the design, and give instructions for making the glass screen and creating split-level planting areas. The view towards the 'false door' is shown below.

The chief factor affecting your roof garden will probably be the wind. Here we look at the construction of the two features in our own design that break the force of the wind and provide shelter for both you and your plants.

Making the canopy
The canopy protects the relaxation area from the wind and is built in three stages (see diagram on next page). First you construct a framework of beams and supports; then you add the slatted screen that acts as the principal windbreak; finally you top the whole structure with a clear, rigid corrugated PVC roof.

Use 150 × 25mm (6 × 1 in) timbers, planed all round, to construct the main framework. Make it in the form of a box, and bolt it to the two load-bearing walls with special expanding masonry bolts. The beams should finish flush with the top of the wall, allowing the corrugated PVC sheet to continue to the gutter beyond.

These PVC sheets, such as Novolux, are normally available in a standard width of 75cm (2½ ft), and can be bought with a tinted finish that is useful for cutting

Below: section of main canopy showing framework topped with rigid PVC sheet

down glare. To ensure adequate fixing, you should space the 150mm (6 in) beams at 35cm (14 in) centres, but remember to drill through the high ribs of the corrugated sheets before screwing them into position. Standard fixing accessories – that is, screws, washers and caps – are usually sold along with the PVC sheets.

Use a 100mm (4 in) softwood post for the single down support, and fix it to the roof with either angle brackets or a single shoe. An important point to remember when about to drill a hole in your roof is that you might cause dampness, or even leaks in the room below if you are not careful. Therefore, make as few holes as possible, and be sure always to use a sealer like mastic or bitumen. Should you have any doubts, call in professional help: it's best to play safe in such a situation.

For the horizontally-arranged wooden slats of the screen on the open side of the canopy, you can also use 150 × 25mm (6 × 1 in) timbers; screw them into the down support at one end, and to a simple 50 × 50mm (2 × 2 in) batten (screwed into the wall), at the other.

Erecting the glass screen
Erecting the glass screen at the front of the garden is a comparatively simple job. A handrail and hardwood posts were already in position on our roof-top area, so we simply had to fit brass lugs to accept the carefully-measured 6mm (¼ in) plate glass panels. A glazier will be able to bevel the edges and drill the glass for you. Use brass nuts and bolts with fibre or plastic washers to protect both sides of the glass from abrasion.

Building the raised beds
Timber will not be the best material for building the raised beds, for it is expensive and involves complicated constructional techniques. Lightweight concrete blocks, such as Thermalite, are what you need. Buy them measuring 80 × 230 × 450mm (3 × 9 × 18 in), and lay them in a stretcher bond (lay blocks lengthways and stagger the joints). Where corners are involved a 'closer' cut to fit will be needed to adjust the bonding. An advantage of these blocks is that they can be sawn, producing neat joints.

The main feature in our garden comprises the seat and split-level beds, and is built up from blockwork two, three and four courses high respectively; the tops of the walls are neatly finished with glazed paving bricks, 25mm (1 in) thick. As lightweight blocks are porous you will have to render them with sand and cement, and then apply a stone paint, such as Sandtex. You needn't render the inside of the bed as three coats of a bituminous paint will be satisfactory.

The highest bed is 90cm (3 ft), but it would be both unnecessary and unwise to fill with soil to this depth: 45cm (18 in) will be sufficient. Fit a false asbestos floor, which you can support with 6 × 50mm (¼ × 2 in) steel strips bedded into the blockwork two courses from the top. Drill 25mm (1 in) holes, spaced at 23cm (9 in) centres, into the floor for drainage, and similar-sized holes through the blocks just above roof level, to allow water to drain into the main gutters.

Insert plugs into the blockwork forming the bottom of the seat, and fit a

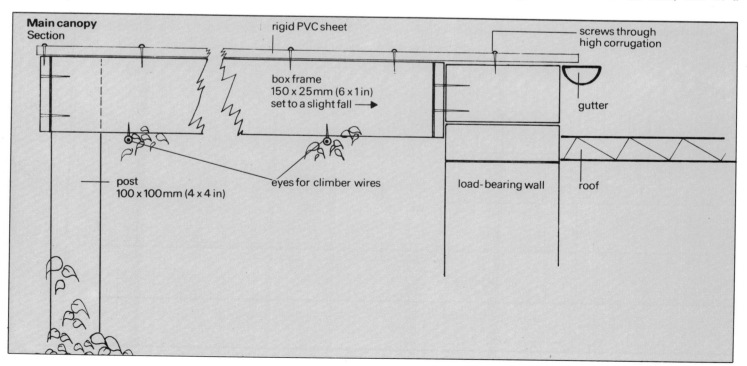

Main canopy
Section

rigid PVC sheet

screws through high corrugation

box frame 150 × 25mm (6 × 1 in) set to a slight fall →

gutter

post 100 × 100mm (4 × 4 in)

eyes for climber wires

load-bearing wall

roof

50 × 50mm (2 × 2 in) timber frame. Screw three 200 × 20mm (8 × ⅞ in) slats into this, and chamfer and carefully sand them, prior to painting.

Bedding the paving bricks
Glazed paving bricks, similar to those used on the top of the beds, are ideal for forming the retaining edges that define the areas of chippings. Bed the bricks in mortar, making sure that the joints are carefully pointed, and leaving an occasional gap to drain any trapped water. Stepping stones through the chippings will need to be approximately 25mm (1 in)

thick to match the bricks, and this rules out most pre-cast slabs that are normally in excess of 38mm (1½ in). Natural stone is often available in thinner gauges, however, and slate in particular will look very handsome against the paler surrounding surface. Bed the stones in mortar in the same way as the paving bricks.

In this design we have placed stepping stones to lead up to the old front door that we screwed to the wall on the left. With a handle fitted, the door to nowhere fools numerous visitors, who either ask what is on the other side, or actually try the handle. We fitted a squared trellis to the wall on each side of the door and trained climbing plants over this.

Soil mixture for raised beds
The soil to use in raised beds in a roof garden is a specially-prepared mix, lighter than that in an ordinary garden.

An ideal mix would be made up (by loose bulk) from 2 parts medium loam and 1 part each of peat, vermiculite granules and well-rotted manure. You

could also add an additional 85g (3 oz) of superphosphate of lime per 50kg (1 cwt) of soilmix, although this is not essential. The vermiculite is a very light insulation material, giving the mixture bulk and reducing the overall weight of the soil.

Before adding the soil to the beds, spread a layer of broken crocks over the bottom, making sure that the holes are protected and won't become clogged with soil. Add the soil in layers, wetting each as work progresses; this will enable the roots of the plants to take up moisture evenly as soon as they are in position.

You can plant in exactly the same way as you would in a garden at ground level, but pay particular attention to the staking and tying of plants, remembering that the wind can easily uproot young specimens. Walls and beams can be neatly wired to take climbing plants, but the wire should be closer to the wall than normal to combat the force of the wind.

Maintenance of a roof garden is very important, water being the key to healthy plant development. Few people realize how quickly beds and pots dry out, and during hot weather it is prudent to use the watering can daily, little and often being a better rule rather than sporadic floods. Try also to water in the morning or evening, avoiding the extreme heat of the middle of the day.

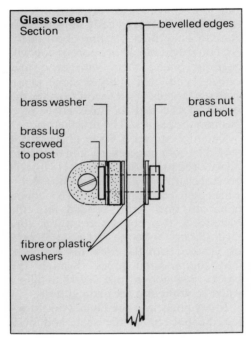

Glass screen
Section

bevelled edges

brass washer

brass lug screwed to post

brass nut and bolt

fibre or plastic washers

Left: section of plate glass screen attachment to post. Below: section of gravel area with chippings and stepping stone retained by glazed paving brick Bottom: seat and split-level raised beds

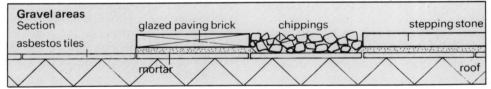

Gravel areas
Section

glazed paving brick   chippings   stepping stone

asbestos tiles

mortar   roof

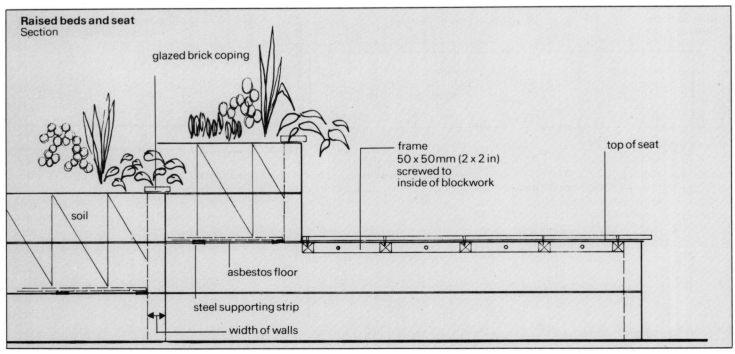

Raised beds and seat
Section

glazed brick coping

frame 50 x 50mm (2 x 2 in) screwed to inside of blockwork

top of seat

soil

asbestos floor

steel supporting strip

width of walls

Herbaceous and Cottage Gardens

There is an old-fashioned ring about the title 'herbaceous and cottage gardens' and here we illustrate some typical ones. We follow up with comprehensive planting plans and lists of plants that would suit both types of garden.

The herbaceous border has been much maligned in the labour-saving cult of recent years, admittedly with a degree of justification. But why condemn something of beauty if there are still keen gardeners prepared to undertake the work involved? A herbaceous border requires plenty of preparation and constant maintenance, but then so does a shrub border.

THE HERBACEOUS GARDEN

The preparation for a border is not complicated and involves straightforward digging, although this isn't everyone's favourite gardening task. If the soil is sandy then you only need to dig out a single 'spit', that is, the depth of the spade being used. You should then incorporate manure in the bottom of this spit; if the soil is heavy, it may be necessary to double dig it (that is two spits deep, see page 17, to give extra drainage required.

Again, incorporate manure into the bottom spit. Before planting, it does no harm to scatter a general chemical fertilizer and rake it in. Spring planting is firmly recommended for herbaceous plants. There is a critical period during late spring (late March and April) when it is best to plant and this can sometimes be extended into early summer (May) if the spring season has been a wet one.

Choosing plants

If you like the idea of a herbaceous border, but have only a vague notion of the types of plants you want, then it would pay you to spend a season visiting nurseries and gardens open to the public. In this way, you will get the 'feel' of how plants are used and placed, in relation to their colouring, height and leaf texture. You can then take a look through a catalogue and place an early order in the autumn to ensure spring delivery.

When you choose your plants, take into account factors such as aspect, damp or dry soil and the length of period during

Above: herbaceous border at Barrington Court in Somerset

which you want a display. The longer the border, the better placed you will be for an extended display of colour. You should also consider whether you take your holidays at a regular time each year, as there is little point in a border looking its best when you are not there.

In the 1950s, the mixed border came on the scene and this combination of shrubs and herbaceous plants was very fashionable for a time. You need an extremely wide border in order to obtain the right effect and you can still see a good example of this at the Royal Horticultural Society's garden at Wisley, Surrey. The 'grand' idea of the mixed border has had to be adapted to the context of today's average-sized garden and the best compromise is to have a herbaceous border in front of shrubs that should ideally be early-flowering and preferably evergreen.

Staking and tying

One drawback to having herbaceous plants is that they need support, and staking not only takes a long time but gives an ugly appearance to the border.

The least attractive form of staking is with canes and string; pea sticks are best and should be used in early summer (May), when growth is just beginning to rise. For a week or two, the border will look as if it is merely a collection of pea sticks. The pea sticks should be inserted close to each clump with the tops bent inwards above the clump, just below the height at which the plant will flower; the plant will continue to grow through the bent-over twigs and eventually conceals them entirely. This style of staking will withstand the onslaught of the worst weather that even a traditional British summer can produce.

An alternative is to use a form of metal support based on the same principle as the bent-over pea stick, with the plants growing through a ringed wire meshing. The rings vary in diameter but may not be large enough for bigger clumps.

The island beds

A modern development of the herbaceous border is where cultivars of herbaceous plants are planted in island beds and so

Herbaceous border, with clumps of varying height and texture merging into each other to create a dense planting effect

we are told do not require staking; in other words, they will stand up unsupported. Opinions vary on this, but in general, provided you make a suitable choice of plants, the idea works. It obviously succeeds best in a large garden, where there is room for a bed to be cut out of a lawn, but as none of the group grow very high, island beds are useful in a small garden with narrow borders.

Planning a herbaceous border

At this stage a precise definition ought to be given as to what exactly is a herbaceous perennial. A perennial plant is one that lasts for an indefinite period, and this applies to trees and shrubs, but they do not die down to the ground each year. Thus it can be said that an herbaceous perennial has an annual stem and a perennial rootstock. However, many plants that are very useful in the herbaceous border, such as kniphofia (red hot poker), do not die down altogether, so, by way of a looser definition, a herbaceous perennial is one that flowers perennially, but has soft stems.

The herbaceous border is probably the most artificial form of gardening that has ever been devised, but if cleverly planned it can be one of the most spectacular and colourful features in a garden. Planning the planting of the border is fairly straightforward provided one or two principles are observed: first, it would be tempting to have in a border, say 7·3m (24 ft) long by 1·8m (6 ft) deep, three rows of plants – tall at the back, medium in the middle and dwarf in the front. But this would give too uniform an effect and so, in our plan, we bring forward some back-row plants to the middle and some middle-row plants to the front to provide a variation. You should have three, five, seven or nine plants in each clump as this enables it to have an irregular rather than a rounded shape; you can also arrange the plants to run into each other rather than leave gaps in the grouping.

In the planning you can organize an early border or an autumn border. However, unless you are especially fond of one particular group of plants, it would be inadvisable to have a border devoted to, say, delphiniums, irises or Michaelmas daisies, as the flowering period would be so brief. You might make an exception of paeonies; they do very well in a shady corner where little else will grow, and there can be few gardens that do not possess such a corner.

THE COTTAGE GARDEN

This is very much a personal form of gardening. The image is of a garden full of colour with hardly a couple of centimetres of soil to be seen, and plants cascading over the edges of steps, paths or walls; aromatic herbs and sweet-scented flowers fill the air with their fragrance and the cottage walls are clothed with colourful and perfumed climbing plants.

Probably the best example of such a garden is at East Lambrook Manor, in Somerset. Here, the late Margery Fish did much to encourage gardeners to cultivate cottage garden plants. It was a very personal garden and has lost something of its personality since her death, even though it is still being cared for.

You can have a jumble of colour in cottage gardens and the eye is not offended if one brilliant hue conflicts with another. There is no definite design and fresh plants are put out wherever there is a bit of space. In a genuine old cottage garden, there is often an established apple tree, with shade-loving plants growing beneath. Invariably, it will contain a few fruit bushes, gooseberries or currants, under which self-sown annuals will flower. The vegetable garden, if there is room for one, probably has the odd row of carrots or peas muddled in with the flowers and is likely to have flowering plants trailing through the turnips or runner beans.

Wild plants and bulbs

Most cottage gardens will be in or near the countryside and are thus likely to have weed seeds blowing into the garden. Some wild flowers are obviously too weedy to allow in but one or two have useful properties. *Sambucus nigra* (elder), although rather invasive, can provide useful flowers for country remedies and cooking, and the berries make delicious wine. Cardamine (lady's smock) is a graceful plant that thrives in a moist place and makes an attractive show early in the year; a double form is obtainable from some nurserymen. Solidago (golden rod) is a bit of a weed, but sometimes you can come across a good or late-flowering form. *Arum maculatum* lords-and-ladies, or cuckoo-pint, has interesting arrow-shaped leaves, occasionally spotted purplish-black, that are useful for spring decoration in the house. *Clematis vitalba* (the wild traveller's joy or old man's beard) has greenish-white flowers, but it is best known for its woolly greyish-white seed-heads that appear in autumn; this thrives on chalky and lime soils. Obviously, your love of wild plants has to be tempered by the size of the garden and the behaviour of the plants in question.

Bulbs are useful in cottage gardens, and these cover not only the usual spring daffodils, hyacinths and tulips, but the summer-flowering lilies, alliums and the white galtonia. The advantage of bulbs is that they can peep through other plants and their untidy foliage is hidden in the general confusion. The difficulty is in remembering where they are when forking through a border.

Planting Herbaceous Borders

Having, perhaps, visited other gardens and assessed the types of plants you would like in your own, you can now look at some catalogues and draw out the plan for your border. Here we detail individual plants and suggest particular border designs, and later we will tell you about plant groupings and their seasonal arrangements.

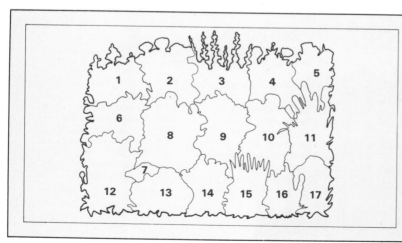

ALL SEASONS BORDER

Allow three plants of each species unless otherwise stated in brackets.

Key to border – 6 × 1.5m (20 × 5 ft)

1 *Anchusa italica*
2 *Rudbeckia subtomentosa*
3 *Delphinium*
4 *Helianthus decapetalus*
5 *Aster novi-belgii*
6 *Monarda didyma*
7 *Gypsophila repens* (1)
8 *Echinops ritro*
9 *Achillea*
10 *Chrysanthemum maximum*
11 *Kniphofia*
12 *Trollius ledebourii*
13 *Sedum maximum*
14 *Potentilla atrosanguinea*
15 *Salvia × superba*
16 *Liatris callilepis*
17 *Achillea filipendulina*

You may find it helpful to have some idea of the number of plants that will be required to fill 30 sq cm (1 sq ft) adequately. For instance, *Anchusa italica* Opel is 1·5m (5 ft) tall, with an individual spread of up to 1·2 sq m (4 sq ft). *Macleaya cordata* is 2m (6–7 ft) and has a 'thinner' style of growth, so you would plant three anchusas as against five macleayas. As a general indication, a border 12 × 1·2m (40 × 8 ft) would need 160 plants, and this can be reduced or increased in proportion as needed: for example, you would require 40 plants to begin with in a border 5 × 1·2m (20 × 4 ft). In order to provide you with a reference, we have compiled a useful chart giving you concise information, and from which the plants have been chosen for grouping in the borders as illustrated here.

As you can see from the chart details, borders can be planned for whatever time you require them and of whatever colour you want, although towards the end of the season the predominant colour, Michaelmas daisies apart, seems to be yellow. Here are three ideas for borders – for all seasons, in shade and late-flowering. If you have a particular colour or combination of colours in mind, it is easy enough to pick out from the list those you like and to make a border plan that will suit your own taste.

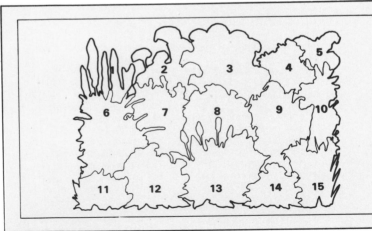

SHADED BORDER

Allow three plants of each species.

Key to border – 6 × 1·5m (20 × 5 ft)

1 *Aconitum arendsii*
2 *Thalictrum glaucum*
3 *Eupatorium purpureum*
4 *Campanula lactiflora*
5 *Thalictrum aquilegifolium*
6 *Dicentra spectabilis*
7 *Campanula persicifolia*
8 *Geranium psilostemon*
9 *Lysimachia clethroides*
10 *Anemone japonica*
11 *Liriope graminifolia*
12 *Doronicum caucasicum*
13 *Polygonum m' iletii*
14 *Doronicum cordatum*
15 *Iris foetidissima*

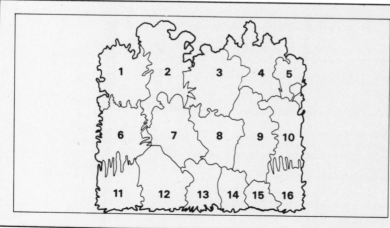

LATE-FLOWERING BORDER

Allow three plants of each species.

Key to border – 6 × 1·5m (20 × 5 ft)

1 *Aster novi-belgii*
2 *Eupatorium purpureum*
3 *Rudbeckia fulgida*
4 *Artemisia lactiflora*
5 *Vernonia crinita*
6 *Solidago × canadensis*
7 *Eryngium × oliverianum*
8 *Campanula × burghaltii*
9 *Heliopsis scabra*
10 *Anemone japonica*
11 *Veronica spicata*
12 *Sedum spectabile*
13 *Stokesia laevis*
14 *Potentilla atrosanguinea*
15 *Anaphalis triplinervis*
16 *Physostegia virginiana*

NAME OF PLANT	FLOWERING SEASON/REMARKS	HEIGHT
Acanthus mollis (bear's breeches)	Late summer to early autumn. White and pink. Architectural' leaves. Does not like winter wet.	1–1 2m (3½–4 ft)
Achillea eupatorium (or *filipendulina*) Coronation Gold	Mid to late summer. Flat yellow heads.	90cm (3 ft)
A.e. Gold Plate	Mid to late summer. Bright yellow.	1·2m (4 ft)
A. ptarmica The Pearl	Mid to late summer. Double white.	1m (3½ ft)
A. taygetea	Mid to late summer. Primrose yellow.	45cm (18 in)
A.t. Moonshine	Mid to late summer. Bright yellow.	45–60cm (18–24 in)
Aconitum arendsii	Mid summer to early autumn.	1·2m (4 ft)
A. napellus Bressingham Spire	Late summer to early autumn. Violet-blue.	90cm (3 ft)
A. variegatum bicolor	Late summer to early autumn. White and blue.	1m (3½ ft)
Agapanthus umbellatus (or *orientalis*)	Late summer to mid autumn. Mid-blue.	60cm (2 ft)
Alchemilla mollis (lady's mantle)	Mid summer to early autumn. Lime yellow.	45–60cm (18–24 in)
Anaphalis margaritacea	Early autumn. White, grey foliage.	45cm (18 in)
A. triplinervis	Late summer to mid autumn. White, sturdy.	30cm (12 in)
A. yedoensis	Early to late autumn. White, everlasting.	60cm (2 ft)
Anchusa azurea (or *italica*) Loddon Royalist	Early to mid summer. Gentian blue.	90cm (3 ft)
A.a. Opal	Early to mid summer. Soft opal blue.	1·5m (5·ft)
A.a. Royal Blue	Early to mid summer. Rich royal blue	90cm (3 ft)
Anemone japonica (or *hupehensis*) *alba* (Japanese anemone)	Early to late autumn. White.	60cm (2 ft)
A.j.a. Profusion	Mid autumn. Soft pink.	60cm (2 ft)
Anthemis tinctoria (ox-eye chamomile) Grallagh Gold	Mid summer to early autumn. Rich golden flowers.	90cm (3 ft)
A.t. Wargrave Variety	Mid summer to early autumn. Sulphur-yellow.	75cm (2½ ft)
Artemisia lactiflora (white mugwort)	Early to late autumn. Creamy-white.	1·2m (4 ft)
A.l. Lambrook Silver	Bright foliage, sprays of grey flowers.	75cm (2½ ft)
A. nutans	Feathery silver foliage. Sunny place.	60cm (2 ft)
A.n. Silver Queen	Silver foliage. Good for cutting.	75cm (2½ ft)
Aster novi-belgii (Michaelmas daisy)	See border plans for selected named species and varieties.	
Astilbe varieties	Mid summer to early autumn. Plant in a damp spot.	
Amethyst	Lilac-purple	90cm (3 ft)
Bressingham Beauty	Rich pink.	90cm (3 ft)
Ceres	Pink and rose.	1m (3½ ft)
Fanal	Bright red.	75cm (2½ ft)
Red Sentinel	Brick-red spikes.	75cm (2½ ft)
White Queen	White.	60cm (2 ft)
Astrantia carniolica Rubra	Mid summer to mid autumn. Crimson-green flowers.	38cm (15 in)
A. maxima	Mid summer to early autumn. Rose-pink.	90cm (3 ft)
Baptisia australis	Mid summer. Blue pea flowers.	90–120cm (3–4 ft)
Brunnera macrophylla	Late spring to mid summer. Blue forget-me-not flowers.	45cm (18 in)
Campanula × burghaltii	Mid summer to mid autumn. Large mauve bells.	60cm (2 ft)
C. glomerata Superba	Mid to late summer. Purple-blue.	45cm (18 in)
C. lactiflora Loddon Anna	Mid summer to early autumn. Pink.	1·2–1·5m (4–5 ft)
C. latiloba Peter Piper	Mid to late summer. Deep blue.	90cm (3 ft)
C. persicifolia	Mid summer to early autumn. Blue. Rather weedy.	90cm (3 ft)
Centaurea dealbata John Coutts	Early summer to early autumn. Clear pink.	60cm (2 ft)
C. macrocephala	Mid summer to early autumn. Large yellow flowers.	1·2–1·5m (4–5 ft)
Chelone obliqua	Early to late autumn. Pink.	60cm (2 ft)
C.o. Alba	White form.	60cm (2 ft)
Chrysanthemum maximum (shasta daisy)	Choose well-established varieties, such as these, from catalogues.	
Dairymaid	Late summer. Cream.	90cm (3 ft)
Esther Read	Late summer to mid autumn.	60cm (2 ft)
Wirral Supreme	Late summer to mid autumn. Reliable double white.	90cm (3 ft)
Clematis recta Grandiflora	Late summer to early autumn. White.	75–90cm (2½–3 ft)
Coreopsis grandiflora Goldfink	Mid summer to mid autumn. Deep yellow.	25cm (9 in)
C. g. Badengold	Late summer to early autumn. Orange-yellow.	90cm (3 ft)
C. verticillata	Mid summer to mid autumn. Starry yellow flowers.	45cm (18 in)

NAME OF PLANT	FLOWERING SEASON/REMARKS	HEIGHT
Crambe cordifolia	Early to late summer. Panicles of white flowers.	1·5–1·8m (5–6 ft)
Crocosmia masonorum	Late summer onwards. Montbretia-like orange.	90cm (3 ft)
Cynglossum nervosum (hound's tongue)	Mid summer to early autumn. Gentian blue.	30cm (12 in)
Delphinium varieties	Mid summer onwards. Good for cuttings. Choose varieties according to desired height and colour. Belladonna group are shorter, require no staking.	
Dicentra formosa Bountiful	Mid spring onwards. Pink 'bleeding heart' flowers.	45cm (18 in)
D. eximia	Late spring onwards. Pink.	45cm–60cm (1½–2 ft)
D.e. Adrian Bloom	Late spring to early summer. Vigorous.	30cm (12 in)
D.e. Alba	Early summer to mid autumn. White form.	25cm (9 in)
D. spectabilis	Late spring. Pink, the true 'bleeding heart'. Needs deep soil.	60cm (2 ft)
Dictamnus fraxinella (or *albus*)	Mid summer to early autumn. Spikes of lilac or white spider-like flowers.	75cm (2½ ft)
Dierama pendulum (wand flower)	Late summer to mid autumn. Pink flowers on graceful stems.	75–90cm (2½–3 ft)
Doronicum caucasicum Miss Mason	Late spring to mid summer. Bright yellow.	45cm (18 in)
D. cordatum	Mid spring to early summer. Golden daisies.	15–25cm (6–10 in)
D.c. Spring Beauty	Late spring to mid summer. Double yellow flowers.	38cm (15 in)
Echinacea purpurea	Early autumn. Rose to crimson.	1m (3½ ft)
E.p. The King	Early autumn. Reddish-purple on stiff spikes.	1·2m (4 ft)
Echinops humilis (globe thistle) Taplow Blue	Mid summer to mid autumn. Dark blue globes.	1·5m (5 ft)
E. ritro	Mid summer to mid autumn. Rich blue.	1m (3½ ft)
Erigeron speciosus (fleabane) Charity	Mid summer. Light pink.	60cm (2 ft)
E.s. Darkest of All	Mid summer. Deep violet-blue.	60cm (2 ft)
E.s. Dignity	Mid summer. Mauve-blue.	60cm (2 ft)
E.s. Foerster's Liebling	Mid summer. Deep cerise-pink.	60cm (2 ft)
E.s. Rose Triumph	Semi-double, deep rose-pink.	60cm (2 ft)
Eryngium bourgatii	Mid summer to early autumn. Silvery-blue.	45cm (18 in)
E. × oliverianum	Mid summer to early autumn. Blue.	90cm (3 ft)
E. tripartitum	Mid summer to early autumn. Metallic blue.	
Eupatorium purpureum	Early to mid autumn. Purple.	1·5–1·8m (5–6 ft)
E. rugosum	Late summer to mid autumn. White.	90cm (3 ft)
Euphorbia griffithii	Mid summer. Orange-red.	75cm (2½ ft)
E. polychroma (or *epithimoides*)	Late spring to early summer. Yellow.	45cm (18 in)
E. sikkimensis	Mid to late summer. Purple shoots, yellow flowers.	1·2m (4 ft)
E. wulfenii	Late spring to late summer. Yellowish-green, evergreen foliage.	90cm (3 ft)
Geranium psilostemon	Late summer. Cerise.	75cm (2½ ft)
G. renardii	Early to mid summer. Light mauve.	38cm (15 in)
Geum × borisii	Early summer. Tangerine-scarlet.	30cm (12 in)
G. chiloense Fire Opal	Early summer to early autumn. Orange-red.	60cm (2 ft)
G.c. Prince of Orange	Early to mid summer. Double orange-yellow.	60cm (2 ft)
Gypsophila paniculata Bristol Fairy	Mid summer to mid autumn. Double white.	90cm (3 ft)
G. repens Rosy Veil	Mid summer to mid autumn. Double shell pink.	25cm (9 in)
Helenium autumnale Bruno	Early to late autumn. Mahogany-red.	1m (3½ ft)
H.a. Butterpat	Early to late autumn. Pure yellow.	90cm (3 ft)
H.a. Mahogany	Late summer to early autumn. Golden brown-red.	75cm (2½ ft)
H.a. The Bishop	Mid summer. Bright yellow, dark centre.	60cm (2 ft)
Helianthus decapetalus Loddon Gold	Late summer to mid autumn.	1·5m (5 ft)
H.d. Lemon Queen	Graceful lemon flowers.	1·5m (5 ft)
Heliopsis scabra Ballerina	Mid summer to early autumn. Warm yellow.	90cm (3 ft)
H.s. Golden Plume	Mid summer to mid autumn. Double deep yellow.	1·2m (4 ft)
H.s. Sunburst	Late summer. Double orange-yellow.	1·2m (4 ft)
Heuchera sanguinea Greenfinch	Early to late summer. Greenish sulphur-yellow.	75cm (2½ ft)
H.s. Pearl Drops	Early to late summer. Almost white.	60cm (2 ft)
H.s. Scintillation	Bright pink, tipped with coral-carmine.	60cm (2 ft)
Inula ensifolia	Mid summer to early autumn. Bright yellow, long-lasting.	25cm (9 in)
I. hookeri	Mid summer to mid autumn. Rayed, yellow flowers.	75cm (2½ ft)

NAME OF PLANT	FLOWERING SEASON/REMARKS	HEIGHT
Iris varieties	Named varieties of *Iris sibirica* and the flag iris, *I. germanica*, should be seen to judge for preference of height and colour.	
Kniphofia galpinii	Late summer to mid autumn. Delicate orange.	45cm (18 in)
K. nelsonii major	Early to mid autumn. Bright orange.	60cm (2 ft)
K. uvaria (red hot poker) Bee's Lemon	Late autumn. Citron yellow.	75–90cm (2½–3 ft)
K.u. Maid of Orleans	Mid summer to early autumn. Ivory-white.	90–100cm (3–3½ ft)
K.u. Royal Standard	Late summer. Bright red and yellow.	1m (3½ ft)
Liatris callilepis	Late summer to mid autumn. Fluffy lilac-purple.	75cm (2½ ft)
L. pycnostachys	Early to late autumn. Rosy purple.	90–150cm (3–5 ft)
Libertia formosa	Mid to late summer. White. Iris-type leaves.	75cm (2½ ft)
Ligularia clivorum Desdemona	Late summer to mid autumn. Orange flower, bronze foliage.	90cm (3 ft)
L.c. Greynog Gold	Late summer to mid autumn. Golden flowers.	90cm (3 ft)
L.c. Sungold	Mid summer to early autumn. Golden-yellow.	90cm (3 ft)
Liriope graminifolia	Mid autumn. Violet, grape hyacinth-like flowers.	15cm (6 in)
Lobelia cardinalis Queen Victoria	Mid to late summer. Good red. Not hardy. Needs a damp spot.	60cm (2 ft)
Lupinus (lupins) varieties	Early to mid summer. Choose variety according to desired colour. Place towards the back, where late-flowering plants can come up in front. Do not over-feed soil with farmyard manure.	
Lychnis chalcedonica (campion)	Late summer to early autumn. Brilliant scarlet.	1m (3½ ft)
L. flos-jovis	Mid summer to early autumn. Delightful combination of pink flowers and grey foliage.	25cm (9 in)
L. viscaria Splendens Plena	Mid to late summer. Cerise.	25cm (9 in)
Lysimachia clethroides	Early to mid autumn. White.	90cm (3 ft)
L. punctata	Mid to late summer. Bright yellow.	60cm (2 ft)
Lythrum salicaria (purple loosestrife) Robert	Late summer to mid autumn. Bright carmine.	75cm (2½ ft)
L.s. The Beacon	Late summer to mid autumn. Rosy-crimson.	1m (3½ ft)
Macleaya (or *Bocconia*) *cordata*	Early to mid autumn. Cream-white.	2·1m (7 ft)
M.c. Coral plume	Early to mid autumn. Buff.	2·1m (7 ft)
Monarda didyma Cambridge Scarlet	Mid summer to early autumn. Red.	90cm (3 ft)
M.d. Croftway Pink	Mid summer to early autumn. Soft pink.	90cm (3 ft)
Nepeta gigantea (catmint)	Mid summer to early autumn. Lavender-blue.	75cm (2½ ft)
N. × mussinii	Mid summer to early autumn. Lavender-blue.	38cm (15 in)
N. × m. Six Hills Giant	Mid summer to early autumn. Deeper blue.	60cm (2 ft)
Oenothera tetragona Fireworks	Mid summer to early autumn. Orange-yellow, red buds.	45cm (18 in)
O. glaber	Mid summer to mid autumn. Golden, bronzy foliage.	38cm (15 in)
Origanum laevigatum	Early to mid autumn. Purple.	38cm (15 in)
Paeonia (paeony) varieties	Late spring to early summer. Single or double, pinks to reds. Adapt to any soil or conditions.	
Papaver orientalis (oriental poppy) Lord Lambourne	Mid summer. Bright red.	90cm (3 ft)
P.o. Mrs Perry	Mid summer. Pink.	90cm (3 ft)
P.o. Perry's White	Mid summer. White with black blotches.	90cm (3 ft)
Phlomis samia	Mid summer to early autumn. Yellow, greyish leaves.	75cm (2½ ft)
Phlox	Late summer to early autumn. Choose according to colour preferences. Prefer good rich soil with plenty of moisture.	
Established varieties	Balmoral (rosy-lavender); Brigadier (brilliant orange-red); Hampton Court (blue); Pastorale (large pink); White Admiral (the best white).	
Physostegia virginiana Summer Snow	Late summer to mid autumn. White.	75cm (2½ ft)
P.v. Vivid	Early to late autumn. Deep rose.	45cm (18 in)
Platycodon grandiflorum	Late summer to early autumn. Blue.	45cm (18 in)
P.g. Snowflake	Late summer to early autumn. White.	45cm (18 in)
Polemonium foliosissimum (Jacob's ladder)	Late spring to early autumn. Lavender-blue.	75cm (2½ ft)
P.f. Sapphire	Early to late summer. Blue.	45cm (18 in)

NAME OF PLANT	FLOWERING SEASON/REMARKS	HEIGHT
Polygonum amplexicaule atrosanguineum (snake weed)	Mid summer to mid autumn. Deep red spike.	1·2m (4 ft)
P. bistorta Superbum	Early summer onwards. Does well in moist places.	90cm (3 ft)
P. millettii	Mid summer to mid autumn. Deep red. Slow-growing, likes moisture.	45cm (18 in)
Potentilla atrosanguinea (cinquefoil) Gibson's Scarlet	Mid summer to early autumn. Brilliant scarlet.	38cm (15 in)
P.a. Mons. Rouillard	Mid summer to early autumn. Deep crimson, orange blotched.	45cm (18 in)
P.a. William Rollisson	Mid summer to early autumn. Semi-double, orange.	38cm (15 in)
Prunella webbiana (self-heal) Loveliness	Early summer onwards. Pale mauve.	25cm (10 in)
Pyrethrum	Early to mid summer; if cut back at once, will repeat in the autumn. Choose from pinks to salmons and scarlets. Useful for cuttings.	
Rhazya orientalis	Mid summer to early autumn. Blue.	45cm (18 in)
Rudbeckia fulgida Deamii	Early to late autumn. Deep yellow; dark centre.	75cm (2½ ft)
R.f. Goldsturm	Late summer to late autumn.	45cm (18 in)
R. laciniata Goldquelle	Early to late autumn. Double yellow.	90cm (3 ft)
R. nitida Herbstsonne	Early to late autumn. Bright rich yellow.	1·8m (6 ft)
R. subtomentosa	Mid to late autumn. Deep yellow.	1·2–1·5m (4–5 ft)
Salvia haematodes	Mid summer to early autumn. Light lilac-blue, grey-green foliage.	90cm (3 ft)
S. × superba	Late summer to mid autumn. Violet-purple.	90cm (3 ft)
S. × s. East Friesland	Similar, except for height.	45cm (18 in)
S. × s. Lubeca	Mid summer to mid autumn. Violet-purple.	75cm (2½ ft)
S. × s. Lye End	Mid summer to early autumn. Blue.	1m (3½ ft)
S. turkestanica	Late summer. Rose and pale blue.	1·2–1·5m (4–5 ft)
Scabiosa caucasica Clive Greaves	Mid summer to mid autumn. Mid blue.	75cm (2½ ft)
S.c. Loddon White	Mid summer to mid autumn. White.	75cm (2½ ft)
S.c. Penhill Blue	Mid summer to mid autumn. Deep blue.	75cm (2½ ft)
Sedum maximum Atropurpureum	Early to late autumn. Deep purple flowers, creamy foliage.	45cm (18 in)
S. spectabile	Early to late autumn. Pale pink.	38cm (15 in)
S.s. Autumn Joy	Early to late autumn. Bright rose-salmon.	60cm (2 ft)
S. spurium Ruby Glow	Late summer to early autumn. Rose-red.	30cm (12 in)
S.s. Vera Jameson	Late summer to early autumn. Pale pink, purplish foliage.	38cm (15 in)
Sidalcea malvaeflora Elsie Heugh	Mid summer to early autumn. Soft pink.	90cm (3 ft)
S.m. Mrs Alderson	Mid summer to early autumn. Large clear pink.	75cm (2½ ft)
S.m. William Smith	Late summer to mid autumn. Warm salmon-pink.	1m (3½ ft)
Solidago canadensis (golden rod) Goldenmosa	Early to mid autumn. Large heads of golden-yellow.	75cm (2½ ft)
S.c. Golden Radiance	Early to mid autumn. Bright heads.	75cm (2½ ft)
S.c. Lemore	Early to mid autumn. Soft primrose.	75cm (2½ ft)
Stachys lanata (lamb's tongue)	Mid summer to early autumn. Pink flowers. The entire plant is woolly-grey and spreads.	30cm (12 in)
Stokesia laevis Blue Star	Late summer to early autumn. Lavender-blue.	45cm (18 in)
Thalictrum aquilegifolium Album	Late spring to late summer. White.	1·2m (4 ft)
T.a. Purpureum	Late spring to late summer. Purple-mauve.	90cm (3 ft)
T. dipterocarpum Hewitt's Double	Late summer to mid autumn. Double mauve.	90cm (3 ft)
T. glaucum	Early to mid summer. Bright yellow, grey foliage.	1·5–1·8m (5–6 ft)
Trollius europaeus (globe flower) Superbus	Early to mid summer. Light yellow.	45–60cm (1½–2 ft)
T. ledebourii Imperial Orange	Mid summer to early autumn. Orange.	1·5–1·8m (5–6 ft)
Verbascum bombyciferum (mullein)	Mid to late summer. Yellow, silvery leaves.	90–120cm (3–4 ft)
V. hybridum Cotswold Queen	Mid summer. Terracotta.	1·2m (4 ft)
V.h. Pink Domino	Mid summer. Deep rose.	1m (3½ ft)
V. thapsiforme	Mid summer. Deep yellow.	1·2–1·5m (4–5 ft)
Vernonia crinita	Mid autumn. Purple.	1·5m (5 ft)
Veronica incana Wendy	Mid summer to early autumn. Deep blue, silver foliage.	30cm (12 in)
V. spicata Barcarolle	Mid summer to early autumn. Deep rose-pink.	45cm (18in)
V.s. Minuet	Pure pink, grey-green foliage.	38–45cm (15–18 in)
V. teucrium Royal Blue	Mid to late summer.	45cm (18 in)
V. virginica Alba	Early to mid autumn. White.	1·5m (5 ft)

No design has been suggested for a cottage garden because of all forms of gardening, this is the most personal. Each site has to be developed according to the aspect and type of soil and the owner's requirements. We have therefore listed a comprehensive selection of plants we think will cater for every need and taste.

The backbone of any garden is formed by the trees and shrubs that are planted in or near it. Some gardens may have the advantage of external planting – such as a wood or common – as a background. This would suit a cottage garden for there is little enough room to accommodate many trees and shrubs. If you can, choose an elder, as it has many culinary advantages, apple trees to provide a natural setting and the odd conifer or two to give a bit of height, background and coloured foliage. The garden will now be set to receive other plants.

Daphne mezereum, with its scented, mauvy-pink flowers, seems an obvious choice for a winter display, and *Fuchsia magellanica* does very well in sheltered parts of milder regions, and it can be used for hedges in very mild corners. *Forsythia × intermedia* is a useful shrub from which to take cuttings of early flowers and hamamelis (witch-hazel) provides scented winter blossom – if there is sufficient room for it. Smaller shrubs, such as the hypericums, but not *Hypericum calycinum* (rose of Sharon), do well

along the edges and buddleia attract the butterflies in summer.

A shrub rose or two, in preference to the more formal hybrid tea, provides scent and colour in mid summer (June). *Viburnum opulus* (guelder rose) supplies not only flowers in the spring, but red berries in the autumn, and its relative *Viburnum tinus* (laurustinus) provides a dark evergreen background of generous proportions, and flowers from late autumn to mid spring (October to March).

Herbs

Herbs are an essential feature of the cottage garden; horehound, penny-royal and wild parsley have a romantic country air about them and are decorative in a garden. As herbs are best known by their common names we list the following decorative and culinary ones in this way.

Angelica, *Angelica archangelica*, is a distinctive and attractive biennial, rising to some 1·5m (5 ft) in height and lending an architectural quality to the garden with its head of greeny-whitish flowers.

Balm, *Melissa officinalis*, has scented leaves that were used to make tea or, when dried, to put with linen.

Bergamot, *Monarda didyma*, is a herbaceous perennial with a beguiling perfume that fills the air around it. It has attractive pink or red flower-heads that are particularly useful in pot-pourri as its scent is retained when the plant is dry.

Chives, *Allium schoenoprasum*, are tasty in salads and in use with a variety of cold vegetables. The flowers are attractive, but should perhaps be cut off to maintain a good clump of leaves.

Comfrey, *Symphytum officinale*, has been valued from early times for its curative properties and for the fritters that can be made from its nutritious leaves. *S. caucasicum* and *S. peregrinum* are about 1·2m (4 ft) tall and produce mauvy-blue bell-flowers from spring to autumn. Their spread equals their height so you should be careful about placing them or, more to the point, note where they have seeded.

Hyssop, *Hyssopus officinalis*, is another perennial and this grows happily in a light, dry soil in a sunny place and is useful for the edge of the border.

Mint or spearmint, *Mentha spicata*, comes in many shapes, forms and scents: apple mint, lamb mint, pea mint – all have their own delicious scents and flavours. Eau de Cologne mint, *M. piperita citrata*, was reputedly used to make toilet water, and it is one of the most refreshing scents when a sprig of the foliage is crushed in the hand. *M. requienii* can be used as a

Above: Monarda didyma *Cambridge Scarlet. Left:* Forsythia × intermedia *Arnold Giant. Below:* Daphne mezereum

carpeting plant and, when walked upon, gives off a peppermint aroma.

Rosemary, *Rosmarinus officinalis*, makes an attractive shrub some 1·2m (4 ft) tall, with pale blue flowers in summer. It is excellent for flavouring meat dishes and stews.

Sage, *Salvia officinalis*, is particularly delicious with pork and for seasoning other dishes; a purple-leaved form is useful as a foil to other planting.

Sweet Cicely, *Myrrhis odorata*, seeds itself about without being a nuisance. It has healthy foliage on a 60–90cm (2–3 ft) stem. The foliage is aromatic and the white flowers an attraction in any garden.

Sweet fennel, *Foeniculum officinale*, is a perennial and has a delicate feathery foliage used for garnishing and for fish sauces. It also has a dark purple-leaved form of some interest.

Thyme is a favourite and well-known aromatic herb, useful for planting in paving where if trodden on the crushed plant will emit an attractive fragrance. Common thyme, *Thymus vulgaris*, is 15–20cm (6–8 in) tall and there are several cultivars of the carpeting species.

Grasses

There is such a generous range of form, texture and colour to be found among grasses that they should not be neglected in a cottage garden.

Milium effusum aureum (Bowles' golden grass) provides a plant that is totally yellow and the delicate 45cm (18 in) flowering stems make a bright splash in mid summer (June); it is suited to a damp shady spot.

A number of annual grasses can be effective and *Briza maxima* (quaking grass) will seed itself about in an acceptably untidy way and its 'quaking' flowers can be cut for indoor decoration.

Helictotrichon sempervirens (or *Avena candida*) is a grass with graceful, silvery, flowering stems some 1·2m (4 ft) long that rise from a tidy clump of stiff, grey foliage.

Lasiogrostis splendens is an effective plant with buff-shaded plumes about 90cm (3 ft) tall, appearing mid summer to early autumn (June to August).

Miscanthus sinensis has several cultivars about 1·2m (4 ft) tall: *M.s.* Gracillimus forms a bamboo-like clump; Variegatus has green and white variegation, while Zebrinus (zebra-striped rush) has bands of yellow at intervals up its stem. The latter does well in any soil but looks particularly good by water.

Cortaderia selloana (Pampas grass) has many named cultivars all of which, in

heights varying from 90cm–3m (3–18 ft), supply the spectacular white plumes that are picked for indoor decoration. Sunningdale Silver is a particularly good cultivar with restrained behaviour and silver plumes.

A number of seed firms offer packets of annual grasses that have varying and interesting shapes and sizes of benefit to the cottage garden.

Plants for a damp site

If the site of the garden is a damp one, do not despair as there are many plants that can be accommodated.

In a really damp site *Astilbe × arendsii* (false goat's beard) would be ideal; there are many cultivars to choose from that will give a succession of colour from mid summer to early autumn (June to August): Amethyst is a taller lilac-rose cultivar at 90cm (3 ft); Bressingham Beauty has 75–90cm (2½–3 ft) spikes of rich-pink; Fanal, an old favourite, has deep red plumes about 60cm (2 ft) high.

Ranunculus repens (the creeping buttercup) is a pest but its double form, Flore Pleno with dark green glossy leaves, whilst mildly invasive can easily be kept in check and is most attractive. *R. bulbosus* Pleniflorus (double buttercup) is less rampant, taller at 45cm (18 in), but has the same attractive double flowers.

Helleborus niger (Christmas rose) would flourish, but *Helleborus orientalis* (Lenten rose), with its colours varying from white and pink through to deep purple, can be more attractive. Other distinctive hellebores include *H. corsicus*, with its large head of white flowers, and *H. foetidus* (stinking hellebore).

Hostas, the plantain lilies, would do well in a damp corner. They come in

Top right: Briza maxima, *the aptly-named quaking grass. Above:* Helleborus orientalis *Below:* Primula vulgaris, *common primrose*

many permutations of foliage variegation and have caused confusion over their naming, some nurseries having not quite accurate names. *Hosta fortunei* Aureomarginata has a golden edge to its leaf; *H.f.* Thomas Hogg has creamy-white edges to the leaves; *H. sieboldiana* Coerulea has good bluish leaves and *H. fortunei* Albopicta attractive green and yellow ones in spring. Hostas are, of course, grown mainly for the variation in their leaf forms, but their lilac flower spikes add further appeal.

Spring planting

To return to the spring – primroses are a good old cottage garden favourite; this is

where the old double varieties could be found. Ever since Elizabethan days, the doubles have grown in British gardens. They are not easy to please and it is by having such safe, undisturbed homes that they have survived until today. The easiest of them all is *Primula vulgaris* (or *acaulis*) Lilacina Plena, a double lilac. There are a number of named cultivars of the coloured primrose but they are hard to come by as well as difficult to grow; they have been given romantic names such as Bartimeus, Mme de Pompadour and Prince Silverwings. It is perhaps best to stick to the familiar primula Wanda along the edges to give an early display of

Top right: Aster amellus *King George. Above right:* Fritillaria imperialis *Lutea Maxima Above:* Meconopsis betonicifolia

colour. The group of garryarde primroses are worth having for their crimson leaves and pink, magenta and crimson flowers.

Polyanthus, one of the primula hybrids, should not be overlooked – some of the old laced varieties are coming back. Closely related are the auriculas, which have developed into a somewhat sophisticated breed of show auriculas, but the one chiefly associated with cottages is the *P. auricula* Old Dusty Miller, or the more frequently-grown variety, Old Yellow Dusty Miller.

Summer planting

Later on in the year, if the garden in question has a damp woodland corner, the candelabra primulas can be allowed to grow and seed about; there are several species and it is difficult to select just a few. The simplest are probably *Primula*

japonica, that varies in colour from pale pink to mauve; *P. aurantiaca* in mainly orange and yellow shades, and *P. chungensis*, orange. *P. pulverulenta* is a bright red, while its Bartley Strain cultivar has a pleasant colour range from pink to red. *P. florindae* has hanging yellow bells and *P. burmanica* is deep purple. These are all 45–60cm (18–24 in) tall.

Meconopsis baileyi (or *betonicifolia*), the Himalayan blue poppy, is often mixed in with candelabra primulas. Unfortunately it is short-lived and has to be replaced from time to time, but its intense blue flowers that appear in mid summer (June) are unsurpassed.

Autumn planting

This is sometimes a neglected time of year in the garden when everything is concentrated on spring and summer.

Anemone hupehensis (Japanese anemone or wind flower) is a simple, honest, white flower that appears in mid autumn (September) and lasts into late autumn (October). It has pink and semi-double

forms but the pure white is the better for its simplicity.

One or two variations on the chrysanthemum and Michaelmas daisy theme can provide interest. *Chrysanthemum* Apollo is an intense brick-red, single type, flowering mid to late autumn (September to early October), and then there are the old favourites Cottage Pink and Cottage Yellow that have inhabited most cottage gardens at one time. Some of the more interesting Michaelmas daisies are: *Aster ericoides* Esther, a pink at 75cm (2½ ft) tall, and *A.e.* Ringdove, violet at 90cm (3 ft). These have much smaller but more profuse flowers. The *Aster amellus* group is most attractive but provides a challenge in cultivation. *Aster amellus* King George is an established cultivar with lavender-blue flowers, and *A.× frikartii* is light lavender-blue, with slightly lax growth, but a charming plant. The neat-growing, wiry-stemmed *A. linosyris* or *Crinitaria linosyris* (goldilocks) supplies masses of small yellow flowers in compact clusters.

Bulbs for all seasons

Lastly, there are the bulbs – the whole garden can sometimes be smothered in hundreds for a winter display when the foliage of the herbaceous plants has been cleared away. Crocuses can start the year in early spring (February) with *Crocus chrysanthus* Snow Bunting, a creamy-white with a golden throat and Blue Pearl, a soft delicate blue – just two from many varieties. If it does not matter about spreading, then *C. tomasinianus* will oblige for many years.

The reticulate irises will flower about the same time, again with many cultivars to choose from: *I. reticulata* Cantab, a pretty, pale blue; *I. reticulata* J.S.Dijt, reddish-purple and scented. *Iris histrioides* Major is excellent value, with large, deep blue flowers.

After the irises come the chionodoxas (glory of the snow) that naturalize well, and scillas, particularly the early *Scilla tubergeniana*.

And then follows the wealth of choice to be found in the daffodil and narcissi groups; only by perusing a catalogue can any choice be made. The tulips and hyacinths come next and the main flush of the spring bulbs. A good choice for the cottage garden is *Fritillaria imperialis* (the crown imperial fritillary). There is something majestic about this bulb that comes in either yellow or orange-red during late spring (April).

For the summer, lilies can push up through the foliage of other plants; the *Lilium candidum* (madonna lily) is a typical type for the cottage garden, but any of the other species or named selections would look equally appropriate and charming.

The plants for a cottage garden are best described in groups – for foliage, as annuals, for situation or just a particular group. Then you can make a selection according to personal taste, guided by requirements for your particular garden.

Silver foliage

The air in the country is much more favourably disposed to grey- and silver-foliaged plants than in towns where the plants tend to accumulate a thick layer of dirt on their hairy leaves. This is not only unsightly but can cause their eventual death unless it is washed off by regular spraying. An occasional grey-leaved plant in the garden enhances other colours and provides a natural and neutral foil to colours that otherwise would clash if planted side by side. In general, silver-greys thrive in a hot, dry situation and dislike cold, wet winters.

Achillea taygetea Moonshine is a dwarf perennial for the edge of the garden. It is only 45–60cm (18–24 in) high at the most and has soft, silver foliage (much beloved by birds for making nests) and harsh yellow flowers.

Several of the anaphalis genus make good perennials but just two are selected here: *Anaphalis triplinervis*, some 38cm (15 in) tall, makes a tidy clump of silver foliage, excellent for cutting, with whitish flowers in early autumn (August); *A.*

Right: informal effect of mixed annuals in a typical cottage garden
Below: Senecio laxifolius likes dry soil

Convolvulus cneorum, *a more manageable relative of bindweed, has evergreen silvery leaves, and flowers from early summer to mid autumn*

nubigena is similar, but smaller at 30cm (12 in) and not so good for cutting.

The British wormwood has developed some interesting garden cultivars of which *Artemisia absinthium* Lambrook Silver is a pleasing form. It reaches some 75cm (2½ ft) when in flower in late summer (July) and is ideal for cutting. It is herbaceous, whereas *A. arborescens* is a semi-evergreen, upright shrub reaching 90cm (3 ft), and although eventually it becomes a graceful specimen it is of little value for cutting. *A. ludoviciana* is rather invasive but useful in the odd corner for ground cover. Its flower stems are about 60cm (2 ft) tall.

Ballota pseudodictamnus is a woody perennial shrub that thrives on being cut for the house. The stems can become 60cm (2 ft) tall and will dry well for winter decoration.

Convolvulus cneorum is a relative of bindweed but behaves much less invasively. It is a sub-shrub technically, and is occasionally cut back by frost but it has superb silver leaves and long, lanky stems that flop nicely over the edge of a path or border; the flowers from early summer to mid autumn (May to September) are typical bindweed flowers with a tinge of pink on the reverse of the petals.

Eucalyptus gunnii is a tall tree, reaching 18m (60 ft) if left to its own devices, but continual clipping will keep it short and ensure a show of the more attractive, rounded, young leaves.

Lavandula (lavender), with its grey foliage, is an obvious choice for the cottage garden. *L. vera* (Dutch lavender) is a well-known bushy shrub some 75cm (2½ ft) tall; *L. spica* (English lavender) is slightly bigger and of course there are smaller cultivars such as *L. s.* Twickle Purple and the really dwarf *L. s.* Munstead Dwarf at 30cm (12 in).

Romneya coulteri (Californian bush poppy) needs a while to become established but when it does it takes a lot of eradicating, yet it remains inoffensive. It bears large flowers in early autumn (August) resembling fried eggs and the glaucous foliage reaches a useful 1·2–1·5m (4–5 ft).

Santolina chamaecyparissus (cotton lavender) is a shrub that needs to be pruned back annually to produce its best grey foliage. The foliage starts off greeny-grey but by summer time the leaves are nicely felted and it forms a 60cm (2 ft) shrub. The flowers are no particular attraction and could well be removed, as they tend to make the plant become coarse. Nana is a small version of this plant as is Weston, which is smaller again.

Senecio cineraria, or *Cineraria maritima*, is one of the most popular plants for summer bedding; it has grey-felt textured leaves and small yellow flowers. It seeds itself about in gravel paths and in the cracks in crazy paving, providing a decorative informality in its behaviour. It can also be pruned quite severely if it outgrows its situation, although frequent cutting for the home might do this automatically. It is often used as a tender sub-shrub annual but, once established, can stand several degrees of frost.

Senecio laxifolius is a popular dwarf shrub with many daisy-like yellow flowers. It can be allowed to romp about in a dry corner or kept under a degree of control in a border by cutting back each spring. In fact this annual pruning is essential to keep the plant in good shape, even if it seems to be cutting away good growth. Do not prune in winter.

Stachys lanata (lamb's tongue) is a good ground-covering perennial that can become rather invasive. It is a good-tempered plant for the front of the border and softens a straight edge. The flowers are a pretty, pinky-mauve. The foliage tends to become ragged but can be removed in late summer (July) to improve its appearance later on. *S. l.* Silver Carpet, a non-flowering form in cultivation, is useful for pure ground cover.

Verbascum bombyciferum (mullein) reaches 1·5m (5 ft) high and provides a spectacular grey spike that shows up well from a distance. The florets are pale yellow and open spasmodically up the stem. This plant is monocarpic, that is, it dies after flowering, but it seeds about the garden easily.

Dianthus

Modern hybridists have introduced some interesting colour variations in dianthus (perennial pinks) but they seem to have lost some of the old scents; for those grown in old cottage gardens, scent was more important than shape or colour.

Mrs Sinkins is probably the best known variety; its white flowers and general behaviour are not altogether tidy but its scent is exquisite; Crimson Clove is rarely seen these days but it probably has the best scent of all. The fringed and strongly-fragrant Bridal Veil is not pure white as might be expected but has a greenish centre and a crimson patch at the base of each petal.

Some dianthus have been in cultivation for centuries. The Chelsea Pink dates from about 1760 and is a small double crimson laced with white. The fringed pinks are typical of cottage gardens and some named cultivars are still in cultivation today. Fimbriata is a large ivory; the Earl of Essex is a double rose-pink with a darker eye, and Sam Barlow a double white with a very dark, almost black, centre. There are many other quite delightful plants to be found still growing in cottage gardens; they invariably have local names but are none the less acceptable and usually sweetly scented.

It will not be easy finding a nurseryman who stocks these pinks but if you search for them diligently enough you will find they are there.

Biennials

Cheiranthus cheiri (wallflower), useful as a biennial to fill in gaps, with perhaps *C. × allionii* (Siberian wallflower) as a preference, for a longer colour display.

Dianthus barbatus (sweet William) is closely related to pinks, and lovely for the cottage garden. Although officially biennial, they sometimes last longer, but are best replaced by sowing each year in early or mid summer (May or June).

Digitalis purpurea (foxglove) is another biennial; this can be rather invasive and do harm to other plants by smothering them. But if there is the space, foxgloves fill it well and produce varying shades of purple flowers, sometimes white, and reaching to 1·5m (5 ft) or so. If you want a more interesting variation, then try *Digitalis × mertonensis*, a hybrid that comes true from seed and whose colour has been described as 'akin to squashed strawberries'. It is not quite as tall as the ordinary foxglove, reaching about 1·2m (4 ft) and it flowers a little later.

Hesperis tristis is a 45cm (18 in) high biennial with whitish-cream, brownish-red, or purple flowers that are scented at night during the late spring and summer. Its cousin, a British native *H. matronalis* (sweet rocket), is more perennial and also has fragrant flowers of various colours. The latter has an excellent double white form, Alba Plena, and another form with

Right: dianthus, or old-fashioned pink, Mrs Sinkins, and below: matthiola (Brompton stocks) — both are strongly scented

double purple flowers, Flore Pleno. These forms do not increase by seed.

Lunaria annua (honesty) has a misleading botanical name as it is sown in one year to flower the next. It is one of those plants that pays its rent twice, producing mauvy flowers in summer (May to June) and silver seed-heads that can be picked later for winter decoration. The variegated-leaved form is quite spectacular and comes true from seed.

Matthiola incana (stocks) are valuable for their sweet scent and seed packets of the mixed Brompton stock can easily be obtained.

Onopordons are worth considering. *Onoporddon acanthium* (common cotton thistle), has large, grey leaves 30–38cm (12–15 in) long that are woolly to begin with. The flowers are not in any way significant but the whole plant has architectural qualities that make it quite distinctive. *O. salteri* is even taller, up to 3m (10 ft), and with its snowy-white stems it makes an attractive display. Like foxgloves, they seed easily, but seedlings can be lifted and planted where required, which is an added advantage.

Annuals

These are very much a question of personal choice as everyone has their own favourites and dislikes.

Antirrhinums will last more than a year in favoured situations. Hollyhocks are listed in seed catalogues as annuals but they can be considered perennial in mild areas such as southern England. Whatever their correct designation, they are an essential feature of cottage gardens, producing 1·5m (5 ft) flower spikes of either double or single reds, pinks, yellows and whites.

Atriplex hortensis Cupreata (salt bush) is a dark-leaved annual ideal for contrasting with grey foliage with deep red leaves and darker stems on a plant 1·2m (4 ft) tall.

Calendulas seem almost too formal for the cottage garden but the ordinary pot marigold, used as a filler here and there, will give a spot of colour.

Of Clarkias, the best double is *Clarkia elegans* Flore Pleno; the flowers come in the bluey-purple-mauve ranges, shading to pale pink and white, and are excellent for cutting.

Eschscholzia (Californian poppy) are mainly in the yellow-orange range and once sown are never lost, coming up each year in an inoffensive manner.

Gypsophila paniculata is an elegant perennial, growing up to 1·2m (4 ft); the well-known cultivar Bridal Veil produces generous, fluffy panicles of white flowers from mid summer to early autumn (June to August); if you want something smaller, *G. elegans* is an aptly-named annual that can tumble over the edge of a path as it is only 30cm (12 in) tall; there are pink forms as well as white.

Helianthus (sunflower) always provides a talking point, with competitions to see who can grow the tallest; but it is not necessary to have the very tall Russian Giant as there are a number of smaller cultivars in seed catalogues.

Lathyrus (sweet pea) look attractive if you have a bare space in the garden where some pea sticks can be inserted. If you wish to combine economy with colour display then it would not be inappropriate to have a wigwam of bean sticks with runner beans trailing up them, as the runner bean was first introduced to cultivation as a flowering plant rather than a vegetable.

Lavatera trimestris Loveliness (mallow) is an attractive annual reaching 60–129cm (2–4 ft) and with a continual display of brilliant pink flowers.

Limonium latifolium (sea lavender), with its fluffy head of minute lavender-blue flowers and rosette of downy leaves, is a good plant to have, otherwise the annual statice is a useful substitute.

Nicotiana (tobacco plant) is strictly a half-hardy annual and needs greenhouse raising before planting out, but this can be done in an unheated house. It has a range of mixed colours including the lime-green much beloved by flower arrangers, and it also releases a delicious perfume at dusk, so find a spot for it near the house.

Nigella damascena (love-in-a-mist) is another useful annual for seeding about; its feathery green foliage is unobtrusive and its blue flowers are attractive throughout the summer.

Petunias, and zinnias for that matter, are seemingly too sophisticated for the cottage garden, but reseda (mignonette) is an important asset; *Reseda odorata*, at 30cm (12 in) high, provides a well-known fragrance for the edge of a path or border.

Several perennial rudbeckias are mentioned in the list of herbaceous plants (see Week 30) and there are also some annuals that are rather colourful; a recent, popular introduction is the 60cm (2 ft) tall *Rudbeckia hirta* Marmalade, with clear, golden-yellow flowers up to 13cm (5 in) across. Again, this is strictly a half-hardy annual requiring greenhouse raising.

Tropaeolum (nasturtium), if they can be kept clear of blackfly, are useful to trail about and fill odd gaps; they thrive in poor soil, flowering profusely.

Above left: Nigella damascena *(love-in-a-mist). Left: mixed annual* Rudbeckia hirta *(black-eyed Susan) Rustic Dwarf and Marmalade.*

Left: brilliant display of the biennial
Dianthus barbatus *(sweet William).*
Above: eye-catching blooms of perennial
climber Tropeaolum speciosum
Below: spikey althaea (hollyhocks)

Sloping Site Gardens

From a design standpoint, a completely flat garden raises problems, for it can so easily become dull and obvious. Slopes are helpful because they give variety and this can be exploited to great advantage. But sloping ground is harder to work than a level site, it can take up a lot of your time and involves a good deal of hard labour. If terracing is introduced it can also be more costly to lay out. It is, however, extremely useful for breaking up and enhancing the shape of the slope. Measuring up the site and assessing the problems of subsidence are explained. We also set out the logical process in building retaining walls, terraces and balustrades – covering the range of landscaping possibilities in a sloping site garden.

The first question you have to decide upon is whether to terrace and so convert the slope into a series of levels, or whether to accept it as it is. In a tiny garden it will have to be either one or the other, but where there is more space to play with it may be better to combine the two, contrasting the obvious artificiality of terraces with the more natural appearance of irregularly-contoured land. This can accord well with the common practice of allowing the garden to become progressively less formal the farther it is from the house.

One or two terraces close to the house may serve the dual purpose of providing comfortable outdoor 'rooms' in which chairs and tables can be placed when required, and at the same time providing a firm setting for the building. If a garden slopes uninterruptedly downward from a house, it will inevitably give it a slight appearance of instability, as if the building itself might one day begin to slip down the incline. An upward slope will give an opposite impression of the garden sliding down into the living rooms (and something of the kind does happen occasionally when freak rain storms

The gardens at Bodnant, looking from the croquet terrace to the rose terrace. Steps divide on either side of a fountain and pool, and the wall provides shelter for a wide variety of shrubs

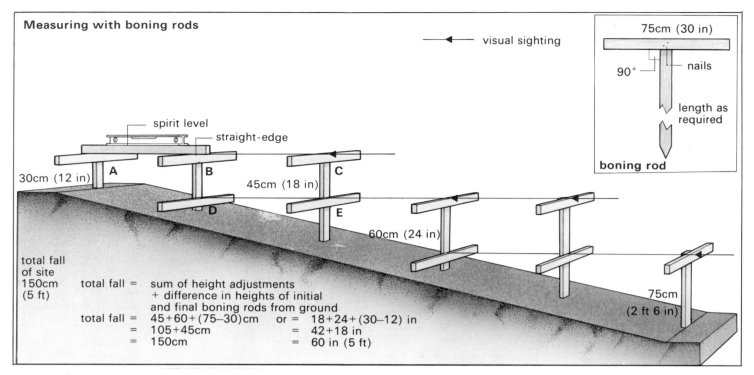

Measuring with boning rods

← visual sighting

75cm (30 in)

90° — nails

length as required

boning rod

spirit level

straight-edge

A   B   C

30cm (12 in)

45cm (18 in)

D   E

60cm (24 in)

75cm
(2 ft 6 in)

total fall of site 150cm (5 ft)

total fall = sum of height adjustments
+ difference in heights of initial
and final boning rods from ground

total fall = 45+60+(75–30)cm   or = 18+24+(30–12) in
= 105+45cm   = 42+18 in
= 150cm   = 60 in (5 ft)

occur). Good wide terraces, solidly retained with masonry, can completely correct either impression.

In making good terraces, especially if there are several of them, it is essential that they should all differ in width, depth and treatment. The advantage of this diversity can be seen very clearly in some of Britain's famous gardens; for example, at Bodnant in north Wales, five magnificent terraces overlook the valley of the river Conway, and at Powis Castle, Welshpool, the slope is even steeper and the terraces more architectural. No one would suggest that in small gardens these grandeurs should be imitated, but they do forcefully illustrate the advantages of variety, and that is possible however modest the scale of the operation.

Terracing with boning rods

To begin with, draw a plan of your site to scale on graph paper. You will invariably find that slopes are steeper than they appear and it is absolutely essential to know what the differences in level are before embarking on any scheme of terracing. There is no need to use expensive equipment such as a theodolite for this preliminary survey. On a small scale it can all be carried out with a straight-edged plank, a spirit level, and some stakes with a short piece of board nailed across the top of each in the form of a letter T. These are known as 'boning rods' and they are very useful for sighting across once a preliminary level, or for that matter any desired angle of slope, has been established (see diagram).

Armed with correct level distances, and the scale plan of the site, you can set about determining how wide each terrace should be, how deep its retaining wall or bank and how much, if any, of the land should be left with its natural slope. If the land falls across the site as well as along its length, it will be necessary for you to take levels in both directions, and then to make the required provisions for soil movement and retention.

To measure slopes for terracing First, drive in a short boning rod (**A**) at the highest point of the slope, and then place one end of the plank on the edge of this and drive in a longer boning rod (**B**) down the slope to support the other end of the plank. Lay the spirit level on the top of the plank and adjust the second stake until the bubble is at dead centre. This means that the tops of the two boning rods will now be level, and by taking a sighting across them you will then be able to drive in a third rod (**C**) farther down the slope, without needing to use the spirit level or plank again.

If the slope is steep, it will quickly become impractical to make boning rods tall enough to maintain the original level, so that instead you measure an identical distance down the last two rods, nail on additional cross pieces at this new lower level, and continue as before. The sum of the height adjustments made in this way, plus the difference in height from soil level to the top of the first boning rod and to the top of the last boning rod, is the difference in level from the top to the bottom of the slope.

Steep banks

Terraces can be retained by steep banks, but they may easily prove a nuisance to maintain. It is difficult to cut steeply sloping banks, and rocky banks take a lot of weeding. Ground cover can be fairly satisfactory, especially if some very soil-binding evergreen is used such as *Hypericum calycinum*, but then you must take care that it does not stray farther than it is required. Some small shrubs also grow well on steep banks, and in warm sunny places, cistus, available in considerable variety, can be very effective. There are also cotoneasters such as *Cotoneaster dammeri*, *C. microphylla*, *C. horizontalis* and *C. salicifolius repens* that thrive on sunny banks and, in the shade, both the

Right: natural approach to a gradient and formal effect (below right) at Dartington Hall in Devon. Below: an effective use of terracing and planting can transform a short, sharp slope into an attractive miniature garden

greater and lesser periwinkles (*Vinca major* and *V. minor*) will grow well.

Retaining walls

You will save labour in the long run by retaining terraces with walls and if they are cleverly designed and well built these also give the best effect. However, walls can be expensive, even when built at home, so it will be wise to check on the quantity of the stone or brick you would require and the probable cost before coming to any decision.

Whatever the material used, walls can be either mortared or unmortared (usually known as 'dry'). Mortared walls are strong and durable, excellent for climbing or trained plants, but useless as a home for plants. For that, dry walls are essential, with plenty of good soil packed between each course and uninterrupted access for roots to the main body of soil behind. In fact well-built dry walls, by simulating more closely the conditions rock plants are accustomed to growing in (often vertical crevices), are better for many of them than rock gardens.

Lewisias, ramondas and haberleas often prove difficult to manage on the flat, but are perfectly at home in the crevices of a good dry wall and this kind of gardening can become an interesting hobby in itself. Alternatively there are easy plants such as arabis, perennial alyssum, aubrietia and

Above: Cytisus × kewensis *on a dry wall*
*Left: sloping garden incorporating varying
styles, with artificial terraces at the
far end and a shrubbery in the foreground*

*Above: front elevation and side section
showing how to build a dry stone and turf
wall using squarish stones bonded with
turf that also acts as a planting medium*

many trailing campanulas that grow profusely in walls either planted on the face or established on top and allowed to cascade downwards. A dry wall need never be dull.

Building a dry wall

These are built in much the same way as mortared walls with the important difference that soil takes the place of cement. They can be made with dressed or undressed stone, or any of the various building blocks available from merchants. Alternate rows of stone must be staggered to give the wall a bond, just as bricks are bonded in any constructional work. The first row of stones must be well bedded into the soil and if the wall is over 1 metre (3 ft) high it is usually best to build it with a slight inward slope, or 'batter', for greater stability. Soil should not only be spread fairly thickly between the blocks but also rammed in behind them so that there are no hollow places left. When mortared walls are made, leave holes every few feet to allow water to drain out of the retained soil; this is not necessary with unmortared walls since every crevice acts as a drainage channel.

Steps and balustrades

Terraces necessitate steps for access and again these permit considerable diversity in style, material and planting. There is no reason why steps should follow the most obvious straight line. Sometimes a change in direction can produce interesting shapes or contrasts of light and shade. Materials can be varied, too, possibly with panels or surrounds of paving brick to contrast with concrete or stone slabs. But steps should always be set in mortar for they are likely to get a lot of wear, and loose or irregular steps can be dangerous.

When steps require balustrades, these may provide additional scope for training plants, particularly soft-stemmed climbers such as vines or clematis that won't catch in clothing or harm anyone.

Terraces

Because terraces are so clearly artificial it is appropriate that their design and planting should be seen to be man-made. They are the wrong place for rock gardens and cascades and the right place for carefully-proportioned beds, fountains and ornamental plant containers. Garden roses look well on terraces as do other highly-developed flowers such as fuchsias, pelargoniums and many bedding plants. If your fancy runs to topiary, a terrace is as good a place as any on which to display it. Here, too, lavender can be used to form little hedges or the shapes of beds can be more sharply defined with clipped edges

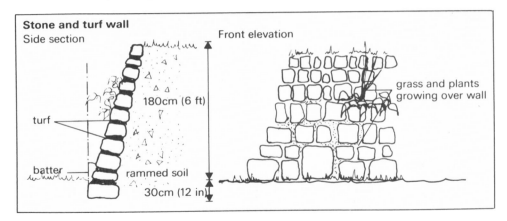

Stone and turf wall
Side section

Front elevation

180cm (6 ft)

turf

batter

rammed soil

30cm (12 in)

grass and plants
growing over wall

Above: 'stagger' steps for a soft effect
Right: patterned brick and stone steps
in an unusual circular arrangement
add a decorative touch

of box, thyme or santolina (cotton lavender). In fact it is only when there are differences of level that the old-fashioned formal style of gardening can be fully appreciated, for you need to be able to look down on a pattern of beds or flowers from above to see it at its best.

Topsoil and subsoil

Terracing involves the movement of soil and it is important when doing this not to leave the relatively infertile subsoil on top and bury the good topsoil. To avoid this danger, remove the topsoil to a depth of at least 20cm (8 in) and stack it in some convenient place. Then make the necessary adjustment of level and when this is done replace the topsoil where it belongs, on top, but not under paving or other areas where there will be no plants.

Problems of subsidence

Soil that has been removed takes a considerable time to settle. This can be shortened by treading and ramming as the in-filling proceeds, but even then some subsidence is bound to occur over a period of weeks if not months. So it is unwise to be in too great a hurry to complete such tasks as permanent planting, lawn making and the laying of paths. It is better to make a temporary display with annuals and bedding plants and to cover paths and lawn sites with cheap, quick-growing rye grass, until the site is firm and no further subsidence feared.

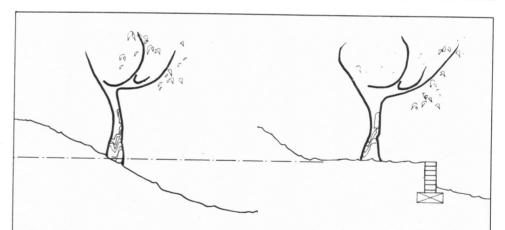

Retaining levels around trees

When terracing a slope, the position of trees is an important factor Most mature trees are very sensitive to any changes in level around the trunk or bulk of the root system.
To overcome this problem, make a shelf around the tree, using the existing level as its base. The size of this shelf should approximate to that of the canopy or spread of branches overhead and it will need to be retained by a wall where it drops down to meet the natural slope of the ground. The type of wall will depend on the
overall design of the area and it can be allowed to blend gradually into the slope on either side.
If you think the wall looks too severe, you can construct a platform using a steep earth bank to regain the lower level. You may need to stabilize this with planting; a rampant ground cover, such as Hypericum calycinum, Vinca minor or Hedera colchica is ideal, as it knits together quickly and prevents long-term soil erosion.
Young trees being far more adaptable, are less troublesome

We have described the methods and merits of terracing a sloping site. Now we will look at other, easier, ways of dealing with a sloping site, from building paths, and planted banks to the new approaches made possible by modern materials.

One method, similar to terracing, is to turn the slope into a series of banks separated by level paths. If the nature of the site permits it, both banks and paths can be curved to give the effect of an amphitheatre, although this may involve more soil-moving than would be necessary with straight banks and paths.

Grassed banks

It is unwise to put banks, straight or curved, down to grass without very careful consideration of the work this will involve. Grassed banks can look very effective, as many old formal gardens prove, but invariably they are difficult and tiring to mow. Since the introduction of light rotary hover mowers such as the Flymo Domestic, bank cutting is easier than it was, as these mowers can be moved freely in all directions, and be swung like a pendulum from the top of a bank. But it is still a fairly tricky job, for a rotary hover mower out of control can be a menace, since it will slide down any slope, cutting everything that comes into its path.

It is also sensible to make fairly shallow banks that you can tend from the adjacent paths with a minimum need to scramble on them. This applies equally, whether the banks are grassed or planted, for even the densest of ground cover will need some attention.

Planted banks

If you decide upon planting, the possibilities are almost endless, with the one proviso that the plants chosen must be able to withstand the sharp drainage and the occasional dryness of such places.

Small shrubs such as cistus and broom are ideal, as well as many creeping or sprawling rock plants such as helianthemum, aubrietia, arabis, alyssum and numerous campanula and dianthus (pinks).

Many grey or silver-leaved plants such as santolina, artemisia, anaphalis and helichrysum thrive on banks, but very rampant plants like cerastium enjoy the conditions so much that they become weeds.

Some sprawling roses such as Max Graf and *Rosa × paulii* grow well on banks, but their thorny stems make it rather difficult to move amongst them when they need pruning and weeding.

This is a case where shallow banks that can be tended from the level paths are almost a necessity.

Annuals and bedding plants usually thrive on sunny banks as many of them come from countries like South Africa and Australia, or areas of Central and South America that have warm, sunny climates. But most of these plants flower exclusively in summer and will leave the banks bare in winter, unless you include some evergreen shrubs as a permanent framework.

Bank gardening of this kind can produce effects just as formal and dignified as those characteristic of walled terraces, but at a much lower cost of construction, since no expensive walling stone is required. But many people do not

Plants for banks: helianthemum Brilliant (below) give a blaze of colour in summer and Artemisia arborescens *with* Senecio greyii *(bottom) give good contrast*

like formal gardens or else they may wish for a gradual transition, from formality close to the house, to more natural styles farther away. This approach can offer numerous interesting variations, and sloping sites are just as suited to it as they are to terracing.

Woodland glade gardening

What is a little misleadingly called 'woodland', or 'woodland glade', gardening can be very satisfactory even on the steepest of slopes. There need be no forest trees in the woodland; indeed, unless the area to be planted is half an acre or more, there almost certainly should be none.

The woodland can be artificially created using small ornamental trees. However, avoid anything larger than a mountain ash or amelanchier (snowy mespilus) and mix in some of the smaller maples and birches, laburnums, ornamental crab apples, Japanese cherries (if the site is not so rural that every bud will be stripped by birds) and magnolias (which never seem to be attacked by anything).

If the soil is lime-free, rhododendrons, azaleas and camellias will thrive under the trees and, whatever its character, it will be possible to grow skimmias and hydrangeas. Below these again, you can grow herbaceous perennials, hostas (green, blue-grey and variegated), foxgloves,

Plants for woodland: Amelanchier canadensis *(left) has a height and spread of 3m (10 ft) when fully grown; woodland hosta (below) likes shade*

cyclamen, polygonatum (Solomon's seal), lilies of the valley, dog's tooth violets, snowdrops and daffodils. Woodland gardens do not produce a lot of weeds because of the tree canopy and so are easy to look after.

Rock gardens

Rock gardens, by contrast, can make a lot of work, for most of the weeding must be done by hand, but a naturally hilly site is ideal for them. It makes construction easy, too, since the rocks can be bedded into the slope to create the effect of a natural outcrop. Stone-chipping paths can be distributed in a natural way through the rocks, providing easy access to the plants. If you desire some more open spaces, they can be created with carpet-forming plants such as *Arenaria balearica*, various acaena and *Cotula squalida*, underplanted with small bulbs such as crocus and narcissus species, chionodoxas, muscari and scillas.

Small shrubs also fit well into the rock garden setting, not simply the dwarf conifers but flowering shrubs such as daphne, cistus, various small brooms, such as *Cytisus kewensis* and *C. beanii*, and shrubs such as *Cotoneaster adpressus* and *C. microphyllus thymifolia*.

Plants for rock gardens: Cistus × purpureus *(above), a vigorous bush of upright habit;* Cistus crispus *(top right) is a native of S.W. Europe and only moderately hardy;* Cistus nigricans *and* Cistus revilii *(above right and right) bear these single, rose-like flowers in profusion in early summer*

Peat beds

Although rocks gardens are ideal for open sunny situations, where there is a fair amount of shade, peat beds may be better, particularly if the soil is naturally acid. Peat beds are built rather like rock gardens, but with blocks of hard peat (known as peat blocks) in place of stones, and a 50/50 mixture of peat and acid loam in place of ordinary garden soil. They are labour-saving because few common garden weeds thrive in such conditions. Equally, many familiar plants will not grow in them either, but there are plenty of plants less well known but just as beautiful that prefer these conditions. These include cassiopes, gaultherias, pernettyas, small rhododendrons, *Astilbe simplicifolia*, *Corydalis cashmeriana*, many (but not all) gentians, meconopsis, *Orchis elata*, ourisias, *Polygala chamaebuxus*, most of the Asiatic primulas, sanguinaria, *Saxifraga fortunei*, trilliums and *Uvularia grandiflora*.

Streams and pools

Streams and pools constitute another possibility. Water that comes tumbling and splashing down over cascades and along stony watercourses is always attractive, and nowadays it is quite unnecessary to have a natural water supply since reliable re-circulating pumps are readily available. Nor, as is sometimes suggested, is there anything inconsistent about having pools on sloping ground. Water will collect in any depression beneath which there is a water-resistant layer of clay or rock. Lakes exist at all levels in mountains and it is not at all difficult to create a very natural-looking sequence of pools in a sloping garden if the right contours are there or can be created by a little soil shifting.

It is natural to think of pools and cascades in connection with rock gardens since this is where they are so often placed, but it need not be an inevitable

Plants for peat beds: Trillium grandiflorum *(top left), a herbaceous perennial that was formerly included in the lily family;* Trillium sessile *(left) produces stemless flowers with upright, faintly-scented petals and looks best in large clumps;* Astilbe simplicifolia Aphrodite *(below) seen against a background of fern*

association or even necessarily the most desirable one. Streams and pools can be placed in a woodland setting also, or used in conjunction with peat beds.

Today, the task of pool construction has been greatly simplified by the availability of plastic or rubber sheets for use as liners. A similar technique can be applied to the construction of streams, but it is not quite so easy. The pre-formed, glass-reinforced plastics (such as Fibreglass) sections offered by many garden centres are hard to disguise and look very artificial. So many garden-makers may still prefer to rely mainly on concrete as a waterproof lining material for streams and cascades, keeping the plastics or rubber sheeting for the pools.

The contemporary approach

All the alternatives so far described are well tried and traditional. Some adventurous garden owners may prefer 'contemporary modern' schemes such as have been brilliantly demonstrated in European gardens and exhibitions. These bear a similar relationship to conventional garden-making that modern sculpture and painting do to traditional art. You could say that they seek to interpret natural shapes in terms of the material being used, with no attempt to disguise it, but rather tending to emphasize its particular characteristics. It would be ill-advised to attempt any such experiments in traditional environments, but in a contemporary modern setting they can be strikingly effective.

An advantage of this ultra-modern approach to modern gardening is that the materials used are cheaper than traditional materials. Concrete is used for retaining walls, steps and paving, and all its potentialities are exploited. Aggregates are selected to produce desired effects and, just before the concrete finally sets, it is heavily brushed to expose the aggregate and give a characteristic finish. Or, at an earlier stage in setting, the concrete may be raked to leave a distinctive pattern of tooth marks. In other schemes, corrugated plastics sheets or asbestos cement have been used to retain terraces in place of bricks or stones.

To put such schemes into effect requires a degree of imagination and there are not many places in the British Isles where effective examples can be studied, but some are to be found in the display garden of the Cement and Concrete Association at Wexham Springs, near Slough in Berkshire.

Water Gardens

When it comes to creating a focal point of interest in a garden there is nothing to beat a pond. It draws the rest of the garden round it, diffusing an aura of calm and rest, and provides a never-ending source of pleasure and enjoyment. Even non-gardening members of the family will be captivated by its charms, whether the sight of gleaming fish or the distant murmuring of a fountain or waterfall. Here we tell you how to make your own garden pond – from choosing a suitable site to selecting the best pond shape.

To make and maintain a garden pond is much simpler than generally realized. A hole must be excavated, certainly, but thereafter modern materials make construction a quick and easy job requiring no hard labour. If the basic rules of design and planting are followed there will be no need for frequent changes of water, or for a total annual clearout. A pond can stay clean, healthy and attractive for years with no more than a little annual tidying up, provided you make sensible decisions initially about size, shape and position. Remember that however much the pond may please you, your family and friends, it must first and foremost satisfy the needs of the plants and fish living in it.

Old wives' tales

Don't be influenced by any old wives' tales. There's one that says a pond must be 1·2–1·5m (4–5 ft) deep in one part to make fish safe in winter: this, as will be seen later, is nonsense. Another says that a pond must be in the shade because sunlight makes the water turn green. The problem of green water exists, but is not solved by putting the pond under a tree.

The sectional shape of a pond will affect the occupants' health. The first two shapes below are poor, with low volume-to-surface-area ratios. The third shape includes a marginal shelf and spawning area, and has a much better volume-to-surface-area ratio

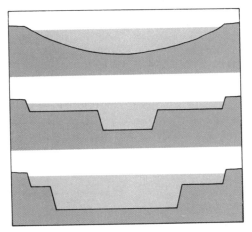

Correct siting

The best site for a pond is the most open you can find. *Nymphaea* (water lily) will flower only sparingly in the shade, and even such tolerant shallow-water plants as *Caltha palustris* (marsh marigold or kingcup), *Iris pseudacorus* (flag iris) and *Mimulus moschatus* (musk) will not give of their best without strong light.

Fish have definite dislikes too, becoming sickly and diseased in water polluted by decaying leaves and twigs. So clearly the last place for a pond is beneath a tree. Both plants and fish will be happier in an open position attracting the maximum amount of sunshine.

If you're considering a fountain pump or underwater lighting remember that you will need to lay a cable for an underwater socket outlet. Bear in mind, too, that you will need a hose for the initial filling and for topping up later.

The best shape and size

The site you decide on will influence the surface shape of the pond. The foot of a rock garden or alongside a curving border calls for informal, natural curves, while on a patio a formal circle or rectangle could be appropriate. But formal or informal, keep the shape as open and simple as possible. When sketching your plan on paper resist the temptation to make it more interesting by the addition of wiggly outlines, serpentine canals, elaborate crosses, pinched waists and quite pointless bridges. Although such designs may look attractive on paper remember that you will not be looking down on your pond from the air. Apart from proving severely cramping to plant growth, narrow arms and canals will become visual nothings when viewed from ground level across the garden.

The need is not for fancy shapes but the broadest stretch of water possible: water to catch light reflections, water to contain the spray of a fountain, water for the free-spreading growth of plants. Squares, egg shapes and broad ovals are all good, and circles—or something very similar—best of all, being visible across their full width from all observation points. The golden

A pond needs only two depths, a main floor 45–60cm (18–24m) deep, which will suit nearly all water lilies (see below right), and a shelf 15–20cm (6–8 in) deep, for marginal plants like flag iris (right) and red mace (far right).

rule is: whatever shape you decide on, be sure to fill up the pond with as much water as possible.

Pond size will depend on how much of the garden you can spare as well as on the cost. Within these limits do make it as large as possible. To start with a small pond and 'see how it goes' is not advisable, because the smaller the body of water the more its temperature fluctuates. The greater the volume, the more stable the environment and the happier the occupants. A surface area of about 5 sq m (50 sq ft) should be the minimum aim. It sounds a lot but in fact it is only a 2·1m (7 ft) square or a circle 2·5m (8 ft) in diameter. If you can stretch it to a 3m (10 ft) square or a circle 3·3m (11 ft) in diameter the surface area becomes 10 sq m (100 sq ft), which has real potential.

Don't finalize your ideas about size and shape until you have marked them out on

the ground with a hose or length of clothes-line. Examine each design from the important viewing points. Figures may seem large on paper, glass-reinforced plastics ponds may look impressive standing on end in a garden centre, but both can prove inadequate in the context of your own garden. Second thoughts about ponds are almost always on the lines of 'I wish I'd made it bigger'.

Green water
The water in a new pond invariably turns green. This is entirely natural, and no danger to fish, being simply unattractive in appearance. The 'pea soup' is in fact no more than a broth of minute single-celled plants, algae.

Algae thrive on two things: mineral salts dissolved in the water, and light. In a newly-filled pond they have both in abundance, there being no surface cover to prevent maximum light penetration, and tap water being rich in dissolved mineral salts. So the water becomes thick as green distemper. Changing it merely brings in a fresh supply of mineral-rich water to start the whole process over

again, while chemical treatment, although possible, is of no more lasting effect than taking aspirin for toothache.

The answer is to introduce natural competition in the form of other plants that will deprive the algae of both nutrients and light. The foliage of water lilies and floating plants will cut off sunlight at the surface, and an abundant growth of submerged oxygenating plants will consume mineral salts. Once these plants are established and flourishing the algae will simply fade away and the water will gradually clear.

Volume-to-surface-area ratio
Sometimes, though, the pond remains green and more often than not this is because of an insufficient volume of water to share the sunlight falling on the surface. A low volume-to-surface-area ratio will also produce sharp fluctuations in water temperature which is not good for fish. Saucer-shaped ponds suffer badly in this respect and should be avoided.

The sectional shape (that is, the shape you would see if you sliced the pond down the middle and looked at it edge on) is all-important.

The main depth of the pond should, for the sake of volume, extend over most of its area and should be sufficient to ensure adequate capacity for every square metre of surface area. An absolutely vertical side is not practicable, but if you can slope it at about 20 degrees to the vertical, and the depth is adequate, a satisfactory volume-to-surface-area ratio of 250, preferably 350 or even 500 litres per sq m (5,

7, or 10 gal per sq ft) is assured.

The right depth for plants
The pool should be deep enough for water lilies, the more vigorous of which will grow in 90–120cm (3–4 ft) of water if necessary, although nearly all will be happy with no more than 25–45cm (10–18 in) over their crowns (root tops).

Allowing for a soil depth of 15cm (6 in), the main pool depth should therefore be 40–60cm (16–24 in), thus ensuring a satisfactory volume/surface area ratio. No greater depth is needed.

While you must obviously take into account the depth preferences of other water plants there is certainly no need to make a staircase of shelves at a dozen levels. For the sake of marginal plants like *Scirpus* (bulrush), *Typha latifolia* (reed mace), flag iris and marsh marigold that like to grow in shallow water, it is only necessary to have a shelf 15–20cm (6–8 in) below the surface. This will allow for containers with 10–15cm (4–6 in) of soil and 5cm (2 in) of water above. A continuous hedge of marginals is not desirable and a total shelf length equivalent to about a third of the pond's perimeter is normally quite enough.

A shelf width of 25–30cm (10–12 in) is ample for plant containers. Anyone interested in breeding fish, however, could include at one end of the pond a shelf approximately 60cm (24 in) wide and 20cm (8 in) deep. Here oxygenating plants thickly planted in fine gravel in plastic seed trays will provide ideal conditions for spawning goldfish.

Above : a small-scale fountain is ample for a formal pond of this size

We have considered the size, shape and depth of the pond, and explained how the right site is vital to the health of plant and fish life. Here we compare the various pond-lining materials available, and tell you how to make your own garden pond using either plastics or concrete.

The successful garden pond is first and foremost a waterproof pond and with the advent of plastics the problems of cracked structures and disappearing water have been virtually eliminated.

Concrete or plastics?
Concrete, for many years the *only* lining available, is still considered by some people to possess the ideal qualities for the construction of a pond. But this is not so for, although it can provide a beautiful finish if skilfully handled, its effectiveness as a waterproof shell leaves much to be desired. The fundamental problem is a fatal lack of 'give'. A gentle subsidence of earth, as can happen in light sandy soils or drought-shrunk clay, is sometimes all it takes to disturb the foundations and precipitate a fracture in the shell. The pressure exerted by a thick sheet of surface ice can be similarly destructive.

It is not really surprising, then, that plastics is now far more popular than concrete for pond-making. Its use involves much less labour, and although you must still dig the hole, at least it is a smaller hole, no allowance being necessary for wall and base thickness. Installation is quick and easy, and stocking can take place immediately afterwards as no seasoning or treatment is required. Ice and soil movement seldom worry plastics, which is resilient enough to absorb stress. Although some plastics may be punctured by accidents that would be harmless to concrete, such damage can usually be repaired very easily.

Choice of plastics
Glass reinforced plastics ponds (such as Fibreglass) will be familiar to many people from the blue, green or brown pre-formed shapes propped against fences at garden centres (and, incidentally, looking twice as large as when sunk in the ground). They are reliable and durable, but expensive compared to other materials, and only the largest designs can be taken seriously as ponds.

Vacuum-formed mouldings are the lightweight, usually grey, ponds that feel so much flimsier than Fibreglass. Although cheap, they are·generally deficient in depth and volume. They are handy as reserve ponds for fry (young fish).

'Pond-liner' is the term normally applied to a flat sheet of flexible plastics used to line an excavation. There are several different kinds, most of which can be supplied in as large a size as you may require. So, unlike preformed designs, you can make the pond whatever size and shape you like – but remember that the more complicated the shape the more material will be wasted out of a rectangular sheet.

Polythene, once much used, is now the least-valued sheet plastics for pond construction. It is very cheap, but also extremely fragile, being easily torn and impossible to repair. It does not stretch and has to be tucked into the hole.

Butyl synthetic rubber is the aristocrat of the sheet plastics group. It is also the most expensive (though cheaper than glass reinforced plastics), and has a useful life of an estimated 50–100 years. It will be some time, of course, before the accuracy of this estimate can be assessed.

For those of you not concerned with looking so far ahead, laminated PVC, with an estimated 10–20 years' lifespan, will probably be adequate. This material looks like polythene but possesses quite different characteristics and chemistry. It is tougher, it stretches, and if damaged is easily repaired. A version is available in which a sandwich of PVC has a centre of nylon or Terylene net, but this reinforcement would seem to offer no advantage in the garden pond context.

Using a flexible plastics pond-liner
The design opposite meets the requirements specified overleaf for a pond of adequate size, simple open shape, and containing a sufficient volume of water in relation to surface area.

Shape and size
The shape derives from two circles, just touching, one of 1·2m (4 ft) radius, the other of 60cm (24 in) radius. The outer extremities of the two circles are joined by easy curves to create an ovoid, or egg shape, whose overall dimensions are $3·65 \times 2·45$m (12×8 ft). The perimeter is about 9·5m (31 ft) round. Approximately 3·5m (11 ft) of marginal shelving is provided, 25cm (10 in) wide and 20cm (8 in) below water-level, plus a wider shelf at the narrow end that can be used for either additional marginals or, as mentioned in Week 9, spawning plants (see also Week 13), or both. Elsewhere the water depth is 60cm (24 in).

The surface area is about 7 sq m (75 sq ft) and volume approximately 3·3 cu m (730 gal), making a very satisfactory volume-to-surface-area ratio of almost 500 lit per sq m (10 gal per sq. ft).

Calculating the liner size
To work out the size of the liner double the maximum pond depth and add the result to the overall length and overall width of the surface shape (the extent, size and shape of the shelves will not affect the calculation).

In this case, 2×60cm (2×24 in) is added to $3·65 \times 2·45$m (12×8 ft), giving a liner size of about $4·85 \times 3·65$m (16×12 ft). You need make no allowance for the surrounding flap (which will be covered by turf or paving stones) as the angled sides of the pond, quite apart from stretch in the liner, will result in a certain amount of spare material when you install the liner.

Laying a measuring tape down the sides, round the shelves and across the bottom of our design would show a total profile length of 4·5m (14 ft 9 in) and a maximum width of 3·3m (10 ft 9 in), leaving 35cm (14 in) to spare each way out of a 4·85 × 3·65m (16 × 12 ft) sheet (even without stretching it), meaning at least a 17cm (7 in) flap all round.

Preparing the site

It is essential that the ground surrounding the pond be absolutely level so that when the pond is filled the water will lap the rim all the way round. A vital tool, therefore, is a spirit level, together with a good length of straight timber.

For easy grass-cutting and a neat appearance the surround, at least part of which will be paved, should be flush with the adjoining ground – or about a centimetre below grass level. So first of all remove 6cm (2½ in) of soil/turf from an area exceeding the size of the pond by 60cm (24 in) all round (or more wherever the layout of your garden makes an extension of the paved area desirable).

When you have levelled this area you will be ready to mark out the shape of the pond. This you can do by using a skewer attached to the end of a piece of string tethered to a centre peg. Scratch out two circles 1·8m (6 ft) apart, and with radii of 1·2m (4 ft) and 60cm (24 in) respectively. Draw the curved sides joining the circles free-hand and delineate the whole outline with pegs and string.

Digging the pond

First excavate the whole pond area to a depth of 20cm (8 in), angling the sides at approximately 20 degrees so that at a depth of 20cm they are 8cm (3 in) in from the vertical. At this level (20cm down) the ovoid should be 3·5m (11 ft 6 in) long and a maximum of 2·3m (7 ft 6 in) wide. Next mark out the shape of the marginal shelves and spawning area, and from these lines excavate the main pool area a further 40cm (16 in), giving a total main floor depth of 60cm (24 in). Whether or not you intend backing the pond with a rockery or waterfall you should still move all excavated soil at least 60cm (24 in) away from the hole, and not pile it right on the pond edge.

Using a hardboard template that you can make yourself (see diagram) check that the sides slope at the correct angle, and that the shelves are at the correct

depth, of the right width, and even-surfaced. Any necessary adjustments can then be made.

Installing the liner

Remove any stones and flints, and also any bits of wire, broken glass and pot. Then cover the pond floor with approximately a centimetre of building sand (or old carpet, underfelt, or several thicknesses of newspaper) to provide a soft and even bed for the liner. Treat the shelves similarly, but not the walls unless the soil is very flinty, in which case damp sand trowelled on will cling adequately.

Now position the pond-liner over the hole and secure it with a row of bricks or paving stones, making sure these weights do not overhang the pond edge but sit firmly on the liner, which should extend some 30cm (12 in) beyond the side of the pond. The liner will then sag into the hole

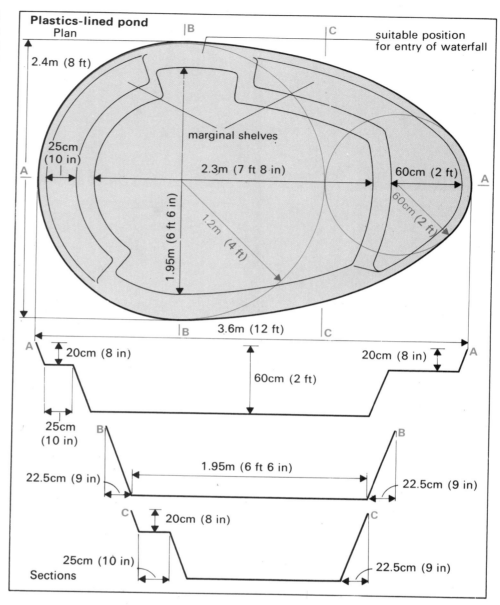

Ovoid shape is ideal for plastics-lined pond. Cross-sections **A** *and* **B** *show longest and widest points, and* **C** *the spawning area*

but will still need to be stretched before it will cling snugly to the pond profile. This is achieved by running water onto the liner. Gradually the growing weight of water forces the liner down, to conform to shape and contour of the excavation.

This process is likely to take nearly three hours to complete, but when the pond is filled to the brim you can remove the weights from the liner edge, and trim off the surplus material with scissors, leaving a flap 15–20cm (6–8 in) wide all round. Water pressure will hold the liner firmly in place and there is absolutely no chance of the flap suddenly slipping.

Finally, nick the flap as necessary where there are folds so that it lies flat, and bed paving stones onto it in a mixture

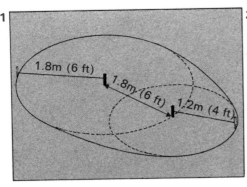

1.8m (6 ft)
1.8m (6 ft)
1.2m (4 ft)

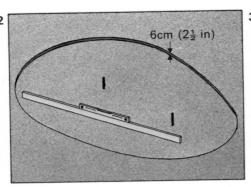

6cm (2½ in)

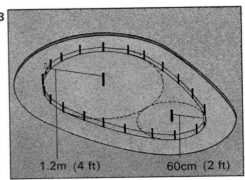

1.2m (4 ft)   60cm (2 ft)

7.5cm (3 in)

20cm (8 in)

25cm (10 in)

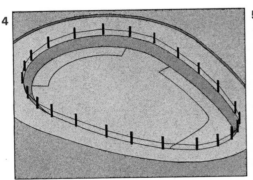

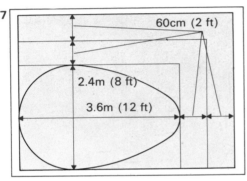

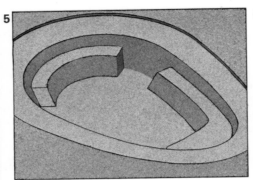

30cm (12 in)

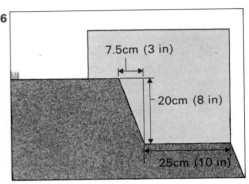

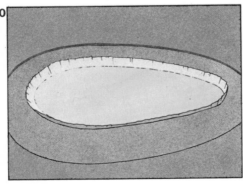

60cm (2 ft)

2.4m (8 ft)
3.6m (12 ft)

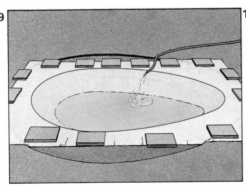

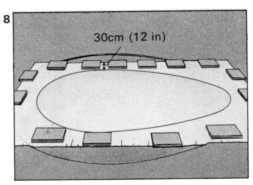

paving slab

3:1 sand/cement

liner

sand

Inserting a plastics liner

1. *Mark out pond surround*
2. *Remove turf or topsoil*
3. *Mark out circumference of pond*
4. *Dig to marginal shelf level*
5. *Dig to full depth*
6. *Check size and angles with template*
7. *Calculate size of liner*
8. *Position liner over hole*
9. *Fill with water*
10. *Trim off surplus liner*
11. *Bed paving slabs around edge*

of three parts sand and one part cement, positioning the stones to project 5cm (2 in) over the water. Small pieces are of no use here as foot pressure will tend to rock them on the edge and break them away. Use the largest pieces possible to ensure that the easily accessible parts of the pond surround, which will inevitably attract most use, are well and firmly paved. You can use turf elsewhere provided you turn down and bury the liner flap virtually to the water's edge to expose adequate soil for nourishment.

Alternatively, the turf can stop several centimetres short of the water, leaving a narrow border to accommodate such plants as aubrietia, alpine phlox, campanula, *Erica carnea* Springwood, *Saponaria ocymoides* and other sprawlers that will drape the edge and conceal the liner.

You can easily modify the pond design illustrated here to suit a smaller liner size. For example, a liner 3·65 × 2·75m (12 × 9 ft) would be adequate for a pond 2·75m (9 ft) long and 1·8m (6 ft) wide overall, with a maximum depth of 45cm (18 in). The circle radii in this case would be 90cm (3 ft) and 45cm (18 in), and the surface area a little over 4 sq m (40 sq ft). The width and depth of the marginal shelf would remain unchanged, but position and extent could be modified as desired.

Building a concrete pond

However, for those of you still determined to proceed with a concrete pond despite the drawbacks and labour involved, we give the following instructions. Apart from digging the hole, your main task will be laying the concrete, and for this you will need to devote a full day if you are to avoid the leaks that result when one stage dries out too much for the next to key into it.

Preparing the excavation

First, then, you must dig a hole large enough to take both a firmly-rammed hardcore foundation 10–15cm (4–6 in) thick (15cm in clay soil), and a lining of concrete 12–15cm (5–6 in) thick, the latter extending up the walls to ground level. This done, you can then insert the foundation, and on top of this place chicken wire, which should also continue up the sides to the surface. It is a mistake to concentrate strength in the base at the expense of the walls, for although the base must withstand the weight of the water, the walls – particularly round the rim – have to bear the brunt of considerable ice pressure.

Concreting floor and walls

You will need three parts coarse, 2·5cm (1 in) down aggregate, 2 parts sand, and 1 part cement. These must all be measured accurately by volume, and then mixed very thoroughly with water to achieve a smooth, even consistency. You could add waterproofing powder, although completely waterproof concrete comes only from really thorough mixing.

To make the floor, add a 10–12cm (4–5 in) thickness of concrete to the hardcore foundation, working part of it through the chicken wire. Then, to form the walls and marginal shelving, lay the same thickness of concrete (10–12cm) onto the sides, having first erected timber and hardboard shuttering to keep the wet concrete in place until it has set. When all the concrete is set hard, apply a rendering coat (3 parts sharp sand to 1 part cement) 2·5cm (1 in) thick overall.

Combating free lime

A new concrete pond cannot be stocked immediately as damaging free lime will soak out of the concrete into the water unless preventive measures are taken. You could paint the pond with either three coats of a coloured plastics paint such as Poolcote, or five coats of a solution of colourless magnesium silico-fluoride. Alternatively (and perhaps more reliably), you can simply fill the pond, leave it for a fortnight, and then empty it. When you have repeated this at least three times the pond should be safe. Potassium permanganate is often recommended as a neutralizer of free lime, but in fact it has no effect at all.

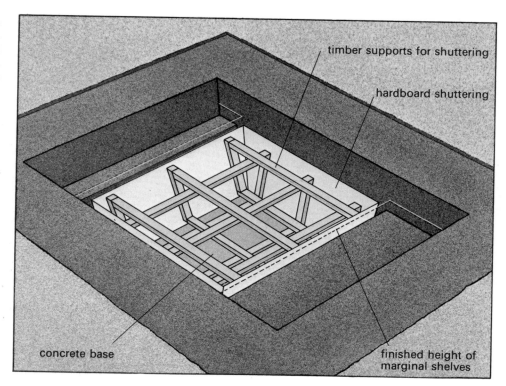

timber supports for shuttering

hardboard shuttering

concrete base

finished height of marginal shelves

Above: erect shuttering for walls as soon as concrete base is set

Below: plan of pond, and cross-section showing construction of base and walls

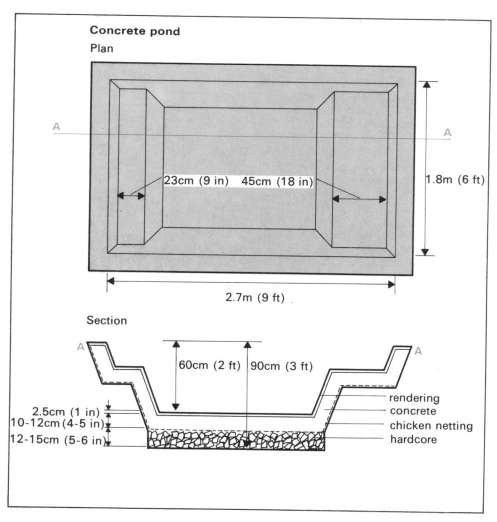

Concrete pond

Plan

A — A

23cm (9 in)   45cm (18 in)

1.8m (6 ft)

2.7m (9 ft)

Section

A — A

60cm (2 ft)   90cm (3 ft)

2.5cm (1 in)
10-12cm (4-5 in)
12-15cm (5-6 in)

rendering
concrete
chicken netting
hardcore

Water Plants

We will now analyze how best to stock your pond – from which plants to choose to how you can provide the best conditions for healthy growth.

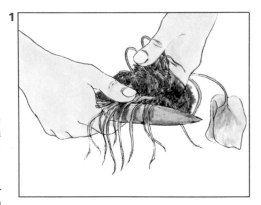

When you have built your garden pond the next thing to consider is which plants to stock it with. Pond plants should be moved only when actively growing, so the ideal time for stocking is early to late summer (May to July), although the planting season for most aquatics can be stretched from late spring to mid autumn (mid April to mid September).

If you build your pond outside this period, stocking will have to wait until the planting season arrives, by which time the water will probably resemble thick pea soup. This condition, examined in detail (on page 143), is quite normal, and intelligent planting of the pond will help control it in the future. But now, at planting time, you will have to remove the water, otherwise submerged plants – particularly oxygenators – will have a struggle to survive, let alone flourish, simply because they lack sufficient light.

Emptying the pond

We have discussed how to install a submersible pump to provide a waterfall, and you can use this now to empty the pond. Simply detach the pump from its delivery hose, pushing a garden hose long enough to reach a drain or other convenient discharge position onto the pump outlet. Assuming no sediment has yet accumulated, you can sit the pump on the bottom of the pond, enabling it to remove all but a few centimetres of water; remember to switch off while it is still covered by water. Once you have refilled the pond you can plant it almost immediately, but it is best to wait three days for the chlorine to be dispersed.

Diet

Most aquatic plants are thoroughly easy-going, requiring no fussing and making few demands on your time once established. They certainly won't want a rich diet, and being immersed in water, obviously don't need watering. Too much growth is likely to be your problem rather than too little.

The ideal planting medium is the heaviest loam you can find, well mixed with chopped turf (but *not* finely riddled). Don't use fertilizer, peat, leaf mould, John Innes or other composts, although you could add well-rotted manure or coarse bonemeal to the mixture for *Nymphaea* (water lily)—but sparingly.

Any fertilizer that dissolves readily into the water will merely encourage algae in the form of green water or blanket weed.

Planting techniques

There are two possible planting techniques. Traditionally, you plant into a thick layer of soil spread over the entire floor and shelves. Although this requires much soil it undoubtedly produces abundant growth, sometimes to the extent of choking the pond. Clearing overgrown plants and mud from such a pond can be a mammoth task, so be warned if you decide to take this course.

The alternative, and nowadays more popular, method is to confine the soil to planting containers, or at least to limited areas of the pond. This way there is no soil lying on the floor for fish to stir up, or to encourage straying roots, and as a result plant growth is more easily controlled. You could buy plastic containers with perforated sides, but these are totally inadequate for robust water lily roots. Your best plan is to build a compartment yourself, using bricks but no cement, and making it about 60cm (2 ft) sq and 20–23 cm (8–9 in) deep. Cement blocks, incidentally, should never be used for this or any other purpose in the pond.

For smaller lilies and all other aquatics, plastic containers have many advantages, keeping growth in tidy clumps and radically reducing the amount of soil that has to be found. They can be rearranged at will, and spring-cleaning the pond is greatly simplified. You should line perforated containers with permeable fabric such as old sheets or curtains. Planting can never be too firm, bearing in mind that soil in a container is bound to loosen up a little when immersed in water. Top the soil with coarse gravel or pebbles so that fish cannot stir it up.

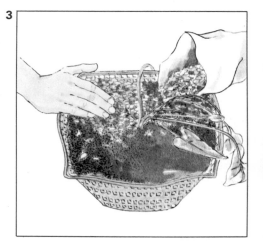

WATER PLANTS

Water plants can be divided into five groups, some purely ornamental, some functionally valuable without being particularly ornamental, and some combining good looks with good works.

To plant in container: **1** *trim roots;*
2 *secure in soil;* **3** *cover with gravel;*

4 *Brick compartment for robust lilies*
Right: Nymphaea × marliacea chromatella

NAME OF PLANT	SEASON (IF GROWN FOR ITS FLOWERS)	HEIGHT	DEPTH OF WATER OVER ROOTS
Aponogeton distachyus (water hawthorn)	Intriguing, forked white flowers (spring and autumn) with black anthers and strong scent. Floating oval leaves. A 'must'.	Surface	10–45cm (4–18 in)
Nuphar luteum (brandy bottle)	Too much leaf and not enough flower. Not recommended.	Surface	Up to 240cm (8 ft)
Nymphoides peltata/Villarsia nymphoides (water fringe)	Small, mottled, heart-shaped leaves and bright yellow flowers in early summer (May) make this plant very like a small water lily.	Surface	10–45cm (4–18 in)
Orontium aquaticum (golden club)	Blue-green leaves, yellow/white flower spikes in mid summer (June). Unusual.	0–30cm (0–12 in)	0–45cm (0–18 in)

Water lilies

The water lily is as useful as it is beautiful. It will flower from early summer to late autumn (May to October), producing gorgeous waxen blooms that fully justify its title of queen of the water garden.

Equally important, the plant helps to maintain clear water (in company with oxygenators) by producing pads that

Above: Stratiotes aloides *(water soldier)*
Below: Nymphoides peltata *(water fringe)*
Right: Aponogeton distachyus *(water hawthorn). All will combat algae*

spread across the surface of the pond, thus cutting off sunlight and discouraging undesirable algae.

Water lilies vary considerably in vigour and spread, some tolerating a water depth of as much as 90cm (3 ft). It should be clearly understood, however, that no lily *needs* this depth, and all except miniatures will grow happily in a pond approximately 45–60cm (18–24 in) deep. It is a pity that so many garden ponds become smothered by cheap vigorous lilies when beautiful varieties of more suitable proportions exist, and cost only a little more.

Deep marginals

These plants grow rooted in soil, and extend leaves and flowers to the surface of the pond or just above, thereby contributing to the control of algae. This group includes *Aponogeton distachyus* (water hawthorn), one of the best pond plants, and the only one with a strong scent.

Floating plants

Floating plants, being surface-coverers, cut down light, and so help control algae, but some spread too rampantly. The safest are *Stratiotes aloides* (water soldier) and *Lemna trisulca* (ivy-leaved duckweed), which float only part of the time, and *Hydrocharis morsus-ranae* (frog-bit).

Oxygenators

Oxygenating plants, although not valued for their ornamental qualities, are vital to the balance and hygiene of the pond, depriving algae of mineral salts, and providing food, shelter, a spawning medium and oxygen for fish. You should plant them at the rate of one every 1800 sq cm (2 sq ft) of surface area for the first 9 sq m (100 sq ft), and half that rate every 9 sq m thereafter. With the exception of *Ceratophyllum* (hornwort), oxygenators must be planted, and *not* just 'dropped in'. Fine gravel will suit them as well as soil.

Marginals

Marginal plants have no important function in the pond and can be omitted if you wish. But as they will grow up above water-level they could add interest to an otherwise flat surface profile, and many are well worth having for their attractive flowers or ornamental foliage.

You can plant marginals in soil in containers positioned on the marginal shelf, but if several plants are grown in one container make sure that they are all of the same variety.

Fish and Pond Life

We have covered stocking your pond with suitable plants – now we examine other forms of pond life, from the ever-popular goldfish – always a welcome addition to any water garden – to the less attractive water beetle.

Although your pond can be successful without fish, keeping a few will prevent it becoming a breeding place for midges and mosquitoes, as well as adding colour, grace and movement.

When to introduce fish

You must allow three, preferably four, weeks for your pond plants to become established before introducing fish to the water garden. This is vital for aquatics, particularly in the case of oxygenating plants, which will be destroyed unless given sufficient time to develop secure roots. And without a healthy growth of oxygenators to compete with algae your pond will probably succumb to green water (see Week 9).

How many?

There is a limit to the number of fish a pond will hold: beyond this, growth will be stunted and disease become likely. To ensure ample room for growth and breeding you should think in terms of one fish for every 2000 sq cm (2 sq ft) of surface area – the size of your fish when you buy them is immaterial.

Which types?

The following list describes different types of fish that can be mixed together, with comments on their desirability.

Goldfish The cheapest and hardiest ornamental pond fish, goldfish are the mainstay of most ponds. Although generally orange-red, they can also be yellow or white, and some may be marked with silver or black.

Shubunkins Mottled with a mixture of several colours, shubunkins – particularly the prized blue form – are attractive, but tend not to show up too well in the pond.

Comets Both comet goldfish and comet shubunkins are graceful variants with

Above: Iris laevigata *(Japanese water iris).* Below: Zantedeschia aethiopeca *(arum lily).* Below left: Mimulus guttátus

NYMPHEAE (WATER LILY) Selection of hardy varieties				
Surface spread	1·5–2·1m (5–7 ft)	1·2–1·5m (4–5 ft)	90cm (3 ft)	45–60cm (18–24 in)
Water depth (above soil)	30–90cm (12–36 in)	25–60cm (10–24 in)	18–38cm (7–15 in)	8–25cm (3–10 in)
WHITE	Gladstoniana *N. tuberosa richardsonii* Virginalis	Gonnere *N. marliacea albida* *N. odorata alba*	Candida *N. odorata minor*	*N. pygmaea alba* *N. tetragona*
YELLOW	Colonel Welch	*N. marliacea chromatella* *N. odorata sulphurea* Sunrise	Aurora Graziella Paul Hariot	*N. pygmaea helvola*
PINK	Amabilis Masaniello *N. tuberosa rosea*	Mrs Richmond *N. marliacea rosea* Rose Arey	*N. laydekeri lilacea* *N. odorata turicensis*	Joanne Pring
RED	Attraction Charles de Meurville Escarboucle	Conqueror James Brydon William Falconer	Froebeli *N. laydekeri purpurata*	*N. pygmaea rubra*

NAME OF PLANT	SEASON	HEIGHT	DEPTH OF WATER OVER ROOTS
Acorus calamus (sweet flag)	A prolifically self-seeding weed. Avoid it.	120–150cm (4–5 ft)	0–5cm (0–2 in)
Acorus calamus variegatus	Leaves striped cream and green. Moderate growth from creeping rhizome.	75cm (2 ft 6 in)	0–5cm (0–2 in)
Butomus umbellatus (flowering rush)	Narrow leaves, rushy stems; red-stamened, pink flower clusters in mid summer (June).	90cm (3 ft)	5–10cm (2–4 in)
Calla palustris (bog arum)	Small, white, arum-type spathes in mid summer (June); shining, dark green leaves.	15–23cm (6–9 in)	0–5cm (0–2 in)
Caltha palustris (single kingcup or marsh marigold)	Late spring to early summer (April–May).	30–38cm (12–15 in)	0–5cm (0–2 in)
Caltha palustris alba (white Himalayan kingcup)	Late spring to early summer (April–May).	30cm (12 in)	0–5cm (0–2 in)
Caltha palustris plena (double kingcup)	Compact, very double, deep yellow; prolific blooms in late spring to early summer.	23cm (9 in)	0–2·5cm (0–1 in)
Caltha polypetala (giant kingcup)	Largest of an invaluable family. Big, single yellow flowers, late spring to early summer.	75–90cm (2½–3 ft)	0–7·5cm (0–3 in)
Cyperus longus (sedge)	Graceful, and needing the control of container planting.	120–150cm (4–5 ft)	0–10cm (0–4 in)
Eriophorum angustifolium (cotton grass)	Grassy foliage; plumes of silvery, silk down.	45cm (18 in)	0–2·5cm (0–1 in)
Glyceria aquatica variegata	Leaves striped yellow, green and white.	60cm (24 in)	5–7·5cm (2–3 in)
Iris laevigata (Japanese water iris)	Violet flowers in mid summer (June). There are also pure white, white/china blue and white-mottled-dark-blue varieties.	60cm (24 in)	5–10cm (2–4 in)
Iris laevigata variegata	Violet flowers in mid summer (June). Showy, green/cream leaves right through summer.	60cm (24 in)	5–10cm (2–4 in)
Iris pseudacorus (yellow flag iris)	A variegated form is more compact and controllable. Flowers in early summer (May).	120cm (4 ft)	5–10cm (2–4 in)
Menyanthes trifoliata (bog bean)	Creeping rhizome throws up spikes of pink-tinted, white blooms in early summer (May).	23cm (9 in)	0–5cm (0–2 in)
Mimulus guttatus (monkey flower or musk)	Cheerful yellow flowers from early summer to mid autumn (May–September).	30–38cm (12–15 in)	0–2·5cm (0–1 in)
Pontederia cordata (pickerel weed)	Glossy leaves. Spikes of violet flowers in late summer to early autumn (July–August).	60–75cm (2–2½ ft)	5–10cm (2–4 in)
Ranunculus lingua grandiflora (great spearwort)	Yellow buttercup: mid to late summer (June–July). Container control essential.	90cm (3 ft)	5–15cm (2–6 in)
Sagittaria japonica (Japanese arrowhead)	Late summer: 3 petals, white, gold eye.	45cm (18 in)	5–15cm (2–6 in)
Scirpus albescens (bulrush)	Creamy-yellow, rushy stems, vertically lined with green.	120cm (4 ft)	5–10cm (2–4 in)
Scirpus lacustris	Not worth growing as an ornamental plant.	150–180cm (5–6 ft)	5–15cm (2–6 in)
Scirpus zebrinus (porcupine quill or zebra rush)	Stems banded green and white.	90cm (3 ft)	5–10cm (2–4 in)
Typha angustifolia (slender reed mace)	Much better for garden ponds than 2·5m (8 ft) native reed mace, *Typha latifolia*.	120–150cm (4–5 ft)	5–10cm (2–4 in)
Typha minima (dwarf reed mace)	Plant all typhas in containers to control spread and help develop brown bosses.	45–60cm (18–24 in)	2·5–5cm (1–2 in)
Zantedeschia aethiopeca (arum lily)	Superb as marginal. In winter, stand container on pond floor. Flowers early summer (May).	120cm (4 ft)	5–30cm (2–12 in)

extra long tails.

Fantails Varieties with short deep bodies and large double tails. They may be red, mottled or black (moors). Less robust than plain goldfish.

Goldfish, shubunkins. comets and fantails can all be interbred, as they are all derived from the carp family.

Golden orfe The most visible pond fish, these colourful and lively surface-feeders will quickly demolish any insect that touches the surface. Rudd and silver orfe, although satisfactory in ponds, are not so showy.

Nishiki koi (fancy carp) These fish are very colourful, but require a great deal of room to develop fully.

Tench Often recommended as scavengers, but not worth having. Tench certainly feed on the pond bottom, but they do *not* act as aquatic vacuum cleaners by sucking up dirt, as many people imagine. They don't do anything that a goldfish won't do equally well (apart from their particular trick of sucking snails out of their shells), and they're quite invisible in the pond.

The fish mentioned so far will all live quite happily together, unlike catfish, which would just as soon eat other fish as anything else, and should therefore never be included in your pond. Roach, chub, carp, and other fish from the wild, as well as being designed by nature to be invisible from above, will almost invariably bring with them parasites and disease organisms that can be harmful to exotic fish – so it is best not to introduce them.

Below: as well as the familiar red or yellow, goldfish can also be mottled, as shown in this group of pond fish

Likewise, avoid perch and pike, both of which are predators.

On the whole it would be better to stock your pond initially with a large number of small fish rather than a small number of large ones, although a mixture of sizes is perfectly in order.

Breeding fish

You can buy fish in sexed pairs, but only at sizes of 13–15cm (5–6 in) or more. However, most mixtures of small fish will include both sexes. If your pond is well planted, breeding size will be reached very quickly, and fish introduced when 8–10cm (3–4 in) long would in most cases be sexually mature the following year.

When breeding time is imminent, you will very likely notice certain fish being chased and chivvied by the others: don't confuse this mating play with fighting and try to intervene. Eggs will be deposited among plants in shallow water, so that 10–12 oxygenators planted in gravel in a plastic seed tray, and placed on the marginal shelf, will help to provide ideal spawning conditions.

Ideally, when spawning has taken place, you should move the plants and eggs carefully to a separate pond, for rearing. In the main pond, many of the fry will be eaten by adult fish, although a fair number may survive, provided you can supply plenty of plant growth in which they can hide themselves.

Some fry are coloured from the start, while others are brown at first but develop colour later. Any that are still brown after 18 months, or when 7cm (3 in long), you should dispose of before they reach breeding size, otherwise they will reproduce more and more offspring that are similarly coloured.

Feeding fish

It is difficult to be exact about how much food you should give your fish, since their appetite will vary with the seasons and with the water temperature. They will eat most in summer, less as the water cools in the autumn, and nothing at all when it is really cold. When fish are active you can feed them daily, but give them only as much as they can consume in five minutes. You will soon get the hang of judging what they need and adjusting the amount accordingly.

Fish are perfectly capable of surviving for long periods without being fed, provided their pond is well established and contains plenty of natural food. If you go on holiday don't ask someone to come in and feed the fish as they will probably give far too much – and an uneaten portion rotting on the bottom is the surest way to pollute the pond and encourage disease. Let the fish forage for themselves for a few weeks; they'll come to no harm.

Other pond inhabitants

Apart from fish there is no form of livestock whose introduction to your pond can be heartily recommended. Snails are of doubtful value. The best kind, *Planorbis corneus*, the Ramshorn snail, probably does little harm, but not much good either. The amount of algae it consumes is insignificant, and when it eats plant waste it produces waste itself. Fish eat its eggs, and tench will eat the snail itself, so it is difficult to maintain a stock. This is not true of *Limnaea stagnalis*, a large snail with a long pointed shell. It is a prolific breeder that does a lot of damage to water plants, so you should never introduce it to your pond. If any do appear (as eggs on plants), hand-pick them to extinction.

Freshwater mussels live by filtering green algae out of the pond water, and so should, in theory, be just what you want. Unfortunately, once they have filtered all the algae in your pond they will simply starve to death – and nothing pollutes a pond quicker than dead mussels. This and the fact that their larvae spend the first months of life as parasites on fish make mussels a distinct liability.

A variety of creatures will turn up out of the blue and make themselves at home in your pond. Frogs, toads and newts short of natural ponds may adopt it as a nursery. There is no harm in this, although a large number of frogs can create a considerable disturbance, and even be a danger to any fish they blunder into – though this is very rare. Once spawning is over they will go, leaving

their spawn behind. Unless you want a pond full of tadpoles, you must net them out. Both tadpoles and newts are harmless, but the latter will eat insects and small fish fry.

Since water beetles can fly, and readily do so at night, it will not be long before your pond is colonized by many different kinds. Nearly all will be small and totally harmless, and can be ignored, but if the Great Diving beetle, *Dytiscus marginalis*, turns up you will have to eliminate it.

This pest will not be hard to recognize. The adult's body is a blunt oval 25–40mm (1–1½ in) long and 12–20mm (½–¾ in) across the back. It will be dark brown in colour, except for an edging of dull gold. The larva may be very small when it first appears among plants, but it will grow into a nasty-looking piece of work with a curved, tapering, segmented body up to 5cm (2 in) long, with a pair of bristles at one end (for breathing), and a pair of pincers at the other. Both the larva (which lives in the pond for 2–3 years) and the adult are carnivorous, attacking snails, aquatic insects, and even quite sizeable fish, when short of easier prey. Fortunately, these pests will need to rise to

the surface periodically to take in air – making it easier for you to net them. Early and mid summer (May and June) is the time they will normally appear.

Another grotesque-looking creature that you may see stalking small insects through the jungle of underwater plants is the larval form of dragonfly. This six-legged larva is capable of catching small fry but will be no menace to grown fish. The adult dragonflies that dart over the pond, and the frailer-looking, fluttering damselflies, are both entirely beneficial, feeding on gnats, midges and similar nuisances. However much of a menace they may be to other insects, dragonflies – and indeed all the creatures mentioned here – are entirely harmless where human beings are concerned.

Pond health

From time to time, particularly during heavy summer weather, you may see your fish gulping at the pond surface. It is often assumed they are hungry, but in fact such behaviour means they are suffocating and that something must be done immediately

A selection of ornamental fish: two golden orfe (top right); a group of shubunkins (top left) and nishiki koi (centre); and fantail goldfish (left).

to help them. The effect is associated with thunderstorms and the sort of sultry, oppressive weather that makes humans gasp and feel languid. It can last a few hours or a few days. Fish may recover without help in mild cases, although in severe ones they could all die overnight.

Fish, of course, use up oxygen and exhale carbon dioxide. Submerged water plants, on the other hand, consume carbon dioxide and produce oxygen, so if you have enough of each you would expect things to balance out. But what is often forgotten is that plants only behave like this under the influence of light. In darkness they work in reverse: both they and the fish use up oxygen and produce carbon dioxide. Nevertheless, during the summer months when the plants are most active, long days and short nights ensure the production of enough oxygen to keep the fish happy.

There does not have to be a precise balance between plants and fish because, in addition, oxygen is absorbed into the water from the air and carbon dioxide escapes into the air from the water. Under most weather conditions this natural process will make good any oxygen deficiency and prevent an excess of carbon dioxide reaching a critical level.

Making your own Rock Garden

Creating a focal point of interest in your garden can be a problem, particularly if you live on one of today's many housing estates. Often there are no fences between sites, and sometimes there are restrictions on having trees, or indeed any plant that grows above a certain height. One answer could be to create your own rock garden, and here we explain how to do it. We guide you in your choice of site and rock and offer many hints to ensure an attractive effect.

Before you make any final decision on whether to proceed with a rock garden, you must first consider the conditions that will most suit rock plants and alpines. Ideally, a rock garden should be situated on a gentle slope, preferably facing south or south-west, and sheltered from strong winds. It should be close enough to any trees to benefit from the sunlight that will filter through the leaves in summer, but not so close as to suffer from the continual dripping of rain. A well-drained, sandy loam is the best soil for this type of garden.

Obviously, many sites will fail to meet at least one of these requirements, but don't worry. In fact, one of Britain's best-known rock gardens, at the Royal Horticultural Society's establishment at Wisley, is on a north-facing slope, but by clever construction parts of it have been 'turned' to face south. How this was done is explained in the section headed: Forming an 'outcrop' rock garden.

The worst places you can attempt to create a rock garden are in a dry corner, near a hedge, or in very dense shade. But the more determined you are, the more you can do to combat difficulties.

Preparing the site

Once you have settled on where to situate your rock garden you must turn your attention to the preparation of the site. First dig the area over and, if it is a heavy soil, trench it. Remove any perennial weeds, by chemical means if necessary.

Clay soils must be drained (see diagram next page), and to do this dig trenches approximately 45cm (18 in) deep and 90–180cm (3–6 ft) apart, according to the state of the clay. Half-fill the trench with rubble or large stones, cover these with upturned turf or very coarse compost, and fill up with soil.

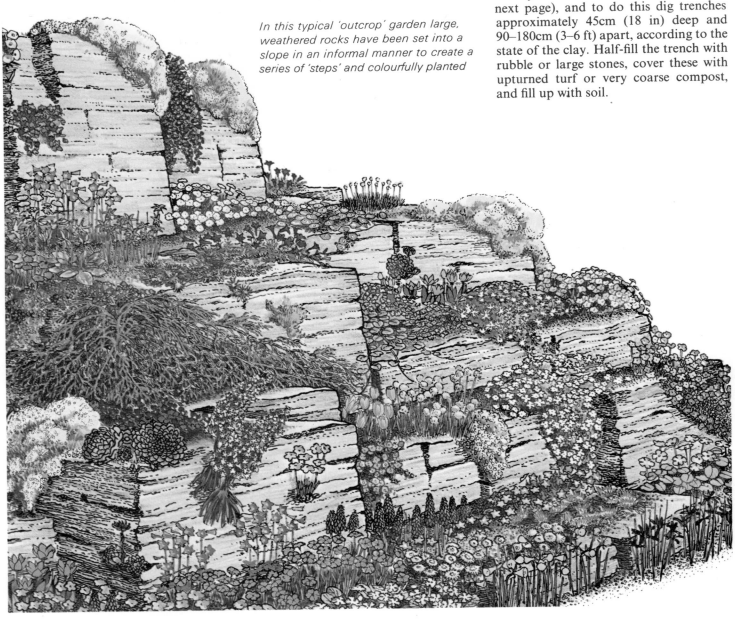

In this typical 'outcrop' garden large, weathered rocks have been set into a slope in an informal manner to create a series of 'steps' and colourfully planted

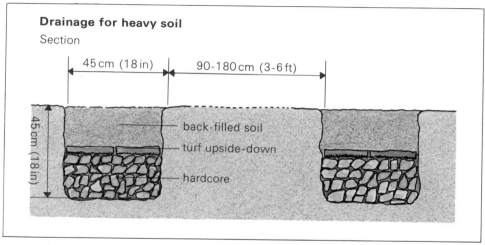

Natural lie of rocks

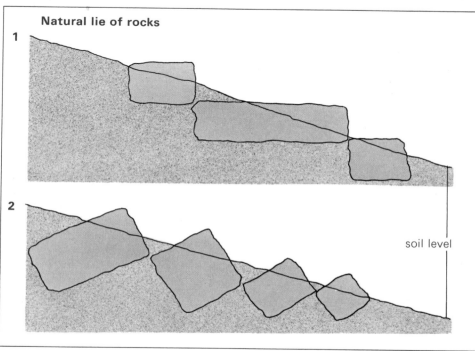

Rock used in the garden includes cold, hard granite (top), mellow sandstone (above) and rough, porous tufa (below)

*Above: an outcrop rock garden should imitate nature to be effective. In **1** rock lies flat in the earth's surface, but in **2** geological upheaval has set it at an angle of about 45 degrees*

Bed the rocks in a soil mound comprising 2 parts 6mm (¼ in) down rock or gravel chippings – to provide drainage – and 1 part each of loam and moss peat. If only 10mm (⅜ in) down chippings are available, these will suffice. The mound will subside after a while, even though you firm the soil down, so keep a reserve of the mixture for topping up after about ten days – or sooner if it rains.

Finally, add a top-dressing of 6mm (¼ in) down chippings, making it about 2–3cm (1 in) deep, and rake flat. The chippings have a three-fold purpose: to retain moisture; to protect the necks of plants from rotting; and to prevent rain

splashing soil onto the flowers, some of which – although hardy – are delicate.

Other badly-drained sites will require the same approach. A rock garden built on chalk should present no problems, provided you follow the same drainage procedure as for clay. But your choice of plants will be limited, and you may need to add a chemical agent to the soil to prevent the foliage turning yellow.

Choice of rock
You should give extremely careful thought to the choice of rock. It is not a cheap commodity, and you will have to balance aesthetic considerations with the availability of the stone you choose.

Two important factors to bear in mind when making your decision are the type of soil in your garden, and whether any local stone is available. Matching the rock with the soil is very important if your

155

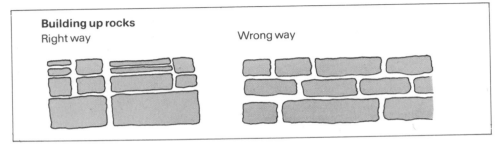

Building up rocks

Right way

Wrong way

Above: don't build on the brick wall principle of overlapping shown on the right
Below: set rocks at an angle to achieve a south- or south-west-facing planting area

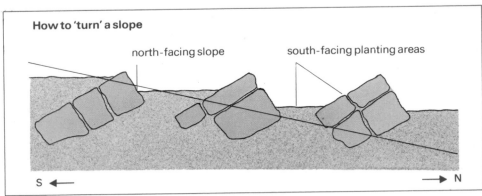

How to 'turn' a slope

north-facing slope

south-facing planting areas

S ←

→ N

rock garden is to look authentic. Nothing looks more out of place than, say, a water-worn limestone in a sandstone area or, indeed, vice versa. In some urban areas limestone tends to wash white and become rather glaring, although it will prove excellent if used in conjunction with a stream, pond or waterfall.

If you are unable to get any local stone, or if none exists, you will have to look around and see what you can find. Sandstone will be kindest to your plants, and is available in the south of England. Sussex sandstone is very popular, and Kentish Rag sandstone is quite easily obtained. Cotswold stone has a warm appeal, but although a sandstone, it contains an element of alkalinity, so a careful choice of lime-loving plants is necessary. Granite is cold, hard and heavy, and plants will not really grow well around it, but it can make quite an attractive garden.

As far as cost is concerned, the amount you will have to pay will be determined primarily by the distance the rock has to travel from the quarry.

Below: informal rock garden in Kent

How much rock will you need?

When you have decided which rock to use, and discovered the cost per tonne, the next thing is to calculate how much you will need. For a rock garden measuring 4·5 × 3m (15 × 10 ft), 1½–2 tonnes of rock should be sufficient. Individual pieces of different types of stone will vary in size, and you will get a slightly larger volume of sandstone per tonne than you will limestone. Ideally, of course, you should be able to pick out the particular pieces of stone that you want, but this is not always possible.

In a small garden, an economical use of stone is essential if you are to keep the overall effect in proportion. Judicious placement can often make the end result appear rather more than the number of stones might indicate.

Rock in nature

All rock starts life as a large lump – be it in the shape of a mountain or a range of mountains. The action of various strains and stresses in the earth's behaviour causes this lump to crack and split. Splitting occurs in parallel lines, vertically and horizontally, but not diagonally. Moisture which permeates into these cracks expands and contracts under the alternating effects of cold and heat, eventually causing the rock to split further and to crumble. Some parts disintegrate to the extent of forming soil, but others protrude from the earth's surface as an outcrop, and it is this that is often imitated in the rock garden.

Forming an 'outcrop' rock garden

The important thing to remember when forming an outcrop rock garden is that it should appear natural. In nature, geological upheavals can mean that rocks lie at an angle in the soil, so when positioning the stones in your garden make them slope gently into the ground.

If you already have a slope suitable for a rock garden then clearly your task will be much simpler than if you don't. However, if your slope faces north, you would be well advised to turn it so that it faces south. This is achieved by setting large rocks into the slope at such an angle that they face north, thus providing a protected area behind them – facing south – where you can place your alpines and rock plants (see diagram on page 203).

If your garden is flat, you will have to create an artificial slope, but at least you can point it in the right direction, and make it an appropriate size.

All rock has strata lines, that indicate successive layers of deposited substance,

Above: densely-planted outcrop rock garden at Dinmore Manor, Herefordshire

formed over millions of years. In some rocks, these lines are barely distinguishable, while in others they are fairly well defined. When arranging the rocks in your garden, try to ensure that the strata lines are horizontal and never vertical.

Remember, too, that if your particular design requires you to place one rock on top of another, you should follow nature's example and avoid the brick wall principle of overlapping.

Forming a tufa rock garden

Another type of rock used for building a garden is tufa. If weathered it will be grey in colour, but direct from the quarry it is bright creamy-white.

It is basically a porous limestone, formed by the action of water passing through limestone rocks and collecting particles that, together with decaying plant life of a primitive nature, form the original tufa. The porosity is brought

about by the decaying and eventual washing away of the primitive plant life.

The advantages of tufa over the other types of rock mentioned are numerous. From the construction point of view, it has little or no strata lines. Many plants will actually grow *on* it, as roots can penetrate its porous form. Saxifrages and draba will both do very well here.

As with an outcrop rock garden, drainage is essential. Tufa should be arranged on an informal basis: you simply 'mould' the stone to the existing contours of your garden, or use it to create a rise and fall on flat ground. When you have laid the rocks and filled in with soil, the ground can be top-dressed with the left-over 'dust' from the rock, or with limestone chippings. The cost per tonne is rather high in comparison with other stone, but its porosity makes it light in weight and, therefore, good value for what you have to pay.

Making your own Scree Garden

We have discussed the building of an informal rock garden and compared the different types of stone available in Britain. Here we look at the use of stone chippings, or scree, in the rock garden, and include a selection of suitable shrubs and alpine plants.

A scree in the context of a rock garden is simply a reconstruction of the conditions in which rock plants grow in their natural habitat throughout the mountains of the world. Plants that will often prove difficult to cultivate in a normal environment positively thrive in a bed of stone chippings. The scree provides perfect drainage, a cool root run, and moisture during dry periods.

A scree can be created on any soil: alkaline or acid, heavy clay or light sand. It can form an integral part of a rock garden, or it can be a feature on its own, but always remember that in nature a scree emanates from a rock formation and usually 'fans out' from a fairly wide fissure or valley in the rocks. Examples of scree can be found in botanic gardens all over Britain, and there is a particularly good one at the Royal Botanic Garden in Edinburgh.

In a rock garden, the most suitable place to form a scree is between two rising outcrops, but it is also possible to lay special scree beds, either as an edge to a rock garden, or as a completely separate bed on a lawn.

Making a scree bed

To make a scree bed you must first mark out the area you propose to use and excavate it to a depth of approximately 90cm (3 ft) on a heavy subsoil, or 60cm (2 ft) on a light, well-drained soil. Slope the floor gently on a well-drained soil, but more sharply on a heavy soil, where you should also add a layer of rough drainage material – something like brick rubble or broken pot would do the job. Over this, place either rough peat, compost, half-decayed leaves or rotted turf, and tread firm. Finally, the scree itself is laid.

Opinions differ on the ideal make-up of a scree, but basically it is agreed that too much drainage is worse than too little. Make your scree of roughly 50 per cent chippings, 25 per cent sandy loam and 25 per cent peat or leaf mould, and you should be all right.

158

To add interest to the surface, as well as create a more natural finish, you could dot a few rocks here and there, building up the scree around them for greater effect. It is a good idea to add a modest top dressing of leaf mould or peat once a year.

The chippings should be no larger than the 6mm ($\frac{1}{4}$ in) variety if possible, although the standard 10mm ($\frac{3}{8}$ in) might be the only one available at your local supplier. If the colour of the chippings does not blend with the stone in your rock garden, you can cover the chippings with a thin top dressing of whatever will match, be it granite, limestone or tufa.

Raised scree beds

One form of rock garden leads to another. A raised scree bed can be constructed from broken paving stone comparatively cheaply, and can, in fact, form quite a feature in a garden that has been terraced. Alternatively, the raised scree can be free-standing, particularly in an environment containing a great deal of paving or concrete.

A raised scree won't usually exceed 45cm (18 in) in height, but a normal raised bed can be up to 90cm (3 ft). It makes an excellent form of gardening for the elderly, or those confined to wheelchairs, as it is not necessary to crouch to reach the planting area. It is also a controlled form of gardening, for the soil mixture can be specially chosen to suit whatever group of plants you plan to cultivate.

The construction of a raised scree bed differs from that of the other forms of rock garden so far described, in that, for strength and rigidity, the rocks or paving forming the wall can be interlocked on the brick wall principle.

The walls should not be exactly vertical; each stone should be set back gradually to form a slight slope. If you can also tilt the stones slightly to cause the rain to percolate through to the centre, so much the better.

You will have to insert plants for the sides of the bed at the same time as you build the wall. For extra security you might decide to cement the stones into

Top right: section of scree bed excavated to total depth of 90cm (3 ft) with a base slope at 20° to horizontal for poorly-drained soil, or 5° for well-drained soil
Centre: make hardboard, triangular template to measure the 20° angle of slope; for a 5° angle, the short side of the triangle should be 5cm (2 in) long
Right: section of raised scree bed with supporting side wall of paving slabs, tilted to allow water to run into bed

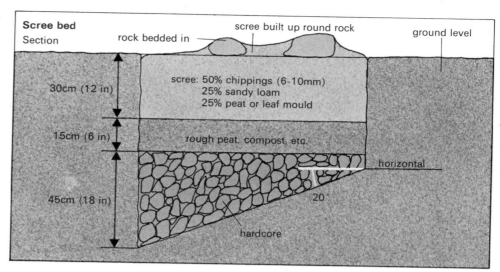

Scree bed
Section — rock bedded in — scree built up round rock — ground level
30cm (12 in)
scree: 50% chippings (6-10mm)
25% sandy loam
25% peat or leaf mould
15cm (6 in) — rough peat, compost, etc.
horizontal
45cm (18 in) — 20°
hardcore

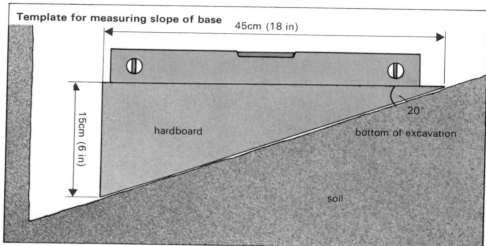

Template for measuring slope of base — 45cm (18 in)
15cm (6 in)
hardboard
20°
bottom of excavation
soil

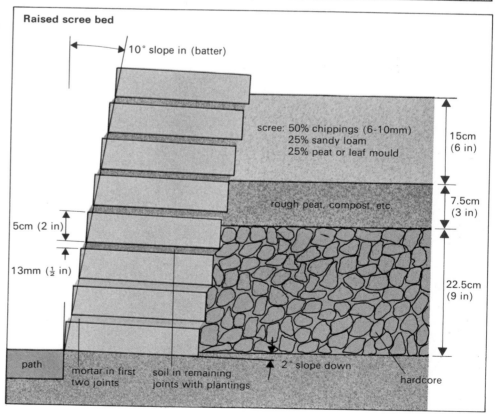

Raised scree bed
10° slope in (batter)
scree: 50% chippings (6-10mm)
25% sandy loam
25% peat or leaf mould
15cm (6 in)
7.5cm (3 in)
rough peat, compost, etc.
5cm (2 in)
13mm ($\frac{1}{2}$ in)
22.5cm (9 in)
path
mortar in first two joints
soil in remaining joints with plantings
2° slope down
hardcore

Top: free-standing, raised scree bed looks attractive in a paved area

Below: Cotyledon simplifolia thrives on well-drained, rocky surfaces

place, but the most satisfactory results will be achieved by setting them in soil, apart from perhaps the first few layers. This will allow plants like ramonda and lewisia to grow happily on their sides in the wall, rather than upright on the flat area below the wall, where they will collect rain in the centre of their rosettes.

Instead of paving or rock, you could use discarded railway sleepers to make the wall of the bed. Lay them one on top of another, to form a square or rectangle, and drive iron stakes into the ground around the edge to keep them in position.

Planting in rock and scree

There is an almost unlimited range of rock plants and shrubs, but it is important that, when making your selection, you

also consider where you are going to put each plant. A visit to a specialist nursery-man is well worth the effort, as he will be able to advise you on what will be best for your particular soil. You will also be able to see the plants in flower. Alpines are always grown in pots and are thus easily transplanted at any time of year, although spring is naturally the best time for planting.

Never put fast-growing plants close to slow growers, otherwise the former will tend to overrun the latter. Try to arrange things so that your rock garden has some colour all through the year, rather than just in one season. The best plan is to plant the miniature shrubs first, and then select the most suitable positions for the other plants.

Evergreen conifers are particularly useful in the rock garden, providing variety in colour, height, form and texture. Often, a conifer can be used to enhance the appearance of another plant, but follow the directions of nature when deciding on the appropriate places for planting. You would never see a tall tree on top of a mountain – it will always be at the base – and so it should be in your garden. On the same principle, a prostrate conifer or shrub would best be planted to fall over the edge of a rock.

To provide a continuous and colourful display throughout spring and summer, you can plant aubrietia, alyssum, iberis, helianthemum, some campanula and the more vigorous dianthus: position them to cascade down a dry wall or bank. If you add *Polygonum affine* and *P. vacciniifolium* to this group, the display will continue through to the autumn.

Bulbs, in general, will not do well on a scree, but a selection of those which are suitable adds interest. Plant them so that they peep through mats of ground cover such as thyme or acaena. Tulips come in all sizes and colours, with the many hybrids and varieties of *Tulipa kaufmanniana* being particularly suitable. Then there are the numerous dwarf species and cultivars of narcissus. Crocuses will make an attractive show early in the year, and *Crocus speciosus* will start again in the autumn.

As already explained, it is not advisable to grow the more vigorous rock plants on a scree because they would soon choke more delicate and choice species. So while, for instance, *Campanula allionii, C. pulla, C. arvatica, C. cochlearifolia* and other small campanulas would all do well, larger plants such as *Campanula portenschlagiana* and *C. poscharskyana* would be out of place and a menace. The latter two would be best situated on a dry wall where it will not matter if they spread rampantly. Kabschia saxifrages are a good choice for a scree, particularly the yellow-flowered *Saxifraga × apiculata* and *S. burseriana*, with its many hybrids. Careful siting is vital, for unless they occupy a shady position in summer, they can be scorched in a single day. Autumn rains will tend to rot them, so glass protection may also be necessary. Otherwise they are completely hardy.

Of the other saxifrages, *S. aizoon* and its forms create silver-encrusted mats of rosettes, while *S. cotyledon* and *S. longifolia*, particularly the form of the latter called Tumbling Waters, provide handsome sprays of flowers, some 30cm (12 in) long.

The alpine aster *Aster alpinus* will thrive, and the alpine catsfoot *Antennaria dioica rosea* makes an attractive grey carpet with short pink flowers. *Armeria caespitosa*, a form of thrift, will form little hummocks and produce heads of pink flowers. The European aretian androsaces would be too vulnerable in this sort of situation and is best kept in an alpine house, but the rock jasmine from Kashmir, *Androsace sempervivoides*, again with pink flowers, would enjoy scree conditions. Some of the gentians will give a good display, notably *Gentiana gracilipes* and *G. septemfida*, two summer-flowering species. The well-known *G. acaulis* and *G. verna* would also be happy, and although the latter is a short-lived plant, it will seed freely. A dwarf flax *Linum salsoloides* Nanum, bears slightly opalescent pearly-white flowers during the summer, and might also be considered suitable.

Among other bulbs that will do well

in scree are the rhizomatous irises, including *Iris innominata, I. cristata* and *I. mellita*. The latter is a miniature flag iris, only 8–10cm (3–4 in) tall, and it can have either smoky-purple or yellow flowers. The other two are 13–15cm (5–6 in) tall, are natives of America, and – like most American iris – detest lime.

Dianthus go well in rock gardens. *Dianthus alpinus*, with its deep green, strap-shaped leaves, and its large, deep-rose flowers that appear in early summer, will like the cool side of a rock. Another European dianthus worthy of your consideration is *D. neglectus*, which has a distinctive light buff reverse to its petals, and will form a dense cushion of fine green linear foliage, almost indistinguishable from grass. *D. freynii* is yet another from Europe, and has more typical greyish foliage, and small pink flowers on 3–5cm (1–2 in) stems. Dianthus will not object to lime and neither will *Linaria alpina* (toadflax), although the latter will be happier on a scree, where it will form a compact mat of blue-grey foliage and produce little mauve snapdragon flowers with orange markings.

Although it tends to seed itself freely, the pink-flowered *Erinus alpinus* and its hybrids will not become objectionable. An interesting miniature relative of the cabbage family is *Morisia monantha* (or *M. hypogaea*), which has a long taproot and will form a flat rosette of glossy, dark green leaves in which will nestle golden-yellow flowers in the spring. *Wahlenbergia serpyllifolia* Major and *W. pumilio* are two cousins of the harebells. They form prostrate mats and produce deep purple and lavender bells respectively in mid summer (June). They are sometimes considered temperamental plants and are often short-lived, but they are still worthwhile.

You can bring a touch of colour to the scree in the autumn by planting two cyananthus. *Cyananthus microphyllus* (also known as *C. integer*) can become over-large for a scree, but *C. lobatus* and *C. l. albus* will both do very well.

Shrubs can also be grown in the spartan conditions provided by a scree. *Daphne arbuscula* is a fragrant-flowered, 15–25cm (6–10 in) tall shrublet that will flower in June. *Juniperus communis compressa* (common juniper) is a greyish-foliaged conifer that will slowly reach to over 60cm (24 in) in a slim, columnar manner. Other suitable conifers are *Chamaecyparis obtusa caespitosa* and *C. o. minima*: both produce dense, dark green foliage, and are very slow growing, taking several years to reach 30cm (12 in).

This, then, is but a small selection of what will grow in rock and scree conditions. As already indicated, a visit to your local nursery will give you a much better idea of what is available and which plants grow best in your area.

Above: the hardy Saxifraga × apiculata
Below: Erinus alpinus *with starry flowers that are borne throughout the summer*
Bottom left: an alpine dianthus hybrid
Centre: Ramonda myconii, *a native of the Pyrenees suited to north-facing slopes*
Bottom right: Linum salsoloides

A Garden for Roses

The idea that roses need to be segregated in beds or even gardens of their own seems to be a relatively modern one. Perhaps Napoleon's Empress Josephine started it all in 1800 with her famous collection of roses at La Malmaison near Paris, where, it is said, 250 varieties of roses grew – all that were then known in the western world. Today, however, there is a return to using roses blended in with other flowers, and there are many fine examples of this type of design to be seen throughout the United Kingdom.

As roses became fashionable in the mid 19th century, growers developed special beds in which their roses could be pruned, fed, and cared for. They could also be prepared for exhibition in the best

Below: modern hybrid tea, Whisky Mac
Bottom: modern floribunda, Anne Cocker

possible way, without any competition from other plants.

The Victorian passion

What really started the fashion for rose beds – and then, by a natural extension, for rose gardens – was the introduction towards the end of the 19th century of the new race of hybrid tea roses. These were followed shortly by the polyantha pompon varieties, and then in the 1920s by the even more spectacular floribundas.

All these races brought a new element into rose-growing. They had a longer flowering season than all but a handful of the old roses and the hybrid teas appeared at a time when the Victorian passion for summer bedding was at its height. All manner of showy plants were then being placed outdoors in early to mid summer (late May-early June) to fill the garden with coloured patterns until the autumn.

Garden design had already been adapted to accommodate the numerous and often very elaborate beds required to contain this conspicuous display. It was, perhaps, natural to see these new free-flowering – and often very showy – roses in terms of this kind of garden-making, but without the necessity for constant replanting since roses, unlike many of the greenhouse-reared bedding plants, were both hardy and perennial.

So rose gardens became fashionable and soon a legend grew up that roses were poor mixers, did not do well with other plants in close company and needed to be kept on their own. To obtain the massed display that this kind of gardening demands they were planted very closely, often no more than 50cm (20 in) apart and were pruned fairly hard in mid spring (March) to develop strong erect stems with all the blooms on top.

Breeding to order

Since this was the kind of rose gardeners wanted, breeders obliged by producing more and more varieties to meet the demand. Growth habits were virtually ignored so long as the plants could hold their flowers erect. Colour, size and form of bloom, and freedom and continuity of flower production, were the all-important and it mattered little what kind of foliage a new rose had, and not at all whether it produced any heps after the flowers had faded.

But there is no reason for roses to be grown in this way and there are still plenty of varieties, including those often referred to as 'shrub roses' (as if all roses were not shrubs) that are delightful to look at as bushes. One of the most famous of British breeders considers that in years to come we could have roses with graceful arching stems, and (almost wholly) evergreen foliage that could be scented like that of the sweet briars. Another breeder believes that many roses of the future will carry attractive crops of heps that will last through much of the winter after the flowers have all gone.

Well, roses with all these virtues do already exist, though there are certainly not enough of them. There are also prostrate roses that can be used as ground cover, as well as all manner of climbing roses, some only capable of covering a short pillar or maybe one side of an arch, others able to climb to the tops of high trees and fall out of the top in wonderful cascades of bloom.

So when I recommend making *a garden for roses* rather than *a rose garden*, what I have in mind is drawing on all these different qualities of the rose and using them, with whatever other plants seem appropriate, to furnish a garden that will be beautiful because of its variety of shapes, colours, textures and perfumes, and not simply because it has, for relatively short periods, more or less flat, featureless masses of colour.

It is untrue that roses do not associate well with other plants, and the proof of this is to be seen in scores of gardens in which they are not segregated in any way.

RHS Wisley Garden

There is a delightful example in the new walled garden in Britain's Royal Horticultural Society garden at Wisley, Surrey, where roses are used with lavender, catmint, hardy geraniums, variegated mint, artemisias, alchemilla, lilies and other plants to create charming colour schemes and contrasts in foliage texture and plant habit.

Hidcote Manor

In the long central walk at Hidcote Manor, near Chipping Campden in Gloucestershire (a National Trust garden open much of the year) roses are used with canna and many other plants in a section that is planned in shades of red and purple.

Kiftsgate

Just a short distance down the hill from Hidcote is Kiftsgate, a privately-owned garden (occasionally open to the public) in which roses are similarly planted with many other shrubs and herbaceous plants to produce what is really a cunningly interwoven tapestry of colour. At Kiftsgate, too, is the original specimen of one of the most magnificent of all climbing roses, *Rosa filipes* Kiftsgate, a rose so vigorous that it is completely unsuitable for small gardens. Here, though, supported by a large tree, it produces a breath-taking display of white blooms during late summer (July).

National Rose Society garden

Even in the Royal National Rose Society's own display garden in Chiswell Green Lane, St Albans in Hertfordshire, a slightly grudging acknowledgment is being made that roses look all the better for having other plants with them. Here one of the main companions is geranium Johnson's Blue, a fine hardy perennial with lavender-blue flowers produced for many weeks in summer. Like catmint and lavender, it is the kind of plant that can be used with almost any rose, whatever its colour. For a background in the same colour range there are few better plants that you could choose than *Campanula lactiflora*. This will grow to a height of approximately 1·5m (5 ft), and displays large loose sprays of flowers in various shades of blue and lilac.

Tyninghame

In Scotland, Tyninghame (a privately-owned garden near Dunbar) provides a fine example of how to make a garden for roses without it becoming a rose garden. Here, one of the main areas chosen for roses was once a hard tennis court. It is enclosed by hedges and walls and its centrepiece is a bower made of light trellis work in which stands a statue of Flora, goddess of flowers, surrounded by roses. The central bower can be seen through very wide arches covered with climbing roses, and around it are large beds containing many lightly-pruned bush roses. But there are many other flowers as well, including delphinium, paeony, alchemilla, phlomis (Jerusalem sage), campanula Loddon Anna, blue flax, rosemary, geranium Johnson's Blue, various honeysuckles, *Cytisus battandieri*, and various lilies including the apricot-coloured martagon lily, Mrs R. O. Backhouse, growing beneath a *Rosa filipes* that is a little less vigorous and certainly more manageable than its variety Kiftsgate. Many of the roses are

Top right: roses among grey-leaved plants in walled gardens at Wisley
Right: original specimen of R. filipes *Kiftsgate at Kiftsgate*

old-fashioned varieties such as Queen of Denmark, Bourbon Queen, Reine des Violettes, Celeste, Rosa Mundi, Empress Josephine, Mme Hardy and Pink Moss, but there are modern roses as well, mainly hybrid teas and shrub roses.

Charleston Manor

Totally different ways of using roses can be seen in other gardens. They can be placed as individual specimens to be seen from all sides, as they are at Charleston Manor, near Seaford in East Sussex. Here, too, a use has been found for a derelict orchard that, cleansed and fairly

Above left: single-flowered Frances E. Lester in foreground, with double-flowered François Joranville behind, in National Rose Society Garden

drastically pruned, provides ideal support for a whole collection of climbing roses, one variety to each apple tree.

Cranborne Manor

At Cranborne Manor, Dorset, roses are used as they often are in cottage gardens, in almost random association with other plants. Design interest is provided by the beds themselves, which are of simple geometric shape hedged with box or lavender – a style called 'parterre'.

Hatfield House

A similar scheme is used most effectively in one of the big parterres at Hatfield House, Hertfordshire. Both these gardens are fine examples of what the late Vita Sackville-West, creator of the lovely gardens at Sissinghurst Castle, Kent, described as her ideal recipe for garden-making, the maximum formality in design combined with the maximum informality in planting.

Sissinghurst Castle

At Sissinghurst Castle, roses are given a degree of segregation in that they dominate one section. But they are allowed to develop freely into big bushes, supported where necessary by substantial timber tripods and revealing their full potentiality as shrubs. Other plants share this section of garden with them, though in a supporting role only. Sissinghurst Castle also has an old orchard that has been made beautiful with roses.

A rose without a thorn? There are, as you can see, endless ways in which roses can be used in the garden. Sprawling kinds such as Max Graf and *Rosa paulii* can be used to cover banks, though it is wise to clear the soil of perennial weeds first because it can be a painful job trying to pull out weeds that have struggled up through a thick cover of thorny rose stems. Not all roses are thorny, however, and some, such as climbing Zéphirine Drouhin, are completely thornless. It would be nice if rose breeders would give some attention to this desirable feature and breed a representative selection of roses, without thorns.

Routine maintenance

There are very few rules to be observed in making a garden for roses. The rose (even the free-growing shrub varieties) will need annual pruning because it is the nature of rose bushes to renew themselves with

Left: roses in herbaceous border at Hidcote Manor

young growth and to allow the old growth to die in time. Pruning allows this natural regeneration to go on without the plants ever becoming unsightly. But because they need pruning the garden must be designed so that the gardener has access to the roses without harming them.

Roses may also need spraying, but that should not create any serious problems since chemicals can be chosen that will not harm other plants growing alongside. Still, it must be possible to get a spraying machine close to them, and the plants in general should not be too far away from a path or other open space. It is physically near impossible to spray big climbers like varieties of *Rosa filipes*, but don't worry as they rarely suffer from anything.

Roses like rich food because they depend on plenty of feeding for the strong annual growth that is so important to them. The best feeding will combine a mulch of manure, spent mushroom compost or decayed garden refuse in spring, supplemented by two or more light top dressings with a rose fertilizer in spring and early summer. The fertilizer presents no problems but the mulch does involve a fairly clear space around the base of each rose bush where it can be spread without smothering small plants. Bulbs can be planted to come through the mulch and after it has been down a few weeks small things such as violas and pansies can be planted to grow over it.

The natural look

It is just as easy to use roses in 'natural' as in formal designs. Even when the beds themselves are geometrically-shaped and symmetrically-arranged it is not essential for the plants within them to be in serried ranks. That is one of the important lessons to be learned from gardens such as Cranborne, Sissinghurst Castle and the new Wisley walled garden; and it can also be learned from engravings of 16th and 17th century gardens, where great formality in design is often accompanied by a very random style of planting.

Whether natural or formal is ultimately a matter of personal preference.

For further information see Choosing and Buying Roses (page 456), Hybrid Teas and Floribundas (page 459), Climbing and Rambling Roses (page 463), Miniature Roses in the Garden (page 466), Shrub Roses (page 469), The History of the Garden Rose (page 474), Routine Care of Roses (page 481), Pruning Roses (page 485) and Rose Pests and Diseases (page 488).

Above: varieties of Amethyste and Auguste Gervais growing on an apple tree in the old orchard at Sissinghurst Castle

Below: roses at Charleston Manor are planted individually, and can thus be seen equally well from all sides.

Herb Gardens

A herb garden can provide a fascinating extra interest. Herbs are beautiful, practical and easy to grow. They are undemanding as regards soil, rarely attacked by pests or diseases and the great majority of them will remain quite happily in the same place for years.

And, of course, herbs are perfect plants for people too busy to grow vegetables but who still want to produce something useful. Here we instruct you on which plants to choose for our Herb Garden that is shown on the next pages.

Herb growing is the oldest form of gardening and was originally practised by those forerunners of modern doctors and chemists, the early herbalists. The writings of these men as they struggled to learn the truth about the properties of plants, with nothing to guide them but fragments of the classics and medieval folklore, appear quaint to modern eyes. In 1629 John Parkinson recommended asters, gentians and mint 'against the biting of a mad dogge', which sounds optimistic – but he was right about the other virtues of mint and of thyme, from which the modern drugs menthol and thymol were derived.

Using your herbs

Keeping a herb garden can be a very satisfying pursuit. The plants not only create a restful atmosphere with their soft colours and aromatic scents, but will also provide a rich source of flavourings for the cook. You can use herbs to improve soups, sauces, meat and fish dishes, and with sweet things like puddings, jams, syrups and creams and sweetmeats such as Turkish delight, traditionally flavoured with rose petals and very easy to make. Herbs will add variety to salads.

Young leaves of cowslip, daisy, dandelion, nasturtium and of the cucumber-tasting burnet and lovage, as well as the flowers of cowslips, pot marigolds, violets and borage, are just some that are pleasant to eat raw. Cowslips, dandelions and elder flowers and berries are among those you can use for making wine. A herb garden will provide raw materials for such other items as pot-pourri, lavender bags, scented sachets (that could save the cost of commercial air fresheners) and hop pillows to help you sleep. Toilet water, excellent hair rinses and cosmetics can also be made from many herbs and flowers.

In the past herbs were grown mainly for medicinal purposes and many people still

An old print of the 16th century showing a formal herb garden in the process of creation. Today's designs may be simpler, but the same basic features still endure

believe it is better to use these old remedies for ordinary ailments than many of the latest drugs. Refreshing herb teas, or tisanes, long accepted in Europe, are made by pouring boiling water on a handful of fresh leaves or a teaspoonful of dried ones. Balm and vervain teas are good nerve tonics, while lime-flower tea with honey makes a perfect nightcap. Rose-hip tea is rich in Vitamin C and comfrey (known as knitbone in the Middle Ages) is a marvellous healing plant if used as a poultice for cuts, bruises and sprains. You can make ointments from herbs simply by simmering them in pure lard.

Once you start, you may find that your herb garden is becoming a profitable hobby, as most people have neither the knowledge nor the space to grow many herbs themselves and unusual ones are difficult to come by in shops. Plants in pots, fresh or dried herbs for cooking, little bags of bouquet garni (a mixture of dried bay, parsley and thyme) to put in casseroles, potpourri, herb pillows and sachets can all be sold or used as gifts.

Where will they grow?

If you've never grown herbs before, first be sure your garden is suitable. While many herbs, like pot marjoram, salad burnet, fennel and creeping thyme are native to Britain and so will grow in any temperate climate, nearly all the aromatic herbs, like lavender, rosemary, rue and most of those with silver foliage, come from the Mediterranean area. Although they will grow in almost any soil, good drainage is essential and they will not survive in heavy, waterlogged clay. They enjoy sun and ideally should be grown in a fairly light soil, sloping gently to the south – but this is a counsel of perfection, not a rule. If you can grow lavender, you can grow most herbs.

Planning a herb garden

Now for the plan. Herbs always look best in a classic setting where the attraction is the total effect. They are simple plants, many having small flowers that would be lost in a border of showy hybrids, but they look beautiful when their varied greens – from the dark, glossy bay to the near white of some artemisias – can be seen together in a pattern of contrasting shapes and heights. A good plan, if it incorporates architectural points of interest, should both pull them together and fit the average oblong plot. To appreciate the classic garden designs it helps if you first know something of how they were originally evolved.

In medieval times all plants were grown

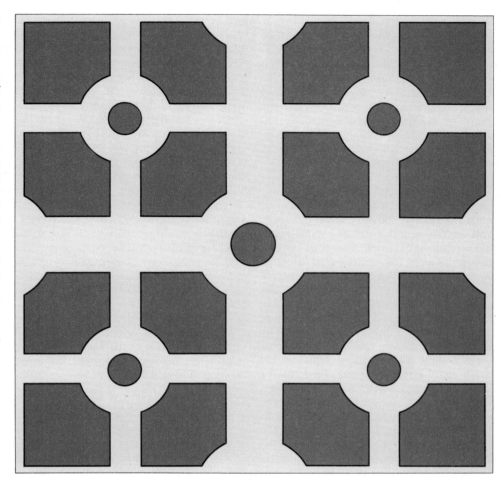

Above: a herb garden design of 1631

strictly for use. Few vegetables, as we know them, were cultivated, and people ate a lot of meat that was flavoured and stuffed with herbs and served with bread and 'sallets'. Gardens were tucked into odd corners of castles and fortified towns, or thickly hedged against wild beasts and robbers. 'Physic' gardens were planted in the grounds of monasteries or abbeys that were sometimes built on top of the ruins of Roman buildings, whose walls dictated squared-off garden plans. The source of water was often a well or fish pond and paths tended to radiate from this, so that, in dry weather, water could be carried to the plants by the shortest route. Thus, in the simplest gardens, cross-paths divided the plot into four beds, the proportions of which could be altered to fit almost any site. Sometimes these beds were cut back to leave more room round the central well or pool and in more complicated designs they were sub-divided for better access and to segregate plants like mint and balm that tend to run rampant and invade others growing nearby.

Water for effect

With time the utilitarian pools and well-heads became increasingly ornamental but even today, when we have hoses and sprinklers to do the watering for us, a small pond still seems the natural centre-piece for a herb garden. You may find it easier to put a decorative cistern or dripping tank against a side wall, with the water falling into it from a dolphin or lion's mask. Even a simple tap, wreathed in creepers, can drip enticingly into a cool, stone basin of very modest size. If you want a water feature decide where it is to go and do not change your mind: the plumbing (and the electricity, if you want a fountain pump) must go in before the paths are laid. Think about lighting points as well at this stage.

Some basic plans are illustrated here. The lines should relate to the shape of the plot and to the house, with paths aligned where possible to the main features. A change of level, even if it is just two steps down from the house terrace, adds a bit of drama to any scheme.

Sunken ponds can be surrounded with paving or kerb stones (see Weeks 9 and 10), but a pond built up from the ground may be safer for children and is easy to construct. A strong, circular or D-shaped wall, 30–40cm (12–16 in) high is water-proofed with a plastics liner, the top edge

167

of which is hidden by a wide stone or concrete rim. This will then act as a seat or garden table. The Roman writer Pliny, about the year 100 AD, describes such a pool-cum-dining table in his garden in Tuscany, where large dishes were placed round the rim and the smaller ones, in the shape of ducks or boats, floated on the water. A summer meal in a sweetly-scented herb garden, round such a pool, is some people's idea of heaven.

What kind of path?

Grass paths are not really suitable for herb gardens as they are tricky to mow and tend to wear in patches. It is better to use paving slabs, brick, gravel or poured concrete, with the main paths at least 90cm (3 ft) wide. While gravel or concrete can be of any width, if you decide to use concrete slabs or brick you must conform to the widths they enforce: bricks measure 23×10cm (9×4 in) and you can buy easily-handled concrete slabs approximately 45cm (18 in) square. You can lay brick in herringbone or basketwork patterns, or lengthwise, bonded as if in a wall. If paths are slightly sunken, the excavated soil can be added to the beds to help with drainage. Later you can plant a few gaps between the bricks with creeping thyme, mint and other plants that release their scent when trodden on.

Somewhere to sit

As the amount of work needed to maintain a herb garden is less than on a vegetable plot, provide yourself with seating to enjoy your leisure. In the days of the troubadors, seating was often merely banks thrown up against the castle wall and carpeted with grass and flowers. Sometimes it resembled a raised, stone flowerbed where people could sit on an upholstery of living thyme or camomile – you can see examples in the reconstructed herb gardens at the famous English garden at Sissinghurst in Kent, and in the Queen's Garden at the Royal Botanical Gardens, Kew. For hot days you could place a wooden seat in a simply con-over it. You can grow wall fruit here: both cordoned stone fruit – like Morello cherries that fruit well on a north wall – and figs, vines, cultivated blackberries, loganberries or pears. Choose climbing roses for their fragrance, bearing in mind that rich reds and deep pinks would be more in keeping than modern orange-reds. Hops are beautiful perennial climbers with decorative leaves and their female flowers develop from the cone-structed arbour or 'herber', set at the end of a cross path and with a paved space in front of it. Jasmine or honeysuckle could be trained over it.

Giving seclusion

For the true atmosphere of an old herb garden you need the seclusion afforded by enclosing walls, fences or hedges. Trellis can be added to a low wall or fence and useful or scented climbing plants trained shaped catkins used for hop pillows and flavouring beer. The strongly-scented old-fashioned sweet pea is also suitable.

The pergola has a history as long as that of the cultivated grape, and if there is room you could run one down a side of the garden or conceal the 'service area' behind it. Early-ripening varieties of grape vines for fruit or wine-making are now on the market and a vine pergola is beautiful in summer and autumn; as vines are deciduous, it will not make the garden dark in winter.

Three interesting old fruit trees in keeping with a classic plan for a larger garden would be mulberry, medlar and quince. Lime trees, to make lime-flower tea, the French *tilleul*, might be pleached (the stems interlaced) to form a screen. The honey that bees make from lime-flower nectar is said to be the best in the world and a bee-hive would be a fascinating addition to a herb garden. There is a medium-sized lime, *T. mongolica*, that seems to be safe for bees and unattractive to aphides.

Lastly the elder, a native British shrub, is the most interesting and historic of all herbs, having a wide range of uses. Try to find space in your garden for an elder bush at all costs as it is an infallible protection against all evils including witches, lightning and rheumatism.

Note Of the many plants mentioned in this series only the berries of lily-of-the-valley and ivy are actually poisonous, but excessive consumption of some herbs can cause ill effects – so do be careful, especially where children are concerned.

Our Herb Garden design faces south west, so the garden has a good mixture of sun and shade. The fountain is on the shady side and the arbour in the sun, but if your garden faces a different direction you can reverse them and adjust the planting. The 9m or 27 ft wide plan on a metre or yard module is not difficult to copy as the circles are centred on the mid-lines of the paths. If your garden is wider you can widen the beds, if narrower you may lose one or both of the side beds. The length of the garden will determine the amount of space beyond the pergola for your service area.

Our Herb Garden layout is based on classic principles and incorporates a greenhouse at the far end beyond a pergola, a fountain flowing into a small pond half-way along the left-hand border, and an arbour with a seat on the opposite side, all connected by stone paths.

Left: rosemary, Rosmarinus officinalis, *for meat flavouring*

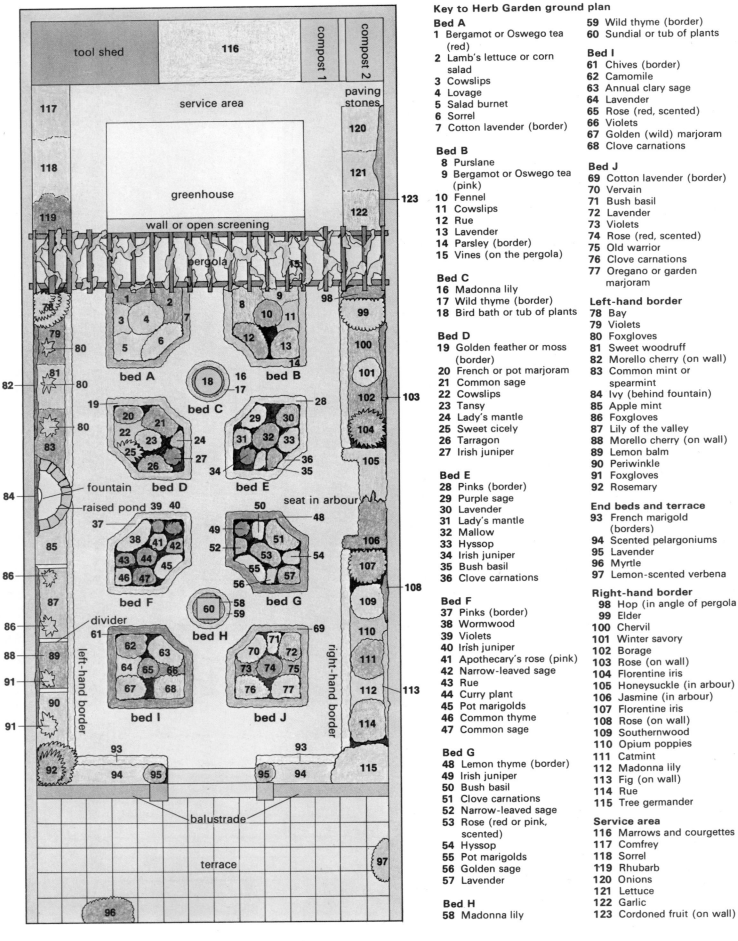

Key to Herb Garden ground plan

Bed A
1 Bergamot or Oswego tea (red)
2 Lamb's lettuce or corn salad
3 Cowslips
4 Lovage
5 Salad burnet
6 Sorrel
7 Cotton lavender (border)

Bed B
8 Purslane
9 Bergamot or Oswego tea (pink)
10 Fennel
11 Cowslips
12 Rue
13 Lavender
14 Parsley (border)
15 Vines (on the pergola)

Bed C
16 Madonna lily
17 Wild thyme (border)
18 Bird bath or tub of plants

Bed D
19 Golden feather or moss (border)
20 French or pot marjoram
21 Common sage
22 Cowslips
23 Tansy
24 Lady's mantle
25 Sweet cicely
26 Tarragon
27 Irish juniper

Bed E
28 Pinks (border)
29 Purple sage
30 Lavender
31 Lady's mantle
32 Mallow
33 Hyssop
34 Irish juniper
35 Bush basil
36 Clove carnations

Bed F
37 Pinks (border)
38 Wormwood
39 Violets
40 Irish juniper
41 Apothecary's rose (pink)
42 Narrow-leaved sage
43 Rue
44 Curry plant
45 Pot marigolds
46 Common thyme
47 Common sage

Bed G
48 Lemon thyme (border)
49 Irish juniper
50 Bush basil
51 Clove carnations
52 Narrow-leaved sage
53 Rose (red or pink, scented)
54 Hyssop
55 Pot marigolds
56 Golden sage
57 Lavender

Bed H
58 Madonna lily

59 Wild thyme (border)
60 Sundial or tub of plants

Bed I
61 Chives (border)
62 Camomile
63 Annual clary sage
64 Lavender
65 Rose (red, scented)
66 Violets
67 Golden (wild) marjoram
68 Clove carnations

Bed J
69 Cotton lavender (border)
70 Vervain
71 Bush basil
72 Lavender
73 Violets
74 Rose (red, scented)
75 Old warrior
76 Clove carnations
77 Oregano or garden marjoram

Left-hand border
78 Bay
79 Violets
80 Foxgloves
81 Sweet woodruff
82 Morello cherry (on wall)
83 Common mint or spearmint
84 Ivy (behind fountain)
85 Apple mint
86 Foxgloves
87 Lily of the valley
88 Morello cherry (on wall)
89 Lemon balm
90 Periwinkle
91 Foxgloves
92 Rosemary

End beds and terrace
93 French marigold (borders)
94 Scented pelargoniums
95 Lavender
96 Myrtle
97 Lemon-scented verbena

Right-hand border
98 Hop (in angle of pergola
99 Elder
100 Chervil
101 Winter savory
102 Borage
103 Rose (on wall)
104 Florentine iris
105 Honeysuckle (in arbour)
106 Jasmine (in arbour)
107 Florentine iris
108 Rose (on wall)
109 Southernwood
110 Opium poppies
111 Catmint
112 Madonna lily
113 Fig (on wall)
114 Rue
115 Tree germander

Service area
116 Marrows and courgettes
117 Comfrey
118 Sorrel
119 Rhubarb
120 Onions
121 Lettuce
122 Garlic
123 Cordoned fruit (on wall)

The service area

First, then, we will consider the vital area between the pergola and the far end of the garden. Here you can place a small shed for tools and storage, and two compost heaps, one for building up, the other for use. The inclusion of a greenhouse behind the pergola will save you money, enabling you to propagate herbs quickly from cuttings or seed; to overwinter tender plants like the scented pelargoniums; and to bring on deciduous herbs in pots for early use, keeping some going after the winter begins. Plants you can grow in your greenhouse include tomatoes, peppers, cucumbers and aubergines.

Between the shed, greenhouse and compost heaps – if you want to branch out beyond herbs – is just enough space for a few easy vegetables – perhaps marrows or courgettes, a root of rhubarb, a few rows of onions or shallots, and some lettuce. Fruits such as cordoned apples or pears, and loganberries or thornless blackberries, can be grown or trained against the walls.

The main garden

Now for the garden proper. Details of walls and pergola plantings are included on page 368 but there are two interesting shrubs you can grow against the terrace walls. One is the lemon-scented *Lippia citriodora* (verbena), which might go against the sunniest side wall. Slightly tender, it will require a little protection in winter, but it is worth the trouble. Its lemon-flavoured leaves can be used in cooking, or dried for pot-pourri. You might also like to try *Myrtus communis* (myrtle), a glossy-leaved, white-flowered little evergreen. Once part of every bride's bouquet, it is aromatic, and likes a warm site, as befits its Greek origins.

When devising the planting scheme you must first differentiate between shade-loving and sun-loving plants, as well as between the different heights involved so as to avoid putting an enormous plant in front of a small one. Note if the plants are evergreen, and the predominant foliage colours, so that you can arrange them in harmonies or contrasts. Some aromatic Mediterranean herbs are silvery or greyish, but shade and damp-loving plants, having no need for protective hairs or 'powder', are usually green.

Flower colour is secondary to leaves and roots, but some medicinal plants do have lovely flowers and can be included. Among them are two shade-loving plants from which heart stimulants have been made: *Digitalis purpurea* (foxglove), a spike of which has the unexpected use of prolonging the lives of other flowers in a vase, and *Convallaria majalis* (lily of the valley), which is deciduous and tends to ramp, although the scent from its white, bell-like flowers is legendary. The best form is Fortin's Giant, which flowers a little later than the more common varieties.

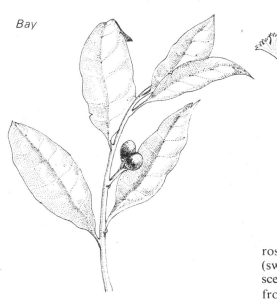

Bay

Parsley

Lilium candidum (madonna lily), is entirely edible, and has a long herbal tradition, as have several of the mallows and *Papaver somniferum* (opium poppy), a useful annual to use as a gap-filler. The white *Iris florentina* (Florentine iris), from whose dried roots orris powder is made, is a beautiful form of *I. germanica* and the fleur-de-lis of French heraldry. *Monarda didyma* (bergamot) is of American extraction, has bright red or pink flowers, and appreciates shade in dry soil. It makes a pleasant tisane, hence its name, Oswego tea. Perhaps the best-loved herbal flower is *Dianthus caryophyllus* (old clove carnation or gilliflower), particularly the dark red one, which was once employed for spicing wines and is still so used in Chartreuse. Its edible flowers, like those of the violet, can be eaten raw in salads, or candied, and the dried petals can be put in scented cushions.

Rose petals have always been put to many uses, especially those of *Rosa gallica officinalis* (apothecary's rose), and *R. centifolia* (old cabbage rose). *R. damascena triginpetala* is grown for attar of roses in Bulgaria, and shrub roses noted for their petals include the scented hybrid musks, the China and Bourbon roses and the hybrids of *R. rubiginosa* (sweet briar), the latter three also having scented leaves. Try to choose your roses from a specialist while they are in flower, look for fragrance and avoid modern hybrids with overlarge blooms and the orange shades that would ruin your soft

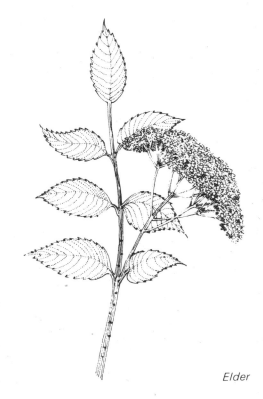

Elder

colour scheme.

A few shrubs to form a 'backbone' to the garden are essential. Rose bushes could be the central features for some beds. *Laurus nobilis* (bay), and a *Sambucus nigra* (elder) – the latter a shrub of many uses – might soften the angles where the pergola meets the boundary. *Rosmarinus officinalis* (a rosemary bush) and *Teucrium fruticans* (tree germander), with similar flowers but blue-grey, evergreen leaves, could serve the same purpose below the ends of the terrace. Four *Juniperus communis hibernica* (Irish juniper) shrubs set towards the inner corners of the four central beds would emphasize the middle of the design, and provide some delicious juniper berries as well.

Asperula odorata (sweet woodruff) and *Vinca major* (periwinkle) are herbs that you can grow in the shade. The former has little white flowers and starry leaves whorled round its stems. Its delicious scent when dried makes it ideal for a linen cupboard. Periwinkle is a rampant growing plant that will gladly occupy the whole of your shady bed. Its historical

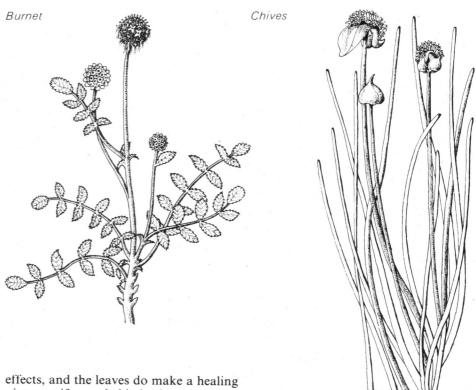

Burnet

Chives

effects, and the leaves do make a healing ointment if pounded in lard.

Plants for edging

The formal design of the herb garden requires formal planting, so edge each bed with neat, low plants and put your taller herbs in the middle. Alternate beds could have silver and green edging. Silver-leaved dianthus are perfect where there is lime in the soil and the woolly, grey *Santolina chamaecyparissus* (cotton lavender), growing 75cm (2½ ft) high, and its dwarf form *S.c.nana*, 23cm (9 in) high, make traditional edgings for knot gardens (old-fashioned, formal, bedding-type gardens). Santolina should be cut back hard in spring to encourage neat growth, and the aromatic clippings dried, to keep moths out of wardrobes. The clippings of the silver-leaved artemisia can be similarly used.

Lavandula spica Hidcote or Munstead Dwarf amethyst-flowered dwarf lavender makes a good grey edging, but is inclined to spread – getting 'leggy' in the process – and so must be replaced. If you try to cut it back very much, you will be in danger of killing it. *Nepeta cataria* (catmint), is another desirable grey and mauve edging plant, although it does tend to flop. *Thymus citriodora* (lemon thyme), which grows to a height of 15cm (6 in) and produces tiny, bright, lime-green leaves, edges well but creeps outwards, rooting as it goes. Purists with electric shears might edge all the beds with *Buxus* (dwarf box), although some would say this carries formality too far, at the expense of

variety – but being neat, box might be suitable for the side beds and service area.

A quick-growing edging plant is *Chrysanthemum parthenium* or *Pyrethrum parthenifolium* (golden feather or moss), the old herbal name of which is feverfew. While perfectly hardy it is usually raised

Common mint

Rosemary

name of 'sorcerer's violet' alludes to the times when its leaves were chewed to stop a nose bleed, its 'young tops' made into a conserve to prevent nightmares, and its long stems twined and tied around a person's legs to allay cramp. It is still used medicinally for its astringent and tonic

Wild marjoram

Fennel

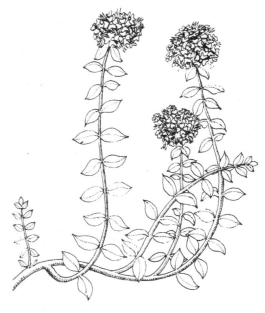

from seed as a half-hardy annual in a temperature of 15°C (60°F), pricked out and hardened off before planting. If you allow it to produce its white daisies and set seed you will never, thereafter, be without its cheerful, lime-yellow leaves that are such a joy in winter.

Another annual edging plant is *Tagetes patula* (French marigold) – choose either lemon or primrose, but not orange, as that will clash with rose pinks and mauves. This old plant has a new reputation for repelling whitefly and other insect pests.

Petroselinum crispum (parsley) makes a perfect green edging, but you must sow it *in situ* every year, and a clump of *Allium schoeneprasum* (chives) can be divided and replanted to make an enchanting grassy green edge with long-lasting, thrift-like flowers.

Herbs for the kitchen
Turning to the formal beds and the herbs, you can start by planting a handful of green salads: the cucumber-tasting perennial *Poterium sanguisorba or Sanguisorba minor* (burnet) from the chalk downs of England; *Valerianella olitoria* (corn salad or lamb's lettuce), producing biennial rosettes, and used as a lettuce substitute in winter; refreshingly sharp-tasting *Rumex acetosa* (sorrel), a perennial for salads or spinach soup; *Myrrhis odorata* (sweet cicely) with lacy, fern-like leaves and edible roots; and *Portulaca oleracea*, (purslane), a half-hardy annual, always popular in salads in France, and once considered a certain cure for 'blastings by lightning or planets and burning of gunpowder'.

Last but not least come the flavouring herbs, listed in alphabetical order of their better-known common names:
Melissa officinalis (balm), a perennial for the shady wall bed, growing up to 90cm (3 ft), with a tendency to ramp. It has lemon-flavoured leaves which, fresh or dried, can be used to flavour stuffings or stews, or to make a tea that is famous for its soothing effect on the nerves.
Ocimum minimum (bush basil), 15–30cm (6–12 in), from tropical India, clove-like and perfect for tomato dishes.
Anthriscus cerefolium (chervil) is delicious in omelet *fines herbes*.
Foeniculum officinale (fennel), 1·2m (4 ft), is handsome and feathery and specially good with fish.
Allium sativum (garlic) is childishly simple to grow – sown in mid spring it will be ripe by early autumn.
Hyssopus officinalis (hyssop), 60cm (24 in), is a shrubby semi-evergreen, with an aromatic flavour, that produces brilliant blue flowers in early autumn (August). At one time it was used to poultice bruises.
Ligusticum scoticum or Levisticum officinalis (lovage), 90–120cm (3–4 ft), is a magnificent, celery-flavoured plant, invaluable in stews, onion soup and salads.
Calendula officinalis (pot marigold), is a hardy annual, whose petals can be eaten in salads, or used for flavouring stews, and substituted for saffron.
Origanum onites (French or pot marjoram) is easily grown, as is *O. vulgare* (wild marjoram). *O. majorana* (oregano, known as sweet, knotted or garden marjoram) tastes best.

Wild thyme

Mentha spicata (common mint or spearmint) a rampant perennial 30–60cm (12–24 in), can be used for mint sauce, but the connoisseurs among you may prefer the woolly-leaved *M. rotundifolia* (apple mint) as it dries well and keeps its colour. There are many other mints, some decorative, some creeping. Examples of the latter are *M. pulegium* (pennyroyal), 2–3cm (1 in) high and *M. requienii* (Spanish or Corsican mint).
Ruta graveolens (rue), stewing herb with unmistakable aromatic blue-green foliage, is a dramatic evergreen.
Salvia officinalis (common sage), the form used in cooking, is an evergreen shrub with grey-green, gold variegated or purple-leaved forms. *S. angustifolia* has large blue flowers and tangy taste. A ravishingly pretty annual, *S. horminum* (annual clary sage), was once used for treating eye complaints, and has leaf-like mauve or pink bracts that last longer in water than any flowers.
Satureia montana (winter savory), is an evergreen used for pork pies and game.
Artemisia dracunculus (tarragon), the best form of which is French tarragon, needs protection in winter but is the perfect herb for chicken dishes, omelets and eggs.
Thymus vulgaris, (common thyme) 30cm (12 in), is a popular bushy, evergreen herb requiring no description. *T. serpyllum* (wild thyme) is a prostrate, and *T. × citriodorus* (lemon thyme) a creeping variety.
Verbena officinalis (vervain), a sacred herb in pagan times, acts as a proven cure for headaches when made into tea.

As you will have seen, our Herb Garden contained not only herbs as such but some of the more conventional fruit trees and flowers that are also used in cooking and confectionery, for cosmetic or medicinal preparations, or as the basis for decorative gifts based on dried herbs.

Here we divide herbs into shrubs, perennials, and hardy and half-hardy annuals. Many shrubs and perennials can be bought from garden centres, but if your choice is not available you can order it from a specialist herb nursery. Hardy and half-hardy annuals, however, must be raised from seed.

A great number of aromatic herbs come from the Mediterranean and so appreciate a sunny position and good drainage. They do best on sandy, limy or chalky soils, so if your soil is heavy and acid you may have to plant them in raised beds (with the soil level above normal level) lightened with cinders or sand and dressed with lime or soil conditioners based on gypsum or alginates. They are marked 'MED' in the following groups.

SHRUBS AND TREES

When planting a shrub or tree, remember that it pays to dig a hole wider and deeper than the size of the shrub might seem to merit; make the hole at least twice as deep and wide as the root system, preferably more. Break up the bottom soil and add compost or other nourishment – a Mediterranean shrub will not need much – and plant it carefully, noting the soil mark on the stem for the correct planting depth. Spread the roots and work in some light soil between them. Fill up the hole and tread firmly, but not too hard. Water in dry weather and the young shrub will soon settle down.

Neat, bushy shrubs will not need staking, but if a shrub looks top-heavy and as if it might be blown loose by the wind, put a stake in *before* planting it, to avoid driving the stake through the roots. Occasionally, you should check that the tie is not too tight.

Bay (*Laurus nobilis*) MED evergreen, up to 4m (12 ft) but it can be trimmed; will stand shade.
Cotton lavender (*Santolina chamaecyparissus*) MED evergreen, 75cm (2½ ft); clip back hard in mid spring (March) to encourage neat growth.
Curry plant (*Helichrysum angustifolium*) MED evergreen, 60cm (24 in); clip over in mid to late spring (March to April).

Elder (*Sambucus nigra*) 2·4m (8 ft). Wild form is rarely sold so you may have to find a seedling near an established bush, or else raise your own plant, either from seed or from hedge cuttings. Nurserymen stock the gold form, *S. n. aurea*.
(Tree) Germander (*Teucrium fruticans*) MED evergreen, 60–150cm (2–5 ft). Needs protection of a wall in cold districts. Prune back after flowering to encourage new growth.
Hyssop (*Hyssopus officinalis*) MED semi-evergreen, 60cm (24 in); clip over in mid spring (March).
Juniper, Irish (*Juniperus communis hibernica*) Evergreen, 3m (10 ft); slow growing. Thrives on lime and chalk soils.
Lavender (*Lavandula spica*) MED evergreen, 45–90cm (1½–3 ft). Trim over in mid spring (March), but do not cut into the old wood.
Myrtle (*Myrtus communis*) Evergreen, 90cm–3m (3–10 ft) depending on situation. Fairly tender. Needs sheltered, sunny position and winter protection in cold districts.
Old warrior (*Artemisia pontica*) MED evergreen, 30-60cm (12-24 in). Grows anywhere.
Roses The apothecary's rose (*Rosa gallica officinalis*), old cabbage rose (*R. centifolia*) and any other red or pink, scented varieties. Plant when dormant during mild weather from late autumn to late spring (October to April). Dig bed well before planting and dress with manure, compost or peat with addition of bonemeal well mixed into soil.
Rosemary (*Rosmarinus officinalis*) MED evergreen, 1·2–3m (4–6 ft). Can be kept in shape with secateurs.
Rue (*Ruta graveolens* Jackman's Blue) MED evergreen, 45cm (18 in). Trim in mid spring (March to April).
(Common) Sage (*Salvia officinalis*) MED evergreen, 45cm (18 in). All sages prefer the sun and do not grow well on acid soil, including the narrow-leaved (*S. angustifolia*), purple-leaved (*S. purpurea*), and golden (*S. o. variegata*).
(Winter) Savory (*Satureia montana*) MED evergreen, 30cm (12 in).
Southernwood (*Artemisia abrotanum*) MED evergreen, 60 cm (24 in). Can be trimmed if out of shape.
(Lemon-scented) Verbena (*Lippia citriodora*) 2·4–3cm (8–10 ft) Tender. Needs the shelter of a sunny wall and, in cold districts, winter protection of straw or bracken secured with light sacking or plastics sheeting. Cut back young shoots near to old wood in mid spring (March).
Wormwood (*Artemisia absinthium*) MED 90–150cm (3–5 ft), can be trimmed.

PERENNIALS

For planting, the ground should be well dug over and free from weeds. Plant 15–23cm (6–9 in) apart and not deeper than the original soil mark. Spread the roots well and fill in with light soil. Firm well and keep watered in dry weather till the plant is established. Spreading plants can be propagated by root division in spring.

Roots and underground stems of some perennials may well spread beyond the confines of the border and intrude between the paving. If you wish to prevent this happening you could build an underground concrete wall along the edge of the paving, extending about 25–30cm (10–12 in) below ground level. Alternatively, you can plant in large pots sunk into the soil, or in an old sink.

(Lemon) Balm (*Melissa officinalis*) 90cm (3 ft). Thrives best in rich, damp soil and shade but ramps exceedingly and if given ideal conditions must be contained.
Bergamot or Oswego tea (*Monarda didyma*) 75–150cm (2½–5 ft) depending on richness of soil and variety. Spreads slowly, prefers damp, rich soil and will grow in light shade.
(Salad) Burnet (*Poterium sanguisorba*, or *sanguisorba minor*) 45–60cm (18–24 in). Likes fairly light soil but is not fussy. Often sown outdoors in late spring (April) and planted out about 30cm (12 in) apart.

Tarragon

Catmint (*Nepeta cataria*) 30cm (12 in). Likes a sunny, well-drained position but add compost if very dry. Cut back dead heads in late spring (April) as they help protect the plant in winter.

(Clove) Carnation (*Dianthus caryophyllus*) 15–45cm (6–18 in). Forms of hardy border carnations, the most suitable for a herb garden being Fingo Clove, Gipsy Clove or Perfect Clove. Well drained sunny position in good, ordinary garden soil but do not bury the stem. Plant 40cm (15 in) apart.

Camomile (*Anthemis nobilis*) Prostrate. Very strong, needs no special conditions.

Chives (*Allium schoenoprasum*) MED 15cm (6 in). Remove flower-heads as soon as formed if using leaves for garnishing. Plant anywhere.

Comfrey (*Symphytum officinale*) 1·2–1·5m (4–5 ft). or **Russian comfrey** (*S. caucasium*) 60–90cm (2–3 ft). Any soil. Very strong with deep taproot and if hoed off will spring again. Excess plants can be controlled by cutting them at ground level and applying a little sodium chlorate to the cut root surface with a paint brush.

Cowslip (*Primula veris*) 15–20cm (6–8 in) Grow as primrose. Keep moist in dry weather. Prefers some shade in summer, likes rich soil. Roots can be divided after flowering.

Fennel (*Foeniculum officinale*) 1·2m (4 ft). Light soil and situation. Remove seed heads as otherwise excess seedlings can be produced.

Foxglove (*Digitalis purpurea*) 90–150cm (3–5 ft). Biennial. Sow in the open from early to late summer (May to July). They prefer dappled shade. The plants are ready to be put in their flowering positions in September.

(Florentine) Iris (*Iris florentina*) 90cm (3 ft). A form of *Iris germanica*, it likes its roots firmly planted but the backs of the rhizomes showing just above surface level; ordinary garden soil. In sun-baked situations increases thickly and can be divided after flowering every third year.

Lady's mantle (*Alchemilla vulgaris*), or silver-leaved *Alchemilla alpina*, 30cm (12 in). An easy plant with no problems except that it may produce many seedlings which should be removed.

Lily of the valley (*Convallaria majalis*) 23cm (9 in). Best form, Fortin's Giant. Prefers shade and rich, slightly damp soil. Has a tendency to ramp.

Elder, Sambucus nigra, *is one of the most interesting and historic of all herbs, and reputed to be protection against such evils as witches, lightning and rheumatism*

Lovage (*Ligusticum scoticum* or *Levisticum officinalis*) 90–120cm (3–4 ft). Sun or shade but prefers moist, rich soil. Will grow in light soil if compost is added. Propagate from seed.

(Madonna) Lily (*Lilium candidum*) 90–120cm (3–4 ft). A temperamental plant. Its main needs are sun, excellent drainage, an occasional handful of leaf-mould and to be left alone. It may die if moved. *L. regale* can be an easier, if not traditional, substitute.

Mallows (*Malva sylvestris*) The common blue mallow, 45cm (18 in), biennial or perennial. The **musk mallow** (*M. moschata* 60–75cm (2–2½ ft) is biennial to perennial, pale pink; **marsh mallow** (*Althea officinalis*) 60–90cm (2–3 ft) prefers the cool back of a border and moist soil.

Marjoram (*Origanum onites*) French or pot marjoram, 30cm (12 in). Ordinary garden soil. **Golden (wild) marjoram** (*O. vulgare aureum*) 30–60cm (12–24 in), needs part shade as the leaves scorch in too hot sun. The best-flavoured is known as **oregano** – sweet, knotted or garden marjoram (*O. majorana*) 30–60cm (12–24 in). It can be kept in a pot in the greenhouse in the winter.

(Common) Mint or spearmint (*Mentha spicata*) and **apple mint** (*M. rotundifolia*) 30–60cm (12–24 in). All mints prefer rich, damp soil and slight shade but are very invasive and must be contained. **Pennyroyal** (*M. pulegium*) is a creeper.

Periwinkle (*Vinca major, Vinca minor* and varieties) 10–15cm (4–6 in). Tough, hardy ground cover, will grow in shade.

Pinks (*Dianthus* hybrids) 23cm (9 in).

Chervil

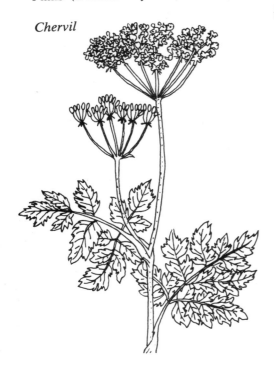

Plant Old World Garden pinks as hardy perennials in sunny positions.

Sorrel (*Rumex acetosa*) 45cm (18 in). Perennial that is grown from seed sown in drills in spring.

Sweet cicely (*Myrrhis odorata*) 90–120cm (3–4 ft). Enjoys damp and shade.

Tarragon (*Artemisia dracunculus*) 45–60cm (18–24 in). Likes a sunny position and good drainage.

Tansy (*Tanacetum vulgare*) 15–30cm (6–12 in). Very hardy in any soil.

Thyme (*Thymus vulgaris*) The bushy, common thyme, 30cm (12 in), and **wild thyme** (*T. serpyllum*), prostrate. Plant any time. The creeping **lemon thyme** (*T. × citriodorus*) 15cm (6 in) spreads slowly Plant in light soil. All these evergreens prefer sun.

Vervain (*Verbena officinalis*) 45cm (18 in) A perennial downland herb, tough and hardy.

Violet (*Viola odorata*) 10cm (4 in). Ordinary well-prepared and dug garden soil. Does not like heavy clay. Can be lifted and replanted if it becomes congested. Stands shade.

(Sweet) Woodruff (*Asperula odorata*) 15cm (6 in). Woodland plant, likes moisture and shade.

Winter savory

Herbs in the greenhouse

Most herbs, whether shrubby, perennial or annual, can be grown from seed, although shrubs and perennials give quicker results if bought from a nursery. Seed sown in the greenhouse in early to mid spring (February to March) produces plants quicker than hardy plants sown later out of doors.

Vervain

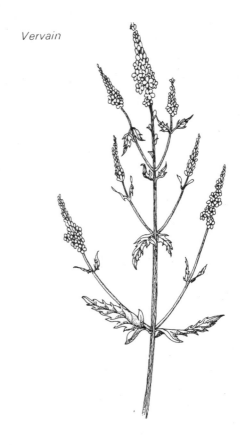

Fill a box to within 13mm (½ in) of the brim with moist seed-growing compost such as J.I. seed compost. Pat down till firm and sprinkle seed thinly all over the surface; then add a thin layer of soil, just enough to cover the seed completely, and water lightly. Cover with a sheet of glass and a sheet of brown paper and leave in the greenhouse until the seeds start to sprout. Remove paper and glass and keep moist but not wet. Prick out when the seedlings are big enough to handle and keep in boxes in the greenhouse as long as frost is expected, then harden off by setting the boxes outdoors or in a frame, watering from time to time until the plants are big enough to plant out. Seed of many hardy perennials may also be sown outdoors in early summer (May) as for hardy annuals.

Half-hardy annuals are propagated in the same way, the difference being that they must be sown in mid to late spring (March to April) in a temperature of 60°F (15°C). If the greenhouse cannot be raised to this temperature use a heated propagator.

HALF-HARDY ANNUALS

(Bush) Basil (*Ocimum minimum*) 15–30cm (6–12 in). Sow late spring (March to April) preferably in sterilized soil. Keep in a pot in the greenhouse in winter.
Golden feather or moss (*Chrysanthemum parthenium* or *Pyrethrum parthenifolium*) 10–13cm (4–5 in). For edging. Hardy but best treated as half-hardy. Sow seeds 3mm ($\frac{1}{8}$ in) deep.
(French) Marigold (*Tagetes patula*) 23–30cm (9–12 in). Pale yellow colour is good for edging.

HARDY ANNUALS

Seed of hardy plants can be sown outdoors. Sow vegetables in drills, flowers in patches. First break down the soil to a fine tilth using a rake and treading down any large lumps. This is not a job for wet weather or for wet, heavy soil. A drill is

Basil

made with the corner of the hoe drawn in a straight line cutting a little channel about 2–3cm (1 in) deep, or with the flat of a draw hoe about 10–15cm (4–6 in) across depending on the seeds. If sowing in a patch the top surface is drawn to one side. Sow the seed thinly and cover with a thin layer of soil so that the seeds are hidden but not deeply buried. Pat the soil down and keep watered and, while the seedlings are at a tender stage, keep them moist. If the weather is dry and very sunny, try to give them some shade. A protective cloche may be used. When seedlings are bigger they should be thinned 15cm (6 in) apart.
Borage (*Borago officinalis*) 45cm (18 in). Sow anywhere in 2–3cm (1 in) holes and thin to 15cm (6 in) apart.
Chervil (*Anthriscus cerefolium*) 30–45cm (12–18 in). Sow in a drill or patch.
(Annual) Clary sage (*Salvia horminum*) 45cm (18 in). Sow where it is to flower late spring to early summer (April to May).
Garlic (*Allium sativum*) 30–90cm (1–3 ft). Treat as an annual. Sow the cloves in a row in mid spring (March).
Lamb's lettuce or corn salad (*Valerianella olitoria*) 15–23cm (6–9 in). Biennial. Sow late summer or early autumn (July–August) for winter's use, putting the seeds

about 13mm ($\frac{1}{2}$ in) deep.
(Pot) Marigold (*Calendula officinalis*) 30–45cm (12–18 in). Sow thinly in patches late spring to early summer (April to May).
Parsley (*Petroselinum crispum*) 15–30cm (6–12 in). Sow in a wide drill as an edging from mid spring (March) onwards. As it is slow to germinate, taking six weeks or more, it helps to pour a kettle of boiling water along the drill before sowing. (Radish seed sown lightly along the row gives you a catch crop and shows you where the row is.)
(Opium) Poppy (*Papaver somniferum*) 75cm ($2\frac{1}{2}$ ft). Sow thinly where it is to grow from mid spring to early summer (March to May). Seeds 6mm ($\frac{1}{4}$ in) deep. Be sure to thin out early. Can be sown in mid autumn (September) for flowering the following year.
Purslane (*Portulaca oleracea*) 15cm (6 in). Sow in early summer (May).

Note Of the many plants mentioned in this series only the berries of lily of the valley and ivy are actually poisonous, but excessive consumption of some herbs can cause ill effects – so do be careful, especially where children are concerned.

Sorrel

Clary Sage

Colour Schemes for Spring Bedding

It is perhaps a pity that a more attractive word than 'bedding' could not have been found to describe the arrangement of brilliant flowering plants in the garden, for this lack-lustre description may well have contributed to the poor image the practice has acquired over the years in some gardening circles. With just a little thought and imagination the most striking effects can be achieved, as we show here and on the following pages for spring bedding.

The image of bedding arrangements was not improved by the Victorians, who displayed an appalling predilection for concentric circles and parallel stripes in primary colours, and committed such flagrant acts of bad taste as planting scarlet pelargonium with yellow calceolaria and rampant blue lobelia.

However, excesses of the past should not be allowed to disguise the fact that bedding can prove most rewarding, provided you display a basic appreciation of form, line and colour. There is an art to successful bedding, but it can be learnt.

Form

The form of the border lies in the contrast between different shapes, textures and plant heights, as well as the more obvious variations in colour.

To achieve an emphatic change in height you could plant ricinus (castor-oil plant), canna (Indian shot) or zea (variegated maize), all commonly used in bedding. Less dominating plants such as grevillea (silky oak), the creamy-yellow and green *Abutilon savitzii*, and many grey-foliaged plants, notably kinds of cineraria and centaurea – the easiest-grown of which is probably cineraria Silverdust – can also be helpful in making a contrast of this type.

Another way you can vary height is to use standards or half standards of certain plants. These are plants grown with the stem kept bare up to a height varying between 45–90cm (18 in–3 ft), where the head (of branches, leaves and flowers) is allowed to form. Pelargoniums, fuchsias and heliotrope are frequently treated in this way, and can look especially effective if they are used with a complementary carpet of their own kind.

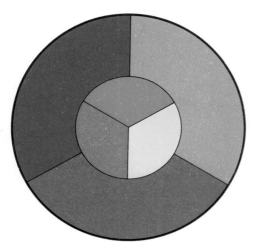

Above: any primary colour (inner ring) combines happily with the results of mixing shown opposite on outer ring
Left: two tulips of differing height on forget-me-not and wallflower carpet

SPRING BEDDING SCHEMES

CARPET		MAIN CONTRAST	
Plant	Colour	Plant	Colour
Wallflower	golden	Tulip	scarlet
Siberian wallflower	golden	Tulip	black or deep purple
Viola (winter-flowering)	golden	Hyacinth	dark blue
Viola (winter-flowering)	golden	Tulip (early spring-flowering)	red/gold (bi-colour)
Wallflower	ruby	Tulip	cream
Siberian wallflower Forget-me-not	golden (40 per cent) blue (60 per cent)	Tulip Tulip	purple orange
Siberian wallflower Forget-me-not	golden (40 per cent) blue (60 per cent)	Tulip Tulip	scarlet gold
Forget-me-not	blue	Tulip	pale pink
Forget-me-not	blue	Tulip Tulip	purple lavender blue
Forget-me-not	blue	Tulip (lily- flowered)	deep pink
Viola	white	Hyacinth	bright blue
Alyssum	white	Tulip (early spring-flowering) Tulip (early spring-flowering)	purple white
Wallflower	pink	Tulip	pink
Polyanthus	pink shades	Tulip	rich pink
Polyanthus	yellow shades	Tulip (late spring-flowering)	scarlet
Polyanthus	yellow shades	Hyacinth	mid-blue

Colour

Tastes in colour differ, so don't be too disappointed if not everybody likes your bedding arrangement. There are areas of broad agreement though, and the accompanying diagram provides a general guide to which colours will mix well together. The three primary colours, red, yellow and blue, are spaced equally around the centre. Combining red with yellow produces orange; yellow with blue, green; and blue with red, purple. These results are indicated in an outer circle. Thus, yellow is opposed by purple; red by green; and orange by blue. These pairings are known as complementary colours.

This is simply a crude diagram, and as such lacks refinement, but it is adequate if you wish to combine complementary colours in a free association.

It is clearly preferable if you have first-hand knowledge of plants and their colouring rather than having to rely on catalogues, as it is impossible to describe some shades adequately in words.

While the delicate art of harmony will often be best appreciated from close by, contrast, being strong, forceful and bold, will usually need to be viewed from a distance. To achieve contrast you must use the more aggressive shades in the primary colour range but always exercise restraint and purpose.

Although not everyone is fortunate enough to be blessed with a good colour sense, an observant eye can help to compensate. Simple but effective colour combinations are all around us, in public parks or the gardens of stately homes you may visit, in your neighbours' gardens, and in flowers themselves.

Spring bedding

The pure joy evoked by the sight of spring flowers is indeed a rare one. The summer garden may be richer and more opulent, but it surely cannot match the surge of flowers that marks the passing of winter.

At its simplest, spring bedding means planting a single subject, usually in mixed colours, in the flowerbed. The winter pansy, for example, comes in many colours, including crimson, gold, sky blue, deep blue and bronze, and each individual flower has a black 'face' imprinted in the centre. It will flower spasmodically throughout the winter in mild spells, but by mid to late spring (late March) will be in full bloom and continue so – provided you remove the seed heads – until mid summer (June), when the summer bedding is ready. *Primula denticulata* (drumstick primula), with its globular heads of lilac blue and strong erect stems, is another early flowerer that makes an unusual small bed.

For a subtler form of spring bedding, you could plant a carpet of, say, aubrietia and add mixed, early-flowering tulips. A little later in the season, mixed cottage tulips would go well against a backcloth of myosotis (forget-me-not). Darwin, and lily-flowered or parrot, tulips will do equally well.

The most complex arrangements have a carpet of two or more harmonizing plants, and a display of two different tulips, chosen either for contrast or harmony as well as to blend with the carpet.

The most sophisticated arrangements consist of a carpet of two or more harmonizing plants, complemented by a main display of two differing tulips. The latter either contrast or harmonize with each other.

For example, you might choose an equal mixture of Darwin tulips in scarlet and pale gold, and a carpet of orange Siberian wallflower with the intense mid-

Above: spring bedding at its best
Right: tulips on forget-me-not carpet

blue forget-me-not, Royal Blue. However, if you opted for a carpet of equal numbers of wallflower and forget-me-not, a heavy preponderance of the more intense of the two colours, orange, would result. For a proper balance you should plant 40 per cent wallflowers to 60 per cent forget-me-nots: this will provide a really magnificent display.

When selecting the two tulips, make sure they differ in height, otherwise one flower will tend to mask the next. Darwin and cottage types are ideal, flowering when the carpet is at its best. Choose varieties with a height difference of 5–15cm (2–6 in), such as the bright scarlet Marshal Haig, 70cm (28 in) and Mrs J. T. Scheefers, an 85cm (34 in) pale gold.

Don't attempt displays incorporating wallflower or forget-me-not if your garden is too northerly, or badly affected by atmospheric pollution.

Colour patch bedding
This is a quite charming system of bedding and particularly suitable for smaller private gardens. What you do is fill any available space with small clusters of spring-flowering plants. Plants used for this type of bedding include separate coloured viola, dwarf forget-me-not, miniature (pomponette) daisies, arabis, aubrietia, alyssum, polyanthus and silene – anything, in fact, that will flower reliably in early summer (May).

These plants are all dwarf and should not be planted with a tall tulip – Triumph would be suitable, being 45–55cm (18–22 in) tall. Choose distinctly-coloured varieties, and plant them 15cm (6 in) apart, in groups of five, with approximately 60cm (24 in) between groups.

Some plants to choose
The following list of plants are all suitable for use in spring bedding arrangements:

Arabis *A. albida* Flore Pleno resembles miniature double white stock. Makes a dense carpet for late spring (April) flowering bulbs. Propagate by division of clumps when lifted to make way for summer bedding. Grows to 15–23cm (6–9 in) height. Plant 23cm (9 in) apart.

Aubrietia Shades of violet, indigo, purple and rose. Best grown in pots plunged in soil or peat for the summer. Plant in autumn with plants touching for maximum effect, as little growth is made.

Bellis (daisy) A large double form of the common daisy. Pink, red and white flowers up to 5cm (2 in) across. Grows to 15cm (6 in) height. Nana or pomponette are attractive, similarly coloured. Flowers 13mm ($\frac{1}{2}$ in) across. Grows to 8cm (3 in) height. Sow seed in mid summer (June) and plant 20cm (8 in) apart.

Cheiranthus (wallflower) Hardy biennial widely used for spring groundwork. Colours: yellow, orange, lemon, red, purple and pink as well as many shades – but avoid blood-red varieties as these are very dull. Sow in mid summer (June) for the following spring. Plant 30–35cm (12–14 in) apart.

C. × Allionii (Siberian wallflower) Quite different in appearance but raised similarly. Its bright orange colour combines happily with forget-me-not. Grows to about 30cm (12 in) in height. Plant about 23–30cm (9–12 in) apart.

Hyacinthus (hyacinth) Stiff-shaped and best planted on its own in a formal setting. Plant each bulb 20cm (8 in) apart.

Myosotis (forget-me-not) One of the most popular of all spring flowers. Excellent Royal Blue variety also comes in dwarf form. Grows to only 15cm (6 in) height. Sow in mid summer (June). Plant 30cm (12 in) apart.

Polyanthus A cross between primrose and cowslip. Bright and long-lasting, it makes an excellent foil for early bulbs. Comes in many colours, individual flowers are bi-coloured, with orange-yellow eye. Strains with extra large flowers are not advisable for bedding as they are inclined to suffer weather damage. Sow in early to mid summer (May to June), treating as a biennial. Needs moist soil. After flowering, it can be divided. Plant 30cm (12 in) apart.

Silene *S. pendula* comes in white, salmon-pink and rose. Grows to 23–30cm (9–12 in) height. Sow in a seed tray in mid summer (June) and treat as a biennial.

Tulipa (tulip) A most important spring flowering bulb. Best size for outdoor use: 11cm (4½ in) circumference. Larger bulbs

are often malformed. Be sure to buy firm and clean bulbs with clear bright chestnut-coloured skin. Plant 23cm (9 in) apart.

Tulips divide into these divisions:
Early single, 30–38cm (12–15 in) height.
Early double, 25–30cm (10–12 in) height.
Late double, 45–55cm (18–22 in) height.
Parrot, striking sports (mutations) of other sections with much-cut petals, 60–75cm (24–30 in) height.
Cottage, 60–85cm (24–34 in) height.
Darwin, 65–85cm (26–34 in) height.
Lily-flowered, attractive reflexed petals, 50–70cm (20–28 in) height.
Triumph, Mendel and Darwin hybrids, flower 7–14 days before Darwins and cottage, and so link early tulips with early summer (May) flowering ones.

Buying for spring bedding

When buying bulbs, to get the best varieties and quality, use a reliable supplier, and purchase them the moment they first appear. Then store in a cool dark place until you need them.

Hyacinth bulbs vary in size, but for bedding choose them firm at the base, plump, and free from scars.

Tulips, too, should be firm, and without mould or scars, although it won't matter if some skin has peeled off.

Polyanthus and wallflowers should have firm green foliage. Do not buy any plants which have dried out on display.

Some overall schemes

There are various terms used to describe bedding schemes. It is assumed that most schemes have a principal 'subject' at low level, and this is known as the 'carpet'. The effect of the carpet can sometimes be enhanced by a surrounding border, contrasting in colour, and called the 'edging'. On the carpet, you can place occasional plants of conspicuous shape or colour for contrast and effect: these are known as 'dot' plants.

Spring bedding schemes

The following list does not include variety names as these are forever changing and your choice will be limited to the selection at your local garden centre. Buying by post from a good firm has much to recommend it but may cost more.

Where proportions in mixtures are not 50/50 the planting ratio is indicated by percentage figures shown after the colour details.

Remember that a dwarf carpet like polyanthus will go best with tulips 45–50cm (18–20 in) high and taller wallflowers with tulips 65–75cm (26–30 in) high.

Colour Schemes for Summer Planting

We have examined the principles of colour schemes in relation to bedding, and showed how every gardener can practise this underrated, but potentially most rewarding, system of planting. Here we consider the care of your flowerbeds, and take a detailed look at summer bedding.

The importance of cultivating your flowerbeds cannot be overstressed if your bedding arrangements are to realize their full potential. Soil constitutes the 'larder' from which your plants must obtain their food, so keep it filled with nourishing ingredients.

Caring for your flowerbeds

Plants take their food in liquid form only, so your best plan will be to mix water-

Right: a small-scale bedding arrangement. Any corner of the garden can be made attractive with a combination of annuals mixed with ornamental grasses

retaining humus into the soil. The simplest method is to single-dig your flowerbeds between spring and summer bedding, and add as much humus or peat as you have available. Every third autumn, double-dig the beds – that is, cultivate to the depth of two spade blades (or two 'spits' as it is commonly called), adding humus to the lower spit. Following this procedure means you remove any tree or shrub roots, as well as providing a well-broken-up growing medium, and good, moisture-holding conditions, both conducive to healthy root development and plant growth.

You would be wise to add 100g per sq

m (3 oz per sq yd) of a long-lasting autumn fertilizer – either a proprietary brand or a coarse bonemeal – at that season, and after or during spring digging, 85g (3 oz) of a good general fertilizer such as Growmore.

Soil height

This is important to both growth and appearance. In general, grass edges should not be less than 5cm (2 in) above soil level, and preferably about 8cm (3 in). A depth of more than 8cm would look unattractive, while below 5cm would make it difficult to use edging shears. An 8cm edge will mean rapid, easy work with the shears, the conservation of moisture, and a neat appearance.

To emphasize the planting it is desirable to have the centre of the bed raised, but not so much as to make it look like a hill, or to throw off rain too rapidly.

Planting the beds

Having prepared the beds properly, as already outlined, created the right consistency by treading the soil down at a time when it does not clog on the boots, and outlined the planting shape with an iron rake, it only remains for you to plant to the best advantage.

By this stage, you should have already planned your scheme and colour arrangement. If you decide to include plants grown on a tall stem as standards, these should be placed first. Make a random arrangement of them while they are still in their pots; then stand back and, walking around the bed, consider it from all angles. You should aim for balance from all viewing points, being particularly careful to avoid straight lines or gaps. Enlisting the help of someone to move the plants as you direct, will prove a great help at this stage.

'Dot' plants go in next, and you can use the same means of obtaining an even distribution without formality as for standards. A strictly mathematical distribution should usually be avoided.

PLANTS FOR SUMMER BEDDING

FOR FOLIAGE

Abutilon	*Helichrysum lanatum*
Beta (beet)	Iresine
Canna (Indian shot)	Kochia
Chlorophytum	Matricaria
Cineraria maritima	Pyrethrum
Coleus	Ricinus
Cordyline	Santolina
Dracaena	Senecio
Eucalyptus	Veronica
Grevillea	Zea

FOR FLOWERS

Ageratum	Gazania	Pelargonium
Alyssum	Gladiolus	(ivy leaf and zonal)
Antirrhinum	Heliotrope	Petunia
Aster	Impatiens	Phlox
Begonia	Lobelia	Salvia
Calceolaria	Mesembryanthemum	Stock
Coleus	Mimulus	Tagetes
Dahlia	Nasturtium	Verbena
Dianthus	Nicotiana	Viola
Fuchsia	Pansy	Zinnia

SUMMER BEDDING SCHEMES
CARPET

Antirrhinum (pink, 60 per cent)
Antirrhinum (purple, 40 per cent)

Verbena venosa (mauve, 40 per cent)
Antirrhinum (yellow, 60 per cent)

Heliotrope (purple, 80 per cent)
Cineraria maritima Silverdust
(foliage, 20 per cent)

Marigold, French (golden)
Verbena venosa (mauve)

Marigold, French (golden)
Antirrhinum (scarlet)

Petunia Blue Bee (violet blue)
Marigold, African (golden)

Ageratum (dark blue)
Tagetes signata pumila (golden)

Cineraria maritima Silverdust
(foliage, 30 per cent)
Verbena venosa (mauve, 70 per cent)

Ivy-leaved pelargonium Galilee (rose
pink)

Pelargonium (rich pink, 40 per cent)
Verbena Loveliness
(light blue, 60 per cent)

Impatiens Balsamina (mixed colours)

Fibrous begonia (mixed colours)

Above: summer bedding carpet, with shades of pink and mauve in the foreground and background, including begonia, ageratum and zinnia, and in the middle, yellow and golden tagetes

Now for the main planting. If you intend using an uneven number of mixed plants – say 10 per cent purple antirrhinums and 90 per cent yellow antirrhinums – first plant the smaller number (the purple ones) evenly over the bed, and then fill in the spaces with the yellow.

If edging plants are to be used, they should go in before the main carpet. Water the whole bed thoroughly as soon as you have completed the planting.

Maintenance
Attend to staking and tying. This is most important, because a sudden gust of wind can break down a plant such as a fuchsia if it is not adequately secured. Stakes and ties should not be visible, so use dark timber and green string.

Remove seed-heads, as their formation will tend to stop flowering. Dead-heading is advisable to avoid the display getting a slovenly appearance.

Keep the hoe going to check weeds and preserve water supplies.

Never let the bed dry out completely.

As the season ends, see that all the plants you wish to keep – fuchsias, tuberous begonias, dahlias, and so on – are correctly labelled while there are still flowers to check by, and store them in frostproof conditions for the winter.

Summer display
The earlier you get your summer bedding plants in, the sooner their colour will be enlivening your garden – but as few of the plants used will be frost-hardy, it is wise to wait until the danger of frost is over in your district. Most local papers have weather records that will help in this respect, and you can usually start planting towards mid summer (late May or early June).

We suggest ideas here for summer combinations of plants, but there is much to be said for making a note of any happy association that you notice on your travels, whether it be in a neighbour's garden, in a park, or anywhere at all.

Here, we concentrate on normal summer bedding, and do not include such specialist practices as sub-tropical bedding or large-scale carpet bedding, and the like.

One of the principal differences between spring and summer bedding is that the latter generally involves plants of hotter, stronger colour, with a greater variety of heights, and a wider range of foliage and form. But you should beware of overdoing the use of strong colours, or of mixing primary-coloured plants like scarlet pelargonium, harsh yellow calceolaria, hard blue lobelia and white marguerites.

The trick is to choose complementary shades. For example, on its own one of the hottest colours of summer is that of the pelargonium Maxim Kovaleski, which is bright orange, but when mixed with the petunia Blue Bedder it can produce a most unusual and striking effect. Unfortunately, petunias are notoriously unreliable flowerers in a cold, wet summer, when *Verbena venosa* would be a more dependable bet. In the same way, yellow antirrhinums can be used to

SUMMER BEDDING SCHEMES

CARPET	DOT PLANTS
Tuberous begonia (yellow, 25 per cent) Lobelia (bright blue, 75 per cent)	*Centaurea candidissima* (silver foliage)
Pelargonium (salmon pink) Antirrhinum (buff pink)	*Lobelia cardinalis* (red foliage, scarlet flowers)
Calceolaria (yellow) Ageratum (deep blue)	*Zea quadricolor* (green, white, pink and yellow foliage)
Pelargonium Maxim Kovaleski (orange red) Petunia Blue Bee (violet blue)	Half-standard pelargonium Maxim Kovaleski (orange red)
Marigold, French (golden)	*Lobelia cardinalis* (red foliage, scarlet flowers)
Pansy (golden, 90 per cent) *Verbena venosa* (mauve, 10 per cent)	*Salvia splendens* (blue)
Petunia (salmon rose, 60 per cent) Petunia (purple, 40 per cent)	*Zea quadricolor* (green, white, pink and yellow foliage)
Verbena venosa (mauve, 90 per cent) Pelargonium Decorator (bright scarlet, 10 per cent)	*Abutilon thompsonii* (mottled green and yellow)

soften the harshness of the crude red pelargonium Gustav Emich. The rosy-purple of *Verbena venosa* would serve the same purpose, and is one of the most useful complements to other colours.

The use of grey foliage is another way you can soften overbearing colours. Scarlet begonias, the brilliant red *Salvia splendens*, and similar plants, if used with silvery plants like the best forms of *Cineraria maritima*, will find a mutual association, the latter softening the former, the former vivifying the latter.

You can provide variety in height by using standards and half-standards. Start your cuttings a few weeks earlier, and pinch out all side growths until the stems reach 45cm (18 in) – half standard height – or 90cm (3 ft) – standard height – and then allow the heads to form. A cutting with a 45cm stem is known as a 'half standard', and with a 90cm stem, a 'standard'. Pelargonium, fuchsia and heliotrope cuttings are all suitable for this treatment.

Zea mays quadricolor (ornamental maize), canna, and *Ricinus communis gibsonii* (the true castor oil), can all be used to relieve flatness.

Use of foliage

There are many excellent plants that lack flowers but whose foliage alone justifies their place in bedding arrangements. It is quite possible to make a most colourful display using such plants, particularly if you create small, contrasting groups like those illustrated on this page.

The following guide to foliage colour will help you in your selection. Remember that the green in variegated plants gives invaluable point and contrast.

Left: summer foliage bedding at the Royal Pavilion, Brighton, with a carpet of silver cineraria and yellow and red coleus, and 'dots' of ornamental maize

SUMMER BEDDING SCHEMES

EDGING	CARPET	DOT PLANTS
Pyrethrum parthenifolium Golden Moss (foliage)	Fibrous begonia (scarlet)	*Cineraria maritima* Silverdust (foliage)
Lobelia (bright blue)	Tuberous begonia (rose pink)	*Centaurea gymnocarpa* (silver foliage)
Pyrethrum parthenifolium Golden Moss (foliage)	Pelargonium Paul Crampel (scarlet)	Marigold, Afro-French (golden)
Tagetes signata pumila (golden)	*Salvia splendens* (blue)	*Ricinus gibsonii* (red or green foliage)
Lobelia (light blue)	Ivy-leaved pelargonium Galilee (rose pink, 80 per cent) Lobelia (light blue, 20 per cent)	

A Garden for Winter

In dark winter months what could be more cheering than the sight of an attractively laid out winter garden? A surprisingly large number of hardy shrubs, plants and bulbs will flower at this time of year, and in many cases the small, jewel-like blooms exude an appealing fragrance.

Here we suggest the form your winter garden might take, and introduce our own garden design and planting plan, and later we will describe some of the trees, climbers and wall shrubs, both evergreen and deciduous, suitable for planting in this garden.

Although delicate winter flowers will make little impact if merely dotted about a large garden, grouped together in just one part or in a smaller garden devoted entirely to winter plants, it can be a different story.

Flowers for the New Year

To watch a series of plants coming into flower very early in the year, when most gardens – at least in Britain – are devoid of any colour is a most enjoyable experience. Such a garden makes home-coming a delight and gives pleasure to neighbours; it even seems to shorten the winter and hasten the arrival of spring.

Flowers will last far longer in winter than in summer, and while frost may brown some, snow will leave most unscathed, and even those that seem to disappear will often reappear with milder weather. The little posies that you will be able to pick in early and mid spring (February and March) will be far more satisfying than bought flowers, and with their fresh, light form they make pot plants seem stuffy by comparison.

A great advantage of the winter garden is that it requires very little in the way of upkeep. Shrubs will need only an occasional mulch and a little pruning to keep them in check – the latter you can do when picking a few sprays of flowering wood for flower arrangements in the house or to give to your friends.

For winter time stay-at-homes

A garden of winter-flowering plants might well be of interest to people with seasonal work or who enjoy a sport, for example sailing, that keeps them busy or away from home in the summer. Owners

of small town gardens with no interest in growing vegetables might consider a winter garden to be just what they need, while country dwellers with large gardens can group all their winter flowers in a small secret garden, perhaps visible from a side window. A winter garden is also a particularly good solution for an awkward but sunny area lying beside a house – especially if there is a warm chimney-stack on the side wall – or for a small front garden between the house and the road.

A winter garden will not be empty in summer. Except for bulbs and plants like anemone and cyclamen that disappear, winter-flowering plants, with their varied foliage shapes, will clothe the garden in a colour scheme of different greens. Plants chosen for their winter foliage, for example hebes, will flower in summer, as will shrubs chosen for winter berries.

The ideal position for a winter garden is one sheltered from easterly and northerly winds, and facing south or south-west. Shade in early morning is desirable for some flowers, like early-flowering magnolia and camellia, because frost can act as a magnifying glass and burn brown patches on petals if the sun reaches them before the frost has melted. Many winter-flowering plants will benefit from good drainage and grow well on chalk or limestone, although others may prefer an acid soil.

EVERGREEN SHRUBS

Evergreen shrubs provide a welcome touch of green in the winter, as well as adding substance to our design.

Buxus (box)

Buxus sempervirens, 1.8m (6 ft) always looks happy and healthy, and is one of the oldest evergreen shrubs in Britain. It is so amenable that it stands hard clipping and is often used for topiary. *B. s.* Elegantissima is a dwarf form with silver-edged leaves, and *B. s.* Latifolia Maculata (also known as *B. s.* Japonica Aurea) is a compact, gold-leaved form.

Camellia

Camellias, 1.5–3m (5–10 ft), have dark, shiny green leaves and can be trained on a wall. The perfect early-flowering shrubs for gardens on acid soil, they can nevertheless be grown in lime districts by putting them in peat beds or tubs – but always water with rain, never tap water. The best early varieties are white *C. japonica* Nobilissima and the pink *C. × williamsii* November Pink, that may start in early winter (November) and carry on to mid spring (March).

C. × williamsii Donation is a very early-flowering pink, while *C. japonica* Debutante is pink and white, and spreading *C. j.* Lady Clare is another early one with large, semi-double, rose-pink flowers.

Choisya

Choisya ternata (Mexican orange blossom), 1.8m (6 ft), looks well in winter with dark, shiny, triple leaves that smell of furniture polish when bruised. It thrives in a shady place, and has masses of white, scented blossom from mid spring to early summer (March to May).

Daphne

Daphne laureola (spurge laurel), 90cm (3 ft), possesses a common name that gives no idea of the attraction of this decorative British plant. It displays glossy, pointed leaves in rosettes set all round with small, bright green, scented flowers in early and mid spring (March and April).

Fatsia

Fatsia japonica (Japanese aralia or figleaf palm), 1.8m (6 ft), is a handsome shrub related to ivy, with dark, palmate leaves. It grows well in shade and produces ivy-

Above: wide-spreading Choisya ternata
Bottom left: Juniperus communis Hibernica

like flowers in early winter (November).

Hebe

Hebe Autumn Glory, 30–90cm (12–36 in), has violet flowers from mid summer to late autumn (June to October), and sometimes until mid winter (mid December). Its attraction for us is its purple-shaded foliage that adds to our winter colour scheme.

Ilex (holly)

Ilex aquifolium Golden King and *I. a.* Silver Queen both grow up to a height of 4.5m (15 ft). These hollies are gold- and silver-variegated respectively, but Golden King is female and has berries, while Silver Queen, a male variety, has none. Hollies are dioecious (that is, they have male and female flowers on separate plants), and you need both male and female plants to produce berries. In the winter garden you can probably cut back their glistening foliage in mid winter (mid December) if they grow too big.

Juniperus (juniper)

Juniperus communis Hibernica (Irish juniper), 3m (10 ft), is an upright juniper that will give some height to the sink bed, but it takes many years to mature.

Apart from this, there are many other conifers that are decorative in winter.

Laurus (bay laurel)

Laurus nobilis (sweet bay), 3.6m (12 ft), is a good background shrub bearing dark, pointed, aromatic leaves that stand clipping well. It is as pleasant to look at as it is useful in the kitchen.

Mahonia

Mahonia aquifolium Atropurpurea, 1.2m (4 ft), is a fine form of the Oregon grape. The leaves turn purple in winter, and soft yellow flowers are produced in mid to late

spring (March to April). *M. a.* Orange Flame, 60cm (24 in), is a dwarf newcomer to Britain (from America), displaying bright orange leaves, and producing yellow flowers between late winter and early spring (January and February).

M. japonica, 1.8m (6 ft), is a handsome shrub with tough pinnate leaves that turn red and orange in winter, and scented, pale yellow flower sprays that appear between early winter and mid spring (November and March). Mahonias are excellent in a dry, shady position.

Pieris

Pieris formosa forrestii, 2.5m (8½ ft) or more, and its varieties have young spring foliage a brilliant red in colour, and white bell flowers. *P. japonica* Christmas Cheer is a compact, slow-growing shrub for the peat bed that displays pink flowers in late spring (April) and coloured leaves in mid winter (December). It needs moisture and will grow in shade.

Rhododendron

Rhododendron Praecox, 1.2m (4 ft), has lilac flowers in early mid spring (early March) that will blend with corylopsis. The variety *R.* Christmas Cheer is low and compact, and will grow in a partially shaded position, producing pink flowers in early spring (February).

Skimmia

Skimmia japonica Foremanii, 90cm (3 ft), has scarlet berries, and white, scented flowers in mid spring (March). It is a female form and is self-fertilizing, although some skimmias are dioecious. *S. j.* Rubella has red buds and large flower-heads. Plant it in groups for pollination.

Viburnum

Viburnum tinus (laurustinus), 3m (10 ft), was unpopular for years after over-use in Victorian shrubberies, altogether it is a superb background shrub. It flowers freely from late autumn to early spring (October to February), and makes perfect ground cover. *V. t.* Eve Prince, with pink flowers, is a good form.

DECIDUOUS SHRUBS

With their dainty flowers, often sweetly scented, and their subtly-coloured stems, deciduous shrubs provide a delicate touch to the winter garden.

Acer (maple)

Acer palmatum Senkaki (coral bark maple), 3m (10 ft), is a breathtaking sight

Young shoots of Salix alba *Britzensis*

in winter, truly deserving its common name, and displaying grace and style in summer, too. It is of Japanese origin.

Cornus (dogwood or cornel)

Cornus alba Elegantissima (red-barked dogwood), 2.4m (8 ft), also known as *C. a.* Sibirica Variegata, has bark a darker red than *Acer palmatum* Senkaki. The 'elegance' in its name refers to the silver-variegated leaves. Prune it in late spring (April) to ensure bright new bark for the following winter.

C. mas (cornelian cherry), 6m (20 ft), is for a bigger garden than our own, but its masses of tiny gold flowers in early spring (February) earn it a mention.

Corylopsis

Corylopsis pauciflora, 1.2m (4 ft), has larger flowers than the more common *C. spicata*, 1.8m (6 ft), and makes a smaller shrub. Both species have flower-bells with the colour and scent of cowslips, in mid to late spring (March to April).

Daphne

Daphne mezereum (mezereon), 90cm (3 ft), can be temperamental, but its pink or white flowers are among the sweetest of winter and early spring (January to March). It grows wild on the edge of woodland and thrives on lime soils. If it dies it may leave you a seedling.

Forsythia

Forsythia ovata, 90–120cm (3–4 ft), comes from Korea and flowers in early spring (February), so qualifying for the winter garden. Its flowers are a more delicate yellow than those of many of the later-flowering forsythias.

Hamamelis (witch hazel)

Hamamelis mollis (Chinese witch hazel), 3.6m (12 ft), is very slow growing. Its fragrant, spidery flowers appear on the youngest shrubs between mid winter and early spring (December and February). *H. m.* Pallida possesses pale sulphur-yellow flowers, and *H. × intermedia* Ruby Glow is red flowered.

Salix (willow)

Salix irrorata, 2.4m (8 ft), has violet-purple stems with a grape-like bloom. *S. alba* Vitellina has yellow stems, and *S. a.* Chermesina (scarlet willow), that is also known as *S. a.* Britzensis, has scarlet stems. If these coloured-stemmed willows are pruned hard in late spring (April) they shoot again with bright new growth for the following winter's colour. There is a large selection of willows, many of which have beautiful catkins.

Stachyurus

Stachyurus praecox, 3m (10 ft), is a fascinating winter-flowering shrub from Japan. It has a reddish bark and displays yellow flowers in pendant racemes from early spring (February) onwards. The flowers are not soft but stiff and rather wiry, which gives the shrub its peculiar character.

Viburnum

Viburnum × bodnantense Dawn, with pink blooms, and *V. × b.* Deben, with white blooms, flower through from late autumn to mid spring (October to March) during mild spells, holding their mass of

Aromatic flowers of Daphne mezereum *(top) are followed by poisonous scarlet berries*
Densely-branched Corylopsis pauciflora *(above) requires shelter from cold winds*

flowers in drooping bunches.

V. fragrans (V. farreri) flowers just as freely as the viburnums already mentioned, but produces smaller flower bunches, that it holds upright.

All of these shrubs have a gaunt habit of growth and are better used as background plantings than as specimens, but their fragrance is superb.

CLIMBERS AND WALL SHRUBS

Climbers and wall shrubs play an important role in the winter garden, softening existing walls and providing an attractive backcloth to the main planting areas.

Chaenomeles (ornamental quince)

Chaenomeles speciosa Aurora, 1.8m (6 ft), is a salmon-pink form of the old japonica or cydonia. It produces quince-like fruit that can be used for jelly, and is the earliest of its family to flower. It may produce occasional apple-blossom flowers from late autumn (October) onwards. As well as growing on a wall, chaenomeles, with its glossy, green leaves, makes a good border shrub. Spring-flowering varieties are obtainable in a colour range from white, through pink and salmon, to orange and crimson.

Chimonanthus (winter sweet)

Chimonanthus praecox, 2.4m (8 ft), that is also known as *C. fragrans*, is one of the most fragrant of all winter flowers. It grows well in any warm position, and seems to enjoy rather poor soil. The fresh green leaves turn gold in autumn, and the flowers start in late winter (January) from buds that resemble little balls of butter, and are stiff, claw-shaped, and almost transparent, with maroon centres. Chinese ladies once used the flowers to scent their hair.

Clematis

The fern-leaved species *Clematis cirrhosa balearica* is lovely in winter when the bell-shaped, primrose flowers hang among deeply-cut, bronze-coloured foliage. It does well on lime soil. Cut it back by a third every spring.

Garrya

Garrya elliptica (silk tassel bush), 3m (10 ft), was introduced to Britain from America in 1828. It has neat, wavy, evergreen leaves, and the male form produces green catkins that are long enough to be used to represent icicles in Christmas decorations. They reach their full length in early spring (February). *G. elliptica* is usually grown as a wall plant except in mild districts. Do not prune too

Male catkins of Garrya elliptica *(top) make attractive Christmas decorations*
Chaenomeles speciosa *(above) can be grown against a wall or used as a border shrub*

189

hard as the catkins are borne on the previous year's wood.

Jasminum (jasmine)

Jasminum nudiflorum (winter jasmine), 3–3.6m (10–12 ft), is the yellow, winter-flowering jasmine. It grows well in any position, even on a north-facing wall, and is all the better for being cut for the house. Its bright yellow flowers clothe the bare stems from early winter to early spring (November to February).

Pyracantha (firethorn)

Pyracantha angustifolia, 4.5m (15 ft), is an evergreen, berrying shrub that can stand free or will make a good hedge or wall shrub. The berries last well as they do not ripen until late winter (January), when they take on orange-yellow tints. This is one good example, but there are many other berrying shrubs that are suitable for the winter garden.

TREES

Provided they are used sparingly and chosen with care, trees will balance the design of your winter garden and make a contrast in shape and height with the surrounding plants and shrubs.

Magnolia

Magnolia stellata, 3m (10 ft), is the earliest of this genus to flower. It produces white, starry blooms, well protected by furry buds, by late spring (end of March). Slow-growing, it can be considered a bush rather than a tree, but it flowers when very young. On chalky soil it benefits from peat mulches and seques-trene fertilizer. *M.* × *loebneri* flowers almost as early as *M. stellata*. It is similarly tolerant, but not quite so pretty, although it grows faster.

Prunus

Prunus cerasifera Nigra, 6m (20 ft), is a purple-leaved cherry plum that flowers early if the birds do not eat the buds. Both single- and double-flowered forms are available.

P. subhirtella Autumnalis Rosea (pink-flowered spring cherry), 4.5m (15 ft), is the best of the winter-flowering cherries. It displays pink flowers from late autumn to late spring (October to April) during mild spells. The foliage colours well in autumn, and there are white, deep rose and weeping forms. *P. s.* Accolade is a lovely early hybrid with rich pink flowers.

P. triloba (*P. triloba* Multiplex), 1.8m (6 ft), is a slow-growing dwarf almond that has pink flowers during mid and late spring (March and April) in almost

Shoots of Jasminum nudiflorum *(top) should be pruned back hard after flowering* Arbutus unedo *(above) produces distinctive berries*

The aptly named Calluna vulgaris Blazeway

artificially perfect rosettes. The bush form, with several stems, would look best if you base your garden on our design.

HEATHS AND HEATHERS

Among the most useful plants in the winter garden are erica and calluna – the heaths and heathers. They are not herbaceous perennials, being small flowering shrubs with woody stems 30–45cm (12–18 in) high, but their habit of growth is low and compact and like many herbaceous plants they spread by layering. Tree heaths such as *Erica arborea* and *E. canaliculata* grow much taller than most heaths and heathers and are therefore unsuitable for our particular winter garden.

Measurements given after the name of a plant indicate its ultimate height.

Calluna (heather or ling)

This will not grow in lime soil but could go in the peat bed. Although it flowers in summer and autumn only, some varieties produce bright foliage that looks wonderful in winter.

For example, there is white-flowered

Calluna vulgaris Gold Haze, that has gold foliage all the year round. Then there is lilac-flowered *C.v.* Blazeaway, with foliage to justify its name, and purple-flowered *C.v.* Robert Chapman, whose foliage slowly turns from gold in spring, to orange and then to red.

Erica (heath)

For winter flowers there is the erica family, that grows in any soil and blooms between mid winter and mid spring (December and March).

E. carnea varieties Springwood White, Springwood Pink, and dark pink King George (Winter Beauty) and Vivellii (Urville) are all reliable. *E. × darleyensis* also flowers in winter, and among its many varieties are Arthur Johnson, that produces lilac-pink flowers, and Silberschmelze, that is white-flowered.

PERENNIAL PLANTS

Some perennials are of the highest importance in the winter garden, providing useful ground cover.

Ajuga (bugle)

Ajuga reptans Atropurpurea, a cultivated form of wild bugle, makes flat mats of

evergreen ground cover that is spread by surface runners. *A.r.* Variegata has green and silver foliage, and *A.r.* Delightful is rose-pink, green and purple. All three give winter leaf colour and produce blue flower spikes in early summer (May).

Bergenia (pig squeak)

Bergenia stracheyi Schmidtii is the earliest-flowering of this genus, producing its blooms in early spring (February), while the flowers of *B.s.* Silberlicht may open in mid spring (March). The strong spoon-shaped leaves of the species bear the cottage garden name 'elephants ear' and often turn red or purple in winter, *B.s.* Abendglut and *B. purpurascens* Ballawley being extra good in this respect.

Cut off rather than pull off the dead leaves, for like those of hellebores and paeonies they are attached so strongly that you could pull away part of the root and even a bud as well.

Epimedium (barrenwort)

Epimedium perralderianum makes handsome, coloured ground cover in winter, having large, shining, heart-shaped leaves on wiry stems rising 45cm (18 in) from the ground. Sprays of yellow appear in mid spring (March), when the old leaves should be cut off.

E. macranthum (*E. grandiflorum*) Rose Queen has quaint, rose-pink flowers crossed with white in spring, and leaves of a papery thinness that turn a true rose-pink in winter.

Helleborus (hellebore)

Helleborus niger (Christmas rose) is the best known of this essential winter-flowering family, starting in mid winter (December) with large white blooms that are sometimes flushed with pink.

H. orientalis (Lenten rose) is a taller plant growing up to 45cm (18 in), and flowering from late winter (January). The petals can be any shade from white, through greenish creams and pinks – sometimes mottled with crimson spots – to dark, purplish-reds and near blacks. Experts can name dozens of varieties.

The common name of *H. foetidus* – stinking hellebore – is unkind and undeserved. This woodland plant has deeply cut, architecturally handsome evergreen leaves, and yellow-green flowers held in bunches, and sometimes edged with red, from early spring to early summer (February to May).

H. niger, *H. orientalis* and *H. foetidus* all grow in shade and on lime, and like a rich soil.

Hepatica

Hepatica triloba, 25cm (9 in), used to be called *Anemone hepatica*, being related to the anemone, and is also known as *H. nobilis* and *H. trifolia*. Its small flowers come out between early and mid spring (February and March), and are blue, pink white in colour. The plant will grow in even that of beeches, and the last well in water. There are forms for the enthusiast.

laris (Algerian iris), 30cm (12 known as *I. stylosa*. It should re it will get plenty of sun in preferably against a wall – a clump of long stringy its mass of flowers the The worst leaves can be ter (December). rs that appear be- and mid spring are white, mauve, d from greyish, ed in water, the you watch.

Evergreen Helleborus corsicus *(above) likes a shady position and well-drained soil*
Primrose Primula vulgaris sibthorpii *(below) adds early colour to the winter garden*

191   also known

as *P. acaulis*, is probably the most beautiful form, and flowers during mild spells from late autumn to late spring (October to the end of April). Many of its descendants and close relatives flower during this period, including a pretty, mauve-coloured sub-species sometimes labelled *P. vulgaris sibthorpii*, and the *P. juliae* group, of which the well-known hybrid Wanda is a member.

Pulmonaria (lungwort)

Pulmonaria saccharata, 30cm (12 in), is often called 'soldiers and sailors' after its flowers that open bright blue and fade to pink – reminiscent of the colours of early servicemen's uniforms. It flowers very early, and often produces a few blooms in autumn as well.

    P. rubra (Christmas cowslip) has brick-pink flowers that open from mid winter to late spring (December to April), while the most attractive *P. angustifolia* (blue cowslip) – also known as *P. azurea* – produces flowers of an intense gentian-blue from early spring (February).

Tellima

Tellima grandiflora Purpurea, 30cm (12 in), is a member of the SAXIFRAGACEAE family. It distinguishes itself in winter when its leaves, whose shape is a cross between a heart and a vine leaf, turn slowly from green to bronze, then crimson and wine-red. It makes good ground cover under trees or shrubs, and sets off galanthus (snowdrops) beautifully.

Vinca (periwinkle)

The evergreen and spreading *Vinca major* (greater periwinkle) and *V. minor* (lesser periwinkle) flower spasmodically throughout the year; they are sometimes covered in flowers in early spring (late February), but open in earnest in mid spring (March).

    V. major, 10–15cm (4–6 in), is far too rampageous for a small garden, but *V. minor*, 15–30cm (6–12 in), that can be obtained in many forms – with blue, white or mauve flowers (sometimes double), or with gold- or silver-variegated foliage – is a useful and attractive ground cover.

Flowering plants for winter: Pulmonaria rubra *(top left), that reaches 15–25cm (6–9 in) in height;* Viola odorata *(top right), that forms tufts of thick rhizomes and spreads by means of runners; and strongly-scented* Crocus chrysanthus Mariette *(right).*

Eranthis hyemalis prefers a fairly moist soil

Viola (pansy and violet)

Viola odorata (sweet violet), 10–15cm (4–6 in), flowers throughout the winter. It shrivels in very cold weather but re-appears with the next mild spell. There are mauve, pink, purple and white forms, and no winter garden should be without a few patches of these favourite flowers.

It is also well worth sowing a packet of seed of the winter-flowering type *V.×wittrockiana* (garden pansy), also known as *V. tricolor hortensis*. From a sowing made in mid summer (June), plants start producing odd flowers in autumn, continue in mild weather all winter, and then cover themselves with blooms in early spring (February).

BULBS, CORMS AND TUBERS

Bulbs, corms and tubers add splashes of welcome colour to the winter garden, and provide ground-level interest.

Anemone (windflower)

Many anemones flower early, one of the prettiest being *Anemone blanda* (mountain windflower of Greece), 15cm (6 in). This is ideal in light woodland where it will increase to cover a wide area, but it can equally well echo the sky as a patch of blue and white in a small garden in early and mid spring (February and March). If the weather is mild, *A.×fulgens* may produce a scarlet head or two in mid

spring (March). The blue-flowered *A.× appenina*, 30cm (12 in), flowers around mid to late spring (March to April).

Chionodoxa (glory of the snow)

Chionodoxa luciliae, 15cm (6 in), comes from Turkey, where its common name also originated. Flowering in early to mid spring (February to March), it can be grouped with scilla (squill) and muscari (grape hyacinth) in a bed of spring blues. Other varieties are *C. gigantea* (*C. grandiflora*), with large, white-centred flowers, and gentian-blue *C. sardensis*. They could well be grown in a trough.

Crocus

Although colchicums are often described as autumn crocuses, there are true crocuses that flower from mid autumn to early spring (September to February). Among them are *Crocus speciosus*, that has large, bright mauve flowers in late autumn (October); *C. ochroleucus*, white-flowered in early winter (November); and *C. laevigatus*, with blooms of a soft violet striped with purple from late autumn to mid winter (October to December).

C. tomasinianus flowers in early spring (February), making sheets of lavender and purple, and also early is *C. chrysanthus* and its varieties such as Cream Beauty, the yellow E. A. Bowles, Blue Bird, and the strongly-scented, striped-

flowered Mariette.

Cyclamen

Collecting forms of wild cyclamen can be a fascinating hobby. To those used to the large indoor plants they appear like Dresden china miniatures. *Cyclamen neapolitanum* (or *hederafolium*), 10cm (4 in), displays pink or white flowers from mid autumn to early winter (September to November), and has beautiful marbled leaves throughout the winter.

There are many cyclamen grouped under *C. coum* that produce crimson, pink or white flowers between mid winter and mid spring (December and March) and have rounded leaves, those of *C.×atkinsii* being marbled.

Wild cyclamen flower in shade and need good drainage.

Eranthis

The gold flowers ruffled with green that are displayed by *Eranthis hyemalis* (winter aconite), 10cm (4 in), and *E.×tubergenii*, also 10cm (4 in), are a winter joy not to be missed. The former is the earliest-flowering aconite, starting in early spring (February), while the latter flowers a little later, in mid spring (March), and is sturdier in appearance. Both combine well with hostas (plantain lilies), flowering before the latter's leaves appear, and disappearing in summer.

Galanthus (snowdrop)

No winter garden would be complete without *Galanthus nivalis* (common snowdrop) and the double-flowered form *G.n.* Flore-plena. Both flower around late winter (January), as do the giant form *G.n.* Atkinsii, 25cm (9 in), that is easily recognizable with its long, occasionally misshapen, petals, and *G.n.* S. Arnott, that has perfect, rounded petals.

G. plicatus (Crimean snowdrop), that flowers in mid and late spring (March and April), has grooved leaves and comes from the Crimea. *G. elwesii*, often the first to flower, has wide, bluish leaves. Although it sometimes dies out, it is certainly worth trying.

Iris

Iris histrioides, 15cm (6 in), is the first of the small bulbous irises to bloom – in mid winter (December). Its flowers are a brilliant blue in colour, and surprisingly large, growing close to the earth on short stalks. It will persist if given a good dressing of bonemeal in summer. This is even more important in the case of *I. danfordiae*, a miniature yellow, that blooms in late winter and early spring

(January and February). The bulbs of this tend to split into bulblets after flowering, but even if you lose this lovely little flower it still costs less than a bunch of tulips from a shop and gives far more pleasure.

I. reticulata is dependable, and returns every year, in early spring (February), with its gold-splashed purple flowers. There are many good hybrids, including *I.r.* Cantab, that has pale blue flowers; *I.r.* Clairette, that is sky-blue with deep blue falls (the downward-hanging part of the perianth) streaked with white; *I.r.* Blue Veil, that is bright blue; and *I.r.* Dijt, that is reddish-purple. These jewels of the winter garden are best grown in a rockery or trough, where they are not likely to be disturbed or lost in summer.

Narcissus (daffodil)

Narcissus cyclamineus February Gold, 25cm (9 in), flowering in early spring (February), is one of the earliest, and possibly the longest-lasting of all daffodils. It has reflexed petals inherited from its early-flowering parent *N. cyclamineus*, 15–20cm (6–8 in), and these give it the air of a little horse with ears laid back.

There are many old early daffodils, notably *N. pseudonarcissus obvallaris* (Tenby daffodil), 20cm (8 in), and a

Iris reticulata *Blue Veil (top) requires protection from the attentions of birds*
Pulsatilla vulgaris *Rubra (bottom) generally performs best on chalky soil*

double variety, Van Sion, 30cm (12 in), that is a deep yellow. W. P. Milner, 25cm (10 in), is creamy in colour, early and very free-flowering. These small narcissus are often more appealing in the winter garden than bigger ones, of which Early Glory, 35cm (14 in), with a soft yellow perianth

and yellow trumpet, is perhaps the best.

The study and collection of narcissus species is a world in itself. Among the earliest-flowering are *N. asturiensis* (*N. minimus*), that produces a perfect, tiny yellow trumpet 6cm ($2\frac{1}{2}$ in) high, but is a martyr to slugs, and *N. bulbocodium* (hoop petticoat): both are candidates for planting in the trough.

Pulsatilla

Pulsatilla vulgaris (pasque flower), 30cm (12 in), displays flowers ranging from deep mauve to white, red and rich purple hybrids. By late spring (April) the flowers are replaced by silvery seed-heads.

Scilla (squill)

Scilla tubergeniana flowers at the same time as the snowdrops and aconites, and has several spikes of pale blue flowers on every bulb. *S. bifolia* is covered with many starry-blue flowers from mid spring (early March). The more common *S. sibirica* flowers in mid and late spring (March and April), but with its rich blue blooms is worth remembering even though it may be a little late for the winter garden.

Tulipa (tulip)

Tulipa kaufmanniana (waterlily tulip) and its hybrids, 15–25cm (6–10 in), flower in mid spring (March) and come in a colour range of creams and yellows streaked with carmine or scarlet. *T.k.* Heart's Delight is pale rose, and *T.k.* Shakespeare is a blend of salmon, apricot and orange.

Violet-pink *T. humilis*, 15cm (6 in), flowers in early spring (February), and is a treasure for a trough or sink.

Flower Garden

We have created this special 'Flower Garden' so that you can follow its development and maintenance during the twelve vital weeks in the gardener's calendar, from February through to March. You can incorporate the unusual design features into your own existing garden and our expert advice will help you to achieve the same visually exciting results.

This long, narrow plot, typical of so many back gardens, calls for an imaginative layout, so we have steered away from the tunnel-like effect of narrow side borders and a central rectangle of grass or paving and created instead a series of curving lines and irregular shapes. In this way the eye is attracted by informal groupings of flowering plants and shrubs (which avoid the considerable upkeep required by more formal herbaceous borders), while the rose-covered trellis acts as a natural break in the length.

We have filled the garden with easy-to-care-for evergreens, flowering shrubs and trees, seasonal bulbs and roses for the paired pergolas. Annuals planted at appropriate times of the year and flowering plants in tubs on the patio provide additional patches of instant colour, as and where they are needed.

The paved patio runs the whole width of the garden, providing a convenient eating-out and relaxation area near the house on sunny days and somewhere to scrape the mud off your boots on the wet ones. There is room for a lean-to greenhouse to be erected against the north wall if you feel tempted to invest in one, and facing the end wall of the garden, screened by the rose-covered trellis, is a sizable shed for all those tools, toys and miscellaneous garden furniture.

Turfing or seeding?

For the lawn, with its attractive curved edges, we opted for turf – which need not be such an expensive outlay as you might imagine (unless you hanker after the bowling-green effect of a really luxury lawn). The great advantage of turf is that it gives you a quicker result than if you had settled for sowing from seed.

Food for compost

If you have not already got a compost-heap, start saving vegetable waste as soon as you can. The compost is vital to the well-being of your garden – as important as a fridge is to a cook. If possible, keep *two* waste bins in the kitchen – one solely for vegetable matter which can be added to your compost. Avoid saving very smelly things like fish bones, though – and meat bones take far too long to break down.

Know your weeds

There are several weeds that produce colourful displays and fill a border quite prettily, but their spreading roots may be doing untold damage beneath the surface. It is important to be able to tell the difference between growing weeds and good plant stock. Forthcoming sections in the book will help you to distinguish the 'good' weeds from the 'bad' ones – and how to control them.

Inheriting the earth

If you are already the owner of a well-cared-for garden, you are spared the trials, and may lose the pleasures, of creating a totally new one. But you still have plenty of room to exercise your talents by redesigning the planting areas,

Some plants grow happily anywhere, such as cotoneaster (shown here) and berberis. Both these shrubs are tolerant of all soils, including chalk or limestone

choosing new shrubs – even reshaping the lawn, and our week-by-week advice will tell you how to do all this.

A little caution is called for, however, if you have recently acquired a garden of unknown quantity. Do not rush ahead with a complete replanting job as there are many perennials that die down and remain dormant underneath the earth for months at a time, and you may not know that they are there. One of the most enjoyable experiences here is being happily surprised as a small shoot in late spring grows unaccountably tall and blossoms, for instance, into a hollyhock come mid summer. If you keep a note in your garden file of the plants that appear out of seemingly bare earth as you identify them, it will be of enormous help to you in any redesigning plans you may have.

During this watchful period you must not neglect basic maintenance such as pruning and so on, as this is of vital importance.

Know your neighbours

Different districts have their own peculiar quirks, and so indeed do individual gardens in the same street. Useful local knowledge can be gathered from conversations over the garden wall. You'll soon find out what grows well in your area by this method and by looking at other nearby gardens.

You'll also be told of great disasters of the past, and so learn by the mistakes of others, and of great successes which you may well emulate.

ACID OR ALKALINE?

Before planting it is necessary to know if your soil is acid (peaty) or alkaline (limey). Some plants, such as heathers and rhododendrons, like acidity; a few, such as clematis and viburnum, like alkalinity; but most prefer a slightly acid-neutral soil.

Soil acidity or alkalinity is expressed in terms of its pH value. This can be measured by using a proprietary soil-testing kit.

Something like pure water is neither acid nor alkaline and has a neutral pH of 7. The higher the pH reading, the higher the alkalinity; the lower the reading, the more acid. pH 6.5 (slightly acid) is the level at which most plants flourish best.

If too acid, lime should be added; if too alkaline, an acid substance such as peat should be dug in.

Don't be afraid to stop and speak to someone working his patch – gardeners are great talkers, and as often as not you'll end up by having cuttings of admired plants bestowed on you.

Starting from scratch?

If you have just moved into a new house with an as yet unplanned space for a garden, this means that you have the opportunity to create your own design from nothing. With the ideas and expert advice supplied throughout this book you will be able to transform a site into a thriving, colourful garden.

When faced with a derelict patch instead of a garden, you must first of all clear the site by removing all the litter and rubbish that is lying about. Some of the bricks, stones and timbers may be useful later on, so pile them into a corner.

If the amount of rubbish is not too great, you can put it into strong polythene bags but don't overfill them, or they become too heavy to move around. For large loads of rubbish you will have to hire a skip for which you will need a licence from the local council.

The next clearance job is to remove all unwanted plants from the garden site, including such things as brambles, weeds, tree stumps and even old, weedy turf.

If you come across any plants worth keeping at this stage, leave them where they are or carefully dig them up, with plenty of soil around the roots, and plant them in a prepared trench that has been well dug over until they can be put into final positions.

Drawing up the ground plan

Having done all this, you can then see more easily how to set about the next task, which is to draw up a rough plan of the available area.

You will need a long measuring tape (borrowed or hired if necessary), a ball of coarse twine, some stakes, a sheet of strong paper clipped to a board and a pencil. Begin by taking the measurements of existing structures such as the walls.

Don't forget to mark on your ground plan where the points of the compass fall, so sun-loving and shade-preferring plants can be given the positions they need. Any existing features should also be marked in, such as the three trees in our garden – laburnum, silver birch and horse chestnut.

Now transfer the details from this

Ground plan, showing the main features of the Flower Garden plot, which measures 22 metres (72 feet) long by 7·5 metres (25 feet) wide

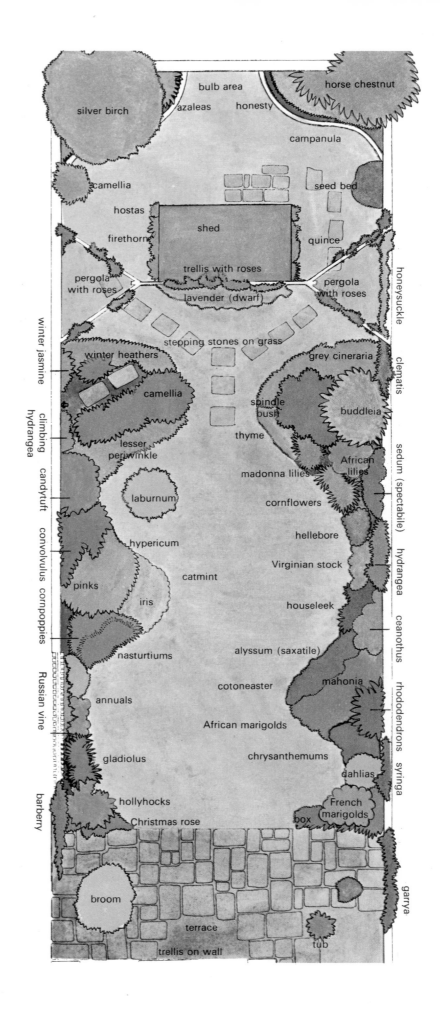

first rough drawing to a sheet of graph paper, using a simple scale. Be sure to allow for the whole garden to be shown on a single sheet. On this ground plan you should have accurate measurements of structures and existing plants.

Outlining special features
First of all decide what special features you want in your garden and list them on a separate sheet of paper. In this design for instance, the paved patio, the shaping of the borders and lawn areas, the shed with its rose-covered trellis and matching pergolas are all important, some for practical reasons, others for helping to break up this long, narrow garden. The sample garden feature plan at right shows how these are indicated on the graph paper, with the essential measurements needed to transfer your plan into reality outdoors.

Whatever you plan at this stage, don't get carried away and make your garden too complicated and overfull. It is always more effective if the design is kept relatively simple and interest maintained throughout the year by your plants.

Once you have finalized your plan in general outline, get the building-type work done before you start making preparations for planting. If you construct the paved patio near the house first, you will have a solid base from which to carry out other work as well as a resting place for sunny days.

Preparing the patio area
From your graph of the garden you will be able to calculate the quantities of materials you require. We chose York stone, for its old-world character and lasting quality, but there are many suitable alternatives, such as pre-cast slabs in various colours and textures.

Before laying the paving, it is essential to peg out and level the site, taking care not to bridge the damp proof course and under-floor ventilation bricks of the house wall.

As the lawn comes right up to the terrace, it makes for easy mowing if you set the paving a little lower than the intended final level of the lawn surface. (If the paving is higher than the lawn, mowing becomes very difficult and you will have to use shears to cut the grass along the edge.) The grass here will help to hide any unevenness in the front edge of the paved patio.

Siting the shed
The next important feature is the shed, centred within the garden's width but towards the far end so as to give a visual

break to the length of the site. It is hidden from the house by a screen of trellis-climbing plants and other perennials in a shaped bed below.

Our shed measures some 3 × 2m (10 ft × 6 ft 6 in) and the door and window face west, with access via the stepping-stone path. If you decide on an easy-to-erect prefabricated one, the only essential is that it should be on a level base, preferably of brick, concrete or wooden sleepers. If possible, allow an air space below to prevent the floor timbers from rotting. You will need to fix guttering and a water barrel or soakaway to collect rain water and prevent puddles forming around the base.

Digging a new garden
Unfortunately, all the heavy work – digging the site and levelling by raking – comes at the beginning. This is also the time to buy in, and spread where

necessary, any extra topsoil you need to mix in with the existing soil. Dig it over to at least the depth of the spade blade or fork tines (prongs). This rule applies to the whole garden.

Digging can be very hard work, and it is advisable not to do too much at one time; take it at your own pace, and dig correctly to minimize aches and pains. It doesn't matter how dry the soil is, but don't try to dig when it is very wet.

If the soil seems to be compacted (very hard and heavy) or very light, such as sandy or chalky, it would be a good idea to dig in some compost, manure, peat or similar soil-conditioning material.

Decide in which direction you are going to dig; in this garden, for instance, it is best to start from the far end and work backwards, trench by trench, to the paved patio. In this way you will avoid treading on the dug soil.

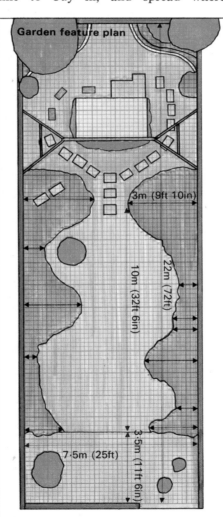

Draw up your ground plan on graph paper, marking in essential features, and measure up the north border to help you work out your plant plan

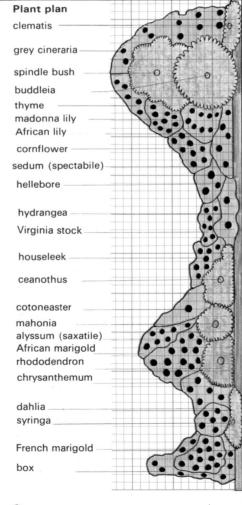

Plant plan

clematis
grey cineraria
spindle bush
buddleia
thyme
madonna lily
African lily
cornflower
sedum (spectabile)
hellebore
hydrangea
Virginia stock
houseleek
ceanothus
cotoneaster
mahonia
alyssum (saxatile)
African marigold
rhododendron
chrysanthemum
dahlia
syringa
French marigold
box

🌼 1 large growing plant
● 1 smaller growing plant
▱ area for small growing or temporary plant

N →

Digging in comfort

Always stand face on to the line of soil to be dug, and never try to dig too large a lump of soil at any one time. The least tiring way to dig is to stand close to the upright spade or fork, and if you are right-handed place your right foot on the cross-piece over the blade or tines, with your left hand on the handle and right one about halfway down. Press the head of the tool into the ground to its full depth by putting your weight onto the foot on the cross-piece. Then place your right elbow on your right knee and use this knee as a fulcrum (leverage point) to lift the soil free from the ground and turn it over and forwards. Another way is to use the edge of the undug soil on which you are standing as the lifting and pivoting point. If the soil is very compacted you may have to cut the edge of each spadeful by pressing the implement in at right angles before digging the soil.

If, manual digging seems too arduous a task, you can hire a powered cultivator (from your local hire service shop) which turns the soil over quickly, rather like a miniature plough.

If time allows, it pays to leave the soil for a week or so to settle naturally. Then, when the weather is fine and the ground not too wet, you should go over the whole site with a rake and roughly level it. If you want slightly raised soil anywhere, as round the silver birch and horse chestnut at the far end of the garden, now is the time to see that it is in position.

Planning for planting

Between bouts of digging, and while the soil is settling, make notes of what plants you intend to grow, and where they are to be placed in the garden. This will enable you to estimate the cost and order in advance.

First draw the shape of each of the planting areas onto separate sheets of graph paper, as this enables you to use a large scale. Then, with the aid of plant, bulb and seed catalogues, select your plants and list them on a sheet of paper. Alongside each plant put down what type it is (perennial, bulb, etc.), the variety, what height and width it will mature to, what colour its flowers and leaves are, when it is at its most colourful, whether it likes sun or shade, and any other points of interest about it. Armed with this information you are then ready to transfer your choice to each planting area graph.

In our Flower Garden, mixed borders of different types of plants predominate, giving variety, interest and plenty of colour all the year round, yet requiring the minimum of upkeep. The plant plan here shows how the border against the north wall (which faces south and is therefore sunny) has been planned, indicating the position of the selected plants and how many of each you need. Don't forget that the taller plants should be at the back and the smaller ones at the front of the border, with an intermingling zone in the centre.

Once you have finalized your basic garden feature and plant plans on graph paper (as described on the previous pages), it is time to make more detailed lists of plants you want and to put your planning into practice.

Marking out borders and features

Clip your plans to a board and protect them with transparent plastic. With your garden feature plan worked out to scale, you already have your basic measurements. You now need to measure out these positions on site. For this you require a long measuring tape, canes and stakes, wooden mallet, and a large ball of string.

At each of the marked points you hammer in a stake. When you want curves (for the border) use canes at intervals of about 1m (3 ft) between the stakes. When these are positioned (see the north border plan here), take the ball of string and tie one end to one of the end stakes. Then twine string round all intermediate marking canes and main stakes until you reach the other end of the border.

Continue marking each of the edge lines of the borders, shed, pergola, trellis and raised borders in this way. These lines will be essential when turfing the lawn and other grassed areas. The final edges of the flower borders will be formed when you cut the turves.

Planning plants for the borders

You will have seen from the illustration of the Flower Garden ground plan overleaf that we selected a wide variety of plants. To help you make your choice we list ours here under the following groupings: trees, shrubs, climbers, herbaceous perennials, bulbs including corms, tubers and rhizomes, annuals and biennials. Additional plants will, of course, be suggested later.

Trees

In our Flower Garden we were fortunate enough to have some mature trees *in situ*: aesculus (horse chestnut), *Betula pendula* (silver birch) and laburnum. To assist in breaking up the long, narrow plot we added three smaller trees, decorative in themselves.

Our selection: acer (small maple); *Euonymus europaeus* (spindle tree); syringa (lilac).

Shrubs

Be they evergreen or deciduous, shrubs help to create perspective and depth in mixed borders. They also make attractive features throughout the year when tub-grown, and add to the overall design of the garden while generally needing little care and attention. The lower-growing types also help to control weeds.

Our selection: aucuba; azalea; berberis (barberry); buddleia (butterfly bush); buxus (box); camellia; ceanothus; chaenomeles (quince); choisya (Mexican orange blossom); cotoneaster; cytisus (broom); erica (heathers and heaths); euonymus (spindle bush); garrya (in area reserved for a lean-to greenhouse); hamamelis (witch hazel); hydrangea; hypericum (St John's wort); lavendula (lavender); mahonia; olearia; pyracantha (fire-thorn); rhododendron; skimmia; viburnum; vinca (periwinkle).

Border measuring plan

■ main stakes

● intermediate marking canes

3m (9ft 10in)

10m (32ft 6in)

Climbers

Both climbers, and shrubs that can be treated as climbers, are ideal for clothing bare walls or helping to hide unsightly objects as well as being highly decorative. In our garden they cover the trellis and pergolas that help to break up the length of the site and give it a broader appearance.

Our selection: clematis; jasminum (jasmine); lonicera (honeysuckle); polygonum (Russian vine); rosa (rose).

Herbaceous perennials

In a mixed border herbaceous perennials give colour at different periods in spring, summer and autumn, and provide cut flowers for the house. Unfortunately, they die down during the winter months, so use shrubs to help hide the bare patches.

Our selection: agapanthus lily (African lily); *Alyssum saxatile*; *Anemone japonica* (wind flower); campanula; chrysanthemum; grey cineraria; dianthus (pinks); helleborus (hellebore); *Helleborus niger* (Christmas rose); hosta (plantain lily); nepeta (catmint); pyrethrum; sempervivum (houseleek); thymus (thyme).

Bulbs

The bulb area (to be at the far end of our garden) should be a riot of colour each spring and provide plenty of flowers for early picking. Allow space for bulbous plants, including corms, tubers and rhizomes, in a mixed border as well, as they give long seasons of flowering.

Our selection in the mixed borders: *Lilium candidum* (madonna lily); gladiolus (sword lily); dahlias; iris.

Annuals

To give splashes of colour during the summer months, and to fill gaps in the borders, annuals are ideal plants – either the hardy forms sown straight into their final positions, or half-hardy ones planted out in late spring. Both forms will be discussed in more detail later.

Our selection: centaurea (cornflower); convolvulus; iberis (candytuft); malcolmia (Virginian stock); papaver (poppy); tagetes (African and French marigolds); tropaeolum (nasturtium).

Biennials

Raised from seed one year to flower the next, biennials have a useful part to play as temporary gap-fillers. In some cases, as with lunaria (honesty) plants, they will seed themselves each spring, flower in summer, and produce unusually decorative seed pods to enliven your winter flower arrangements.

In situ: althaea (hollyhock); lunaria (honesty).

First Work in the Early Spring

Most pruning can be started in early spring (February) in warmer areas, as much as four or five weeks earlier than would be possible in colder regions. Judge by weather conditions rather than the calendar: in cold frosty weather delay pruning until late spring (April).

Roses

This is the usual time to prune established hybrid tea and floribunda bushes, established repeat-flowering shrub roses and climbers, standards and miniatures. Single-flowering climbers and weeping standards are *not* pruned, though any dead or out-of-place stems should be cut out in autumn.

If roses are not cut back every year they become unshapely and suffer from diseased and dead wood. This causes them to produce smaller, shorter-lasting blooms and weak, sparse shoots. Pruning encourages healthy and shapely future growth. Don't be afraid to attack your roses with the secateurs in a ruthless fashion. You will be rewarded by a continuous, successful show of flowers.

Really sharp secateurs are important: blunt instruments will pinch the stems and make a messy cut. Each cut should be made 6mm ($\frac{1}{4}$ in) above a dormant bud, sloping down to the other side of the stem so that the top end of the cut is level with the top of the bud. Pruning at an angle prevents water collecting on the cut which could lead to disease or cause it to become frozen in winter, damaging the wood. Choose a bud growing outwards so that the new growth does not turn inwards and clutter up the centre of the plant, encouraging the breeding of pests and. diseases in the summer, and adversely affecting foliage and flowers.

Any frost-damaged, dead or diseased wood should be cut out. You will notice that when healthy wood is cut it is a creamy-green colour. If it appears brown when cut, then it is diseased or frost-damaged, so make some further cuts until you reach healthy wood, or cut the stem out completely. Dead or frost-damaged wood is much lighter in weight than good, healthy wood and the thorns become brittle and turn brown.

If the leaves are late dropping after a gentle autumn, frozen rain caught in the angle of leaf stalk and stem is liable to damage the dormant bud and again trigger off disease, so watch out for small brown patches in otherwise healthy, green stems. These are signs of disease, so prune well below them. Cut thin, twiggy shoots right back to the main stem, but thicker, healthy stems less ruthlessly. In colder areas paint the cut with a protective compound to stop disease and rotting.

When you are pruning roses wear a tough pair of old gloves or it becomes a painful exercise. Throw the cuttings onto a large sheet of polythene or paper, cutting the larger trimmings in half. It is then a simple matter to tip them onto a bonfire heap.

Trees and shrubs

Newly-planted trees will do better if their side branches are cut back by a good 30 per cent, if this has not already been done by the plant nursery.

Prune laburnum after it has flowered, never before, not forgetting to cut down from an outward-facing bud. The shrubs that need pruning most here are the hydrangeas, buddleia, ceanothus, winter-flowering jasmine, wisteria, lonicera (honeysuckle) and large-flowered clematis.

Do not be afraid to cut back quite drastically as the emerging plant will be stronger and healthier as a result. Cut back to healthy buds on growth made the previous season. The wisteria, lonicera and large-flowered clematis can be pruned less vigorously, with just the over-crowded and unwanted shoots being removed, if you prefer.

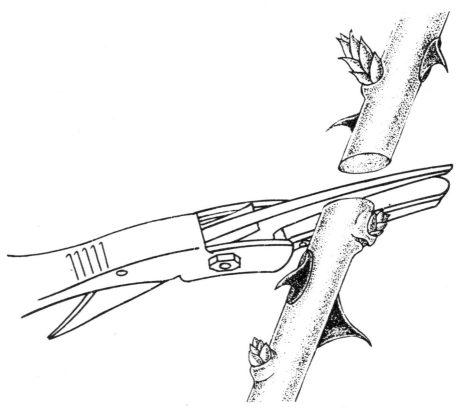

Top end of cut is level with top of bud

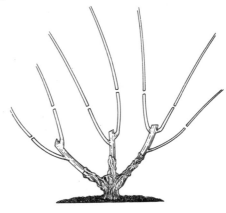

Prune new buddleia shoots hard back

Annuals for Colour

Annuals – hardy, half-hardy or tender – are old favourites that have a place in every garden. On the following pages we tell you how to sow hardy annuals and help you make your choice, but meanwhile there are certain things to be done in the garden at this time – mid spring.

First clear the mixed flower border of dead leaves and weeds. Then give a dressing of a general purpose fertilizer such as Growmore, at the rate recommended by the manufacturers, that will help new spring shoot and root growth. Hoe this in lightly, taking care not to disturb the roots near the plants. A layer of mulching material – peat, bark fibre, compost, hop manure and suchlike – will help to improve soil conditions, retain moisture during drought periods and suppress weeds; if any of the latter do appear, they are easy to pull out of the mulch layer.

Plant gladiolus corms now in warm parts of the border, where they will get sun and be protected by other plants. With a hand trowel, dig out a hole 10cm (4 in) deep (or a little deeper if there is still danger of frost), put in a small handful of silver or coarser garden sand and then place the corm, root disc downwards, on the sand and replace the soil. For most effective results, plant the corms in clusters of 5–10, each about 12cm (5 in) apart. Mark each batch with a label or stake so you remember where they are.

While planting the gladiolus, take the opportunity to fork over the soil (to a depth of the tines) where chrysanthemums and dahlias are to be planted next month. Mixing in some bonemeal (at the manufacturer's recommended rate) will help the plants make a good start in life.

Annual Borders

When making a new garden it is virtually impossible to produce a finished result in one year, unless you are going to spend a small fortune on buying container-grown plants of a fairly large size.

It is generally best to plan first for your major trees, shrubs and perennial plants and to get them into position. For the first year or two, while these are growing to their more mature size, fill up the gaps between with annual plants which will give welcome splashes of colour during the summer months. It may even be that in your first year of a new garden you will not be able, for various reasons of timing, design and final selection decisions, to do much permanent planting. In such cases the borders can consist entirely of annuals for the first summer. For an explanation of the different types of annuals, see our Plant Categories section on pages 380–381.

However, as there is going to be plenty of ground work to be done in the first year of preparation, it is not very practical to add to your chores by raising half-hardy and tender annuals yourself, as these need to be grown under heated glass (greenhouse, frame or propagation unit). Buy some packets of hardy annual seeds instead, and sow these from mid spring to early summer (March to May) directly into the borders where you wish them to flower. In addition, you can always purchase, quite cheaply, boxes of young half-hardy annuals for planting out in early summer when all danger of frost is over.

It is best to select from some of the more popular hardy annuals likely to be found in most seed catalogues, shops or garden centres. Choose ones that will give you a variety of heights and colours.

Sowing hardy annuals

When the soil is not too wet and sticky it should be dug over lightly with a fork, and weeds removed, then trodden down to firm it. To do this, simply walk up and down with your footsteps close together. Then rake it lightly backwards and forwards so that the surface soil is as crumbly and flat as possible. If the soil is not in very good condition (lumpy and hard, for instance) add a 13mm ($\frac{1}{2}$ in) layer of moist peat and a handful of a general fertilizer, such as Growmore, per square metre (or square yard) while raking.

The seeds are best sown in fairly bold patches, with the taller-growing annuals

towards the back of the borders and the lowest along the front edges. An easy way to plan a layout is to get a stick and draw the outline of the clumps on the soil. Then scatter the seeds as thinly as possible over the soil in the designated areas. Very fine seeds will require a sprinkling of fine soil over them (some topsoil through a sieve is easiest) but the larger seeds can be covered by careful raking. The biggest seeds of all, like sweet peas and nasturtiums, can be sown separately by pushing each one down about 2–3cm (1 in) into the soil – each seed approximately 15cm (6 in) apart.

The seeds should germinate and start poking their noses through the earth any time in the next four weeks. When the seedlings are large enough to take hold of, thin them out by pulling some out completely – roots as well – so that those left behind are about 10–30cm (4–12 in) apart, according to the instructions on the packet and their ultimate height. After that, except for removing weeds, watering with a sprinkler in very dry weather and dealing with pests, there should be nothing to stop a fine display of colour through the summer. (Incidentally, removing the dead flowerheads promptly will help to encourage the plants to keep on producing more and more blooms.)

POPULAR HARDY ANNUALS

alyssum (madwort)
amaranthus (love-lies-bleeding)
Anchusa Blue Bird
bartonia/*Mentzelia lindleyi*
calendula (pot marigold)
centaurea (cornflower)
chrysanthemum (annual varieties)
clarkia
delphinium, annual (larkspur)
dianthus (annual pinks)
eschscholtzia (Californian poppy)
godetia   gypsophila
helianthus (sunflower)
iberis (candytuft)
lathyrus (sweet pea)
lavatera (mallow)
linum (flax)
lupinus (annual lupin)
lychnis (silene)
malcolmia (Virginian stock)
nemophila (Californian bluebell)
nigella (love-in-a-mist)
Papaver rhoeas (shirley poppy)
Phacelia campanularia
reseda (mignonette)
Salvia horminum
tropaeolum (nasturtium)

If you want to add *half-hardy* annuals, such as althaea (hollyhocks), antirrhinums, petunias, verbena, nicotiana (tobacco plants), nemesia, zinnias, tagetes (African and French marigolds), these should be planted out in early summer.

Down with slugs
These pests are the main enemy of your flower border. They must be destroyed or they will, in turn, destroy the plants. The small, grey slug loves to munch his way through the leaves, especially if the weather is warm. Operating mostly at night, slugs leave a tell-tale trail of white, mucous film behind them. This is the sign of all types of slugs, and snails too. Put down proprietary slug pellets; remember to carry out this eliminating operation regularly.

Beware birds – and cats!
Both birds and cats love newly seed-sown areas of the garden and to prevent them wreaking havoc among your annuals anchor down some nylon netting over the beds, and place a lot of twiggy sticks and branches, or gorse, over the areas. Remove these protective barriers when you thin out the seedlings. Alternatively, treat these areas with a proprietary animal repellent that will help to deter both birds and rodents.

Laying the stepping stones
York stone slabs were selected for the stepping stones here. Once the positions of the flower beds, trellis and pergolas have been marked out it is easy to estimate the number of slabs required. Laying them is also a simple matter and it is advisable to position them before making the lawn. (See Laying Turf on page 62.)

Stepping stones should be level and the best way to achieve this is to remove approximately 5cm (2 in) of soil, put down a layer of coarse sand to replace it and lay the paving slab in position. Then, using a spirit level, ensure it is level by raising or lowering it by adding or removing sand. It is particularly important to ensure the slabs by the shed door are all level, not only with the ground but also with each other, so there are no jutting-up edges to trip over. When the lawn turfs are laid, these should come slightly above the level of the slabs, thus making it easy to cut the grass with a lawn-mower. If the slabs are above the turfs, then it will involve the onerous task of cutting grass round the paved areas with hand shears. The turfs will be about 3·5cm (1½ in) thick and you can always adjust the paving slabs later so that they are at the correct height to the grass.

Popular hardy annuals: (top) annual chrysanthemums and tropaeolum

Know Your Plant Categories

Plants are allotted to convenient categories according to their hardiness and the following descriptions will help you to understand these classifications.
All plants exhibit varying degrees of hardiness, or tolerance towards cold and damp, and this tolerance is directly related to the climates of their countries of origin.
We will explain the differences between trees, shrubs and climbers and divide the confusing bulb group into bulbs, corms, rhizomes and tubers.

A lot of the terms used to describe plant categories are usually abbreviated in catalogues and plant references, and we give these initials following the full name, where appropriate.

Hardy perennials HP
This term denotes plants that will live and grow outside from year to year in all but extreme climates. Although this group includes shrubs and trees, the term 'hardy perennial' commonly refers to hardy herbaceous border perennials.

Examples of: (right) half-hardy perennials, pelargoniums; (far right) tender or greenhouse perennial, the house plant dizygotheca; (below) hardy perennials, the true geranium psilostemon

Herbaceous perennials
These overwinter by using various forms of rootstock. The top growth dies down in the autumn and more new shoots emerge the following spring. This group of plants may be propagated from seed, although it is advisable to increase them by dividing the roots or taking cuttings. Familiar examples are delphinium, dianthus pinks, phlox and geum (avens).

Half-hardy perennials HHP
This group includes some of the well-known summer bedding plants, for example pelargonium and begonia. Dahlias, chrysanthemums and some bulbous plants like gladiolus are also represented

here. Although some of these plants will survive outside during mild winters, they stand a much better chance of living if they are taken out of the ground and over-wintered in a dry place where temperatures remain above freezing.

Certain 'tender' or 'greenhouse' perennials also fall into this category. An example of this is abutilon, which is often used as a 'dot' plant in summer bedding schemes, but originates in a warmer climate and requires a high winter temperature to ensure survival. Other plants, such as antirrhinum (snapdragon), petunia and nemesia, although often referred to as half-hardy annuals and indeed treated as such by being raised

from seed each year, are also in fact half-hardy perennials.

Tender/Greenhouse perennials GP
Natives of hot and often humid zones, these plants require constant protected cultivation, although some of them may be placed outdoors in sunny positions during good summer weather. A few members of this group are used in elaborate summer bedding schemes.

Annuals A
All annuals are characterized by completing their life cycle within a twelve-month period. They germinate, grow, flower and produce seed all during the favourable growing period.

Hardy annuals HA
Hardy annuals are the familiar flowering plants of the summer cottage gardens. Plants such as calendula (pot marigold),

(Above) hardy annuals, calendula (pot marigold), not to be confused with tagetes (French and African marigold)
(Below) half-hardy annuals, double zinnias

clarkia, godetia and centaurea (cornflower) may be grown from a spring sowing in open ground and will be flowering profusely in early summer. Seeds of hardy annuals may be sown during autumn and the young plants will stand the winter outside to give an extra early flower show during the following spring. Lathyrus (sweet pea) is often treated in this way.

Half-hardy annuals HHA
The colourful bedding plants, half-hardy annuals, brighten many gardens in summer. They are natives of warm climates and so will not reproduce naturally outdoors in countries that experience cold, wet winters. The gardener has to intervene in the plant's natural cycle and either collect seed in autumn and store it in a dry warm place in winter, or purchase fresh seed every spring. To obtain maximum showiness from these plants, seedlings should be raised in a warm environment, such as a greenhouse or heated frame, and planted out when all danger of frost is passed. Tagetes (African marigolds), zinnias and lobelia are familiar examples in this group. Seed of half-hardy annuals may be sown outdoors when all danger of frost is passed, but generally this method does not give such a good show of blooms.

Tender annuals
Although generally requiring constant greenhouse cultivation, tender annuals can safely go outdoors at the height of

(Below) tender annual example, a group of greenhouse-grown dwarf cinerarias

summer when they are already in bloom. Schizanthus (butterfly flower), cineraria and celosia are all good examples.

Biennials B
These plants grow one year to flower the next. Cheiranthus (wallflower), *Dianthus barbatus* (sweet William), bellis (daisy) and myosotis (forget-me-not) are all familiar spring bedding plants which are biennials. They are all hardy and seed is sown in early summer so that the plants will be large enough to plant out in their spring flowering quarters during the autumn. There are several greenhouse biennials, such as calceolaria. In addition, some tender perennials such as cyclamen are often treated as biennials.

Trees
These are usually defined as perennial plants that are woody, with one main stem (trunk), and a mass of branches and stems above. Trees usually grow over 4m (13 ft) tall. They are generally sub-divided into two categories: the broad-leaved kinds which can have a variety of different shaped leaves showing a network of veins – such as the tilia (lime), aesculus (horse chestnut) and laburnum – and the conifers, like taxus (yew) and picea (Christmas tree) which have needle-like or 'scale' leaves.

Trees can take many years to mature. They can also be either hardy, half-hardy or tender, and obviously it is only wise with such a long-term plant to buy a hardy type. Trees and shrubs are often referred to as evergreen (that is, they retain their leaves in winter) or deciduous (that is, they shed their leaves in autumn

and produce new ones in the following spring).

Shrubs

Unlike trees, these are woody perennials that branch naturally from the base and have more than one main stem. They can grow as tall as 8m (26 ft) or be only a few centimetres (1–2 in) high. Like trees, they can be hardy, half-hardy, or tender. Again it is sensible to plant only the hardy kinds outdoors. There are innumerable examples suitable for gardens, such as rhododendron, camellia, syringa (lilac) and buddleia. Shrubs are sometimes called bushes, and this term can also refer to a cluster of shrubs.

Climbers

True climbers are a group of plants that grow upwards naturally and are able to support themselves against an object such as another plant, trellis, wall, string, netting, pergola and so on. They can do this by various means, such as tendrils

One of the many shrubs — or bushes — a rhododendron with a profusion of ball-shaped blooms

Below: a characteristic fall of laburnum, one of that broad-leaved trees

208

Left: a pair of popular true climbers
from the favourite clematis genus
Below: lilies are among the true bulbs

(short, twisted leafless growths), aerial roots (short stems with little roots), sucker pads (self-adhesive growths), leaf stalks which twist round the support, hooked spines, or by the twining growth of their stems. Examples of some of the different methods are lonicera (honeysuckle), by twining; hedera (ivy), by aerial roots; clematis, by tendrils; parthenocissus (Virginia creeper), by sucker pads; lathyrus (sweet pea), by tendrils; blackberry, by hooked spines; and convolvulus, by twining of the stems.

Climbers may be perennials or annuals, hardy, half-hardy or tender. In addition to the climbers, there are other plants, such as 'climbing' and 'rambling' rosa (rose), quince, ceanothus, some pyracantha (firethorn) and cotoneasters that are basically shrubs but grow in such a way that they can be trained against supports, provided they are given a helping hand by twisting or tying in the shoots to the supports, and in some cases by careful pruning.

Bulbs

Many people when they refer to bulbs also include plant organs which are similar in function (as food stores), but which should strictly be referred to as corms, tubers, or rhizomes. A true bulb is an underground 'bud' that has fleshy or scaly leaves around it, all growing upwards from a basal 'plate'. These are plant food storage leaves. Inside are the rudiments of flower, flower stalk and leaves. When conditions are right, roots grow down into the soil from the basal plate and the rudimentary flowers and leaves grow upwards to give the above-ground parts of the plant. The leaves and roots absorb plant foods during growth and feed these back into the bulb or a 'daughter bulb', before they die back at the end of their season. In this way, they prepare for the next growth period by again forming rudimentary flowers and leaves. Sometimes several bulbils or 'daughter bulbs' are formed around the original parent, and these can be used to increase the plants.

True bulbs include lilium (lily), hyacinth, narcissus (daffodil), tulipa (tulip) and galanthus (snowdrop). All bulbs are easy to grow and have the advantage of rapid growth when conditions are suitable. Some are hardy and can be left

209

in the ground all the year round (tulips and daffodils) whereas others (nerine and vallota) are half-hardy and are best lifted from the ground, dried and stored in cool, frost-free conditions (or well protected with straw outdoors). Yet others are tender and require greenhouse conditions throughout the year, such as amaryllis and lachenalia.

Tubers

Tubers are thickened parts of underground stems or roots which store food

and carry buds for leaves and flowers above ground, and roots below. Typical examples of these are dahlias and some begonias. Such plants are usually treated as half-hardy annuals and can be sown from seed. Usually, however, the tubers are stored in cool, dry conditions during the winter months, cut up into sections and started into growth in a cool greenhouse in spring, for planting out when hardened off.

Corms

These are fleshy, swollen and solid underground stem bases with scales (outside leaves) that can be round (crocus) or flat (gladiolus). Like bulbs, they are food storage organs and contain embryo flowers and leaves that grow from the upper surface, while roots grow from a 'disc' below. They can be considered annuals because each year a new corm is formed above the old one.

Hardy corms, like crocus, can be left in the ground all year, but half-hardy ones, such as gladiolus, are best dug up, dried and stored carefully each autumn for planting the following spring. Propagation is by the small 'cormlets' also

produced, but these may take a year or two before they flower.

Rhizomes

A rhizome is a fleshy underground or creeping, root-like food storage organ from which leaves, stems and flowers grow upwards and roots downwards. It tends to be scaly and look 'jointed'. Typical examples are flag irises, convallaria (lily of the valley) and polygonatum (Solomon's Seal), all hardy plants.

The Garden in Spring

Deciduous trees, shrubs and roses can be planted in mid spring (March) if the soil is dry and workable and the weather reasonably mild. If the plants you ordered earlier arrive during a bad weather period, either store them in a frostproof place still in their root packaging, or open them up and put them into a temporary trench outdoors. If your planting sites have been previously prepared, all you have to do now is dig a hole large enough to take the roots comfortably without squashing them. Examine any existing trees and shrubs with stakes to check that both are securely in the ground and haven't been moved by winter gales. Look at any tree ties to make sure that they aren't strangling the plants in any way or chafing the stems.

Check your trellis work and pergola timbers. Any rotting timber is best removed, or at least reinforced, and nails and screws should be examined to make sure that they are still firmly in position.

Existing lawns need their first mow in mid spring (March), but the grass should not be cut too low at this time of the year: cutting back to 5cm (2 in) is quite sufficient. To cut the grass cleanly the lawn-mower must have sharp blades.

Below: for a broken lawn edge, cut a square, move it up and trim the bad edge, filling gap with new turf

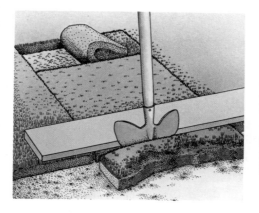

For this first cut it is always advisable to collect the cuttings in a grass-box or bag while mowing; they can be added to the compost heap or used for mulching (unless a wormkiller has been applied).

After this first cut of the season, any mossy areas should be very apparent. So now is the time to apply a lawn moss-killer at the rate recommended by the makers. As moss is usually a sign of badly drained soil, it is wise to aerate the lawn's mossy patches by sticking in the tines of a fork every 10–15cm (4–6 in), wiggling it backwards and forwards to enlarge the holes slightly and then brushing in a 50/50 mixture of soil and peat to aid drainage. Once the moss has been killed, rake it out and, if necessary, re-seed the area with suitable grass seed.

You can also deal with any worn areas or broken edges now. Cut out worn patches and replace them with pieces of turf cut from areas which are not much used or not visible from the house. To make good the resulting bare patches, fill up the holes with soil, firm it with the feet, level it and sow with grass seed.

Cover the Trellis and Pergolas with climbing roses

Do your boundary walls look bare and uninteresting? Are they high enough to grow all the plants you would like? Do you wish to hide, as we do, an unsightly feature? In our garden where the shed is fully visible from the house, an attractive disguise is required. Here the designer has made full use of trellis work extending at either side of the shed, as well as the two pergoldas leading to the utility end of the garden, providing ideal places to grow climbing and rambling roses.

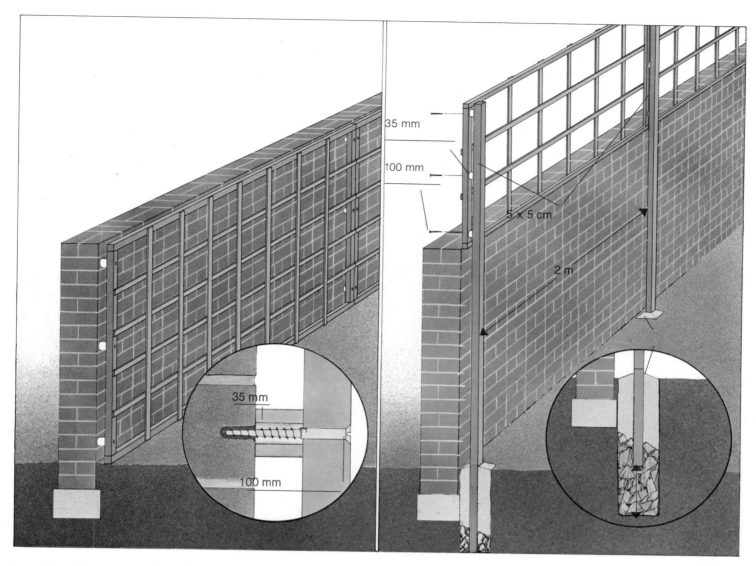

A trellis will give your boundary walls additional height and you more privacy.

If you are erecting trellis work against the walls, it is always advisable – and a friendly gesture – to inform your immediate neighbours beforehand. Furthermore, make sure the trellis doesn't interfere with their garden designs or cut out what is known as 'reasonable light and air'. (There is no definite ruling as to what height a trellis may reach, but 2·5–3m (8–10 ft) from ground level is generally acceptable.)

Buying the trellis
Although trellis is easy enough to make, it is quicker and generally far preferable to buy it ready-made. It can be bought in various patterns, lengths and heights and, if you are armed with the measurements, it should present no problem to get just what you want, in the form of prefabricated panels. You will also need some timber supporting posts, which should preferably be 5×5cm (2×2 in); add a further 60cm (2 ft) onto the required

length, to allow for sinking the posts into the ground.

Before erecting the trellis posts and panels, paint them with a wood preservative that is not harmful to plants. The supporting posts, too, need similar treatment and, as an extra precaution, soak the bottom ends in creosote to a height of 60cm (2 ft) to give added protection against rotting in the ground.

Fixing to the walls
Use the normal type of plastic wall plugs and screws to fix the top, middle and bottom of each main vertical lath of the panel. To prevent contact between the wall and the timber (which could cause rotting) use 100mm (4 in) long fixing screws with a 35mm ($1\frac{1}{2}$ in) long plastic tube spacer over the screw shank.

Fixing above the walls
For this type of trellis support posts are necessary, sunk into concrete at 1·80m (6 ft) intervals. First dig a hole 90cm (3 ft) deep, fill the bottom 30cm (12 in)

Above: how to fix a trellis against, and above, a wall
Overleaf: the Flower Garden pergola
When extended, a diamond-shaped trellis will not reach its full height
Rigid trellis is available in either wood or plastic-coated wire

with rubble (hardcore), place the post in position, put more rubble around it and tread it firmly into place.

Make a cement mix, using either a ready-mix type according to manufacturer's instructions, or 1 part cement to 4 parts coarse sand and enough water to make it sufficiently liquid to handle. Shovel this into the rubble-filled hole, and check that the post is vertical with a spirit level. Finally, smooth the cement surface to form a slightly convex top, so that rainwater will fall away from the post. Repeat this for all the posts and allow several days for cement to set.

It is then a simple matter to screw the trellis panels to these upright posts, inserting 100mm (4 in) screws with

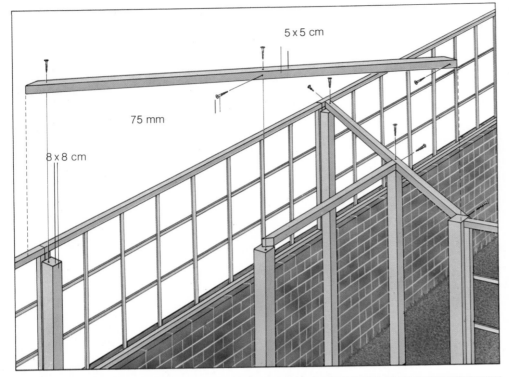

5 x 5 cm

75 mm

8 x 8 cm

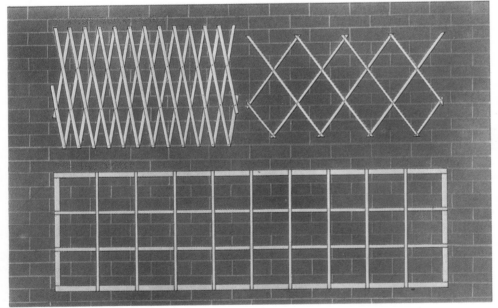

Mid spring (March)

If any buxus (box) edging plants have become straggly or died away at the base by mid spring, it is time to dig them up. Divide the clusters by pulling them apart and then trim the best portions of each plant – both roots and branches – with secateurs. Replant them 15cm (6 in) apart, treading them in firmly. The newly set-out plants will quickly re-establish themselves and give a much more satisfactory result later in the season than if you had just cut them back with shears.

Hoe carefully between your spring and early summer flowering biennial plants, such as wallflowers, forget-me-not, sweet William, Canterbury bells, and honesty, so as to catch and kill the weeds in an early stage of growth. If antirrhinums are overcrowded, or you have any left from last year that have overwintered outside, a good place to plant them is among the tulip bulbs that are now pushing their noses through the soil. This will give a second splash of colour to the tulip areas once your bulbs have finished flowering.

If you have not yet prepared the planting areas for new trees and shrubs, do so as soon as weather conditions allow – when the temperature is above freezing and the soil not so wet that it sticks to your boots or shoes. Don't forget to dig the area as deep and as wide as possible and add plenty of humus-forming matter, such as well-rotted compost or manure, to the lower soil. You should also prepare supporting stakes for the trees and shrubs and make sure you have suitable ties for holding the two together.

If your garden is relatively warm and sheltered, it is quite possible in mid spring (March) to sow some sweet pea seeds outdoors in a patch of light soil to which sand and peat have been added. Sow them in clusters and transplant them to their flowering positions later on.

If any new plants arrive during a frosty period, when the ground will be hard or very cold, don't attempt to plant the newcomers but keep them wrapped in a cool but frost-free place. For extra protection cover them with straw or sacks. If the cold spell is very prolonged, you may have to uncover the branches to let light and air get to them, but keep the roots covered. Only when the ground has warmed up and is workable should the new plants be set outside. If they are evergreens it pays to give them a protective sheeting of polythene or sacking from north and east winds after planting.

35mm (1½ in) spacers 30–45cm (12–18 in) apart as previously described.

To give the trellis and posts an attractive, finished appearance, convex wood capping pieces on each end post and above the top laths of trellis are effective, as well as useful in discouraging rainwater from accumulating.

Fixing trellis against the shed

This length of trellis in our garden is 3·65m (12 ft) long and so will require three supporting posts and probably two 1·8m square (6 ft square) panels of prefabricated trellis. Erect them as previously described and make sure the vertical laths of the panels abut each other for a clean and tidy finished appearance.

Erecting the pergolas

The vertical 8 × 8cm (3 × 3 in) painted poles can be erected in the same way as the trellis posts. Fix the supporting cross pieces by nailing or screwing them into position, as indicated in the construction diagram above. In our garden the pergolas have been designed in triangular form, see above, to hide the utility area behind and to create interesting walk-ways through from one part of the garden to the other.

As the trellis in front of the shed is designed to render it invisible from the house, an evergreen climber is ideal.

Unusual evergreens

Although there are only a few evergreen roses, they are an unusual and attractive choice for this purpose in the garden. From the point of view of flowers, easily the most spectacular is the single yellow Mermaid which blooms from mid summer (June) onwards and although it is only semi evergreen, it does retain some leaves throughout the winter. On the other hand, it is slightly tender and the stems can be killed right down to ground level in very severe weather.

The thickest-leaved evergreen rose for this situation is *R. wichuraiana* which has attractive glossy leaves and heads of bunched smallish flowers. Its greatest attraction, however, is its piercing fragrance – and the fact that it does not start flowering until early autumn (August), when most climbing roses are past their best. It also has a second season of

Below: Pink Perpétué flowers in summer and winter. Bottom: semi-evergreen, Mermaid, with large single blooms
Right: Rosette-shaped Dorothy Perkins is prone to mildew. Below: Crimson Shower bears trusses of flowers from late July

colour when the small red heps (fruit) cover it in late autumn (October). There are many handsome *wichuraiana* hybrids, but none is completely evergreen.

There are two hybrids from the evergreen Mediterranean rose (*R. sempervirens*) which, although only semi evergreen, could be considered for this situation. The first is Adelaide d'Orléans, whose flowers are much the colour of strawberries and cream, with rather more cream than strawberries; they are small and very double, like a Japanese Cherry bloom, and open in mid summer (June). With rather more persistent leaves is Adelaide's sister, Félicité et Perpétué, which has white flowers opening from crimson buds in late summer (July). Once these two have flowered they have finished for the year, but the display is dazzling. these have the advantage of flowering from early summer (May) until autumn, although they do have a tendency to have two main bursts, with a few odd flowers in between.

There are also a number of vigorous climbing sports of HT roses that have the large flowers of their type, but only flower once and tend to make rather gaunt plants. However, they mingle happily with the pillar roses. A favourite is Guinée, with very fragrant flowers that are almost black when they open. New

Dawn tends to keep on flowering and has silvery pink blooms, while Climbing Crimson Glory has large crimson flowers.

Finally there are some large-flowered hybrids of *R. wichuraiana*, characterized by glossy leaves and flowers in size between the HT and the ramblers. Of these, one of the best is Albéric Barbier, with yellow flowers that turn to cream and a sweet scent. Emily Gray is an old favourite with buff-coloured flowers, while those of François Juranville are coral pink. Paul Transon has salmon-pink flowers and usually blooms again in the autumn, while May Queen has lilac-pink ones. All these are a blaze of flower at mid summer, but usually that is the full extent of their contribution to the garden, although the glossy, dark green leaves are attractive for long periods. They need little pruning, except to be thinned out when the growths get too crowded. This is most easily done in winter.

All these climbing roses have to be tied in to the pergola, but otherwise they require little attention – except for the ramblers, from which you have to remove the flowering growths once the flowering is over and then tie in their new growths later on.

Some of the interesting varieties described here may be difficult to obtain, but are well worth searching out. Also illustrated are some of the more popular and readily available varieties of climbers.

The Trees in Your Garden

Trees are the most attractive and rewarding features of a garden. They add height and interest, and give a touch of elegance to even the very simplest of plots.

There are two types of trees: evergreen or deciduous; they may be tolerant of acid or alkaline soil. The varied shapes include widespreading, weeping and columnar.

In addition to contributing height and interest to a garden, they can be put to many practical uses, from providing shade or acting as a windbreak to hiding an obstinate eyesore. It is a pity to remove existing trees unless absolutely necessary, as they may have taken years to mature.

Making the right choice
The majority of trees will grow happily in a soil that has an almost neutral pH or is slightly acid. Some, such as birches, trees of heaven (ailanthus), elms and some poplars, have a definite preference for acid soils. Others, for example the decorative members of the apple and cherry genera, maples and crataegus (thorns), prefer some free lime.

Waterlogged or boggy ground suits very few trees, such as weeping willows and alders; dry or shallow soils do not worry many except the moisture-loving ones, provided the lower soil is not composed of solid chalk. (If chalk is a problem dig it out as deeply as possible and replace with good topsoil.)

For the best results with all varieties make sure the soil is deep, friable, well-drained and well-manured. A specific tree may prefer acidity or alkalinity and either can be provided for when preparing the ground for planting. If necessary, top dressings or feeds of special fertilizers can be given each year.

When to plant
It is best to buy and plant trees during the autumn and spring months when the weather is reasonably mild and the soil is not too wet or frozen. Some can be planted in winter if conditions are suitable, but generally trees do not pick up and grow as well in the first season, as their roots are in their most active state during that period.

The Common Laburnum that was already in existence in our Flower Garden

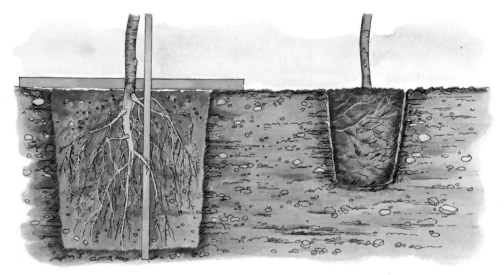

Trees must be planted to the correct depth and their roots well spread out; damaged or broken parts must be removed

Trees for planting in autumn and spring are often in the 'bare-rooted' state. This means there is little or no soil on their roots, or that the roots are in polythene or sacking containing a little loose soil. Bare-rooted trees are ideal for planting during their dormant period of non-active growth but *not* at any other time of year.

'Container-grown trees' – most nurseries and garden centres supply them – have been grown in soil-filled plastic, metal, whalehide or polythene containers from an early age, and their roots are well-established in the soil. The object of container-grown trees is to lengthen the planting season, so that they can be set in the garden at any time of year.

In theory this seems to work quite well, but in practice, after planting during the summer months, you must be especially careful to ensure that the roots get plenty of water during a dry spell and the leaves are sprayed every day for four to six weeks to help overcome any possible transitional shock.

If both bare-rooted and container-grown trees are available, you can plant at virtually any time of year, and have no excuse for a bare area. It also allows for impulse-buying should you see a specific tree you have not been able to obtain previously.

You will have to pay rather more for container-grown trees or plants of any kind, as they are more expensive to raise and transport to retailers.

Considering the many years a tree spends in the ground, it pays to prepare its site thoroughly. Begin by digging out the soil to the depth of a spade or the fork tines, and make a hole 1–1·5m

(3–5 ft) in diameter. Then dig over the next layer to the same depth and add to this as much well-rotted manure or compost as you have available. Tread it firm and follow this with a light scuttling of the top 5–7cm (2–3 in) of soil with the fork or a large rake.

During preparation remove any large stones or weeds.

Planting bare-rooted trees

Trees must be planted to the same depth as they were previously growing; this is shown by the soil mark on the stem above the roots. Place the tree in the hole and check the depth by the level of the soil mark. If the hole is too shallow remove more soil; if it is too deep, put back some topsoil and lightly firm it.

Then get a wooden stake, about 4cm (1½ in) square, preferably with a sharpened end, and firmly hammer it into the centre of the hole. It should be long enough to reach as high as the first set of branches.

Put the tree back in the hole, carefully placing the roots around the stake. If there are any broken roots .cut off the damaged portions with a sharp knife or secateurs. Make sure all the other roots are spread out.

If you can get someone to hold the tree in position the planting will be easier. If not, tie the tree to the stake. Shovel the topsoil back into the hole so that it gets well round the roots (slightly shaking the tree will help). Return all the soil, firming it from time to time, and make sure the tree remains upright.

Planting container-grown trees

First water the soil in the container and leave it to drain. Then place the tree, in its container, into the prepared hole to ensure the correct depth.

Next remove the container either by

slitting the sides or tipping out the soil-ball round the roots. Hold the tree in position, return the topsoil and firm it. A stake of suitable length is again required, but in this case it is advisable to hammer it in *after* planting, taking care not to disturb the soil ball.

Caring for young trees

First tie the trunk of a new tree to its stake. Use one of the proprietary tree ties available or, if that is not possible, a nylon stocking. Don't use coarse string as it may chafe the bark. Fix a tie about 10cm (4 in) above soil level and another at about the same distance from the top of the stake.

After planting, a good watering is advisable and, especially in spring, the plants should be sprayed daily for about a month. A layer of mulch over the whole planting area will help to conserve moisture and provide food for the roots.

Until the trees are established, which could be up to three years after planting, keep the soil area free of weeds and grass that might inhibit healthy growth.

IN OUR FLOWER GARDEN

We 'inherited' two large and mature trees – silver birch (*Betula pendula*) and an Indian horse chestnut (*Aesculus indica*) – at the far end of the garden. They are both deciduous and, mainly because of their size, commonly associated with woodlands or parks. They can, however, look equally right in a garden, provided they are carefully sited (if being newly planted) or incorporated into the landscaping as in this instance – where they form features with underplanting for added interest.

Birches

Silver birch trees are most elegant in form with golden-yellow diamond-shaped leaves in autumn and white peeling bark, which develops as the trees mature, the final height being about 8m (25 ft).

Because of the tracery framework of their branches, silver birches do not cast dense shade, but they are rather shallow-rooting and plants set beneath them should not have roots that penetrate too deeply (hence our choice of azaleas). The only soil they don't like is a chalky one (again, like the azaleas).

There are a number of other fine birch trees. For example, *Betula costata*, with white peeling bark in summer that turns orange in winter; *B. pendula* Tristis, tall and slender with hanging branches; *B. pendula* Youngii, a smaller tree with weeping branches of delicate leaves that reach the ground; and *B. utilis*, with its greyish trunk and russet-brown branches contrasting with each other.

Horse chestnuts

Among the horse chestnuts, *Aesculus indica* is one of the most attractive, with its 'candles' of white, pink and yellow flowers in mid to late summer (June to July), followed by smooth-coated 'conkers' later in the year.

Other horse chestnuts are *A. flava* (sweet buckeye) which has yellow flowers and finely toothed, smallish leaves that colour attractively in autumn; *A. carnea* Briottii with deep rosy red flowers and smooth 'conkers'; and *A. hippocastanum* (common horse chestnut) with its summer 'candles' of white flowers up to 30cm (12 in) high followed by the 'conkers' loved by children. All horse chestnuts grow freely in most soils, except very chalky ones, and they create dense shade beneath, so underplants have to be carefully chosen.

Laburnums

We also inherit a laburnum sited on the south edge of the lawn. There are few smallish, drooping-shaped trees – they grow to about 6m (20 ft) – that are more attractive. They beautify a garden in late spring to mid summer (April to June) by their long, pendulous yellow pea-like

Right: slow-growing Japanese maple, Acer palmatum, *with glorious autumn foliage*
Below left: common horse chestnut, Aesculus hippocastanum, *bears 'candle' blooms and conkers. Below right: spindle* Euonymus europaeus, *has flowers and fruit*

flowers, followed in autumn with brown seed pods and in winter with green twigs.

All parts of the plant are poisonous, particularly the seeds, so obviously care should be taken where there are children.

The most common laburnum is *L. anagyroides* with various forms, such as *L. anagyroides* Aureum, with golden yellow leaves; and *L. a.* Autumnale, which often flowers for a second time in autumn. *L. vossii*, also very popular, is later-flowering than most, has darker glossy green leaves and is more erect in habit.

In our mixed flower border we added three small garden trees: a spindle, miniature maple, and a lilac.

Spindle tree

The spindle is one of the few trees among the Euonymus family of shrubs and is correctly called *Euonymus europaeus*. It grows to about 6m (20 ft), and its inconspicuous yellow-green small flowers are followed by a wealth of clusters of pinkish-red fruits, which open to reveal orange-coloured seeds. In autumn the leaves turn beautiful yellow and red hues. It is one of the easiest of trees to grow in almost any position.

Maples

The small maple, *Acer palmatum*, slowly grows to a height of about 4m (12 ft). We chose it for its attractive lobed leaves, which are pale green in summer and gorgeous orange and red tones in autumn. It is sometimes commonly called the Japanese maple and there are many cultivars of it, all equally attractive and easy to grow, if the soil is not too chalky.

There are several other forms of maples which are mainly much larger trees and more suitable for bigger gardens, or for planting in a far corner for shade or to hide an unpleasant view.

Syringas

Our lilac tree is more correctly called Syringa. The many trees and shrubs in this genus produce a mass of fragrant flowers in early to mid summer (May to June), and remain shapely green-leaved plants from early spring to late autumn (February to October).

Lilacs grow well in all but the most chalky soils, and they give their best in a sunny position. The most common varieties grown in gardens are those of *Syringa vulgaris*. They provide a wide colour range of flowers – from white, pale pink, dark red, mauve, purple, yellow to greenish-tinged – and can be either single or double flowered. There are so many that it is advisable to choose a colour to harmonize with other blooms in the immediate vicinity.

Some good ones are *Syringa vulgaris* Clarke's Giant (lavender-pink); Olivier de Serres (mauvish-pink); Esther Staley (carmine-pink); Charles Joby (purple-red); Mrs. Edward Harding (red); Maud Notcutt (white); and Souvenir d'Alice Harding (alabaster – off-white).

Left: the graceful birch, Betula pendula, *has attractive leaf shapes, such as heart or diamond, as well as some splendid stem colours. Below: the lilac tree,* Syringa vulgaris, *has many varieties which happily mix with other surrounding plants.*

Heathers for Winter Colour

Winter colour in the garden is often considered a problem, but a never-failing source of coloured leaves and flowers comes from winter heathers. The designer has created a special corner for them at the end of the south mixed flower border so that not only can they be given the soil conditions and aspect they prefer, but also you then have a delightful area to look at, and flowers to pick, during the so-called 'dead' months of the year. The winter jasmine arching on the trellis behind adds to the overall pleasing picture.

Heather is the common name generally taken to include the true heathers (erica), the heaths (daboecia) and ling (calluna), as each genus is very similar in appearance and requirement. They are rightly popular and with careful selection they provide colour and form throughout the whole year. They are not, however, as widely grown as they might be, for many people seem to think they need the conditions of their native habitat, moorlands. In fact, heathers are among the easiest plants to grow and require little

attention. They prefer a sunny position but will thrive in partial shade, though flower colour may not be as good. They are not unduly fussy about soil, provided it is on the peaty, acid side without lime, but even so there are some cultivars and hybrids, for instance *Erica carnea, E. × darleyensis, E. mediterranea, E. arborea* and *E. terminalis*, which will grow as happily in soils containing free lime (but not solid chalk) as in acid ground. The ideal pH to aim for is 5.6 to 6.0.

Planting preparation
All the heathers are best planted in late spring to early summer (April to May) or late autumn or early winter (October to November). Even if you have good, suitable soil it still pays dividends to prepare it thoroughly and weed it in advance of planting, by forking in plenty of peat and leaf mould (rotted leaves). If the ground is at all limey, then it is advisable to dig out the soil to the depth

of two spade blades and replace it with lime-free topsoil (brought in if necessary) mixed with plenty of peat. The surplus soil can be used elsewhere in the garden or heaped somewhere for future use.

After digging, it pays to allow the soil to settle naturally for a week or so if time allows. If it doesn't, then tread the soil firm and rake it over afterwards.

Planning for heathers
When planted individually among other plants, heathers never look their best, except possibly the tree forms. It is far better to mass them in one place where they can set each other off to best advantage. It is also far easier to take care of their few requirements when they are all together in one spot.

In our garden the heathers have been selected for winter flower and leaf colour throughout the year. They have been massed together in part of the mixed flower border on the south side of the

For a colourful mixed border choose heathers in white-tinged pale pinks to deep mauves

garden, facing to the west, where they will get the open conditions they like. On the other hand, because it is possible to produce a mass of colour throughout the year, either from flowers or leaves, many people prefer to put them in an 'island' bed – a flowerbed that stands on its own and can be seen all round from a variety of angles. In this case, 'dot' (individual) specimens of other acid soil-loving plants such as dwarf rhododendrons, azaleas and conifers are often added to give even further interest. A heather edge to a border or low hedges along paths are other effective ways to use these plants.

Before buying your plants, it is wise to draw on paper a scale plan of the types and varieties you want. By doing this you can ensure that there are no colour clashes, you get the right plants of the correct heights in the places you want them, and you can work out in advance how many plants of each variety you need. Again, with the exception of the tree heathers, it is more effective visually to put a number of plants of the same type in one clump, and to blend the clumps into one another. In this way you get bold hummocks and mats of flowers and leaves that create a most attractive appearance.

Most heathers are generally best kept to a height of 60cm (24 in) or less, except of course, tree heathers which will grow up to 3m (10 ft) or more. But even the latter can be kept smaller by pruning. It is advisable to purchase small plants that have been raised from cuttings (rather than division), as these grow more quickly and reach maturity sooner. The average distance between each plant should be about 45cm (18 in). This may make them look thin on the ground initially but they will soon grow to intermingle with each other and cover the ground to act as most useful suppressors of annual weeds.

Putting in the plants
From your scale plan, draw out with a stake the areas where each group of heathers is to be planted. Then place the plants, still in their pots if possible, or with a minimum of disturbance to the soil ball if not, on the surface of the 'clump' areas to finalize where each plant is to go. Next plant each heather by digging out a hole of the right size with a trowel (or spade for larger areas) and removing the pots (if plastic), or tearing down one side (if they are peat pots). Make sure the soil level is where it was originally on the plant, and firm it with your fingers (or feet, if a larger plant).

Planting should only take place when the soil is suitably dry and workable, and

afterwards the plants should be watered in carefully. During a dry period they may need watering and spraying regularly for a month or so in order to get them well established.

After-care of heathers
The only attention required by heathers after planting should be careful, shallow hoeing to remove the weeds until the plants have spread sufficiently to smother them for you. You must remove dead heads with shears immediately after flowering. (Incidentally, these can be most attractive used in dried flower arrangements.) The tree heathers, es-

Five cultivars of Erica carnea: *(left to right, top) Springwood White, Pink Spangle; (centre) Winter Beauty, Vivelli; (bottom) Ruby Glow,* E. arborea Goldtips

pecially if they get too big or straggly, should be cut back hard into the old wood some time in late spring (April).

The only other attention that may be required is if your heathers are growing on a soil that is not sufficiently acid for them. In this case they may show their displeasure by poor growth and unusual leaf discoloration. These symptoms are caused by the lack of certain essential plant foods in the soil. To overcome the problem, apply a special fertilizer containing the necessary nutrients (such as Sequestrene) once or twice a year.

Choice of heathers

The two groups with winter flowers that compliment each other well are *Erica carnea* and *Erica × darleyensis*. The former grow about 15 to 30cm (6–12 in) high and are ideal for planting in front of the latter which grow about 60cm (24 in) tall. Both groups contain cultivars and hybrids and flower through from early winter to late spring (November to April), with the majority being mid-season (January to March). Both are tolerant of a certain amount of lime in the soil and are thus suitable for growing in most gardens and are rightly among the most popular of low-growing shrubs.

In our garden, we have selected four cultivars of *Erica carnea*, namely:

Ruby Glow – rich carmine-red flowers rising from bronze-coloured foliage.
Springwood Pink – rose-pink flowers with dense leaves and branches that trail over the ground and smother weeds.
Springwood White – a fine white-flowered heather with a similar growing habit to Springwood Pink.
Vivellii – flowers the deepest red of all winter heathers and superb dark bronze leaves (which are dark green in summer). Makes a good foil to white-flowered forms.

To give height to this part of the border, we planted at the back two clumps of hybrids of *Erica × darleyensis*:
Arthur Johnson – free-flowering sprays of magenta pink standing up from light green leaves; excellent for cutting. Alba (sometimes called Silberschmelze) – also produces dense sprays of sweetly-scented white flowers for a long period.
There are a number of other varieties of *Erica carnea* and *E. × darleyensis* that flower during the winter months. Among those worthy of note are:

E. carnea Eileen Porter – deep rich carmine and pale pink flowers for a long period.

E. carnea Gracilis, compact plants with rose pink blooms.
December Red, purplish flowers and low spreading growth.
King George (sometimes called Winter Beauty) with bright carmine, brown-tipped flowers.

Of the *Erica × darleyensis* hybrids, outstanding is Darley Dale, which produces pink blooms for a very long period.

GENERAL WORK
Late spring (April).
Continue to remove dead heads of spring flowering bulbs regularly.

Finish planting gladiolus corms if not already completed in mid-spring (March).

Complete the clearing of mixed and other flower borders of leaves and general winter debris.

Pruning of roses should be completed immediately if not already done. Also complete pruning of shrubs that have flowered during the winter by cutting out all old, dead, diseased or crossing plants. This includes hedging plants.

If moss and wormkiller treatments were not applied to lawns in mid spring (March), do so now. Repeat the treatments if either appears not to have been fully effective. Mow the lawn as necessary, still keeping the height of cut about 5cm (2 in). Apply a general lawn fertilizer at the rate recommended by the manufacturer.

Tread firm any soil loosened by frost.

Heather garden at the Royal Horticultural Society garden at Wisley, ablaze with Erica × darleyensis *Furzey,* E. arborea, *and* E. mediterranea *W. J. Rockliff*

223

Shrubs and Climbers

Shrubs and climbers are ideal for all gardens (including paved areas, as many can be grown in containers), for they supply colour, framework and form all year round. They act as useful low-growing weed-suppressors as well as ornamental screens. They can be an endless source of interest, require little attention and mix well with other plants that may be of only seasonal interest.

Budgeting ahead

One point to bear in mind when planning for mixed borders is that shrubs and climbers are generally more expensive to buy initially than many other types of plants. However, they more than compensate for this over the years. If you don't wish to get involved in too great an outlay when making a new garden, or renovating an existing one, it is advisable to plan for all the shrubs and climbers in advance, so that you know exactly where they are to be positioned, and then buy a few each year until you have completed your original design.

Planning ahead

Apart from varying shapes and sizes, shrubs can be evergreen or deciduous and have a variety of features such as variegated or different-coloured leaves, colourful and/or fragrant flowers, decorative bark or aromatic leaves. They can change leaf colours in autumn, produce interesting and colourful fruits, and be suitable for planting in all types of soil, sun or shade.

Always remember to keep down the number of shrubs and climbers in your garden and not plant too many, otherwise they grow into a tangly mess and swamp other plants in the border. The best policy is to put young plants close together and then, when the selected ones are reaching maturity, pull out and discard the remainder; but this is expensive and unnecessary with mixed flower borders.

As with all plantings it is wise to plan the borders on paper beforehand and draw them out on graph paper, as we described for the Edible Garden.

List your choice of shrubs and climbers—most good plant catalogues describe them in detail—and alongside each add its ultimate height and diameter, the colouring of leaves, flowers and fruit, their timing, whether evergreen or deciduous, soil preference, sun-or shade-lover, and any other specific requirement.

When and how to plant

As with trees, deciduous shrubs and climbers are best planted in autumn or spring, and evergreens in spring. Both types are available in bare-rooted and container-grown forms, the latter being suitable for planting at more or less any time of year provided the necessary precautions are taken. The preparation for, and the planting of, shrubs and climbers are essentially the same as for trees.

Stakes are not likely to be required except for large specimens, shrubs that have a floppy habit of growth and need some form of control, and those that are to be trained as climbers and will require a form of permanent framework up which to grow. After-care of the newly planted shrubs is also similar to that of trees.

IN OUR FLOWER GARDEN

We selected a variety of shrubs for different purposes here and, after the initial planting as shown in the ground plan we added shrubs that can be planted almost anywhere in the mixed borders—aucuba, choisya, skimmia and viburnum—and olearia, which likes a sunny position. They are described in alphabetical order.

Aucuba

Really hardy and versatile evergreens that grow to about 1·5m high and spread to 1·5m (5 × 5 ft), in sun or shade, town or country, and any type of soil. *Aucuba japonica*, the common form, has glossy, oval leaves and brilliant scarlet berries on the female plants.
Aucuba japonica Crotonifolia (male) and *A.j.*Variegata (female) are both variegated forms.

Azalea

Here there is a wealth of hybrids from which to choose including some deciduous ones that are 2–3m (6–10 ft) tall, and evergreens 1–1·5m (3–5 ft) tall. In many catalogues these are listed under rhododendron as they belong to the same family and have the same requirements, of which an important one for both types is that the soil should have an acid pH and contain no free lime. If your garden does not have a naturally acid soil you must prepare the ground before planting as you did for heathers, that is either providing lime-free topsoil with plenty of peat, or forking in adequate quantities of peat and leaf mould.

As the azaleas in our Flower Garden are growing under the shade of the deciduous silver birch, we have selected a mixture of evergreen cultivars (varieties) to give interest all year round, with the emphasis on different coloured flowers in early summer. A few popular evergreen ones from which to choose are:

Addy Wery	vermilion
Blue Danube	purple-blue
Hinodegiri	bright crimson
Orange Beauty	salmon-orange
Rosebud	pink
Palestrina	ivory
Mother's Day	rose-red

The deciduous forms of azalea, although without the advantage of being

Top left: silver-flowered azalea
Above left: Aucuba japonica *Variegata*
Left: blue berries of Berberis darwinii
Above: sweet-scented Buddleia globosa

evergreen, do have special attractions in that they produce an even wider range of flower colours and are usually fragrant, and the leaves turn to beautiful red tints in autumn. They are, however, rather larger than the evergreens and so require more planting space. Among the best deciduous ones to choose are:

Knap Hill Exbury hybrids	single colours or mixed
Directeur Moerlands	gold and orange
Coccinea Speciosa	orange-red
Aida	peach-pink
Koster's Brilliant Red	orange-red
White Swan	white
Narcissiflorum	pale yellow

Berberis (barberry)

Another family of plants with both deciduous and evergreen forms that can vary enormously in habit from horizontal ground cover growth to dwarf bushes 60cm high, 60cm spread (2 × 2 ft) or medium ones 1·5m high, 1·5m spread (5 × 5 ft). They can be planted as individuals or hedges, are easy to grow in any soil and tolerate shade; the evergreens will thrive in the shade. The flowers in spring and summer are usually yellow or orange, and the autumn fruits are very showy. Many berberis species also produce brilliant leaf tints in autumn and winter; all of them are more or less spiny, so you will need your gloves when clipping back.

In our garden we needed a low-growing form that would help visually to break the edge of the paved area near the house, but would also blend well with both the mixed border and the paving stones. For this purpose we selected *B.candidula*, an evergreen variety.

Berberis candidula Leaves with silvery undersides, yellow flowers and purple oval-shaped berries. Grows only about 45cm (18 in) high, 1–1·5m (4–5 ft) spread.

B. darwinii and *B.stenophylla* Bear their flowers and berries on arching stems and make ideal, unusual hedging plants.

B.verruculosa White undersides to evergreen leaves that colour well in autumn; golden yellow flowers on arching branches followed by rich purple berries. Grows to about 1m high, 1m spread (4 × 4 ft).

Two attractive deciduous types are:

B.thunbergii Brilliant leaf colours and scarlet fruits in autumn; mainly compact bushes.

B.wilsoniae Almost evergreen leaves that turn rich red and orange in autumn, and blend well with the clusters of coral-coloured berries. Smallish in size, tending to form mound-shaped bushes.

Buddleia (butterfly bush)

Quick-growing deciduous shrubs producing panicles (elongated branches) of flowers in late summer and mid autumn. As their common name indicates, they are much loved by butterflies for the sweet fragrance produced by most species. They thrive in any soil, and particularly love sun. For our garden we have chosen the very popular *B.davidii*.

Buddleia davidii Grows quickly anywhere to a medium size and flowers freely even in its second year. There are many varieties of this shrub with flowers colours varying from the usual bluish purple to white, rose, lavender and shades of purple.

B.alternifolia Almost tree-like in form, with fragrant lilac flowers in long, thin sprays. Grows freely, particularly against a warm wall.

B.globosa Virtually evergreen buddleia that produces in early summer sweetly scented flowers, round and orange in colour, on short stems; long tapering leaves that are grey underneath.

B.fallowiana Silvery-leaved with sweet smelling lavender-blue flowers in late summer. Alba is a white-blooming form.

Buxus (box)

Very useful shiny green evergreens that are ideal for hedging, edging borders and paths or, as in our garden, forming a link between the north side mixed flower border and the paved area. They grow anywhere and withstand hard treatment. The larger boxes can be used for hedges or topiary (clipping of trees or hedges to make 'sculpted' designs). For our garden we chose *B.sempervirens*.

Buxus sempervirens Often sold as a low-growing shrub, 60cm high, 60cm spread (2 × 2 ft). Other popular boxes are:

*B.s.*Aurea Variation of *B.sempervirens*, with yellow-edged leaves. This dual coloration does not always make a good contrast to other plants.

B.s.suffruticosa Common edging box normally seen in small formal gardens. Its medium-sized leaves of bright green set off other plants to advantage.

Camellia

These beautiful shiny-leaved evergreen winter- and spring-flowering plants are not nearly as difficult to grow as is frequently thought. They are, in fact, as hardy as the common laurel. However, they do like the same acid, peaty soil conditions as azaleas, rhododendrons and heathers, hence in our garden we have planted them by the azaleas and heathers on the north-facing side, so all these plants can have the same treatment. They like protection from north and east winds and not too much direct winter and early spring sun, which can damage the flowers following a frosty night. An ideal position, if you have it, is a lightly wooded part of the garden that offers frost protection. Camellias grow from 1·5 to 3m (5 to 10 ft) high 1·5m (5 ft) spread.

There is a vast range of camellias from which to choose, many with different flower shapes, and we have selected one of the early-flowering *C.williamsii* hybrids to grow by itself at the far end of the garden, and two of the later *C.japonica* hybrids to complement the heathers at the lower end of the flower border.

Camellia flowers may be in any shade of white, pink, red, peach or multi-coloured and some of the best to select from are:

Camellia williamsii Donation	orchid pink
C.w. J. C. Williams	pale pink
C.w. November Pink	pink
C.japonica Mathotiana	crimson
C.j. Elegans	salmon-rose, splashed white
C.j. Adolphe Audusson	blood-red, yellow centre
C.j. Lady Vansittart	pink and white striped
C.j. Mercury	light red
C.j. Lady Clare	pale pink

Ceanothus

Sometimes called California lilac. The most appealing feature of these evergreen or deciduous shrubs is that they are among the best hardy blue-flowering ones available. They vary in size, and do best in a sunny position where the soil is well-drained and not too chalky. Gloire de Versailles, a popular deciduous type, is the one we have selected for our south-facing wall and we suggest a few others:

Gloire de Versailles, with sky-blue flowers borne on arching branches in late summer or late autumn.

Topaz (deciduous), with deeper blue flowers.

C.thyrsiflorus (evergreen) is one of the hardiest, with bright blue blooms in early summer.

C.thyrsiflorus repens (evergreen), a very attractive weed-suppressor, growing only up to about 1m (3 ft) high, but spreading to 2·5m–3m (8–10 ft).

Far left: well-trimmed Buxus sempervirens
Left: ceanothus Gloire de Versailles
Below left: camellia D. Olga Anderson
Bottom left: Camellia japonica *C. M. Wilson*
Right: chaenomeles bears edible berries
Below: C. japonica *Hearn's Pink Dawn*

Chaenomeles (quince, japonica)

Sometimes called *cydonia*. Very easy deciduous shrubs to grow either in natural form or to train as a climber. They do well in any soil and any position, regularly produce a mass of flowers from mid spring to early summer and tend to produce further blooms intermittently all year round. After saucer-shaped flowers in shades of red, pink, orange or white, they all bear edible quince fruits.

To grow up the north-facing end of our garden shed, we selected the crimson-flowering variety, *Chaenomeles superba* Rowallane. Other varieties worthy of note are:

C.superba

Knap Hill Scarlet	orange-scarlet
Pink Lady	rose-pink
Crimson and Gold	crimson with gold centres
Boule de Feu	orange-red

C. speciosa

Moerloosii	pink and white in clusters
Nivalis	pure white
Umbilicata	deep salmon-pink
Rubra Grandiflora	extra large, crimson
Eximea	brick-red

Choisya (Mexican orange blossom)

Choisya ternata, the only species in this small genus of evergreens, is virtually essential for all gardens. As its common name implies, it comes from Mexico and has sweetly fragrant, white flowers of orange blossom; its foliage is also aromatic when crushed. Useful on most soils and in sun or shade, it flowers spasmodically throughout the year, but most profusely in summer. It forms a rounded bush of about 2m (6 ft) spread and can be grown against a wall.

Cotoneaster

A large genus of plants that can be evergreen or deciduous; low-growing creepers, bushes or trees. They survive well in varying soils and positions, and they all produce white or pink-tinged flowers in summer, attractive autumn leaf colours and brilliant fruits. The ground covering plants are excellent weed-smotherers. For our purpose we selected a prostrate-growing evergreen form, such as *C.salicifolius*, for the front of the south-facing mixed border. *C.s* Autumn Fire, has longish, willowy leaves and orange-red berries. Other good examples are:

Cotoneaster dammeri	scarlet berries
C.microphyllus	crimson berries
C. Skogholm	coral-red berries
C.conspicuus	bright red berries carried on arching branches

A popular deciduous form for low-growing or training up walls is *C.horizontalis*, the 'fish bone' cotoneaster (its branches grow herring-bone fashion), whose berries and leaves produce a riot of colour in autumn and look very effective.

Most of the taller-growing varieties are semi-evergreen; *C.lacteus* is one of the popular, though few, fully evergreen forms for hedging or screening, with its fruits lasting well after mid winter. Other good taller types are:

Cotoneaster bullatus	red cherry-like berries
C.divaricatus	superb scarlet in autumn
C.rotundifolius	upright, small-leaved, berries last until late spring
C.franchetii	sage green leaves, scarlet berries

Cytisus (broom)

Varying in size from low-growing plants to small trees, all cytisus have pea-shaped flowers (usually yellow) and most of them like a sandy, rather acid soil and plenty of sun. In general they flower in spring and summer but some produce blooms in early autumn thus providing a long season of colour and interest.

For the planting space in the paved area of our garden we selected *C.purgans*. This dense, almost leafless shrub with fragrant yellow flowers in spring will give colour and fragrance near the house in the early part of the year. It grows to about 1·2m (4 ft) high maximum, and 45cm (18 in) spread. Other pretty low-growing species are:

Cytisus purpureus	lilac-purple flowers in summer
C.× beanii	golden-yellow, early summer

Others of note are the hybrid forms with flowers of yellow, red, white or pink, and species such as:

Cytisus × praecox	very floriferous
C.battandieri	beautiful leaves, pineapple scent
C.nigricans	late summer and early autumn
C.grandiflorus	grey woolly seed pods

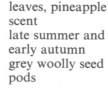

Opposite page, far left: Cotoneaster conspicuus *bears bright red berries in autumn. Opposite page, left: glossy-leaved evergreen* Cotoneasta microphyllus
This page, left: dwarf Cytisus × beanii
Above: low-growing Cytisus purpureus, *known as purple broom*
Below left: the common broom, Cytisus scoparius *Canary Bird*
Below: the tall Cytisus battandieri *has unusual pineapple-scented flowers*

Euonymus (spindle)

Mainly evergreen and deciduous shrubs, but *E. europaeus* and its forms make attractive small trees for gardens. Spindles are easily grown and especially useful where the soil is chalky. Special attractions lie in their autumn leaf tints, the colours of the berries on the deciduous forms and the fact that they tend not to grow too large.

In our Flower Garden we wanted a spindle bush that would harmonize with the buddleia behind it and the grey cineraria alongside, and also give colour throughout the year. For this we chose the pretty evergreen *E. fortunei* Silver Queen variegata. Most of the *E. fortunei* forms are very hardy, trailing or climbing evergreens with a variety of uses.

Euonymus fortunei Silver Queen variegata Compact with silver variegations to the leaves and attractive rose tints in winter.
E. japonicus Another hardy type; does well in town, country or by the sea. There are a number of variegated-leaved forms.
E. alatus Superb deciduous spindle with corky bark, feathery leaves in spring turning to rich red in autumn, and purple berries with orange seeds.
E. sachalinensis Handsome shrub that is also highly colourful in autumn.

Garrya

A fascinating and decorative, quick-growing evergreen that we have planted to be trained as a climber against the north wall of our garden (unless you plan to put up a lean-to greenhouse here). It is available in male and female forms; the latter are the more popular for their long-dangling, grey-green silky catkins produced during winter.
Garrya elliptica Most common species; does well in all soils provided they are not heavy and are well-drained. It does not need a sunny site.

Hamamelis (witch hazel)

Produce the most fascinating winter and early spring clusters of flowers that withstand the coldest weather; and they enchant with fragrance and curious strap-like bright yellow and red petals borne on leafless branches. As a genus they are

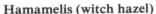

Top: Hamamelis mollis *(witch hazel) flowers throughout winter and spring*
Above: Hydrangea paniculata *flowers through summer and early autumn*
Left: Euonymus alatus *deciduous spindle*

shrubs or small trees, and we have put one against the house wall in the south-east corner, but it can be grown in almost any position. Being deciduous it is a useful plant as it produces hairy, hazel-like leaves during spring which turn golden yellow in autumn, thus giving the plant a second season of attraction. *H. mollis* is the best and most popular of all the witch hazels, other species, such as *H. × intermedia*, *H. japonica* and *H. vernalis*, are not so frequently found in catalogues:
Hamamelis mollis Pallida Dark yellow flowers.

Hydrangea

Highly prized plants in many gardens for their prolonged display of flowers during summer and early autumn. All of them like a sunny position, but not where the soil dries out round their roots, so it pays to give them a deep, well-manured site and regularly mulch them every spring.

Top: Hypericum calycinum *(St John's wort) in flower, a semi-evergreen plant*
Above and above right: Mahonia aquifolium—*its berries are good for jam*
Top right: Hypericum Elstead *in fruit*

They are all deciduous, but grow in a variety of forms from small to medium-sized bushes, 60cm–2·5m (2–8 ft) high, and some are genuine climbers, such as the one we have growing on the north-facing wall:

Hydrangea petiolaris Climber with flat heads of white flowers.

Hydrangea flower-heads are of three types: large and rounded (known as hortensias or mop-heads); large and flat or dome-shaped (known as lacecaps); and species (with heads of various shapes). These last are easy and rewarding shrubs to grow, and we have chosen *H. involucrata* for the south-facing wall:

Hydrangea involucrata Late-flowering dwarf bluish-purple and white blooms.
H. arborescens Grandiflora Greeny-white flowers that turn bronze-brown in winter.
H. villosa Pale blue flowers, grey-green leaves.
H. paniculata Grandiflora Creamy white to pink semi-arching branches of flowers.

As their name implies, lacecaps have flat, lacy flower-heads with pink or blue flowers and among the most popular are: Bluewave, Mariesii, Veitchii and White-wave.

The hortensias are the hydrangeas most frequently seen as pot-grown specimens in florists' shops, and there are a large number of cultivars, mainly with shades of pink or blue globular flowers. It is an interesting fact that on acid soil blue flowers will appear, whereas on chalky alkaline soil pink blooms will be produced.

Hypericum (St John's wort)

Semi-evergreen shrubs. Some are low-growing, and have mat-forming and weed-suppressing growth; others have a delicate, and more branching habit, growing to about 1·2m (4 ft) high. They grow easily in any soil, sun or shade, and have attractive brilliant yellow flowers lasting from mid summer to late autumn. Some, too, have the added advantage of autumn leaf tints or coloured berries. One of the most popular is *H. calycinum* as a spreading plant that keeps weeds under control. It forms a dense mat and the leaves turn a purplish colour in autumn.

For our garden we have chosen a beauty: *Hypericum* Hidcote (*H. patulum* Hidcote). Forms a delightful bush with saucer-shaped golden flowers that blend well with surrounding catmint and iris. Other good species are:

Hypericum elatum	rose-red berries
H. androsaemum	red and black berries, autumn leaf tints
H. × moseranum Tricolor	pink, cream and green variegations

Lavandula (lavender)

Much favoured, mainly for their soft grey permanent foliage and delightful fragrance. We have planted a whole border of this in front of the shed trellis so that it makes an attractive spot throughout the year. Lavenders also have a long season, providing their flower spikes from summer to autumn, and they enjoy any well-drained soil and as much sun as possible. They are excellent by the sea and for making dwarf hedges. Forms of *Lavandula spica* are those most commonly grown and in our garden we have a mixture of:

Hidcote	deep purple-blue flowers
Nana Munstead Dwarf	lavender blue
Twickel Purple	purple
Loddon Pink	pinky-blue
Vera	soft blue

Mahonia

Often confused and listed with berberis, but the essential difference is that they have compound leaves (leaves with several lobes) and no prickly spines on the stems. They are all evergreen, grow about 60cm–1m (2–4 ft) high and produce flowers in winter or spring followed by berries which are usually blue-black. They grow in almost any soil, but prefer a well-drained one, and are happy in the shade. We chose *M. japonica* for our garden against the south-facing wall:

Mahonia japonica is similar to *M. bealei* but bearing clusters of two flowers during winter and early spring.

Two of the most popular species are:
M. bealei Scented like lily of the valley.
M. aquifolium Holly-leaved, of bronze colour in spring, purple-red in winter and berries that are excellent for making jam.

Olearia

Attractive and easy to grow when on

chalky soil in sunny position, these evergreens (often called daisy bushes) have daisy-like flower-heads usually of a whitish colour, and grow between 1–2m (3–6½ ft) high. They flower from early summer to early autumn and are excellent by the seaside. Our choice is *O. × haastii*, one of the hardiest forms:

Olearia × haastii. Also good by the sea or in industrial areas. Has delightful fragrant flowers and is ideal in a mixed border.

For olearias with pink, lavender or blue flowers, choose forms of *O. stellulata* Splendens.

Pyracantha (firethorn)

True shrubs but frequently trained as climbers up walls and garden supports so that they are very often listed in the climbing plant section of catalogues. They are the most useful of hardy evergreen, berrying shrubs, growing freely in all positions and soils. They can reach a height of about 4·5m (15 ft), though only half this, particularly if the long shoots are kept cut back, is more customary. Firethorns bear masses of hawthorn-like white flowers in early summer, and clusters of berries in autumn that often last through to spring.

We selected a free-fruiting hybrid, *P.* Watereri, which has dense clusters of bright red berries, to grow against the south side of the garden shed. Other fine varieties are the free-branching:

Pyracantha rogersiana	red berries
P.rogersiana Flava	yellow berries
P.atlantioides Aurea	yellow berries
P. Orange Glow	orange-red berries

One of the most popular, *P. coccinea* Lalandei, has rather broader leaves and bears clusters of orange-red berries throughout autumn and winter.

Rhododendron

One of the largest and most varying groups of shrubs and, as we have mentioned these include azaleas. They both need the same type of acid soil and general treatment. Most are evergreen, they can be prostrate, shrubby or tree-like in habit and usually flower from late spring to late summer. Broadly, they can be classified into hardy or pedigree

hybrids and species. We wanted a rhododendron in our garden to go between the mahonia and syringa, but were restricted for space. We therefore selected the hardy hybrid Britannia with its glowing crimson flowers for good contrast and its semi-dwarf habit as it grows only to about 1·2m high and spreads to 1·2m (4 ft × 4 ft).

Skimmia

Small evergreen shrubs with aromatic, long, glossy leaves and fragrant flowers in late spring and early summer. If male and female plants are grown together (as these shrubs bear all male or female flowers on separate plants) then you can expect a profusion of coloured berries on the females in the autumn.

Skimmia japonica Most popular and hardy anywhere and in almost any soil. It is available in a variety of forms and the male Rubella (red buds in winter, white flowers in spring) grown alongside the female Foremanii (brilliant red berries in autumn) make an attractive combination.

Viburnum

Large genus of shrubs in evergreen or deciduous form. Most produce white, often sweetly scented, flowers followed by autumn leaf tints and/or coloured berries. They can be grown in almost any position. The plants grow about 1–3m (3–10 ft) high. As they vary so much in

their season of attraction, the easiest way to describe them is to divide them into three groups: winter-flowering. spring/early-summer flowering, and autumn colour:

WINTER-FLOWERING

Viburnum tinus (Laurustinus) Highly sought after, has pink-budded white flowers from late autumn to early spring among evergreen dark glossy leaves, and blue-black berries from late summer.

Another good variety is *V. fragrans* with bronze-coloured young leaves, fragrant winter flowers and scarlet berries.

SPRING- AND EARLY SUMMER-FLOWERING

V. tomentosum Very popular with its large clusters of snow-white flowers and pendant green leaves that turn plum-colour in autumn.

V. × *burkwoodii* (evergreen) Large fragrant white flowers opening from pink buds and leaves that are dark shiny green above with brownish-grey 'felt' beneath.

AUTUMN COLOUR

V. betulifolium One of the best of all the berrying shrubs, producing berries in redcurrant-like form after small white flowers in spring.

V. opulus (guelder rose) White flowers in mid summer followed by autumn leaf colour and translucent berries.

V. davidii (low-growing evergreen) If male and female forms are planted together, the female produces exceptional turquoise-blue berries.

Above left: Viburnum betulifolium *with berries that last through into winter*
Far left: Lavandula *Nana Munstead, dwarf fragrant lavender, good for hedges*
Left: Viburnum davidii, *low-growing evergreen with bright berries contrasting well with rich-toned branches*
Below, far left: Olearia × scilloniensis, *profusely flowering, evergreen daisy bush*
Below: Viburnum tomentosum, *whose leaves turn plum-colour in autumn*
Above, and below right: pyracantha (firethorn) in fruit and flower. This evergreen shrub trains well as a climber

Vinca (periwinkle)

Most popular of low-growing glossy, evergreen shrubs for planting as weed-suppressors, in shady or sunny sites, on banks, or any difficult spot where nothing else wants to grow.

Vinca major These forms flower in early summer; *V. m.* Maculata has yellow-blotched leaves and *V. m.* Variegata creamy-white ones that set off the blue blooms to advantage.

V. minor Its forms are smaller versions of *V. major*, flowering in late spring and early summer and intermittently until autumn, in various shades of blue or white and some with variegated leaves.

CHOICE OF VINE CLIMBERS

Climbing plants are ideal for adding an extra dimension to the back of mixed flower borders or for growing naturally up trellis or other supports, to give additional height, or to act as a screen to partition the garden into interesting sections.

Clematis

Among the most versatile of climbers. As long as the soil is well-drained and the site sunny, but with a shady root area, clematis rarely fail to give endless pleasure. They support themselves with curling leaf stalks and except for pruning need little attention.

Clematis are a large genus and for easy distinction you can divide them into the species and large-flowering groups. Of the species we suggest the following:

Clematis tangutica Mass of yellow flowers in mid summer, followed by silky old man's beard berries (superior form of those seen in hedgerows).

C. montana (white) and *C. m. rubens* (rose-red) have scented flowers which smother the plant in early summer.

If you want an evergreen clematis, two good species are:

C. armandii White.

C. balearica Pale yellow with bronze fern-shaped leaves.

Of the large-flowered group we suggest the following:

Right: Clematis montana, *favoured for its scent.* Below: C. patens *Barbara Dibley* Bottom: Jasminum officinale, *common white jasmine, a fragrant semi-evergreen*

Nelly Moser	pale mauve and carmine
Barbara Dibley	bright violet
Comtesse de Bouchaud	rose pink
Gravetye Beauty	cherry red
Lasurstern	lavender blue
Marie Boisselot	white

Jasminum (jasmine)

Always popular, especially the winter-flowering one *J. nudiflorum*.

Jasminum nudiflorum Bears yellow trumpet-shaped flowers from early winter to late spring on naked green branches. During the remainder of the year it is clothed with small, shiny green leaves.

J. officinale Common white, summer-flowering jasmine that is sweetly scented and opens from pale pink buds; it has many-lobed leaves.

J. × stephanense Another summer-flowering hybrid that requires plenty of space to show off its sometimes variegated leaves and pale pink flowers followed by glossy black berries.

Lonicera (honeysuckle)

Love to ramble over pergolas, arches or old tree trunks and are best given their freedom rather than trained against walls or other supports. Most flower in summer, but some continue blooming until late autumn; they all grow in almost any soil and aspect but, like clematis, prefer to have their roots in the shade. With the exception of *L. japonica* and its forms (which are evergreen), the remainder are all deciduous, though *L. × purpusii* is winter-flowering.

Among the most popular are the early and late blooming Dutch honeysuckles:

Lonicera periclymenum Scented tube flowers of rose-purple and yellow.

L. tellmanniana Produces 5cm (2 in) long trumpet flowers but no perfume.

L. × americana Spectacular hybrid with large trusses of white to yellow, sweetly fragrant flowers.

Polygonum (Russian vine)

Sometimes known as mile-a-minute vine, this rampant climber grows rapidly in any position and will completely smother a wall or building in one year. The most commonly grown is:

Polygonum baldschuanicum Often confused with *aubertii*, its pale heart-shaped leaves and froth of creamy-pink flowers make a wonderful sight each year from late summer to late autumn.

Left: Jasminum nudiflorum,

Above right: Lonicera sempervirens (honeysuckle),

Right: Vinca major Elegantissima (periwinkle) a good weed-suppressor

Bulbs in the Garden

Now is the time to start planning your bulb display for next year. Bulbs in friends' gardens and in public display are still in full bloom and, seeing them in the open air and in natural surroundings (rather than the isolation of the bulb-grower's catalogue), you can more easily decide upon the varieties and colours that you would like to have.

GENERAL WORK
Late spring (April)

If weather conditions are favourable and the soil is dry enough to work without it sticking to the rake or your boots, make the first outdoor sowings of hardy annual seeds (see page 377). Thoroughly prepare the ground for chrysanthemums, add a general fertilizer, such as Growmore, and set the plants in position within two weeks.

Finish planting bare-rooted trees, shrubs and hardy herbaceous plants. Container-grown types can be planted at any time of year provided conditions are suitable and the plants are regularly watered.

Pot-grown clematis can be planted now. The soil level from the pot should be set 2–5cm (1–2 in) below ground level and the roots firmly pressed down. Prune the new plants back to about 30cm (12 in).

Carefully tie in to their supports new shoots of shrubs trained as climbers or those climbers that need assistance. Keep an eye open for greenfly and blackfly and spray as soon as they appear with malathion or a systemic insecticide.

It is at the far end of our Flower Garden that we have decided to make a special feature of bulbs, where they can be seen at their best during spring from the upper windows of the house. The word 'bulb' is, of course, used here rather loosely, as the term is intended to cover also corms and tubers.

The function of the bulb itself (or corm, or tuber) is to be a form of food storage, to help the plants survive not only the long cold winter, but also the hot dry summer that is common in the parts of the world where these plants grow wild. Most

bulbs are found naturally in mountainous regions, where they are covered with snow for much of the winter. Directly the snow melts the leaves and flowers appear; and during this period, although they get plenty of water, the soil in which they grow drains quickly.

There are, of course, exceptions to this. The various members of the narcissus family often grow in alpine water meadows, and there are one or two bulbs that have no objection to quite marshy conditions, such as the spring and summer snowflake, *Leucojum vernum* and *L. aestivum* and the big summer-flowering Peruvian squill (*Scilla peruviana*).

Where to plant

Generally, however, it is safe to assume that bulbs do best where the soil is reasonably light and well-drained. In practice, they will thrive in most gardens. And since bulbs will have made most, if not all, of their growth by early summer (mid May), they will be perfectly happy under deciduous trees and shrubs, where they can get enough light for their growth before the leaves have developed too much. They should not be planted beneath evergreens, however, as they will not get enough light to produce food to store for the coming year.

How to plant

There are a lot of old gardeners' tales about the correct planting depth for bulbs: one of the favourites is that the top of the bulb should be the same distance from the surface as the length of the bulb. But in the wild, bulbs are almost always considerably deeper than this, and you can safely say that the tops of small bulbs should be at least 10cm (4 in) below the surface, while larger bulbs should be 15cm (6 in) below. If they are less deep there is always a risk that hoeing or some other operation will bring them to the surface. Small bulbs can be planted close together, say 5–8cm (2–3 in) apart, but the larger ones should have 15–20cm (6–8 in) between them.

Most spring bulbs should be put in the ground as soon after early autumn (August) as you can obtain them, and they will start making roots within a month. Narcissus, in fact, are scarcely ever without roots and must inevitably receive a slight check if they have been lifted and dried off, although it may be barely noticeable.

The main exception to this generalization is the tulips, which can well be left until early winter (November) before planting.

Above: Galanthus miralis *(snowdrops), one of the earliest flowers of the year*
Bottom right: crocus, easy-to-grow and free-flowering for several years
Bottom left: the scented Iris reticulata, *Harmony has prominent gold markings*

Soil or sand?

If your soil is very damp and heavy there is probably some advantage in planting your bulbs on a layer of sharp sand, which drains fast and will prevent water from lodging immediately around the basal plate of the bulb, the part most suscep-

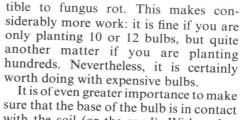

tible to fungus rot. This makes considerably more work: it is fine if you are only planting 10 or 12 bulbs, but quite another matter if you are planting hundreds. Nevertheless, it is certainly worth doing with expensive bulbs.

It is of even greater importance to make sure that the base of the bulb is in contact with the soil (or the sand). With rather large bulbs it is only too easy to take out a trowel full of soil and put your bulb in so that it lodges halfway down the hole with its base suspended in air. When the roots emerge they are unable to find any nourishment, and they may well perish. There is enough nourishment stored in

Above: Narcissus pseudonarcissus *(daffodil) Penrose and (below) narcissus White Lion*

the bulb to produce leaves and possibly even a flower, but the bulb cannot renew itself and will eventually die. Seeing that plants get off to a good start is one of the main secrets of success in gardening.

Dividing the clumps

If your bulbs are doing well they will, in the course of five or six years, form clumps. These will eventually get so crowded that flower production suffers.

When this happens you must lift the clumps and divide them up. The best time to do this is in the early summer, when you see the leaves just starting to yellow. The bulbs should be good and plump by then and the new corms should have been formed. Some bulbs, most notably snowdrops, never seem to become overcrowded and there is no need to lift and divide them unless you wish to increase the area of these bulbs. To help you plan your 'calendar of bulbs' for the early spring we suggest a selection of winter aconite, snowdrops, iris, crocus, narcissus and tulips.

Winter aconite

The first to appear is usually the winter aconite *Eranthis hyemalis*. This has a tuber from which springs a little ruff of leaves, in the centre of which is a yellow flower not unlike a buttercup. The plant grows wild in woodland and does best in a shady position. If it is happy it spreads quite extensively and will also seed itself, but it is not happy everywhere. It seems to like the sort of woodland soil that has plenty of leaf mould and if you have either a very sandy or a very clayey soil you may well find that it does not persist for more than two or three years. *E. × tubergenii* is a hybrid between the ordinary winter aconite and the larger species from western Asia, *E. cilicica*. It has larger flowers which, however, never set seed, and is somewhat more expensive.

Snowdrop

After the winter aconite come the snowdrops. There are many species of these, all looking rather similar and chiefly distinguished by the way their leaves emerge from the ground. The one most widely grown is *Galanthus nivalis*, that is available with either single or double flowers. We are always told that snowdrops should be moved when they are still in active growth. This is fine if you are moving them from one bed to another, or if you can get some from your friends, but firms only sell the dried-off bulbs and when you are buying new snowdrops you will have to make do with these. They seem to grow adequately, although the display the first spring after planting may not be quite as good as you would expect. However, do not lose heart, it will almost certainly be much more satisfactory the following year.

Among other species, *Galanthus elwesii* is supposed to be a much larger-flowered snowdrop, but the large flowers are seldom maintained for long in cultivation and after a few years you can only distinguish *G. elwesii* from the ordinary snowdrop by its broad glaucous leaves. If you can obtain *G. caucasicus*, particularly in its double form, you will find that it flowers earlier than *G. nivalis*, usually in late winter (January), and has the added advantage of increasing faster.

Iris

We come now to the dwarf bulbous iris, of which three are worth having. The most spectacular is *Iris histrioides* Major. This produces blue flowers up to 10cm (4 in) across, which usually open in late winter (mid January) and, although they look very exotic, are completely unmoved by the worst that the winter can unleash. They are often frozen and covered with snow without showing any ill effects. They are not, alas, cheap, but they persist and increase, although not very rapidly.

Then there is the charming little yellow *I. danfordiae*. In most gardens, after flowering, it splits up into several smaller bulbs which take a long time to flower again, so frequently they have to be replaced each year. It is said that if the bulbs are planted very deeply, at least 23cm (9 in), they are less liable to split up.

The commonest of the early iris is *I. reticulata*, which flowers usually in early spring (February). It has rather narrow violet flowers (although purple or blue in some forms) with an exquisite violet scent. Provided they have well-drained soil all these bulbous iris are very easy to grow. An infection to be watched out for is the dreaded fungus disease known as ink-spot, which causes the bulbs to rot. There is no simple cure for this, if indeed there is any. It has been suggested that if the bulbs are lifted, dried off completely and then soaked for two hours in a very weak solution of formaldehyde (one part in 300), they can be protected, but this only applies to healthy bulbs, not to infected ones.

Crocus

Perhaps of all the spring bulbs the crocus is the favourite, and here we have an enormous choice. For many of us the first sign of spring is the Dutch yellow crocus. This is a sterile form of the eastern Mediterranean *Crocus aureus*, which has been known in gardens for nearly 300 years. Since it never sets seed it increases rapidly by producing extra corms, and soon makes large clumps. The true *C. aureus* flowers slightly earlier and has rather richer coloured flowers, as well as increasing by seed.

However, if you want a crocus that increases by seed the best is *C. tomasinianus*, a very slender plant with grassy leaves and a thin flower, which is nearly invisible until the sun opens the lavender petals. There are also some darker purple varieties, such as Taplow Ruby, Barr's Purple and Whitewell Purple. *C. tomasinianus* increases at a prodigious rate, both from extra corms and from self-sown seedlings, which may flower the second year after germinating. Very similar, but with a larger flower, is *C. dalmaticus*.

C. chrysanthus has a large number of forms, all characterized by bunches of rather globular flowers, mainly in varying shades of yellow, but including some very good blues, which unfortunately are usually very slow to increase, while the yellow and cream forms are vigorous.

The Cloth of Gold crocus, *C. susianus*, is prodigal with its rather small yellow flowers which have dark brown stripes on their outside. A very attractive crocus is *C. etruscus*, that is usually only obtainable in the form known as Zwanenburg and that flowers in early spring (late February). The flowers are quite large and a very fine shade of lavender-mauve. Another very popular crocus is the deep mauve *C. sieberi*. Finally there are the huge Dutch hybrids, that flower in mid spring (March) but some people find rather gross. Best of these is the showy silver-lavender Vanguard.

Narcissus

Daffodils (with a trumpet centre) and narcissus (with flatter, cup centre) all belong to the genus *Narcissus* and they all like ample water when they are growing. They are exquisite in flower, but they have very long leaves, which persist until mid summer (June) and tend to look unsightly. They are probably best placed between shrubs, where their leaves will not be so noticeable. Whatever you do, do not cut the leaves off or plait them into dainty bundles, as that will wreck your chances of good flowers in the next season. You must just make up your mind that when you grow narcissus, you must put up with these disadvantages.

Tulip

Most tulips come rather late, but the water-lily tulip, *Tulipa kaufmanniana*, is usually in flower by mid to late spring (March–April) thus linking early and late spring displays. Many tulips tend to deteriorate after a year or so, but *kaufmanniana* is fairly reliable, although rather slow to increase. The wild plant has a flower that is long and pointed, cream outside, with a broad crimson stripe down each petal, and ivory inside. The flower opens nearly flat in sunlight. It has now been hybridized, producing blooms in deep yellow, pinks and even scarlets.

The Darwin hybrid variety Apeldoorn, up to 75cm (2 ft) tall, is good for display

Bulbs in bowls

Early bulbs planted indoors can bring added colour to your home in winter. Order them in early autumn (August) to plant in bowls or pots indoors or in the greenhouse in mid autumn (September). Bulbs, corms and tubers that are generally grown in pots for early flowering are hyacinths, daffodils (narcissi), tulips, crocuses and cyclamen.

Always plant top-size bulbs as you will get more and better bulbs from these and they are well worth the extra cost. You can buy 'prepared' bulbs. These are treated with refrigeration to speed up the period before flowering.

Plant in potting compost so that the upper third of the hyacinth bulbs are exposed and the noses of crocuses and daffodils.

After planting, place the bulbs in darkness and in a cool place. Leave for six to eight weeks until they produce shoots. To start with keep the bowls in a subdued light, then, after a week, transfer them to a full light and a temperature of 10°C. Keep the compost or fibre moist but do not over-water and they should flower beautifully.

Herbaceous Plants

Our gardens would look rather sad places without the herbaceous plants that flower, most particularly in the late summer (from mid July onwards), when there are few flowering shrubs left and we must depend on perennials and roses for colour in the garden.

All annuals and biennials are strictly speaking herbaceous – all the word means is that the stems are of only annual duration and die down each autumn, so that in that sense even bulbs are herbaceous – but the term is usually used of herbaceous perennials. Perennials are plants that go on growing for many seasons, increasing in dimensions as they

do so. They are normally planted either in the autumn or in the early spring, although there are one or two exceptions.

When to plant
Ideally autumn is the best time to plant, if you do so early enough. This enables the plants to root into the fresh soil before winter comes, so that they will be in a good condition to grow away as soon as the days lengthen and the air warms up. Plants that are transplanted in the spring have to start to grow away at once, so that if the spring is exceptionally cold or exceptionally dry their initial growth can be checked quite considerably. However there are one or two plants which seem to make very little growth after being transplanted in the autumn, with the result that they often die during the first winter and for these spring planting is obviously better. The most well-known of

these is that large scabious, *Scabiosa caucasica*, one of the best herbaceous plants to grow for cutting.

When to transplant
There are a number of plants that really loathe any root disturbance, either because they have long tap roots, which may cause the death of the plant if they are damaged, or for less recognizable reasons. There seems no obvious reason why hellebores should dislike being moved, but they certainly do and may sulk for a year or so after they are transplanted. We find the same thing with paeonies, but this may be because they have such a vast amount of tubers underground that it is almost impossible

to move a good-sized plant without seriously damaging the root system. Plants with long tap roots, such as lupins or oriental poppies, should only be moved as young plants and once planted should be left.

In any case it is always best to start off with small plants, whether they be seedlings or divisions from other plants. Such plants usually arrive with their roots more or less undamaged and soon grow on to make vigorous specimens.

Caring for herbaceous plants
You can find herbaceous plants to fit any soil or situation, but the majority will be perfectly happy in a soil that is reasonably deep and not inclined to water-logging. Most like full sunlight, although it is possible to grow bog plants and shade-lovers where conditions allow.

After a time some herbaceous plants may become very large, in which case they should be lifted and divided up. Some plants get their roots so interlocked that it is by no means easy to divide them; the answer is to get two garden forks and insert them back to back in the clump and then lever them apart. The centre of the clump is probably impoverished, due to the fact that it will have exhausted the soil where it was originally planted; also the centre tends to get overgrown by the stronger outside parts which are in fresh soil; so when clumps are split up the centre is usually discarded and the plantlets on the outside are preserved.

There are many hundreds of herbaceous perennials to choose from, so for our Flower Garden we have selected a number of plants which are easy to grow and which will establish themselves in the border quickly.

Hellebore
Helleborus niger (the Christmas rose) is the earliest-flowering of our selection. It grows on the edge of woodlands in the wild, so a position giving dappled shade is ideal. Almost all the hellebores are somewhat greedy plants, so the soil cannot be too rich. The white flowers will emerge from the ground at any time from early winter to early spring (November–February) and the new leaves start to emerge at the same time. Later the leaves are going to be quite large, so a position among or just in front of shrubs should prove very suitable. Some Christmas roses have the unfortunate habit of producing only very short stems, so that the flowers easily become splashed with mud in bad weather. If you are ordering plants by mail there is not much you can do about this; but if you go to a nursery, pick out the long-stemmed plants.

Otherwise you might prefer to grow one of the hybrids of *H. orientalis* (the Lenten rose). These all have long-stemmed flowers, which usually do not open before early spring (February). There are a few whites among them, but most are some shade of pink or greenish-pink, while a few are a very deep maroon. They require the same treatment as the Christmas rose, but have very much larger leaves, which take up a lot of room later in the season. There are also a number of hellebores with green flowers.

Hellebores may be transplanted in the autumn (September), and the earlier the

better. The old leaves of the Lenten rose often persist while the flowers are opening, but the plants seem to come to no harm if you cut these off before the flowers open: the leaves begin to look rather tattered by that time. This is not a problem with the Christmas rose.

Alyssum
Our next plant is *Alyssum saxatile*, which flowers in late spring (April). Strictly

Above: double dianthus. Pink Diane
Top: Helleborus niger, *the Christmas rose*
Above left: delicate Scabiosa caucasica
is best planted in the spring
Left: the leaves of Alyssum saxatile *give winter interest, the flowers appear in late spring. Right:* Hosta albo-marginata, *the plantain lily, thrives in shade*

speaking it is not herbaceous at all, but a small shrub, which carries its grey leaves throughout the winter and makes the border interesting during the dreary season. In the spring it covers itself with golden, sweet-smelling flowers. It likes full sun and has no objection to rather poor soil. After about four years it gets somewhat leggy, but it is very easily propagated by cuttings or by seed.

Senecio cineraria
The grey-leaved cineraria (which you might otherwise know as *Cineraria maritima*) is a good example of the sort of plants that are grown for their foliage colour rather than for their flowers. Such plants are very valuable since they remain attractive for more than six months; this is more than can be said for most flowering plants, which seldom carry their flowers longer than three weeks and

often considerably less. The grey (or, in the variety White Diamond, the silvery-white) leaves are very attractive, and they gain much of their appeal from their contrast with more usual green leaves. Don't try to overdo this effect, because unfortunately the cineraria bears rather crude yellow daisy-like flowers which are not very appealing.

Most grey or silver-leaved plants will not survive in soils that retain too much wet and our grey cineraria is also liable to perish during particularly severe winters. Fortunately cuttings root very easily, so it is always a good idea to root a few in late summer (July) and keep them in pots under cover during the winter, in case disaster strikes. In any case, the plants become rather gaunt after a few years and are best replaced.

Hosta

Another plant with unusual foliage but also with quite attractive lily-like flowers, is the plantain lily, a species of hosta (sometimes known as funkia). This vanishes completely during the winter

and the new shoots can often be wrecked by slugs, so it is as well to mark their positions and put down bait in late spring (April) when young leaves are emerging.

The leaves vary in size and in colour and some are variegated with ivory, but they are all handsome plants, which get more effective as they get larger. There is

Above: peach-leafed Campanula persicifolia Telham Beauty *is easy to grow*

really no need to split up their clumps at any time, as they can go on getting larger and larger without any ill effects. In summer (June–July) they send up spikes of lily-like flowers, usually about 5cm (2 in) long, trumpet-shaped and white or mauve in colour. These plants thrive in dense or partial shade.

Dianthus (pinks)

These plants also have pretty grey leaves, but they are grown mainly for the sake of their small, fragrant, carnation-like flowers. They prefer a limey soil and, if you have the sort of soil that will grow rhododendrons, you will probably have to add some lime before you plant your dianthus. These again are evergreen and look interesting during the winter, but they very soon become gaunt and need frequent replacing. This is done by means of cuttings, usually known as pipings, which are ready in late summer or early autumn (July and August).

Dianthus are not particularly showy flowers, but their heady scent makes them worth all the trouble. They look attractive

*Bottom left: pompon
chrysanthemum London Gazette,
give welcome autumn colour
Bottom right: pyrethrum chrysanthemum
with daisy-like flowers in early and
mid summer*

massed together or along the front of a border. The flowers are usually white, pink or crimson, and popular varieties are Mrs Simkins, Red Clove, and the newer Imperial Pink.

Campanula

Two species of these nice trouble-free plants are generally grown in borders. One is the peach-leafed *Campanula persicifolia*, which grows about 45cm (18 in) high and has flat blue or white flowers in mid summer (June). These are only slightly bell-shaped and reach about 5cm (2 in) across. The other is the tall *C. lactiflora*, which can grow to 1·2m (4 ft) and has a huge head of small mauve, rather spidery flowers in late summer (July). Although the individual flowers are only about 2–3cm (1 in) across, they are borne in large numbers and a plant in full flower is a wonderful sight. There are shorter forms of *C. lactiflora* and also some pinky-purple ones.

Agapanthus (African lily)

An attractive plant flowering in late summer (July and August). The plants to

obtain are called Headbourne hybrids and are all hardy, whereas the larger *A. africanus* generally requires wintering under cover. The Headbourne hybrids have quite small strap-shaped green leaves, but throw up stems to 75cm (2½ ft), bearing at their tops heads of blue trumpet-shaped, lily-like flowers about 5cm (2 in) long. They like as warm a position as you can give them and full sunlight, but they are very tolerant about soil, so long as it is not waterlogged.

Chrysanthemum

For late autumn (October) we have chrysanthemums. The cut flower types, *C. maximum*, are not the most beautiful plants and are best raised each year from cuttings, but the Korean chrysanthemums are excellent for the border. These bear daisy-like flowers in the greatest profusion, usually some shade of red in colour, and are completely trouble-free. The little pompon chrysanthemums add needed colour in autumn (early October) and are now available in various pastel shades which are preferable to the rather dull colours which they used to be. The ordinary chrysanthemum can be grown as a border plant, if the flowers are not disbudded, but it is less attractive than either the Korean or the pompon types.

Japanese anemone (wind flower)

The Japanese anemone, in pinky-purple or in white, is a marvellous plant, being completely trouble-free and increasing with ease, and always flowering well in mid to late autumn (September–October). It does not really like being moved, so it is best left undisturbed as long as possible.

Pyrethrum

Botanically derived from *Chrysanthemum*

roseum, these are invaluable for their single white, pink or carmine daisy-like flowers on long stems in early and mid summer (May–June). They like a sunny position and deep well-drained soil.

Lupins

Excellent companions for the pyrethrums are *Lupinus* (lupins) which like the same conditions and produce their spires of pea-like flowers above decorative leaves about the same time. They are available in a wide range of colours of white, pink, yellow, red and lavender-blue, and are often bi-coloured. The Russell hybrids are a good strain but there are many varieties from which to choose. If you remove the old flower-heads as they fade, you will encourage a second season of blooming.

Oriental poppy

A third perennial to plant with the two foregoing is *Papaver orientalis* (the Oriental poppy), which also likes the sun and flowers at about the same time. It is available in pink, white, scarlet or crimson flower shades. Incidentally, it likes water if there is a drought period immediately prior to its flowering season in early to mid summer (May–June).

Thyme

This, the first of our two dwarf plants, is the creeping *Thymus serphyllum*, which makes a mat of aromatic foliage covered with crimson or purple flowers in mid summer (late June). These are also fragrant. Thyme spreads rapidly and the plants should be at least 30cm (12 in) apart to avoid congestion.

Sempervivum (houseleek)

Looking like a little cactus with rosettes of fleshy leaves, which are often attractively coloured, this dwarf plant has rather odd looking daisy-like pink flowers

on 10cm (4 in) stems. The houseleek produces numerous offshoots each year, so do not place new plants too closely together. The cobweb houseleek has its leaves covered with cobwebby grey hair.

Nepeta (catmint)

A spreading plant, catmint has feathery masses of small, grey-green fragrant leaves, with lavender-coloured feathery flower spikes in summer and autumn (June–September).

These last three plants like rather gravelly soil and it is worthwhile incorporating some gravel if the soil is rather slow-draining.

Papaver orientale, *the poppy with pronounced colour contrast in its markings*

Dahlias, Lilies, Gladiolus and Iris

Some of the most popular flowers in the garden are tuberous – dahlias, which give a glorious show of colour throughout the autumn, as well as lilies, gladiolus and iris. This week we tell you how to care for these plants so as to get the best display.

GENERAL WORK

Early summer (May)

Continue to remove all the dead flower-heads from bulbs to save the plants wasting energy on seed production and encourage them to build up strong bulbs for next year.

Put stakes in position alongside herbaceous perennial plants for tying in the young shoots as they grow.

Plant evergreen trees and shrubs, water in thoroughly and put a mulch over the root area. Keep the soil moist and spray the plants each day until they start making new growth.

Tie in climbing plants, and shrubs treated as climbers, to their supports as the young shoots grow.

Roses may produce too many spindly shoots so cut some out to prevent a tangled mass of unprolific stems.

Clip evergreen hedges, such as privet, to keep them tidy. Repeat as necessary.

Mow the lawn regularly, each week, cutting it to 2·5–4cm (1–1½ in).

Pests, particularly greenfly, blackfly and red spider mite can start attacking many plants now. Spray with insecticide regularly according to manufacturer's instructions.

Certain plants in our garden are characterized by some sort of underground swelling that acts as food storage. In the dahlia it is a swollen root, called a tuber; in the lily it is swollen leaves that form a bulb; in the gladiolus it is the swollen base of the stem, which is called a corm; while in the case of the iris it is a creeping underground stem, the rhizome, which bears roots on its underside.

Popular dahlias

Of these plants the dahlia is probably the most important and popular so far as garden ornament is concerned.

There are a vast number of varieties in each group from which to choose and it is essentially a matter of personal preference for shape and colour, and the area they are to occupy in the garden.

The main types of dahlia grown are:
decoratives (flat broad petals)
cactus and semi-cactus (quill-like petals)
show or pompons (globular heads of

tubular petals)

collerettes (single flowers with the larger outside rays set off by inner 'collars' of petals in contrasting colours)

anemone-flowered (central coral-coloured disc florets)

singles or dwarfs (single circles of petals).

In the case of the first three types, the size of the flower-heads can vary considerably and the heads are often referred to in catalogues as giant (over 25cm/10 in), large (20–25cm/8–10 in), medium (15–20cm/6–8 in), small (10–15cm/4–6 in), or miniature (less than 10cm/4–6 in), or miniature (less than 10cm/4 in). Some useful varieties are listed or shown here.

DECORATIVES

Lavender Perfection (giant)	lavender pink
Majuba (large)	deep red
Snowstorm (medium)	pure white
Terpo (medium)	scarlet
Gerrie Hoeck (medium)	pure pink
Glory of Heemstede (small)	deep yellow
Procyon (small)	scarlet and yellow
David Howard (miniature)	orange-bronze
Rothesay Pippin (miniature)	deep scarlet

CACTUS AND SEMI-CACTUS

Colour Spectacle (large)	red and white
Golden Crown (large)	orange and yellow
Clarion (medium)	orange-red
Golden Autumn (medium)	golden yellow
Morning Kiss (medium)	pink and white
Orfeo (medium)	deep purple
Rotterdam (medium)	blood red
Hit Parade (small)	scarlet
Popular Guest (small)	lavender pink
Preference (small)	salmon-pink
Park Princess (miniature)	bright pink

Top left: dahlia Symbol, large decorative
Top right: dahlia Twiggy, medium decorative
Right: single dahlia, Coltness, is available in a good mixed colour range

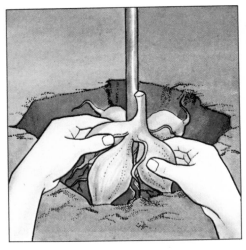

Above: planting dahlia tuber in ground previously dug and manured
Below: digging up tuber with fork

Above: cutting stem after frost
Below: storing tubers in boxes, with stems uppermost, at end of season

Below: cactus dahlia, Klankstad Kerkrade

Starting from seed

Single or dwarf dahlias are mainly grown from seed sown in heat as early in the year as possible, pricked out when large enough and gradually hardened off, to be planted out in mid summer (June). They flower fairly freely from early autumn (mid August) until the frosts come, but often they fail to produce any tubers, so cannot be kept from one season to the next unless the plants are lifted before the frosts come, potted up, and kept under cover. They are very useful plants for late flowers, but they do require heat in the early stages, although a warm airy room may be sufficient if you haven't a greenhouse.

Starting with plants

All the other types of dahlia can be considered together because they all require the same treatment, and in the first year it is best to start by buying plants. It is difficult to overfeed dahlias, so there is every advantage in preparing the place where you intend planting them by thorough digging and incorporating plenty of humus or, alternatively, very well-rotted manure.

As they are susceptible to even slight frost—they are always the first to suffer in the autumn—they should not be planted out until all risk of frost can be considered past and even mid summer (June) is not too late. Dahlias are somewhat brittle plants so they will probably require staking and it is a good idea to put the stakes in at the same time as you plant. They make large plants and can be planted at least 90cm (3 ft) apart, although a little less will be all right for the smaller pompons.

At one time people used to grow enormous dahlias, such as Crawley Beauty, which made plants 2m (7 ft) high with flowers up to 25cm (10 in) across, but these are not so popular now as they used to be. Such giant plants have to be put 1·80m (6 ft) apart.

Routine care

Although the dahlias will branch naturally many people pinch out the growing point when the plant is about 15cm (6 in) high to encourage branching to take place earlier. This should not be done until the new plant has clearly rooted into the soil. Then all you have to do is tie in the branches as they elongate, so that the plant is always kept fairly rigid.

Dahlias do not care for prolonged drought and should be watered copiously and the leaves sprayed well during dry spells. Otherwise your only worries are

POMPONS	
Brilliant Eye (medium)	glowing scarlet
Pride of Berlin (medium)	lilac-rose
Amusing (small)	orange-scarlet
Little William (small)	red and white
Nero (small)	velvety-red

COLLERETTES	
Grand Duc	red and yellow
La Cierva	purple and white
Libretto	velvety-pink and white

ANEMONE-FLOWERED	
Fable	dark red
Guinea	pure yellow
Roulette	pink

SINGLES OR DWARF	
Coltness hybrids	many colours
Firebird	bright red
Sneezy	pure white
Murillo	pink

pests. Greenfly can be a bore in the early stages of growth but your worst pest will probably be earwigs, which attack the flowers just as they are about to start. Straw or hay in an inverted flowerpot at the top of the stake is a useful way of trapping them, but this must be inspected daily and the earwigs burnt.

End-of-season care

With the first autumn frosts your dahlias will blacken. This is when you remove as much soil from the roots as you can and put them in a place that is dry and frost-free. Some people dust the tubers with a copper-lime dust to keep off a sort of mildew that sometimes attacks resting tubers, although provided they are kept perfectly dry there seems to be little risk.

In the second year

In the spring you have three choices. You can just replant the tubers as you lifted them and this is probably best done about early summer (mid May). Alternatively you can bring the plants into a cool greenhouse or warm room in early summer (May) with the roots in soil or peat, which is kept moist; after a time shoots will start to appear around the rootstock (but not from the tubers themselves) and you can cut the plant up into as many plants as there are shoots.

The way that is most preferred, provided you have the facilities, is to bring the tubers into heated greenhouses in early spring (February), again with the roots in moist soil or peat, and wait for shoots to appear. Once they have two joints they can be detached and rooted but quite considerable heat is needed for this. Since shoots are continually produced you can get a large number of plants from a single rootstock. Once rooted, the cuttings are potted up individually, if necessary potted on, and gradually hardened off to be planted out in mid summer (June) when the whole cycle starts up again.

LILIES

Of all the bulbs that beautify the herbaceous department it is arguable that the lilies are the loveliest. They are certainly the most difficult to manage successfully. In nature they are usually found in open scrub, where their lower leaves are shaded, while the flowers emerge in full

Above: Lilium tigrinum; *the popular tiger lily is unfortunately prone to virus disease. Right: modern hybrids –*
Golden Splendour, Emerald Strain,
Black Dragon, Pink Perfection

249

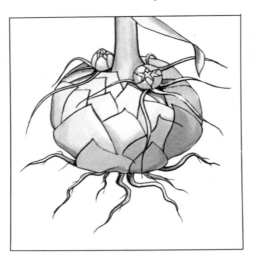

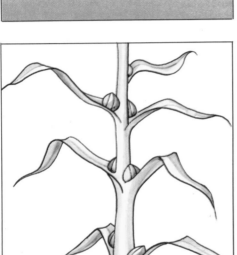

Top: planting lily bulb on sand
Top right: lily bulb with offsets
Above: lily plant with bulbils

sunlight sometime between mid summer and early autumn (June to August). Also, unlike other bulbs, the underground portions of the stems are liable to produce roots. This means that they do best in a fairly open soil with ample compost or leaf mould and that they should be planted fairly deeply, so that there is a good length of stem underground. It is probably best if the top of the bulb is 15cm (6 in) below the surface.

Preparing the ground
Since lily bulbs are expensive it is best to take considerable trouble, digging out the soil to a depth of 30cm (12 in), breaking it up well and incorporating compost or leaf mould, levelling out at a depth of about 20cm (8 in) and putting down a good layer of sharp washed garden sand to improve the drainage immediately around the bulb, and then filling up with the rest of the soil.

In the garden, lily bulbs scarcely rest at all and there is often ample root growth

going on at times when nothing can be seen above ground, so the bulbs should be planted as early as possible, say in late autumn (October), if the bulbs can be procured at that time. The bulbs may have travelled a long way – even from as far as Japan – so that the roots will have dried off altogether and the plants may take some time to get going again. It is not unknown for a whole season to pass before any leaves are seen, so don't despair until the second year.

Some varieties to choose
Lilium candidum (madonna lily) – pure pearly white – and its popular hybrid *L. × testaceum* (Nankeen lily) – pale yellow – are exceptional in that they are more or less evergreen and should be planted in early autumn (August or the first week in September). Once they have been planted in suitable soil there is little you can do, except wait and hope for the best. If it likes you, the madonna lily will thrive, but it is a choosy plant and it is not clear quite what it needs, but it seems to do best where the roots are crowded.

Virus disease is very common in lilies, although less common with plants that have been raised from seed. It is apparently always present in *L. tigrinium* (tiger lily) – orange red with black spots – so if you grow that you will probably be wise not to grow any other lily. The lilies that seem easiest to grow are *L. regale* – white, *L. henryi* – orange, and the Mid-century, Harlequin and Bellingham hybrids – mixed colours, followed by *L. umbellatum* (now called *L. × hollandicum* but frequently listed under *L. maculatum*) – in many varieties and different colours. Also easy and rewarding to grow are *L. hansonii* – orange-yellow, *L. pardalinum* – orange-red, and *L. speciosum* – pure white.

Of the modern lilies raised in recent years that are generally reliable, hardy

and free-flowering, the following offer a good selection:

Citronella	golden-brown
Connecticut Dream	yellow
Connecticut Yankee	orange
Earlibird	apricot
Enchantment	red
Firebright	currant-red
Geisha Girl	lemon-yellow
Golden Splendour	gold
Green Magic	white and green
Limelight	yellow
Orange Light	orange
Pink Champagne	yellow and pink
Redstart	wine
Red Velvet	deep maroon
Shuksan	light orange
Tabasco	ruby-red
White Princess	ivory

Increasing your stock
Lilies are very slow to produce offsets, but some come rapidly from seed, notably *L.regale*; and some produce bulbils on their stems, which can be grown on outdoors in a specially-prepared seedbed. Otherwise you have to remove bulb scales, put them upright in a box of sand and peat with only the tip protruding, and keep in a temperature of 15°C (60°F) until a bulblet forms at the base; this can then be grown on.

GLADIOLUS
Gladiolus present few problems. They like to be in full sun and can be planted from mid to late spring (March to April); even later will be quite satisfactory. The top of the corms should be about 10cm (4 in) below the surface and slightly deeper will do no harm at all. There is no point in purchasing the very large corms as the smaller ones will give just as good flower spikes from mid summer to late autumn (July to October) and are cheaper to buy.

By and large they are fairly trouble-free, but it is possible that they may be attacked by thrips, which distort the leaves. They are pests easily controlled by malathion or other insecticide.

Once the leaves begin to yellow, which is some time after flowering, the corms should be lifted and dried as fast as possible, as by hanging up in an airy, frost-free situation. Later they can be cleaned and stored in open slatted trays until the time comes to plant them again. You clean them by removing the old growths above the corm as well as the old corm and roots below it.

Large-flowered gladiolus

Early:

Bon voyage	azalea pink
Flower Song	yellow and carmine
Life Flame	vivid scarlet
Mabel Violet	velvet purple
Peter Pears	orange and red
White Friendship	cream

Mid season:

Albert Schweitzer	salmon-orange
Blue Conqueror	violet blue
Deciso	salmon-pink
Green Woodpecker	lime green
Hochsommer	orange and yellow
Memorial Day	rose magenta
Snow Princess	white

Late:

Bloemfontein	apricot-pink
Trader Horn	crimson-scarlet
Tropical Sunset	red and purple
Zenith	shell-pink

Primulinus varieties

Early:

Canopus	cyclamen pink
Harmony	lilac-purple
White City	white

Mid season:

Apex	scarlet
Comic	smoky-brown
Yellow Poppy	yellow

Late:

Pretoria	coral-red

Miniature varieties

Delphi	rose, salmon shading

Butterfly varieties

Early:

Red Spot	yellow and red
Riante	peach-rose

Mid season:

Greenwich	greeny-yellow

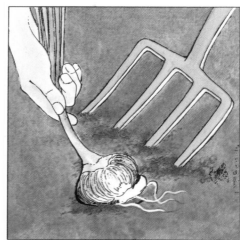

Top right: lifting gladiolus corm with fork
Above: corms drying fast, hanging up
Right: storing corms over winter
Bottom left: large-flowered mixed gladiolus Atlantic, Memorandum, Shakespeare. Bottom right: large-flowered gladiolus Red Cascade

Melodie	pink and orange
Southport	ivory white
Late:	
Bright Eye	yellow and red
Dancing Doll	yellow and pink

FLAG IRIS

Flags or, as we now call them, tall bearded iris, are among the most spectacular of all garden flowers, although their season is disappointingly short – only early and mid summer (May and June).

Left and below left: planting iris, with top of rhizome showing above soil
Above: flag iris Amethyst Flame
Bottom: flag iris Golden Alps

They have fans of leaves springing from a fleshy underground stem, which should never be completely buried, and flower on stems about 1m (3 ft) tall. Although they appreciate good soil, they will grow in ground that is rather poor.

Routine care

Their treatment is easy enough. The best time to move them is after flowering and new plants should be received in late summer (late July) or early autumn (August). If the rhizomes are bearing roots, just these should be buried, leaving the rhizome on the surface; if the rhizome has no roots, you must half-bury it, so that the top half is above the ground. As you want to encourage rooting, after planting you must water if there is a very dry spell, until the rhizome has anchored itself well. The plants can then be left for three years, after which lift them, break up the clumps and start again.

Your only real cause for concern is rhizome rot, which is caused by bad drainage or by the rhizomes getting buried. If you see the rhizomes rotting and the fans dying off, lift the plant, cut off the infected parts, dust the cut ends with powdered charcoal and replant in a new situation. This must be done as soon as you see symptoms, whatever time of the year it is.

Some varieties to choose

There are so many excellent tall bearded iris now on the market that it is difficult to recommend what to buy to begin with. Many gardeners start with a mixed selection, and then gradually add to their collection. Among some of the outstanding modern hybrids are:

Blue Shimmer	blue and white
Braithwaite	lavender and purple
Cleo	chartreuse green
Cliffs of Dover	milk-white
Golden Planet	golden yellow
Green Ice	greenish-cream
Headlines	white and purple
Helen McGregor	clear, light blue
Lady Mohr	oyster, yellow and red
Lothario	bi-colour blue
Mabel Chadburn	yellow
Mulberry Rose	mulberry
New Snow	snow-white
Pinnacle	white and yellow
Prairie Sunset	pink, apricot and gold
Ranger	crimson
Sable	blue-black
Zantha	golden yellow

There are other forms of iris, such as the beardless, cushion and bulbous-rooted, but these flower at various times of the year and require different cultural conditions. They will be described later.

Chrysanthemums

The specialist will spend endless time over his chrysanthemums to get large and perfectly-shaped blooms, probably for exhibition, but there is no good reason why you should not have more, though smaller, flowers to decorate the border in the autumn and early winter (September to November). There is a choice of four different groups.

GENERAL WORK
Early summer (May)
Continue to hoe weeds regularly to prevent them getting a hold and making the borders unsightly. Take care not to damage any shallow-rooting cultivated plants.

Dig a spare corner in the garden, firm it by treading, and rake the soil to a fine tilth to make a seedbed for sowing biennials for flowering next year.

To help healthy growth of hardy herbaceous perennials, as well as spring-flowering bulbs, water them from time to time with liquid fertilizer.

Start planting out chrysanthemums in positions prepared for them previously.

Climbers that have finished producing their spring flowers should have their flowering wood pruned out.

If there are any weeds on the lawn, either treat it overall with a weedkiller or spot-treat individual weeds if there are only a few.

Complete the sowing of hardy annuals where they are to flower.

Single
True singles have only one row of outer petals (called ray florets) – which are long and thin – and an eye (which consists of disc florets). The species that forms this group is *Chrysanthemum rubellum*, sometimes known as *C. erubescens*. It covers itself with masses of pink daisies about 5cm (2 in) or more across. Each flower is on a long stem, so that the plant is also

*Above and top right: two decoratives —
anemone-flowered Raymond Moundsey
and spider-flowered Martha, excellent for
town use and giving welcome autumn
colour
Above right: a true single, Clara Curtis*

useful for cutting. The whole plant may
grow about 90cm (3 ft) high. There are a
number of different coloured forms now
available.

Korean
The Koreans are similar to singles in that
they have a central eye, but in fact they are
semi-doubles – that is, they usually have
more than one row of outer petals.

The flowers are again about 5cm (2 in)
wide, and come in a number of colours, of
which crimson and dark purple are the
most common, though shades of apricot,
salmon pink, yellow and bronze are also
available. These are not always easy to
obtain but if you can get them they
usually make a very brilliant display in
mid autumn (September).

Pompon
As far as display in the border goes, you
probably cannot do much better than the
pompons. These produce large numbers
of small, tight flowers, looking rather like
powder puffs, that can be obtained in
almost all colours from white to pink, red,
purple and yellow. There are now some
very attractive pastel shades in pale shell-
pink. It is a little difficult to suggest
particular varieties as so-called 'improved' types are constantly being introduced and any list of names can soon
become out of date. It is best to visit a
chrysanthemum show, join a chrysanthemum society, or visit a specialist
nursery. You can also study catalogues,
so long as you bear in mind that
nurserymen tend only to mention the
most desirable features in their parti-
culars. If you live in a town, a talk with
someone in the Parks Department could
well prove informative.

Decorative
Ordinary chrysanthemums that are
grown for border ornament are becoming
increasingly hard to obtain and you may

well find that you have to get the outdoor
decoratives. These have actually been
bred to make many-petalled, large show
blooms, which must be specially grown
and disbudded. On the other hand, if you
do get a chance to get hold of varieties
such as Garden White or Memento
(white), Golden Orfe or Solley (yellow),
and Hilde or Pink Glory (pink), then do
so without hesitation.

Routine care
Whatever plants you select the treatment
is the same. The nursery will supply
rooted cuttings, preferably in late spring
(April). These will have come out of a
greenhouse and so will be very soft and
particularly appetizing for snails and
slugs. Pot them up separately and harden
them off by standing the pots outside
where slugs cannot reach them. Be sure to
sprinkle slug pellets around the pots as an
added precaution. After about three
weeks they should be ready to go into the
border – and ideally should be there
before mid summer (by the end of May).

Although the cuttings are small the
plants will get quite large, so plant them at

least 75cm (2½ ft) apart. About a week after you have planted them out, remove the growing tip *only*, so as to encourage the plant to throw out side growth. Do not remove any of the stem, however, as this will reduce the amount of sideshoots that a plant will produce. Removing the tips of the new sideshoots about a month later will encourage further bushing. After this all you have to do is sit back and wait for the plants to come into flower.

Chrysanthemums are fairly greedy plants, so top-dressing with a chrysanthemum fertilizer in late summer and early autumn (July and August) can do nothing but good, although it is by no means essential. Apply the fertilizer in the evening and give the plants a good soaking directly afterwards if the soil is at all dry. If you have a sprayer with a really fine spray, use a foliar feed instead. In any case you should stop feeding the plants during early autumn (after the second week in August).

Plants from cuttings
Once flowering is over, cut the stems down to within about 5cm (2 in) of the ground and leave them over the winter. You now have two choices: you can either leave the plants as they are, thinning the new growths out to about four per plant, or you can take cuttings and do exactly as you did the year before.

To root cuttings all you have to do is to pull up the shoots, which will appear in late winter or early spring (January to February), and cut them off just below a node (where you will see one or more leaves). The cuttings should be about 8cm (3 in) long. Dip the ends into a rooting powder and put them in a potful of cutting compost, which can either be purchased or made up of equal portions of peat and sharp garden sand.

Very little heat is needed to root the cuttings, so if you have no greenhouse you can do it perfectly well on a windowsill in a warm room. You can envelop the pot in a polythene bag, but in that case you should turn the bag inside out every three days. The compost should be watered after you have inserted your cuttings, to ensure it is in contact with the base of the cuttings, but after that no further watering should be necessary unless the compost dries out.

The cuttings should root in two or three weeks and if you give a gentle tug and find that they do not feel loose, you can be fairly sure that they are rooted. Once they are, pot them up in 8cm (3 in) pots in either J.I. No 1 or any growing compost and gradually harden off as before.

If you choose the easy way and leave your clumps in the border, you will need to lift them about every three years and split them up. This is best done in mid spring (March) when you should replant the new, outside growths in another part of the border.

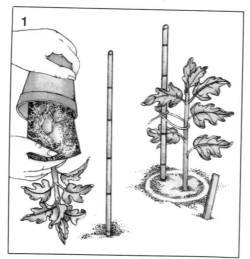

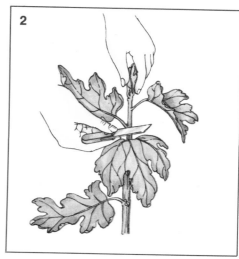

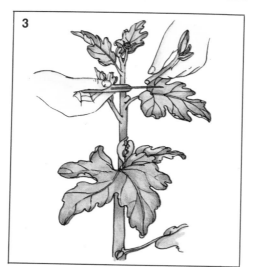

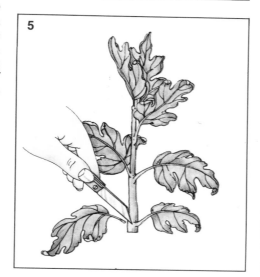

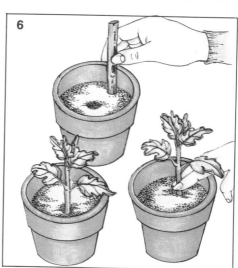

1 *Planting out from pots;* 2 *cutting out top shoot and* 3 *sideshoots;* 4 *thinning out new growth to four plants* 5 *Cutting off new shoots below the node for propagation;* 6 *planting cutting with dibber — one centrally, or first of several cuttings around the pot*

Above right: pyrethrum Evenglow
Above and right: double and single types
of shasta daisy, C. maximum *Esther Read*

If the leaves are discolouring in patches, then eventually yellowing and turning limp, the plants have probably got chrysanthemum eelworm pest. In this case you might just as well give up growing chrysanthemums altogether for at least three years. Dig out all the plants and burn them. However, eelworm attacks outdoor chrysanthemums comparatively rarely, although it likes the more showy types.

SOME OTHER CHRYSANTHEMUMS

There are a number of other chrysanthemums that you can grow in the garden.

Shasta daisy

Esther Read, such a stand-by of the flower arranger, is a double form of the shasta daisy, which used to be called the Edward VII chrysanthemum and is, botanically, *Chrysanthemum maximum*. This is so easy to grow that if anyone you know has it, they can probably let you have some of their divisions (see Division and layering, Week 12). All you have to do is plant them in the border and divide the clumps every three or four years. The shasta daisy itself is just an enormous white daisy, but there are quite a few double forms besides Esther Read.

Pyrethrum

There is also an old friend, *Chrysanthemum coccineum*, but you may not recognize the name. This is the pyrethrum, that crimson daisy which is so much used for cut flowers in mid summer (late May and June). This is not quite so easy to grow as *C. maximum*, as slugs are likely to do great damage when the new leaves appear in the spring; but if you use plentiful slug pellets or surround the plants with soot, you will find them quite trouble-free. They appear to exhaust the soil rather quickly, so many people split the clumps up and transplant every other year. At one time there were many forms of pyrethrum, both single and double, in various colours from deep crimson to pale pink and white, but the choice is now much less and you will probably have to settle for either the deep crimson or the semi-double pale pink.

Annual chrysanthemums

Finally there are the annual chrysanthemums, which have been bred from three wild species, *C. carinatum*, *C. coronarium* and *C. segetum*. These can be started from seed sown in warmth in mid spring (March), pricked out in boxes and eventually planted out, or sown outside in late spring (after the middle of April). There are both singles and doubles and they range in colour from white to sulphur, yellow, pink and red. They grow to about 60cm (24 in) high and may be expected to flower from mid summer to mid autumn (late June until September). They are thus useful for filling up any gaps or for inserting between spring bulbs, so as to give a display after they have died down. They like sunny situations, and will thrive in all soils, although they prefer it to be fairly dry and well-drained.

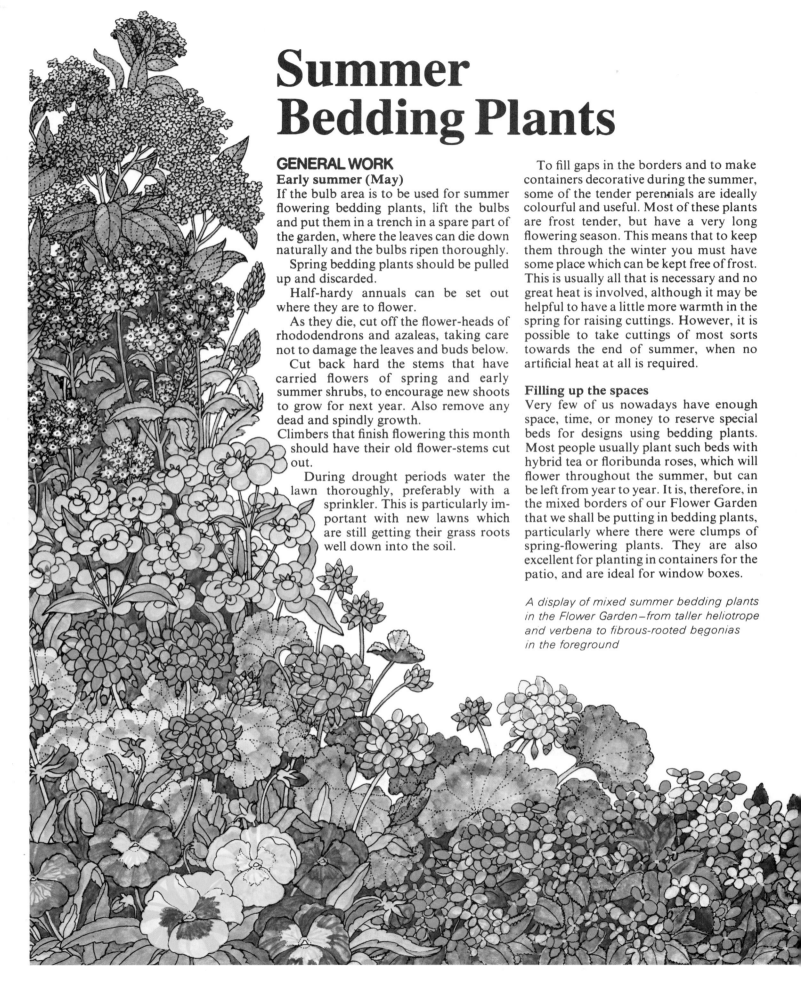

Summer Bedding Plants

GENERAL WORK

Early summer (May)

If the bulb area is to be used for summer flowering bedding plants, lift the bulbs and put them in a trench in a spare part of the garden, where the leaves can die down naturally and the bulbs ripen thoroughly.

Spring bedding plants should be pulled up and discarded.

Half-hardy annuals can be set out where they are to flower.

As they die, cut off the flower-heads of rhododendrons and azaleas, taking care not to damage the leaves and buds below.

Cut back hard the stems that have carried flowers of spring and early summer shrubs, to encourage new shoots to grow for next year. Also remove any dead and spindly growth.

Climbers that finish flowering this month should have their old flower-stems cut out.

During drought periods water the lawn thoroughly, preferably with a sprinkler. This is particularly important with new lawns which are still getting their grass roots well down into the soil.

To fill gaps in the borders and to make containers decorative during the summer, some of the tender perennials are ideally colourful and useful. Most of these plants are frost tender, but have a very long flowering season. This means that to keep them through the winter you must have some place which can be kept free of frost. This is usually all that is necessary and no great heat is involved, although it may be helpful to have a little more warmth in the spring for raising cuttings. However, it is possible to take cuttings of most sorts towards the end of summer, when no artificial heat at all is required.

Filling up the spaces

Very few of us nowadays have enough space, time, or money to reserve special beds for designs using bedding plants. Most people usually plant such beds with hybrid tea or floribunda roses, which will flower throughout the summer, but can be left from year to year. It is, therefore, in the mixed borders of our Flower Garden that we shall be putting in bedding plants, particularly where there were clumps of spring-flowering plants. They are also excellent for planting in containers for the patio, and are ideal for window boxes.

A display of mixed summer bedding plants in the Flower Garden—from taller heliotrope and verbena to fibrous-rooted begonias in the foreground

257

Top right and above right: two varieties of zonal pelargonium, Paul Crampel and Mrs Quitter, like poor soil and full sun
Top left: mix heliotrope with calceolaria
Above: ivy-leaved pelargonium L'Elegante, free-flowering, long-stemmed trailing species, effective in hanging baskets
Opposite: combined pelargonium hybrids, variegated regal and zonal varieties

There is a very large choice of bedding plants, including a number of annuals which will require some heat in the spring to raise the seedlings. Alternatively, you can buy young plants from a nursery, although this is rather more expensive. To begin with, we have chosen plants that can be kept going from year to year.

Heliotrope

An old favourite is heliotrope, or 'cherry pie'. This is around 45cm (18 in) high with rather dark leaves and large heads of violet or bluish flowers with one of the loveliest scents of all garden plants. You will probably have to start by buying in some plants and there is no point in doing this much before mid summer (June) as you cannot plant them out until all risk of frost has gone. They can be raised from seed sown in gentle heat, around 15°C (60°F) in mid spring (late February or early March), but the results may be a rather mixed bag, although Lemoine's Giant is said to come true from seed.

In early autumn (mid August) side-shoots or growing tips may be taken for cuttings. Make them about 5cm (2 in) long, from just below a leaf joint and put them

in a cutting mixture, either a ready made-up bought compost or equal parts of peat and sharp garden sand. If only a few are being taken, insert the cuttings in a pot and put the potful inside a polythene bag. The cuttings should be put in a position shaded from direct sunlight and should root in two or three weeks. Once rooted they are first hardened off by removing the polythene bag and leaving them for a few days, and then either potted up separately in 8cm (3 in) pots or planted out about 8cm (3 in) apart in trays. At this stage you should use either a soilless growing compost or J.I. No 1.

Before there is any risk of frost bring them under cover, in a frame or a greenhouse if possible, otherwise into the house, and keep them as dry as possible. Water only when the leaves wilt and always use water warmed to 15°C (60°F) when you do. Towards late spring (at the end of March or early April) you will need to water more frequently. You can put your plants outside during the day to harden them off, but remember you will have to bring them back under cover if there are any late frosts. Plant them out in mid summer (June).

Zonal pelargoniums

The most popular bedding plant for over a hundred years has been the geranium, which should really be called the zonal pelargonium. This is one of the most useful of all garden plants, although in very wet summers it may produce masses of leaves and only a few flowers. You also have to be somewhat selective as to what sorts you obtain as some of the most handsome only give of their best in a cool greenhouse and do not flower very freely out of doors.

Some of the blazing scarlets, such as the ever popular Paul Crampel and the double-flowered Gustav Emich, are somewhat harsh in colour and not too easily combined with other plants, but if you find this you can always go in for the delightful salmon-pink King of Denmark or the orange-tinged Maxim Kovaleski or Orangesonne. Doris Moore is an attractive cherry red, Vera Dillon is almost magenta and Hermione is pure white. All these are old and trusted varieties, but fresh ones are brought out each year.

There is also a race of zonals with showy leaves that are their main attraction. These include the yellow-leaved A Happy Thought and Golden Harry Hieover and the astonishing Henry Cox, in which the leaf is variegated in deep maroon, red, green and cream. The flowers of these variegated types are not produced particularly freely and they are not very attractive in any case; the interest lies in their leaves.

Ivy-leaved pelargoniums

Very different in habit, but flowering very freely, are the trailing ivy-leaved pelargoniums, which are splendid for putting around the sides of containers or in hanging baskets, as the growths hang down and hide their containers. Although there is quite a range of colours, you will have to find a specialist nursery if you require anything other than the pink Madame Crousse or the purple-veined white L'Elegante. The latter has the advantage of leaves margined with pale cream and purple, so that it is handsome at all times of the year.

Assuming that you have to start by buying in pelargonium plants, it is usually best not to plant them out at once, as they have probably been growing in a fairly warm greenhouse. So leave them in their pots for a fortnight, bringing them in at night if there is a risk of frost. The beginning of mid summer (June) is a good time to plant them out, so early summer (mid May) is a good time to purchase plants. One of the great advantages of pelargoniums is that they do best in very

poor soil, so see that they have the poorest soil in your border and full sunlight. If the soil is too rich they grow prodigiously, but concentrate too much of their energies on stems and leaves and not enough on flowers.

Cuttings are taken in early autumn (mid August). Take growing points about 8cm (3 in) long, remove any flower buds if necessary and let them lie in the sun for 24 hours. Now cut them off just below a leaf joint and insert them in a cutting mixture. There is no need to envelop the pot in a polythene bag.

The cuttings usually root fairly quickly and they can be potted up singly. During the winter they should be kept just free of frost, on the dry side and in as much light as possible. Sometimes the cuttings produce flower buds very soon, but these must be removed. About mid spring (the end of March) you will have to start giving more water, and this is quite a good time to nip out the growing point to encourage a bushy plant.

Stand the plants outdoors in late spring (the end of April), but remember to bring them back in if late frosts are expected. Plant them out finally towards mid

summer (June). Provided they have been hardened off, pelargoniums will take a degree or so of frost without damage, but is not advisable to expose them to it. It is possible to pot the plants on in late spring (early April), but not really necessary.

Viola

A bedding plant that is rather rarely seen nowadays, even though it is hardy, is the viola. This is much like the pansy to look at, but has the advantage of a much longer flowering season. These are sown in early spring (February), pricked out when large enough in boxes, hardened off and planted out usually in early summer (May). Alternatively it is possible to buy named sorts such as the mauve Maggie Mott or the yellow Golden Bedder. You can also buy the apricot Chantreyland but this will come true from seed as will the reddish Arkwright Ruby.

With named sorts, or with any seedlings you want to perpetuate, you take cuttings in late summer or early autumn (July or August). To find the cuttings you have to lift the plant up, when you will see small shoots coming from the rootstock. These are detached from as near the root as possible when about 5cm (2 in) long, and treated like any other cutting.

Once rooted they are pricked out in boxes and then planted out either in their permanent positions or in some reserve ground. The original plants will survive the winter, but they never flower so well the second season. All these violas are about 15cm (6 in) high.

You may well be wondering why so excellent a plant should be so rarely seen and the answer is that there is one snag. Once the viola has set seed it will stop flowering, so you have to keep on nipping off the faded flowers, which can be quite tedious and time consuming. However, if you do this you have flowers all through the summer so it is worth it if you can find the time.

Verbena

Verbenas are usually treated as half-hardy annuals, being sown in gentle heat, around 13°C (55°F) in early spring (late February), pricked out into boxes, hardened off in early summer (early May) and planted out about two or three weeks later. Most of the seeds produce mixed colours so that if you want to preserve a particularly good form you will have to resort to cuttings.

These are taken from sideshoots in early autumn (August) and usually root readily enough. They can then be planted out in boxes, kept frost-free throughout the winter, brought back into gentle heat towards mid spring (the end of March) and then treated as the seedlings were. You start to harden them off at the end of

Below: Viola × wittrockiana *Jungfrau useful for bedding out and edging paths*
Right: verbena *Lawrence Johnston*
Below right: Viola cornuta *Dartington*

and stopped by pinching out the growing tips in early spring (February). As soon as you see sideshoots appearing you can pot the cuttings up in 8 or 10cm (3 or 4 in) pots, and once established they are gradually hardened off and planted out. They like a rather rich soil and often resent prolonged drought. On the other hand they will do equally well in full sun or in partial shade. They are becoming scarce, so are worth cultivating.

Fibrous-rooted begonia

Finally we should mention *Begonia semperflorens* (the fibrous-rooted type), a dwarf plant, often with deep purple leaves and flowers of some shade of red, pink or white. It can be treated as a half-hardy annual, but needs at least 25°C (70°F) to start the minute seeds and it is probably best to buy in plants. Shoots growing from the base of old flowering stems of plants lifted in the autumn (October) can be used for cuttings in the spring (March or April), but the plants need a temperature of around 10°C (50°F) throughout the winter. The cuttings are cultivated in the same way as the others.

Begonia semperflorens may be a bit expensive to keep over the winter, but it does have the advantage of continuous flowering, whether the weather be wet or dry, and does equally well in full sun or in shade, so it can be a really useful plant. spring (the beginning of May), as usual seeing that they are not damaged by late frosts, and plant them out before mid summer (at the beginning of June).

Verbena are trailing plants with round heads of flowers in various shades of red from scarlet to pale pink, or with white or violet flowers; often the flowers have a white eye. It is also possible to keep plants through the winter in the greenhouse and continue to take cuttings in mid and late spring (March and April) if you want to build up a large stock. With all these bedding plants it is a great help to have a frame in which to harden off the plants. It can be kept open at all times except when late frosts are forecast.

Calceolaria

Verbena is seen only rarely nowadays, but it is more common than the so-called shrubby calceolaria. This may be slightly woody at the base, but looks like a herbaceous plant about 30–45cm (12–18 in) tall with purse-shaped flowers that are usually yellow, though at one time a deep brown form was popular. The variety Sunshine is a good hybrid. The plants will take a few degrees of frost without damage, but prefer to be protected.

Colourful display

If you prefer a show of colourful flowers, choose ones that will flower over a long period. Begonias will last from year to year if you bring them under glass during the winter.

Heliotrope is not very showy, but it diffuses an exquisite perfume and does flower over a long period. Zonal pelargoniums are not confined to the rather fiery-coloured Paul Crampel; you can also obtain delightful salmon-pink ones, such as King of Denmark, the orange Maxim Kovaleski, the almost magenta Vera Dillon, the white Hermine and the red-edged white Lady Warwick. Nor should you overlook those with variegated leaves, such as Henry Cox, whose leaf is shaded black, red, green and cream and is very showy. Happy Thought has a large yellow zone in the leaf, while Golden Harry Hieover has a gold and red leaf. They produce red or crimson flowers, though not very freely, and it is their leaves that are the main attraction.

If the containers are quite high off the ground, ivy-leaved pelargoniums trailing over the sides, with perhaps a fuchsia in the centre, make a pleasant planting. One of the best is L'Elegante, with silvery variegated leaves and white, purple-striped flowers. The more popular pink Mme Crousse, or its purple sport Claret Crousse, are also attractive and both of them are easy to grow.

All of these plants would do best planted directly into a soil that is not too rich: J.I. No 1 is quite sufficient. The first hard frost will kill all the pelargoniums and heliotropes, at which time you can just pull them up and throw them on your compost heap. However, with both these flowering plants it is very easy to root cuttings in early or mid Autumn (August or September) and they can be over-wintered on the kitchen windowsill. Fuchsias can also be rooted then, but most people prefer spring-struck cuttings.

The marguerite, *Chrysanthemum frutescens*, with grey-green leaves and white daisies that seem to go on flowering for ever, is not often seen nowadays, but if you can obtain it from a nursery it is still excellent value for money. Here again cuttings root easily, but if you lift the plant and pot it up, it will probably go on flowering all through the winter indoors.

Half Hardy Annuals

Annuals are the great stand-by in our Flower Garden. With careful planning, they help to provide that 'riot of colour' throughout the flowering season that every gardener dreams of. Although slightly more difficult to raise, the half-hardy annuals are particularly valuable for colour in the borders.

Half-hardy annuals can be very useful in the garden, especially for summer bedding and filling up gaps in the border. The only conceivable objection to them is that they need some heat when the seeds are germinating, so that if you have no greenhouse, you will have to raise them in the home, or sow them outside rather late in the season, or buy plants in.

Why 'half-hardy'?
The reason we call a plant half-hardy is that it is liable to be damaged by frost. This means that in most parts of the United Kingdom, for instance, it will not be safe to put the plant out in the garden before the last week in early summer (May) or the beginning of mid summer (June). As the plant is also an annual it is in a great hurry to flower and set seed. Since, once its seeds are ripe, it is going to die in any case, it is not much concerned with making a large root system; the important thing is for it to flower and set seed before the winter comes.

Buying plants
What this means in practical terms is that once an annual starts to flower it has, almost certainly, ceased making growth, so do not choose any plants that show either buds or flowers. It is possible to encourage further growth by taking off all the visible flowers and buds, but they will

Left: Cleome spinosa *need a warm spot*
Top right: callistephus Milady Blue, a single species of half-hardy annual that likes a loamy soil; decorative as pot plants
Above: dimorphotheca, or African daisy, whose flowers do not open in the shade

never make really satisfactory plants.

Half-hardy annuals are liable to come into flower quickly if their root space is at all constricted, so you will be wise to avoid boxes of seedlings with a crowded mass of plants growing closely together. Look for a box where the plants are at least 5cm (2 in) apart in each direction. This gives the roots room to expand and so will stop the plant coming into flower prematurely. The point is that although annuals can come into flower with very few roots, if they are given the opportunity to make a sizeable root system they will make larger plants and produce more flowers, and so continue flowering over a longer period. Thus, ideally, you want to purchase plants that are well-spaced in their boxes and not showing any signs of flowering.

The best time to buy
The next question is when to buy them. As you will probably not want to plant them out before mid summer (end of May), take no notice of anyone offering you plants in late spring (April). (This, of course, only applies to half-hardy annuals, since hardy annuals can be purchased at any time if you are unable to grow them from seed.)

The plants will probably have come out of the nurseryman's greenhouse and will be what some gardeners call 'lishy'. The leaves are very soft and practically irresistible to slugs and insect pests, and you will need to harden them off before you plant them out. This usually takes 10–14 days, so around the middle of early summer (mid May) is an excellent time to purchase the seedlings of half-hardy annuals. All you have to do is stand the boxes outside, preferably propped up on some support to keep the slugs away, water the soil if it gets at all dry (but not otherwise), and put the plants wherever you want them after 14 days.

Of course, if there is a risk of frost during this fortnight, you will have to bring the boxes indoors overnight. Anywhere in the house will be frost-free at that time of year, so it does not matter where you put the boxes, which can go out again during the daytime. If you have a frame you can, of course, harden your plants off in that, opening the lights at all times, except when frost is expected.

Raising from seed indoors
With the exception of *Begonia semperflorens*, most half-hardy annuals require very little heat to germinate. About 15°C (60°F) is quite adequate so, if you lack a greenhouse, you can probably germinate them on a windowsill indoors. In this case sow the seed in mid spring (towards the end of March) in a seed compost. When the seedlings have produced about two pairs of leaves, prick them out 5cm (2 in) apart in trays in a growing compost, either J.I. No 1 or a soilless mix, and put them in a slightly cooler place after ten days.

Then harden them off as already described. There is not much point in starting the seeds too early, as either the weather is too cold or the plants get too advanced by planting out time. The same routine applies if you have a greenhouse.

Sowing 'in situ'
One other possibility is to sow the seeds in position outside in early to mid summer (the end of May), for flowering in late summer and early autumn (July and August). This will not be possible with plants that flower in early and mid summer (May and June). as they will not have enough time to make their growth.

Care after planting out

Once they have been planted out – with tall plants about 30cm (12 in) apart and the shorter ones 15–25cm (6–9 in) apart – there is not much that needs doing. You should bear in mind that the annual's main object in life is to set seed, so if you can find the time to nip off all flower-heads as soon as they have finished flowering, you will encourage the plant to produce more flowers and so prolong the season. If, at the same time, you give a very light dressing of a balanced fertilizer or a foliar feed you will aid this process, although probably not very significantly.

Some plants to choose

The first four plants in the following list are all known as 'everlastings', that is, they can be dried and used for flower arrangements throughout the year.

Acrolinium, Helichrysum, Lonas and **Xeranthemum** have mixed colour, single or double, daisy-like flowers and grow up to 60cm (24 in). They can all be started early or sown direct out of doors, and flower from late summer to late autumn (July to October).

Ageratum These are usually low-spreading plants rarely more than 15cm (6 in) tall, although there are some taller ones. They bear heads of small bluey-mauve powder puffs over a long period, if regularly dead-headed. Seed sown outside in early to mid summer (the end of May onwards) produces good, autumn-flowering (August to October) plants.

Alonsoa A rather unusual plant about 30cm (12 in) tall with masses of small bright red flowers. Sow outside early to mid summer (late May) for late summer to late autumn (July to October) flowering.

Antirrhinum The popular snapdragon is not strictly half-hardy at all, but the plants need quite a long growing season, so seedlings must be raised early. There is little point, therefore, in sowing in early to mid summer (late May), but you can sow outside in early autumn (August) and let the plants overwinter *in situ*. In fact you can treat antirrhinum as a biennial.

Begonia semperflorens A marvellous little plant about 20cm (8 in) tall, sometimes with purple leaves and an endless succession of red, pink or white flowers from mid summer (the end of June) onwards. There is no objection to buying flowering plants as it is really perennial and can be kept through the winter in heat. Nor is it necessary to remove the faded flowers. It will also, rather unusually, grow in semi-shade, whereas most annuals require full sun. A temperature of at least 22°C (70°F) will be needed to germinate the dust-like seeds, so most gardeners will have to buy plants at the appropriate time.

Callistephus (Chinese aster) This decorative plant is highly popular. The flower-heads, usually in various shades of pink and blue, yellow or white, come in a number of shapes – daisy-like blooms, doubles, quills, pompons or chrysanthemum shape – and are always interesting. It will grow to a height of approximately 15–60cm (6–24 in), and can be sown outdoors in early summer (May). Its flowering season lasts from late summer (May) onwards.

Celosia (cockscomb or Prince of Wales feathers) This plant possesses rather odd, feathery heads that are coloured crimson or yellow. It can grow up to 90cm (3 ft) tall, and it will flower from late summer (July) onwards.

Cleome (spider flower) This grows as a tall bushy plant with pink and white flowers. It can reach a height of 1·2m (4 ft), although usually it will grow to less than this. It produces flowers from late summer (July) onwards.

Cosmea (cosmos) This has fern-like leaves and dahlia-like flowers that come usually in some shades of pink or red. It will grow up to 75cm (2½ ft) in height, and its flowering season occurs in the autumn (August and September).

Dimorphotheca (star of the veldt) Probably best left until early summer (May) and sown where you want it to flower. It grows about 30cm (12 in) tall and has masses of bright orange, yellow or white daisies which appear right through summer and into autumn.

Felicia bergeriana (kingfisher daisy) Is again best left until near mid summer (late May) and sown *in situ*. It only reaches a height of 10cm (4 in) and has daisies of a brilliant kingfisher blue from mid summer to mid autumn (June to September).

Gaillardia The annual variety. Has large daisies in various shades of yellow and orange with almost black cones in the centre. Grows about 60cm (24 in) tall, and flowers from mid summer to late autumn (June to October).

Lobelia Has such tiny seeds that it is almost essential to start them in pots, although you will get nice plants from seed sown in early summer (May). Mainly blue flowers but some red or white, from late summer (July) onwards. The plants grow about 10cm (4 in) tall.

Mesembryanthemum (Livingstone daisy) Has fleshy leaves and daisy-like flowers in a bewildering assortment of colours. Grows only about 10cm (4 in) high, but spreads widely and flowers from late summer (July) until the frosts come. It also likes dry conditions. Seed sown outside in early to mid summer (late May) starts to flower rather later, but is quite satisfactory.

Nemesia Showy South African plants growing about 25cm (10 in) tall with clusters of flowers in varying shades of red, orange, yellow, and even blue. The flowering season is rather short, so late-sown seeds will provide you with a second display.

Nicotiana The popular tobacco plant, usually 45–90cm (1½–3 ft) tall has white or red night-scented flowers from late summer to mid autumn (July to September).

Perilla This is grown not for flowers, but for its dark purple, almost black, indented leaves. Grows to about 60cm (24 in).

Petunia Possibly the most reliable half-hardy annual for continuous display. It does require starting fairly early in the year, but is usually trouble-free, flowering through summer and autumn until the first frosts. The flowers come in a wide range of single or bicolours and may be simple and bell-like or a mass of petals (multifloras). It grows to a height of 10–25cm (4–10 in).

Far left, above: Cosmos Sunset loves sun
Above right: celosia Belden Plume, a fiery tropical plant, thrives in warm conditions
Right: ageratum North Sea, its clusters of neat flower-heads last for a long time

Above left: Salpiglossis sinuata blooms in profusion and has beautiful veined markings. It originally came from Chile .
Above right: Lobelia erinus, a dwarf spreading plant, flowers from early summer
Top: Phlox drummondii should be planted out in a moist, sunny border

Annual phlox A very attractive annual with heads of flowers from deep crimson to white and yellow. Can well be sown outside at the end of May. Grows to 15–20cm (6–8 in) and flowers from late summer (July) through the autumn.

Portulaca Rather rarely seen nowadays as it can be unsatisfactory in wet summers, but gorgeous in a dry, warm one. Grows to 15cm (6 in) with large single or double red and yellow flowers from mid summer to mid autumn (June to September).

Ricinus (castor oil plant) Grown for its ornamental bronze, dark purple or green leaves and stately habit, it reaches 1·2m (4 ft). You will probably have to grow this yourself, as nurserymen rarely offer it in plant form.

Salpiglossis The plants are unpleasantly sticky to touch but the flowers, which are trumpet-shaped and about 8cm (3 in) long in many rich colours, are amongst the most spectacular of all annuals. The plants grow to 60cm (24 in) and flower from late summer to mid autumn (July to September).

Salvia The bedding salvia, well known for its scarlet flowers, though there are now forms with the spiky flower-heads in purple or pastel shades. Grows between 23–30cm (9–12 in), flowering in late summer and early autumn (July and August).

Statice About 30–45cm (12–18 in) tall with large heads of everlasting flowers in a wide selection of colours. Can be sown outside, and flowers in late summer (July).

Tagetes French and African marigolds. The French makes perfectly good plants from seeds sown in mid summer (June), but the African, which is taller, needs a rather longer season, although it flowers from mid summer seeding in a good year. Usually yellow and orange flowers from late summer (July) onwards; the bushy plants grow to about 15cm (6 in).

Ursinia Another orange South African daisy, best sown outside in a sunny position. Grows to 23cm (9 in) and flowers from mid summer to early autumn (June to August).

Venidium (monarch of the veldt) Large daisy in pastel shades, with a dark blotch in the centre. Height-wise, it will grow up to 75cm ($2\frac{1}{2}$ ft), and its flowering season lasts from mid summer to late autumn (June to October).

Verbena (vervain) Still a valuable bedding plant with heads of bright flowers in pink, crimson, scarlet or violet from mid summer (June) until the first frosts. Height about 30cm (12 in).

Zinnia One of the showiest annuals for late flowering either in tall forms up to 60cm (24 in) or in dwarf forms not taller than 30cm (12 in). The flowers are multi-petalled in shades of orange, yellow, red or white. They should not be planted out before mid summer (mid June), long after most other half-hardy plants, and even so may prove unsatisfactory should the summer be either cold or wet.

266

Raising Annuals under glass

When you grow your own plants from seed you have better control of their quality and timing. Most of the favourite bedding plants can be sown in the greenhouse from about mid to late spring (March to April). It is a good idea to sow seeds from the packet over a period of time so you can enjoy a long flowering period.

How you sow can be varied to suit the cost, quantity and size of the seed. Large seeds (like zinna) should be sown individually in small pots. Finer seed should be sown in a tray or pan; prick out the seedlings into more trays when they are large enough to handle. Instead of pricking out you can then thin the seedlings by pulling out the excess and discarding them.

For germinating seed use a sterilized seed compost such as John Innes Seed Compost and make sure that it is moist. A useful rule is to cover the seed with its own depth of compost. Very fine or dust-like seed, however, should not be covered.

After sowing cover the seed containers with glass and then a sheet of brown paper or newspaper. Some form of propogator will be most helpful for germinating the seeds. For bedding plants high temperatures are undesirable. Too much heat will force the seedlings and they will become spindly, pale and weak. A temperature of 7–18°C (45–65°F) is adequate for most plants. There are inexpensive small electric propogators for warming only one or two seed trays, and designs that are heated by paraffin oil lamp. Many people manage to germinate the odd trays of seeds in their homes on the window-sill of a warm room.

Germination time may vary from a couple of days to several weeks depending on the type of seed and temperature. Remove the containers cover when the first seedlings are through – but exposure to bright sunlight in the early stages can be harmful.

Pricking out should be done as soon as

the seedlings are big enough to handle easily. In the case of very tiny seedlings such as lobelia, small groups can be 'patched out' since it is impossible to separate them. When pricking out be generous with your spacing so the roots do not become entangled and damaged when the young plants are divided for planting out. After pricking out, water the seedlings with a Cheshunt compound to help prevent damping-off disease.

All bedding plants must be given a

Above left: Nemesia strumosa suttonii, *whose cut flowers last well in water*
Above right: clarkia, *used mainly as border decoration, or can be grown for cutting*
Top: Zinnia elegans, *Envy, a showy plant*

period of gradual acclimatization to the open air before planting out – 'hardening off'. In the greenhouse itself move the seed trays to cooler spots and move the trays to frames outside three weeks before you intend to bed them out.

Hardy Biennials

Biennial flowering plants can be the stand-by of every judicious gardener as their extended life cycle enables you to organize your bedding schemes and keep design and colour in mind for the following year.

True biennials are plants that grow one year, overwinter, then flower, seed and die in the following year. Among them are many of the popular garden plants such as Canterbury bell, honesty and foxglove, also a number of plants usually grown as biennials which are really perennials, such as wallflower, pansy and sweet William.

Some have such large seeds that it is possible to sow them in their flowering positions, but others will need to be sown in a part of the garden reserved for raising seedlings, such as in our seedbed in the north-west corner. They can be thinned out subsequently into rows where they can remain until it is time to plant them in their flowering positions in mid autumn (September). With very fine seeds, like those of foxglove, it is probably better to sow in a flowerpot left outside; once they have germinated they can be transplanted 15cm (6 in) apart into rows in the seedbed and then planted into their flowering positions in the autumn.

When to sow

The time for sowing depends to a large extent on when the plant will flower the following year. Plants that flower fairly early in the spring, such as wallflower, honesty and pansy, have to make all their growth before the winter so the longer they are given the better it will be. Later-flowering plants, such as hollyhock, stock, sweet William or Canterbury bell, will make some further growth after the winter before they start producing flowers so they can be sown somewhat later.

Far left: Echium plantagireum *Blue Bedder (viper's bug loss); above:* Cheiranthus cheiri *(wallflower) with profuse showy blooms*
Below: richly-coloured giant pansies

GENERAL WORK

Mid summer (June)

Hoe weeds regularly in all parts of the garden where there is bare earth, to prevent the weeds getting established, seeding and spreading. Always take care not to damage any shallow-rooting cultivated plants.

Continue to plant out half-hardy annuals and sow some in positions where they are to flower to give a longer season of colour.

As climbing plants, and those shrubs treated as climbers, continue to grow and produce new shoots, tie in to the supports where necessary.

From now until early autumn (August) the lawn will probably require mowing twice a week. Cut the grass to 13mm ($\frac{1}{2}$ in) high. Unless the lawn has been treated with a weedkiller, the grass cuttings should be added to the compost heap.

269

Above and above right: Lunaria annua (honesty) flowering, and seeding in autumn to leave flat silver pods that can be used to make excellent winter decoration

Keep an eye open for any attacks of pests or diseases on plants and take prompt action by spraying or dusting with the appropriate pesticide according to the manufacturer's instructions. Watch out for signs of reinfestation.

Annuals treated as biennials

There are also some hardy annuals that will produce much larger plants if they are treated as biennials and sown in the autumn (September). The plants that like this treatment include godetia, calendula, candytuft, echium (viper's bugloss), sweet pea, cornflower, larkspur, Shirley poppy, eschscholtzia and annual clary sage. Just sow the seeds in rows in drills and leave the young plants until the following spring, when you can transplant them to wherever you want them to flower.

Preparing to sow

Before considering sowing times, you should first think of preparing the ground. The most important things for a young seedling are plenty of light, so that it can manufacture energy, and a fairly light soil so that the roots can penetrate quickly and anchor the plant.

The light will normally be there, unless you sow in the shade of evergreens, but you will have to prepare the soil. It will need loosening up, even if it is a light, sandy one. A very stiff soil is hard for the roots to get into so, if your soil is heavy, dig it, break it up and incorporate some sand or peat into this broken-up soil. If the soil is dry, give it a thorough soaking with water before you start your sowing. If the soil has been well soaked the young roots will soon get down to the moisture, even though it may be dry on top.

How to sow

Having got your soil prepared, make a small drill, not more than 2–3cm (1 in) deep and sow your seeds as thinly as possible. Rake some soil over them and sit back and wait.

After sowing, biennial seeds usually germinate rapidly enough and you should not have to wait more than a fortnight before you see the seedlings appear; usually you will get results even sooner.

With the large-seeded plants, which you can put where they are expected to flower, it is wise perhaps to put two seeds in every place and pull out the weaker of the two if both germinate. The distance between the plants when you line (plant) them out will vary according to type and the recommended distances are given below under each plant individually.

Thinning and transplanting

Apart from those seeds sown *in situ*, you now have two choices. If you do not want

many plants, you can just thin the seedlings out and leave them where they are. Alternatively, you can transplant them as soon as they are large enough to handle and leave them in rows until about the middle of autumn (mid September) when you lift them and put them where you want them to flower.

Be sure that the young plants do not dry out when you line them out. The simplest way is to puddle them. You dig a hole to the required depth with a trowel – the required depth will be such that the roots can be as deep in the soil as they were before you moved them. Then pop in the plants, fill the hole with water and then push the soil back around the roots. This enables your small biennials to get away without much check, and you want to keep them growing with as few checks as possible.

The plants should be in their final positions by mid autumn (mid September), to give them a chance to make a little growth and anchor themselves in the fresh soil before the onset of winter. However, this may not always be possible. You may, for example, want to put wallflowers where you now have dahlias. These will not be lifted before late autumn (the end of October), so it may well be early winter (November) before you put in your wallflowers.

The result will be that you won't get quite such a good display in the spring as you would have done if you could have

moved the plants earlier, but, failing an absolutely appalling winter, you should still get quite good results.

Some plants to choose

Here we list some good biennials, in order of flowering.

Pansy Sow in late summer (July) and prick out 15cm (6 in) apart. They start to flower in late spring (April) and can go on until late summer (late July). The blooms come in a variety of rich shades, either single or bi-coloured.

Wallflower Sow either in mid or late summer (June or July). Line out 15cm (6 in) apart. In flower from late spring (late March) to mid summer (June) in reds, oranges and yellow colours.

Honesty Should be sown in mid or late summer (June or July), preferably where the plants are to flower. If you do prick them out they should be 25cm (9 in) apart. The purple or white flowers appear in early to late summer (May to July). The flat and round silver seed pods which follow are very sought after for winter flower decorations.

Top left: the familiar digitalis (foxglove)
Below and bottom right: two Papaver
nudicate *(iceland poppies), suitable for
rock gardens as well as mixed borders*
Bottom left: Verbascum bombyciferum
(mullein)

Sweet William Sow in late summer (early July) and prick out to 25cm (9 in) apart. They flower mid to late summer (June to July) in mixtures of red, white, pink or salmon colours.

Stock It is the Brompton and East Lothian strains that are biennial; the ten-week and the night-scented are annuals. Sow in late summer (early July), and prick out 30cm (12 in) apart. It is possible to leave them in the rows until the following spring, in which case they must be put in their final positions in mid spring (March). Flowers are shades of pink, red, lilac, yellow or white, with the Bromptons appearing in early summer (May) and the East Lothians during summer and early autumn (July and August).

Foxglove These digitalis seeds are so minute that they are best started in a pot. Prick out the seedlings to 30cm (12 in) apart and, again, they can be left in the rows until late spring (early April) if it is more convenient. The flower spikes of white, pink, purple and yellow appear in mid summer (June).

Canterbury bell Sow in summer (May or June). The seeds are very small, so it may be easier to start them in a pot. Prick out

Below: matthiola (Brompton stocks)
Left: Althaea rosea (hollyhock)

the seedlings at least 30cm (12 in) apart and once more you can wait to plant them in their final positions until the following late spring (April). They flower in summer (June and July) in white, pink, blue or mauve shades.

Iceland poppy This needs rather different treatment. All poppies (or papavers) dislike transplanting so you can either sow them where they are to grow, or start them in a pot, prick out or transplant about 5cm (2 in) apart into trays and then put them in their final positions the following spring (April). The trouble with sowing them *in situ* is that the seeds are very tiny, so it is not easy to differentiate between the young seedlings and weeds when thinning them out. Some people treat these poppies like any other biennials with complete success, but it can be a bit tricky. Sow in mid to late summer (late June or early July). They flower from mid summer (June) until the frosts come, in various shades of pink, orange, red or yellow.

Mullein The one you find catalogued most often is either called *Verbascum* Broussa or *V. bombyciferum*. It makes an enormous silver rosette of leaves the first year and the following year sends up a great golden spire 1·2m (4 ft) high. Sow in mid to late summer (June to July) and prick out 30–45cm (12–18 in) apart. These again can be left until the spring before being put in their final positions. They flower from mid summer to early autumn (June to August). There are other mulleins which are perennials, but they all want the same treatment.

Hollyhock These have such large seeds that you can put them where you want them to flower. Sow in mid to late summer (June or July) and, if you are pricking out, put the plants 30cm (12 in) apart. They flower in shades of pink, white, red, yellow or purple from late summer to mid autumn (July until September).

Herbaceous Perennials

Herbaceous perennials form the basis of your summer flower display. Rooted cuttings are expensive but some varieties are simple to grow from seed.

GENERAL WORK

Mid summer (June)

Spring-flowering bulbs that have finished flowering and whose leaves have yellowed, and which are in positions required for summer bedding plants, should be dug up now, placed in a box containing soil or peat in a dry place and left to complete ripening and drying.

Herbaceous perennials, annuals and bulbous plants that are tall growing and have not already had stakes or twigs put alongside them, should have this done now. Tie in as the plants grow.

Put a 2–5cm (1–2 in) layer of mulching material such as compost or peat round the root areas of gladiolus and lily if not already done. This will help to discourage weeds and conserve essential moisture.

Sow seeds of herbaceous perennial plants in the open ground or in pots outdoors.

With a rake, preferably a spring-back wire one, rake the lawn now to lift up creeping stems of weeds for cutting off with the mower. If possible, rake twice, once in each direction.

Water all plants, including the lawn, regularly and thoroughly once or twice a week during periods of dry weather.

It is an obvious economy to grow as many plants as possible from seed and hardy herbaceous perennials are usually both easy and profitable to treat in this manner. And you don't have to wait any longer to get results than if you had bought rooted cuttings. Seed sown one year will produce flowering plants in the following season, provided they have been sown early enough.

If you have delayed somewhat in sowing the seeds, you may have to wait an extra season, but that will be the only delay. There are, too, some plants – such as paeony or flag iris – that take longer to arrive at a flowering size, but even these will generally give you some flowers the year after sowing. What's more, the plants will grow larger in each succeeding year, so they are what might be termed a 'growth investment'.

Here we advise you on plants that can be sown outdoors in mid to late summer (June to July), but there is nothing to stop you sowing the seeds earlier – from late spring (April) onwards, if it is more convenient: and you will end up with

Above left: Anthemis tinctoria, *a daisy-like perennial that requires well-drained soil and a sunny spot in the border*
Above: Achillea taygetea Moonshine *flowers in late summer*

larger plants if you do.

How to sow

Sow the seed outdoors as thinly as possible in rows in the seedbed. As soon as the seedlings are large enough to handle, either thin the rows out or transplant them so that they are farther apart. Alternatively, you can sow the seeds in a pot of seed compost and then either prick the seedlings out directly into the open ground or first prick them out 5cm (2 in) apart into trays containing J.I. No 1 or a soilless mix, and then line them out (transplant them) when they are more established. This second method obviously entails more work but you can look after the seedlings more easily at their most delicate stage. Moreover, even if you sow the seeds in the open ground, you have to be sure that they are kept free of weeds – and this at a time when there is often a lot of other work going on in the garden.

Special cases

Plants with very small seed, such as campanula, are certainly best started in pots and the same would apply to plants that are hard to transplant when large, such as *Lathyrus latifolius*, the everlasting sweet pea (although this can perfectly well be sown where it is to grow). There are a few plants, such as hellebore and gentian, which take a long time to germinate, and for these pots are certainly necessary.

In the case of lupins, either the Russell hybrids or the tree lupins – both of which have nice large seeds – it is probably best to put the seeds singly or in pairs where you want the plants to flower. It is

possible to move lupins, but they send down a long tap-root, like a thin carrot, and if this is damaged the plant may die, so the less they are disturbed the better. An alternative is to sow the seeds singly in 8cm (3 in) pots and then move them on to their permanent positions. In this case do not use a seed compost but J.I. No 1 or the equivalent soilless compost. If you have plenty of seed, put two together and throw the weaker one away if they both germinate.

Preparing the seedbed

If you do sow directly outdoors, you want to make your seedbed what is termed 'friable'; that means that the soil should be aerated and easily penetrable by the young roots of the seedlings. If your soil is naturally rather heavy, incorporate some peat or coarse sand into the top 15cm (6 in) of it; this will have good results. You should also give it a good soaking about two days before you sow your seeds unless, of course, there has been a heavy rainfall (remember that light showers do not penetrate very deeply into the soil).

Draw out a shallow drill 2–3cm (1 in) deep and sow the seeds as thinly as possible and then cover them with raked earth. Keep the seedbed moist until the roots have had a chance to get fairly well down in the soil, which is usually about a fortnight after germination.

After-care

No garden operation is trouble-free, and in this case you must keep the spaces between the drills well hoed and take precautions against slugs and insects; especially if you see evidence of damage. After three or four weeks the young plants will be ready to be lined out. With most herbaceous plants a distance of 25cm (9 in) between the plants will be adequate. Here again, water the soil well (if it needs it) before you transplant your seedlings and see that they do not dry out during the following ten days. This is sufficient time for the plantlets to take root in the new soil.

Final planting

During mid or late autumn (September or October) or mid or late spring (the end of March or early April), lift the plants and put them wherever you want them to flower.

Some plants to choose

Some of the plants that this kind of outdoor treatment will suit include:
Achillea (yarrow) Makes plants up to 75cm (2½ ft) high with flat heads of minute yellow, white or cerise flowers in late summer and early autumn (July and August).

Above: Anchusa azurea, *a short-lived perennial best treated as a biennial and whose flowers are attractive to bees*
Below: Gaillardia grandiflora Dazzler *is a good border plant but not reliably hardy in wet or cold localities*

Anchusa Rather a short-lived perennial and best, perhaps, treated as a biennial, but not to be confused with the annual varieties. The perennials have bristly leaves and tall spikes of flowers which reach a height of 25–120cm (9 in–4 ft), according to variety. The flowers are a wonderful blue colour and open from mid summer (June) onwards.
Anthemis Somewhat spreading plant up to 60cm (2ft) in height, covered from mid summer (June) onwards with quite sizeable yellow daisies or, in the case of *A. sancti-johannis*, orange ones. They are very useful plants for cut flowers as well as for giving a long display in the garden.
Aquilegia (columbine) Splendid decoration for mid summer (June) when the plant opens its long trumpet-shaped flowers of many colours. It grows 30–90cm (1–3 ft) high.
Aubrietia This delightful creeping plant, about 10cm (4 in) high, is a mass of mauve, pink or purple from mid spring

*Above left: summer-flowering
lupins, easy to grow in moderately
good soil
Above right:* Echinops ritro,
*useful in herbaceous borders or
in a wild garden
Below:* Helleborus niger *benefits from a
top dressing of compost after flowering*

until early summer (late March to May).
The earlier it can be sown, the larger the
plants will be.

Bellis The old-fashioned pink and red
double daisy may have been around a
long time, but that is because it is such an
excellent plant and so easy to raise. It
grows up to 15cm (6 in) high and flowers
from late spring (April) onwards.

Delphinium A main stand-by of the
border, with its spires of blue, mauve,
purple or white flowers. Unfortunately
slugs find the plant irresistible, so take
precautions by scattering slug pellets. It
grows up to 1·5m (5 ft) and flowers from
mid summer (June) onwards.

Dianthus This group includes pinks and
carnations and they all grow readily from
seed. However, you may find many of
them produce single flowers only (instead
of doubles), so it is as well to let them
flower in the drills the first year and then
throw out the unsatisfactory ones. There

Above, top: Kniphofia uvaria *Royal Standard*
Above: Dianthus allwoodii *Doris, a hybrid created by crossing pinks with carnations*
Above right: Linum narbonense *Heavenly Blue likes well-drained soil and full sun*

are also some dwarf pinks such as *Dianthus allwoodii, D. deltoides, D. gratianopolitanus* (the Cheddar pink) and *D. plumarius* that come true from seed: that is, they flower as expected and do not revert to their original single-flowered form. The colour range is generally white, pink or red and the height 10–30cm (4–12 in). They flower from early to late summer (May to July).

Echinops (globe thistle) Grows up to 1·2m (4 ft) with heads of blue globular flowers in late summer and early autumn (July and August).

Eryngium (sea holly) Useful plants with heads of teazle-like blue flowers, but they may take an extra season before they flower. Grow up to 60cm (24 in).

Euphorbia (spurges) Produce green and golden flowers in mid summer (June) as well as having interesting leaves. They grow about 25–90cm (9–36 in) tall and about the same across.

Gaillardia, helenium and rudbeckia The perennial varieties are all useful. North American daisies with a mixture of flower colours in late summer (July) onwards. Height up to 90cm (3 ft).

Hemerocallis (day lily) Grows very rapidly from seed, though most varieties will need an extra season before they flower prolifically. Grows 30–90cm (1–3 ft) with flowers in shades of pink, red, purple or yellow.

Kniphofia (red-hot poker) Usually flowers the year after sowing, though some may take a year longer. It is a very effective plant with a long flowering season from late summer to late autumn (July to October). The tall spires of flowers are normally shades of red or yellow, reaching up to 1·2m (4 ft). It is often listed in catalogues as 'tritoma'.

Liatris Throws up spikes of rose-purple flowers about 30cm (12 in) long, which, rather unusually, open from the top downwards in late summer (July). Grows up to 90cm (3 ft).

Linum (flax) Produces myriads of large yellow or blue flowers on very thin stems, so that they seem to float in the air. They open from mid summer to late autumn (June to October). Reaches between 30–90cm (1–3 ft) in height.

Scabiosa Rather slow from seed, but produces heads of purple flowers from mid summer to late autumn (June to October). Grows 60–90cm (2–3 ft) in height.

Sidalcea Enchanting plant like a miniature hollyhock, with mallow-like flowers of pink or red produced in late summer and early autumn (July and August). Grows up to 1·2m (4 ft).

Veronica Has spikes of brilliant blue flowers from mid summer to early autumn (June to August). Can grow up to 60cm (2 ft) high.

Some Late Bulbs in the Garden

Mid summer is the time to think about growing a few late-flowering plants that will provide welcome splashes of colour in the bulb area of your mixed borders in the latter part of summer and also during the autumn.

You can make your choice from a range of bulbs that includes amaryllis and tiger flower, hardy nerine and acidanthera – and don't forget that there are even species of the popular crocus that will flower in the autumn.

Some bulbs seem to do much better when planted in mid summer (June) than when grown earlier in the year. Here we give a full description of each, and provide detailed instructions about planting times and distances, and cultivation.

Acidanthera

First among these, *Acidanthera bicolor murielae*, you may well find offered as either *A. bicolor* or *A. murielae*. There will be no doubt concerning the 'acidanthera' part, although botanists have now decided that the differences between acidanthera and gladioli are not great enough

Tiger flower

to warrant making a fresh genus, and that the correct name should now be *Gladiolus bicolor* (though the plant is not like the generally-recognized gladioli).

Whatever its name, it produces a very handsome and striking flower, with a spike of large trumpet-shaped blossoms, each with a long tube and expanding at the ends to as much as 6cm (2½ in) across. The flowers are white with a brilliant purple blotch at the mouth and they exhale an intoxicating perfume. They open in early and mid autumn (August and September). The leaves are like those of gladioli. There is also *Acidanthera tubergenii*, very similar, but with a

maroon red blotched centre, that flowers a little earlier.

Planting The only real secret in growing them successfully is to wait until the soil has warmed up before you plant the corms. If you plant them too early (which is easily done since the corms look so much like the ordinary gladioli corms that you may well feel they need the same treatment) you could easily find that they just sit in the soil and rot off before they start growing. But if you wait until mid summer (June), or slightly later where there have been frosts in early summer (May), they start to grow immediately, and get away without any checks.

Their habit is like that of the ordinary tall gladioli; they grow to a height of 60–90cm (2–3 ft), and the corms are best

Acidanthera

Nerine

planted about 20cm (8 in) apart, with the tops of the corms approximately 8cm (3 in) below the surface of the soil, provided that it is well-drained. These are best grown in full sun, but they may well succeed in lightly-dappled shade. While they are making their first growth they should not be allowed to dry out for any length of time, but it is the roots that need water, so do not worry if the surface of the soil looks dry, so long as it is still moist below. In late autumn (beginning of October) they should be lifted and treated in the same way as gladioli or else hung up to dry, cleaned off, and stored in a dark frost-proof place.

Tiger flower

Tigridia pavonia (or *ferraria*), known as tiger flower, is not that tall, being from 25–30cm (9–12 in) in height, but it bears wide-open flowers up to 10cm (4 in) across, that are coloured in the most brilliant shades of red, pink, orange and yellow, with the centre of the flower speckled with dots in contrasting colours. Although the flowers rival the most

Amaryllis

gorgeous tropical orchids in their shape and colours, they only last for a single day. Since each flower spike will produce from four to six flowers, this is not as serious as it sounds; in fact, a clump will show attractive flowers for a month or more, therefore the display could not be described as short-lived. They are not expensive, even though spectacular, as they come readily from seed, often flowering the same year as sown, making it simple to increase your stock; moreover, the bulbs will produce offsets.

Planting   The bulbs should be planted 15cm (6 in) apart, with the tips 5–8cm (2–3 in) below the surface of the soil. They will flower from early autumn (August) to late autumn (end of September).

It is probably well worth your while to save some seed and raise further plants. You sow the seed in a pot in spring, either in J.I. No 1, or in a soilless growing compost. If you can start the seed in early spring (February), either on a warm windowsill or in a greenhouse, you may well have a few flowers in the autumn and you will in any case have plenty of bulbs for next year.

As you will be leaving the plants in the pot for the whole growing season, you must take great care to sow the seeds thinly, if possible 2–3cm (1 in) apart, so you will only want 12 seeds or so to a 13cm (5 in) pot. If you put in any more, the seedlings will be too crowded and the bulbs won't develop adequately.

Once flowering is over, treat the bulbs like gladioli; lift them in late autumn (October), dry them off and store them somewhere dark and frost-free. You can leave your seedling bulbs in their pots if you so wish, but it may be more convenient to store them in the same way. In this instance, stop giving the bulbs water in late autumn (October) and let them dry off in the pots. This sometimes takes a surprisingly long time with young plants and you may still have green left in the leaves in early winter (November).

Hardy nerine

One of the real joys of the autumn is the hardy nerine, *N. bowdenii*, that produces its clusters of shocking pink, spidery flowers in mid and early winter (September and November). Usually nerines produce their flowers before their leaves, but some plants seem to be practically evergreen. Even so, the best time to move them is in late summer (July), and this is also the best time to buy them in. They are rather expensive for some reason, but they produce offshoots very freely, so it is not long before you can have a good clump from just a few bulbs. Later in the

season, if they have not already done so, they produce a number of slightly floppy, strap-shaped, bright green leaves.

Planting   The bulbs are best placed at least 30cm (12 in) apart, with the tip of the bulb only just below the surface. As most nerines are frost-tender, they are usually best placed against walls facing south or west, but this is not completely necessary if the garden is a warm one.

Nerines do not like to be disturbed so, once planted, it is as well to leave them until the clumps become too congested, when they can be lifted and split up. Otherwise they are generally quite trouble-free. If seed is set (and this does not happen every year), it can be sown at once and takes about three years to reach bulbs of flowering size.

Crocus

Amaryllis

Another autumn-flowering bulb, that wants planting in late summer (July), is *Amaryllis belladonna* (sometimes catalogued as *Hippeastrum equestre*). In temperate climates like Britain, this needs south-facing wall protection and even then can be shy of producing its umbels (clusters) of pale pink, fragrant, lily-like flowers in mid and late autumn (September and October). The strap-like leaves come after the flowers and last until mid summer (June or July). The amaryllis is no trouble to keep alive, but getting it to flower can be difficult. However, if it is grown against a south-facing wall, and the plants are protected from frost by straw or polythene in winter and early spring, lovely flowers should result.

Planting It has large bulbs and it is probably a wise policy just to purchase one to begin with and see how it fares. The top of the bulb should be about 8cm (3 in) below the surface of the ground. If it does well with you, and you plant more, place the bulbs about 30cm (12 in) apart.

Crocus and colchicum

There are a number of autumn-flowering crocus, but two are most commonly grown. These are *Crocus speciosus*, which produces its long, blue-mauve flowers in mid autumn (end of September), and *C. medius*, which has violet flowers in late autumn and early winter (October and November). *C. speciosus* has very handsome flowers, but a light shower of rain may well flatten them. This is not a problem with *C. medius*. There are some colour forms of *C. speciosus*, including a pale blue and a handsome white, and in some gardens you may well find self-sown seedlings coming up. *C. medius* never sets seed, but produces great clumps of corms, so to increase, just lift and divide them. There are many other attractive species and good mixtures can be easily bought.

Colchicum (meadow saffron), has flowers that look just like a large pink, purple or rosy-purple crocus, but the following year they produce enormous leaves that are rather unsightly, so the best place for them is probably the front of the shrubbery. There are quite a few to choose from, the cheapest being the British *C. autumnale*, but the most handsome is *C. speciosum*. These usually flower in mid autumn (September), although *C. autumnale* can be out by the early autumn (end of August).

Planting You also want to plant autumn crocus and colchicum in late summer (July). Grab them as soon as they appear in the shops or the moment you get your bulb catalogue. The crocus are quite cheap, as they increase fairly readily, but the colchicum, which have very large corms, are normally somewhat more expensive. They do produce side corms, but not very freely, and they take years to reach flowering size from seed.

Colchicum corms should be put 25cm (9 in) apart in the late summer (July) and the top of the corm should be 10cm (4 in) below the surface of the soil. The autumn crocus should be 10–15cm (4–6 in) apart and the tops of the corms should be 5–8cm (2–3 in) below the surface. The crocus need full sun, but the colchicum have no objection to dappled shade. Once planted, both may be left in position for years, although you can split clumps.

Colchicum speciosum *(meadow saffron) adds a touch of colour to the autumn garden*

GENERAL WORK
Mid summer (June)
Spring-flowering bulbs that have been lifted for drying and storing until replanting time in the autumn should now have the old soil and dried leaves removed. The cleaned bulbs are then stored in boxes in an airy, dark place. Any bulbs that are soft or diseased should be burnt.

All tulips, except the species, should be lifted and placed in a trench in a spare part of the garden where they can ripen and remain until replanted in the autumn.

Hardy annual plants that were sown *in situ* should be thinned now. Thin tall-growing plants to 30cm (12 in) and shorter ones to 15–25cm (6–9 in).

Prune early-flowering clematis species by removing shoots that have finished flowering. Well-established plants with a mass of growth are best cut back as necessary to keep them within bounds.

The lawn will benefit from an application of a proprietary lawn fertilizer applied now according to the manufacturer's instructions. Be sure to apply it evenly.

Keep an eye on all plants for attacks by pests and disease; take remedial action with pesticides at the first sign of trouble.

Above: half-hardy Tigridia pavonia *(tiger flower)*, notable for its brilliant-coloured flowers; *right: sweet-smelling* Acidanthera bicolor murielae; *below:* Amaryllis belladonna *will need the protection of a south-facing wall against cooler climates*

Above: Crocus speciosus, *one of a number of crocus that will flower in the autumn. Unfortunately, its handsome flowers can be spoiled by a light shower of rain*
Far left: Colchicum autumnale *(meadow saffron) will grow in dappled shade, unlike the crocus, which needs full sun*
Left: hardy Nerine bowdenii *should be planted against a wall facing south or west unless it is in a warm environment*

Choosing and Buying Roses

The first step towards growing first-class roses is to select the right plants. It's something that deserves time and thought – your roses may be with you for many years, so don't rush into buying inferior plants simply because they are cheap and easy to get.

Choosing the right rose varieties for your garden is best done after seeing the plants in garden conditions. If you can be patient, follow their progress in a friend's garden over an entire season. In this way you can judge how big and strongly they will grow, how well and often they will flower, how resistant they are to disease, and how well they will stand up to the elements.

Your friends may have some roses that you like in their garden but by restricting yourself to these you can miss something better. A good local nursery will always be helpful with advice, but as most nurseries stock only a limited range, your choice may still be restricted. Also, you may not be able to see the roses in their mature state. It is particularly unwise to choose shrub roses in this way unless you have already seen them in a garden. It is quite impossible to visualize the sheer mass of a large shrub without having actually seen it. You could buy a rose

60cm (24 in) tall and end up with one 1·8 × 1·8m (6 × 6 ft). Actual size may not be so important if the habit of growth is light and airy, but a very leafy, dense-growing bush will make its presence felt in no uncertain manner. It's worth remembering that some of the bigger nurseries and many of the specialist rose nurseries have display beds – as distinct from nursery fields – where well-established bushes can be seen.

Where else can you see a variety of roses growing? Many city parks have beds of roses properly labelled and there are fine displays in public gardens elsewhere, and at stately homes and houses owned by the National Trust, many of which are famous for their collections of old roses. Examples include: Hardwick Hall in Derbyshire, Hidcote Manor in Gloucestershire, Mottisfont Abbey in Hampshire, Nymans in Sussex, Sissinghurst Castle in Kent, Wallington in Northumberland.

The Royal National Rose Society has special display gardens in Cardiff, Edinburgh, Glasgow, Harrogate, Norwich,

Far left: a flourishing rose garden with floribundas Iceberg and Evelyn Fison at front, climbers Golden Showers and Chaplin's Pink at back
Above: Royal National Rose Society garden at St Albans, essential viewing for any serious rose buyer
Left: a true container-grown rose has moss or algae growing on soil surface

Nottingham, Redcar, Southport and Taunton, and in these you can see the latest and best varieties. But the finest collection of all is at the Society's headquarters near St Albans in Hertfordshire. Another fine place to visit in order to 'pick' your favourites is the famous Queen Mary's Rose Garden in Regent's Park, London.

Container-grown roses

Another popular way of buying roses is to get them as container-grown plants from garden centres and nurseries. The advantage of this is that roses can be planted out at almost any time and with the minimum of root disturbance; but they must be container-*grown*. The roots must also be well-established and a good way to determine this is to lift up the container and see if any have worked their way through to the bottom; if they have, it is a good sign. The presence of moss and algae on the soil surface is another way of seeing that your chosen rose has not recently been pushed into the container with a bit of earth rammed over the roots. An unscrupulous supplier may simply take the bare-root roses, usually the weakest ones that he was unable to sell in the autumn, and chop off enough of the roots (which can mean most of them) to fit them into the container, putting them on sale in the spring as 'container-grown'. If in doubt, always make sure by asking, as you will be paying quite a bit more for roses grown in this way. Do not be misled by a show of leaves, or even flowers; any rose that is not actually dead will produce some of these, but the plant itself may be second rate and take ages to establish itself properly, if it ever does.

Choosing from catalogues

If you order from a catalogue through one of the big, specialist nurseries you will be fairly sure of getting good-quality plants. But picking what you want from a catalogue alone has its hazards. The colour printing may not be top quality, and therefore misleading, and often the descriptions are far too brief. Only a few of the big growers mention if a particular rose is prone to disease; this is because the incidence of disease varies enormously in different parts of the country. One area may be terribly bad for black spot, strangely enough because of the purity of the air; another may be quite free of it because the air is polluted by sulphur fumes from factory chimneys. Or again, one variety may suffer from mildew on one type of soil or in one situation in a garden, but not in another. No nursery will want to put customers off by warning them against something that may never happen. However, there is no excuse for not warning about a rose that will not stand up to rain, and, regrettably, there are roses like this on many lists. If you see the words 'good under glass' beware: it really means that a downpour will reduce the flowers to a sodden mass.

Bargain buys?

Hundreds of thousands of roses are sold each year through stores, supermarkets, and greengrocers' shops. They are usually cheaper and you can find real bargains in this way, but you can also get rubbish and even dead plants if you don't know what to look out for. Some of the varieties sold in this way may never have been very good while others have long been superseded by better ones, but are sold because it is easy to propagate from them.

Unless temperature and humidity are right, the polythene packs in which the roses are sold can act like miniature greenhouses, forcing some of the buds into premature growth. These white and sickly-looking shoots will be killed off as soon as the rose is planted out. Avoid roses like this, along with any that look dried up or have wrinkled bark on the stems. This means they have spent too long in a dry atmosphere and, if they survive, will be a long time recovering.

You must be very cautious in following up the 'bargain' offers in newspapers as you are most unlikely to get first-rate plants. Special offers in growers' catalogues are another matter. These are usually made up of ten or a dozen roses chosen by the seller. The grower can market them at a cheaper rate as he can make up the selection in advance instead of having to pick out varieties according to customers' orders. These offers are most useful to a beginner who wants the minimum of trouble in choosing and ordering his roses; they also make good presents for a young couple just starting out with a garden.

However, it is worth checking the varieties against the description of them in the main part of the catalogue to make sure that they are not too disparate in size and character. Selections have been offered ranging from Queen Elizabeth, which can top 2·4m (8 ft), to Zambra, an orange floribunda at 30cm (2 ft), and taking in on the way Lavender Lassie, which is generally reckoned to be a shrub rose. There is nothing wrong with these roses individually, but planted as a group by somebody who did not know them they would look strange to say the least.

How to recognize a good rose

We have given the black side of choosing and buying roses and emphasized the pitfalls simply to ensure that you will know whether you are getting the best and what to complain about if you are not. At most times you will obtain good roses from all

Vigorous floribunda Queen Elizabeth

sources mentioned but it is safest to go to one of the big, specialist growers. They may be a little more expensive but you will get quality and there are few suppliers of any kind who will not exchange bad or wrongly-labelled plants.

You will only learn to recognize good or bad varieties by experience, by seeing them grow, or by reading about them. Knowing a good rose is not enough. You also want to make sure that you are getting a healthy plant, and there are certain points to look out for.

No good rose bush should have less than two firm, green, wrinkle-free and unbroken canes, *at least* as thick as a pencil. Preferably they should have three or four canes and they should not be discoloured by greyish or brown patches of disease.

There should be a strong root system with plenty of fibrous roots and you may have to unpack the rose to check this. Despite the disapproving frown of the sales assistant, you are perfectly entitled to inspect what you are buying, and if in any doubt you would be wise to do.

There is even a British Standards Institution specification for roses, stipulating, in addition to the above, that the neck between the roots and the point where the canes branch out should be at least 16mm ($\frac{5}{8}$ in) thick. This is only applicable to plants sold as First Grade, although if you keep your eyes open you will generally find some plants that comply with this BSI specification, even if they are not so described.

The top awards

Awards won by roses are sometimes shown in catalogues, but the only ones of real value to growers in Britain are those given by the Royal National Rose Society and the Royal Horticultural Society. The Rose Society is the main body concerned with roses, but you occasionally see the RHS awards, FCC, AM or AGM (First Class Certificate, Award of Merit or Award of Garden Merit) after the description of a rose. The Rose Society holds most thorough trials over a period of three years and in ascending order of merit the awards they give are: Trial Ground Certificate, Certificate of Merit and Gold Medal. In some years, a really outstanding rose may win the President's International Trophy, in addition to the Gold Medal; but any rose with even a Trial Ground Certificate would be a sound choice for your garden. Overseas awards have little relevance in Britain where growing conditions and, in some cases, judging rules are very different.

Hybrid Teas and Floribundas

Anyone interested in roses will want to be able to recognize the various forms and to be aware of their advantages and disadvantages. Here we tell you about the famous hybrid tea and floribunda roses.

Hybrid teas (HT) are the most popular roses in Britain because of the size, scent and beauty of their flowers.

It is often said that modern roses lack scent. This is true of floribundas, to a large extent, but they make up for this with their extra vigorous character and profuse flowering.

HYBRID TEAS

The first hybrid tea rose, raised in 1867, was the silvery-pink La France. This was the result of crossing the older hybrid perpetual roses with tea roses from the Far East, thus combining the greater refinement of shape and more recurrent blooming habit of the latter with the robust constitution of the hybrid perpetual. Few tea roses could survive the climate of the British Isles except under glass. Their name, rather a strange one, supposedly comes from the fact that they smelled like the newly-opened tea cases that arrived from the East.

Their colour range is probably only exceeded by that of the iris, for there are no blues among the roses, nor is it likely there ever will be, for they lack the necessary pigment – delphinidin. The lilac-mauve of the HT Blue Moon is the nearest approach there is. Unlike the floribundas, there is an abundance of HT varieties that are just as strongly-scented as any rose of the past. Several come to mind, such as Alec's Red, Blessings, Bonsoir, Ernest H. Morse, Fragrant Cloud, John Waterer, Lily de Gerlache, Mala Rubinstein, My Choice, Prima Ballerina, Red Devil, Wendy Cussons and Whisky Mac, and there are many more. The HT Peace, the most popular rose ever raised, seems scentless, although some people claim to detect a trace of something in it.

Advantages of the hybrid tea

Hybrid teas are most often used in the garden for bedding, and for this they certainly have advantages over other plants. They are permanent, or at any rate they should last for twenty years or more, so that you do not have to replant each year as you do with annuals. Their range of colour has already been mentioned, and they will bloom for five to six months with only the briefest of resting periods. Some varieties have coppery-red foliage when they first come out, so the beds can look appealing even before the first flush of bloom in mid summer (June). There is even a modern HT called Curiosity, a red and yellow bi-colour and 'sport' (chance variation) of the older Cleopatra, that has variegated leaves of deep green, splashed yellowish-white.

Finally, they make wonderful flowers for the house, though it is largely true that those lasting longest in water are often the most prone to rain damage outside. Gavotte, Red Devil and Royal Highness come into this category, but Alec's Red,

Right, and below: vigorous, upright HT varieties Alexander, and Fragrant Cloud

Fragrant Cloud, Gail Borden, Grandpa Dickson, Piccadilly and Troika are a few that can be recommended for both indoors and out.

Planting distances

It is impossible to be exact about how far apart HT types should be planted for bedding; 45cm (18 in) is a good average,

but some varieties, Peace for example, are far more vigorous than others and need fully 75cm (2½ ft). Others, like Perfecta, are strong growers but tall, narrow and upright, and yet others, like Josephine Bruce and Percy Thrower, tend to sprawl outwards. The important thing is that the roots should not be so close as to rob one another of nutrient and water, and there should be room between them for hoeing, mulching and proper spraying. The beds should not be so densely packed that air cannot circulate freely as this would encourage disease and probably insect pests as well. On the other hand, nothing looks worse than a rose bed with huge spaces of bare earth between the plants.

If you have seen your chosen types of rose growing before you buy them, you will probably know their spacing requirements, but some people favour ground-cover plants between their roses and space must be left for sunshine to reach these. Violas and pansies, particularly the blue varieties, are the most frequently recommended, and there is no doubt that they can look very attractive. On the other hand, it is hard to reconcile the use of these with good rose cultivation. Roses need to be well mulched to give of their best, or, failing this, the beds should at least be hoed regularly to keep them free of weeds, and neither of these activities would make violas or pansies very happy about their living conditions.

Plants for edging rose beds

The use of edging plants is another matter. Small, or smallish, grey or silver-leaved kinds like anaphalis (pearl everlasting), lavender, nepeta (catmint) and dwarf sage, most of which have reasonably discreet mauve flowers, are excellent for this purpose. They blend in beautifully with roses and there is no colour clash, but you may wish to use plants that flower earlier and so give colour to the bed before the roses are out. In this case, polyanthus and primroses are hard to beat.

You can also use miniature roses; many are almost evergreen in a mild winter and most start flowering before the HT. They are best suited to the edge of a south-facing border, or at least where their bigger neighbours will not overshadow them and keep the sun away. Even the greatest rose enthusiast could not claim that a newly-pruned rose bed was a thing of beauty and some form of edging does divert the eye from unsightly stumps.

Mixing varieties and heights

It is generally supposed that you should not mix several different varieties or colours of roses in one bed. It is really a matter of choosing what you like. The plants of one variety will be more or less uniform in height and can look marvellous in the mass, but with some roses there may be quite a long rest period in the middle of summer, when little or no colour is showing. A mixed bed can look spotty, with some varieties blooming and some not, but there will be long periods

Left: small mixed border with HT roses and a floribunda in the background
Below: Whisky Mac, a strong-growing HT

when all are out together and a spectacular riot of colour can result. Plant
mauve, white or cream roses between any
two colours that might otherwise clash.
You can divide a round bed into segments
like an orange, each one planted with a
different variety of rose, and possibly
add a standard or half-standard HT in
the centre to give height.

The question of height is an important
one, particularly if your garden is flat.
Trees and shrubs carry the eye upwards
and break up something that could
otherwise seem rather monotonous. Standard roses, either in the centre of a round
bed, or spaced out at about 1·8m (6 ft)
intervals along the centre of a long one,
can have the same beneficial effect. Use a
rose of a contrasting colour for these.

Varieties for hedges and shrubs

The standard HT can also be used to line a
path or a drive, which suggests another
use for the bush varieties. Not nearly
enough use is made of rose hedges, and
tall robust kinds, like the vermilion
Alexander, Peace, Chicago Peace, and
many others are first-rate for this. Some,
if not pruned too hard, can be built up
into fine specimen shrubs to stand on
their own, perhaps in the middle of a lawn
or by the corner of a patio.

FLORIBUNDAS

Most of the general principles outlined
for the hybrid tea rose apply equally to
floribundas, so with these it is enough to
point out where they are better or worse,
how they differ, and to recommend
varieties suited to different purposes.

The floribunda, as opposed to the HT,
grows with large heads or trusses of
comparatively small flowers. These are
often only single or semi-double, and
open to show their stamens. Modern
breeding tends towards larger, HT-shaped
flowers with fewer in a truss so that in
some instances it is difficult to say to
which class a rose belongs. Pink Parfait
and Sea Pearl are examples of this and
have the rather clumsy official
classification of 'floribunda – hybrid tea
type'. In Germany, its country of origin,
Fragrant Cloud is classed as a floribunda,
though it is rather difficult to see the
justification in this case, as the flowers are
so large. Floribundas have a different
ancestry from the HT and, because of the
scentless roses in it, few have a
worthwhile fragrance. Arthur Bell,
Chinatown, Dearest, Elizabeth of

*Above right: this low-growing floribunda,
Paddy McGredy, is a good edging variety
Right: Iceberg, a bushy floribunda*

Glamis, Escapade, Harry Edland, Michelle, Orange Sensation and Pineapple Poll do have scent, but breeders are conscious of the lack in most others and are trying, with mixed success, to remedy it.

Advantages of the floribunda

As a race, floribundas are very vigorous and make more new growth in a season than most HT types. They flower more continuously and are very quick to repeat should they rest at all, which gives them an advantage for bedding. And because most have fewer, smaller and tougher petals, they will open better in wet weather. This also means that most floribundas make good cut flowers. The bright vermilion Anne Cocker, with its blooms in tight little rosettes on the truss, will last fully ten days in water – central heating permitting – and many others are almost as good.

Varieties for edging

It is probably best not to mix floribunda and HT in one bed because of the difference in their growth. However, there are a number of low-growing, bushy floribundas coming onto the market that will make excellent edging for a rose bed. Meanwhile, the brilliant scarlet Topsi (rather prone to black spot in some areas), dark red Marlena, pink Paddy McGredy and the brand new orange-scarlet Stargazer are all suitable for this, or for lining paths or drives. They are excellent, too, for a small bed.

For some years now, both types, HT and floribunda, seem to have been getting taller and taller and, in some cases, even lankier; so this new breeding tendency towards what might be called the rounded, cushion effect is welcome, especially in the smaller garden. It almost constitutes a return to the poly-pom roses from which the floribundas are descended, but the flowers are much better and the plants healthier.

Varieties for hedges and shrubs

The stronger-growing floribunda has a particular advantage over their HT counterparts as hedges and as shrubs. Their growth is more branching and bushy as a rule and the sheer mass of flowers they produce is difficult for anything else to match. Some have tremendous vigour and will reach 1·2–1·5m (4–5 ft) in two seasons, if not overpruned. If you want a tall, narrow hedge, try yellow, disease-free Chinatown, the equally healthy Queen Elizabeth, Southampton or Dorothy Wheatcroft. The Queen Elizabeth can be kept quite bushy and between 1·5–1·8m (5–6 ft) in height if you prune it to about 90cm (3 ft) each year, and this will avoid the 2·2 or 2·7m (8 or 9 ft) specimen that you see so often with all its flowers at the top.

There seems no way to prune the supremely beautiful Fred Loads to curb its reach for the sky. Unlike Queen Elizabeth, it has huge trusses of large flowers in soft vermilion-orange, not all at the top. Although it might be more rightly classed as a shrub rather than a floribunda, officially it is known as a 'floribunda-shrub'.

The following lists of recommended varieties will serve as a guide but go and see them growing before you decide which ones to buy.

Some varieties to choose

HYBRID TEAS

Alec's Red	cherry red
Alexander	vermilion
Blessings	light pink
Ernest H. Morse	turkey red
Grandpa Dickson	pale yellow
John Waterer	deep red
Just Joey	coppery-orange
Pascali	white
Peace	pale yellow, pink edges
Piccadilly	scarlet, yellow reverse
Troika	apricot-orange
Whisky Mac	orange-yellow

FLORIBUNDAS

Allgold	yellow
Anne Cocker	vermilion
City of Leeds	salmon-pink
Elizabeth of Glamis	salmon-pink
Escapade	lilac-mauve, white reverse
Evelyn Fison	scarlet
Iceberg	white
Lili Marlene	dusky scarlet
Matangi	orange-vermilion, white eye and reverse
Orange Sensation	vermilion
Orangeade	orange-vermilion
Queen Elizabeth	pink
Southampton	apricot-orange
Topsi	orange-scarlet

Right: Peace, the most successful HT cultivar ever grown

Climbing and Rambling Roses

The important thing to understand straight away is the difference between a rambler and a climber. Their habit of growth is different and, in some cases, their uses are too. They are not always interchangeable and, to make matters a little more complicated, there are two main groups of ramblers.

Ramblers

Most ramblers are either wild or species roses, and their fairly close relatives. By far the greatest number of those grown in the garden are hybrids of *R. wichuraiana*. They produce massed clusters of small flowers, single, semi-double or double, and they bloom in late summer or even early autumn (July or August) and they do not repeat later on. The leaves are attractive and very glossy before mildew claims them as it does with so many ramblers. Like the wild roses of the hedgerows, ramblers send up long, pliable canes from the base of the plant each year. It is on these that the flowers grow so it is best to remove the old canes when blooming is over. Examples of the first rambler group are American Pillar, Crimson Shower, Dorothy Perkins, Excelsa and the very lovely and relatively healthy Sander's White.

Ramblers like the scented Albertine are different. They are also once-flowering, but the blooms are larger and appear much earlier in mid summer (June). While new canes may come from the base, enormously long and vigorous ones will also grow from some way up the main stems; these stems should be shortened back above one of these new growths after flowering. It is much harder to tell this kind of rambler from a climber that flowers only once a year.

Because of the likelihood of mildew, never plant ramblers against a wall or a close-boarded fence, as air circulation there will be poor. Instead, use them for arches or pergolas.

Climbers

Purists maintain that climbing roses are misnamed and that they are not climbers at all. They have no tendrils, certainly, and do not twine round their supports, or cling to the trunk of a tree in the way that ivy does. In nature, they reach aloft by thrusting their way into shrubs, hedges and trees, hooking their often formidable thorns over the twigs and branches. They get up there somehow, even if in the garden they usually have to be tied in to their supports.

Climbing roses, whether incorrectly titled or not, have larger flowers than ramblers as a rule. Once again, they can be single, semi-double or double, but are often as big and shapely as those of a hybrid tea. They may appear in small clusters (though there may be hundreds of these) or they may come out singly, and a large number of climbers are repeat-flowering. This is particularly so with the newer varieties such as Bantry Bay, Casino, Compassion, Danse du Feu, Golden Showers, Grand Hotel, Handel, Pink Perpétue, Schoolgirl and Swan Lake; but old favourites such as Caroline Testout, Gloire de Dijon, Mme Grégoire Staechelin and Mermaid, come into this category, too.

Climbers only occasionally send up new canes from ground level and in some cases virtually never. From this they form a sturdy main framework and concentrate on producing sideshoots and laterals from this. Sometimes a climber can become very bare and gaunt looking at the base but proper training can help to keep it clothed with leaves and flowers low down. With some of the more pig-headed varieties it may be necessary to plant a low-growing bush, preferably an evergreen, in front of it to hide the often rather ugly, gnarled bare stems.

Apart from natural climbers, you should be able to identify the climbing sports of a number of the HT and floribunda races. A 'sport' occurs when a quirk in a bush rose's make-up, probably due to its mixed ancestry, causes one of two things to happen: it will either produce flowers on its stem quite different from those on the rest of the bush (Super Sun, an orange-yellow sport of the red and yellow bi-colour Piccadilly, is an example of this), or else the flowers stay the same but the habit of growth will change. Suddenly the odd bush will develop the long canes of a climber and, as it is possible to propagate from both kinds of sport, a new rose is born. The prefix 'climbing' appears in catalogues before the variety name if the rose is a climbing sport, e.g. Climbing Iceberg.

These climbing sports used to be much more popular than they are today, although they are still sold in large quantities. It has been found that a very large number of them flower with far less freedom than their bush equivalents and some, whether from HT or floribunda, only flower once. So be careful when

Glossy-foliaged and large-flowered Chaplin's Pink Climber

making your choice and ask your supplier about the variety you are thinking of choosing before you commit yourself. Roses that usually do come up to expectation as climbing sports include Allgold, Crimson Glory, Ena Harkness, Etoile de Hollande, Fashion, Iceberg, Lady Sylvia and Shot Silk. Climbing Peace can grow to an enormous size yet have only one flower in five years; this is typical in Britain though it will flower better in a warmer climate.

Use in the garden

How can you best use climbing roses in the garden? Climbers, as distinct from ramblers, can be trained on walls, but however good the repeat performance of a rose, there will be periods when it is out of flower. Many climbers are described as 'perpetual flowering' but few, if any, really are; at best they are recurrent, so why not grow them up through some other wall shrub that will bloom before they do or when they are resting?

Forsythia suspensa or *Chaenomeles japonica*, for instance, will give colour to the walls of your house in mid and late spring (March and April). Or you can choose a shrub that flowers when the roses do, but in a contrasting colour. The

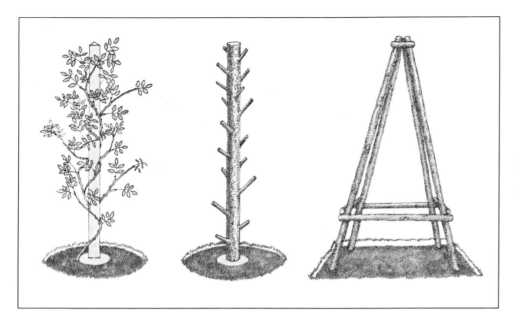

soft blue of a ceanothus looks wonderful combined with the pale, primrose yellow of the repeat-flowering rose Casino, or with white Swan Lake. Mid summer flowering clematis, grown up through roses, is another way of achieving extra colour in between the first and second flush of rose bloom. Choose kinds that are cut hard back each early spring (February) and do this without fail, or you will end up with the rose struggling pitifully to peer through an impenetrable tangle.

Training the less vigorous climbers and ramblers on pillars is an effective way of using them, provided that the pillar is a substantial one and preferably set in concrete so that its base will not rot. It should be round, or at least have any sharp corners planed away, so that the rose stems are not chafed.

A variant of the straight up-and-down pillar is to use part of the trunk of a small tree, such as a larch, that has branches coming out of it at fairly regular intervals all round. If these branches are sawn off about 30cm (12 in) from the trunk, they are very easy to tie the rose to. For either sort of pillar, train the canes around it in a spiral; this will make it more likely to send out flowering sideshoots low down.

Training techniques

The secret of training climbers and ramblers is, paradoxically, to keep the main growths as horizontal as possible. If they go straight up, the sap flows up them freely, and most of the new growth and flowers will be at the top. If, when used against a wall or fence, the canes are fanned out to each side and tied in to horizontal wires, the effect of bending the

canes will be to restrict the sap flow and to divert it into the side buds along their entire length. These buds develop and form flowering laterals, which in turn are fanned out and tied in, so that the rose moves upwards, gradually, and is covered with flowers and leaves from tip to toe.

The supports should consist of strong, galvanized wire, the strands about 30–45cm (12–18 in) apart, threaded through 15cm (6 in) vine-eyes, so that, allowing for a few centimetres of the eye to go into the wall or fence, the wires will be 13cm (5 in) from the wall surface. This allows some air to circulate between the wall and the rose. You should tie the canes not too tightly (so as to allow for growth) to the outside of the wires with plastic-covered garden wire.

Up pillars Training roses in a spiral on a pillar has something of the same effect as fanning them out, but start the training straight away, as some climbers have very stiff canes that, once developed, are quite difficult to bend.

Up pyramids Probably even better than a pillar is a 2m (7 ft) tall, upright pyramid of either three or four rustic poles, joined at the top and with crosspieces bracing the sides about half-way down. The rose will be much less restricted in its growth on a pyramid than on a pillar, and it is even possible to grow two roses of blending colours at the same time on one support.

As hedges You can form a hedge of almost any height you like with climbers and

Above: climbers can be trained up a pillar (left) or larch trunk (centre), but vigorous varieties will prefer a pyramid (right)
Right: free-flowering rambler R. wichuraiana Excelsa

ramblers. Link upright posts at approximately 1·8m (6 ft) intervals with galvanized iron wires 30cm (12 in) apart, and on these the roses are trained. In time, they will make a fine and very colourful screen, but only in the summer, for in winter the leaves will fall.

As weeping standards Rambling roses make the best weeping standards if you choose them from the first group previously mentioned. Their canes are pliable and hang down all round as they should, laden with blossom, but whatever rose you use, make sure it is supported above the ground by a very strong stake, about 1·8m (6 ft) tall. Wind pressure on a weeping standard can be very great, so something substantial is needed to keep it upright. Nurseries supply suitable wooden stakes, but an old metal gas pipe, painted green, is a good alternative and it will last almost for ever if galvanized as well as painted. The top should go right up into the head of the rose to give it extra support and the rose should be tied to it with plastic ties, one at the top and two equally spaced further down.

Sometimes a wire 'umbrella' frame on the top of the stake is recommended. This should not be needed with ramblers like Excelsa, but with the more rigid canes of Albertine, that is frequently sold as a weeping rambler, you may need an umbrella to persuade its canes to go in the right direction.

Up trees A very lovely way of using the more strong-minded ramblers and climbers is to train them up trees. Many of the old species such as *R. filipes* Kiftsgate and *R. longicuspis* are first-rate for this, as are the old ramblers Rambling Rector, Seagull and Wedding Day. With a little guidance at the beginning, they will ramble quite happily on their own with no tying in, and produce waterfalls of

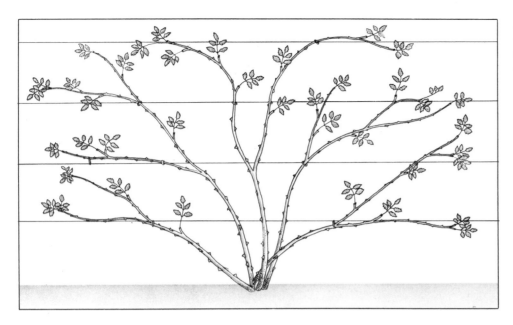

Left: to restrict sap flow and encourage flowering, canes of climber growing against a wall should be trained outwards
Below: climber, Alchymist

immensely fragrant, small white flowers in mid summer (June). Don't plant them too close to the trunk of the tree, because the rain must be able to reach the roots.

However, a warning is needed about the kind of tree you choose. If your rose is described as reaching 9m (30 ft), it is obvious that you must not pick a tree of 4.5m (15 ft) up which to grow it. An old apple tree can be ideal, but it must not be too old or have rotting branches, for after a year or two the weight and wind resistance of the rose may bring the whole lot down in a gale.

Covering up and ground cover Climbing and rambling roses are invaluable for covering old, unsightly sheds (as well as new, unsightly houses), and ramblers belonging to the *wichuraiana* group can be used for ground cover. *R. wichuraiana* itself will grow quite flat along the ground, spreading out in all directions, rooting as it goes and covered in late summer (July) with star-like, single white flowers. A similar hybrid called Max Graf has pink flowers and in time both roses will grow dense enough to smother weeds. Wandering over a bank that you have been wondering how to cover and that is difficult to keep tidy, they make a really different and attractive feature in the garden.

Some varieties to choose

CLIMBERS

Allen Chandler	bright crimson
Aloha	pink
Altissimo	blood-red
Compassion	apricot
Danse du Feu	orange-scarlet
Golden Showers	daffodil yellow
Handel	cream, edged pink
New Dawn	pale pink
Parkdirektor Riggers	blood-red
Pink Perpétue	pink
Schoolgirl	apricot-orange
Swan Lake	white

RAMBLERS

Albéric Barbier	creamy-white
Albertine	coppery-pink
Excelsa	red
Sander's White	white

Miniature Roses in the Garden

Miniature roses need to be well displayed to look their best, and can be grown in beds by themselves or be put into window boxes or pots.

Miniature roses are thought to be related to the long-flowering China roses, and their Latin name is *R. chinensis minima*. They are sometimes referred to as Rouletii after a Dr Roulet who found some, quite by chance, growing in pots at a village called Onnens in Switzerland in 1918. Nobody remembered seeing anything like them before or could find out how they got there, though one theory is that they were a lost offspring of a much older French rose known as Pompon de Paris.

Yet another species name for the miniatures is *R. lawrenceana*, after the 18th century writer on roses, Miss Molly Lawrence, and this multiplicity of names reflects the uncertainty as to where they really originated. However, they are first-rate little plants; *R. rouletii* itself is only about 13cm (5 in) tall, with small, delicate rose-pink flowers.

In the true miniature rose, everything should be on the same scale. The flowers, the leaves and the stems should be in the same proportion to the rest of the plant as those on a hybrid tea or floribunda, but with a number of recent varieties, such as Gold Pin, this is not so. Miniatures are gaining in popularity all the time, particularly in the United States, and in the

race for more and more novelties, a number of full-sized floribundas are being crossed with the miniatures, and the result is that the flowers are relatively too large for the plant. This does not always happen, but depends on which strain comes out on top in a particular cross.

This inter-breeding with floribundas can have another effect, too, as seen in a rose such as Baby Masquerade, that will certainly reach 38cm (15 in) and sometimes more. The flowers and leaves are still small, duplicates of the floribunda Masquerade on a tiny scale, but the whole plant in itself is not small as a miniature

Miniature roses massed in a bed at the Royal National Rose Society's gardens

should be. In fact, though appearing in most nursery catalogues as a miniature, Baby Masquerade is classed officially as a floribunda-dwarf.

One other thing can affect the size of miniature roses, and that is whether or not they are grown on their own roots. Miniatures take very easily from 8cm (3 in) cuttings, planted out in mid autumn (September), which is most useful if you want to increase your stock. Grown in this way, they make good, strong plants, but they will be considerably smaller than if they are budded onto a vigorous rootstock. They will be the size they should be, and the closer in their ancestry to the original *R. rouletii* the likelier they are to keep small.

General characteristics

Each leaflet on a miniature rose will probably be no more than 13mm ($\frac{1}{2}$ in) long, the flowers no more than 3cm (1 in) in diameter. The blooms can be single or semi-double, but they can also be as packed with petals and as fully double and shapely as a hybrid tea. The minute blooms of Cinderella, for instance, have up to 60 petals, each as perfectly formed as a baby's toenail.

Some miniatures are fragrant, though this only really becomes significant when they are grown in pots at eye-level. The colour range is as wide as for any other class of rose, and there is an extremely good selection of those in the mauve and lavender shades, like Lavender Lace. They all last well in water.

Miniatures are, in the main, very rain-resistant and recurrent flowering, repeating quickly. They also flower early, and the first blooms will probably show colour in early summer (mid to late May). By this time the plants will be fully clothed with leaves, for these will start to develop in mid to late spring (February or March). In fact, in a mild winter, many miniatures are practically evergreen.

The health of these tiny roses is probably better than that of larger ones, due perhaps to the healthy China rose strain in their make-up, but such spraying as may be needed is very quick and easy. One or two squirts deal with each plant.

No real pruning is needed, but with some varieties there is so much growth that the shoots can become rather congested and will benefit from thinning out in early spring. Otherwise it is simply a matter of removing, as and when necessary, the small number of twigs that may die back each year, and perhaps having to shorten the odd vagrant, extra-vigorous growth that throws things out of balance. It is easier to use sharp scissors rather than secateurs for thinning.

Growing outdoors

There are many attractive ways of growing miniature roses in the garden, but probably the way that most people see them first is when they are sold as pot plants in shops and garden centres. This has given rise to the myth that they are pot plants for the house, not suitable for growing out of doors, and that they are more delicate than other roses. They are, in fact, every bit as tough, and are sold in pots because they are small and easy to handle like that; they can also be kept alive indefinitely, unlike bare-root roses.

Miniatures are not house plants. If they are kept indoors all the time, the dry air will cause the leaves to drop, and the plant will be weakened. Bring the roses into the house when they are coming into flower, and take them out again immediately afterwards. Stand them in a spot shaded from the midday sun, or plunge the pots into damp ashes or peat, and keep them well watered at all times. Leave them out of doors for the winter, or they can be

Below: terraced beds display miniatures well on a slope. Bottom: they can also be used to advantage as edging plants

brought into a cool greenhouse in late autumn (October), when slight heat (and good top ventilation) applied in spring will bring them into flower in late spring (April) or even a week or two earlier. After this, stand them out of doors once more to build up their strength again in their natural environment. Use J.I. No 2 potting compost for your pots.

For the rockery They make excellent rockery plants, but they must have reasonably large pockets of good soil, 30cm (12 in) deep at least, for they will not thrive on the starvation diet that suits some rock plants. On a rockery, they are likely to have good drainage, which they like, and the big stones will give them a cool root-run, which they possibly like even more. One rose on its own may look a little lost on a big rockery but groups of three or four together make a good show.

As edging If you are looking for something with which to edge your rose beds and give you early – or fairly early – colour, miniature roses can be the answer. The important thing to remember here is that they need sun to give of their best, so that the other roses must be far enough back from the border edge not to over-shadow them. You can use miniatures, too, for edging paths, but for something as wide as a drive, it is probably best to plant some of the taller-growing, stronger-coloured of the miniature varieties. Orange-salmon Coraín or yellow Rosina would be suitable. These roses look well in front of (and on the sunny side of) other shrub plantings.

In raised beds If you do want to smell your roses and appreciate the tiny beauty of their individual blooms as well, grow them in a raised stone sink at least 30–38cm (12–15 in) deep, perhaps placing it on a patio or using it as a backing for a garden seat. As an alternative, try long, narrow, terraced beds, built up with dry-stone walling or brick, and planted entirely with miniatures, each bed rising one tier above the last and perhaps planted with a contrasting colour. This is a good way to use a bank where the garden changes its level, but drainage in both a properly-constructed sink or on terracing is likely to be better than roses like, so water regularly.

Miniature rose garden

Each of the terraces described above will form a complete miniature rose bed, but it is possible to try something even more ambitious than this – a complete miniature rose garden. For these there are nowadays not only bush varieties but miniature standards and climbers,

though both the latter tend to be on the large side. In America even miniature moss roses have been developed.

Mark out the beds in whatever pattern and to whatever size takes your fancy or that you have room for, but remember that miniature roses are relatively expensive in comparison to their larger relatives and that you will not need more than about 20cm (8 in) between each bush. A bed 1·2 × 1·2m (4 × 4 ft) may not seem large, but it would take about 36 of the smaller-growing miniature roses, that are the best for this kind of planting.

You should not need to double dig the

ground. In time, miniature rose roots can go quite deep, but not as deep as this. However, the soil should be well broken-up to a depth of 30–38cm (12–15 in), and some fertilizer added before planting.

Paths between the beds can be either very narrow, to be in proportion to the roses, or as wide as an ordinary garden path, so that you can stroll along them more easily. The wider paths, if they are of grass, can be easily cut with a lawn-mower. Narrow grass ones may create problems in keeping them neat, and the grass itself, if it is anything other than very closely shaved, may actually look out of scale with the roses. Nothing looks better than grass for surrounding rose beds, but this is one case where small paving stones or fine gravel (contained within thin, damp-proofed, wooden edging) may be the most practical solution, and is a very good second best. A paved, sunken garden of miniature roses makes a most pleasing feature for any garden.

The following selection of varieties is divided into the dwarf and the taller-growing kinds. Dwarf here means about 15–20cm (6–8 in) and taller means

23–25cm (9–10 in), but remember that height will depend a lot on the conditions in which the roses are grown.

Some varieties to choose

DWARF

Baby Gold Star	yellow, flushed apricot
Colibri	orange-yellow, flushed pink
Frosty	white
Humpty Dumpty	carmine-pink
Lavender Lace	lavender-mauve
Pixie	white, tinted pink
Pour Toi	creamy-yellow
Peon (or Tom Thumb)	crimson, white centre
Simple Simon	deep pink
Toy Clown	white, edged pink
Yellow Doll	yellow

TALLER

Cinderella	shell-pink
Coralín	orange-salmon
Little Flirt	flame-yellow, red reverse
Maid Marion	scarlet
Oakington Ruby	crimson
Perle de Montserrat	rose-pink
Rosina	golden-yellow
Starina	red, flushed gold, carmine reverse

Shrub Roses

All roses are shrubs, so why is the term 'shrub rose' used, and what exactly does it mean? It is not easy to give a precise answer to either of these questions, and perhaps the nearest you can get is to say that 'shrub roses' are not normally used in the way that hybrid tea and floribunda roses are. Some shrub roses can be so used but they are the exception and are quite different in appearance from the more modern varieties. What shrub roses are, as opposed to what they are not, should become clear from the descriptions that follow.

They are made up from a number of families or groups, the oldest being the wild or species roses and their near relatives. Next in historical order come the gallicas, the oldest family of cultivated roses, and then follow the damasks, albas, centifolias, moss roses, Bourbons, hybrid perpetuals, China roses, rugosas, hybrid musks and the modern shrub roses.

Examples from any of these groups can be bought today without great difficulty and they add a dimension to rose-growing undreamed of by those who have never tried them. Think of the charm of the single rose or huge, many-petalled blooms, rich in scent, their soft pastel or rich purple colours often changing as the flower ages, and with their petals infolded or quartered in a way that recalls the prints from Victorian albums. Their informal growth contrasts strongly with the sergeant-major uprightness of the hybrid tea; in some cases they display great beauty of foliage and in autumn have branches laden with heps like drops of scarlet sealing wax. They also mix happily with shrubs.

After each of the following groups, we suggest a few varieties from which to choose and give first the ultimate height and then the spread for each plant.

Species

The species native to Britain, like the dog rose, have very fleeting flowers but many from overseas, particularly from the Far East, make excellent, if rather large, garden shrubs, flowering early and staying in bloom for weeks on end. Only one or two are recurrent, and they are not perhaps the first choices for garden display, unless you are forming a compre-

Above: Rosa gallica versicolor
Below: the alba Königen von Dänemark

hensive collection. All but one of the true species have single flowers of five petals, but a number of what you could term 'sub-species' (natural crosses made by species in the wild) have semi-double or double flowers. Generally, they are carried in enormous profusion along the whole length of great arching canes and smother the shrubs with colour in early and mid summer (late May and June). Plant them as specimens in a lawn, or in general shrub planting, always in full sun.

No pruning should be carried out or the natural shape of the shrub will be spoiled. A little trimming to develop a balanced bush is allowable early on, but avoid drastic cutting later simply because you have not left enough room for the rose to reach its full size. Just remove the dead branches as they occur.

Diseases and pests are rarely a problem to species. They are tough and shrug off any mild touch of mildew or black spot they may get without needing spraying.

Here are a few varieties to help you make your choice.

Canary Bird. Brilliant, single yellow flowers in early and mid summer (May and June). $2 \times 2m$ (7×7 ft).

Complicata. Huge, single pink flowers with white eye and gold stamens. Very vigorous and will scramble into surrounding shrubs. $1\cdot8 \times 2\cdot4m$ (6×8 ft).

R. moyesii Geranium. Crimson-red, single flowers and tall, open growth; huge heps. $3 \times 2\cdot4m$ (10×8 ft).

R. × paulii Rosea. Pink, single flowers. Low and spreading for ground cover. $1\cdot2 \times 4\cdot5m$ (4×15 ft).

Gallica

Most gallicas are small, upright shrubs, not often exceeding $1\cdot2$–$1\cdot5m$ (4–5 ft), and they carry their single crop of flowers well above the foliage. They make a very pretty showing if used in small clumps in front of a planting of other shrubs, or they can be used effectively for a low hedge to line a drive or path, where their tendency to sucker if on their own roots does not matter too much. A great advantage is that they can be clipped over – though not too drastically – rather than pruned. The canes have few thorns, but are covered with stiff, hairy bristles. Some mildew is likely on most of them.

As will become clear from the descriptions that follow, there are some gallica hybrids that do not conform to type and are much larger and lax-growing.

Belle de Crécy. Very fragrant flowers, cerise-pink, turning to Parma violet. $1\cdot2m \times 90cm$ (4×3 ft).

Camaieux. Crimson-purple flowers, striped white and fading to lilac-grey.

Below: species rose Canary Bird
Above: Pink Grootendorst, a hybrid musk

$90 \times 60cm$ (3×2 ft).

Cardinal de Richelieu. A lax grower with dark, maroon-purple, double flowers. $1\cdot5 \times 1\cdot2m$ (5×4 ft).

Charles de Mills. Flat, quartered blooms in cerise-crimson to wine-purple. $1\cdot5 \times 1\cdot2m$ (5×4 ft).

Rosa Mundi (*R. gallica versicolor*). Deep pink, striped palest blush. $1\cdot2 \times 1\cdot2m$ (4×4 ft).

Scarlet Fire. Massed, single scarlet blooms in late summer (July). $2 \times 2m$ (7×7 ft).

Below: Henri Martin, with characteristic 'moss' on the stem and calyx

Damask roses

It is difficult with damask roses to pinpoint specific characteristics for the whole group, except for scent, the fact that they form large, bushy shrubs, and that none of them is the rich, damask purple that you associate with the name. Their colour range is from white to deep pink, and they should be used for general shrub plantings or as specimens.

Little pruning is needed, except for the removal of dead wood and the shortening of laterals before flowering, though even

this is not essential. Of this comparatively small group the following are typical:
Celsiana. Flowers large, loose and blush-pink. 1·5 × 1·2m (5 × 4 ft).
Mme Hardy. Flat, pure white, double and quartered flowers with a green eye. 1·8 × 1·5m (6 × 5 ft).

Alba

Some of the alba roses, despite their name – meaning white – have pink flowers. As a group, their characteristic and attractive grey-green foliage makes them distinctive additions to a general shrub planting. The more vigorous varieties, that can be very large, scramble happily up through their neighbours quite happily. Some degree of suckering is possible.
Alba Semiplena. Double, ivory-white flowers against typical alba grey-green leaves. The white rose of York. 3 × 1·5m (7 × 5 ft).
Céleste. Soft pink. 1·8 × 1·2m (6 × 4 ft).
Félicité Parmentier. Pale yellow buds, opening to flowers of soft, blush-pink. 1·5m × 90cm (5 × 3 ft).
Königin von Dänemark. Buds scarlet-pink on opening, turning soft pink, quartered. 1·5 × 1·2m (5 × 4 ft).

Centifolia and moss

The centifolia and moss roses can really be taken together, as the latter, in its original form, was a sport from the former and, apart from the mossy, glandular growth on the flower-stalks and calyx of moss roses, they are similar in habit. All of them, except for a few very

Above: the Bourbon La Reine Victoria
Below: Rosa damascens *Mme Hardy*

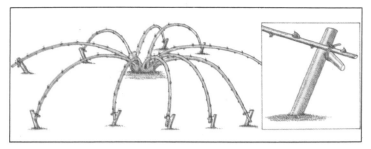

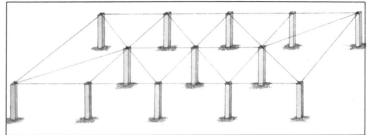

Above: peg down a hybrid perpetual for an ordered display in early summer
Above right: fasten canes of several hybrid perpetuals to a wire cage
Below: Roger Lambelin, a hybrid perpetual

small ones that can be used as rockery plants, will need the support of stakes. They are lax, rather untidy growers if left on their own and have big, drooping leaves. The weight of the very beautiful, many-petalled flowers will weigh down the canes. The taller varieties can be used as pillar roses.

The centifolia was the origin of the term 'cabbage rose', though the cupped blooms do not much resemble the cabbage as we know it today.

Chapeau de Napoleon. Deep-centred, globular, scented pink blooms with a unique 'cockade' of greenery around the bud that makes it look like Napoleon's hat. 1·5 × 1·2m (5 × 4 ft).
Fantin Latour. Very lovely, soft pink flowers in clusters opening flat. 1·8 × 1·5m (6 × 5 ft).
Henri Martin (moss). Green moss and pure crimson double flowers. 1·5 × 1·2m (5 × 4 ft).
Common Moss. Pink, globular blooms in great profusion. 1·2 × 1·2m (4 × 4 ft).

Bourbon

Most Bourbons are large, vigorous shrubs with sumptuous double flowers, that in a number of cases flower again in the autumn when they may be even better than in the first flush. The support of a pillar or a tripod will probably be needed, particularly with the more lax growers. Little pruning is needed, except for the shortening back of the sideshoots in early spring.
Honorine de Brabant. Blooms pale lilac-pink, spotted and striped mauve and crimson; recurrent. 1·8 × 1·8m (6 × 6 ft).
La Reine Victoria. Pink, cupped, shell-like, fragrant blooms; needs support; recurrent. 1·8m × 90cm (6 × 3 ft).
Pierre Oger. Sport of the last, paler creamy pink, deepening in hot sun. 1·8m × 90cm (6 × 3 ft).
Mme Isaac Pereire. Huge, richly-scented, cerise-crimson blooms. Will reach 3–3·3m (10–11 ft) when trained up wall or pillar. 2 × 1·5m (7 × 5 ft.)

Hybrid perpetual

The hybrid perpetuals are in many ways like the Bourbons, though more of them flower again well in the autumn. At that time they send up very long canes that, if left to themselves, will bear flowers mainly at the top in the following year. These can either be shortened back at pruning time in spring to encourage branching lower down or, if you have room for it, they can be pegged down. To do this, remove the soft tips and simply bend the canes over in an arch, tying the ends to wooden pegs driven into the ground all round the bush. This has the same effect as training the canes of a climber on horizontal wires, and in the early summer all the sideshoots will develop and produce flowers.

If you have a whole bed of hybrid perpetuals, as an alternative to pegging them, you can make a low 'cage' of galvanized iron wire, strung between stakes about 30cm (12 in) long, and tie the rose canes down to the wires. This may not be the most beautiful structure in the winter, but in summer the effect is spectacular.

Pegging down can also be done with many of the Bourbons and other tall-growing roses.
Frau Karl Druschki. A lovely, pure white rose that, unfortunately, has no scent. 1·5 × 1·2m (5 × 4 ft).
Georg Arends. Strawberry pink with a cream reverse to the petals. 1·5m × 90cm (5 × 3 ft).
Mrs John Laing. Silvery-pink very recurrent; fragrant. 1·5m × 90cm (5 × 3 ft).
Reine des Violettes. Scented, lilac-purple flowers, recurrent, opening flat and quartered with a button eye. 1·8 × 1·5m (6 × 5 ft).
Roger Lambelin. Double, crimson-purple fragrant flowers. 1·2m × 90cm (4 × 3 ft).

China

The China roses are distinguished by their light and airy growth, pretty flowers that repeat well right through to the autumn, and by attractive, pointed leaves that are exceptionally healthy. Some of the smaller varieties can be used for bedding, but as their colours are mostly pastel pinks to white, expect a restrained rather than an eye-catching display. Because of this,

small beds probably suit them best. The bigger varieties can reach 1·8–2m (6–7 ft) and mix well with other shrubs. Little if any pruning is needed.

Bloomfield Abundance. Tiny, pearl-pink, hybrid tea-shaped blooms in enormous flat-topped clusters. 1·8 × 1·8m (6 × 6 ft).

Cécile Brunner. Flowers like the last. The climbing form is, surprisingly, enormously vigorous, but not so recurrent. 90 × 60cm (3 × 2 ft).

Perle d'Or. Not unlike Cécile Brunner in habit, but with egg yolk-yellow flowers. 90 × 60cm (3 × 2 ft).

Rugosa

The name of this type of shrub, the most versatile of roses, derives from *rugosus*, the Latin for wrinkled. Mostly large and bushy, with magnificent, disease-proof, wrinkled foliage that colours in the autumn, they can be mixed with other shrubs, make (very thorny) hedges, or can be used as specimens, and are resistant to the salt-laden winds of the seaside. They will grow well even in poor soil and carry their flowers, scented in most cases, from mid summer to mid autumn (June to September). The kinds with single flowers form large red heps that look like small tomatoes and the ones from early flowers appear on the bushes alongside the later blooms; if you want heps, don't dead-head.

One or two hybrid rugosas, like Conrad F. Meyer and its sport Nova Zembla are not really typical of the family. Lovely in bloom, they can become bare at the base and need something else planted in front of them. They are also less healthy than the others, and are susceptible to rust.

Alba. Single white flowers on a dense shrub; orange-red heps maturing to tomato red. 1·8 × 1·8m (6 × 6 ft).

Frau Dagmar Hartopp. Single, pale-pink flowers and huge, crimson heps. 1·5 × 1·5m (5 × 5 ft).

Roseraie de l'Hay. Velvety, wine-red, scented flowers all summer; no heps. 1·8 × 1·5m (6 × 5 ft).

Pink Grootendorst. Small, clear, pink flowers in big clusters, the petal edges frilled like a carnation; no heps. 1·8 × 1·5m (6 × 5 ft).

Hybrid musk

Many of the hybrid musk roses are like giant floribundas in a way. However, they are much more widespreading, reaching in some cases 1·8–2m (6–7 ft) tall and wide. The scented blooms come in large, free-ranging sprays or trusses, and they make wonderful colourful hedges if you have the space. They can also be used for bedding in a large plot, but do not expect the regularity of growth that you get with a floribunda. There is a fine autumn flowering as well as one in early summer and some flower in between.

Buff Beauty. Apricot-yellow blooms, fading to cream. 1·8 × 1·8m (6 × 6 ft).

Cornelia. Coppery-apricot, fading to cream. 1·5 × 2m (5 × 7 ft).

Penelope. Penelope Semi-double flowers, creamy-pink, shaded light orange in colour; very robust. 1·8 × 1·5m (6 × 5 ft).

Modern shrub roses

These are very diverse in appearance and habit. Some, like Chinatown and Fred Loads, are actually extra-vigorous floribundas and grow in exactly the same way. Others, like Constance Spry, are hybrids of old roses and usually take after one or other of the parents in habit of growth or flower form.

Cerise Bouquet. Cerise-crimson flowers in large sprays. 2·4 × 3m (8 × 10 ft).

Chinatown. Very large, scented, canary-yellow double flowers in clusters. 1·5m × 90cm (5 × 3 ft).

Constance Spry. Huge, pink cupped blooms in old style. 1·5 × 2·4m (5 × 8 ft).

Fred Loads. Huge trusses of semi-double, pale vermilion-orange flowers; prune hard and regularly to restrain growth. 2·4 × 1·2m (8 × 4 ft).

Fritz Nobis. Clove-scented, blush-pink, semi-double flowers; very free. 1·8 × 2·1m (6 × 7 ft).

Frühlingsgold. Huge, arching canes, bearing 10cm (4 in), semi-double, light yellow blooms. 2·4 × 2·1m (8 × 7 ft).

Golden Wings. Non-stop flowers with single, yellow, scented blooms; very healthy. 1·8 × 1·5m (6 × 5 ft).

Marguerite Hilling. Sport of Nevada, pink. 2·1 × 2·4m (7 × 8 ft).

Above: Buff Beauty, a fragrant hybrid musk
Below: the magnificent arching habit of Fruhlingsgold, a modern shrub rose

Nevada. Completely smothered in ivory-white, semi-double flowers in mid summer (June) and later. 2·1 × 2·4m (7 × 8 ft).

History of the Garden Rose

Modern roses bear little resemblance to the original wild roses – with their rather fleeting flowering season – that go back millions of years to a time long before Man inhabited the earth. Fossils of some have been found in France, the Middle East and in America.

Many of these old species roses survive today. There are probably about 150 true species, but a number of roses that appear to be species because they have been given Latin names are really hybrids that have crossed by chance with other roses in the wild. Many of them have semi-double or double flowers whereas, with one exception, genuine species roses have simply five single petals.

Accidental crossing was responsible for the creation of all the early families of rose, for it was not until the late 18th century that anyone began to realize that cross pollination between plants by bees and other insects was the way in which new varieties were created. The intentional breeding of new plants by man is a comparatively new science and in the case of roses, because of their very mixed ancestry, a very unpredictable one. The poet Keats knew about this when he wrote in his 'Ode to Psyche':

With all the gardener Fancy e're could feign,
Who breeding flowers, will never breed the same

Gallica

The gallica or French rose is the oldest cultivated rose we knòw and the first records of it go back to the 16th century though they were not then grown as garden plants in the way they are now.

Much earlier the gallica, and possibly a form of damask rose, was grown in enormous quantities at Paestum in Italy to decorate and perfume Roman feasts and other festivities. Damasks, and another race of roses, the albas, were also grown on a massive scale for the production of attar of roses in the Balkan countries and Turkey and, to a lesser extent, in France. Dating back hundreds of years, this industry still exists.

As can be seen from a reading of the old herbals, the rose was long considered a plant with almost unlimited medicinal properties. The Romans thought that a

HYBRID TEA ROSE—"LA FRANCE"

preparation made from a British wild species, *Rosa canina*, was a cure for hydrophobia, a symptom of rabies, and this is how the dog rose got its name.

One of the early gallicas, *R. gallica officinalis*, was cultivated near the town of Provins in northern France as well as in other places, for the medicines and magic potions to be distilled from it. Thus it earned the popular name of the apothecary's rose. To this day it is known as the rose of Provins and has also gained fame as the red rose of Lancaster, from England's 15th century Wars of the Roses. Its lasting qualities are such that it is still stocked by nurseries.

Alba

The gallica, of course, was far from being the only one chosen as a symbol. *R. × alba*, another you can still buy, was the white rose of York, and variety Alba Maxima was the Jacobite rose of Bonnie Prince Charlie. Heraldry featured the 'Tudor' rose, and the rose has long been a symbol of purity in many religions.

Opposite page: La France, the first hybrid tea, from an 1896 botanical book. Top left: the dog rose, R. canina, was known to the Romans. Top right: R. chinensis Old Blush, one of the repeat-flowering China roses. Right: hybrid perpetual Reine des Violettes dates from 1860. Far right: Zigeunerknabe (Gypsy Boy), Bourbon rose raised in 1909. Below: one of the earliest known, R. gallica officinalis

19th century development

Napoleon's wife, the Empress Josephine, was a dedicated gardener and at Malmaison, her villa near Paris, she collected together all the roses then known to be in cultivation, making what was probably the first rose garden. Such was its attraction that the idea caught on amongst her fashionable contemporaries and the rose, as a popular garden plant, had arrived. From about this time, you can begin to see the breeding lines that were to lead to the modern hybrid tea, though the first step came about purely by chance.

At this time, many missionaries and government and trade officials worked in China and other parts of the Far East. A number of them, fascinated by the strange plants they saw, became keen collectors and sent specimens and seeds back to interested friends and botanical gardens in Europe.

Almost all the roses known in the West were once-flowering – in early summer – but a number from China were fully recurrent and when these began to arrive there was great excitement in the gardening world. In themselves, the roses were not the most spectacular varieties to look at, or particularly robust, but they were welcomed for their long flowering period alone. Nobody knew how to pass this quality on to the existing Western roses, but Nature did it for us.

Bourbon

On the Ile Bourbon (now Réunion) in the Indian Ocean, some China roses were planted in a hedge with a rose called the Autumn Damask. This was a very ancient and strong-growing Western rose that had gained its name because it usually did produce a few flowers after the first flush but could not really be called recurrent. Insects, flitting from one rose to another in the mixed hedge on the Ile Bourbon, fertilized the flowers, and seedlings resulted that were strong-growing, strong in constitution, and flowered well into the autumn. They combined the best qualities of both parents and were noticed in the first quarter of the 19th century by a visiting botanist called Bréon. He took some back to France and the Bourbon rose, with its characteristic huge, many-petalled flowers, was born. Its merits quickly made it popular.

Portland

Almost at the same period a similar chance cross between a China rose and a damask – nobody knows if they were actually the same varieties – was taking place in Italy, and produced a small group called Portland roses, named after the Duchess of Portland of the time. They did not catch on to the same extent as the Bourbons but nevertheless they are an important group in the history of the hybrid tea rose.

Hybrid perpetual

Bourbons, crossed with the Portlands, resulted in the hybrid perpetual roses so loved by the Victorians that the catalogues of large growers might contain well over 1000 varieties. This may seem difficult to believe and it is probably as well to be sceptical. Even in nurseries cross pollination was still taking place largely at random and it is pretty certain that many of the so-called new varieties were as nearly identical to those already in existence as makes no matter. Two rival nurseries might well call exactly the same rose by different names of their own choosing.

Hybrid tea

The early hybrid perpetuals had short centre petals that made for a flower of globular form. This faded out and the high-centred bloom we admire today began to appear after the introduction of the recurrent tea rose from China. Not really hardy in the northern European countries, this was a rose of great elegance of form, with long centre petals and with the outer ones reflexing symmetrically all round. Crossed with hybrid perpetuals, it produced the first hybrid tea, named La France, in 1867.

The yellow rose

Some of the tea roses were of a pale, creamy-yellow colour but, apart from a few species, there were no bright yellow ones. One of these species, the Persian *R. foetida*, had – and still has – glowing yellow single flowers. A sport from it, *R. foetida bicolor*, was brilliant scarlet, with the petal reverse yellow, and there was also a double yellow form. A French nurseryman from Lyons, called Pernet-Ducher, worked for many years trying to cross the latter with hybrid perpetual roses and at long last his great patience was rewarded by the production of Rayon d'Or, leading in turn to the better Soleil d'Or, a double yellow rose, flushed with orange and red, and this was put on the market in 1900. From this rose all our yellow, flame and orange roses are descended, and our bicolours from crosses with *R. foetida bicolor*. These early yellow roses were known as Pernetainas after their raiser but as they became merged with other roses the name was dropped.

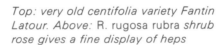

Top: very old centifolia variety Fantin Latour. Above: R. rugosa rubra *shrub rose gives a fine display of heps*

The susceptibility of *R. foetida* to black spot disease was also, unfortunately, passed on to its many grandchildren and through interbreeding with other-coloured roses this same tendency has been firmly established in practically all modern varieties.

Floribunda

As we know, floribundas have a different habit of growth, the blooms being smaller and coming in trusses as they do on many ramblers, unlike the large blooms, one to a stem, of many hybrid teas. It is not surprising, therefore, to know that floribundas have come down to us as a result of crosses between China roses and the rambler *R. multiflora*. Crossed with bush roses, these produced first of all the poly-pom roses that were quite popular before World War II. They were small, bushy plants with small flowers in clusters that made a colourful display before succumbing to mildew – something they were very prone to do.

In 1924, the Danish hybridist Svend Poulsen put Else Poulsen and Kirsten Poulsen on the market; he had bred them

by crossing poly-pom roses with hybrid teas, and they became known as hybrid polyanthas or simply as polyanthas. They were the first to resemble floribundas as we know them today, though it was not until after World War II that they became really popular and the name floribunda was adopted. Present breeding tendency is towards floribundas with bigger, HT-shaped flowers, with fewer on a truss, and they are known as floribunda-hybrid tea type. It is getting more and more difficult to distinguish some of them from hybrid teas and this development is so marked that the World Federation of Rose Societies is debating the use of a new term – 'cluster-flowered' – that will embrace all those roses that do not have single flowers to a stem.

Other types

So much for hybrid teas and floribundas, but there are a few strands of rose development that have not been mentioned. Rambling roses came from species like *R. wichuraiana*, sometimes crossed with hybrid teas and other roses, and climbers from the Chinese *R. gigantea* and other natural climbers.

The centifolia roses, that were enormously popular at one time, are thought to have been the result of a cross between an alba rose and the dog rose. They were developed largely in the Netherlands and appear with their globular, 'very double' blooms in the pictures of many of the old Dutch flower painters. A centifolia sported the first moss rose, a group pretty well identical to the centifolias except for the mossy, glandular growth on the pedicals and calyx. The novelty of this appealed greatly to the Victorians and in our thinking the moss rose is closely linked with that period. There has been little recent development with them except for the production of a yellow moss rose and, in the USA, miniature moss roses.

Rugosa roses, the Ramana rose of Japan, have gone their own way producing a number of first-rate shrub roses but, strangely for something so good, playing a very small part in the history of the rose.

The Royal National Rose Society

Earlier on, we left the Empress Josephine spreading the word about the rose as a garden plant. But, for many years, rose gardens were the preserve of the rich and in Britain it was not until the foundation of the National Rose Society (now Royal) in 1876 by Canon – later Dean – Reynolds Hole and the Reverend H. Honeywood D'Ombrain that the rose began to be the flower for everyone, rich or poor. Beginning by encouraging rose shows all over the country, they worked hard to popularize the flower they loved so well. How well the society has succeeded in the 100 years it has been in existence, can be seen in every garden today.

Modern breeding programmes

Looking forward, what pointers are there to the way the rose will go? Healthier roses must and will come and this is something to which many of the best breeders are giving thought. However, it can take up to eight years to breed and market a new rose, so a great deal of patience on the part of both growers and the public is called for.

There is a constant striving for a blue rose. Whether or not this would be a good thing must remain a matter of opinion but one is only likely to develop through a freak of nature. The make-up of the rose does not include delphinidin, that essential ingredient of blue flowers, so it is most unlikely that we will get anywhere nearer the target than, say, the present-day hybrid tea, Blue Moon, which is really lilac-mauve in colour.

Comparatively few of the species and old roses have played much part in the breeding programmes of modern hybridists. Using them can be a long and frustrating job, especially for a firm that has to make money to stay in business, but the constant search for novelties has brought a few into the picture recently.

The floribunda Picasso, with unusual deep cerise blotches on the petals of its light cerise flowers, has a species in its recent pedigree. News, another floribunda, is beetroot-purple, its colours coming from the gallica rose Tuscany. These two are just beginnings: before long we may see yellow garden roses with a red eye, grandchildren of the Iranian species rose *R. persica*, and currently the subject of experimental breeding programmes.

Above: R. foetida bicolor, *ancestor of modern bicoloured varieties*
Left: Blue Moon, nearest yet to a true blue rose

Above: R. foetida bicolor, *ancestor of modern bicoloured varieties. Left: Blue Moon, nearest yet to a true blue rose.*

Choosing the Site and Planting Your Roses

Having looked at the roses themselves we now tell you where and how to plant the various groups for best results and we go on to routine care and propagation.

Roses like plenty of sun, though there are some climbers that will do quite well on a north-facing wall. They will grow in most types of soil, though are far from their best on chalk. A good, medium loam suits them best of all, so you can help them on light soils by adding as much humus as possible, and peat and other materials on heavy ones, both to lighten them and to improve drainage. The latter is important, for no rose likes being waterlogged. They should have plenty of water if they are to flourish as they should, but they will survive drought far better than they will constant flooding.

Choose, if possible, an open but not a windswept site. Avoid narrow, draughty wind-tunnels such as you find between houses, or shady places under trees, where the roses will grow tall and spindly looking for the light and have to compete with the tree roots for water and food.

How many roses you will need to fill your chosen beds depends not only on how many you can afford, but also on the varieties you select. If you have seen the same varieties growing elsewhere beforehand, you will know just how large they get, and whether they are spreading or upright growers. As a rough guide, it can be said that an average distance between plants of about 45cm (18 in) will suit most hybrid teas and floribundas. This will allow for air circulation, and make spraying and hoeing between them not too difficult a task.

Do not plant new roses in a bed that has grown other roses for some years. The soil will have become what is known as 'rose sick' and the new roses will never do well. You must either replace the soil from another part of the garden, which is a job few people care to tackle if the bed is a big one, or else choose another spot altogether. However, if you are simply replacing a rose that has died in the middle of an established bed, it is not too big a job to dig out a 45cm (18 in) hole, about 30cm (12 in) deep, and put new soil in – still hard work but it should be done.

Preparing the site
Roses will give you twenty years or more of their beauty, so it is only fair and

A fine display of mixed roses resulting from careful siting and planting

sensible to give them the best home possible to live in. The preparation of the site will vary to a greater or lesser extent according to your type of soil. In extreme cases where, for instance, drainage is almost non-existent and the ground waterlogged, it may be necessary to put in land drains, or at the very least put in materials to make it more porous. Light, sandy soils need the opposite approach for, though good drainage is essential, a correct balance must be struck between this and some degree of water retention. Roots need air as well as water to function properly, which is the reason heavy soils need to be broken up so as to make them more friable.

This breaking-up should be done by double digging and keeping the fertile topsoil where it should be, at the top. It is a good idea to put chopped-up turfs, grass side downwards, along the bottom of each trench and, when filling in, add well-rotted compost, leaf mould, granulated peat or stable manure – or a mixture of all of them – whatever organic material you can get hold of, together with a generous dressing of bonemeal.

All this digging and manuring should be done some time in mid autumn (September), about three months before your roses arrive. The ground will have time to settle down and you can recover from a back-breaking job. Heavy work it may be, but you will be more than glad in years to come that you faced up to it, for with good cultivation roses will not only grow and bloom well, but will be much more resistant to diseases.

Finally, a few tips for special conditions. About 1½kg per sq m (3 lb per sq yd) of gypsum (calcium sulphate) added to the bottom of a double-dug trench will help to break up a clay subsoil, though only over quite a long period. On very light, sandy soils, deep digging should not be needed, as both water and roots can penetrate it easily in its natural state. In fact, disturbance of the lower spit will make it even easier for the water to get away, which is the last thing needed on this kind of soil. Plenty of humus in the top spit is the answer here.

If you are gardening on solid chalk, with only a few centimetres of soil over it, it will be necessary to dig out the chalk to a depth of at least 45cm (18 in), and to add plenty of peat to the soil that replaces it. Roses do best in a slightly acid soil, of a pH value between 6·0 and 6·5.

When and how to plant
Your roses will probably arrive from the nursery in early winter (November). This is the best month for planting them, as the soil will still be warm enough for the roots to get established.

If you have to wait a few days before planting, either because you are too busy with something else, or the ground is frost-bound, or soggy from prolonged rain, do not unpack the roses but keep them in a cool, frost-proof shed. If there is likely to be a longer delay, heel them in as soon as weather conditions permit. To do this, unpack the plants and put them along a trench in a spare corner of the garden, burying them so that at least 15cm (6 in) of soil covers the roots. They can remain like this for some weeks if absolutely necessary, but it is always best to get them into their final quarters with the least delay so that they can start to make themselves at home.

Whether you are planting straight away or heeling in, inspect the roses carefully as soon as you have unpacked them. Check the labels to make sure that they are what you ordered, as even the best of nurseries can make mistakes and will always exchange a wrong variety. If the plants are described as being First Grade, they should have a minimum of two firm, healthy canes (stems), at least as thick as a pencil and with smooth, unwrinkled bark. The neck joint between the rootstock and the budding union should be at least 16mm (⅝ in) thick, and there should be a good, fibrous root system. Cut off any leaves remaining on the canes, and cut back any of the latter that are diseased or broken to a point

1 Dig hole wide enough to spread roots

2 Carefully remove wrapping material
4 Work planting mixture around roots

3 Settle roots in hole and check level
5 Fill in and firm down before watering

just below the damaged portion. Shorten any very long, thick roots by a third; this will encourage the thinner, feeding roots to grow from them. If the roses look dry, put them in a bucket of water for at least an hour.

While they are sucking up the water, you can make up your planting mixture which, while not absolutely essential on good soil, will certainly help to give your roses a good start. You will need about one large shovelful for each rose, consisting of equal parts of soil and moist granulated peat, with a handful of bonemeal or rose fertilizer per plant mixed well in. It is advisable to wear gloves when handling fertilizers.

Dig your first planting hole wide enough for the roots to be spread out as evenly as possible all round, and deep enough so that the budding union comes about 13mm ($\frac{1}{2}$ in) below the soil level. Carry your bucket of roses to the rose bed so that you can lift them straight from it and the roots have no chance to dry out again. Put your first rose in its hole, spread out the roots and check the level by putting a cane across the top of the

hole. Put a shovelful of planting mixture over the roots, tread lightly, and then fill in the hole with soil, treading again rather more firmly. Finally, give each rose at least 8 litres (2 gal) of water. It may be as well to tread the soil once more after a few weeks, especially if there has been a frost that may have loosened the plants.

Climbers
Climbing roses against a house wall, where the soil is certain to be very dry, need slightly different treatment. Plant them at least 45cm (18 in) out from the wall and fan out their roots *away* from it towards the damper ground. If they are long enough, tie in the canes straight away to the lowest support wire to help prevent wind-rock.

Standards and shrubs
Standard roses should have the stake that will support them driven into the hole before planting, so that it will not damage any roots. The stake should be long enough so that it just goes into the head of the bush to give it extra support, but should not show above it. Tie the two together with plastic ties that have a buffer between the plant and stake to prevent chafing, but only fix them loosely at first as the rose may sink a little as the soil settles. After a week or ten days, you can tighten up the ties enough to hold the stem firmly, but not to strangle it.

When planting the larger-growing shrub roses, make sure that you really have left room enough all round for them to achieve their full size.

Container-grown plants
Many people buy container-grown roses from nurseries and garden centres, and these plants should be carefully inspected before buying to make sure that they are up to standard and have genuinely been grown in a container and not just put in one for selling purposes. They have the

Left: a good soaking helps dry plants
Above: standards should be firmly tied

great advantage that they can be planted at any time, even in full flower, provided the rootball is not disturbed too much.

However, don't just dig a hole big enough to take the container, particularly if your soil is heavy. By doing this you might simply be making a sump, that would fill with water after rain and whose sides the roots might find it hard to penetrate. Dig a hole at least 30cm (12 in) across, breaking up the subsoil for drainage. Water your rose well while still in its container, and put it in the hole to check that the depth is right. If it is, slit down each side of the container with a sharp knife, ease it out from under the rootball, fill the hole with planting mixture, tread firm and water well. Should the container be of metal, you will, of course, have to remove the rose before putting it in the planting hole.

Growing under glass
Roses are not hothouse plants, but they can be grown successfully in a greenhouse, at least for part of the year, so that you can have spring blooms long before the garden roses are out.

Use 20 or 25cm (8 or 10 in) pots with 2–3cm (1 in) of broken crocks in the bottom; their size depends on the vigour of the variety. J. I. potting compost, either No 2 or No 3, is a suitable growing medium, with perhaps a small amount of well-rotted garden compost or small pieces of chopped turf immediately on top of the crocks.

Plant the roses in early winter (early November), making sure that the soil level is about 2–3cm (1 in) below the pot rims to allow for watering and liquid fertilizers if you wish to use them. You may well have to cut the stronger roots back quite hard to fit the whole thing into the pot, but they will soon form new, finer ones. Firm planting is important, and all leaves and flower-buds should be removed and long shoots shortened a little.

Leave the pots out of doors until mid winter (early December), and then bring them into the greenhouse.

A cold greenhouse will produce flowers in early summer (May), but some heat will be needed for flowers earlier than that. Good ventilation is important at all times, particularly from above, and some form of shading will be needed if the sun is hot. Prune them at the end of mid winter (December), and do not introduce heat into the house until at least ten days after it has been done.

Prune hard, to the first two or three eyes (buds) or you will get tall, straggly plants. Watering should not be too generous at first, but gradually increased as the plants start into growth. Give a thorough weekly soaking once they are really away, with a liquid feed added to the water two months after pruning.

Pests such as caterpillars and greenfly can be removed by hand if you only have a few roses. Mildew can be largely avoided by good roof ventilation, but if any spraying of the plants has to be done, it is much safer to take them out of the greenhouse so that you do not breathe harmful chemicals.

When the plants finish flowering, towards the end of early summer (May), turn off the heating if this has been used, and open the ventilators to prepare the roses for a move outdoors in two weeks or so. Once outside, sink the pots to their rims in ashes in a sheltered spot, where they can be left until brought indoors again in early winter (December), when re-potting should be done if necessary.

Routine care of Roses

If you are to get the best results from your roses, whether they be tiny miniatures or giant ramblers, then regular attention is most important. Here we tell you about the routine jobs, such as when to add fertilizer and how to disbud.

Starting with winter, when there is least to do by way of maintenance, your first job is to spray the dormant roses at least once, but preferably two or three times, with Bordeaux mixture to kill over-wintering disease spores. It has been found that this spraying makes quite a difference to the health of roses later in the year.

Fertilizing and mulching
After spring pruning, apply a proprietary rose fertilizer round each bush at the rate recommended by the supplier, probably between 70–140g per sq m (2–4 oz per sq yd), and hoe it in lightly so that the fine, surface-feeding roots are not disturbed or severed. Water well afterwards if there is no rain about.

Late spring (mid April) when the soil has begun to warm up, is a good time to mulch the rose beds, but there is no point in putting on a mulch in the middle of a dry spell. A mulch serves three purposes: to keep the weeds down, to fertilize the soil when it breaks down, and to form a blanket to keep in the moisture. But it cannot do the latter if there is little or no moisture there in the first place, and if the mulch itself dries out, it will absorb an enormous amount of rainwater before any moisture penetrates to the soil beneath. Grass mowings in particular, unless spread very thinly, form an almost impenetrable mass.

Remove any persistent perennial weeds before mulching, and then spread a layer about 5–8cm (2–3 in) thick of well-rotted farmyard manure over the whole bed, keeping it just clear of the rose stems. This is the ideal mulch as it has in it many of the nutrients that roses need, and makes good humus as well. If you cannot get

Looking after your roses pays off with a colourful display such as the one below

manure, use well-rotted compost or leaf mould, which is almost as good. Other alternatives are hop manure or granulated peat (the most attractive-looking, but getting more and more expensive), but these have no manurial value, though peat is an excellent soil conditioner when it is eventually hoed in. It helps to lighten heavy soils and to make light soils more water-retentive.

Early summer (mid to late May) is the time for a second application of fertilizer, and if you wish to add a third to boost the

Left: identifying parts of the rose bush
Below left: as with all flowering plants, dead-heading will encourage a rose to continue blooming; on a floribunda cut off the entire truss down to a good bud
Below right: pinch out side buds to get one large bloom on each stem
Bottom: suckers come up around the stem

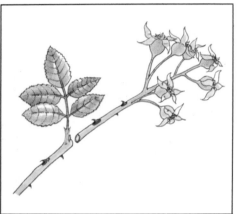

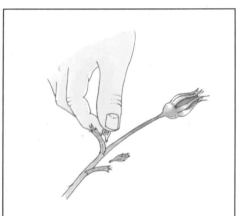

roses for autumn blooming, this should be done no later than late summer (the end of July). Otherwise growth will be encouraged that will not have time to ripen before the winter and is likely to be killed by frost.

When and how to dead-head
In the natural way of things, roses produce seeds after flowering, and a good deal of the plant's energy goes into this rather than into the production of new flowers. If the seed-heads (heps) are removed the rose tries again and more flowers are the result. This removal is known as dead-heading or summer pruning, and serves a double purpose in that it also removes the sometimes unsightly, dying blooms of the varieties whose petals do not drop cleanly or those that may have become sodden with rain.

Do not just pull the heads off, however. It is far better, and will produce new flowers more quickly, if you cut back to a good strong bud below the old flower or below the spent truss of a floribunda. Remove as little wood and as few leaves as possible in doing this, however, or the rose will be weakened.

How to recognize suckers
Roses, unless they are growing on their own roots (which is unusual with nursery-bought plants), will have been budded on to an understock or rootstock of a more vigorous species or near species, such as *Rosa canina* in one of its many forms. Suckering is an attempt by the rootstock to start a life of its own by sending up shoots. These shoots are called suckers, and if they are not dealt with promptly, all the strength of the roots will be diverted into them. The rootstock will take over, and your own chosen rose will die.

How to distinguish a sucker growth presents problems for a beginner, particularly as a number of different roses are used as rootstocks, and their shoots vary in appearance. Sometimes a sucker is easy to recognize, as some stocks produce very light green shoots that will probably have several leaflets. They look entirely different from the growth of hybrid tea or a floribunda, but this is not an infallible guide. After you have had some experience, you will be able to recognize any sucker immediately, but to be on the safe side until you are sure, trace the suspected sucker back to its source.

This will probably mean scraping a little soil away from the base of the plant to see where the sucker comes from. If it comes from below the budding union (a thickening of the main stem just above the roots, from which the canes of your rose

Above: always plant roses so the budding union (that you can see clearly on new shrubs) is beneath the soil surface
Left: suckers grow from the rootstock and should be removed by clearing away soil to their start point and pulling hard

sprout) it is a sucker. It should be pulled away from the root rather than cut, stopping short, of course, of pulling your rose up in the process.

This is the only way of making sure that no dormant buds are left behind to form new suckers. Never just cut a sucker off at ground level. All you will be doing then is pruning it and encouraging more strong growth.

Treated like this, they should come away quite easily, provided that they are dealt with promptly and not allowed to mature. The only real problem is when one comes from right under the rose, or from the middle of a tangle of old roots. Then there is probably nothing to be done except to cut it back as far as possible and to keep an eye open for it emerging again – as it is certain to do.

The stem of a standard rose is part of the rootstock, and any shoots that appear on the stem are the equivalent of suckers and should be broken off.

Disbudding for bigger blooms

Many HT roses have clusters of buds at the end of each cane. For general garden display, this does not really matter, but if you want to get bigger blooms (and fewer of them), remove some or all of the side buds as soon as they are large enough for this to be done without damaging the main bud. If you are going to show your roses, you will have to disbud them. One or two varieties, like Pink Favorite, have so many closely-packed buds that, to get the best of the rose for garden display, at least some of the buds should be pinched out carefully between finger and thumb.

Autumn pruning

This is not pruning to encourage new growth. It simply means shortening the canes of HT and floribunda types by about one-third early on in winter (early November) to prevent the bushes being rocked by the winter winds and probably loosened in the soil. This is especially important for tall-growing varieties.

Tidying up

This is another autumn job, consisting of raking up and burning the fallen rose leaves from the beds, to help destroy disease spores that may winter on them. Also, pick off the plants and burn all remaining leaves that are showing signs of black spot disease. This may be quite a job if you have a lot of rose bushes and is really a task that should be started earlier in the summer if you want to keep it under control, and continued right through to this stage of the autumn. If you can face up to this programme, it pays dividends the following summer.

Finally, hoe the beds lightly to destroy weeds and to accelerate the breaking down of the spring mulch into the soil.

Taking cuttings

You can increase your stock of roses by taking cuttings, but it should be remembered that not all types of rose take equally well and some, even if they do take, will not have the same vigour on their own roots as when budded onto rootstock. As a compensation, you will not have to cope with suckers from the roses, and they will cost you nothing.

A large number of HTs are reluctant to root from cuttings, though it is always worth a try. Floribundas, generally speaking, are much easier and miniature roses take readily. So do most climbers, ramblers, and shrub roses. Among the latter, families like the gallicas, albas, rugosas (if on their own roots when bought), and species like the spinosissima group, sucker quite freely, and root cuttings can be taken by easing out the sucker and cutting off a portion that has roots attached.

For the other roses mentioned, cuttings can be taken any time between mid autumn and early winter (September and November). Choose a strong, well-ripened and unbranched shoot – one that grew early in the summer – and make a clean cut immediately below the lowest eye. Make another cut directly above a bud about 25cm (9 in) away from the first, sloping the cut downwards and away from the bud as you would in pruning. Remove all but the top pair of leaves, and your cutting is ready for planting. From long shoots, you can obtain two or even three 25cm (9 in) cuttings. Do not try to take one from the very soft, pithy tip of the shoot however.

Once you have a selection of cuttings label them if they come from different roses and put them in a polythene bag so that they will not dry out.

Dig a narrow trench about 15cm (6 in) deep and, if your soil is at all heavy, sprinkle a mixture of sharp sand and granulated peat along the bottom. Place your cuttings in this, about 15cm (6 in) apart and so that 15cm of their length are below soil level, fill in the trench and firm well. If you moisten the ends of the cuttings before planting and dip them into a hormone rooting powder their chances of rooting will be increased.

On light, sandy soils it may not be necessary to dig a trench or even to use sand or peat. Simply make a long, straight, 15cm (6in) deep slit by pushing a spade into the earth and working it backwards and forwards. The cuttings can be inserted into this, and treading along the sides of the slit will push the earth back into place around them.

Leave the cuttings until the following autumn, when those that have taken can be transplanted to their final quarters, but do not expect to have fully-grown plants for two or three years. Taking cuttings is an easy but not a very quick way of increasing your stock.

For miniature roses, the cutting can be about 8cm (3 in) long and everything else is scaled down in proportion. Miniatures will grow to full size relatively quickly.

Propagation by budding

This is a much speedier method of increasing the number of your roses. It is the way nurseries create new plants and consists of inserting a bud or eye from one of your existing roses into the neck of a rootstock, where, with luck, it will grow away. It is a rather more complicated process than taking cuttings, and the actual budding does require a knack, though this is not too hard to acquire (see Budding and Grafting, page 41).

Your local rose nursery may well be prepared to let you have a few rootstocks, or there are several specialist firms that supply them, though often in quantities of not less than twenty-five. In the autumn, plant your stocks about 60cm (24 in) apart in a spare piece of ground. During the winter, they will settle in and, in the spring, start to grow. Late that same summer prepare to do your budding and choose a showery spell of weather if possible.

Cut some ripe shoots with strong, plump, dormant buds from the roses you wish to increase. Shoots that have flowered in mid or late summer (June or

To propagate a rose from a cutting, cut off a new shoot below the lowest eye, then cut above a bud 25cm (9in) away. Trim off all but top two leaves. Place 15cm (6 in) apart in a narrow trench 15cm deep and leave until following autumn

July) should be ripe in mid autumn (early September) and are very suitable. Place all but one of the shoots in a plastic bag while you work on the first one, to prevent them from drying out.

With a very sharp knife, make a scooping cut into the shoot, starting about 13mm ($\frac{1}{2}$ in) above a bud and coming out about the same distance below it. Trim off the leaf but leave the leaf-stalk to act as a handle for holding the bud. With your thumbnail, twist out the small, boat-shaped piece of pith and wood behind the bud, trim the bottom and top ends of the bark, and put the bud carefully to one side.

Now prepare the stock. Scoop away a little soil at the neck, where it enters the earth, and wipe the neck clean with a damp rag. With the sharp point of your knife, make a T-shaped cut in the bark of the neck with the down-stroke of the T about 19mm ($\frac{3}{4}$ in) long. Very gently, taking care not to damage or detach them, ease out the triangular flap of bark on either side of it.

Now, holding it by the leaf-stalk, slide the bud downwards into the T-cut, under the bark flaps. Bind the whole thing gently but firmly with raffia, except immediately over the bud itself. As an alternative to this you can buy special budding ties that are very easy to use. They are flexible and expand when the bud does. Raffia will simply rot away at about the time when the bud has taken and it is no longer needed.

By the following spring, the bud should have taken, though you must allow for a number of failures – at least until you have mastered the knack of preparing and inserting the bud. When the new shoot is growing strongly, you can cut away the whole top growth of the stock immediately above it, and all the strength from the roots will go into the new rose. For a while, even though it is growing from it, the shoot will not be very firmly anchored into the stock, so it is wise to support it by tying it to a short cane pushed into the ground beside it to guard against the buffeting of the wind. Be very careful when doing this, or you may snap off the shoot. By the following autumn your new rose should be growing strongly and be ready for transplanting to its permanent home.

If you are budding standard roses and want to get a balanced head, insert two buds (double budding) at least, each about 2–3cm (1 in) above the last and on different sides of the stem. This applies to rugosa stock; for canina stock, insert the buds into good strong lateral growths, as close to the stem as possible.

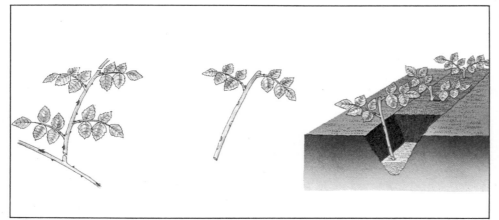

Pruning Roses

The profusely-flowering floribunda Iceberg responds well to good pruning

It is unfortunate that when writing about pruning it tends to sound so complicated. There is no doubt that the best way to learn is to get an experienced rose grower to show you how to do it, provided that he takes the time to explain just why he is doing each operation. If you understand what you are doing and why, pruning all at once loses its mystique and suddenly you wonder what all the fuss was about.

So, first of all, why do we prune? In the wild (and you can see this for yourself in the hedgerows) roses send up new canes each year from the base of the plant or from very near it. The old canes will gradually deteriorate and eventually die off. The best blooms come on the new growth, and all you are doing when you prune is speeding up this natural process of replacement. Also, some of the old canes may very well be diseased, so you are getting rid of these as well.

There are two other things to aim for in pruning. One is to achieve a reasonably balanced bush, though this may not be too important if the roses are growing close together in a bed, and the other to keep the centre of the bush fairly open so

that light and air can reach it. A thick tangle of canes in the middle should be thinned out and, if two are crossing so that they will rub together, one of the pair should be removed or at least shortened enough to prevent this happening.

It pays to buy a good pair of secateurs as they will last you for many years. They should always be kept clean and sharp. If they are not, you will bruise the stems of the roses and make rough, ragged cuts, that will encourage the entry of disease spores.

Hybrid teas
The first thing to do is to cut away all weak, twiggy growth – everything, in fact, that is thinner than a pencil. This includes the very small, matchstick-like twigs that often sprout from the main canes, and that will produce no more than a few undersized leaves if left. Cut right out any dead wood, including stumps and snags that may have been left from poor pruning in the past. Some of these may be too tough for secateurs and for them you should use a fine-toothed saw. Dead wood will be brown or greyish, with

gnarled and wrinkled bark.

Next, remove any diseased canes, or shorten them back to the first healthy bud below the diseased portion. If you cut through a cane and the centre of it is brown, this is a sign of die-back, so move down, bud by bud, until you reach healthy white wood.

You may find some quite thick and apparently healthy canes that were pruned the previous year, but from which only a few spindly twigs have grown below the old pruning cut. If this is all the canes have produced in a season, they will do no better in the next, so remove them.

All of what might be termed 'rubbish' has now been disposed of, and the remaining green and firm, healthy canes should be shortened to about 15–20cm (6–8 in). The cuts should be made about 6mm ($\frac{1}{4}$ in) above a bud, and at an angle, sloping down away from the bud. If you cannot find a bud where you want one, choose the nearest, preferably an outward-facing one, to encourage the new shoots to grow away from the centre of the plant. But once again, if you cannot find an outward-facing bud, do not think that inward growth will make the rose moody and introspective. In fact, it is not unusual, even if you do cut to an outward-facing bud, for the one below it, facing inwards, to be the one that starts away first and makes all the running. You try to point the way, but the rose does not always follow.

That is really all there is to the yearly pruning of HT roses for the average gardener. Harder pruning will produce larger flowers, but fewer of them. Rather lighter pruning is probably advisable on poor, dry soils. Unless these have a regular and massive application of fertilizer and humus, there will not be the goodness in them to promote vigorous new growth on the same scale.

Newly-planted roses
Always prune these more severely, to perhaps 8–10cm (3–4 in). This will ensure that top-growth starts later and there is more time for the energy of the plant to go into developing a sound root system early in the year. If you plant your roses in the spring, prune them at the same time.

Everybody argues about the best time to prune. Each expert has his own theory, so who is right? The answer is, of course, everybody. As long as the bushes are dormant, or nearly so, which will probably be from early winter to mid spring (end of November to end of March) in mild areas, and provided that there is no frost about, it does not matter very much

Top left and right: pruning rules for a standard depend largely on whether it is an HT or floribunda variety; be sure to keep the head a good, even shape
Above left: hard pruning will produce larger blooms on HT varieties
Bottom right: cut out old wood at source

when you prune. If there is a severe winter, autumn pruning may mean that you lose a few canes through frost damage; these can be trimmed back later. But this can happen with a bad spring frost, too. In colder districts, it is wiser to leave your pruning until well into mid, or even late, spring (late March or April).

Floribundas

These are grown mainly for their mass effect and continuity of bloom rather than, as with an HT, the beauty of their individual flowers. For this reason, and because they naturally make more new growth than an HT without the encouragement of hard pruning, they can be treated more lightly.

Basically, however, the approach is the same. Weak, dead or diseased wood is removed, and then healthy growths shortened by between one-half and one-third, cutting just above a bud as before.

Strong laterals or sideshoots should be shortened to the first or second bud.

With very strong and tall-growing varieties, like Iceberg or Chinatown, which may be wanted for specimen planting or for the back of a border, a strong framework of wood can be built up over several years. If the main canes are cut back only moderately, they will produce strong laterals that are shortened in turn the following year, producing yet further branching. Gradually, a very large bush takes shape, from which the main shoots need only be removed as they lose their vigour and are replaced by others.

Ramblers and climbers

As the methods of pruning are different, it is as well to be able to distinguish between the two, but the position is complicated by the fact that there are two types of ramblers, one being much closer to a climber in its habits than the other.

Ramblers With a few exceptions, these only flower once, some varieties doing so as late as late summer or even early autumn (July or August). The first group, that includes varieties like American Pillar, Dorothy Perkins, Excelsa and Sander's White Rambler, have large

clusters of small blooms, and throw up new canes 2m (6 ft) or so long from the base of the plant each year. Pruning consists of cutting the old canes to the ground as soon as they have finished flowering and tying the new ones in their place. With a vigorous, thorny rose, this can be a rather fearsome job, and strong, thorn-proof gloves will be needed. It is often easier to remove the old canes by cutting them into short lengths and pulling these out individually.

If new growth is poor one year, a few of the old canes can be shortened by about one-third and left in place. They will produce some flowers but not with the profusion of new ones.

The second type of rambler, that includes varieties like Albertine, has rather larger flowers and tends to produce enormously vigorous new canes, branching out from anywhere along the length of the old ones. Prune after flowering by cutting away the old just above where a new cane has sprouted. Remove unproductive or diseased old wood as and when it occurs.

Climbers As a class, climbers generally have larger flowers than ramblers, some as big and as shapely as HT roses. Many of the newer introductions and a number of the older ones flower twice. Do not prune any of them until the first year after planting. This is especially important with the climbing sports of HT and floribunda, as hard pruning then may cause them to revert to their bush form.

Many climbers do very well with little or no pruning except what is needed to keep them in bounds, but all will do much better if the laterals are shortened by about two-thirds in winter. Some varieties are extremely stubborn about producing new growth low down, and can become very bare at the base. Apart from training the canes as horizontally as possible to encourage new sideshoots to break, strong cutting-back of a main cane may help to produce others from the bottom. If this does not work, there is nothing for it but to plant something else in front of it, though not so close that it will rob the rose of the goodness in the soil.

Standard roses

Usually these are varieties of HT roses or floribundas, and pruning should be done in the same way as for the equivalent bushes. It is always important to bear in mind the balance of the head and to keep it as even as possible, as with a standard you are more likely to be seeing the rose from all sides.

Weeping standards Both of the rambler

Guide to pruning roses

HYBRID TEA **FLORIBUNDA** **STANDARD**	**Hard pruning** Newly-planted, and HT roses for exhibition blooms	**Moderate pruning** Established HT and floribunda	**Light pruning** Roses growing on poor, dry soils

RAMBLER **WEEPING STANDARD**	**Small-flowered** Cut old canes down to ground after flowering Treat head of standard as small-flowered rambler	**Large-flowered** Cut out old flowered wood to base of new lateral

CLIMBER	Don't prune when first planted, but shorten laterals by two-thirds in subsequent years
MINIATURE	Thin out dense, twiggy growth and discard dead wood; trim to shape
SHRUB	Thin out dense growth, discard dead wood, trim to shape; shorten laterals up to two-thirds

groups are used for these standards, though there is no doubt that the first, small-flowered, group are the best as their long, pliable canes weep naturally. Once again the pruning is the same as if they were growing in their natural rambling form. That is, completely remove old canes after flowering for group one; for the second type, cut back old wood above – or, perhaps, below as the canes should be hanging downwards – the point where a strong side-growth has sprouted.

Miniatures
This involves the thinning out when needed of the varieties that produce dense, twiggy growth and the removal of the few shoots that may die back each year. Some of the more vigorous varieties may send up extra-strong shoots oc-

casionally that unbalance the bush, and these should be shortened. Nail-scissors are best to use for pruning miniatures.

Shrub roses
Species roses, except in their formative years when a limited amount of cutting back may be needed in order to produce a reasonably balanced shape, should be left alone apart from the removal of dead wood. This can be taken out at any time. Pruning would destroy the natural habit of growth and this is one of the main charms of a species rose.

Apart from the removal of diseased or dead wood (that applies to all of them), most other shrub roses – damasks, albas, centifolias, moss roses, Bourbons, hybrid musks, hybrid perpetuals and modern shrub roses – need their laterals shortened

by about two-thirds at the most after flowering to encourage new growth, though they will do quite well even without this attention. Occasionally a strong main shoot can be cut hard back to encourage new growth low down.

If used in hedges, both rugosas and gallicas can be clipped over lightly in winter, rather than pruned, but this should be done following in the main their natural outline. If you are using roses you cannot expect (and should not want) the squared-off regularity of a privet or box hedge.

Varieties of shrub roses that bear heps, other than species, can be trimmed in early spring if they need it, and the pruning of tall floribundas that may be used as shrubs has already been described under the floribunda heading.

Rose Pests and Diseases

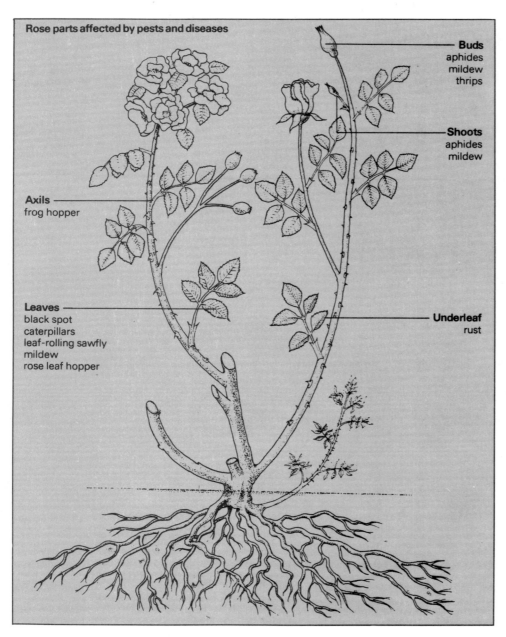

Rose parts affected by pests and diseases

Buds
aphides
mildew
thrips

Shoots
aphides
mildew

Axils
frog hopper

Leaves
black spot
caterpillars
leaf-rolling sawfly
mildew
rose leaf hopper

Underleaf
rust

could be added to the list given above, based on individual growers' experience in particular gardens or in particular districts. Even moving a variety as prone to mildew as Rosemary Rose from one part of a single garden to another has been known to bring about a cure. Dryness about the roots and lack of proper air circulation often encourages mildew, and the purer the air the more black spot flourishes. In industrial areas, where there is sulphur in the atmosphere from factory chimneys, black spot will be no problem, and it is ironic that the creation of smokeless zones, so beneficial to most things, has caused this rose disease to spread into areas where it was not known before.

So the experience of a grower of a particular variety in one part of the country may be very different from one elsewhere, but the roses named above have been found to be some of the best in all conditions.

Not everyone, however, will want to grow just these varieties, and if you have an established garden, you will have to deal with the roses already growing there, that may not be so disease resistant.

Chemical fungicide sprays are expensive, and spraying itself is not the most enjoyable of occupations. Many people feel, too, that it is risky to use chemicals, about whose long-term effects we really know very little. One has only to think back to the time, not so long ago, when DDT was used on a world-wide scale against insect pests and then was suddenly found to be harmful and withdrawn from sale, to see the force of this argument. All of which adds up to not spraying more than you have to.

If there is no sign of black spot in your garden, do not spray against it; or wait until you see the first signs of mildew before you take action. In some years it will be much less prevalent than others and only touch one or two roses.

However, there are areas, and the south-west of England is one, where black spot is always a serious problem, and there it is usual to have to carry out preventative spraying each year before the disease appears, and probably to top up regularly as often as every ten days or so for the rest of the summer. In other places, rust is the trouble, but find out from local growers what diseases your roses are likely to get, and judge from your own experience before acting.

How and when to spray

Wherever you live, you are unlikely not to have to spray against anything at all, be it insects or disease spores, so a few general

There are a number of roses that, under most garden conditions, can be said to be reasonably or almost completely free from disease. The hybrid tea roses in this category include: Pink Favorite and Honey Favorite (both outstanding), Peace, Grandpa Dickson, Wendy Cussons, Rose Gaujard, Ernest H. Morse, Red Devil, Fragrant Cloud, Chicago Peace and Gail Borden.

Some healthy floribundas are: Southampton, Matangi, Sarabande,

Escapade, Chinatown and Evelyn Fison, and among the climbers are Aloha, Mermaid and Golden Showers.

The rugosas, Chinas and a number of the species are outstanding among the shrub roses, but many of the others are so tough that they can shrug off attacks by mildew and black spot without coming to any harm, though this will not prevent them looking rather unsightly in late summer if they remain unsprayed.

Quite a large number of other roses

points about spraying should be born in mind. It is best to use a spray that produces a fine mist. Do not spray in hot sunshine, or the leaves of the rose may scorch – evening is the best time; spray sufficiently to wet the plants all over, but not to the extent of leaving them dripping, which is an awful waste of. expensive liquid. Do spray the undersides of the leaves as well as the upper surfaces.

Systemic sprays

These penetrate into the tissue of the plant. In some cases they will circulate with the sap, but not all sprays do this equally well, which is why it is important to wet the whole rose. Systemics have the great advantage, of course, that they are not washed off by rain and so will remain effective for several weeks.

Pesticides and fungicides

Great strides have been made in recent years with pesticides and fungicides. Greenfly infestation should not be a serious problem any more; mildew is largely under control; an oxycarboxin spray such as Plantvax 75 is a certain treatment for rust, and black spot, while not mastered, can at least be controlled to a large extent in all but the worst areas.

Our chart, based on one prepared by the Royal National Rose Society, should prove a useful guide as to the best sprays to be used for the different diseases and insects. As indicated, many of these chemicals can be mixed together, so that you can spray against everything (if you are unlucky enough to suffer from everything) at one and the same time. The warning given in our Note below should, however, be stressed. Make quite sure that your particular sprays are compatible. Otherwise you run the risk of losing all the leaves from your roses.

Mildew

This is the most prevalent of the rose diseases, and is carried by airborne spores from one plant to another. The first signs are generally small, grey, powdery-looking patches on the leaves and on the flower-stalks and undersides of the buds. In bad cases, the mildew will spread over the entire plant, distorting growth and preventing the second crop of flowers from opening properly. Mildew will not kill a rose, but it will ruin its appearance.

If treated promptly, mildew can nowadays be controlled, but the spraying of vigorous climbers can be a problem if they are high up on the wall of a house. Ramblers, which as a class are subject to mildew, should preferably never be planted against house walls

Aphides massed on rose stems

where air circulation will be poor.

Black spot

This is also carried by airborne spores, and usually appears first around the middle of the summer on the older, lower leaves of rose bushes. The small, circular black spots rapidly grow in size, the rest of the leaf yellows, and eventually dies and drops off. Bad attacks can completely defoliate a rose and this lack of leaves, apart from being unsightly, weakens the plant and can kill it over several seasons of repeated attacks. Spraying will help control, but no real cure has been found. Ideally, affected leaves should be picked off and burned to prevent the black spot spores from spreading.

Spores of both black spot and mildew can overwinter on leaves left on the ground, and also on the rose stems and stumps that have not been properly pruned back.

Rust

Fortunately, this is not as widespread as mildew or black spot, and only certain varieties are usually liable to attack, for a serious invasion of your garden by rust can kill the roses. Until quite recently it was recommended that badly-affected plants should be dug up and burned, but now a spray of oxycarboxin gives complete control. Rust can be recognized by

Rust affects leaves

the formation of orange pustules on the undersides of the leaves, and it should be dealt with without delay.

These, then, are the rose diseases that most rose growers will have to deal with at some time. There are also insect pests, against which modern insecticides give very good protection, but as with diseases, you also need to be able to recognize. the insect enemies to be able to deal with them. The following are the most common and troublesome.

Aphides or greenfly

Probably too well known to need description except to say that those that infest the young shoots and buds of roses can be brown and pink as well as green. They suck the sap of the plant and exude a sticky substance known as honeydew, on which a sooty mould forms. Increase is incredibly rapid, so spray promptly.

Thrips

Small, black insects that move with great

Black spot appears only in clean-air districts

speed over the plant and drop off if disturbed, only to climb back later. Hot, dry summers seem to suit thrips; nibbled-looking buds are likely to be their work and distorted flowers the outcome. Some varieties of rose are, for some reason, much more prone to attack than others, notably Ophelia and its descendants, Mme Butterfly and Lady Sylvia. One cure for thrips is said to be the covering of the beds under the roses with metal foil, as the thrips do not appear to like the reflected light coming from below! Hardly the ideal solution for most gardens.

Frog hopper or cuckoo spit

Small, green insects that hide themselves in a blob of white froth, usually at a joint between a stem or leaf and a side shoot. The nymph sucks the sap of the rose. Either the fingers (if the attack is limited), or a jet of water, should be used to remove the froth before spraying.

Rose leaf hopper
Very small, pale yellow insects, that leap high in the air if disturbed. They cause mottling of the rose leaves, and the presence of their cast-off white skins on the undersides of the leaves is a sure sign that leaf hoppers are about.

Caterpillars
In a mild attack, these can be removed by hand but Dipterex is a most effective spray. It will penetrate the leaf, and so will deal with caterpillars that have doubled a leaf round themselves, as some do when they are feeding on it.

Leaf-rolling sawfly
This pest appears to be on the increase. The name is very descriptive, for the sawfly lays its eggs on the leaves that then curl up lengthwise, protecting the grub feeding within. This makes it difficult to reach with sprays, which are only really effective if applied before an attack, which in itself is difficult to predict. Otherwise, tedious though it may be, removal of the rolled-up leaves is recommended to prevent the larvae moving on from one leaf to another when they have had enough of the first one.

Note Capsids, scale insects, chafer grubs and leaf miners can also be a problem on roses and should be controlled with the appropriate insecticide.

Roses: guide to fungicides and insecticides

FUNGICIDES FOR OUTDOOR ROSES

Active ingredient	Proprietary name	Powdery mildew	Black spot	Rust
maneb	Maneb WP		★★	★★
zineb	Dithane		★★	★★
thiram	ICI Garden Fungicide		★★	★★
captan	Orthocide or Captan		★★	
dinocap	Karathane or Dinocap	★★		
folpet	Murphy Rose Fungicide	★	★★	★
benomyl	Benlate	★★★	★★	
triforine	Gesal Rose Mildew Treatment	★★★	★★	□
oxycarboxin	ICI Plantvax 75			★★★
thiophanate-methyl	Mildothane	★★	★★	
mancozeb	Dithane		★★	★★

Home greenhouse insecticides
For all pests except mites, either: resmethrin+pyrethrum (Sprayday), or bioresmethrin (Copper Garden Spray). Against red spider mites, only water or white oil (e.g. Volck) are recommended. The following have systemic action: formothion, dimethoate, menazon and fenitothion (e.g. Fentro, Accothion). Trichlorphon (Dipterex), while not systemic, can penetrate the leaf-blade.

Compatability guide
Any two wettable powder (WP) fungicides can be mixed with one liquid insecticide, or two if one is Dipterex 80 (a solution).
More than two liquid pesticides should not be mixed together unless a trial has shown them to be compatible. For this generalization ICI Garden Fungicide (a colloidal liquid) can be considered a WP. When three or more pesticides are to be sprayed together they should be diluted separately and mixed together immediately before spray application.

INSECTICIDES FOR OUTDOOR ROSES

Insecticide	Aphides	Thrips	Capsids	Leaf hopper	Scale Insects	Caterpillars	Leaf-rolling sawfly	Chafers	Leaf miners
formothion dimethoate	★★★			★★★	★				
malathion diazinon	★★	★	★	★★	★★	★			
menazon	★★★			□					
gamma-BHC	★	★	★★	★		★		★	★★
trichlorphon						★★★	★★		★★
fenitrothion	★★	★	★	★★	□	★★	★★	★	★□

★★★ very active   ★★ moderately active   ★ slightly active   □ more evidence required   WP wettable powder

Roses for Exhibition

We end this section on roses with a look at growing for exhibition. By showing your best blooms you share their beauty with others as well as competing for perfection.

Everyone who grows roses in their garden can exhibit them at a local show and, if they are prepared to take just a little bit of trouble, win prizes with them. Getting your roses ready for showing, and eventually staging them on the day, gives an added interest to your gardening and provided that you do not take it too seriously, it can be great fun. Our advice for preparing hybrid teas and floribundas is given separately.

Hybrid teas

For local showing it is not even necessary to grow special roses. It is often said, in some cases rightly, that you should not choose HT roses for your garden from the varieties in competitive classes at shows. This is because a number of fine exhibition roses either do not stand up to rain well, or perhaps only produce a very limited number of flowers at one time. Dedicated exhibitors do not mind this and use special bloom-protectors when necessary to keep off the rain. Varieties such as Bonsoir, Gavotte, Isabel de Ortiz, Memoriam, Montezuma, Red Devil and Royal Highness only give of their wonderful best when the sun shines continuously, and Princess has fine show blooms, but not too many of them.

However, there are many roses that will produce flowers that will win in any company and are good garden roses as well. Some of these are: Alec's Red, Chicago Peace, Embassy, Ernest H. Morse, Fragrant Cloud, Fred Gibson, Grandpa Dickson, Honey Favorite, Peace, Pink Favorite, Silver Lining and Wendy Cussons. Rose Gaujard can also be a winner but has a lot of split-centred blooms, and Gail Borden and My Choice are fine if you get your timing right, as they tend to open quickly. The blooms of Perfecta, a rose that has won countless show awards, stand up to rain in themselves but tend to have some rather weak flower-stems. In the 'very double' flowers these may bend over or even snap with the weight of water after a heavy shower. A show rose should have good, strong stems and hold its flower upright.

The actual growing of your exhibition roses needs no special skill for anything other than the biggest shows. Obviously,

if they are well looked after, they will produce bigger and better blooms, so do not neglect to use the fertilizer recommended in the feature on routine care and garden cultivation in Week 34. Keep the roses well-watered and spray regularly, if this is needed, against insect pests and diseases. Healthy foliage is important in a show, as it is in the garden.

Disbudding

The only other thing that you may have to do with some varieties to get the best out of them is to disbud. A single bloom to a stem, with no side branches, is required in almost all classes for HT roses at a show. Some kinds grow naturally like this, but others – Pink Favorite and Stella are examples – often have clusters of buds at the top. Other roses do this, more in the second flush than in the first, so if you want to exhibit them, pinch out all but the main, central bud as soon as the others are large enough for you to do so. You can leave a second bud to develop a little

A magnificent show rose – this perfectly formed hybrid tea Blessings

lower down the stem if it looks as if the main one will open long before the show.

The perfect show bloom

For the actual exhibition, the bloom of an HT rose should be half to three-quarters open at the time of judging. A blown bloom will not win a prize. It should have a high, pointed centre of petals, with no sign of splitting, and the other petals should reflex as evenly as possible all round it. It should be fresh, true to colour for the variety, and as free as it can be of blemishes from weather or other damage. The size should be typical of the variety, though many judges, wrongly, give an oversized bloom preference over a typical one. Extra size should only really count where the class is for specimen blooms. Foliage should be healthy, and the stem should be firm and straight. This is the ideal but if you have days of rain before

Ceanothus Dentatus

Type	deciduous and evergreen shrub
Family	RHAMNACEAE
Flowering season	early summer to late autumn (May–October)
Planting date	bare root: mid autumn or late spring/early summer (September or May/June); from container: any time between late spring and mid autumn (April–September)

The word ceanothus comes from the Greek for a spiny plant, and dentatus (toothed) speaks for itself. The Ceanothus genus is native to California where it forms part of the Chapparal, a dense impenetrable scrub similar to the Mediterranean *maquis*. They are plants of great beauty, but are by no means always hardy except in a mild climate and may be badly damaged or even killed during severe winters.

The ceanothus are a confusing group and a plant of uncertain parentage known as *C. × veitchianus* is often met with under the name of *C. dentatus floribundus*; this is more vigorous and proving quite hardy in the milder parts of the British Isles, and it has equally brilliant flowers. It was sent home as a natural hybrid by the collector William Lobb (who had previously shipped back the *C. dentatus*) in 1853.

C. dentatus is an evergreen shrub about 2·5m (8 ft) tall, but it is often higher against a wall. Its stems are densely set with alternate narrow, resinous leaves that are about 13mm ($\frac{1}{2}$ in) long, dark green on top and grey beneath. In early summer (May), clusters of very brilliant blue flowers appear from the axils, making this one of the most attractive of all spring-flowering shrubs.

The hardiest of the evergreen ceanothus is *C. thyrsiflorus*, but the flowers are a rather pale blue and lack the richness of *C. dentatus*. It is also a much taller plant, occasionally reaching 9m (30 ft) in height, although one 6m (20 ft) tall is regarded as a fine specimen. There is a hybrid between this and *C. dentatus* known as *C. × lobbianus*, which is sometimes confused with *C. dentatus* in gardens. This has the bright blue flower of the true *dentatus*, but is hardier and more vigorous.

Ceanothus never thrive in shallow chalky soil, preferring a soil that is slightly acid and well-drained. They must have sun and do best against a south- or west-facing wall. On the other hand they do not require a particularly rich soil and it is probably the chalk rather than its lack of depth that prevents them from growing well. Although

habitually trained against a wall, the ceanothus have survived in the open in places that might be considered quite unsuitable, so you can afford to be more adventurous.

The leaves of the ceanothus are resistant to salt spray, so they are well suited to gardens near the sea that have the additional advantage of being comparatively free from frost. If they are being grown against a wall it may be necessary to prune them slightly; this is best done as soon as the flowering is over. There is nothing to be gained from pruning the evergreen type (necessary training apart), although the deciduous ones that flower in the autumn are usually pruned back in the early spring.

They are rapid growers and are generally easy to propagate from cuttings, so it is sound policy to take a few each year. They are taken at a node and should be firm but not too woody, and are normally ready by late summer or early autumn (July or August). By this means you have a reserve in case disaster strikes in the winter.

Left: ceanothus hybrid Cascade bears its flowers in elongated clusters
Above: C. thyrsiflorus, *hardiest of the evergreens*
Top: the species C. dentatus *flowers in early summer (May)*

Clematis Montana

Type	deciduous, woody climber
Family	RANUNCULACEAE
Flowering season	early summer to early autumn (May to August)
Planting date	late autumn to early summer (October to May) in mild weather
Mature size	up to 12m (40 ft)

Clematis montana is an extremely vigorous, deciduous climber, easily capable of reaching 7m (23 ft) and can, on occasion, extend even higher if trained into large trees. It ascends by means of its twisting leaf stalk that surrounds twigs in the wild. In cultivation, if you want to grow it up a wall, it is best to provide a trellis or plastic netting.

The plant is native to the Himalayas and was brought into cultivation in 1831 by that enterprising traveller Lady Amherst. When E. H. Wilson visited Szechwan, a province of China, in 1900, he sent back seed of the variety *C. m. rubens*. This has purplish petal-like sepals, known as 'tepals', and flowers a little later than the type. In addition to the purplish flowers, its young stems also have a purple colour and the young leaves have a purple-bronzy tinge. The leaves are somewhat downy while the Indian plants are more or less glabrous, or smooth. Wilson also sent back the variety *C. m. wilsonii* that bears smaller white flowers that do not open before late summer (end of June or early July). There are one or two named forms as well: Tetrarose has pink flowers up to 8cm (3 in) across; Alexander, with white flowers, and Elizabeth, with pink flowers, have the advantage of being fragrant.

The plant bears leaves made up of three leaflets; these are lance-shaped, slightly lobed and each about 5cm (2 in) long, although there is some variation in their size. The flowers arise from the leaf axils of the previous year's growth and come in clusters of about six; each flower is on a stalk that may be 10cm (4 in) long and is made up of four white tepals. The flowers each measure about 5cm (2 in) across, produce very freely and open in early summer (May).

The plant is easy to cultivate and thrives in any soil, flowering well even if trained against a north-facing wall. Like all clematis, it is very intolerant of root disturbance, so you should only purchase pot-grown specimens. If possible, the roots and the base of the stem should be kept in the shade. The plant looks very effective if trained up into a tree and allowed to ramble at will. In some positions, its vigour may be excessive, but you can prune it hard each summer as soon as flowering is

Left: Clematis montana rubens, *one of the best forms of this vigorous grower*
Top: C. montana *produces its mass of flowers in early summer (May)*
Above: brought into cultivation at the same time as C.m. rubens, C.m. wilsonii *bears its smaller flowers towards late summer (July)*

over and remove all flowered shoots. *Clematis chrysocoma*, which looks much like *C. montana*, with rather large pink flowers and young leaves covered with yellow down, is far less vigorous, although equally attractive; it can be recommended as an alternative in cases where *C. montana* might prove too vigorous.

Propagation by cuttings is easy, but slightly different from the cuttings of most woody plants. These are generally finished just below the node, that is to say where the leaf joins the stem. Clematis cuttings on the other hand are called inter-nodal and are cut half-way between two leaves. Cuttings should be taken in late summer (late June or early July) and the stem should be firm, although not woody. It is probably sufficient to allow only one full-grown leaf to each cutting and it is not necessary to have a growing point on your cutting; as soon as the cutting is well rooted, a shoot will arise from the leaf axil and they should then be potted separately in 8cm (3 in) pots either in a soilless mixture or in J.I. No 1, and subsequently potted on into a 13cm (5 in) pot. Once this pot is filled with roots, the plant can be placed in its final position.

Cotoneaster

Type	evergreen and deciduous flowering and fruiting shrubs
Family	ROSACEAE
Flowering season	mid summer (June)
Fruiting season	early autumn to late winter (August–January)
Planting date	late autumn to early spring (October–February); from containers: anytime
Mature size/shape	prostrate to 7m (23 ft); spreading, round or erect shrub

Above: Cotoneaster microphyllus, *a low-growing evergreen*

Right: C. Hybridus Pendulus, *a low-growing shrub,*

The cotoneaster genus contains a little over 50 species of shrubs all of which – with the exception of a comparatively few rarities – are obtainable without much difficulty. Among them are some of the most indispensable of hardy ornamental shrubs and even small trees. There is a cotoneaster for almost every site in the garden no matter what its environment. Large, medium, small and prostrate ones are available, evergreens and semi-evergreens, and varieties suitable for a warm, sunny position or a cold exposed garden, be it inland or on the coast. In tree form as standards and half-standards they are invaluable because they are almost the only evergreens available at this size.

Although they are an extensive and diverse race, most cotoneasters nevertheless have a strong family likeness. They all have hawthorn-like white or pinkish flowers that are either flattened or cupped in shape and often carried in clusters, mainly in mid summer (June). These blossoms are most attractive to bees, although almost insignificant compared with what, in most cases, follows them. The foliage often acquires the most beautiful rich autumnal colourings and, most striking of all, the branches become laden with attractively-coloured berries of different sizes and shapes, which can be scarlet, orange-red, purplish-red, yellow, pink-tinged yellow, crimson or black. It is in these lovely berries that the real glory of cotoneasters is to be found.

With some exceptions, the native habitat of these various species is the Far East – mainly China – while a few hail from places farther to the west – the Himalayas, Assam, Tibet, Burma, East Turkestan and Afghanistan. There are one or two species that are thought to have originated in areas still farther to the west: *Cotoneaster orbicularis* from the Sinai Peninsular and *C. lucidus* from the Altai Mountains in Mongolia – which would indeed be a testimony to its hardiness. Among the earliest to be raised successfully in Britain was *C. tomentosus*, now a very rare shrub indeed; it was taken from the European Alps in 1759.

C. simonsii, *C. horizontalis* and *C. microphyllus* can be found growing wild in the British countryside, but these are probably escapees from cultivated gardens, through birds eating the seeds and later spreading them in their droppings. There is, however, one species – *C. integerrimus* – which seems to be native to Britain. It was found growing wild on Great Orme Head above Llandudno in North Wales in 1783, but there are records of it growing in gardens in the 17th century, so even this might be a stray.

Understandably, there have been numbers of cultivars raised in Britain, but two of particular interest are *C. St Monica*, which was found in a convent garden in Bristol, and *C. splendens* Sabrina, which was raised in a garden in Somerset.

Apart from their attraction in any garden, the species have characteristics and variations that make them most valuable. They range in height from about 5–8cm (2–3 in) above the ground up to an ultimate height of about 4–5m (15 ft), with a few small trees reaching 6m (20 ft) tall. Among them there is a wide range of habits, such as prostrate, spreading, erect, arching, pendulous

and so on, that make them indispensable in any planting scheme. The trailing forms make excellent ground cover and also help to suppress the growth of weeds. Some species and their cultivars, particularly the evergreens and semi-evergreens, are excellent for hedge-making and with their rich autumn tints and colourful berries they give a most pleasing ornamental effect on the boundary of the plot or as a division between two sections of the garden. Probably they are best of all used in a shrub or mixed border where their colour will prolong some of the fading glory of the summer.

Several species and hybrids, for instance *C. buxifolius vellaeus*, *C. franchetii*, *C. horizontalis*, *C. lacteus*, *C. salicifolius* Autumn Fire, *C. salicifolius rugosus* and *C. simonsii*, make excellent wall plants. Because of their tolerance of a wide range of conditions, the aspect of the wall does not disturb them at all; they are therefore particularly valuable for growing against a north wall.

Cultivation

On the whole, cotoneasters are so robust and undemanding that they will survive and flourish in almost any soil and conditions. Most are tolerant to the environment of an industrial area and by the same token they all grow well in town gardens, where the smaller ones are especially acceptable because of space restrictions. There are some, such as *C. simonsii*, that can be planted in full shade and still prosper. On the other hand, all of them will grow well in both partial shade and sun. Many of these most accommodating shrubs and trees also grow well in coastal areas, where they will stand up to a certain amount of exposure.

As far as their soil requirements are concerned, any planting guide will tell you that cotoneasters will grow well in 'ordinary' garden soil. But if your soil is out of the ordinary, you may need a little more guidance.

All species will grow in clay soil providing it is well drained and there is no possibility of it becoming waterlogged. As this is the risk with very heavy clay, it is important to prepare such soil very thoroughly before planting this shrub. Dig it well, to a depth of one spit, removing the topsoil so that the subsoil can be broken up to ensure good drainage. Mix the excavated topsoil with sand or grit to lighten it and help the free passage of water through it, and then replace it. This should stop water remaining on the surface in wet weather.

All species are quite happy in dry acid soils. They will flourish in a shallow soil covering a chalky subsoil, which will almost certainly be alkaline in reaction. There is just one place where a cotoneaster should not be planted, and this is on a damp site: the best course is to choose some other plant that likes the conditions. The alternative (particularly as many other choice plants also dislike a permanently damp soil) is to drain the land either by digging a trench across the site, almost filling it with rubble and replacing the topsoil, or, if the condition is very serious, you may have to resort to a more elaborate scheme involving laying drainage tiles.

When and how to plant

It is only natural that the space to be allowed between cotoneasters and their neighbouring shrubs in a border depends upon the ultimate size they are likely to reach in maturity. The correct planting distance can be calculated by adding the spans of two shrubs that are to be planted alongside each other and dividing the sum by two.

Soak the rootball well before planting. Dig a hole wide enough to allow the roots to be well spread out, and of such a depth that the previous soil level will be at the surface of the soil in the new quarters. Mix a little garden compost or manure into the soil at the bottom of the hole and put the plant in position. Place a layer of similarly-enriched soil over the roots and tread it firmly in with your heel. Then add a further layer of soil, tread it in and finally fill up the hole, levelling off the soil surface.

For planting as a hedge *C. franchetii*, *C. frigidus*, *C. henryanus*, *C. lacteus*, *C. simonsii*, *C. wardii* and *C. × watereri* all make excellent berried hedges. They are planted as described above for bushes in shrubberies, the first two at 45cm (18 in) and the remainder at 60–90cm (2–3 ft) apart respectively.

For use as wall plants, those suitable should be planted about 40cm (15 in) in front of the wall and trained back to it, because very often the soil at the base of a wall keeps excessively dry.

Generally speaking cotoneasters need little attention, but do keep the soil around them free from weeds with regular hoeing. In dry weather they appreciate being watered and mulched with an 8cm (3 in) layer of garden compost, manure or damp peat. The evergreens particularly like being sprayed with water during the evening.

No regular pruning is necessary. When the large-growing shrubs have outgrown their allotted space they can be pruned back: evergreens in late spring (April) and deciduous ones in early spring (February). Trim back evergreen hedges as necessary immediately after flowering by cutting out the more vigorous shoots and side growths. Prune back the current season's shoots to the berry cluster nearest to the tip of the branch. Hedges composed of deciduous cotoneasters should be trimmed in early or mid autumn (August or September).

The evergreen C. conspicuus, *decorus in flower*

Evergreens C. Rothschildianus

Opposite:
Top: evergreen C. Exburiensis
Centre: evergreen C. Cornubia
Bottom: deciduous C. horizontalis

Propagation

Fruiting cotoneasters can be propagated by removing the seeds from the ripe berries in autumn and sowing them in pans of J.I. seed compost or a soilless seed compost and placing them in a cold frame. They normally take about 18 months to germinate. After pricking out the seedlings, first into trays or pots and then into a nursery bed, allow them to grow on for 2–3 years before transplanting them.

Remember that only seeds from species will come true; cultivars must be propagated by cuttings. Take heel cuttings of ripe evergreen shoots, about 10cm (4 in) long, in early or mid autumn (August or September), and of semi-mature deciduous shrubs in late summer or early autumn (July or August). Plant them out in a nursery bed in the following late spring or early summer (April or May) and then leave them for 2–3 years before planting out in their final positions.

An alternative method is to layer shoots in late autumn or early winter (October or November) that will root within a year.

Pests and diseases

Apart from being infested with greenfly and scale insects in the summer, cotoneasters are fairly free from pests. Possibly the most frustrating are birds, that steal their berries in wintertime. Being members of the ROSACEAE family, cotoneasters are subject to possible infection with fireblight, which blackens the flowers and kills the branches. Other diseases that might possibly affect them are honey fungus disease and silverleaf.

Some varieties to choose

Of the total number of species of fruiting cotoneasters and their varieties that exist, a very large proportion are readily obtainable from good nurseries, but the less common ones may be difficult to find in garden centres. The following list will help you to choose the best cotoneasters and their cultivars for your purpose. Many of these shrubs have fruits in varying shades of red, and any exceptions are indicated. Of the dimensions given, the first is the ultimate height, the second the ultimate spread.

PROSTRATE OR LOW-GROWING (EVERGREEN)

C. congestus	Attractive, densely-foliaged shrub, which forms mounds of small bluish-green leaves; red berries. 30cm × 2·7m (12 in × 9 ft).
C. dammeri	Very prostrate, trailing shrub, ideal for covering banks and ground cover; sealing-wax red berries. 5cm × 1·8m (2 in × 6 ft).
C. Donald Gem	Low, rounded, spreading bush with greyish leaves and long-lasting berries. 23cm × 1·5m (9 in × 5 ft).
C. microphyllus	Dwarf glossy-foliaged, spreading shrub; large, round scarlet berries. 5cm × 2·4m (2 in × 8 ft).
C. microphyllus cochleatus	Charming, slow-growing, creeping shrub with bright green leaves and scarlet berries. 2·5cm × 1·8m (1 in × 6 ft).
C. salicifolius Autumn Fire	Rather taller-growing, pendulous *semi-evergreen* shrub. Produces abundant quantities of bright orange-red berries. 30cm × 3·6m (12 in × 12 ft).
C. salicifolius Repens	Prostrate plant with very narrow leaves and small red berries, 30cm × 2·7m (12 in × 9 ft).
C. Skogholm	Vigorous, trailing hybrid with rather dark foliage and coral-red berries. 25cm × 1·8m (9 in × 6 ft).

PROSTRATE OR LOW-GROWING (DECIDUOUS)

C. adpressus	Dwarf, wide-spreading shrub, excellent for the rockery; bright red berries. Leaves turn scarlet in autumn. 40cm × 1·5m (15 in × 5 ft).
C. horizontalis Variegatus	Small, cream variegated leaves becoming suffused with red in autumn; red berries. 45cm × 1·8m (18 in × 6 ft).

MEDIUM-GROWING (EVERGREEN)

C. buxifolius vellaeus	Low, arching, spreading habit, with small leaves of frosted grey; bright red berries. 1·2 × 3m (4 × 10 ft).
C. conspicuus Decorus	Somewhat low-growing shrub, good for covering banks. Profuse red berries. 75cm × 2·7m (2½ × 9 ft).
C. Hybridus Pendulus	Prostrate, moderately low shrub; red berries. When grafted to a tall stem makes a beautiful weeping tree: 60cm × 3·6m (2 × 12 ft).

MEDIUM-GROWING (DECIDUOUS)

C. adpressus praecox	Vigorous, arching shrub with extra large, orange berries and brilliant autumn tints. 90cm × 1·8m (3 × 6 ft).
C. horizontalis	Branches in herringbone pattern. With its red berries and autumn colour it is invaluable for north- and east-facing walls and banks. 60cm × 3m (2 × 10 ft).

TALL-GROWING (EVERGREEN) – RED BERRIES

C. Aldenhamemsis (Watereri group)	Wide-spreading shrub with long, fan-like branches that bear bright red berries. 3·6 × 4·6m (12 × 15 ft).
C. Cornubia (Watereri group)	Vigorous, *semi-evergreen*. Its large red berries are so profuse that they weigh down its branches. 4·6 × 3·6m (15 × 12 ft).

TALL-GROWING (EVERGREEN) – RED BERRIES *continued*

C. conspicuus	Graceful, wide-spreading, arching branched species with abundant bright red berries. 2·1 × 2·4m (7 × 8 ft).
C. henryanus	Large, spreading evergreen or *semi-evergreen* with long, dark green corrugated leaves and crimson berries. 6 × 3·6m (20 × 12 ft).
C. John Waterer (Watereri group)	Large, *semi-evergreen* shrub with bunches of red berries. 6 × 7·6m (20 × 25 ft).
C. lacteus	Large, oval, leathery leaves with a grey, hairy underside. Its red berries last long after mid winter (December). 3 × 2·4m (10 × 8 ft).
C. pannosus	Long, slender, arching branches, and sage-green leaves. Its berries are small, rounded and deep red in colour. 2·4 × 1·8m (8 × 6 ft).
C. salicifolius	Tall and graceful, bearing heavy crops of small bright red berries. 3·6 × 3·6m (12 × 12 ft).
C. salicifolius flocossus	Graceful, with small, polished, shining green leaves, white underneath, and masses of small red berries. 2·7 × 2·7m (9 × 9 ft).
C. salicifolius rugosus	Larger flowers than usual and red berries. 6 × 6m (20 × 20 ft).

TALL-GROWING (EVERGREEN) – YELLOW BERRIES

C. frigidus Fructuluteo (or Xanthocarpus)	*Semi-evergreen* with large clusters of creamy-yellow berries. 3 × 3·6m (10 × 12 ft).
C. Rothschildianus (Watereri group)	Wide-spreading habit. Creamy-yellow berries, borne in large bunches. 3 × 2·4m (10 × 8 ft).
C. salicifolius Fructuluteo	An interesting form with yellow berries. 3·6 × 3·6m (12 × 12 ft).

TALL-GROWING (EVERGREEN) – APRICOT BERRIES

C. Exburiensis (Watereri group)	Recognizable by its apricot-yellow berries, that become pinkish in winter. 3 × 2·4m (10 × 8 ft).

TALL-GROWING (EVERGREEN) – SALMON-PINK BERRIES

C. Inchmery (Watereri group)	This shrub produces clusters of big berries, yellow turning salmon-pink. 3·6 × 3·6m (12 × 12 ft).

TALL-GROWING (DECIDUOUS)

C. bullatus	Handsome, corrugated leaves, becoming richly tinted in autumn. Large, red berries produced early. 2·4 × 1·5m (8 × 5 ft).
C. bullatus Floribundus	A form with larger clusters of flowers and berries than *C. bullatus*. 2·4 × 1·5m (8 × 5 ft).
C. Firebird	Spreading shrub with dark green leaves and dense clusters of large orange-red berries. 1·8 × 2·4m (6 × 8 ft).
C. franchetii	*Semi-evergreen* or deciduous with sage-green foliage and orange-scarlet berries. 2·1 × 1·8m (7 × 6 ft).
C. simonsii	*Semi-evergreen*, sometimes deciduous, erect shrub with large scarlet berries. 2·7 × 2·7m (9 × 9 ft).
C. wardii	Erect-growing, with dark glossy green leaves, white underneath. Berries are top-shaped and orange-red. 2·4 × 1·5m (8 × 5 ft).

SELECTION FOR WALL PLANTS

C. conspicuus Decorus, *C. Cornubia*, *C. divaricatus*, *C. franchetii*, *C. henryanus*, *C. horizontalis*, *C. microphyllus*, *C. salicifolius* Autumn Fire, *C. salicifolius flocossus*, *C. salicifolius rugosus*, *C. simonsii*, *C. wardii*.

SELECTION FOR HEDGING

C. franchetii, *C. frigidus*, *C. lacteus*, *C. simonsii*, *C. wardii*.

Berberis

Type evergreen and deciduous flowering and fruiting shrub

Common name barberry

Family BERBERIDACEAE

Flowering season spring

Planting date outdoors: deciduous varieties late autumn to mid spring (October–March; evergreen varieties mid to late autumn (September–October) or early to late spring (February–April); anytime from containers

Mature size/shape prostrate to 3·6m (12 ft) high; round, dome-shaped, pyramidal or erect

Left: Berberis thunbergii *Harlequin forms a rounded and compact deciduous shrub*
Below left: Berberis darwinii *is chiefly grown for its outstanding display of abundantly-borne spring flowers*
Below: Berberis darwinii *fruiting in autumn*

Although only a fraction of them are widely available, berberis (barberries) are members of a large genus containing over 400 species. Some of these are deciduous, while others are evergreens but, irrespective of this, most of them have similar rosette-like clusters of leaves and generally spiny stems. In some instances the evergreens have holly-like leaves, and despite their smaller size, they can be equally uncomfortable to the touch.

Some of the evergreen species and their cultivars are grown for their very handsome glossy leaves. The deciduous species, on the other hand, are more particularly cultivated for the autumn colour of their foliage and their brightly-coloured berries (or fruits). These usually last well into the winter to enliven the somewhat duller garden scene. The production of berries in autumn is not, however, entirely the prerogative of the deciduous shrubs because many of the evergreens also have them. With several important exceptions, the evergreen shrubs generally yield berries of black, blue, purple and violet while those on the deciduous types are brilliant scarlet, orange-red, coral-red, crimson, pink and, in at least one instance, orange.

Apart from a few species that come from South America, all berberis are hardy and can be grown in most gardens without difficulty.

Most berberis flower in the spring and at that time their blossoms vary in colour largely from pale yellow to orange, occasionally with a touch of red. They are often borne singly, when they sometimes wreathe the arching branches of the shrubs, but can also grow in panicles, spikes or racemes or in flat or dome-shaped flower-heads. Whatever their form, they are always beautiful, but the loveliness of their spring blossoms is only a curtain raiser to the brilliance of their autumn tints and the plethora of vividly-coloured berries of varying shapes and sizes that follow later.

Most berberis are excellent for present-day gardens, being reasonably small in stature, labour-saving and largely trouble-free. They range in size from dwarf – up to 30cm (12 in) in height – to large shrubs – but most of these do not exceed 3·6m (12 ft) in height. A large number of them have ultimate heights and spreads from 60cm to 1·5m (2–5 ft), which makes them fairly reasonable for planting in somewhat restricted spaces. It is usually possible to find a berberis to suit almost any situation, be it sunny or shady, by the sea, in country or town and whatever the soil might be (as long as it is not waterlogged).

The native habitats of the various species of this large family are pretty widespread. Many were brought to Europe from China and Japan; others were carried from central Asia by plant explorers; a few valuable species originated in South America and at least one, *B. chinensis*, hails from Russia. The latter was first cultivated in gardens in 1808. The name berberis comes from the Arabic word for berries. There is one species which is native to the British Isles (or possibly was naturalized a long time ago). This is the common barberry, *B. vulgaris*, which grew widely in hedgerows until it was discovered that it acted as a host plant to the wheat fungus disease, black rust. Since then farmers have so effectively attacked it that it has become very scarce.

While dealing with the origins of the various species, there is one group of very valuable and colourful berberis that came into being as the result of a crossing between *B. aggregata* and *B. wilsoniae* that was made in the Royal Horticultural Society's gardens at Wisley. It produced a hybrid, *B. × carminea*, which in turn has given rise to a number of clones, several of which will be described later. These cultivars are categorized as the Carminea group.

Apart from the wide height range, berberis also come in a range of shapes – rounded, pyramidal, domed, compact, prostrate – all of which are valuable for giving interest and variation in a garden. Similarly, they display between them a number of different habits, such as elegant, arching branches (often weighed down in autumn under enormous crops of berries), drooping branches, or upright growth. Some have dense growth, while most of their shoots bear sharp spines. There are some berberis that are dwarf and wide-spreading, making good ground cover, such as *B. tsangpoensis* and, in particular, *B. sieboldii*, which suckers freely and spreads rapidly.

Berberis are excellent for shrub borders and mixed beds, where the changing colours of their foliage, flowers and berries give a beautiful display. Many of them make good hedges – either dwarf for interior divisions or taller for the boundary. For the former there is little better than *B. thunbergii* Atropurpurea Nana. While excellent subjects for higher hedges are *B.* Buccaneer, *B. darwinii*, *B. julianiae*, *B. stenophylla* (which makes a tough, dog-proof hedge), and *B. verruculosa*.

Cultivation

It is doubtful whether there is any race of plants more tolerant of their environment than berberis. The evergreens flourish in sun and light shade, but to get the fullest development of the autumn tints and vivid berries, the deciduous ones are better in the sun. They are happy in industrial areas and town gardens. Some, particularly *B.* Buccaneer, *B. darwinii*, *B. × ottawensis* Superba and *B. × stenophylla* thrive beside the sea, even if there is some exposure.

Berberis grow easily and are not fussy about soil. All of them grow in clay, providing it is not so heavy that it becomes waterlogged. In such a case, take steps to improve the drainage. They will grow well in dry, acid soil and, equally, with no objection in a shallow topsoil over chalk, which will be alkaline in reaction. Their only real dislike is permanently damp soil, which would have to be drained for them. Usually this defect can be corrected by digging a trench across the ground, partially filling it with rubble and finally filling it up with some of the excavated topsoil. If this action fails, then a more drastic scheme of drainage will have to be introduced.

The deciduous species and their cultivars are best planted any time in the winter from late autumn to mid spring (October–March), when the weather is mild and the ground not excessively wet. The evergreens should be planted either in mid or late autumn (September or October) or else from early to late spring (February–April) so that the risk of exposing them to too much severe weather is lessened. Container-grown plants, of course, can be planted at any time.

Planting distances

To get an idea of how far apart shrubs should be planted, check on the ultimate spread of each (usually from a nurseryman's catalogue). The distance that two shrubs should be planted apart can be calculated by adding their two spreads together and dividing by two.

Dig a hole large enough in diameter to allow the roots of the shrub to be spread out in it, after cutting away any extra long or broken roots. To determine its depth, examine the stem of the new shrub for a mark or stain a few centimetres above the point where the roots start to spread out. This is where the soil reached to when the shrub was growing in the nursery. Make the hole to such a depth that when the roots are spread out, this mark will once again be just at the soil surface.

Careful planting makes a lot of difference to the well-being of a shrub. When the hole is dug, work some garden compost or manure into the soil at its bottom and put in the shrub, spreading out its roots. Mix more compost or manure with some of the excavated soil and cover the roots. Gently move the plant up and down a little to remove any air pockets that might have been formed and gently firm in the soil with your heel. Put in a second layer of soil, tread that in, and then fill the hole with the remaining soil. Level the surface, but do not tread the last layer of soil down.

The method of planting each shrub for a hedge is exactly the same. In order to form a good solid hedge, the planting distance between shrubs should be 45–60cm (18–24 in). The most effective-sized plants to use for this purpose are 30–38cm (12–15 in) high. After planting, give the plants about a fortnight to settle down and then prune each shrub back by about a quarter. This will encourage them to make really bushy growth and quickly produce a solid base to the hedge.

Fortunately most berberis need very little attention in order to flourish.

About 14 days after planting check that the wind has not made them loose in the soil. If it has, tread them in firmly again. (This attention should be given to *all* shrubs at the end of each winter, because frost, wind, snow and rain are likely to loosen them in the ground.)

Hoe regularly round the shrubs in order to eliminate the weeds. In dry weather particularly, berberis must be kept well watered. Give each one about 4 lit (1 gal) of water once a week during dry weather. While the soil is still moist give it a mulch with an 8cm (3 in) layer of garden compost, farmyard manure, damp peat or spent hops. A spray with cold water in the evening is also a help, particularly for the evergreens.

Berberis need no regular pruning. It is beneficial, however, periodically to remove old branches by cutting them down to the ground or a healthy bud. This encourages the growth of new wood from the base. All cutting back should, in any case, be directed towards keeping the bush an attractive shape by shortening any lengthy, untidy shoots and to maintaining it at a size appropriate to the space allotted to it. Deciduous varieties should be pruned in early spring (February), while evergreens should be cut back soon after flowering.

Trim hedges annually to keep them in shape: evergreens after flowering, deciduous ones in early or mid autumn (August or September).

Propagation

Although all species can be readily raised from seed, the resulting plants show considerable variation as berberis hybridize freely and hybrids do not come true from seed. In consequence it is more satisfactory to propagate them by rooting cuttings or layering. Some species like *B. sieboldii* that sucker freely can be reproduced by cutting off rooted suckers and replanting them where they are to grow, preferably between late autumn and mid spring (October–March).

To raise new plants from cuttings, take heel cuttings 8–10cm (3–4 in) long from lateral shoots in early or mid autumn (August–September). Plant them in a cold frame in an equal mixture of peat and sand. The following spring plant them out in a nursery bed, where they should be allowed to remain for one or two years before being transplanted to their final positions. Often cuttings of evergreen berberis are better if they are initially rooted in small pots of J.I. No 2 and then plunged in the soil outdoors, from which position they can be planted out.

The alternative method of propagating is by layering which consists of selecting a low-growing, non-flowering, flexible shoot that can be pulled down to the ground. Make an incision behind a bud at the point where it touches the ground, bury this point in the soil, firming it well in and holding the tip upwards. Fix the bend in position by means of a stone and hold the tip vertically by tying it to a stake. A shoot should be layered in mid autumn–early winter (September–November). In about a year's time, roots will form and the shoot can be severed at a point close to the root on the nearside and planted out.

Pests and diseases

Berberis are fairly free from pests, nor are they very prone to disease, but they are sometimes attacked by honey fungus, which can be detected by the presence of honey-coloured toadstools in the vicinity and by digging the surrounding soil and finding long black threads like bootlaces. The latter give this fungus its popular name of 'bootlace fungus'. If a plant is badly affected, dig it up and burn it.

Right: Berberis aggregata *heavily laden with coral-red berries; this shrub originated in W. China*

Some varieties to choose

As can be appreciated with such a large plant family as that of the berberis, only a small number of them are readily available. The first figure given under each variety description is the ultimate height and the second figure the ultimate spread of the plant.

EVERGREEN

B. candidula	Dome-shaped shrub with dark green leaves with silvery white beneath. Bright yellow flowers, blue-black berries. 60 × 60cm (2 × 2 ft).
B. verruculosa	Compact, slow-growing shrub with dark leaves, white underneath, golden-yellow flowers and black berries. 1·2 × 1·2m (4 × 4 ft).
B. hookeri	Compact shrub with leaves, glaucous underneath. Berries green at first, turning black. 1·5 × 1·5m (5 × 5 ft). Nana is a dwarf form. 75 × 75cm (2½ × 2½ ft).
B. gagnepainii	Erect branches and black berries. Good for hedges. 1·8 × 1·4m (6 × 4½ ft).
B. darwinii	Holly-like leaves, clusters of rich yellow or orange tinged with red blooms. followed by blue berries. 2·7 × 2·7m (9 × 9 ft). Prostrata is a useful dwarf form.
B. stenophylla	Outstanding shrub with arching branches laded with golden flowers in spring, followed by somewhat sparsely-produced purple berries. 2·7 × 3·4m (9 × 11 ft).
B. linearifolia	Erect shrub with rich orange-red blooms, followed by black berries with a white bloom. 3 × 1m (10 × 3½ ft). Orange King is an outstanding form. 1·8 × 1·2m (6 × 4 ft).

DECIDUOUS

B. wilsoniae	Dense, mound-forming shrub with sea-green leaves, giving autumn tints and coral-red berries. 90 × 90cm (3 × 3 ft).
B. sieboldii	Compact, suckering shrub with bright green leaves, borne on red stems, turning rich carmine in autumn. Yellow flowers and red berries. 1 × 1m (3½ × 3½ ft).
B. thunbergii	Compact bush with brilliant autumn foliage and bright red berries. 1·2 × 1·8m (4 × 6 ft). Atropurpurea has reddish-purple leaves that become more intense in autumn. Atropurpurea Nana is a charming dwarf form of the last named. 38 × 38cm (15 × 15 in). Erecta is an upright-growing version. 1·5m × 45cm (5 × 1½ ft).
B. aggregata	Dense shrub with yellow flowers in late summer (July) with red and orange leaves and coral-red berries in autumn. 1·5 × 1·5m (5 × 5 ft).
B. buxifolia	Dark green leaves, grey underneath, yellow flowers, purple-black berries. 1·8 × 1·8m (6 × 6 ft). Nana is a dwarf variety. 45 × 45cm (1½ × 1½ ft).
B. dictyophylla	Leaves, white beneath, are carried on white bloom-covered red stems and turn red in autumn. Yellow flowers are followed by large red berries. 2 × 1m (7 × 3½ ft).

CARMINEA GROUP

B. Buccaneer	Erect-growing shrub with large, deep red berries. 1·2 × 1·2m (4 × 4 ft).
B. Pirate King	Dense-growing bush with fiery orange berries. 1·8 × 1·2m (6 × 4 ft).

Galtonia

Type	bulbous perennial
Common name	summer hyacinth
Family	LILIACEAE
Flowering season	late summer–early autumn (July–August)
Planting date	mid spring (March)
Mature size	1·2m (4 ft) flower spikes

The *Galtonia candicans* (originally called *Hyacinthus candicans*) is a showy though rather elegant plant from south-west Africa and is named after the widely-travelled anthropologist and geneticist Sir Francis Galton (1822–1911).

The plant is cheap and easy to grow. Its large bulbs – that you buy at the same time as gladiolus corms – should be planted in mid spring (March) about 10cm (4 in) deep and 30cm (12 in) apart. They throw out a rosette of strap-shaped leaves that may be as much as 60cm (2 ft) long. In late summer and early autumn (July and August) it releases a stem up to 1·2m (4 ft) in height, and the top 30cm (12 in) is composed of bell-shaped white flowers about 4cm (1½ in) long that have a faint fragrance.

Galtonias will survive outside at all times but in cold districts it is better to plant them about 15cm (6 in) deep for added protection. They need well-drained soil and full light.

Galtonia princeps is a species that has come back into cultivation owing to its popularity with flower arrangers. Smaller than *Galtonia candicans* and bearing pale green flowers, it is just as easy to grow. It is not, however, conspicuous while it is growing and you should put it into the cutting border, if you indulge in such a refinement.

The delicate, bell-like flowers of Galtonia candicans, *that appear towards the end of summer, give off a light fragrance that is especially evident when the plants are grown in a clump*

Hamamelis

Type	hardy, deciduous shrub
Common name	witch hazel
Family	HAMAMELIDACEAE
Flowering season	mid winter–early spring (December–February)
Planting date	late autumn–mid spring (October–March); from containers, anytime
Mature size	1·8–3m (6–10 ft) high, 1·8–2·5m (6–8 ft) spread

The name hamamelis is said to come from *hama* and *mela*, the Greek words for together and fruit, because flowers and fruit can sometimes be found side by side on the same plant. It was discovered in China by the plant collector Charles Maries in 1878 but was relatively unused in Britain for about 20 years after this.

These deciduous plants need not be pruned, although if the side branches are cut back in the formative years a small 'trunk and tree' effect is produced, rather than the natural bush shape. The plants will withstand cold conditions and even the flowers will not be damaged by a touch of frost. A light, loamy soil suits them best, with an addition of peat or leaf mould at planting time.

Propagation is easiest from seed but they often do not germinate for two years. Sow seed in boxes of soil, peat and sand mixture. The Chinese and Japanese varieties of hamamelis are often grafted onto *Hamamelis virginiana* to give them a vigorous root-stock, as cuttings of these varieties are difficult to root. Grafting should be done under glass in the spring.

Hamamelis japonica from Japan has slightly-fragrant yellow flowers. The variety *H. j. arborea* is more vigorous and has darker-coloured flowers, while *H. j. zuccariniana* has lemon-yellow flowers that do not appear until mid spring (March).

Hamamelis mollis from China is often said to be the most beautiful. It has a primrose-like fragrance with golden-yellow flowers that proliferate from mid winter to early spring (mid December to mid February). *H. m.* Pallida, a recent variety, produces large, sulphur-yellow flowers in clusters.

Hamamelis virginiana, the American witch hazel, flowers in the autumn before the leaves fall, and as the flowers are altogether smaller than their Asian counterparts, they are not easily seen. The bark and leaves of this plant are the source of a medicinal oil used in the preparation of bay rum.

There are now several new forms and hybrids. Successful varieties include *Hamamelis × intermedia* Diana, a red-flowered cultivar, and *H. × i.* Jelena with large, coppery flowers and spreading habit; the leaves of both colour well in autumn.

Above: Hamamelis japonica arborea, *a tall-growing variety, flowering in spring*
Below: Hamamelis mollis, *most popular of witch hazels, in flower during winter*

Ilex

Type	evergreen and deciduous, green and variegated, berried trees and shrubs
Common name	holly
Family	AQUIFOLIACEAE
Flowering season	late spring – early summer (April–May)
Fruiting season	early winter – early spring (November–February)
Planting date	late spring – early summer (April–May), or mid – late autumn (September–October)
Mature size/shape	height 45cm–9m (18 in–30 ft), spread 1–9m (3–30 ft). Various, from conical to weeping

To many people, holly bushes are merely plants that grow wild, with their brilliant red berries set deep among the rich green, spiny leaves providing the most lovely, colourful, welcoming decorations for our homes each Christmas. There are also moments when these same bushes, seen growing without any berries, are deadly dull. Yet when laden with fruit, particularly when it peeps through their leaves whitened with glistening snow, holly can present a beautiful sight.

However, this large genus – composed of 300 species of tender and hardy, deciduous and evergreen, trees and shrubs – provides many elegant specimens that are hardy in a temperate climate. It is doubtful whether any genus of trees and shrubs presents greater variety or is more versatile than ilex; beyond the bounds of the very popular green-leaved, red-berried species and their cultivars there are others with a wide range of leaf colorations and markings; berry tints, shapes, stem colourings and other variations give almost infinite opportunities for ringing the changes in the garden scene.

It is as well to mention at the outset that their somewhat inconspicuous white and green flowers that appear in late spring and early summer (April and May) display very little beauty and are likely to pass unnoticed. Male and female flowers are usually borne on separate trees; when these are planted side by side, the females yield masses of berries that last well into the winter until they are ultimately eaten by birds. Some cultivars, however, are self-fertile (or hermaphroditic); examples of these include *Ilex × altaclarensis* J. C. van Tol and *I. aquifolium* Pyramidalis.

As far as shape is concerned it is possible to find ilex that grow as tall and wide pyramids, or miniatures, such as *I. crenata* Mariesii that makes an excellent subject for rockeries, and *I. c.* Golden Gem that grows to a height of 30–60cm (12–24 in) with a spread of 60–120cm (2–4 ft). Between these limits, there are round bushes, ones of conical and columnar shapes, and others with weeping and fastigiate habits.

In terms of size there is also a wide selection. Two of the smaller hollies have been mentioned already. At the other end of the scale are found heights of up to 9m (30 ft) and spreads of the same dimensions. Fortunately most hollies do not mind being pruned so that size can be largely controlled; although most hollies are naturally pyramidal, the shape too can be modified to a certain extent by judicious cutting back.

Much of the attraction of members of the ilex genus lies in the variously-sized coloured berries they produce that are so evident in winter. In the majority of species and hybrids they are red, but on *I. aquifolium* Amber they are bronze-yellow; *I. a.* Bacciflava's are yellow, while those of the deciduous *I. decidua* and the evergreen *I. latifolia* are orange. The berries of *I. crenata*, *I. glabra* (the inkberry) and *I. macrocarpa*, another deciduous

species, are all shiny black.

Although holly trees and shrubs are both evergreen and deciduous, the evergreen types are far more common.

Many of the holly cultivars have splendid foliage so varied in character that it is hard to do them credit in a few words. Some, such as *I. × altaclarensis* Camelliifolia, have reddish-purple hues in their green leaves when they are young. Quite a number of plants have reddish or purple stems. Among these are *I. × altaclarensis* Maderensis Variegata and *I. aquifolium* Madame Briot. There is at least one species, *I. serrata*, that is deciduous and has attractive tints in autumn.

Perhaps the most exceptional species is the Canary Island holly, *I. platyphylla*, that has dark green, leathery, short-toothed leaves, sometimes 13cm (5 in) long and 7cm (2¾ in) wide. These are closely rivalled by the large, bold leaves of *I. latifolia*. It is striking how holly leaves vary in shape. The most intriguing leaf forms are the bat's wing shapes of *I. pernyi*, rivalled only by the kite-shaped leaves of *I. cornuta* O. Spring. Most holly leaves have sharp spines but a few are spineless, or almost so, such as *I × altaclarensis* Camelliifolia and *I. aquifolium* Pyramidalis. Another curiosity in this respect is the silver form of the hedgehog holly, *I. aquifolium* Ferox Argentea, that has spines arising from the surface of the leaves. Lastly, and perhaps the most unholly-like of all, is the dwarf *I. crenata* Mariesii that is crowded with tiny round leaves.

The species and cultivars that have variegated foliage possibly constitute the crowning glory of the ilex genus. Many claim that it includes among the best of the variegated shrubs. A great number of shades and patterns have been woven on the leaves of this type of holly and the many combinations include splashings, mottling, blotching, stripes and, very often, edgings. These may consist of any of the following colours: green, pale green, gold, yellow, creamy-white, white and grey.

Hollies are very tolerant as a group. While *I. crenata*, *I. aquifolium* and their cultivars are content in dry-acid soil, all will grow in clay soil; in fact, *I. aquifolium* and its varieties are happy in both extreme acidic and alkaline conditions. One holly at least, the deciduous *I. verticillata*, with its autumnal, yellow-tinted foliage, flourishes on a damp site. Deep shade does not worry either *I. × altaclarensis* or *I. aquifolium* and their cultivars. Both the latter, together with *I. cornuta* and its hybrids, withstand atmospheric pollution in industrial towns. Exposure at the seaside is no problem to *I. × altaclarensis* and *I. aquifolium* and their cultivars; *I. × altaclarensis* Maderensis is especially resistant to strong winds.

I. aquifolium, the common holly, has a very widespread habitat throughout the world stretching from Europe to North Africa and China. It has been in cultivation since ancient times. Over the

Left: I. a. Aureomarginata, an ornamental variety

years it has been used to decorate cottages and mansions in the depth of winter, particularly at Christmas when so many other shrubs are leafless and colourless.

Many of the forms and cultivars grown today are of garden origins, but there are still a large number of species that have originated in widely-separated parts of the world: China, Japan, the Himalayas, North America and the Canary Isles.

With such variation and brilliance of colour, these plants are obviously of value to present-day gardens. They are fairly slow-growing and most of them can be readily trimmed, so size will not become a problem for a long time. Another great asset they possess is their ability to offer a wide range of shapes that help so much in creating a harmonious garden scene. They can be splendid when planted as specimens in a long stretch of grass. The more columnar forms make excellent markers for a gateway and might well supersede some of the conifers of similar habit. In a shrubbery, or simply a shrub border, you can use some of the brilliantly-coloured varieties most effectively to brighten up dark spots and create interest with their variety of size and shape.

Several species and their cultivars make good hedges that are easily kept in shape – and with the sharp spines of the leaves they are almost impenetrable to man and beast. *I. aquifolium* and its cultivars Argenteomarginata and Madame Briot make excellent hedges of this sort, while *I. × altaclarensis* Camelliifolia, *I. × a.* Golden King and *I. × a.* J. C. van Tol make very beautiful but less prickly ones. *I. crenata* Convexa, reaching 1·2m (4 ft) in height, makes a superb low hedge.

Cultivation

We have already referred to the tolerance shown by the ilex genus. Practically all its members are hardy so when they are established there is little fear of their meeting disaster. They will grow quite well in both sun and shade. However, it must be remembered that the variegated types need plenty of sun to colour well.

They can be grown in any ordinary garden soil but if something a bit moist and loamy can be provided the results are better.

The best times to plant hollies are late spring (late April), early summer (May), or mid to late autumn (September to October), although if the weather is good you can plant them at any time during the winter. You can, of course, plant containerized plants at any time of the year.

You calculate the distance that must be allowed between a holly and its neighbour in the normal way by adding the ultimate spread of each together and halving the sum. When planting a hedge, place hollies 60cm (24 in) apart.

It is best to plant holly (particularly the variegated forms of *I. aquifolium*) by digging a hole of such a diameter that it will take the rootball intact and of such a depth that the main stem is buried to the same extent as when it was growing in the nursery. When replacing the soil, firm it well by treading it in. When it is dry you must water the

plants frequently. Always use young plants as larger ones very much resent root disturbance. If they are exposed to high winds during winter give them some protection by erecting a screen of sacking, polythene or wattle on the windward side, until they are established – after which they will need little attention. No regular pruning is required but if you want to clip holly to size and shape it, this should be done in late summer or early autumn (July or August). Hedges should be trimmed every year in late spring (April).

Keep a watch to check that no shoots on variegated hollies revert to green. If you find any, remove them immediately.

Holly is fairly free from disease but may be attacked by leaf miners. The larvae of this pest tunnel into the holly leaves. They should be sprayed regularly with BHC between mid summer and late autumn (June and October).

Propagation
Hollies are propagated by means of cuttings taken in early autumn (August). In addition they may be layered in late autumn (October). (For detail on these techniques see Weeks 11 and 12.)

Some varieties to choose
The following is a selection of the most popular of the hollies grown today. The first figure given in the dimensions is the ultimate height, and the second is the spread.

I. × altaclarensis
Has dark green leaves. Produces red berries. Has many beautiful cultivars, some of which are given below. 7·5 × 4·5m (25 × 15 ft).

I. × a. Balearica	Erect tree with almost spineless green leaves. Berries quickly. 7·5 × 3m (25 × 10 ft)
I. × a. Golden King	One of the best variegated, golden hollies. Red berries. 7·5 × 4m (25 × 12 ft)
I. × a. Hodginsii	Strong, vigorous male clone with purple stems. 7·5 × 4·5m (25 × 15 ft)
I. × a. Silver Sentinel	Erect, creamy-white and grey variegated, berry-producing tree. 7·5 × 2·5m (25 × 8 ft)
I. × a. Wilsonii	Dome-shaped tree with large clusters of red berries. 7·5 × 3·5m (25 × 11 ft)

I. aquifolium
Common holly, with an ultimate height and spread of 7·5 × 3m (25 × 10 ft); has numerous cultivars.

I. a. Angustifolia	Neat, pyramidal tree. Tiny red berries. 4·5 × 2·5m (15 × 8 ft)
I. a. Argenteomarginata	Perry's silver weeping
Pendula	holly has bright red berries. 3 × 4·5m (10 × 15 ft)
I. a. Aureomarginata	Has golden-edged leaves. Female trees bear red berries. 5·5 × 3m (18 × 10 ft)
I. a. Bacciflava	Has bright yellow berries. 5 × 5·5m (16 × 18 ft)
I. a. Golden Queen	Gold-margined leaves. No berries. Columnar 4·5 × 2·5m (15 × 8 ft)
I. a. Handsworth New Silver	Modest-growing tree with purple stems and grey and creamy-white colouring on leaves. Red berries. 4 × 2m (12 × 6 ft)

I. cornuta Burford Variegated
Leaves edged gold and suffused with varying shades of green. 3 × 3m (10 × 10 ft).

I. crenata
Small, slow-growing holly. Females have black berries. Excellent as a hedge. The cultivars are dwarf or modest growing. 2·5 × 2m (8 × 6 ft).

I. c. Convexa	100 × 75cm (3 × 2½ ft)
I. c. Golden Gem	45 × 100cm (1½ × 3 ft)
I. c. Mariesii	45 × 100cm (1½ × 3 ft)

I. pernyi
Has dwarf, pyramidal growth, near-triangular in shape; pale green leaves and small bright red berries. 2 × 1·2m (6 × 4 ft).

Left: Ilex aguifolium *Handsworth New Silver, a female clone with long, deeply-variegated, spiny leaves*
Below: Ilex crenata mariesii, *an unusual dwarf-growing form, compact, round-leaved and suitable for growing in a rock garden or trough*

Paeony

Type	deciduous, flowering, herbaceous and shrubby perennials
Family	PAEONIACEAE
Flowering season	early–mid summer (May–June)
Planting date	mid–late autumn or mid spring (September–October or March)
Mature size/shape	herbaceous perennials: height and spread 75cm (2½ ft); shrubby perennials: height and spread 1.8m (6 ft); mainly rounded and erect

Paeonia was so called by the Greeks after Paen, a physician of the gods mentioned in Homer's 'Iliad', who was changed into a plant in gratitude for his cures by Pluto, god of the underworld.

These superb plants, that are counted among the aristocrats of the garden, are members of a genus comprising 33 species. For a long time they were part of the very large RANUNCULACEAE family, but now they have been reclassified, forming their own family called PAEONIACEAE.

The species are either hardy herbaceous perennials or woody shrubs. They are grown for their very beautiful, colourful flowers and for their most attractive leaves. Two of the shrub species, *Paeonia potaninii* and *P. lutea*, are renowned for their splendid foliage that is distinctly architectural in quality. The appeal of their leaves is a characteristic that persists to a great extent throughout the whole genus. For this reason many paeonies are cherished by flower arrangers.

Their leaves vary in colour from the pale green of *P. lutea* to the dark green of *P. obovata*, and in form from the lacy leaves of *P. × smouthii* to the deeply-cut foliage of *P. officinalis*. In the case of *P. delavayi* in particular, the flowers are followed by large, black-seeded fruits surmounted by distinctively-coloured, persistent sepals. In the case of many other species, the pods open wide in autumn to reveal their glossy, blue-black seeds. Both the herbaceous and shrubby plants are deciduous. Many of the herbaceous type are notable for the autumn tints of their leaves.

The greatest attraction of paeonies lies in their glorious large, showy flowers that range in shape from globular to bowl-shaped, sometimes like those of the giant kingcup or marsh marigold. Often they open out flat when mature, revealing in many cases the brilliance of their golden stamens. Sometimes they are single, sometimes double. It is regrettable, with such a display, that they do not remain in flower for a longer period.

The herbaceous and shrubby paeonies present a wide range of colours. Among their ranks are found white, blush white, yellow, flesh, silvery-pink, apple-blossom pink, cherry-rose, rose-pink, brilliant crimson, deep red and black-crimson, and some with centres of a different colour such as sulphur yellow. Others have scented flowers.

So far no account has been taken of the division of the genus between herbaceous perennials and shrubby plants. This must be done, of course, because at some points in their cultivation they differ. The physical difference is that the herbaceous paeonies are softwood plants, whereas the shrubby types, often called 'tree paeonies', have hardwood stems and branches. Possibly the other main difference exists in the height to which they grow. This influences the manner in which they are employed in a garden. The average height of the herbaceous perennials is 75cm (2½ ft) while the hardwood shrubs are taller, reaching up to a height of 1.5–1.8m (4–6 ft).

Paeonies are quite hardy and will pass uninjured through all but the harshest winters. However, it is as well to protect them when they are young; tree paeonies in particular need to be guarded against spring frosts because their new season's growth appears quite early.

Herbaceous perennials take a while to become established and they very much resent being disturbed after they have settled in. But once this has happened they are so hardy and durable that they last for a long time. This is probably why the well-known crimson-flowered, herbaceous paeony, *P. officinalis*, is so often seen going from strength to strength in gardens of historic manor houses, cottages and sometimes, with an air of great superiority, inner-city terraced houses. If historians could trace their records, it is highly probable that they would be found to have been in those same places for several hundred years.

Although the common red paeony and its pink counterpart is frequently found in gardens in Britain, there is no real evidence that any of the species are native to the country. One in particular, *P. mascula* (also known as *P. corallina* because its ripe seed pods open in autumn to show their rose-red seed) has been found growing wild through the ages in parts of southern England. It is, however, more likely that these are strays from cultivation, particularly as some can be seen close to the sites of ancient monasteries.

Like so many of our garden plants, the places of origin of the various species of paeony are quite widespread. *P. lutea* hails from Tibet, *P. delavayi* from western China, *P. mlokosewitschii* comes from the Caucasus and *P. cambessedesii* was introduced from the Balearic Isles. Other places that can claim to be the habitat of paeony species are Asia Minor, south-eastern Europe, the western Himalayas, Manchuria, Mongolia and Siberia.

Historically, much is due to French hybridists such as Calot, Dessert, Crousse, whose name crops up in some of the present-day varieties, and Lemoine; during the 19th century these men developed the cultivars that have led to the wonderful varieties we know today. Outstanding examples are the very fine, highly-scented, cream Duchesse de Nemours that Calot raised in 1855, and Lemoine's Edulis Superba.

Both tree and herbaceous paeonies are excellent subjects for a mixed border as neither grows very tall. The rather rounded form of the latter and the more upright, tall shape of the former make valuable contrasting shapes, not only between each other, but also by comparison with the other occupants of the bed. Both types are valuable because they like semi-shade and can be used to enliven a somewhat less interesting border devoted to shade-loving plants. The herbaceous paeonies, because they are so long lived, are extremely valuable if planted in a forward position in a shrubbery where they can display their large, gorgeous blooms during early and mid summer (May and June) against a background of variously-coloured foliage that later in autumn acts as an excellent foil to their rich, red-bronze leaves. Similarly, in spring, the new leaves of the deciduous shrubs display a matching tint, giving interest to what might otherwise be a dull scene. Paeonies grow quite well under mature ornamental cherries and other flowering trees, where they are very good ground cover.

Planting

Paeonies will grow in sunny positions or half-shade, although the shrubby paeonies like more sun. They are, however, best planted in a position

Left: Paeonia mlokosewitschii, *set in a mixed border; its seed pods make a striking display in autumn*
Below left: Paeonia suffruticosa, *a bowl-like single-flowered species, filled with golden stamens, that does well on chalk*
Below: Paeonia officinalis Rubra Plena; *this double-flowered, crimson cultivar makes a handsome addition to the border*

away from early-morning sun to avoid any possible damage following a night frost. A sheltered situation is also helpful.

All paeonies will grow in any moist, well-drained garden soil; it should be deeply dug before planting and have a liberal amount of decayed farmyard manure or compost mixed into it.

The bushy herbaceous paeonies should be planted about 75–90cm (2½–3 ft) apart and tree paeonies with about 1.8m (6 ft) between them. Both types can be planted in mid or late autumn or mid spring (September, October or March).

Do not place the crowns of herbaceous perennials deeper than 25cm (10 in) otherwise they fail to flower. The union graft of shrubby paeonies should be put 8cm (3 in) deep.

Cultivation and propagation

Water paeonies freely when they are dry and protect them against severe frost. Mulch them annually with well-rotted manure or compost in late spring (April) but do not disturb their roots. Dead-head them regularly and cut down the foliage of herbaceous paeonies in late autumn (October). They require no pruning except for the cutting out of any dead wood on tree paeonies in the spring.

You can raise both types from seed by sowing them in pots put into a cold frame in mid autumn (September). Then plant them out into a nursery bed the following early summer (May), from which they can be transplanted during the winter three or four years later. Only species come true from seed. You can also divide and replant root clumps during mid autumn (September).

The shrubby species can be layered in mid spring (March) and will take two or more years to form roots. Cuttings of tree paeonies 15–25cm (6–9 in) long can be taken in late autumn or early winter (October or November) and planted in a shady nursery bed where they should remain for about two years before being planted out. Named varieties can be grafted onto herbaceous stocks from late summer through to early autumn (mid July to August).

Some varieties to choose

The following selection of paeonies is divided between shrubby types and herbaceous perennials. The dimensions given after the species listed correspond to height and spread respectively.

Shrubby species (tree paeonies)

P. delavayi
An attractive shrub that produces deep crimson flowers with golden anthers and has large, deeply-cut leaves. 2m × 2m (6½ × 6½ ft).

P. lutea
This shrub has beautiful, deeply-cut leaves. During early or mid summer (May or June) it produces large, golden blooms. 1.8 × 1.8m (6 × 6 ft).

P. lutea ludlowii
A more robust, splendid form, yielding large golden-yellow, saucer-shaped blooms. 1.8 × 1.8m (6 × 6 ft).

P. suffruticosa (moutan paeony)
This species has white single flowers 15cm (6 in) across, with a magenta-pink blotch at the base, that open in early summer (May). 1.8 × 1.8m (6 × 6 ft). It has given a range of the most attractive varieties that are popular nowadays. A selection of these includes: Comtesse de Tudor, large double, salmon-pink; Lactea, single, white blooms with blotched purple centre; Hanadaijin, double, purple; Louise Michelet, double, rose-shaded salmon; and Osiris, very dark, purplish-red flowers.

P. × lemoinei
This cross between *P. lutea* and *P. suffruticosa* is a handsome shrub producing enormous yellow flowers in early summer (May). 1.8 × 1.8m (6 × 6 ft). Very attractive varieties are Alice Harding, double, canary-yellow; Chromatella, double, sulphur yellow; and Souvenir de Maxime Cornu, fragrant, very large, bright yellow, edged with carmine.

Herbaceous perennials

P. lactiflora
This is a very important species, the forerunner of the Chinese paeony, that is rarely grown nowadays and has been superseded by its numerous varieties. They mainly have heights and spreads of 75–90cm (2½–3 ft). A recommended selection is: Albert Crousse, delicate pink, crimson centred; Duchesse de Nemours, cream to white, scented; Felix Crousse, fully double, brilliant crimson; Lady Alexander Duff, rose-scented, pale pink with golden anthers; Mons Martin Cahuzac, fragrant, black-crimson, and – perhaps the most popular – Sarah Bernhardt, apple-blossom pink.

P. officinalis
This is the favourite of cottage gardens. It has single, crimson flowers that are produced during early and mid summer (May and June). Although it is found growing in many old gardens it cannot be bought easily today and it has been replaced by several most attractive cultivars. 75–90cm (2½–3 ft). Among the best are: Alba Plena, double white; J. C. R. Wegulin, single, garnet with crimson-yellow anthers; deep pink, double, Rosea Plena; and Rubra Plena, double, crimson.

P. cambessedesii
The gem among paeonies. Its leaves are green on top and purple beneath. Its flowers are deep rose and pink 6–10cm (2½–4 in) across with red filaments. They are produced in late spring and early summer (April and May). 45cm (18 in).

Calendula

Type	hardy annual
Common Name	pot marigold
Family	COMPOSITAE
Flowering season	early summer to late autumn (May–October)
Sowing date	outdoors mid to late spring (March–April) or mid autumn (September)
Mature size/shape	30–60cm (12–24 in)
Special use	petals in cooking

Calendula originated in southern Europe, but had travelled to the north of the continent by the 14th century, when it was widely known in England. It was often used in cooking as a kind of poor man's substitute for saffron, when colouring was needed, and the petals added flavour to a stew – hence the term 'pot' marigold. It was also popular as a herbal remedy for a number of ailments, including measles. Today it is rarely grown for its medicinal properties, but as a hardy border annual, although adventurous cooks still find uses for the petals in the kitchen. To dry the petals, first separate them and then put them in a slow oven until they crumble when touched. Store them in an airtight jar and use them to add colour to rice or soups. As with dock leaves, the flowers rubbed over a wasp sting are said to ease the pain.

The calendula colour spectrum goes from pale gold and chrome yellow to subtle tawny and darkest orange
Top: Beauty Pacific
Centre: Monarch Mandarin
Bottom: Radio

The calendula's typical marigold shades of orange and yellow add a really bright splash of colour to your border or tubs. Some varieties are quite tall for bedding plants, so plan to have a ground-hugging plant with them. The newer dwarf varieties look particularly good in window boxes with nasturtiums trailing below them. Popular varieties include Orange King and Radio – both doubles – and the more traditional single-flowered Golden King. The new Baby Orange is especially good.

If planting out in beds, allow about 30cm (12 in) between each one. Deadheading will encourage new blooms throughout the summer, and calendulas are good for cutting too – though watch out for the multibranching varieties.

These hardy annuals can be sown *in situ* in mid autumn (September), for flowering the following summer. This is a very simple operation nowadays, with the pelleted seeds currently available. Alternatively they can be started in a cool greenhouse (about 13°C, 55°F) or cold frame in mid spring (March) and pricked out into individual pots. They will then be ready for transferring to your border or tubs when daffodils and tulips are dying down towards early summer (early May).

Rhododendrons

Type	evergreen and deciduous flowering shrubs
Family	ERICACEAE
Flowering season	late winter to late summer (January–July)
Planting date	outdoors: mid to late spring (March–April) or autumn (September–October); from containers: anytime
Mature size/shape	prostrate to 12m (40 ft) spreading or bushy
Special use	Permanent ornamental foliage and flowering shrubs or small trees

Between them, the rhododendron and the rose have revolutionized British gardens, and it has all happened in the last hundred years or so. Rhododendrons were grown long before that but they were a rather dull lot and made no impact on ordinary gardeners. The first to arrive from Asia Minor in 1763 was *Rhododendron ponticum*, and it liked the British climate and soil so much that it soon escaped from gardens and began to naturalize itself. It is now the common rhododendron of many woodlands and some moorlands, a shrub much used as cover for game and also as a windbreak or hedge, but seldom nowadays as an ornamental garden shrub. Its purplish-mauve colour is too restricted, its flowers insufficiently impressive, to stand competition with the beauties that have since arrived. Nevertheless it is still a very common rootstock for other rhododendron cultivars. The name is derived from the Greek *rhodon* (a rose) and *dendron* (a tree).

The revolution began with the discovery in the mid-19th century of previously unknown rhododendrons in the Himalayas and in the mountain ranges and valleys of Burma, Assam and southern and south-western China. What started as a trickle became a flood and today botanists recognize 500–600 distinct species.

Not all the newcomers were beauties or even of much use to gardeners, but a great many were. What was really remarkable was the astonishing range of shapes, sizes and colour to be found among them. There were prostrate rhododendrons that crept along the ground and, at the other extreme, tree rhododendrons that could reach 10–12m (up to 40 ft); some with huge, and some with tiny, flowers in all manner of colours including scarlet, crimson, pink, salmon, apricot, yellow, purple and very nearly pure blue.

Because of the parts of the world from which they came, a good many of the new species were rather tender. Some needed greenhouse protection

in winter, some grew well in places where the climate was exceptionally mild. But many were completely hardy everywhere and even the tender kinds provided the plant breeders with some magnificent material on which to work.

Looking back to the latter part of the 19th century it is possible to distinguish two distinct types of hybrid. One came from the nurserymen who kept their breeding programmes completely secret and crossed species and existing hybrids with the sole object of producing hardy, reliable, free-flowering shrubs. The other came from wealthy amateurs willing to record and publish the crosses they made and anxious to outvie one another in size of bloom, novelty of colour, richness of scent and everything else that made the new rhododendron so exciting.

The amateurs cared little if some of their seedlings were tender. The nurserymen, by contrast, concentrated on utility, and since, even in the hardiest rhododendron, the flowers and opening flower-buds can be completely spoiled by frost, they selected in the main varieties which flowered only in summer (mid May to mid June). So the amateurs produced hybrids of great beauty and variety with a flowering season from mid winter to late summer (January to July) and the nurserymen produced hardy hybrids which tended to look much alike in shape and size, had a concentrated flowering season, and differed chiefly in flower colours and quality.

The two races are still with us, the pedigree hybrids and the hardy hybrids, plus a great many species just as they grow in the wild. But we now know a great deal more about rhododendrons than we did, can select for gardens from all three groups with every expectation of success, and have developed means of growing rhododendrons even where it would have seemed impossible to do so a generation or so ago. The rhododendron has arrived as a shrub which does for the ordinary garden in spring and early summer what the rose can do so well for it from midsummer to autumn—fill it with colour and perfume and do it with a minimum of trouble or risk of failure.

In one respect rhododendrons are still at a disadvantage to roses. Most of them dislike alkaline soils so much that they can only be grown in chalk or limestone soils with special precautions or treatments. But those precautions are now fully understood and the treatments are available, and anyone can grow rhododendrons today.

Nearly all the shrubs that gardeners would regard as 'true' rhododendrons are evergreens, but botanists extend the genus to include what gardeners know as azaleas, some of which are evergreen and some deciduous. Most garden centres follow this horticultural practice and list azaleas separately, but a few adopt the botanical classification and put them under rhododendron, though with the garden varieties in a separate group under appropriate sub-headings. It is quite likely that botanists will one day also give the azaleas generic rank (they already fill a separate

section or 'series' of the huge rhododendron genus) and there is so much to be said about them that we shall devote a separate Plant Profile to them.

All rhododendrons prefer acid soils but they differ in their sensitiveness to it. For most, pH 5·0 to pH 6·0 is ideal, but many will grow well even up to pH 6·5 and some, including *Rhododendron ponticum* and some of the hardy hybrids, will get along quite nicely in neutral soils (pH 7·0) without special help. But usually, beyond pH 6·5, it will be necessary either to import acid soil and peat to make up beds for the rhododendrons, or to feed them two or three times a year with 'chelated' iron and manganese.

Chelates are complex chemical compounds

Left: magnificent view of hardy hybrid Mrs Furnival
Above: flower detail of hardy hybrid Gomer Waterer

which are now available in most garden shops, ready for mixing with water according to label instructions and applying to the soil. If special beds are prepared it is an advantage if they can be built up 30cm (12 in) or more above the level of the existing soil so that lime does not wash from this into the rhododendron bed. However, this means that another danger must be guarded against; raised beds can become very dry beds in summer. Rhododendrons can be watered, but if the mains water is 'hard' (alkaline), as it may well be in a chalk or limestone locality, this can introduce the very element you are trying to exclude. Rainwater is the ideal solution, and it is worthwhile putting a rain barrel where it can collect water from something like a shed or greenhouse roof.

All rhododendrons make masses of fibrous roots which bind the soil together into a tight ball. This makes them very easy to move even when they are quite big – a bonus for the gardener who can move them to other places if the original arrangement proves unsatisfactory, or can deliberately overplant at the outset to get a quick effect and then thin out later on.

If rhododendrons are to be moved from open ground, autumn (September–October) and mid to late spring (March–April) are the best planting seasons, but if they are obtained in containers rhododendrons can be planted at any time of the year provided they are properly looked after. But they should never be planted in exposed positions during wintry weather.

341

Bushes do not normally require pruning, but if they grow too large the branches can be cut back even to within a few inches of the soil level, although this will prevent flowering for at least one year. The best time for such hard pruning is in early summer (May) or immediately after flowering.

Rhododendrons, especially the species, usually set seed freely. This is almost dust-like and a pod can contain thousands of seeds, which is why the breeders were able to produce new varieties so quickly. But such tiny seeds are rather difficult to manage, seedlings take a number of years to reach

R. wardii, *an early summer-flowering species*

flowering size, and those raised from hybrid plants are likely to differ greatly both from their parents and from one another. So in practice seed is not much used as a method of propagation except by specialists and breeders.

Nurserymen propagate mainly by grafting, usually onto seedlings of *Rhododendron ponticum*, and to a lesser degree by cutting and layering. Grafted plants have good roots and grow well, but if they produce suckers (shoots direct from the roots), these will be of the same character as the stock, not of the garden variety grafted on it. This accounts for many of the big bushes of *Rhododendron ponticum* to be seen in gardens. Their owners have failed to notice and remove the suckers which, because of their greater vigour, have gradually swamped and killed the garden variety. Ponticum suckers have narrower, darker green leaves than most of the hybrids, but the important point to watch for is any growth that is clearly of a different character from the rest of the bush. Trace such stems to their source and if this is at the roots or very low down on the main stem, more or less at soil level, they are almost certainly suckers and should be cut out with a sharp knife or secateurs.

By contrast rhododendrons raised from cuttings or layers are 'on their own roots' to use the gardener's phrase. The whole plant, stems and roots, is of the same kind, and suckers will bear

HARDY HYBRIDS

These average 3–4.5cm (10–15 ft) in height and diameter when fully grown, or considerably more in moist, sheltered positions. Most of them flower in early to mid summer (May to June). The flowers are widely funnel-shaped, and measure 5–7.5cm (2–3 in) across.

Beauty of Littleworth	Rose-red buds opening to large rose-pink flowers.
Blue Peter	Violet-blue, the best of its colour.
Britannia	Scarlet with wavy-edged flowers. Slow growing and compact.
Christmas Cheer	Pink buds opening to white flowers in mid spring (March).
Cynthia	Rose-red, very vigorous, hardy and reliable.
Doncaster	Crimson-scarlet, below average height.
Goldsworth Yellow	Apricot-pink buds opening to primrose-yellow flowers.
Gomer Waterer	White flushed mauve with yellow blotch.
Loder's White	Mauve-pink buds opening to pure white flowers in early summer (May).
Mrs Charles E. Pearson	Mauve-pink becoming nearly white.
Mrs Furnival	Rose-pink blotched with brown and crimson.
Mrs G. W. Leak	Similar to last in colour but a little earlier and a looser flower truss.
Pink Pearl	Rose buds opening to very large pink flowers. Rather lax habit.
Purple Splendour	Rich deep purple.
Sappho	Mauve buds opening to white flowers with almost black blotch.
Souvenir de Dr S. Endtz	Rose buds opening to pink flowers. Vigorous in growth.
Susan	Lavender-blue.

SPECIES

As with the pedigree hybrids, species are best planted in light shelter such as thin woodland.

R. arboreum	Red, pink or white flowers from late winter to late spring (January to April). To 12m (40 ft).
R. augustinii	Blue or mauve flowers in late spring (April–May). 2 to 3m (6–10 ft). Electra is a fine blue form.
R. cinnabarinum	Cinnabar-red (vermilion) tubular flowers in early summer (May–June). To 3m (10 ft). The variety Blandfordiflorum has flowers yellow outside, and the variety Roylei purplish-red flowers.
R. decorum	White or pale pink scented flowers in early summer (May–June). 3–4m (10–13 ft).
R. discolor	Large pink flowers in mid summer (June–July). 3–4m (10–13 ft).
R. falconeri	Huge leaves and large cream flowers blotched with purple in late spring (April–May). 4–6m (13–20 ft).
R. fortunei	Scented lilac-pink flowers in early summer (May). 4–5m (13–17 ft).
R. leucaspis	Saucer-shaped creamy white flowers in early spring (February–March). About 50cm (20 in).
R. moupinense	White or pink flowers in early spring (February–March). Up to 1m (3 ft).
R. racemosum	Small pink flowers in mid to late spring (March–April). Up to 2m (7 ft). Forrest's Dwarf is a shorter form.
R. russatum	Small violet-blue flowers in late spring (April–May). Up to 1m (3 ft).
R. thomsonii	Blood-red flowers in late spring (April). 4–5m (13–17 ft).
R. wardii	Saucer-shaped yellow flowers in early summer (May). 3–4m (10–13 ft).

just as beautiful flowers as stems from above ground and should be retained.

Most rhododendrons like to grow in dappled shade—the kind of shade provided by fairly thin woodland. If the cover trees are mixed deciduous and evergreens, say some oaks and some pines, this is ideal. But these conditions are not essential and the hardy hybrids in particular will usually grow well even in full sun, provided the soil does not get too hot and dry in summer. One of the advantages of digging-in plenty of rotted leaves or peat before planting is that they both help to keep the soil cool and moist without making it too wet in winter; this should also be done each spring.

In addition to the 500–600 species there are now thousands of hybrid rhododendrons. Some nurserymen specialize in them and all garden centres. offer quite a good selection. Here is a short selection of pedigree species and hybrids, together with some non-pedigree hardy hybrids which are still the toughest and easiest to grow (they are certainly the best where the air is smoke-polluted).

Top right: Hawk Crest, a
pedigree hybrid that flowers in early summer
Above: Souvenir de Dr S. Endtz,
a hardy hybrid
Below: R. falconeri *without flowers in the autumn*

PEDIGREE HYBRIDS

These are best planted in thin woodland where they are provided with dappled shade (sharp de-frosting caused by early morning sun may damage buds) and shelter from cold winds.

Angelo	Huge, sweetly-scented white flowers in mid summer (June). 3–4m (10–13 ft) when full grown.
Blue Diamond	Clusters of small lavender-blue flowers in late spring (April). 1m (3 ft).
Elizabeth	Large, deep red flowers in late spring (April). 1m (3 ft). Very hardy.
Fabia	Funnel-shaped orange-red flowers in early summer (May). Up to 2m (7 ft).
Hawk	Large pale yellow flowers in early summer (May). Up to 3m (10 ft). Crest is a particularly fine form.
Lady Chamberlain	Clusters of drooping, almost tubular orange-red flowers in early summer (May). Up to 2m (7 ft).
Loderi	Huge trusses of white- or pink-flushed, richly scented flowers in early summer (May). 3–4m (10–13 ft).
May Day	Brilliant red flowers in early summer (May). About 2m (6 ft).
Naomi	Large pink- or mauve-tinted sweetly scented flowers in early summer (May). To 3m (10 ft).
Polar Bear	Large white flowers in late summer (July). 3–4m (10–13 ft).
Praecox	Magenta flowers in early spring (February–March). To 1·5m (5 ft).
Tally Ho	Colour of May Day but flowering mid summer (June). 2m (7 ft).
Temple Belle	Bell-shaped rose-pink flowers in early summer (May). 1m (3 ft).

Salvia

Type	half-hardy annual, hardy and half-hardy perennials; half-hardy sub-shrubs
Common name	salvia
Family	LABIATAE
Flowering season	summer
Sowing date	late winter to early spring (January–February)
Mature size/shape	15cm–1·5m (6 in–5 ft)
Special uses	some species are used as dried flowers

The name salvia is derived from *salvus*, the Latin word for safe or well. Salvias were once thought to have medicinal and curative properties. The half-hardy exotic salvias from the New World first appeared in Europe in 1744, when seeds were sent from Florida and Mexico. The familiar red *S. splendens*, used for summer bedding, came from Brazil in 1822. *S. fulgens*, of Mexican origin, did not arrive in Britain until 1827, although it was grown on the Continent before this. Also from Mexico came the brilliant blue *S. patens* in 1838. Salvias are well-behaved garden plants, even though they have not been extensively bred or developed since their introduction.

Salvias are a very diverse group, comprising 700 species of hardy, half-hardy and tender annuals, perennials and mainly evergreen sub-shrubs. The most popular species are the familiar half-hardy annuals, including the fiery summer bedding plant *S. splendens*. The Victorians loved bedding plants and used this species to make a splash of colour wherever they could. *S. splendens* and the bright red Blaze of Fire still bring colour into the garden every summer. Strictly speaking, *S. splendens* is a half-hardy perennial, but in mild districts like south-west England it sometimes grows outside from year to year. However, it is best to treat it as a half-hardy annual, starting from fresh seed each year. An attractive variation is the similar Purple Blaze, which grows in the same habitat and produces violet-purple flowers. *S. patens*, a perennial, bears clear blue flowers during the summer and early autumn.

Although it is still not well known, *S. Horminum* is becoming more popular. This true annual is a native of southern Europe and grows to 45 cm (18 in). During the summer, tiny pink or purple flowers appear, but it is the brightly-coloured 4cm (1½ in) long bracts (flower-bearing leaves) that make the most show. Monarch Bouquet, which produces a splendid mixture of white, rose, red, blue and purple bracts, is an excellent variety.

All half-hardy annual salvias are usually raised in heat under glass during the late winter and early spring. They should be planted out during late spring and early summer.

The hardy and half-hardy perennial salvias are very attractive garden plants. *S. argentea*, originally from the Mediterranean, is short-lived and often grown as a biennial. It has delicate rosettes of triangular-shaped leaves covered in silvery-white hairs. The white flowers flushed with mauve are 4cm (1½ in) long and appear in late summer and early autumn (July and August).

A salvia of garden origin is *S. virgata nemorosa*, which grows to a height of 60cm (24 in). The profusion of blue-purple flowers make a welcome display during the summer.

Hardy perennial salvias should be planted in late autumn and mid spring (October and March) in well-drained garden soil. They should be cut down to ground level every year during November.

Once popular as conservatory plants, the half-hardy sub-shrubs are no longer as well known as the other groups. An interesting variety, *S. fulgens*, produces a wonderful show of red flowers during the summer. The leaves are white and woolly

The most commonly-seen salvia is the popular bedding annual Salvia splendens, *of which there are many cultivars. Here we show three: top left,* S. splendens *Pink Rouge; above left,* S. splendens *Blaze of Fire; above,* S. splendens *Flamenco*

on the undersides. This plant will spread about 45cm (18 in) and reach 60–90cm (2–3 ft) in height.

Sub-shrubs are equally happy planted in pots or in greenhouse soil. They prefer large pots and grow best in J.I. No 2 or No 3. Gross feeders, they appreciate liquid feeds every week during the growing season; and they should never be allowed to dry out. It is advisable to ventilate the greenhouse when temperatures exceed 13° C (55° F), as these plants are not lovers of heat.

S. neurepia and *S. rutilans*, two summer-flowering half-hardy sub-shrubs, will thrive inside. They may be encouraged to grow at the base of a south-facing wall outdoors, provided they are protected with straw or other litter during the winter.

Most salvias are propagated from seed, but the half-hardy sub-shrubs are increased by taking cuttings from the non-flowered lateral shoots in late spring or early autumn.

Salvias are rarely bothered by pests and diseases, so they should grow quite well, provided they are adequately fed and watered.

S. officinalis is the common herb sage, which is available in green or decorative leaved form.

Magnolia

Type	hardy deciduous shrub
Common name	magnolia
Family	MAGNOLIACEAE
Flowering season	mid to late spring (March–April)
Planting date	late autumn to mid spring (October–March) for bare-rooted; anytime from containers
Mature size/shape	height 2·5–3m (8–10 ft), spread up to 2m (7 ft)

The magnolia is native to Japan, where it grows wild in certain areas, but has long been cultivated in gardens there. It was named after the 18th-century French botanist, Pierre Magnol professor of botany and director of the botanic garden at Montpellier. Introduced into American gardens in 1862, it reached the British Isles some 15 years later.

Magnolia stellata is a deciduous shrub of rather rounded shape, reaching 3m (10 ft) or occasionally more, although being slow growing it is often seen at little more than 1·25m (4 ft). It is usually much wider than high and a plant 1·25m (4 ft) tall may have a spread of 2m (over 6 ft). The starry white flowers, which have 12–18 petals, open before the leaves in mid spring (March or early April). One of the advantages of this magnolia is the fact that it flowers while still a very small plant; indeed plants under 30cm (12 in) high will produce flowers. There is a so-called 'pink' variety known as Rosea,

Magnolia stellata *bears very distinctive flowers, consisting of 12–18 petals. Like all magnolias, its flowers open before the tree comes into leaf*

346

whose buds are indeed pink, but whose open flowers are white as in the usual form. However, plants of Rosea are quite liable to set seed, which the ordinary type of magnolia practically never does. After the flowers have gone the plant produces narrow oblong leaves up to 10cm (4 in) long.

So far as winter frost is concerned it is perfectly hardy, but the opening flowers are liable to be damaged by frost or by the wind. This is a risk that you will have to take with all the early-flowering magnolias. Such frosting of the flowers, although infuriating, does no harm to the shrub itself.

M. stellata requires full light and a good soil, and is suited to a small garden. It is unsatisfactory on chalky soils, although it seems not to resent some alkalinity. However, it does rather better on neutral or slightly acid soil such as rhododendrons enjoy.

When planting young magnolias remember that they require a lightener such as well-rotted manure

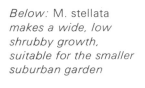

Below: M. stellata makes a wide, low shrubby growth, suitable for the smaller suburban garden

or peat in the soil immediately around the roots. Mix it in with the garden soil to give a rather light mixture into which the new roots can run easily. All magnolias have rather thick fleshy roots and it is usually advisable to defer any planting until late spring (April).

However in certain districts where spring is normally dry, this may be dangerous and here, autumn planting is better. If you plant in spring, the shrub must be thoroughly watered in and then a mulch of straw, dried bracken, or farmyard manure placed around its base to prevent the soil drying out at this crucial time. If your soil is rather poor, much may be done by digging a hole 45cm (18 in) deep and up to 2m (6 ft) across and filling this with a special mixture. This will ensure the plant getting off to a good start and, since it should remain in the garden for ever, there is every reason for you to take a little trouble to help it get started successfully.

The plant is closely allied to *M. kobus*, a quite rapid grower which reaches up to 12m (40 ft) tall, but often takes a very long time before it begins to flower freely. *M. stellata* is frequently grafted on this plant, although *M. stellata* is one of the few magnolias that can be raised fairly easily from cuttings; choose firm but not yet woody growths. *M. stellata* and *M. kobus* have been hybridized to give *M. × loebneri*, which combines the early flowering of stellata with the larger dimensions of kobus; some grow to 7·5m (25 ft) and are slightly more across.

Tagetes

Type	half-hardy annual
Common Name	marigold
Family	COMPOSITAE
Flowering season	mid summer to late autumn (June–October)
Sowing date	under glass: mid to late spring (February–March)
Mature size/shape	15–90cm (6 in–3 ft) bushy plants
Special use	as pot plants

This plant was named tagetes in honour of the handsome Etruscan deity, Tages, who taught the Etruscans the art of divination.

There are four species of tagetes that are grown in gardens. The African marigold (*T. erecta*) and

Above: Tagetes patula *Naughty Marietta*
Above left: T. signata *Lemon Gem*
Left: T. patula *Petite Orange, and Lemon Gem*

the French marigold (*T. patula*), which are the most used, travelled to Spain from Mexico with the conquistadores. *T. erecta* was first known in southern Europe as Rose of the Indies; however, it was already growing wild in North Africa by the 16th century and, following the Emperor Charles V's successful expedition against the Moorish stronghold of Tunis in 1535, it was renamed 'flos africanus', leading northern Europeans to believe that it was native to that part of the world.

T. patula, on the other hand, was traditionally believed to have been brought to England by Huguenot refugees following the 1572 St Bartholomew's Day Massacre and so gained its name of 'French' marigold. Both plants were well established in Britain by the early 17th century and greatly admired for their colourful display, if not their scent: one botanist complained of their 'naughtie strong and unpleasant savour'.

The other two species, *T. lucida* and *T. signata*,

are less well known than either the African or French marigold. *T. signata* is the more common of the two and is represented in cultivation by the varieties Ursula and Lemon Gem; both grow in bushy fashion to 23–25cm (9–10 in) in height.

The traditional African marigold is a tall plant, branching just two or three times, which grows up to 90cm (3 ft) in height. The solitary yellow or orange flowers can reach 10cm (4 in) across. These rather stately plants have attractive feathered leaves and look especially good in the border planted in groups of three or four, some 30cm (12 in) apart. Nowadays dwarf varieties are rapidly gaining popularity, especially for windswept gardens – look for types like First Lady, 35–45cm (15–18 in) and Gold Galore, 30–35cm (12–15 in).

The French marigold is much smaller, growing to a height of 15–30cm (6–12 in). Assiduous deadheading will encourage this plant to spread quite widely, so allow at least 30cm (12 in) between plants when putting them in your border. They are excellent as ground cover, and so are particularly useful in a new garden if you want a display of instant colour. All types like as much of the sun as possible, and grow well in an indifferent soil.

A number of Afro-French hybrids, with flowers

Above: dwarf African marigold, Tagetes erecta *Gold Galore; above right:* T. signata *Orange Gem; right:* T. patula *Sunbeam*

up to 8cm (3 in) in diameter, are now available; these are sterile and therefore deadheading is not so essential to maintain flowering. Varieties Red Seven Star, 23–25cm (9–10 in), and the bright yellow Showboat, 30–35cm (12–14 in), both flower freely over many months.

Propagation of all types is the same. Sow in a warm greenhouse (15–20°C, 60–68°F) at any time throughout the spring, then transplant singly into small peat pots or 5cm (2 in) apart in trays of potting compost, ready for hardening off. The seedlings can then be transferred straight to your flowerbeds or window boxes in early summer when all danger of frost is past.

Seed can also be sown directly into a sunny bed in early summer (May), but this will not usually give such good results as marigolds are particularly influenced by temperature during their early growth period. They will flower prolifically all summer until touched by first autumn frosts.

Caring for Your House Plants

For people who have neither garden nor window box, house plants often provide the only chance of getting close to growing things. From a single pot of chrysanthemums to a massed display of foliage plants, there is always scope to exercise your indoor gardening talents and widen your plant knowledge if you follow the basic rules.

'House plants' are what we call any of those plants that live indoors either permanently or for short periods, and it is important to be able to recognize the two different types.

There are the 'short stay' (or 'florist') plants, which are suited to indoor conditions only during their flowering period and the true house plants, often called 'foliage plants', usually natives of warm climates. These last will live indoors quite happily for years, provided certain rules are followed.

The conditions in which we grow our house plants are often far from ideal, as conditions that suit human beings may not be the ones that plants would select

for themselves, and most of us cannot send our ailing specimens to recuperate in a greenhouse. But once you have learned to cope successfully with the plant's requirements of **air**, **light**, and **soil**, your major problems are over. Anything else is pure commonsense or the learning of simple techniques.

AIR

The atmosphere in which a plant grows is of vital importance. Some plants, such as cacti, are adapted to life in deserts, where the air is extremely dry and little or no rain falls. Such plants have evolved thick leathery leaves that prevent water evaporating too quickly; they are also able to store water to see them through the dry periods. These adaptations came about by a gradual process of natural selection over millions of years; plants that have evolved these special traits are more successful than those that have not, so they have thrived while their relatives have died out.

Other plants have had to adapt to very different atmospheric conditions from those found in deserts – such as the many

species that live in tropical rain forests. Here the atmosphere is always saturated with moisture, so that the plants have no trouble in obtaining enough water. On the other hand, they may grow so densely that smaller ones are shaded by their more vigorous neighbours – thus cutting them off from the vital sunlight without which green plants die. Many, however, have overcome this problem. Instead of growing in the soil, they live on the upper branches and trunks of trees, where they can obtain plenty of sunlight. Plants that do this – such as bromeliads and many vines – are called epiphytes, but unlike parasites they do not harm their hosts.

Different plants have thus evolved so that they can thrive in different environments, and it is often very helpful to their successful cultivation if you know their native habitat.

The actual temperature at which the plants are growing is important, too. It should remain steady, though slight fluctuation will not cause serious damage. One of the snags of growing plants in the home is that, while in nature the night is cooler than the sunlit hours, in the home (at least in winter) the opposite may be the case. If you have the house warmed throughout the day (or if you have no central heating) the temperature remains relatively constant. On the other hand, if you go out to work, and you light a fire or turn up the central heating when you get back in the evening, the room temperature will be considerably higher at night.

This is the complete reverse of what plants need, but fortunately they make very little growth during the winter months, so the damage is much less than might be expected.

As we have seen, desert plants such as cacti can live in very dry conditions, but most plants like the air around them to be moist. Houses are generally too dry for plants, especially when heating systems are being used. Paraffin heaters add some moisture to the air, but a good deal of the moisture is removed from the air with solid fuel or gas fires, and central heating produces a very dry atmosphere (unless some form of humidifier is used). The answer is to create a 'microclimate' around your plants. The easiest way to do this is by putting the plant pot inside another container – either a larger pot or a more ornamental container. The space between the sides of the pot and the walls

'Pot in a pot' method helps to create a microclimate, with vapour rising from the moistened filling between the pots

remember that even these require as much light as you can give them.

Plants tend to grow towards the window as it is their main source of light, and if left to their own devices will become lop-sided. The answer is to turn them around once a week. Plants are often put onto windowsills to give them as much light as possible and, in theory, this is admirable. However, even if you have double glazing, windowsills can become very cold as the outside temperature falls, so bring your plants into the room before you draw the curtains.

WATER
More house plants die from being over-watered than from any other single cause. The proper use of water is a hard thing to

Far left: mixed arrangements of plants can be very effective, as grouped here
Below: without light, leaves of Monstera pertusa *change their shape*

of the larger container is filled either with peat or sand and this must then always be kept moist. As the water evaporates the plant is bathed in the vapour, so that its leaves are an oasis of moisture in the surrounding dry air.

Alternatively, you can fill a rather shallow, flat dish with a layer of attractive pebbles and let these stand in water, while the plant pot stand on the pebbles. The bottom of the pot should never actually be in the water, and the pebbles are there to prevent this happening.

Even with these precautions there are still a few places in a room which are quite unsuitable for plants, such as chimney pieces or immediately over a radiator, because they are far too hot. Other spots are unsuitable because they are far too draughty. Although the room temperature may be satisfactory for your plant, a constant stream of cold air on it will have a disastrous effect. The plant will start to shed its leaves and may eventually die, so watch out for the first sign of trouble.

House plants may also be damaged by the fumes from solid fuel or town-gas fires and paraffin heaters. Natural gas fumes do not affect plants, however.

LIGHT
No green plant can grow without light and from the plant's point of view even the best-lit room is rather shady. For one thing the light has passed through the glass of a window pane and this is very different from natural light. You can get around this problem by growing some of the many plants that thrive in rather shady situations, but it is as well to

Above: Saintpaulia *do not like water on their leaves.*

master, and it is complicated by the fact that plants do not grow at the same rate throughout the year. They need most water when they are actively growing, which is usually between late spring and mid autumn; if you have central heating, however, you will find that the plants tend to go on growing for longer.

During this period you should give your plants water whenever the soil in the pot becomes dry. However, soil on the surface dries out before it has become dry at the base of the pot, and it is a good rule of thumb to wait 24 hours after the soil on the surface looks dry before watering.

If the plant has been properly potted there should be a gap of 1–5cm ($\frac{1}{2}$–2 in) between the soil level and the rim of the pot, depending on the size of the pot. When you water, fill the pot to the brim and always ensure that the water has reached the bottom of the pot. Dribs and drabs will never get to the roots, and it is there that the water is needed. Allow the plant to stand in the excess water for about 20 minutes and then tip the water away. Plants should *never* be allowed to stand in water for long periods.

If the soil should dry out completely, place the pot in a container with sufficient water to reach the top of the pot and leave it to soak for about an hour. Then lift the pot out and let it stand until the surplus water has drained away.

How often you have to water depends on how rapidly the plant is growing – and this in turn is affected by the temperature and the brilliance of the light. If it is very dry the plant will flag, but wilting is not altogether a reliable sign that the plant needs watering, as leaves sometimes wilt if

they are exposed to fierce sunlight – especially through a window. If this is the problem a fine spray of water applied to the leaves will soon bring them back to normal.

Ideally you should use rainwater, but unfortunately not many people are able to store it. A good substitute is the water that comes from defrosting the refrigerator (warmed to room temperature first), but there will probably not be enough of this and you will have to rely on tap water. Never water your plants with very cold water; it should be around 12–15°C (55–60°F), so add a little hot water if necessary. No plant relishes ice-cold water around its roots.

SOIL

As a general rule, house plants are either potted in a mixture of loam, peat and sand – of which John Innes No 2 compost (usually abbreviated to J.I. No 2) is the best known – or else in so-called 'soilless' composts, based on peat with added fertilizers. Both are perfectly satis-

factory, but they should not be mixed.

Sooner or later you will have to pot your plants on – that is, transfer them to larger pots – so you should try to find out what the original mix was. The John Innes composts look much like garden soil, whereas soilless compost looks very peaty and feels very light when dry. Plants in J.I. No 2 should be potted on to more J.I. No 2, while plants in soilless mixtures should go into more of the same.

Whatever basic mixture is used it will be necessary to feed the plants throughout the growing season (early summer to mid autumn) and this is usually done at weekly or fortnightly intervals. There are a number of different feeds available, all of which are good. Whichever one you decide to buy, follow the directions implicitly. Too much at any one application may be harmful.

Another point to bear in mind is that the feed should not be added to dry soil. Even if it is a liquid feed, it should be given when the compost is moist – preferably within two days of watering.

WHAT'S IN A NAME?

Have you ever failed to find Michaelmas daisies in a nurseryman's catalogue because you were unaware of their true name – *Aster novi-belgii*? This is the problem with botanical names that defeats so many amateur gardeners, who shy away from unfamiliar Latin, or other foreign, names and stick to the few plants they know.

The international system initiated by the famous Swedish botanist Linnaeus in 1753, known as binomial nomenclature, is a standard way of classifying all the different plants.

Every plant belongs to a **family** (usually printed in SMALL CAPITALS) which may be very large or quite small, but it is the name – of the **genus** (the generic name printed in *italics*) – that identifies a group of closely-related plants. Within the genus there are a number of different **species** (printed in *italics*), each of which also has its own name. The genus and the species together instantly identify the plant to botanists, horticulturists and gardeners all over the world. After the species name there often follows a third one (also printed in *italics*) that identifies the **variety**. 'Variety' used to refer loosely to botanical varieties and garden **hybrids**, but now denotes only botanical varieties. Garden hy-

brids are now referred to as **cultivars**.

The common name can be the same as the genus name (as in *Clematis*); or, as with Michaelmas daisies, it is quite different – *Aster novi-belgii*.

Many of the plants we grow today are *hybrids* – that is, they are the result of intensive breeding, or 'crossing', of two or more different varieties or species. They are usually indicated by an '×', as in *Clematis × jackmanii* (species cross between two different species).

The example below follows the usual botanical style, and our additional notes may help you track the origins of many other plant names.

Common name	Clematis
Family	RANUNCULACEAE
Genus	*Clematis*
Species	*Clematis montana** *Clematis vitalba*** (old man's beard)
Variety	*Clematis montana wilsonii****
Cultivar	*Clematis* George V
Hybrid	*Clematis × jackmanii*****

* *montana* from the Latin for mountain, as it was found in the Himalayas.
** *vitalba* so-named by Linnaeus from *vitis alba* (white vine).
*** *wilsonii* named for Ernest Henry Wilson, American explorer and botanist.
**** *jackmanii* for the Jackman of Woking nursery, where it was raised in 1860.

Some Easy House Plants

Many people assume that the most attractive house plants are not easy to cultivate. Unfortunately this false impression deprives them of some extremely attractive varieties that are quite simple to grow. The basic secret for success is to understand your plants and their needs for survival.

Among the most decorative house plants that are easy to grow are the silver and golden tradescantias and the similar zebrina. These are rather sprawling plants with succulent stems from which spring egg-shaped leaves ending in a point about 4cm (1½ in) long. Plants with variegated leaves need plenty of light and, if their situation is often too shady, the variegations will be less.

Tradescantias and zebrinas

Rochford's Quicksilver (botanical name *Tradescantia elongata*) has silver-striped leaves which means that it will keep its variegations even in the shade and is, therefore, an ideal plant for a fairly dark position. Since the leaves grow to about 7–8cm (3 in) long and 2–3cm (1 in) wide, it is rather more upright and compact than the golden and silver tradescantias.

These and the zebrinas are best put in a raised situation so that as the stems elongate they will fall down over the sides of the container. With zebrinas the leaves are silver and purple and the plants look most attractive if placed high up to show both colours.

The ordinary silver tradescantia and the whiter one, Tricolor (which also shows traces of pink on the leaves), can be grown at eye level, and should be watched to see that no shoots with plain green leaves are produced. If they are, remove them immediately or they will grow vigorously at the expense of the variegated portions. The same applies to the golden tradescantia, whose dark leaves have, in fact, creamy-yellow stripes. There is no cause for worry with zebrinas as they retain their markings.

No house plant is entirely problem-free, but tradescantias are nearly so.

Right: the tradescantia Quicksilver is ideal for a shady corner
Top: a grouping of easy-to-grow house plants, with (left) a Rex begonia, (centre) Saintpaulia and (right) spider plant

353

They can take overwatering without rotting and, similarly, will stand up to a period of drought. Indeed, those with pink or purple in the leaves show more colour if kept on the dry side.

Zebrina pendula is much more handsome if kept on the dry side, although if its position is too sunny the purple tends to turn rusty-brown.

Winter temperature is no problem. The plants will be quite happy if just kept frost-free; but they will also do well in a warm room. They are also extremely easy to propagate and, when old plants tend to become leggy, they are usually replaced.

Propagation

The plants should be propagated either in spring or summer. Fill a 13cm (5 in) pot with J.I. No 1 potting compost or a soilless potting compost and water it well. Some soilless composts are not easy to water thoroughly, so it is best to use a fine rose on your can to get all the way down. Leave the pot for 24 hours.

Take several ends of shoots, 5–8cm (2–3 in) long, from just below leaves of the old plant and strip the bottom leaves off to allow about 20mm ($\frac{3}{4}$ in) of bare stem. These cuttings are rather brittle so do not try to push them in. Make a hole in the compost with a pencil and then insert five to seven cuttings around the edge and two or three in the centre, so that their base is in contact with the soil. Firm around the top with your fingers so that they are well set. Do not firm soilless potting composts unless they are wet. Keep the compost moist and the cuttings will quickly root.

If you have a plant that looks nice around the edges but has become rather bare in the centre, keep the old plant and insert two or three cuttings in the middle. These will soon fill an unsightly gap.

Spider plant

Another attractive and easy indoor-grower is the spider plant (chlorophytum). It comes from South Africa and should not be kept too warm during winter, although a temperature 12°C (55°F) will not harm it. It has tufts of cream-striped green leaves that grow up to 20cm (8 in) long; in summer it may throw up stems bearing small white, lily-like flowers but more likely a tuft of leaves. If these stems are brought down so that the base of the tufts rests on the surface of the soil, they

Top left: Zebrina pendula *prefers its soil to be kept fairly dry.*
Left: Chlorophytum comosum, *the spider plant, throws out tufts of leaves which can be rooted to make new plants*

The variegated leaves of Rex begonia add colour and interest to your display of house plants

good watering and the potting on is complete. Since the roots have plenty of new soil to penetrate, it may not be necessary to water again for some time.

Asparagus fern

A lesser-known plant, but equally easy to grow, is *Asparagus meyeri*. It is not unlike the popular *A. sprengeri* (sometimes known as Spring Rye), although the stems do not trail but stand upright like miniature Christmas trees. Below ground are a lot of knobbly tubers that store water, which means the plant can be kept rather dry. These roots are quite bulky and need a fairly large pot. It will grow in shady conditions and likes to be fairly cool in winter.

The plant can be increased by division: Cut it in half with a sharp knife and make sure that each part has shoots and some tubers.

Rex begonia

Some of the showy Rex begonias, with large roughly triangular leaves, are somewhat more tricky to grow. They need well-lit situations, but must not be in direct sunlight. They are sensitive to gas fumes, so should not be placed in a gas-heated room or near a gas cooker. They need warmer conditions than the other plants mentioned here. Winter temperature should be no lower than 12°C (55°F).

Since they have very fine roots they do best in a soilless compost. John Innes potting compost is rather coarse and a mixture of leaf mould and sand, with only a little loam, is usually recommended as an alternative. They like a moist atmosphere but not much water around the roots. They will probably need to be potted on from an 8cm (3 in) pot to a 13cm (5 in) after a year and thereafter at two-yearly intervals.

will soon root, when they can then be detached and you have another plant. It is a good idea to secure the tufts in position with a hairpin round the stem.

The soil should always be on the dry side, and the plant itself should be watered fairly sparingly until it is well-rooted, when it can be treated like any other house plant. It needs a well-lit situation; and as it grows it becomes pot bound and must be moved on to a larger pot.

Potting on of house plants

Plants should only be potted on during spring and summer when they are growing. To check if a plant is ready for potting on place thumb and forefinger at the base where it enters the soil, turn the pot upside down and tap the edge on to a flat surface, such as a potting bench or draining board. The whole soil ball should come out easily. Only if it is full of roots is potting on necessary. If it is not well-rooted potting on will do no good at all.

Water the plant well before you pot on.

Generally, plants are moved on to the next size of pot. For instance from an 8cm (3 in) size to a 13cm (5 in) to a 15cm (6 in) and eventually to a 20cm (8 in) pot. Make sure the new pot is clean. Wipe out clay ones with newspaper; it is advisable to wash plastic pots.

If you are using a loam-based John Innes potting compost you will need drainage material; cover the bottom 2–3cm (1 in) of the pot with broken crocks or small pebbles. Remove any of these that are in the soil ball. Cover the base of the pot with the compost. Stand the plant on this and if it is about 2–3cm (1 in) below the rim of the pot add more compost; if it is above, remove some. Plants that are potted too low do not have sufficient soil, and those potted too high do not get thoroughly moistened when watered. Once the level is correct stand the soil ball in the centre of the pot and fill up around the sides, firming it down with your thumbs. Give the plant a

Aphelandria

Type	greenhouse perennial
Common name	zebra plant
Family	ACANTHACEAE
Flowering season	early to late autumn (August–October)
Mature size	20cm (8 in) to 90cm (3 ft)
Special use	as house plant

Aphelandra squarrosa, the aptly-named zebra plant, is a popular house plant. With a little effort it can be persuaded to produce a dramatic head of golden-yellow bracts.

The name aphelandra, deriving from the Greek *apheles*, simple, and *aner*, male, refers to the plant's anthers that are one-celled.

The aphelandra came from Brazil and was obtained there by the nursery firm of Linden in the 1860s. There are many aphelandras in South America, but none seem to have the manifold attractions of *A. squarrosa*, although *A. fascinator*, with its brilliant scarlet flower, could be usefully re-introduced. *Squarrosa* is from the Latin for curved, referring to the leaves.

Aphelandra squarrosa makes a rather stocky plant, with slightly leathery, elliptical leaves that may be as long as 25cm (9 in) and half as wide. They are of a dark shining green colour and the main veins are picked out conspicuously in ivory.

A few named varieties are now available, of which Brockfeld has exceptionally large leaves, but it practically never flowers. To compensate for this, the leaves contain far more ivory than the originally imported stock, and so the foliage is more striking. Before Brockfeld came Silver Beauty, with leaves containing as much ivory as green, but this is hard to obtain. Dania, a rather dwarf form rarely over 20cm (8 in) high, has smaller leaves that are held horizontally, not drooping as is usually the case; it is quite free-flowering.

Once the plant has become pot-bound it produces a four-sided pyramidal head of yellow bracts, from which the long, two-lipped, yellow tubular flowers emerge over a two to three week period. Since the bracts hold their colour from the time when they are first seen until about a week after the last flower has faded, the floral display is maintained for a long time. Eventually the bracts turn green and then the whole flower-head should be removed. Once this has been done, sideshoots will start to appear at the leaf axils and these can be taken off when sufficiently firm, and rooted as cuttings. For this, however, a temperature of 21°C (70°F) is wanted, so it is not easy without a greenhouse.

The aphelandra is greedy and requires a rich soil mixture such as J.I. No 3, but it should not be fed until the flower buds have been formed. If fed, it will be encouraged to produce more and larger leaves, so if the plant is being grown only for the sake of its foliage, you can go on feeding. Should your objective be blossom, however, you have to let the plant become pot-bound and withhold any feeding until you see that it is going to bloom. Even with these precautions it is not easy to persuade the plant to flower well in the home, as the amount of light available is often insufficient, unless you have a sunny room. If you have a greenhouse there should be no difficulty at all.

The aphelandra needs a humid atmosphere, so if it is kept in the house, plunge the pot into a large container with the gap between the two filled with some absorbent material that is always kept moist.

It requires fresh soil every year, but is not potted on into a larger pot. Instead, you remove the soil-ball from the pot and wash off the existing soil, leaving the roots intact. You then put fresh soil into the same pot and replace the aphelandra; this should be done in late spring (April) or early summer (May), when the days are reasonably long. But the plant needs extra warmth for about ten days after this operation, so you may prefer to complete it before turning off your central heating.

Give the aphelandra water at all times, although less is required in winter when this native of the Brazilian jungle should be kept warm; 15°C (60°F) is best, but 13°C (55°F) is adequate. The aphelandra grows slowly under 15°C (60°F) but speeds up as the temperature rises.

Cissus Antarctica

Type	woody greenhouse climber; tender perennial
Common name	kangaroo vine
Family	VITACEAE
Mature size	up to 3m (10 ft), but can reach higher

The name *Cissus antarctica* is derived from *kissos*, the Greek word for ivy, and *antarctica*, meaning the South Polar region. The *Cissus antarctica*, or kangaroo vine, grows wild in southern Australia and was brought into cultivation in 1790 by the distinguished botanist, Sir Joseph Banks.

The plant's leaves are basically triangular, but have a characteristically scalloped edge and are dark, shining green in colour. They may reach a length of 10cm (4 in) and be 5cm (2 in) across at their widest. The leaf stalks are reddish in colour and provide an effective contrast; they are also slightly hairy.

The kangaroo vine is a natural climber, attaching by means of tendrils and, if left to itself, will produce a single, very long, growth. But if the tip of this growth is nipped out in the spring (April or May), the plant will throw out numerous sideshoots from the leaf axils, so that an attractive bushy plant will result. In the following year these sideshoots can be stopped in turn, so that eventually an extremely shrubby effect is achieved.

The plant will require some support and a fan made of three canes with plastic mesh between them will soon shape a handsome specimen, but this will not happen in the first year. To start with it is probably easiest simply to train the plant up a single cane. This vine is one of the easiest and most accommodating of house plants, requiring very little heat to keep it in good condition during the winter and growing well both in shady and in brightly-lit situations; it will not be happy where it is very dark. No harm will come to it if the temperature falls as low as 7°C (45°F), although 10°C (50°F) is a safer limit. It will tolerate higher temperatures, but it does prefer to be fairly cool during its resting period. Southern Australia has definite seasons and these should be observed.

Kangaroo vine is a fairly greedy plant and will appreciate feeding from early summer to early autumn (May to September) and will also take ample water during this time. Reduce the amount of water in mid autumn (October) and until the early spring (mid February), give it just enough to prevent the plant drying out. Then increase the amount gradually as root action starts up again

and the soil dries out more rapidly. In late spring (mid April) it may be necessary to move the vine into a larger-sized pot.

Assuming you purchase the plant in an 8cm (3 in) pot, you will move it into a 13cm (5 in) pot the next year, into a 15cm (6 in) pot the year after that and finally into the 18cm (7 in) pot. This is really the optimum size of pot for the kangaroo vine, and after this you must rely on regular feeding to maintain it in good health. It is best to wait two or three weeks after the potting on has been completed before stopping the leading shoots. If, when you inspect the rootball, you find that it is not yet full of roots, do not pot the plant on, but keep it in the same pot for a further twelve months.

In the home the leaves are liable to attract dust, so clean them at regular intervals with cotton wool dipped in lukewarm water; this not only makes the plant look more attractive but also helps it grow better as the leaves do their job more efficiently.

During the summer it is quite easy to take root cuttings which should be about 10cm (4 in) long and taken just below a leaf joint. The wood should be firm, but not too woody. Remove the soft new growth at the tip of the shoots so that when the cuttings root they will produce sideshoots from the leaves already on them.

Above: Cissus antarctica, *the kangaroo vine, is a natural climber, seen here supported by a cane. Keep its decorative scalloped leaves glossy by regular cleaning*

Coleus Blumei

Type   greenhouse perennial

Common name   stove nettle or nettle leaf

Family   LABIATAE

Mature size/shape   45cm (18 in) high, 30cm
                               (12 in) or more across

Grown for its leaves rather than its flowers, the
coleus can be relied on to produce a magnificent
display of colour almost the whole year round.
The leaves come in many varied shades of bronze,
yellow, apricot, pink and crimson, and make a

*Kimono — a recent and successful strain; this easy-
to-care-for house plant displays a spectacular
range of multi-coloured foliage*

Right and bottom right: new coleus hybrids of unusual appearance in frilled, and standard-leaved, forms
Above: antlered Fantasia type, Red Cascade

striking change from the more usual foliage colours. In recent years even more colourful strains have been developed such as the Japanese variety, Kimono, with its attractive fluted and divided leaves. It is no wonder that coleus is often known simply as 'the foliage plant'.

Coleus is a native of Java, but was well known in Europe by the 19th century, when it was widely used by the thousand in formal bedding arrangements. Its name derives from the Greek *koleos*, meaning sheath, a reference to the way the stamens are enclosed.

Pinching out the growing tips will encourage the plant to produce more leaves and bush out to really good effect. One plant can achieve a spread of up to 30cm (12 in), so that a group of three or four together will fill your windowsill with colour for most of the year. The flowers – that are pale blue and rather insignificant and appear at the tips of the stalks – should be nipped off as soon as they start to show. If the flowers are allowed to remain, the growth of the plant suffers and it will die prematurely.

Coleus is sometimes propagated from cuttings, rather than seed. Take about 7–8cm (3 in) from the top of non-flowering shoot, cut it just below a leaf joint, remove all except the top two leaves and root it in a small pot filled with J.I. No 1 or an even mixture of peat and sharp sand. Move it to successively larger pots as it grows, until settling it finally in the ideal size – an 18cm (7 in) pot.

Cuttings can be taken either in early autumn or mid spring, but in both cases care must be taken that the winter temperature does not fall below 15°C (60°F). Don't be alarmed if the leaves of your cutting fade during the winter – the colours brighten again with longer hours of daylight.

Euphorbia Pulcherrima

*Above: the creamy-white bracts of this well-tended poinsettia may retain their colour for several months
Right: an attractive display of contrasting, coloured poinsettias at their best*

Type	greenhouse perennial
Common name	poinsettia
Family	EUPHORBIACEAE
Flowering season	mainly from early winter to early spring (November to February)
Mature size	1.5–1.8m (5–6 ft) when roots are confined to large pots

The name euphorbia is said to derive from Euphorbus, a physician in ancient times to the king of Mauretania. However, the plant – a native of Central America – is more popularly known as poinsettia and was so-called after Joel R. Poinsette (1775–1851). This botanist and diplomat was the first American ambassador to Mexico in 1825, and brought the plant back with him when he returned to Charleston, South Carolina.

Listen to any of the old gardeners and you will know that they still find it difficult to believe that the once-dreaded poinsettia can be grown today with what seems a casual ease; or certainly casual in comparison with what they had to put up with when tending these exotic tropical subjects. In the old days poinsettia plants required high temperature, good light, careful watering and feeding, and almost nursemaid-like attention.

Without the advantage of the growth-restricting chemicals used today even the best-grown older varieties were frequently tall, leggy things that were of little value as indoor plants. It was the habit of the plant to grow up to 1.5–1.8m (5–6 ft) before producing its colourful bracts (leaves that surround the flowers). The modern varieties develop into compact, multi-headed plants after their growing tips are removed when they reach a height of 15–20cm (6–8 in). Thanks to the facility for branching freely and easily, and the benefit of chemical growth-depressants (applied periodically by the grower in carefully-measured doses), the present-day plants are compact, easily transported and ideal subjects for the living room.

Recalling past experiences in the more troubled days of poinsettia growing, it is astonishing that poinsettias given as presents at Christmas time can still be in flower when the owner departs on holiday in early autumn (late August).

Poinsettias should enjoy the lightest possible window position in the house, a temperature in the region of 18°C (65°F), and a watering programme that allows the compost to dry out a little between visits with the watering can. Also, a little weak liquid fertilizer given occasionally does no harm. If you want the plant to retain its colour for nine months this would seem to be the best advice to follow. Short-lived flowers are seen in the centre of the plant at the top of the stem, but these are insignificant and are surrounded by the bracts that give the plant its colour.

Bracts may remain colourful for anything from a few weeks to many months; once the bracts begin to 'shatter' there will be a general deterioration in the plant as leaves begin to turn yellow and eventually fall. When this happens allow the compost to dry out gradually, by which time there will be few, if any, leaves on the stems. You should then cut the branches back to 8–10cm (3–4 in) from the main stem and store the plant in a warm, dry place. In four to six weeks following the cutting-back operation you will see new growth developing along the main stem – this will be the signal that the plant needs to be given enough water to soak the compost through. Watering will stimulate growth and once there is evidence of this

you pot the plant on into a slightly larger container, carefully removing some of the old soil before doing so. Put a few crocks in the bottom of the new pot to ensure good drainage, and add a mixture of two parts J.I. No 3 compost and one part sphagnum peat. Firm the plant well in with your fingertips and water well.

When the plant has produced a reasonable amount of growth, remove the tips of each shoot to encourage the plants to branch. If the plant is well endowed with branches it will do no harm to take off a few to improve its overall appearance. As with all members of the EUPHORBIACEAE family,

the stem will exude a milky sap when cut, but this should not give cause for concern as the wound quickly heals. If you want to, you can use the pieces that are removed to rear new plants.

Ideally, you should prepare the cuttings from the top section of plant with some three or four leaves attached to each section. Dip the cuttings in a rooting hormone powder or liquid before you insert them in small pots filled with clean peat to which a little sharp sand has been added. Small, 8–10cm (3–4 in) cuttings are likely to produce more suitable and attractive plants than taller, developed ones. When you propagate cuttings

Above: a brilliantly-coloured poinsettia of fine, compact form
Right: dusty pink poinsettias look good against a light-painted brick wall and mix well with green foliage plants

indoors or in the greenhouse it will be a great help if you are able to use a heated propagating frame that generates a close, humid atmosphere. Avoid the tendency to get the compost too wet, but at the same time it is important that the plant should be surrounded by a high degree of humidity. Few cuttings root well in dry, airy conditions.

Of all the varieties available today, *E.p.* Mikkelrochford, with its compact habit and brilliant red colouring, is probably the best. The growing conditions in respect of light and temperature in the nurseryman's greenhouse will have some influence on the bract colouring, so it

will pay you to shop around a little in order to find plants with the brightest red colouring, if that is what you prefer.

As well as the reds there are limited quantities available of the lovely dusty pink variety *E.p.* Mikkeldawn. This is an excellent shade of colouring when you come to arrange poinsettias with green foliage plants – the reds tend to be a little harsh and are usually best left in isolation. Also, from the same group, comes *E.p.* Mikkelwhite; this is a pleasing ivory white in colour and is very useful for decoration in church around Christmas time.

Ficus

Type   greenhouse perennial

Family   MORACEAE

Flowering season   foliage plant

Propagation   sow seed in early spring (February); take cuttings or air-layer mid to late spring (March–April)

Mature size/shape   30m (100 ft) trailing, climbing or single-stem specimens

Ficus is a diverse genus ranging from *F. benghalensis*, the spectacular banyan that extends itself from the main trunk by means of aerial roots that themselves become trunks, to *F. carica*, the edible fig. Several of the tender species are grown as house plants for their attractive foliage.

Ficus elastica (India rubber tree) This most popular species is native to tropical Asia where it grows into a 30m (100 ft) forest tree, but as a house plant it makes a single erect stem, clothed with large and leathery evergreen leaves. It will grow rapidly enough if given warm and moist conditions, and it also tolerates cool, dry atmospheres although this reduces its rate of growth. Its adaptability to so many climatic conditions means that the ficus will suit anywhere that has a minimum winter temperature of 10°C (50°F); it can even survive

at 7°C (45°F) though some of the lower leaves will be lost under these conditions.

The commonest wild form of *F. elastica* grows outdoors in southern Spain. There are several cultivars that are used as house plants.

Decora has large rounded leaves that are up to 30cm (12 in) long. These leaves have a large reddish midrib on the underside and a bright red, almost scarlet, sheath that protects the growing point. When the plant is making its new growth, usually in early summer (May), this sheath is thrown off, but make sure that it falls right away, otherwise it may rot and damage the young leaves.

Robusta lacks this red sheath, but has even larger leaves, up to 45cm (18 in) long and half as wide; it also makes a more compact plant. For most of the time, the India rubber tree can be put in any position. It will never be happy in very deep shade,

but when new leaves are coming out it doesn't want to be directly in the sun's path either. Young leaves are soft and are easily scorched and distorted in a hot sun, while mature leaves are tough and leathery.

Variegated forms Besides the green-leaved Decora and Robusta, two cultivars with variegated leaves are also available. Variegated plants are often rather more delicate than the green-leaved forms and this is especially true of *F. elastica*. The variegated plants like a winter temperature of 15°C (60°F) with a minimum of 13°C (55°F). The leaves need good light for the variegation to become pronounced, but here too you must ensure that the newly-emerging leaves are not subjected to scorching sun.

The cultivar known as Schryveriana has a cream margin to the leaves, while the centre is mottled cream and dark green; the mottling is more or less rectangular in shape. The leaves of Tricolor are mottled with light and dark green and yellow. The old variegated Doescheri has been superseded by other variegated forms, but you might possibly come across it; it has small, elliptical leaves that are pink when young and have light and dark green mottling with an ivory margin.

Black Prince is a newly-introduced form with black leaves.

Other species

At one time, a large number of other ficus were grown in the home, but not so many are available these days.

Ficus lyrata (fiddleback fig) A very imposing plant, it has large, rather light green leaves about 30cm (12 in) long and 25cm (9 in) across, and is shaped like the body of a violin.

Ideally, it likes a minimum winter temperature of 18°C (65°F), but will survive in 15°C (60°F). When syringeing the leaves of this plant, it is fascinating to observe how all the water is channelled down the leaves and trunk, to emerge around the roots. This shows that it is native to a dry region and so, occasionally, it will not mind drying out completely, although naturally it will resent being too wet. Otherwise, treat it in the same way as *F. elastica*, but always give it full light.

Ficus benjamina Not all ficus have large leaves and this species is a very different-looking plant. It makes a small and graceful pendulous shrub (eventually becoming a tree) that has thin wiry branches. These are thickly covered with leaves that are bright green when young and the colour of privet leaves when old. They are elliptically shaped, about 10cm (4 in) long and 3cm (1¼ in) wide, and end in a long thin point. This evergreen plant is almost certainly going to shed some leaves during the winter, but do not be unduly alarmed about this, unless it becomes excessive, as they will all be replaced when growth starts again.

The winter temperature should not fall below 13°C (55°F). If the plant becomes too dry, it wilts, but will quickly recover when watered. During the late spring and summer it will take plenty of water (but do not overdo this) and every two years it will

Below left: Ficus elastica *Decora with its familiar shiny leaves is one of the most adaptable varieties*
Below: variegated Ficus elastica *Tricolor, that sometimes flushes pink. The sheath protecting the growing point can be seen in the centre of the plant*

need to be potted on. It likes a well-lit position without too much direct sunlight.

Ficus diversifolia (mistletoe fig) *F. diversifolia*, that you may encounter as *F. deltoidea*, is interesting as it is the only ficus that normally fruits at home. This small twiggy shrub has thick, dark green leaves, nearly circular in shape and only about 2·5cm (1 in) long and wide. Little round berries, pale yellow or red in colour and on thin stalks, appear from the leaf axils; they are fig-shaped, but you need a magnifying glass to appreciate this fact. These fruits appear on quite small plants and persist throughout the year.

This native of India and Malaya requires a fairly moist atmosphere, but it is surprisingly hardy and will survive happily with a winter temperature as low as 10°C (50°F). If the tips of the twigs are just pinched out in mid spring (March) it will further the production of sideshoots – and also seems to encourage fruiting. The plant is usually purchased in an 8cm (3 in) pot and should be moved into a 23cm (5 in) pot after a year, where it can remain for two or three years before it needs a bigger one.

Ficus radicans You may still see occasionally the plant known as *F. radicans* Variegata. This has the same creeping habit as *F. pumila*, but larger leaves, up to 6cm (2¼ in) long and 2·5cm (1 in) wide, that are triangular in shape, coming to a long thin point. They have a cream margin that may sometimes take over most of the leaf surface.

This ficus needs a warm moist atmosphere and is unlikely to thrive in the home where the air will probably be too dry. The winter temperature should be around 15°C (60°F) and the plant should never be allowed to dry out entirely, even during the winter. It requires ample light, but must be shielded from any burning sun.

Ficus pumila Finally, we come to a plant that breaks all the usual rules for house plants. This trailing or climbing species will survive out of doors in south-west England in places such as Cornwall and so only needs to be kept frost-free indoors and is not suited to very warm rooms. It will support itself on a wall by means of aerial roots in the same way as an ivy, but is normally used as a trailing plant in the home. The thin wiry stems are densely covered with heart-shaped leaves only 2·5cm (1 in) long and 13mm (½ in) wide, that set so thickly that the stems are invisible.

This is a plant that should never be allowed to dry out, as once the leaves shrivel, they are unlikely to revive. It is possible, but not easy, to overwater this plant and the soil should always be kept moist.

Far right: Ficus
elastica *Doescheri*
*needs good light
for its variegation to
remain well-defined*
Right: Ficus radicans
*Variegata likes a humid
atmosphere*
*Above right: the
distinctive leaf of*
Ficus lyrata
(fiddleback fig)

It does not like direct sunlight on its leaves for long and has the advantage of being tolerant of deep shade, though naturally some light is essential.

Cutting and propagation

In the case of *F. elastica*, take leaf-bud or terminal cuttings in the spring (see page 35). These will need a high temperature of 21°C (70°F), if possible, until rooted. Air-layering, when the stem has lost its lower leaves due to over-watering, or grown too tall, is another suitable method of propagation.

For *F. benjamina*, take heeled leaf cuttings; these will need a temperature of 18°C (65°F) when rooting. Once the plants are established you should stop them, to promote branching.

Propagate *F. radicans* Variegata and *F. pumila* by taking leaf-bud or terminal stem cuttings. These will root quickly if kept at a temperature of 21°C (70°F).

All these ficus can be rooted in a peat-sand medium using a propagator, or else pots kept in a warm place.

Potting on and pruning

Ficus are normally purchased in 13cm (5 in) pots and grown in J.I. potting compost. The soilless composts are perfectly adequate, but light, and as India rubber plants grow they are liable to become unstable in such a light mixture. They should stay in this size pot for several years, provided that they are fed regularly in the growing season.

When they do have to be potted on, they should go into an 18cm (7 in) pot with J.I. No 2 or No 3 compost; this soil should be firmly compressed.

If the plant becomes too tall it can be pruned back, but this will release the latex, a milky juice from which rubber was extracted by the Aztecs and the Haitians at the time of the European discovery of the New World (commercial rubber is now obtained from the genus *Hevea* and from synthetics). Have some powdered charcoal ready to sprinkle immediately onto the wound. The plant, as a result, will probably produce about three stems where you had only the single trunk before, giving it a fuller and more attractive shape. The best time to prune is in late spring (April) when the roots are starting to make fresh growth before the new leaves appear.

Care of ficus

The ficus is straightforward to treat. Like most house plants, it appreciates a moist air around its leaves and benefits from being syringed in hot weather, but the soil ball should be kept on the dry side except in times of new growth when it will need plenty of water. On the other hand, it is inadvisable to let the soil dry out completely; water it well, wait until a day after the soil appears to be dry again and then give it another good soak.

The large leaves attract dust, so it is a good idea to sponge them once every ten days, using water and cotton wool. However, you must bear in mind that the newly-unfurled leaves are soft and tender and should not be sponged until they mature.

Impatiens (Busy Lizzie)

Type	sub shrub grown as tender perennial
Common name	busy Lizzie
Family	BALSAMINACEAE
Flowering season	late spring to late autumn (April–October)
Mature size/shape	25–60cm (9–24 in)

The name *Impatiens* comes from the Latin for impatient, a suitable description of the British yellow balsam that discharges its seeds with great violence when ripe. The famous 19th century naturalist Sir J. D. Hooker, when in his eighties, spent nine years studying the balsam genus and pronounced it to be 'deceitful above all plants, and desperately wicked' – an opinion echoed by many an amateur gardener when faced with the more than 700 species it contains. The confusion is reflected in the numerous classifications still given today to busy Lizzie – that can be found listed as a hybrid of *Impatiens sultanii*, *I. petersiana*, *I. holstii*, or *I. walleriana*. It was in Zanzibar in 1896 that Hooker found the species he named *I. sultanii* in honour of the sultan of that island.

A very popular house plant, the busy Lizzie will flourish equally well outside when used as a summer bedding plant. It is aptly named in that indoors it will flower steadily from late spring to late autumn (April to October); in the garden its flowering season is curtailed by temperature and weather conditions. The blooms, single or double and about 5cm (2 in) across, are quite delicate and come in a variety of shades ranging from white, through pink and orange, to magenta and scarlet; variegated blooms are also quite common. Many forms have variegated foliage as well, notably the New Guinea hybrids.

Busy Lizzie is a fast grower and its appearance is greatly helped by pinching out the main growing tip when the plant is about 25cm (9 in) high. This induces it to branch out into a more shapely bush, and you will have more flowers on it as well. However, some of the new hybrid varieties, such as the Imp strain developed at RHS Wisley, are dwarf types that only reach heights of 25cm (9 in) and so do not need to be pinched out.

Busy Lizzie enjoys a light situation, although if you are growing it indoors avoid placing it on a south-facing windowsill where it will be in danger of being scorched by direct sunlight. Water it generously during the growing season, with a weekly feed of appropriate fertilizer according to the manufacturer's instructions.

The plants can be propagated equally well from seeds or cuttings. They grow very well in a compost such as J.I. No 2. A 13cm (5 in) pot is ideal for a busy Lizzie, and it only needs to be repotted every other year, preferably in the spring (February to April). It will overwinter indoors or in a greenhouse quite happily, so long as the temperature is not allowed to drop below 13°C (55°F) and the soil is kept just moist. Don't be alarmed if the plant loses several leaves; they will grow again in the spring.

Busy Lizzie does have a tendency to become 'leggy' and rather unattractive after two or three years, and when this happens you must be ruthless – take a couple of cuttings and throw it out!

Here we show just a few of the many varieties of busy Lizzie. Right: variegated flower Impatiens *Harlequin Orange; centre: variegated leaf* Impatiens *Variegata; far right:* Impatiens *flourishing outdoors; below: brightly variegated leaves of* I. Variegata *contrast with its delicate blooms*

Philodendron

Type	greenhouse perennial
Family	ARACEAE
Mature size	up to 4·5m (15 ft) tall when confined to pots
Special use	indoor foliage plant

The philodendron, whose name comes from the Greek *phileo*, to love, and *dendron*, a tree, in reference to the tree-climbing habits of the plant, originates from the tropical regions of South America. It has recently come into its own with the steady increase in popularity of plants for home and office.

In the warm, steamy heat of the jungle where humidity levels reach saturation point, the philodendron produces majestic leaves that would be quite out of proportion in the average living-room. However, the prospective purchaser should not be deterred by these references to size as indoor conditions are generally far less humid and plants in such an atmosphere will produce leaves that are very much smaller and easier to manage.

Among the philodendrons are climbing types such as *P. hastatum* with broad, arrow-shaped leaves, and those with leaves that radiate in the shape of a shuttlecock from stout central trunks. The latter contains the truly superb *P. wendlandii* that has glossy, green leaves on short petioles or leaf stalks, tightly grouped on short central stems.

P. echlerii is commonly known as the king of the tree philodendrons. If its roots are confined to a large pot or tub, it will have a radius of some 3·6m (12 ft) and a height of 4·5m (15 ft) when grown in a well-heated greenhouse with a minimum temperature of 21°C (70°F). Without doubt, this is one of the most superb indoor foliage plants in cultivation today.

P. bipinnatifidum is the best known of the radiating philodendrons and most certainly the easiest to obtain. The nurseryman finds them a practical and profitable proposition because new plants are easily raised from seed and are not too space-demanding. Deeply-serrated green leaves are supported on slender leaf stalks that may be 60cm (2 ft) or more in length. When space permits, place the philodendron on a pedestal where it gives a superb impression and its architectural appearance can be seen to full advantage.

Mature plants of the larger-leaved philodendrons will usually produce inflorescences (flowering heads) that consist of the spathe (or enclosing bract) that is gently, almost protectively, curled around the central spadix (or flower-spike) from which seed is often harvested; spathe colours vary from a creamy-white to a delightful pale burgundy in the case of *P. echlerii*. Individually these remain colourful for only a few days before they fade and die.

There are many other fine plants among the philodendrons, the best known of which is probably *P. scandens*, the sweetheart plant, which has heart-shaped leaves and is one of the easiest of plants to care for. Any of the philodendrons that you may be fortunate enough to acquire will respond well to the same treatment.

As the larger-leaved philodendrons mature, as well as taking on a more robust appearance, they will develop aerial roots along the main stem or trunk; in nature these roots are used to support the plant almost in the same way as guy ropes are used to support a tent. Although some may be removed with little harm to the plant, it is inadvisable to remove too many; the best practice is to tie the roots to the stem of the plants or to the supporting cane, and to direct the tip of the root into the compost in the pot when the roots are long enough. Alternatively, you can direct the roots into an adjacent water receptacle; treated in this way the roots will draw up moisture as and when required by the plant.

The conventional bamboo stake is seldom strong enough to provide supports for these larger plants. It is much better to get something stouter – such as hazel – and to cover it with a thick layer of sphagnum moss tied securely in position with nylon fishing line or plastic-covered wire. The aerial roots will then find their way into the moss provided it is kept moist by regular spraying with water. Use of moss-covered supports can be of particular benefit to plants that are being grown indoors; the constant spraying of the moss will help to create a certain amount of humidity in rooms that are frequently all too dry. Indoors, in any event, it is essential that you should provide shaded, moist and warm conditions in order to succeed with these ARACEAE family members.

When potting, the compost should be open, peaty and well drained; although damp conditions are vital it is equally important that the soil in the pot does not remain sodden for long periods as this will assuredly result in root damage and subsequent failure with the plant. A suggested mix is two-thirds J.I. No 3 potting compost and add one-third fresh sphagnum peat. You should press the compost firmly into position but must never ram it hard. Feed established plants regularly with liquid fertilizer; you can keep larger plants in 25cm (10 in) pots in good fettle by this means. Large pots are often impractical indoors, but where space is no problem you can then pot plants on into even larger containers and they will usually benefit from this kind of treatment.

Right: Philodendron scandens, *the popular sweetheart plant, can climb vigorously up to 3m (10 ft) or more*
Far right, above: Philodendron wendlandii *should be carefully tended as leaf loss spoils its looks*
Far right: Philodendron bipinnatifidum, *with incized leaves, makes a good subject for a hanging basket*

Saintpaulia

Type: perennial flowering house plant

Common name: African violet

Family: GESNERIACEAE

Flowering season: almost continuously through the year

Mature size/shape: rosette; 7–10cm (3–4 in) high, 10–23cm (4–9 in) across

The first saintpaulias, or African violets as they are commonly called, were introduced from tropical Africa in 1893 by Baron von Saint Paul-Illaire, after whom they are named. Today, the offspring from those plants are among the most popular of all indoor plants, and deservedly so. They are ideally suited for use in the home and are particularly valuable for people without a garden or for those who wish to concentrate on the growing of small plants. Equally they are valuable additions to a collection of general greenhouse or conservatory plants and with the introduction into the horticultural world of the fluorescent tube they can now be used in positions that only a short time ago would have been considered quite unsuitable for any type of plant.

Saintpaulias fit neatly into small spaces – especially narrow windowsills – and because they never grow tall and their spread can be controlled by the removal of outer leaves, they can be grown in the same space for years. They are easily propagated from leaf cuttings (that you can receive swiftly through the post). Old crowded plants can be divided although, ideally, plants should not be allowed to become crowded, or the top rosette may be cut off and re-rooted when plants become old and develop a trunk-like main stem. All of these methods of increasing plants are easy if undertaken at the right time of year and providing that a little care is taken.

Some people seem instinctively to know what type of treatment to give their plants; others quickly learn a plant's particular preferences but, alas, a few must resign themselves to the fact that they just do not have the time or the type of accommodation needed for these plants. For the latter there is always the possibility of using artificial lighting. Reasons for disappointment include following instructions for culture written for one situation in a totally different set of circumstances. Sometimes recommended treatment appropriate to the greenhouse is quite wrong for growing in the home, also many houses differ

in such important features as light intensity, degree of humidity and temperature.

The choice of varieties available is wide and the number is regularly being increased. A great deal of work is being done in the United States and Canada with new varieties and each year new plants pass each other in mid-Atlantic for trial on the other side. There are now plants with single, semi-double and fully-double blossoms. Flower colour ranges from white, through soft pink to so-called red, from palest blue to deepest purple. Some plants have flowers of two colours, some are striped and others have frilled petal edges of a different colour or shade. Flower shape has also been extended and there are now types which are known as 'stars'; these have flowers with five equal-sized petals and have overcome the distressing habit of most of the single-flowered sorts of dropping their flowers while still in their prime. Perhaps the most interesting recent development has been the introduction of the miniature and semi-miniature varieties. These are small editions of the standard forms but usually with no reduction of flower size.

Growing in the home

Taking first the needs of saintpaulias grown in the home, the following treatment will ensure that they thrive. Good light is absolutely essential. Strong and prolonged sunlight falling directly onto plants placed right in a south-facing window could cause scorching of the foliage, but usually some form of curtaining will overcome this problem. No such problem will exist in an east- or west-facing window. A short spell of bright sunshine will often bring into bloom a plant that has been shy to flower. Between 12 and 14 hours of daylight are necessary for the continued production of flower-buds and plants getting a much shorter day length will not flower or will do so only sparsely.

Good light should be coupled with fairly high humidity and this can best be supplied by standing the plants on trays or saucers of damp shingle or moist peat. Grouping several plants together also tends to supply a microclimate that is suitable. Saintpaulias enjoy all the good things in life and particularly a warm steady temperature – around 18°C (65°F) is ideal; at much higher temperatures buds will drop and at lower ones they will not be produced. When a temperature falls much below 15°C (60°F) for any length of time it may be advisable to rest the plant until better times return by keeping it on the dry side. As with all potted plants saintpaulias should only be watered when they need it, which is just as they are about to dry out. The use of tepid water is a refinement but some people regard it as essential. A fairly dry period at the end of winter will encourage the production of flower-buds for the late spring display. Do not under any circumstances over-water saintpaulias or the result will be a small heap of 'mushy' leaves – never to recover. Always water from below – the leaves dislike being doused.

Feeding is essential for healthy plant growth and the steady production of flower-buds. A number of people ring the changes with their liquid fertilizer and this is an excellent idea. Do not use just a general purpose house plant fertilizer, which is most probably rich in nitrogen for healthy leaves, but alternate this with one with a high potash content (a tomato fertilizer). Stick strictly to the maker's instructions – or dilute the mixture and use slightly more regularly – but do not use a strong mix. Double-flowered sorts need more regular feeding than the singles.

Small pots encourage flowering and large pots filled with unoccupied soil lead to root rot and eventual collapse. The soilless composts, provided that they are well nourished, are excellent because they provide exactly the right sort of consistency demanded by these plants: a light, quick-draining compost. The plastic pot retains moisture longer than that of clay but apart from this point there is nothing to choose between them.

Plants should be kept clean and can be gently washed under the tap during reasonable weather; allow them to drain and do this early in the morning so that they dry out thoroughly before night. All spent flowers should be taken off to prevent them producing seed. Stems which have finished flowering should be removed entirely, right back to the main stem, otherwise the remaining section will cause rot. In essence saintpaulias like to be cared for, to have warmth, good light and a buoyant atmosphere, to be just right for water, and well fed but not over-indulged.

They will then respond with an almost continuous display of attractive foliage and beautiful flowers.

In the greenhouse or conservatory

In the greenhouse, humidity can be more easily controlled than in the dryness of the average home; water can be splashed about to evaporate during the day and benches tend to be much damper than the normal room surface. Otherwise much that has been said about growing saint-paulias in the home is appropriate in the greenhouse: soilless composts (or a loam-based compost such as J.I. No 2 with additional grit and peat), pot size, watering, feeding and temperature. What is different is the quality of the light. All greenhouses in which saintpaulias are grown will need some form of shading (or a part of them must be so adapted) otherwise the plants will noticeably yellow or scorch. Dappled light is exactly right for these conditions.

Under artificial light

For some years now a number of plants, particularly begonias and saintpaulias, have been grown under fluorescent lights. Although it is possible to grow them exclusively under artificial light it is more common to use fluorescent tubes to supplement the natural light available and thereby give the plants a longer day. They will respond with flowers out of season. If other growing conditions are right – temperature, humidity, compost and feeding – an additional six or eight hours under the lights every day will persuade the plants that it is summer when in fact it is mid winter. Young plants about to come into bloom will, with this treatment, bloom from late autumn to late spring (October to April) when their flowers are most sought after. If you place 40 watt bulbs 20–25cm (8–10 in) above the tops of the plants and light them for, say, 4–6 hours each evening they will most probably give flowers throughout the winter. Tubes of different colours are available; Daylight and Warm White are two and anyone contemplating installing this very successful aid to winter flowers should consult specialist help or literature on the subject. If natural light is poor, increase the period of illumination by the tube.

Training

You hardly ever read about the subject of training saintpaulias into a particular shape but it is a very important aspect of displaying them to best advantage and vital for exhibition. Saintpaulias are rosette-shaped plants, their leaves are arranged around a central crown as in a posy. Small side shoots are produced as plants mature but you should remove these as soon as this is possible, otherwise they will develop and cause a crowded centre with each one fighting for space and forcing the leaves of the others in all directions. Unwanted growing points can be removed by being gently pushed aside with the blunt end of a pencil, when they will easily leave the axils of the leaves, or tweezers may be used. Be careful to see that the shoots are growth points and not embryo flowers.

*Left: Candy with semi-double flower from the rhapsody group, originating from Holland, trained to give a rosette of leaves around central cluster of blooms
Below: Midget Valentine, a miniature with single flower and attractive variegated foliage*

Propagation

By far the easiest method of propagation is that of leaf cuttings. Carefully remove medium-sized leaves from the parent plants and neatly trim their stalks with a sharp razor-blade to 2–3cm (1 in) long. Then insert the leaves in compost (peat and sand, or a soilless compost) at a 45 degree angle, burying the leaf stalk about 6–13mm ($\frac{1}{4}$–$\frac{1}{2}$ in). Use a tiny pot or, if many leaves are being used, shallow trays. Carefully water the whole thing and put it in a polythene bag and ignore for 6–8 weeks. Given suitable temperatures, leaves will begin to produce clumps of new plantlets that, when of sufficient size, you should divide into individual plantlets and pot up and grow on. New plants will begin to flower when about 8–12 months old. Old plants can be beheaded and the central rosette, after reducing it to, say, about 12 leaves, can be re-rooted in suitable compost, in close conditions (such as in a polythene bag) in the spring of the year. Should a multi-crowned plant be allowed to develop, it can be pulled apart and each individual rosette of leaves potted separately; any crowns that have no roots attached, or very little root, should be given the polythene bag treatment.

Groups and varieties

A few basic facts can be learned about different groups and individual varieties.

Single-flowered These forms tend to drop their blossoms for no apparent reason and most people find it distressing that blooms fall while still fresh. Some varieties are a great deal easier to grow than others. All of the Englert's Diana strain are robust, with large flowers held in large clusters on strong stems well clear of the foliage.

Rhapsodies Another important group which came from Holland that does not drop flowers the

Above: Little Red, a single-flowered miniature with mahogany-green 'quilted' foliage; below: Inge, one of the ballet series, showing unusual reverse leaves

Some varieties to choose

RHAPSODIES
Elfriede	dark blue
Birgit	bright pink
Ruby	deep ruby-red
Gigi	white, edged with light blue
Lila	two-tone violet

BALLET SERIES
Inge (single)	deep blue, ruffled petals
Eva (semi-double)	medium blue
Marta (single)	lavender-blue, ruffled petals
Anna (single)	pale pink, ruffled petals
Erica (single)	cerise-red, frilled petals, bright yellow pollen sac
Lisa (single)	salmon-pink, large flowered wavy-edged petals

SEMI-DOUBLES
Calumet Beacon	lavender-blue, with white edging
Peak of Pink	pink, with a white edge
Jolly Giant	frosty-pink and huge
Crown of Red	crimson, with very prominent pollen sacs

DOUBLE-FLOWERED
White Lady	white
Double Delight	white
Blue Bounty	blue
Pink Rococco	pink

MINIATURES
Window Blue (double)	medium blue
Wee Willie Winkle	white, lavender-edged
Davy Crockett	light blue, star-shaped
Little Red	deep red
Midget Valentine	fuchsia

SEMI-MINIATURES
Dancing Doll (double)	deep pink, star-shaped
Icicle Trinket (double)	ruffled white
Mingo (double)	red, star-shaped
Gay Border (single)	violet with white edge, star-shaped

TRAILING
Violet Trail (single)	reddish-mauve, star-shaped
Mysterium (double)	pale pink

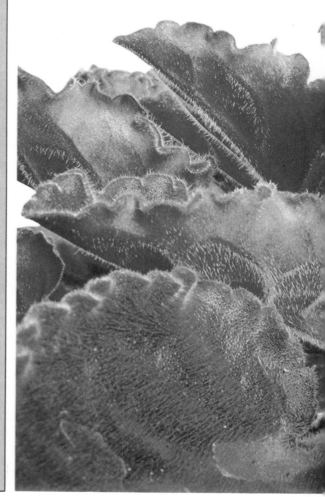

second it is moved. Several named varieties of this group are available.

Ballet Quite new on the scene, this series of single or semi-doubles does not drop its flowers.

Semi-doubles This type holds its flowers very well and the extra petals in the centre add substance to the flower.

Double-flowered These hold their flowers until they dry up, when they should be removed as they fade and would detract from the appearance of the plants. The doubles need a little more regular feeding than the other sorts.

Miniatures The official classification of a miniature is one under 15cm (6 in) in diameter. They are very suitable for people with severely limited space as their flowers are just as freely produced and often there is very little reduction in flower size.

Semi-miniatures These are a little bigger but should not exceed 20cm (8 in) in diameter when the plant is fully grown.

Trailing Bound to become popular when they are better known to a wider public, these trailing forms need a little 'drop' in which to trail but are very effective.

Hundreds of varieties are available, although unlike many other plants, the would-be grower cannot just walk into any florist's shop and ask for a particular variety of saintpaulia. A small number of specialist growers offer a large selection of forms but these must be sought out. Enthusiasts do of course exchange leaves and plantlets and, with only a little trouble, it is possible to import leaves from growers overseas.

Finally, a word of caution: flower colours vary considerably under different growing conditions and it must be borne in mind that colour descriptions do not always mean the same thing to different people.

Flower forms

single

double

semi-double

Cacti and Succulents

Succulents are plants that have evolved with the ability to store water in their leaves, bodies and roots to enable them to survive periods of drought. They are more common than most people realize – in fact, most countries in the world have some form of succulent plant in their native flora. Even in Britain, sempervivum (houseleek) and sedum (stonecrop) are quite often seen even though the climate does not seem to warrant succulent growth.

One of the largest families in the succulent flora is the CACTACEAE, or cactus family. Cacti differ from succulents in having areoles from which their spines grow and from which, in many cases, the flowers are produced. These areoles look rather like small felt pin cushions; the spination of the other succulent plants resembles thorns.

It is believed that both cacti and other succulents originated from a common source before the continents of Africa and America parted in the continental drift many millions of years ago. Today cacti are native to North and South America, but succulents, though mainly indigenous to Africa, can be found growing native in many other parts of the world.

Types of cacti

There are two completely different types of cacti: the epiphytes and the so-called 'desert' cacti. Both groups require separate forms of cultivation as their habitat is so different.

The epiphytes (or 'jungle' cacti) that include such well-known plants as schlumbergera (formerly zygocactus), the Christmas and Easter cacti, epiphyllum, rhipsalis and so on, are flat-stemmed plants growing in the tropical rain forests of Central America. They do not live on the ground but on the branches of forest trees, in crevices and joints that have accumulated leaf mould and bird droppings. Their stems and roots obtain moisture from rain and they are continually shaded from the tropical sunshine by overhanging branches.

The second type is the so-called 'desert' cactus; the name is slightly misleading as the true habitat of these plants is not desert but a form of heathland with grass and small shrubs. They are native to North and South America but seem to adapt well in other places; too well in

Serried ranks of cacti bristling with protective spines (previous page) or a mixed group of succulents (opposite) form a unique display. Above: opuntia (prickly pear) with seed pods. Left: schlumbergera, an attractive jungle cactus

some cases – as in Queensland, Australia, where the opuntia (prickly pear) invaded vast areas of farmland and defeated all efforts at eradication until its natural predator, the caterpillar of the cactoblastis moth, was imported. These cacti inhabit areas of little rainfall but have powers to absorb water when it is available and retain it for future use when times are dry and hard. Sometimes they can absorb moisture from morning mists through their stems and spines.

General cultivation
In Britain most cacti are grown in greenhouses or garden frames, as the winters are too damp and humidity causes the plants to rot if they are planted outdoors. Cacti will withstand a habitat that has very cold, but dry, nights and winters, but cannot survive a damp, cold atmosphere.

Some gardeners still use clay pots for growing cacti, but most have now changed over to plastic, as these are lighter on the greenhouse staging and easier to keep clean, especially for exhibition purposes. Also, plants in plastic pots do not require watering so often.

Composts used for growing cacti and succulents must be particularly porous, such as J.I. No 2 or 3, to which you should add some very sharp sand, grit, or broken brick to ensure good drainage. This is very important, especially when growing in plastic containers. The pot size should be as large as the diameter of the plant with its spines plus a further 13mm ($\frac{1}{2}$ in) all round. The epiphytic cacti will require the addition of humus to the potting compost in the form of leaf mould, peat or well-rotted manure, and again the soil must always be well drained.

Whereas the 'desert' cacti will grow well in full sun provided there is sufficient ventilation, epiphytes, being 'forest' cacti, require shading from sun from early summer to mid autumn (May to September), and can only be grown on top of the greenhouse staging during the winter months. Evidence of sunburn shows as red pigmentation on the stems; affected plants should be shaded at once. Never stand the pot in a container of water as they cannot tolerate bog-like conditions.

How much water?
How much water to give and how often to water are key questions with this group of plants, and it is difficult to give an easy answer. Common sense plays a great part here: if it is hot and sunny, plants growing under glass require a great deal of water. Those growing in clay pots may need water each evening. Be careful when

A mixed group of succulents form a unique display

watering not to leave any droplets on the crowns of the plants, as this could cause scorching when the sun comes out, and badly damage a plant; this is one reason for watering in the evenings and not during the day. If the weather is overcast or damp the plants will not require much water. Desert cacti rest during the winter months and need very little water then, although overhead spraying from time to time can be beneficial. Some succulents can grow in the winter and rest in summer, and it is as well to know the plant's habits and treat it accordingly.

Cacti and succulents grown indoors should be treated as ordinary house plants; they will require watering during the winter (especially if there is central heating) otherwise they will dehydrate. Also if they are kept on a windowsill, and there is frost, bring them into the room, inside the curtains; cacti and succulents will not withstand damp frosts. A quite large plant will go to pulp overnight and is a heartbreaking sight next morning when the curtains are drawn back.

How much heat?
Cacti and succulents require heat during the winter, but remember that they hate a stagnant, stale atmosphere because it causes fungus and rot. So even during the winter provide the plants with some fresh air on a sunny day.

If you heat by paraffin, remember that for every 5 lit (1 gal) you burn, the same amount of water vapour is produced. Even so, many people find heating by this method satisfactory, providing that the appliance is well maintained, and not in a draught. It is very sad to see a collection covered in black, oily soot

where a stove has flared. This is also very difficult to remove and it takes years for the plants to grow out of the effects.

Electricity is clean and easy, but unfortunately very expensive. Under-soil cables are very good, but costly to run and install for a complete collection; this method is favoured for seed-raising and for the propagation section, where plants are put to root. Fan-heaters create a very dry heat, so spraying will have to be done occasionally during the winter when it is sunny or the plants become dehydrated. With a special type of electric water heater that gives off steam when it boils, spraying is not required. Should there be a power failure for any reason, a certain amount of heat will be retained in the pipework, providing the power cut does not go on for too long.

Gas heating for the greenhouse is becoming very popular but be sure that you can obtain spare parts should anything go wrong. Laying a gas supply to the greenhouse could prove to be costly if it is any distance from the house, especially if it necessitates taking up cement paths as well.

Lining your greenhouse with sheet polythene provides a form of double glazing during the winter, and cuts down heating costs appreciably. If you do decide to fit this, make sure that the sheets are overlapped in such a way that the condensation will not drip onto your plants and cause rot, but run down safely out of harm's way.

Window Box Planning

A window box, or a group of boxes, can often be the focal point of the front of a building. A bright splash of colour or the subtle blending of shades of green will draw the admiring eye of the passer-by. It is important that your box is properly planted and cared for, otherwise you may not achieve a pleasing effect.

Unlike those in a garden or growing wild, plants in a window box cannot survive without periodic care. In the growing season, and especially in hot weather, they will need attention two or three times a week. Unless the soil is watered and fed regularly, it will dry up quickly.

Soil and pests

A good way to tackle the soil problem is to fill the box with a mixture of one part peat and two parts sterilized soil with John Innes fertilizer. Subsequently feed the plants regularly with either a liquid or a granular fertilizer, following carefully the instructions supplied. Remember that organic fertilizers are generally safer than chemical ones, as incorrect overfeeding is less harmful to plants.

As your window box soil is in fairly intensive use, it is a good idea to change it every few years, before it is exhausted. In addition, pests and diseases can build up

in the soil if the same types of plant are used each year.

The main pest to look for is greenfly, as the extra shelter a window box affords often allows them to overwinter in the adult stage, especially on such plants as hebe. The cineraria and petunia are also attractive to greenfly. These can be treated with proprietary insecticides but check to ensure that these do not harm any of the other plants you may be using. It is safer to spray with soapy water.

As a box is often sheltered from rain, most plants, especially conifers, will greatly benefit from a fine spray of water once a week, not only to clean them but also to stop any build-up of insecticide on the leaves. Change the brand you use occasionally to cut down the chance of fly building up an immunity to it.

Seasonal schemes

As all plants have a limited growing season, the flowering plants chosen should be changed about five times during the year if all-year colour is required. This need not be very costly, especially if you have a small greenhouse and grow the plants yourself. Move the plants to the box just as they reach the bud stage. For a well-balanced display,

about 40 per cent of the plants in a box can be chosen from the shrub list. The main point to remember when deciding which flowering varieties you will use is to combine shades that blend or complement each other as far as possible, and to see that all the flowers are not the same height so as to give only a narrow band of colour. This problem can be overcome with some species by planting them slightly deeper and by setting some plants at an angle to give a bank of colour against a background of greenery. Trailing plants, such as nasturtium, can be used to fall over the front of the box. Almost any plant can be angled to achieve a special effect as long as the rootball is still embedded in the soil. Cinerarias are often angled at the back and ivy leaf geranium can be spread both front and back to make a cover almost three times the height of the box. Here we list five planting schemes.

Early autumn (August onwards)

Pompon chrysanthemum Denise, Fairie.
Tagetes erecta and *T. patula*.
Coleus blumei Victoria. This variety seems particularly hardy and less liable to leaf-drop than others.
The coleus is a foliage plant with maroon and yellow leaves that blend splendidly with the other recommended plants, all of which are in autumnal shades.

ALL-YEAR-ROUND PLANTING

An effective selection of evergreen plants can provide a pleasing display of greenery for up to four years and requires little attention. If you want an all-year-round display, rather than changing your window box with the seasons, then the evergreens can provide a time-saving, economical answer.

The small conifers, being slow-growing and compact are most suitable for window boxes, but remember to spray the leaves occasionally. When the conifers grow too tall they should be transplanted rather than pruned.

Late autumn (October onwards)

Erica carnea Gracilis or *E. hyemalis*. Both are upright-growing heathers with many flowers.

Solanum capsicastrum Red-berried plant known as Christmas cherry.

From late autumn until the bulb-flowering period is a drab time of year. But window boxes can be planted to look very cheery with this mixture.

Late winter (January onwards)

Daffodils; hyacinths, narcissus; tulips. Beware a yellow/pink or pink/orange clash with this late winter selection.

Mid spring (March onwards)

Cineraria; *Genista hispanica* (Spanish gorse).

The delicate form and colour of the genista contrast well with the somewhat solid and deep-coloured cineraria.

Early summer (May onwards)

Pelargonium domesticum, P. Hortorum, P. P. peltatum; petunia; fuchsia; lobelia; *Begonia semperflorens*; *Salvia splendens*; viola.

Don't plant your choice from this selection until all possibility of frost is over. If you pick off dead flower-heads with the seed pods each week, flowering should continue for about four months.

Late winter planting scheme (top right)
Good contrasts for mid spring (above right)
Long-lasting early summer scheme (right)

379

Gardening Equipment

Forks and **spades** have either a D- or T-shape handle. Many gardeners claim that a D handle allows for better gripping. Try them out in the shop before you buy.

Forks are usually four-pronged and are useful for winter digging, especially on heavy soils.

Spades vary in blade width, from 16–19cm (6–8 in), and blade length, from 26–29cm (10–12 in). You'll find smaller sizes easier to use on heavier soils because less weight is lifted with each spade-load. Lighter, smaller forks and spades are made for women.

A **Dutch hoe** takes the backache out of weeding, and saves time.

When making seed drills you will find a **draw hoe** invaluable. A hand version, known as an **onion hoe**, has a narrower blade and is ideal for cultivating small patches, raised beds, and plants in pots and tubs.

No gardener can do without a **hand fork** and **trowel**. The forks have long and short blades of varying widths; the long, thin ones are excellent for prizing out long-rooted perennial weeds.

You will need a **rake** for breaking down clods to a workable tilth. They range between 30–40cm (12–16 in) wide; when buying ensure that the metal rake is well fixed to the handle.

Wooden ones are wider and are recommended only for very large gardens.

Stainless steel tools cost about twice as much as others, but they are a worthwhile investment. They last much longer, are quick to clean and don't rust. They also slip easily into soil. The handles are made of polypropylene or wood, the former being much lighter.

Pruning can be done with a **pruning knife** or **secateurs**. Well-versed gardeners recommend a sharp knife for most jobs, but many people prefer to use secateurs for trees, shrubs and roses.

The knives must be made of well-hardened steel; cheap ones or pen knives will tear at plant stems and invite infection.

There are two types of secateurs: parrot-billed (scissors action), and anvil (the single blade cuts against a metal block). They should be well-made with sharp blades; blunt ones will only crush plant tissue and frustrate the pruner.

You will need a **reel** and **line** and a **measuring rod** or **tape** in the vegetable garden and for marking out borders.

Wooden or **plastic labels** are best for marking seed-sowings.

Use **gardening gloves** for heavy work and pruning roses.

Your tool shed will not be complete without a **watering can**. Get a 7–9 litre (1½–2 gallon) size with a rose. It is advisable to have a second can for weedkillers.

A **hose** saves time when watering

plants. Invest in a frost-proof one. A **hose reel** will also cut watering time and save wear and tear on the hose.

A **bucket** will serve to carry odds and ends until you acquire a **wheelbarrow**. When you choose a wheelbarrow don't forget to consider its weight when filled and its size in relation to your garden paths.

For hedges, lawns and mixed borders you will require a good pair of **shears**. All but the smallest lawns need to be cut with a mower, but before you decide which type to buy compare the various models and list your requirements (this also applies when buying other lawn

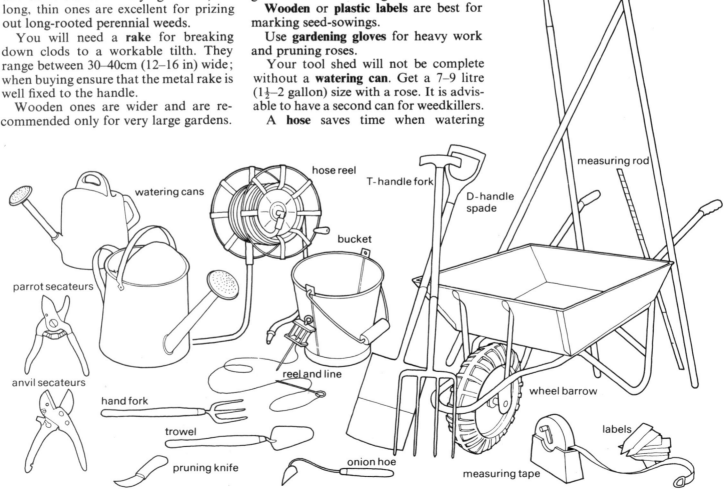

draw hoe
rake
Dutch hoe
measuring rod

watering cans
hose reel
T-handle fork
D-handle spade

parrot secateurs
bucket

anvil secateurs
reel and line
hand fork
wheel barrow
trowel
labels
pruning knife
onion hoe
measuring tape

care equipment). Certain mowers work better on short grass and edges, others on long grass, and all grass boxes are not equally efficient. Choose a lightweight model with adjustable handles if you have steps to negotiate or storage problems.

Hand lawn-mowers

Although it can be tiring to hand mow a large lawn, it is certainly very economical to use a hand machine for small and medium-sized ones. They are also considered to give a better finish than power-operated machines.

Nowadays, due to skilful engineering, cylinder hand mowers are very easy to push and operate. They come in two types: roller and sidewheel and each has its advantages.

Roller types have a small roller in front of the cylinder and a large one behind. The two rollers help to give lawns the striped effect for which many people aim. They also make it easy to cut edges and narrow strips of grass as they simply overhang where necessary. However, these roller types do not operate well if the grass is more than 5cm (2 in) long.

Power lawn-mowers

Power lawn-mowers are precision instruments and often have to stand up to years of rough usage, so you should always buy the best you can afford.

Mains-powered electric mowers are cheap to run and noiseless; but mains-operated types are not suited to large lawns or rough ground. Petrol-driven mowers give more power but can be difficult to start, and require a regular maintenance programme. Apart from the choice between electric and petrol power, the mower may cut by the cylinder or rotary method; the former type cut with a scissor-like action, the latter by beheading the upstanding grass. Cylinder types are good for fine lawns, but not so efficient for grass longer than 5 to 8cm (2 to 3 in) high. The rotary type deal better with long grass and are easier to handle though they do not give a striped lawn effect.

Sidewheel mowers have only the small roller in front of the cutting cylinder and are better for cutting long grass, but they require a balancing act to cut lawn edges, and on soft ground the two side wheels can leave track marks.

Roller mowers cost about twice as much as the sidewheel types and always have the grass box attachment in front. Grass boxes may be fitted to the front or rear of sidewheel models, according

to the make. They are usually more efficient when the box is fitted in front of the cutting cylinder.

With cylinder mowers the grass is cut between the cylinder blade and a fixed blade. The effective cutting width, known as the cylinder length, is usually 25 or 30cm (10 or 12 in), although one sidewheel model is available with a 40cm (16 in) cylinder.

The cutting height adjustment and ease of altering it varies according to the model, so compare these facilities before buying. Both power and hand-driven cylinder mowers are available, but rotary ones are always petrol-driven or electrically operated.

Shears for cutting

The first item for your list is a good pair of shears. There are long-handled and short-handled, edging and cutting shears. Blade sizes vary from 15–25cm (6–10 in); handles can be wooden, metal or plastic, and some models are available with rubber buffers to absorb jarring and reduce fatigue when cutting.

The traditional short-handled shears are invaluable for cutting long or short grass. To avoid having to bend, you can get the same blades attached to long handles. There are two basic models in

this range, one for edging and the other for general cutting. You can also buy spring-loaded hand shears which allow for one-handed operation; one type comes with an orbital handle so that it can be adjusted to cut at any angle between horizontal and vertical.

The lawn edge trimmer, a modification of edging shears, has spring-loaded blades and you push it along to cut overhanging grass. It has a broad, non-slip rubber roller that guarantees easy guiding and balancing, even on undulating ground.

Brushing and raking

All lawns require brushing and raking to keep them looking well-groomed and pleasant to sit on. A besom, or birch broom, is ideal for sweeping off leaves, but a good stiff broom is required for getting rid of wormcasts.

Steel, spring-tined lawn rakes are essential for removing debris and for scarifying the lawn surface. You can get fixed, or adjustable, tined models, the latter being preferable as they can be used for any job from moss-collecting to leaf-raking.

There is also a lawn comb – a cross between a lawn rake and a garden rake, but it has no particular advantage over other rakes.

381

Sprayers and Dusters

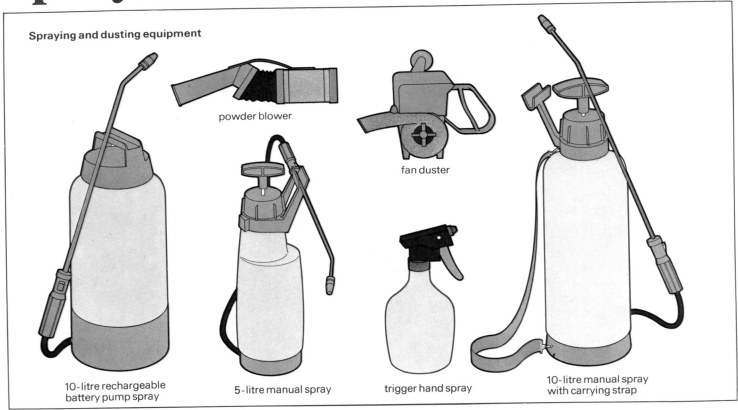

Spraying and dusting equipment

powder blower

fan duster

10-litre rechargeable
battery pump spray

5-litre manual spray

trigger hand spray

10-litre manual spray
with carrying strap

To keep your plants and crops healthy you have to keep spraying at certain times to prevent—or counteract—the adverse effects of weeds, pests and diseases. It saves you time and trouble if you use the right spray for the job.

Many manufacturers of pesticides (both liquids and dusts) produce their chemicals in a pack which itself is the dispenser.

Dusts are sold in puffer-packs made of opaque polythene, with a small plastic nozzle-type orifice. To spray the dust you simply squeeze the sides of the pack. Other dust packs have pepper-pot tops.

Liquids are sometimes sold in inexpensive transparent plastic bottles with a manually-operated spray mechanism as the closure. It is not advisable to refill.

The most popular pack today is the aerosol can. This system is very effective and convenient to use, but must be stored away from heat.

Both aerosol sprays and dust packs are ideal for small gardens or limited applications, but prove very expensive for large areas or prolonged use.

Permanent sprayers
The capacity range here goes from $\frac{1}{2}$lit (1 pt) to several litres. Sprayers over 5lit (10 pt) capacity can be awkward and heavy to handle when full and are not recommended. On large areas it pays to refill, rather than struggle with a larger sprayer.

Traditionally, spraying equipment was made from metal and proved to be extremely heavy. Today, virtually all sprayers are made from lightweight but strong polythene and plastic with stainless metals in some of the working parts.

Trigger sprayers
The smallest sprayers are suited for use on house plants, greenhouse plants and limited use outdoors. They are appropriately called hand sprayers because they are held in the hand and operated by simply pressing a trigger rather like a pistol. Naturally, the range of these models is limited and the operator has to be close to the plant to be sprayed.

Pump sprayers
These consist of a container, a short length of hose and a lance. They require two hands for operation. The container is held in one hand while the lance is directed towards the target with the other hand. The spray container has a maintenance-free pump fitted through the top. The pump is primed by pushing in and pulling out the handle several times

to build up pressure. Everything is then ready for spraying and all you do is depress a simple trigger fitted to the hand end of the lance.

Spray patterns are basically cone shaped and are altered by rotating the nozzle fitment at the end of the lance.

Many of these sprayers have a useful shoulder strap so they may be carried around the garden with ease; this also allows you a free hand to pull the odd long branch or shoot out of the way. The carrying handle itself is usually dual purpose, enabling the lance to be slotted in when the sprayer is not in use.

Battery-operated sprays are convenient because they avoid the need for pressure-pumping. The batteries are re-chargeable and sealed so they are not affected by wet weather. Life between charges is about $1\frac{1}{2}$ hours. Units are made in 5lit (10 pt) and 10lit (20 pt) sizes.

Dusters
Two types of dusting equipment are made: a cheap bellows type with handle which, when shaken, operates the bellows and expels the dust from the attached canister; and a more sophisticated piece of equipment in which you turn a geared handle to operate a fan and distribute the powder from a hopper.

Maintaining Equipment

Rust is the enemy of tools – few garden sheds or garages are totally proof against the all-pervasive midwinter damp – so before being stored away all those tools that will not be needed until the spring should be carefully cleaned, thoroughly dried and their metal parts (if not stainless steel) wiped with a thin film of oil, or even wrapped in oily rags.

It is a good practice to clean a fork or spade after every use. Hoses should be coiled and hung up and lawn mowers, especially electric ones, should be found a place off the ground. In fact tools generally are the better for being kept well above ground level, and some sort of wall rack provides the best type of storage.

This is also a time when tools should be overhauled and repaired. Replace handles and sharpen edge tools like shears, lawn-edging irons, and hoes. Even spades and forks can be sharpened.

Garden shears These should be checked if they seem to have been cutting less efficiently. They may need not only sharpening but also setting. You can sharpen them – provided they are not hollow-ground – with a medium-fine file, using it on the bevel side of the cutting edges. Hold each blade in turn in a vice and file away from the edge, that is *into* the edge. The stroke of the file should not be at right-angles to the blade but somewhat oblique to it. Work until you have achieved a clean, sharp, notch-free edge on each blade. Hollow-ground shears must be professionally sharpened.

Properly-set shears have slightly bowed blades but they should overlap fairly tightly at the tips. If the blades of your shears are not properly bowed you can bend them a little by holding the end of each blade in a vice. If they do not overlap enough you will have to file away a little of the 'heels', the flat metal surfaces down near the handles that butt together when the blades are closed. File both of the butting faces by equal amounts in turn.

Hoes, lawn edge irons and spades All these are improved by occasional sharpening. Hold the tool firmly in a vice and before actually sharpening it file away any notches that the edge has sustained. When the edge is smooth and free of notches start sharpening, filing away from the edge, as with the shears.

New handles Rakes, hoes and the like have a tapered metal socket to receive a new handle. These will be ready-tapered, but may need some further whittling to make them fit properly. Tap the new handle in firmly, spike through the hole in the metal with a bradawl, then drive home a new retaining screw.

Of course, you have to get the old broken handle out first. The handles of some tools are held in with rivets and these may have to be drilled out before the old wood can be removed. Centre-punch the rivet head, drill out the head, then tap out the rivet. The new handle need not be riveted but can be fixed in place with a new round-head screw.

Spades and forks may have an integral cylindrical socket or a pair of metal 'straps'. In either case a new handle may need trimming to fit. Measure the new handle carefully against the old one and mark it so that you can saw off the right amount for your size.

If the old handle has broken off flush with the metal socket the old wood may be difficult to remove. The best way is to drive a large screw part-way into the end of the wood, then hold the screwhead firmly in a vice and tap the tool-head free of the handle.

Garden hose If your rubber hose has sprung a leak you can repair it by applying a band of adhesive such as Copydex about 2–3cm (1 in) wide so that it covers the hole, and then binding a strip of cloth tightly round the adhesive. When the cloth bandage is dry cover it with a second generous coating of the adhesive.

A damaged section of the standard 13mm ($\frac{1}{2}$ in) plastic hose is best cut out and the two ends joined together with a simple patent jointing device such as the Hozelock hose-mender.

Staking and Tying Equipment

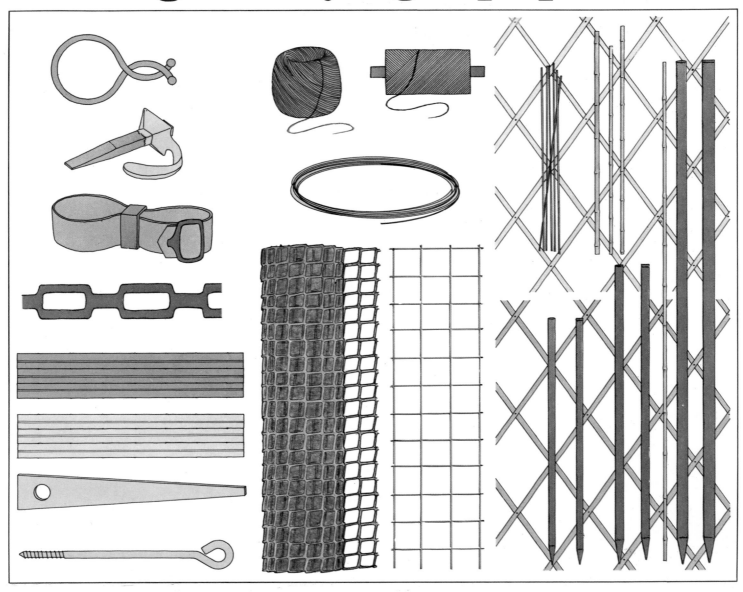

Bamboo and split canes The longer the cane the thicker the diameter. From 30cm–3·6m (1–12 ft) lengths.

Chestnut, cedar or pine stakes Treat with horticultural wood preservative, if not pre-treated.

Plastic buckle ties and buffers Be sure to place the buffer between trunk and stalk to prevent chafing.

Plastic tree or rose ties These can be adjusted each year to allow for increase in girth.

Plastic or wire plant ties Paper-covered wire type only needs the ends twisting together to hold stem to stake; pliable plastic-coated wire type bends around stem and stake.

Plastic clips Ideal for quick support. Long-lasting if stored each winter.

Galvanized, heavy-gauge wire Fixed on a wall, can be used instead of trellis.

Vine eyes Hammer-in or screw-in types, useful for tying in light branches against walls with garden twine or string.

Lead-headed nails Hammer in to wall and bend round flexible arm, or use with garden twine or string.

Garden twine or string Usually green and treated for weather resistance, but can stretch under wet conditions. Tarred garden string is durable, but has an unpleasant smell.

Polypropylene garden string Tough and does not stretch in wet weather.

Raffia Good tying material. Can be torn to any thickness.

Traditional trellis Made of treated cedar, or hardwood for heavier, rustic types. Can be bought ready-made, rigid or expanding, in natural or painted finish. (See Week 6 for fixing details.)

Plastic-coated trellis Rot-proof and long-lasting, rigid or expanding, usually in green or white.

Plastic mesh/nylon netting Convenient but more expensive than chicken wire; easily stored at end of season. Available in different width rolls or packs of specific sizes. Needs stretching between posts or supporting by metal or wood frame structure.

Power Lawn Mowers

All but the smallest lawns need to be cut with a mower, but before you decide which type to buy compare the various models and list your requirements (this also applies when buying other lawn care equipment). Certain mowers work better on short grass and edges, others on long grass, and all grass boxes are not equally efficient. Choose a lightweight model with adjustable handles if you have steps to negotiate or storage problems.

Hand lawn-mowers

Although it can be tiring to hand mow a large lawn, it is certainly very economical to use a hand machine for small and medium-sized ones. They are also considered to give a better finish than power-operated machines.

Nowadays, due to skilful engineering, cylinder hand mowers are very easy to push and operate. They come in two types: roller and sidewheel and each has its advantages.

Roller types have a small roller in front of the cylinder and a large one behind. The two rollers help to give lawns the striped effect for which many people aim. They also make it easy to cut edges and narrow strips of grass as they simply overhang where necessary. However, these roller types do not operate well if the grass is more than 5cm (2 in) long.

Sidewheel mowers have only the small roller in front of the cutting cylinder and are better for cutting long grass, but they require a balancing act to cut lawn edges, and on soft ground the two side wheels can leave track marks.

Roller mowers cost about twice as much as the sidewheel types and always have the grass box attachment in front.

Grass boxes may be fitted to the front or rear of sidewheel models, according to the make. They are usually more efficient when the box is fitted in front of the cutting cylinder.

With cylinder mowers the grass is cut between the cylinder blade and a fixed blade. The effective cutting width, known as the cylinder length, is usually 25 or 30cm (10 or 12 in), although one sidewheel model is available with a 40cm (16 in) cylinder.

The cutting height adjustment and ease of altering it varies according to the model, so compare these facilities before buying. Both power and hand-driven cylinder mowers are available, but rotary ones are always petrol-driven or electrically operated.

Power lawn-mowers are precision instruments and often have to stand up to years of rough usage, so you should always buy the best you can afford. The following guide to the various types should help you to make your choice.

Electric or petrol?

Mains-powered electric mowers start up immediately, require little maintenance, are cheaper to run than their petrol-driven counterparts, and do not make a lot of noise to upset the neighbours. Many models have TV/radio interference suppressors and standard safety equipment. However, mains-operated types (cylindrical or rotary) are not suited to large lawns or rough ground and their mobility depends on their cable length. You can also cut the power cable accidentally but with the inbuilt safety factors of modern machines this is not a danger. With battery models (only available with cylinder cutters) you are also restricted by their operating time before recharging becomes necessary.

Petrol-driven lawn-mowers, generally speaking, give more power than the electrically-operated ones (which are usually one-speed). They have variable speeds, unlimited mobility and the advantage of working well on rough ground. On the other hand, petrol mowers can be tricky to start, especially at the beginning of the season, and require a regular maintenance programme. It is surprising how many owners of petrol mowers neglect even to keep a regular check on the oil level.

Self-propelled or push-along?

All power mowers either have motorized propulsion – that is, the power source turns the wheels as well as blades (and they cost more) – or you have to push them along, in which case only the blades

easy starting. With ordinary use and regular servicing, the engines should last for many years. Two-stroke engines are slightly lighter than their more usual four-stroke counterparts and are better suited to rough spots and slopes. Having fewer parts, two-strokes should be less prone to breakdowns but they tend to be more difficult to start.

Petrol-driven rotary models are fitted with a metal or plastic grass-collecting box, or a flexible bag. On rough grass it is usual to let the cuttings fall back to the land and some models provide a better spreading pattern than others. You must beware of using this type on stony ground without a collecting box (unless fitted with a deflector correctly positioned) because stones may shoot out at high velocity as you mow. Wherever possible, sweep stones out of the way before you start mowing, and never mow with children standing nearby.

Cutting widths of most rotary lawn mowers vary from 38–60cm (15–24 in), and cutting heights from 13mm–15cm ($\frac{1}{2}$–6 in), with independent adjustment on each of the four wheels or by one central mechanism.

Some newer models have rollers fitted behind the blade to give a striped effect

are powered from the engine. The power source is connected to the moving parts by belts or chains.

Cylinder or rotary?

Apart from the choice between electric or petrol power, the mower may cut by the cylinder or rotary method.

Cylinder types cut by slicing the grass between one of their curved blades and a fixed cutting plate, cutting the grass with a scissor-like action. They are good for fine lawns but not so efficient on grass longer than 5–8cm (2–3 in) high, so you must be prepared to mow at least once a week.

Rotary types have a whirling, horizontal blade (that does not require sharpening) rather like a propeller, that beheads the upstanding grass. The cut grass is thrown out of the back of the machine by the fast-moving air current. Rotary types deal better with long grass than cylinder ones and are very popular, with their emphasis on easy handling rather than achieving a striped lawn effect at all costs.

Petrol mowers (rotary)

All engines of this type have recoil starters – you need to pull a cord to start action, and many models are decompressed for

of a kind and they incorporate clutches and varying speeds. Most rotary types have fold-down handles for easy storage.

Petrol mowers (cylinder)
These are the popular, traditional mowers that produce well-striped lawns and a fine cut. It cannot be emphasized enough that a petrol cylinder mower is a precision tool and should be treated as such: Due respect and regular maintenance will pay dividends.

Cylinder mowers are usually self-propelled, although some models have a switch to disengage the roller, converting it to a push-along type. On some types you can also disengage the cylinder for moving the machine from place to place. The engines tend to be four-stroke but, as the cubic capacity varies, so does the horsepower. Most cylinder types have a system of gears, clutch and a brake.

Cutting heights vary from 3–30mm ($\frac{1}{8}$–1$\frac{1}{4}$ in), and it should be easy to adjust to the one you want. You can choose from cutting widths of 30–60cm (12–24 in). Grass-collecting boxes are usually made of steel. The number of blades on the cylinder varies from 5–10, the more blades, the finer the cut, and they must be well-adjusted to ensure a clean cut.

A big roller, or side wheels, support the cylinder. Those with a large metal roller are good for fine turf and enable you to cut right to the lawn edge. Side-wheel types are better for rough spots.

Hover types (rotary)
These, such as Flymo, come with choice of petrol or electric power. They are ideal for steep banks as they are kept afloat by a current of air, gliding along effortlessly about 6mm ($\frac{1}{4}$ in) clear of the ground. But you have to rake up the grass cuttings after use.

Tractor types (rotary or cylinder)
If you have 2,000 sq m ($\frac{1}{2}$ acre) of lawn or more, you might consider a 'sit-on' petrol-driven mower. These larger machines are like small tractors and make the job very easy: you simply drive around to cut the grass. The cylinder type is more suited to exceptionally large, fine lawns.

Electric mowers (cylinder)
This type does give a finer striped finish than the rotary, and the smaller models are very easy to manipulate, rather like a vacuum cleaner. One-handed operation is all that is required for most of the time.

Most models have 5–6 cutting blades on the cylinder and operate on one speed, although there are new, larger models

with 2–3 speed operation. Cylinder sizes start at 30cm (12 in) and go up to 45cm (18 in). Cutting height adjustments are easy to make with a screwdriver and the range is similar to that of petrol models. Some types have a pivoting handle that automatically adjusts to your height.

Battery-operated models, although they are obviously convenient to use, are heavier than mains mowers and slightly more difficult to manoeuvre. They are only available with cylinder blades and the battery needs re-charging overnight after each mowing.

Electric mowers (rotary)
This easy-to-use type is clean, quiet and fitted with every convenience. The main disadvantage is a tendency to burn out if used non-stop for long periods. Some models are fitted with a waterproof, double-insulated switch that cuts off automatically if the motor overheats or

stalls. When using one of these mowers, you must make sure that you do not accidentally cut through your supply cable. It pays to develop a system of walking that ensures you cut in a direction which pulls the cable rather than allowing it to go slack. Never mow downhill, or pull the machine towards you, or wear open-toed sandals. You've only got one pair of feet, so take care not to let them get under a rotary mower.

Blade sizes vary from 30–45cm (12–18 in) and height adjustment is either independent on each of the four wheels, or by one central arm on the handle which raises or lowers the whole cutting system. Adjustable handles are quite common on these models.

Most types have steel or plastic grass-collecting boxes, some with extra-large capacity that allows for more mowing time between visits to the cutting pile. There is very little to go wrong and these

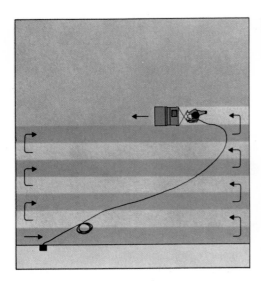

Start mowing nearest your power point so as to avoid accidentally cutting the cable

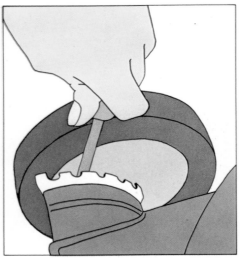

Top: on rotary mowers raising and lowering wheels adjusts the blade height

Easy-to-handle petrol-driven rotary hover mower floats along on a cushion of air

mowers should last for years.

Basic maintenance

For hand mowers the basic maintenance required after a season's work is fairly straightforward and service agents will do it for a reasonable fee. Unless you intend to undertake all your maintenance yourself, you should take your power mower to a reputable firm after the last winter cut, so that it will be in good shape for the first one the following spring. It may need anything doing to it, from blade-sharpening and spark plug-cleaning, to a complete overhaul. If you have a mains-operated electric machine you must be sure that both its insulation and your earthing system are efficient, so check them regularly every year.

On a battery-operated machine the batteries should be kept fully charged throughout the non-mowing season.

In addition there are many small jobs that, if done at the proper time, will save money and ensure continuing good performance from your machine. To start with, one of the greatest enemies of the lawn mower is rust. Even if you cut only in dry weather there is still sufficient water in the grass at any time to cause rust. Wiping the cylinder and fixed blades thoroughly with an oily rag after every mowing will help to keep them keen and free from rust, and postpone the need to sharpen. At the end of the mowing season be sure to oil all blades, gears, chains and bearings. Any component with signs of rust should be removed, scraped clean, oiled and replaced.

Some screws, especially those on the fixed blade and ones that have been left for years, may prove difficult to remove. Be patient and don't get heavy-handed.

First scrape away any rust, dirt and paint from around the screw and then apply some special penetrating oil. Allow a few minutes for it to seep into the threads, and then try to undo the screws with the largest-sized screwdriver that will fit (an under-sized one will just damage the screwhead). If this does not work, play a blowlamp gently over the obstinate screw or use a cold chisel and hammer. At any rate, when you replace the screws, be sure to grease them thoroughly so as to ensure easy extraction next time.

For professional sharpening, blades are removed from the machine. However, if you are going to tackle this job at home, there are a few ways of sharpening the blades without removing them. There are proprietary sharpeners available, but

the cheapest and simplest method is to use coarse grade grinding paste (as for valves in a car engine), which gives a sufficiently good result. Smear it onto the blades quite thickly and turn the cylinder backwards; when you have finished, clean the blades thoroughly.

Above all, it is essential to store your mower in a dry place, not just during the non-mowing season, but all year round.

Shears for cutting

The first item for your list is a good pair of shears. There are long-handled and short-handled, edging and cutting shears. Blade sizes vary from 15–25cm (6–10 in); handles can be wooden, metal or plastic, and some models are available with rubber buffers to absorb jarring and reduce fatigue when cutting.

The traditional short-handled shears are invaluable for cutting long or short grass. To avoid having to bend, you can get the same blades attached to long handles. There are two basic models in this range, one for edging and the other for general cutting. You can also buy spring-loaded hand shears which allow for one-handed operation; one type comes with an orbital handle so that it can be adjusted to cut at any angle between horizontal and vertical.

The lawn edge trimmer, a modification of edging shears, has spring-loaded blades and you push it along to cut overhanging grass. It has a broad, non-slip rubber roller that guarantees easy guiding and balancing, even on undulating ground.

Brushing and raking

All lawns require brushing and raking to keep them looking well-groomed and pleasant to sit on. A besom, or birch broom, is ideal for sweeping off leaves, but a good stiff broom is required for getting rid of wormcasts.

Steel, spring-tined lawn rakes are essential for removing debris and for scarifying the lawn surface. You can get fixed, or adjustable, tined models, the latter being preferable as they can be used for any job from moss-collecting to leaf-raking.

There is also a lawn comb – a cross between a lawn rake and a garden rake, but it has no particular advantage over other rakes. Wooden lawn rakes are prone to breaking and so are not

recommended. The traditional garden rake is best for spreading top dressing on lawns.

Rolling the lawn

It is worth borrowing or hiring a roller each spring to put a new face on your lawn. Winter frosts often lift the turf and rolling will consolidate the surface. It need only be done in spring. It is important to sweep off all wormcasts and debris beforehand and to roll only when the surface is dry and the soil below is damp. Don't roll when the grass is thin or wet and never use a roller weighing over 2 cwt. Bumps should be levelled out properly because rolling will not squash them down.

Tools for aerating

For this you need only use a garden fork. Push it in 7–10cm (3–4 in) deep, at 7–10cm intervals. Easier to use is a fork-like tool fitted with hollow, or solid, tines (sometimes called mechanical spikes), and it gives better results. Wedge-shaped blades can also be attached and are good for compacted areas as they prune the roots and so encourage stronger root growth. For larger areas use an aerator with spiked wheels and inter-changeable tines.

Feeding and weeding

Fertilizer-spreaders ensure an even distribution of lawn feeds and lawn sands. Fertilizers and 'feed and weed' mixes come in several forms and should be

applied with the spreader in strict accordance with the manufacturers' instructions.

A certain number of weeds eventually die as a result of constant mowing but a few stubborn types will remain and must be dealt with by other methods. Apply spot weedkillers from a small bottle with a squeezy-type top, or dig out stubborn weeds with a hand fork, or a long, narrow trowel.

Tidying up the edges

Finally, to ensure that your lawn never encroaches on the flower borders you should edge-up with a good half-moon edging iron at least twice a year.

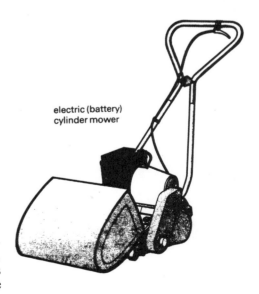

electric (battery) cylinder mower

Seasonal Workplan

LATE WINTER

Mixed flower borders

There is little work that can be done outside this month, but plan ahead to make sure you are ready for seed sowing and planting later by ordering seeds and plants, seed and cutting composts and other essentials. Also clean all pots and trays to be used for seed sowing and check all equipment.

Helleborus niger, the Christmas rose will still be flowering, also *H. foetidus* should start producing flower buds now.

Trees, shrubs and climbers

Provided weather conditions are suitable for working outdoors and the soil is not too wet, frozen or snow-covered, it is possible to plant new deciduous trees, shrubs and climbers.

Ensure the planting hole is dug large enough to accommodate the roots without cramping them and deep enough so that when finally in position the plant is at the original soil mark on the stem. The planting site is best prepared in advance, but if not, dig in well-rotted manure or compost below root level. Remember to insert stakes for those trees or shrubs requiring them, and trellis or other supports for climbing plants.

If weather conditions are unsuitable for planting, keep the wrapped trees, shrubs and climbers in a cool but frost-free place until the soil is workable. Alternatively, unwrap the plants carefully and put in a shallow trench in a sheltered part of the garden.

To prevent branches being broken by the weight of snow, remove as much snow as possible by hand or with a cane.

Bulbs

Bring forced bulbs in pots and bowls into the house as they reach the correct stage of growth. Narcissi (daffodils) should be about 10cm (4in) tall with the flower bud showing. Hyacinths should also have the leaves about 10cm (4in) high with the flower bud well developed in the centre. Other forced bulbs, such as tulips, snowdrops and crocuses are best left until the flower buds are showing colour, to ensure the flowers open properly and give a good display. All forced bulbs brought into the home

should be kept in a cool, not too sunny position for a week or so. The temperature should not be more than about 10°C (50°F) initially and 16°C (60°F) finally at which time the plants can be placed in full light, but not over a radiator or fire.

Water the bulbs when the fibre or compost needs it, and include liquid fertilizer about once weekly to encourage the formation of plump healthy bulbs for planting in the garden next autumn.

For flowering next month in the home, plant hippeastrum bulbs singly in pots of moist J.I. No 2 or soilless mixture. Keep in a tmperature of about 16°C (60°F) and water occasionally until the leaves and flower stem appear. Then water with added liquid fertilizer regularly.

Lawns

Double dig any area proposed for a lawn to be grown from seed next year. Incorporate well-rotted manure or compost into the lower spit of soil and leave the top layer rough for frosts to condition it.

If soil drainage is likely to be a problem, construct soakaways, or a herringbone drainage system of tile drains, in the second or third spit of soil. Order the grass seeds now. If the weather is very mild, it is possible to create a new lawn from turfs this month, provided the soil has been well-prepared.

Fruit, vegetables and herbs

Order your vegetable seeds, including seed potatoes, and when they arrive keep them in a cool and mouse-free place.

Check all gardening equipment and stock up with soil or soilless composts, seed trays, pots, labels and similar odds and ends.

Where the vegetable garden requires liming, now is a good time to do so. If in doubt, test the soil with a pH kit to get a reading of alkalinity or acidity and calculate how much lime to apply. Further sowings of suitable varieties of peas and broad beans may be made under cloches this month.

Herb plants and seeds should be ordered now for delivery in the spring.

Sow tomato seeds in a heated greenhouse for forcing for early fruiting.

Complete pruning of fruit trees and bushes. Also spray them with tar oil winter wash, according to manufacturer's instructions, to kill any eggs.

General

Keep paths, mowed areas and patios clear of leaves by raking or brushing.

Make a note of any repairs or alterations required to hard surface areas to prevent future puddles or icy patches.

Tread firm any soil round plants that has been raised by frost.

EARLY SPRING

Bulbs

Make sure the forced hyacinths and narcissi still flowering indoors are kept moist. If they are ready, bring the bowls of early tulips indoors but keep them in a cool place for a few days so that they can acclimatize before moving them to the warmer living rooms where they are to flower.

If the weather is mild you can plant healthy, plump lily bulbs where they are to flower. Mulch them with peat or leaves to protect them from frost damage.

Place cloches over iris you plan to use for cut flowers; this will improve the quality of the flowers and hasten the flowering dates.

Trees, shrubs and climbers

Remove any snow that may settle on branches to prevent its weight breaking or damaging them. Tidy up by cutting out all dead, diseased, broken or very twiggy branches and burn them.

Order new trees and shrubs and, if weather is suitably mild and the ground dry, prepare planting sites if this has not already been done. Prepare site for any new hedge.

Lawns

Examine the lawn mower and make sure it is in good working order. If new parts are needed, order them now. Oil and clean it thoroughly, sharpen all the blades; the grass will soon need its first cut. Inspect the lawn surface and if not too wet, use spiker, fork or hollow-tined fork to improve drainage and air penetration. Then brush in a 13mm (½in) layer of a 50/50 mixture of coarse sand and peat.

If you are planning a new lawn from seed, dig over the area, incorporating plenty of well-rotted manure or compost.

Flowerbeds

Make sure you will be ready to sow and plant when the time comes by finishing the ordering of seeds and plants, and seed and cutting composts. If you are starting a new border, plan it carefully

on paper and dig over the area concerned – working in plenty of well-rotted compost or manure, plus some bonemeal.

If the soil is workable, hoe it lightly and work in a general-purpose fertilizer.

Start dahlia tubers into growth in damp peat in a warm place for production of suitable cuttings next month.

Fruit

Continue to prune fruit trees and bushes. Also spray them with tar oil winter wash, according to manufacturer's instructions, to kill any overwintering eggs.

Dig up and burn all diseased bushes. Fruit trees and bushes can still be planted provided weather conditions are suitable, the soil workable (not waterlogged and frosty) and the planting sites have been well prepared in advance. Stake securely. If the soil is right you can still prepare for mid spring (March) planting.

Check stored fruit and remove any that appear diseased or damaged.

Vegetables

Early spring (February) is the time to finish the sowing plan and planting schedule; make sure that all the seeds have been ordered.

Test the soil and correct the pH by liming the plots dug in the autumn, particularly where brassicas are to be grown. Place cloches in position to warm up the soil.

Bend leaves over winter broccoli heads to protect from damage.

If the soil is warming up, sow the first broad beans, and early peas.

Start chitting potatoes as soon as you get them.

Examine stored vegetables for soundness and remove and that appear diseased or damaged.

Harvest winter crops such as parsnips, leeks and brussels sprouts when required.

Under glass
Clean out the greenhouse thoroughly. Mend any broken glass or gaps in the structure. Examine cloches and frames and treat likewise.

Scrub all seed trays with a disinfectant.

Start tomato and cucumber seeds in peat pots in the propagator for greenhouse crops. Sow sweet peas, three to a peat pot, for early transplanting.

Make a first sowing of leeks in trays of seed compost to go out into a frost-free greenhouse.

General
Inspect all tools and make sure they are in good condition; clean and oil them well. Make sure you have a good supply of nets, stakes, pots, composts, fertilizers and chemicals.

Check dates of any flower shows you may wish to exhibit at, and plan your planting dates accordingly.

WEATHER VARIATIONS
Early spring in the British Isles has the most variable weather of the year. The map shows how spring arrives one to four weeks earlier in the south-west than in central areas, and again up to four weeks later in north-eastern England and most of Scotland

The Gardener's Seasons

early spring	(February)	early autumn	(August)
mid spring	(March)	mid autumn	(September)
late spring	(April)	late autumn	(October)
early summer	(May)	early winter	(November)
mid summer	(June)	mid winter	(December)
late summer	(July)	late winter	(January)

In the North
In this section we will be highlighting any gardening points particularly relevant to the north of England and Scotland due to the colder climate in those regions. At this time of year the ground is still frozen, so be patient. Do all the work that is to be done off the ground, such as planning and ordering, pruning and tidying up.

MID-LATE SPRING
Spring bulbs
Continue to remove dead flower heads from spring flowering blubs in the bulb area and any other areas where they may be growing. If in bare ground, not

a grassy area, remove the weeds from around the bulbs.

Mixed flower borders
Plant lily bulbs in the mixed borders and stake to show positions and to provide suppot later. Continue to plant gladiolus corms; if not already put in last month, plant them now. Plant out unsprouted dahlia tubers in the positions they are to flower, and protect with a layer of mulch against frost.

If the mixed flower borders have not already been cleared of winter leaves and debris, do it now. Lightly hoe between all the plants. Remove weeds, hoe in a general fertilizer and put a 2·5 to 5cm (1–2in) layer of mulching material round the perennial plants, trees and shrubs. Sow hardy annuals in their final positions. If the weather is suitably dry and warm, the first of the chrysanthemums should be planted out.

To deter slugs and snails, scatter slug-killing pellets, or water with liquid slug-killer.

Trees, shrubs and climbers
Finish pruning roses if not completed last month. Also prune out dead, diseased, crossing branches from trees and shrubs that have just finished flowering. This includes hedging plants. Cut back evergreen trees and shrubs to near their base if they are overgrown and straggly. Complete planting of trees, shrubs and herbaceous plants. Plant out evergreen hedging plants, water them regularly if the weather is dry, and hoe to control weeds.

Lawns
If moss and wormkiller treatments on lawns were not carried out, or completed, last month, do so now. Prepare new lawn site and sow or turf it. Apply fertilizer to an established lawn after the first mowing.

General
Firmly tread any newly dug ground that may 'heave' (raise up) following late

frost. Spray all decorative plants with a systemic spray to prevent insect attacks.

Fruit, vegetables and herbs
Prepare the soil in the seed bed for continuation sowings of brassicas, brussels sprouts, winter cabbage, purple and green sprouting broccoli, red cabbage and winter cauliflower and leeks. Sow dwarf French beans and runner beans in the greenhouse. Regularly water seedlings and young plants in the greenhouse. Hoe to remove weeds wherever possible, or apply chemical weedkillers. Mulch along rows of raspberry canes and tie in canes to supports.

Thin bulbing onions, lettuces, swedes, turnips and summer cabbage sown outside where they are to mature. Fill gaps in broad bean rows and stake the rows. Protect early potato shoots from frost, and plant maincrops. Spray apple trees and bushes at pink bud stage to control pests.

Now is the time to harden off young plants from the greenhouse for later planting outside. Sow tomato seeds in the greenhouse for planting outdoors. Transplant cucumber seedlings in the greenhouse into their final positions of pots. At the end of this month prepare the ground for, and sow, dwarf French beans in the open or under cloches. Also sow parsnips and parsley. Prepare the 'rings' in the greenhouse for transplanting tomato plants next month, which are to be grown by the ring culture method. Arrange for methods of shading the roof of the greenhouse to prevent too strong sunlight burning the plants.

Give potatoes their first earthing-up to protect stems against buffeting winds. If a pea weevil attacks young peas, dust with derris. Put in supports for pea plants to grow up. Harden off young onions for planting out next month. Finish preparing ground outside where they are to be planted. Transplant lettuce from indoor or outdoor sowings to their final positions, sow further seeds for successional cropping. Also sow short rows of radishes.

EARLY SUMMER
Bulbs
Remove dead flower-heads by cutting off each stem from near the base.

If bulb area is required for summer bedding plants, after all spring bulbs have finished flowering carefully fork them out and put in a trench in spare part of the garden, where they can ripen, before lifting for planting again in autumn.

Mixed flower borders
Continue to hoe weeds regularly, taking care not to damage shallow roots on stems of cultivated plants.

After hoeing, scatter and rake in general fertilizer such as Growmore and apply mulch layer.

When they have finished flowering, pull up spring bedding plants such as forget-me-nots and wallflowers.

Complete sowing of hardy annuals in the positions in which they are to flower. Towards the end of month, start setting out half-hardy bedding plants where they are to bloom.

Prepare soil in spare corner of garden and sow biennials such as wallflower, sweet William, forget-me-not, canterbury bell, honesty, evening primrose, and hollyhock, for flowering next year.

The taller growing herbaceous perennials should be staked now, and stems tied in as they grow. To help

healthy growth, water with liquid fertilizer from time to time.

Plant out chrysanthemums.

Trees, shrubs and climbers
Evergreen trees and shrubs can be planted at the beginning of the month. After planting, water thoroughly and put mulch over root areas.

Remove rhododendron and azalea flower-heads as they die, taking care not to damage leaves and buds below.

Prune shrubs that complete their flowering period in late spring and early summer. Cut back hard the stems that have carried the flowers, to encourage new shoots to grow for next year's flowering. Also remove dead and spindly growth.

Climbers that finish flowering this month should also have their old flower stems cut out.

Continue to tie in other climbers, and shrubs treated as climbers, to their supports as necessary.

If roses produce too many young shoots, cut out unwanted ones to prevent bushes becoming too entangled with unprolific stems.

Clip hedges, such as privet, from now on as necessary.

Lawns
Mow the lawn at least weekly; cutting to 2–3cm (1–1½in). During drought periods water thoroughly, preferably with a sprinkler.

If necessary, apply weedkiller over whole lawn or as spot treatment.

General
Regularly spray with insecticide against pests, particularly greenfly, blackfly and red spider.

Fruit, vegetables and herbs
Water thoroughly all outdoor vegetables and apply 'booster' feeds in the form of liquid or soluble fertilizers.

Remove cloches from all crops except those susceptible to late frosts. As soon as first flowers appear on greenhouse tomatoes, start liquid feeding and keep soil moist. Cut out sideshoots as they appear. Harvest the first of the shallots. Prepare ground, and sow marrows outdoors where they are to fruit. Make a first sowing of beetroot outdoors. If night frosts appear imminent cover potatoes and dwarf French beans. Thin summer cabbages and cauliflowers; protect against pests. Thin parsnips and tread soil firm. Start transplanting young plants of cabbage and brussels sprouts to final positions. Sow sweet corn in blocks outdoors. Make last outdoor sowing of runner beans against the supports erected earlier. Hoe regularly throughout.

In the greenhouse tie in cucumber shoots to their supports. Remove male flowers as they appear, also tendrils. Apply insecticides to control greenfly, blackfly and whitefly outdoors and in the greenhouse. Sow another row of broad beans. Ventilate the greenhouse according to weather conditions.

MID SUMMER
Bulbs
Lift overcrowded spring-flowering bulbs when leaves have yellowed, put in a box in a dry place and remove old leaves and outer bulb scales when dry.

Dig up tulips and replant them in a trench for ripening, but leave species types *in situ.*

Mixed flower borders
Continue to hoe weeds regularly. Take care not to damage stems or shallow roots of cultivated plants.

If not done already, stake and tie taller-growing plants.

Continue to plant out half-hardy annuals and sow some *in situ,* for flowering later in the season.

Sow biennials in a prepared seedbed if not done last month.

Mulch gladiolus and lilies to conserve moisture in the root area.

Thin out hardy annuals that were sown in the positions in which they were to flower. Thin tall ones to 30cm (12in) apart and smaller ones to 15–25cm (6–9in).

Sow seeds of herbaceous perennials in prepared seedbed or in pots containing J.I. seed sowing compost.

Early-flowering chrysanthemums can still be planted out about 45cm (18in) apart and staked.

Trees, shrubs and climbers
Continue to clip hedges.

For good rose blooms, remove the central flower-buds of each cluster. Dead-head early-flowering roses by

cutting off finished blooms with a 10–15cm (4–6in) length of stem.

Continue to tie in climbers and shrubs trained as climbers to their supports.

Prune early-flowering clematis species by removing shoots that have borne blooms. Well-established plants with a mass of growth can be cut back as necessary.

Prune chaenomeles (quince) by cutting new growths back to 3–4 buds from the main stem.

Lawns

Start mowing twice weekly from now until early autumn (August), cutting the grass to 13–25mm (½–1in) high.

Use a lawn rake before mowing to lift up creeping stems of weeds for cutting with the mower.

Apply weedkiller as overall or spot treatment if required.

Apply general-purpose proprietary lawn fertilizer this month.

General

Regularly spray all plants with appropriate insecticides and fungicides. Water all plants regularly during dry periods, also lawns.

Fruit, vegetables and herbs

Spray potatoes and tomatoes with fungicides to prevent blight fungus.

Protect strawberries from birds, weeds and slugs by netting and laying straw or black polythene around the plants. Destroy runners or use them to increase stock.

Ventilate and damp down the greenhouse daily.

Thin bunches of greenhouse grapes by about one-third.

Picking of tomato fruits under glass commences this month. Keep the plants well-watered and feed with fertilizer weekly.

Plant young tomatoes outdoors, where they are to flower and fruit.

Plant out hardened-off, self-blanching celery and leeks.

Make late successional outdoor sowings of lettuce, summer spinach, radish, carrots, beetroot, early peas and broad beans. Also sow swedes and chocory for winter use.

Start lifting early potatoes.

Plant out from the seedbed brussels sprouts, savoys, autumn and winter cabbage and purple-sprouting broccoli. Water well and regularly, and add fertilizer towards end of month.

Start picking currents; net to protect from birds if necessary.

Plant out thyme and sage sown earlier and make sowings of other herbs in a well-prepared seedbed for transplanting to their permanent positions in the autumn.

Sow alpine strawberry seeds.

If apple fruitlets do not drop naturally, remove the central one from each cluster.

Ensure female marrow flowers are pollinated by removing male flowers and dusting female with pollen.

Support dwarf French beans.

LATE SUMMER
Mixed flower borders

Support annuals with thin sticks. Cut the flowering stems of everlasting annuals as soon as they come into bloom and dry them in a cool airy place.

Many plants, such as delphinium, lupin, paeony and bedding plants, benefit if the flower-heads are removed as they die. This will encourage further flower production.

Gladioli require plenty of moisture, and even if the wet area is mulched, there should be generous watering during drought periods.

Border carnations can be increased by layering non-flowering stems.

Trees, shrubs and climbers

Shrubs that were planted this spring, or have been newly set out from containers, should be watered regularly and mulched to conserve moisture. Overhead spraying is also beneficial. Provided lawn mowings are weed-free, or weedkillers have not been used for at least six weeks, the mowings make useful additional mulching material.

Shrubs that have finished flowering should be pruned to encourage new shoots for next year's blooms. Limit the pruning of shrubs that flower on one-year-old wood, to the removal of unwanted shoots. Hedges should be cut back whenever necessary. Remove dead flower-heads to encourage further blooms.

Bulbs

Finish lifting late-flowering tulips, not forgetting those put in a trench for ripening last month. Clean and store in a dry, dark and cool place.

Commence planting bulbs and corms, such as amaryllis, colchicum, autumn crocus and nerine, for autumn flowering. Start making list of spring-flowering bulbs for autumn planting

and place orders if buying from specialist firms.

Lawns

Continue to mow regularly (about twice weekly), cutting the grass to 1–2·5cm (½–1in) high. 'Spot' treat isolated weeds with weedkiller according to manufacturer's instructions.

Water the lawn thoroughly, preferably with a sprinkler, during dry weather. Keep the edges well trimmed and tidy. If the edges are uneven and crumbling, cut them straight with a turfing iron.

Fruit, vegetable and herbs

Sow endive, fennel, quick-maturing lettuce and carrots, and winter radish in the open ground.

Net ripening raspberries unless grown in a fruit cage, and spray the fruits with derris if you see raspberry beetle or greenfly. If grey mould fungus appears, spray with captan.

After fruits have been picked, prune the plants and tie in new canes to the supports. Hoe and mulch the root area. After cutting cabbage heads, make a cross-cut at the top of the stem to encourage baby cabbages to grow.

Pick vegetables and fruit as they mature – they taste better when young and fresh.

Continue daily to damp down, shade and ventilate the greenhouse, keeping the atmosphere buoyant.

Feed greenhouse tomatoes regularly,

and use sulphate of potash occasionally to encourage fruiting. 'Stop' the plants after the eighth truss has formed. Spray against brown and grey moulds in the greenhouse if necessary. Thin ripening fruits on outdoor peaches to about one per 1000 sq cm (1sq ft). Spray apple trees with BHC and derris if you see tortrix or codling moth caterpillars. Summer prune apple and pear trees.

Lift shallot bulbs and leave sound ones on the ground to ripen, or put them in a sunny, dry spot. Use at once any that are soft and destroy the diseased ones.

Clean the fruited strawberry beds of old leaves and burn straw if used to protect the fruit. Tip propagate black-currant stems if new bushes are re-quired. Water and feed runner beans to prevent flower-drop.

General
Remove weeds by hand, hoeing or weedkiller, as necessary. Check all plants and treat them with pesticide at the first sign of attack by insects or fungus.

EARLY AUTUMN
Bulbs
Check bulb catalogues and list bulbs required for planting later in the autumn, to flower next spring.

Mixed flower borders
All herbaceous plants, such as lupin, dephinium and paeony, as well as annual and biennial bedding plants, should have dead flower-heads re-moved as they fade. This will en-courage the plants to produce further flowers.

With chrysanthemums that are re-quired to produce large blooms, remove the weakest stems to leave about eight strong ones for flowering. If single blooms for cutting are wanted, remove all buds except the terminal one from each stem. Tie stems to cane supports as necessary.

Cut back herbaceous perennials that have finished flowering to half their height. Even where plants are muched, water thoroughly and at regular inter-vals all flowering varieties, especially those herbaceous perennials that flower in the autumn, such as helenium,

chrysanthemum, golden rod, and michaelmas daisy, as well as annual bedding plants. Lilies can be increased by lifting and removing the firm, healthy outer scales from the bulbs and planting them in pots of J.I. No 1 com-post. Put a plastic bag over each pot and keep in a frost-proof place over winter.

Trees, shrubs and climbers
Take cuttings of heathers by pulling off young sideshoots with a 'heel'; cut off the tip to make the cutting aout 2−3cm (1in) long, and place in a pot of peaty compost covered with a polythene bag. Keep in a cool frame or greenhouse until next spring.

Dead-head roses as necessary and feed with sulphate of potash at 35g per sq m (1oz per sq yd).

Continue to prune out stems of shrubs, climbers and trees as they finish flowering, and remove any diseased or unwanted wood to encourage new wood for next year's flowering.

Hedges should be cut back as neces-sary.

Lawns
Continue to mow regularly (about twice weekly), cutting the grass to 1−3cm (½−1in) high.

Water the lawn thoroughly, prefer-ably with a sprinkler, during drought periods. Keep the edges well trimmed and tidy, and apply weedkiller as 'spot' or overall treatment.

General

Remove all weeds by hand, hoeing or weedkiller, and mulch round perennial plants with lawn mowings (provided these have been free of weedkillers for six weeks).

Check all plants and at first sign of insect or disease infestation, apply the appropriate pesticide according to manufacturer's instructions.

Fruit, vegetables and herbs

If broad beans are infested with black-fly, spray with liquid derris on the underside of the leaves.

Use all waste material from the vegetable garden for the compost heap.

Earth-up the stems of brussels sprouts to prevent loosening in wind.

Sow spring cabbage in the seedbed if space for the plants will be available in the spring.

Continue to pick peas and beans regularly, and cut cauliflowers and cabbage heads as they mature. Pull carrots and beetroots as required.

Loosen onion bulbs with a fork to encourage leaves to bend over and help bulbs to ripen; a fortnight later, lift for drying and storing.

The first of the eating and cooking apples should be ready for picking.

Plant out young strawberries raised from runners previously pegged down, and water regularly until growing freely. If necessary, buy in and set out new young plants of strawberries that are of certified stock.

Take out growing-tip of runner beans when the plants reach the top of their supports and remove weeds from the soil between the plants.

Sow winter spinach.

On paper, prepare a vegetable crop-rotation system to benefit the soil and the plants.

In the greenhouse, continue to water and feed tomatoes and cucumbers, damp down each morning and ventilate well on hot, sunny days.

MID AUTUMN

Bulbs

Plant spring-flowering bulbs such as narcissus, daffodil, hyacinth, scilla and muscari in the positions in which they are to bloom. The smaller bulbs should be 5—8cm (2—3in) deep and the larger 10—15cm (4—6in). Tulips are best planted next month.

Plant specially prepared forced bulbs in bowls of moist bulb fibre for early flowering indoors. Place containers in a cool dark place for 6—8 weeks.

Mixed flower borders

Continue to tie in as necessary late-flowering herbaceous perennials.

Cut and dry seed heads for winter indoor flower decoration. Certain trees and plants can have stems of autumn-coloured foliage cut and preserved by placing the bottom few centimetres in one part of glycerine to two parts boiling water. Some evergreens and ferns can be treated similarly.

Continue to dead-head plants as the flowers fade and remove dead stems of perennials.

Start planning and preparing new mixed flower borders now for planting next month. Herbaceous plants that can be put out now include paeony, the various forms of iris, Canterbury bell, and hardy carnations and pinks.

Trees, shrubs and climbers

This is a good month to plant hedges of evergreen shrubs such as conifers (including yew), holly, box and privet. The ground should be well prepared in advance by deep digging and the addition of well-rotted manure or compost.

Mature hedges will benefit from a final trimming towards the end of this month. The aim should be to make them rather wider and thicker at the base than at the top.

Prepare sites for planting decorative trees and shrubs next month by double digging and adding plenty of well-rotted manure or compost to the soil. Dead-head roses to ensure further flowers. Tie in shoots of climbing plants and shrubs treated as climbers to thin supports.

Lawns

The rate of grass growth starts to slow down this month and longer intervals between mowing can occur. The height of the cutting blades should be raised by about 6mm (¼in).

Towards the end of the month rake the lawn to remove old matted growths and trailing weeds. If the lawn is very compacted, aerate it by forking or using a scarifier. If bare patches are visible, sow grass seed, of the same species as the existing lawn, at the rate of 15−30g per sq m (½−1oz per sq yd).

Earthworms may begin to become active at this time and will damage the lawn if not prevented by the application of a proprietary wormkiller.

General

Apply pesticides if any sign of insects or diseases is seen. Water plants and lawn thoroughly during dry periods.

Remove weeds regularly, especially before they start seeding, but take care to hoe shallowly so as not to disturb plant roots.

Fruit, vegetables and herbs

If not already prepared, plan next season's crop rotation of vegetables now to ensure each group of plants benefits from soil conditions, enjoys the most suitable fertilizer level and is in soil free from pests and diseases.

Sow winter spinach where it is to mature. Also sow winter lettuce in the greenhouse or under cloches, spring and Welsh onions in the open, and cauliflowers under glass for next year. Store beetroot, carrots, marrows and maincrop potatoes. Only perserve those roots that are sound and healthy and keep them in a cool, frost-free place.

Also pick and store sound apple fruits.

Remove the pea and bean haulms, and pull up, clean and store thin supports for use again next year.

In the greenhouse, gradually reduce water and feeding and clean the glass to allow maximum light penetration.

Pick green tomato fruits from outdoor plants to ripen indoors.

Where the ground is clear of crops, put a layer of well-rotted manure or compost over it and turn the soil, leaving it rough dug.

Plant out the spring cabbage seedlings.

Prepare the ground thoroughly — order fruit trees and bushes for planting next month.

LATE AUTUMN

General

Sweep or rake up fallen leaves as necessary and either add to the compost heap or make a separate heap for them to rot down and form leaf mould.

Mixed flower borders

Summer-flowering bedding plants should be lifted and put on the compost heap. Lightly fork over the soil and set out spring-flowering bedding plants.

Herbaceous perennials can be cut down to soil level in all but the coldest parts of the country, where they are best left as protection against frost. The cut-off tops can be composted. After cutting, lightly fork over the soil round the plants and remove the weeds.

If herbaceous perennial plants have become overcrowded and formed clumps that are too dense, dig them up and divide them into smaller pieces by pulling them apart, replanting the younger outer portions and discarding the older central sections. If doing this to many plants, label them to ensure replanting in correct positions. Pull up plant supports and store for use next year. Having prepared the ground last month, newly-purchased herbaceous perennials can be set out this month. Lift half-hardy plants used for summer bedding such as pelargoniums, fuchsias and heliotropes, put them in pots and keep them in a cool place over winter, watering only surfficiently to keep the soil slightly moist. Take cuttings of these plants as well, if not already taken.

Trees, shrubs and climbers
If not already done, prepare the ground for the planting of new shrubs, particularly evergreens and roses, that can be set out towards the end of this month or the beginning of next. Deciduous shrubs can also be planted any time during the winter provided the soil is workable and the weather conditons suitable for working outdoors.

Lightly fork over, or hoe, between shrubs to remove weeds and work into the topsoil the mulch applied during the spring.

Cut back hard hedges of deciduous shrubs planted in the spring. This will encourage a bushy base. Roses will probably continue to bloom during this period, but if frost threatens cut the buds and let them open indoors.

Check plant supports of trees, shrubs and climbers to ensure they are sound, and tie in shoots where necessary to prevent damage by winter gales.

Lawns
The last 'tipping' of the grasses will probably take place this month. Bumps and hollows in the lawns can be rectified by cutting back the turf and adding or taking away soil as necessary to get the area level. If worms are still a problem, apply wormkiller.

Bulbs
If not completed last month, continue to plant outdoor spring-flowering bulbs in the positions in which they are to bloom. Planting more bowls of specially-prepared forced bulbs this month will help to give a succession of flowers in the home in late winter and early spring.

Lift half-hardy bulbous plants such as gladioli, ixia, acidanthera and sparaxia. Cut off the leaves close to the storage root organs, dry them quickly and then rub off soil and old roots. If necessary, as with gladioli, also remove the old corm.

Store in boxes in a cool, frost-free place and examine all at regular intervals during the winter for rot or other infestation.

Dahlias and tuberous-rooted begonias should be cut down by the end of this month, be dried, have the old soil rubbed off, then be stored in boxes of peat in a frost-free and cool place.

Fruit, vegetables and herbs
Prepare thoroughly the planned sites for soft fruits such as raspberries, blackberries, loganberries, gooseberries, black, red and whitecurrants, and plant them towards the end of this month. Erect the necessary support for these fruits.

Tie into the supports the canes of existing soft fruits to prevent winter damage.

Check the posts of the supports to ensure soundness. If weak, reinforce or replace.

Thin the winter spinach seedlings from sowings made last month.

Store chicory in a trench in the garden until required for forcing later.

If not already done, lift, cut off tops, rub off soil and store carrot roots in boxes of moist peat.

EARLY WINTER
Lawns
If the weather and soil conditions are suitable, continue to lay turfs, but complete by the end of this month. Any renovation can be done now.

If planning a new lawn from seed next year, double dig the proposed area, incorporating well-rotted manure or compost into the lower spit. If soil drainage is a problem, construct soakaways or herring-bone drainage system alsoat this time. After replacing the topsoil, leave it rough for winter weather to break it down to a friable tilth.

Apply an autumn fertilizer to an established lawn if not done last month. Apply wormkiller if necessary. Get the lawn-mower overhauled.

Mixed flower borders

Finish forking over the borders, also cutting down herbaceous perennial plants if you plan to do this before cold weather sets in.

Complete planting of newly-purchased herbaceous plants, also spring-flowering subjects, such as wallflowers, forget-me-nots and polyanthus.

Border carnations and pinks can be planted now, perferably in soil that has an alkaline pH of about 6−6·5. Add hydrated lime to the ground if necessary.

Hardy herbaceous perennials raised in the seedbed can be set out in the positions in which they are to flower, provided the soil and weather are suitably mild and not too wet or frosty. In in doubt, leave until mid spring (March).

Trees, shrubs and climbers

Plant roses and evergreens before the end of this month, also deciduous trees and shrubs provided soil and weather conditions are suitable. The ground should have been prepared 3−4 weeks prior to planting. If there is a delay, leave plants wrapped for a few days and

then soak roots in water before planting; or unwrap and set them temporarily in a V-shaped trench in a sheltered spot.

If the soil round plants, especially newly set-out ones, has lifted due to frost, firm it back into position by treading it down carefully.

Young trees and shrubs that are not completely hardy until established, and those mature ones that cannot withstand extremely cold weather, should be given some protection. This can be hessian supported on posts, or sacking and straw covering.

General

Continue to sweep or rake up leaves and add to the compost heap or pile up separately to make leaf mould.

Hoe as necessary to remove weeds, composting annual ones and burning deep-rooted perennial weeds.

Any empty ground should be dug now and left rough for the winter.

Bulbs

The beginning of this month is the last opportunity to plant outside tulip and hyacinth bulbs.

Look at bulbs planted in bowls

earlier in the year. Any showing 2−3cm (1in) or more of tip growth should be moved from darkness to a cool shady position in the home or greenhouse. Water as necessary to prevent the growing medium drying out.

If lily bulbs arrive this month, and the soil is not too cold or wet, plant them in the garden where they are to flower. If the ground is unsuitable, put the bulbs, with the tips just above the surface in slightly damp peat pots or boxes and keep in a cool place until they can be planted out next spring.

Pick flower stems of *Iris unguicularis* as soon as the buds are seen so that the blooms open indoors and do not suffer bird damage.

Fruit, vegetables and herbs

Lightly fork between the rows of spring cabbages, apply sulphate of potash fertilizer, and stake each plant in windy areas.

After clearing the garden of debris, leaves and annual weeds, complete the compost heap with a layer of soil and polythene covering.

Thin winter lettuces sown in mid autumn (September) to 25cm (9in) apart. Protect the plants with cloches. Lift celery roots as required. Make regular sowings of mustard and cress in trays or punnets in the greenhouse.

Make a sowing of broad beans for early picking next year. Protect the plants with cloches in exposed areas.

Plant new rhubarb plants this month when weather and soil conditons allow.

Inspect all stored vegetables and fruit a regular intervals and discard any that are rotting or infected to prevent the problem spreading.

MID WINTER

General
Sweep or rake up leaves from all parts of the garden. Burn diseased ones and compost others.

Any area of ground that has been raised by frost action should be trodden firm.

Look through catalogues to select plants for next year, and prepare planting plans for new areas of the garden.

Mixed flower borders
This is a good month to prepare the soil for new flower borders. The ground should be double-dug if possible and plenty of well-rotted manure and compost added to the lower soil. The topsoil should be left rough-dug to allow the frost to break it down naturally.

Scatter slug pellets around delphiniums and lupins, two herbaceous plants particularly prone to slug attack. Putting a shallow heap of well-weathered cinders or coarse sand around the root area also helps.

To protect leaves and flower-stems of *Helleborus niger* (Christmas rose) from weather damage and to encourage early blooms, put straw or dry peat around the root area and cover the plants with cloches.

Chrysanthemums left in the ground to overwinter should have dry peat lightly forked into the soil above the root area to prevent waterlogging.

Bulbs
Specially forced Christmas-flowering hyacinths and narcissi start blooming this month. Water these pots of bulbs regularly to keep the compost moist. Examine other pot bulbs being forced in darkness and bring them into the light when the stems are a few centimetres (inches) high.

Lily bulbs received or bought now should be plump and firm. If the weather is open and the ground workable they can be planted outdoors where they are to flower. Put shrivelled bulbs in damp peat for 10–14 days before planting. If weather conditions are unsuitable leave the bulbs in the

pots, with their tips just above the surface, and keep in a cool place until ready for planting next spring (February).

Trees, shrubs and climbers
Finish forking over or hoeing between shrubs to remove weeks and work into the ground the mulch applied earlier in the year.

All supports and ties of trees, shrubs and climbers should be examined to ensure they are sound. Renew broken ones to prevent plant damage during winter gales.

If the planting of deciduous trees, shrubs and climbers was delayed by bad weather and soil conditions last month, the plants may still be set out when the weather is suitable.

Lawns
If the edges of the lawn or grass paths are worn and patchy, cut them into longitudinal sections with a sharp spade or turfing iron, lift them by cutting into the root area about 5cm (2in) below the surface, and turn them around so that the inner edge goes to the outside. Fill in any gaps by adding topsoil. Do not

work on a lawn that is waterlogged or frosty.

Fruit, vegetables and herbs
Sow suitable varieties of broad beans and peas outdoors and protect with cloches in very cold or exposed positions.

In the greenhouse, sow cauliflower for early cropping next year. Sow seeds singly in peat pots.

Make regular sowings of mustard and cress in trays or punnets in the greenhouse.

Check all stored vegetables and fruit at regular intervals. Discard any rotten ones to prevent infection spreading.

Prune greenhouse vines and paint with tar oil winter wash.

Prune established and newly-planted fruit trees and bushes, such as apples and pears. Also root-prune any trees that require it.

Remove any rotten fruits and burn them to prevent disease spreading. Spray with tar oil winter wash to kill overwintering insects.

Mulch newly-planted fruit trees and bushes with well-rotted manure or compost.

Generally clear the vegetable garden of leaves and rubbish. Obtain seed and plant catalogues so that orders can be placed in good time for next year.

INDEX